PRACTICAL
SOFTWARE
TESTING

Springer
New York
Berlin
Heidelberg
Hong Kong
London
Milan
Paris
Tokyo

PRACTICAL SOFTWARE TESTING

A
PROCESS-ORIENTED
APPROACH

ILENE BURNSTEIN

Springer

Ilene Burnstein
Department of Computer Science
Illinois Institute of Technology
10 West 31 Street
Chicago, IL 60616
USA
burnstei@babbage2.cs.iit.edu

Library of Congress Cataloging-in-Publication Data
Burnstein, Ilene.
    Practical software testing : a process-oriented approach / Ilene Burnstein.
        p.   cm.
    Includes bibliographical references and index.
    ISBN 0-387-95131-8 (hc : alk. paper)
        1. Computer software—Testing.   I. Title.
    QA76.76.T48 B87   2002   2002024164
    005.1′4–dc21

ISBN 0-387-95131-8   Printed on acid-free paper.

Printed in the United States of America.

9 8 7 6 5 4 3 2 1   SPIN 10779083

www.springer-ny.com

Springer-Verlag   New York   Berlin   Heidelberg
A member of BertelsmannSpringer Science+Business Media GmbH

CONTENTS

3 DEFECTS, HYPOTHESES, AND TESTS

4 STRATEGIES AND METHODS FOR TEST CASE DESIGN I

5 STRATEGIES AND METHODS FOR TEST CASE DESIGN II

6 LEVELS OF TESTING

7 TEST GOALS, POLICIES, PLANS, AND DOCUMENTATION

8

THE TEST ORGANIZATION

9

CONTROLLING AND MONITORING
THE TESTING PROCESS

REVIEWS AS A TESTING ACTIVITY

A MEASUREMENT PROGRAM TO SUPPORT PRODUCT AND PROCESS QUALITY

12

EVALUATING SOFTWARE QUALITY: A QUANTITATIVE APPROACH

13   DEFECT ANALYSIS AND PREVENTION

14   THE TESTERS' WORKBENCH

15 PROCESS CONTROL AND OPTIMIZATION

16 THE TESTING MATURITY MODEL AND TEST PROCESS ASSESSMENT

PREFACE

Software development is evolving into an engineering discipline. Indications of this new direction can be found, for example, in the "Software Engineering Body of Knowledge (SWEBOK)" and the code of ethics that have been developed recently through the efforts of joint IEEE/ACM task forces [1,2]. Licensing procedures for software engineers are also under development. Software testing is a subdiscipline in this emerging field. The software industry is actively seeking and promoting professionals who are educated and trained in the areas of testing and quality assurance, and who will promote the development of high-quality software.

Graduate schools have slowly been responding to this industry need, and a growing number are offering courses focused on software testing and quality assurance as part of advanced degree programs in software engineering. To support these programs, as well as the educational needs of practicing professionals in the industry, a new type of book on software testing is needed. The book should have an engineering/process orientation, and promote the growth and value of software testing as a profession. This text was developed to meet these needs. It has been designed to serve as (i) a text for students enrolled in a graduate-level testing/quality assurance class, and (ii) a knowledge source and learning tool for professionals currently working in the field.

The text is unique in its approach to presenting the field of software testing. It introduces testing concepts that are managerial, technical, and process-oriented in nature. Process is emphasized because of its essential role in all engineering disciplines. The widespread application of the Capability Maturity Model (CMM)® and other process improvement models attests to the importance of process in today's software development industry. Unfortunately, discussions of this topic are lacking in the majority of books on software testing.

The author makes use of the Testing Maturity Model (TMM)^{SM}, which was developed to support organizations in assessing and improving their testing processes, as a guiding framework for presenting testing concepts, and as a context for introducing the reader to test process issues. The text uses TMM levels and goals to support a structured presentation of fundamental and advanced test-related concepts to the reader. The TMM structure highlights the important relationships between the testing process and key players such as managers, testers, and client groups. The reader should note that adaptation of the Testing Maturity Model is not a necessary condition for using this text to learn about software testing. Using this text, you can learn about good testing practices and test process issues and apply them in the context of your individual and organizational needs.

Finally, the author believes that educational material developed for software engineers should be guided by the contents of the Software Engineering Body of Knowledge (SWEBOK). In this context this text endeavors to cover many of the topics outlined in the "Software Testing" chapter of the SWEBOK. It also covers material from the chapters on "Software Quality" and "Software Engineering Process"

Goals

In view of the growth of the software engineering profession, the educational requirements of a software testing specialist, and the need for emphasis on process issues, the author's goals for this text are to:

- introduce testing concepts, techniques, and best practices in a systematic way that reflects an orderly evolution of testing process growth on both an individual and organizational level;

- introduce a view of testing as a process that goes through a set of evolutionary stages to an optimal state of continuous improvement;

- introduce software quality concepts, standards, measurements, and practices that support the production of quality software;

- enable a software professional to build an individual testing process of the highest caliber that is integratable with an organizational testing process;

- enable a software professional to serve as an agent for change when an organization decides that its overall testing process needs improvement;

- introduce the concepts of test process evaluation and improvement and their importance to the software industry;

- support the growth of the profession of software test specialist by providing the educational background necessary for a professional in that field.

Organization and Features

Each chapter in this text covers a managerial, technical and/or process-related topic related to testing. The topics are designed to support the reader's growth as a test specialist. Within each chapter, the relationship of chapter contents to one or more TMM maturity goals is described. The first nine chapters contains basic material that allows the reader to master fundamental testing concepts on the technical level, and to learn about basic managerial concepts that promote a repeatable and defined testing process. These chapters also highlight the importance of an independent test group, and promote monitoring and controlling of the testing process. Maturity goals at levels 2 and 3 of the TMM are integrated into the chapter material .

Chapters 10–15 cover more advanced topics related to levels 4 and 5 of the TMM. These chapters support reviews as a testing activity, and the automation of testing activities with tools. They also promote qualitative and quantitative evaluation of the test process and its continuous evolution. Qualitative and quantitative evaluation of the software product under test is also addressed. Chapter 16 provides a discussion of test process assessment using the TMM Assessment Model, and describes some applications of the TMM in industry.

The last sections of the text are its appendices. Appendix I, called "Supplementary References," contains a collection of test-related references which the reader will find useful to supplement the material in the text. In this appendix a complete bibliography, organized alphabetically by author is presented that includes all references in the book chapters. It also contains a listing of additional textbooks, papers and Internet sites that are rich sources of material for the test specialist. They support continual professional growth in a rapidly evolving field. Appendix II contains a sample test plan to illustrate the typical contents of such a document. Appendix III contains the TMM Questionnaire, ranking algorithms, and the full set of TMM Activities, Tasks, and Responsibilities (ATRs) for those readers interested in test process assessment.

Other features to note in this text include definitions of key terms in each chapter which are shown in italics. At the end of most of the chapters the reader will find exercises that will help him/her to learn the concepts that are discussed. Some exercises provide hands-on experience in applying the concepts. A set of references is included at the end of each chapter for the reader who would like a more in-depth discussion of the topics.

This text is one of the tools you can use to develop as a professional software tester. To use the text effectively you should have a background in basic software engineering concepts, and some experience in software development. The best approach to learning the material is to read the chapters carefully and work out the exercises in the back of each chapter. Feedback from an instructor with respect to homework exercises and examinations is also very valuable. Discussions with instructors, classmates, and/or colleagues will also help you to integrate and clarify concepts. It is the author's objective to assist you in accumulating the knowledge and expertise you need to develop as a professional software tester.

Intended Audience

Readers who would benefit from this text are senior undergraduates and graduate students in computer science and software engineering programs, and software professionals who are interested in improving their testing skills and learning more about testing as a process. For students, the text is a tool that can be used to develop the testing skills necessary to become a professional software tester. For those in the software industry it can help to enhance testing skills, and provide guidelines for evaluating and improving organizational testing processes. To use the text effectively, readers should have a background in basic software engineering concepts and some experience in developing software.

Notes to Educators

This text can be used for several types of graduate courses including those in software testing, software quality assurance, software verification and validation, and systems engineering. It can also be used as a text for an undergraduate two-semester software engineering course.

For educators using this book as a text for a one-semester course in software testing, covering the first ten chapters and Chapter 14, will give your students a solid foundation in testing fundamentals so that they can develop into professional software testers. Chapters covering more advanced topics, including the TMM, can be discussed if time permits. Students should be assigned homework problems from the chapters and receive feedback on their results. A suggested team project for the course is the development of a system test plan with attachments for a simple software system. Students will need a requirements and/or design description depending on the nature of the requested test plan.

For software professionals using this text, there is much material that can help to enhance your knowledge of the testing field. The material relating to the TMM can be applied to evaluate and make changes in your testing process in a manner consistent with organizational goals.

Permissions

IEEE term definitions, test plan components, and steps in a software quality metrics methodology reprinted with permission from:

IEEE Standard Glossary of Software Engineering Terminology (IEEE Std 610.12-1990), copyright 1990 by IEEE

IEEE Standard for Software Test Documentation (ANSI/IEEE Std 829–1983), copyright 1983 by IEEE.

IEEE Standard for a Software Quality Metrics Methodology (IEEE Std 1061–1992), copyright 1993, by IEEE.

The IEEE disclaims any responsibility or liability resulting from the placement and use in the described manner.

Pearson Education has granted permission for use of material from "Software Metrics: Establishing a Company-Wide Program" by Grady and Caswell.

[1] A. Abran, J. Moore, P. Bourque, R. Dupuis, editors, "Guide to the Software Engineering Body of Knowledge, Trial Version," IEEE Computer Society Press, Los Alamitos, CA, 2001.

[2] D. Gotterbarn, K. Miller, S. Rogerson, "Computer Society and ACM Approve Software Engineering Code of Ethics," *IEEE Computer*, Vol. 32, No. 10, 1999, pp. 84–88.

Acknowledgments

In preparing this text I have had support from many people including family, colleagues, students, and publishers. The support has been in many different forms. I would first like to thank my university, Illinois Institute of Technology, for granting me a sabbatical leave that enabled me to complete a good portion of this text. Colleagues who have been supportive of my work include Professor Anneliese A. Andrews, (Colorado State University), Professor Robert Carlson (Illinois Institute of Technology), and Professor Martha Evens (Illinois Institute of Technology).

I have used drafts of this text in my "Software Testing and Quality Assurance" class over the last two years and I would like to thank the students in these classes (CS 589) for their comments about the text. Ms. Yachai Limpiyakorn, who was the teaching assistant for the course, has also provided useful comments.

I would like to acknowledge the major contributions of Drs. Taratip Suwannasart, and Ariya Homyen (Wichitnuntakorn) to the development of the Testing Maturity Model during the course of their doctoral studies. The model provided the framework for the development of this text. My editors at Springer-Verlag, in particular, Wayne Wheeler and Wayne Yuhasz, have been very patient, and have provided suggestions and useful comments that I have incorporated into the text. Anonymous reviewers have also been very helpful in suggesting changes that improved the text quality.

Finally, I would like to thank my husband, Ray Burnstein for his encouragement, and advice in the writing of this text, and for always "being there" for me. I would like to thank my sons Kenneth and Jonathan who have expressed enthusiasm for this authoring project. Thank you one and all!

Ilene Burnstein

INTRODUCTION TO TESTING AS AN ENGINEERING ACTIVITY

1.0 The Evolving Profession of Software Engineering

This is an exciting time to be a software developer. Software systems are becoming more challenging to build. They are playing an increasingly important role in society. People with software development skills are in demand. New methods, techniques, and tools are becoming available to support development and maintenance tasks.

Because software now has such an important role in our lives both economically and socially, there is pressure for software professionals to focus on quality issues. Poor quality software that can cause loss of life or property is no longer acceptable to society. Failures can result in catastrophic losses. Conditions demand software development staffs with interest and training in the areas of software product and process quality. Highly qualified staff ensure that software products are built on time, within budget, and are of the highest quality with respect to attributes such as reliability, correctness, usability, and the ability to meet all user requirements.

In response to the demand for high-quality software, and the need for well-educated software professionals, there is a movement to change the way software is developed and maintained, and the way developers and maintainers are educated. In fact, the profession of software engineering is slowly emerging as a formal engineering discipline. As a new discipline it will be related to other engineering disciplines, and have associated with it a defined body of knowledge, a code of ethics, and a certification process. The movement toward this new profession is the focus of the entire November/December 1999 issue of *IEEE Software*.

The education and training of engineers in each engineering discipline is based on the teaching of related scientific principles, engineering processes, standards, methods, tools, measurement and best practices as shown in Figure 1.1. As a reflection of the movement toward a software engineering profession, and these educational needs, the IEEE Computer Society and the Association of Computing Machinery (ACM), the two principal societies for software professionals, have appointed joint task forces. The goals of the task force teams are to define a body of knowledge that covers the software engineering discipline, to discuss the nature of education for this new profession, and to define a code of ethics for the software engineer [1]. Foreseeing the emergence of this new engineering discipline, some states are already preparing licensing examinations for software engineers [2].

This text is based on the philosophy that software development should be viewed and taught as an engineering discipline and that quality in both the process and the product are of prime importance to professionals in this field. Using an engineering approach to software development implies that:

- the development process is well understood;

- projects are planned;

- life cycle models are defined and adhered to;

- standards are in place for product and process;

- measurements are employed to evaluate product and process quality;

- components are reused;

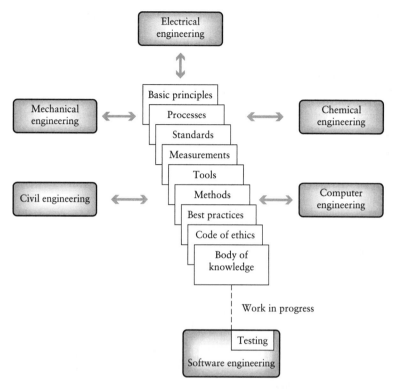

FIG. 1.1

Elements of the engineering disciplines.

- validation and verification processes play a key role in quality determination;

- engineers have proper education, training, and certification.

The aim of this text is to support the education of a software professional called a test specialist. A test specialist is one whose education is based on the principles, practices, and processes that constitute the software engineering discipline, and whose specific focus is on one area of that discipline—software testing. A test specialist who is trained as an engineer should have knowledge of test-related principles, processes, measurements, standards, plans, tools, and methods, and should learn how to apply them to the testing tasks to be performed.

This text aims to educate the reader in the testing discipline. Testing concepts, instead of being presented as an isolated collection of technical and managerial activities will instead be integrated within the context of a quality testing process that grows in competency and uses engineering principles to guide improvement growth. In this way all of the elements of the testing discipline emerge incrementally, and allow the tester to add knowledge and skills that follow a natural evolutionary pattern. The integrating framework for presenting testing concepts in this text is the Testing Maturity Model (TMM)SM [3–7].* An explanation of the value of this process-oriented approach to presenting the discipline of software testing follows in the succeeding sections of this chapter.

1.1 The Role of Process in Software Quality

The need for software products of high quality has pressured those in the profession to identify and quantify quality factors such as usability, testability, maintainability, and reliability, and to identify engineering practices that support the production of quality products having these favorable attributes. Among the practices identified that contribute to the development of high-quality software are project planning, requirements management, development of formal specifications, structured design with use of information hiding and encapsulation, design and code reuse, inspections and reviews, product and process measures, education and training of software professionals, development and application of CASE tools, use of effective testing techniques, and integration of testing activities into the entire life cycle. In addition to identifying these individual best technical and managerial practices, software researchers realized that it was important to integrate them within the context of a high-quality software development process. Process in this context is defined below, and is illustrated in Figure 1.2.

> **Process, in the software engineering domain, is the set of methods, practices, standards, documents, activities, policies, and procedures that software engineers use to develop and maintain a software system and its associated artifacts, such as project and test plans, design documents, code, and manuals.**

---

*Testing Maturity Model and TMM are service marks of Illinois Institute of Technology.

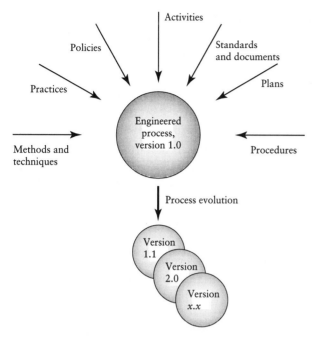

FIG. 1.2

Components of an engineered process.

It also was clear that adding individual practices to an existing software development process in an ad hoc way was not satisfactory. The software development process, like most engineering artifacts, must be engineered. That is, it must be designed, implemented, evaluated, and maintained. As in other engineering disciplines, a software development process must evolve in a consistent and predictable manner, and the best technical and managerial practices must be integrated in a systematic way. Models such as the Capability Maturity Model® (CMM)* and SPICE were developed to address process issues [8,9]. These models allow an organization to evaluate its current software process and to capture an understanding of its state. Strong support for incremental process improvement is provided by the models, consistent with historical process evolution and the application of quality principles. The models have re-

---

*The Capability Maturity Model and CMM are registered trademarks of the Software Engineering Institute and Carnegie Mellon University.

ceived much attention from industry, and resources have been invested in process improvement efforts with many successes recorded [8].

All the software process improvement models that have had wide acceptance in industry are high-level models, in the sense that they focus on the software process as a whole and do not offer adequate support to evaluate and improve specific software development sub processes such as design and testing. Most software engineers would agree that testing is a vital component of a quality software process, and is one of the most challenging and costly activities carried out during software development and maintenance. In spite of its vital role in the production of quality software, existing process evaluation and improvement models such as the CMM, Bootstrap, and ISO-9000 have not adequately addressed testing process issues [3–7,10]. The Testing Maturity Model (TMM), as described throughout this text, has been developed at the Illinois Institute of Technology by a research group headed by the author, to address deficiencies these areas.

1.2 Testing as a Process

The software development process has been described as a series of phases, procedures, and steps that result in the production of a software product. Embedded within the software development process are several other processes including testing. Some of these are shown in Figure 1.3. Testing itself is related to two other processes called verification and validation as shown in Figure 1.3.

> **Validation is the process of evaluating a software system or component during, or at the end of, the development cycle in order to determine whether it satisfies specified requirements [11].**

Validation is usually associated with traditional execution-based testing, that is, exercising the code with test cases.

> **Verification is the process of evaluating a software system or component to determine whether the products of a given development phase satisfy the conditions imposed at the start of that phase [11].**

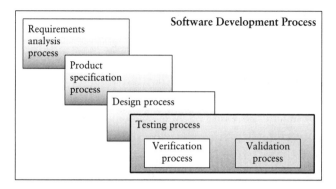

FIG. 1.3

*Example processes embedded in the
software development process.*

Verification is usually associated with activities such as inspections and reviews of software deliverables. Testing itself has been defined in several ways. Two definitions are shown below.

> **Testing is generally described as a group of procedures carried out to evaluate some aspect of a piece of software.**

> **Testing can be described as a process used for revealing defects in software, and for establishing that the software has attained a specified degree of quality with respect to selected attributes.**

Note that these definitions of testing are general in nature. They cover both validation and verification activities, and include in the testing domain all of the following: technical reviews, test planning, test tracking, test case design, unit test, integration test, system test, acceptance test, and usability test. The definitions also describe testing as a dual-purpose process—one that reveals defects, as well as one that is used to evaluate quality attributes of the software such as reliability, security, usability, and correctness.

Also note that testing and debugging, or fault localization, are two very different activities. The debugging process begins *after* testing has been carried out and the tester has noted that the software is not behaving as specified.

> **Debugging, or fault localization is the process of (1) locating the fault or defect, (2) repairing the code, and (3) retesting the code.**

Testing as a process has economic, technical and managerial aspects. Economic aspects are related to the reality that resources and time are available to the testing group on a limited basis. In fact, complete testing is in many cases not practical because of these economic constraints. An organization must structure its testing process so that it can deliver software on time and within budget, and also satisfy the client's requirements.

The technical aspects of testing relate to the techniques, methods, measurements, and tools used to insure that the software under test is as defect-free and reliable as possible for the conditions and constraints under which it must operate. Testing is a process, and as a process it must managed. Minimally that means that an organizational policy for testing must be defined and documented. Testing procedures and steps must be defined and documented. Testing must be planned, testers should be trained, the process should have associated quantifiable goals that can be measured and monitored. Testing as a process should be able to evolve to a level where there are mechanisms in place for making continuous improvements.

1.3 An Overview of the Testing Maturity Model

Several important test-related issues have emerged from the previous discussion. We have learned that

1. there is a demand for software of high quality with low defects;
2. process is important in the software engineering discipline;
3. software testing is an important software development sub process;
4. existing software evaluation and improvement models have not adequately addressed testing issues.

An introduction to the Testing Maturity Model is now presented to the reader as a framework for discussion of these issues, and as a means for addressing them. The model is discussed in more detail in later chapters of this text. The focus of the TMM is on testing as a process in itself that can be evaluated and improved. In the testing domain possible benefits of test process improvement are the following:

- smarter testers

- higher quality software

- the ability to meet budget and scheduling goals

- improved planning

- the ability to meet quantifiable testing goals

Test process improvement is supported by the set of levels and maturity goals in the TMM. Achievement of the maturity goals results in incremental improvement of an organization's testing process. The TMM Assessment Model supports test process evaluation. Section 1.3 gives the reader an overview the set of levels and maturity goals. The levels and goals serve as guidelines for the organization of this text and define the sequence for introduction of testing concepts.

The development of version 1.0 of the TMM was guided by the work done on the Capability Maturity Model for software (CMM), a process improvement model that has received widespread support from the software industry in the United States [8]. The CMM is classified architecturally as staged process improvement model. This type of process improvement model architecture prescribes the stages that an organization must proceed through in an orderly fashion to improve its software development process. Other process improvement models can be described as having a continuous type of architecture, for example, the SPICE model. In this type of architecture there is no fixed set of levels or stages to proceed through. An organization applying a continuous model can select areas for improvement from many different categories.

The CMM has five levels or stages that describe an evolutionary pattern of software process maturity and serve as a guide for improvement. Each level has a set of Key Process Areas (KPA) that an organization needs to focus on to achieve maturity at that level. There are also key practices associated with each level that provide support for implementing improvements at that level. The CMM also has an assessment procedure that allows an organization to evaluate the current state of its software process and identify process strengths and weaknesses.

Other input sources to TMM development include Gelperin and Hetzel's Evolution of Testing Model [12], which describes the evolution of the testing process in industry over a 40-year period; Beizer's testing model, which describes the evolution of the individual tester's thinking [13]; and the Software Testing Practices Survey Report [14], which identifies best test practices in industry as of 1993. More details relating to these items as well as the TMM maturity goals and the TMM Assessment Model are found in later chapters of this text.

1.3.1 TMM Levels

As in the case of the CMM, the TMM also follows what is called a staged architecture for process improvement models. It contains stages or levels through which an organization passes as its testing process evolves from one that is ad hoc and unmanaged to one that is managed, defined, measured, and optimizable. The internal structure of the TMM is rich in testing practices that can be learned and applied in a systematic way to support a quality testing process that improves in incremental steps. There are five levels in the TMM that prescribe a maturity hierarchy and an evolutionary path to test process improvement. The characteristics of each level are described in terms of testing capability organizational goals, and roles/responsibilities for the key players in the testing process, the managers, developers/testers, and users/clients.

Each level with the exception of level 1 has a structure that consists of the following:

- *A set of maturity goals.* The maturity goals identify testing improvement goals that must be addressed in order to achieve maturity at that level. To be placed at a level, an organization must satisfy the maturity goals at that level. The TMM levels and associated maturity goals are shown in Figure 1.5.

- *Supporting maturity subgoals.* They define the scope, boundaries and needed accomplishments for a particular level.

- *Activities, tasks and responsibilities (ATR).* The ATRs address implementation and organizational adaptation issues at each TMM

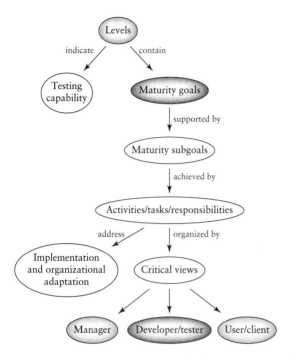

FIG. 1.4

The internal structure of TMM
maturity levels.

level. Supporting activities and tasks are identified, and responsibilities are assigned to appropriate groups.

Figure 1.4 illustrates the TMM level structure. Each maturity goal at each TMM level is supported by a set of maturity subgoals. The maturity subgoals are achieved through a group of activities and tasks with responsibilities (ATR). Activities and tasks are defined in terms of actions that must be performed at a given level to improve testing capability; they are linked to organizational commitments. Responsibilities are assigned for these activities and tasks to three groups that TMM developers believe represent the key participants in the testing process: managers, developers/testers, and users/clients. In the model they are referred to as "the three critical views (CV)." Definition of their roles is essential in developing a maturity framework. The manager's view involves commitment and ability to perform activities and tasks related to improving testing capability. The developer/tester's view encompasses the technical activities and tasks that, when applied, constitute quality testing practices. The user's or client's view is defined as a cooperating, or supporting, view. The developers/testers work with client/user groups on quality-related activities and tasks that concern user-oriented needs. The focus is on soliciting client/user support, consensus, and participation in activities such as requirements analysis, usability testing, and acceptance test planning.

The maturity goals at each level of the TMM are shown in Figure 1.5. They are fully described in published papers and are also listed below along with a brief description of the characteristics of an organization at each TMM level [2–6]. The description will introduce the reader to the evolutionary path prescribed in the TMM for test process improvement. Additional details are provided in subsequent text chapters.

Level 1—Initial: (No maturity goals)

At TMM level 1, testing is a chaotic process; it is ill-defined, and not distinguished from debugging. A documented set of specifications for software behavior often does not exist. Tests are developed in an ad hoc way after coding is completed. Testing and debugging are interleaved to get the bugs out of the software. The objective of testing is to show the software works (it is minimally functional) [1,5]. Software products are often released without quality assurance. There is a lack of resources, tools and properly trained staff. This type of organization would be at level 1 of the CMM.

Level 2—Phase Definition: (Goal 1: Develop testing and debugging goals; Goal 2: Initiate a testing planning process; Goal 3: Institutionalize basic testing techniques and methods)

At level 2 of the TMM testing is separated from debugging and is defined as a phase that follows coding. It is a planned activity; however, test planning at level 2 may occur after coding for reasons related to the immaturity of the testing process. For example, there may be the perception at level 2, that all testing is execution based and dependent on the code; therefore, it should be planned only when the code is complete.

The primary goal of testing at this level of maturity is to show that the software meets its stated specifications [2,5]. Basic testing techniques

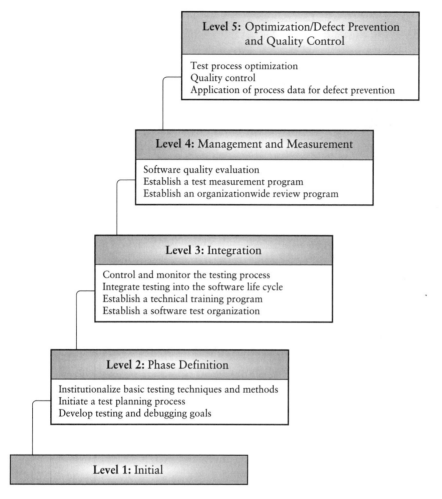

Level 5: Optimization/Defect Prevention
and Quality Control

Test process optimization
Quality control
Application of process data for defect prevention

Level 4: Management and Measurement

Software quality evaluation
Establish a test measurement program
Establish an organizationwide review program

Level 3: Integration

Control and monitor the testing process
Integrate testing into the software life cycle
Establish a technical training program
Establish a software test organization

Level 2: Phase Definition

Institutionalize basic testing techniques and methods
Initiate a test planning process
Develop testing and debugging goals

Level 1: Initial

FIG. 1.5

*The 5-level structure of the testing
maturity model.*

and methods are in place; for example, use of black box and white box
testing strategies, and a validation cross-reference matrix. Testing is multi-
leveled: there are unit, integration, system, and acceptance levels. Many
quality problems at this TMM level occur because test planning occurs
late in the software life cycle. In addition, defects are propagated from
the requirements and design phases into the code. There are no review

programs as yet to address this important issue. Postcode, execution-based testing is still considered the primary testing activity.

Level 3—Integration: (Goal 1: Establish a software test organization; Goal 2: Establish a technical training program; Goal 3: Integrate testing into the software life cycle; Goal 4: Control and monitor testing)

At TMM level 3, testing is no longer a phase that follows coding, but is integrated into the entire software life cycle. Organizations can build on the test planning skills they have acquired at level 2. Unlike level 2, planning for testing at TMM level 3 begins at the requirements phase and continues throughout the life cycle supported by a version of the V-model (see Section 8.7) [2]. Test objectives are established with respect to the requirements based on user/client needs, and are used for test case design. There is a test organization, and testing is recognized as a professional activity. There is a technical training organization with a testing focus. Testing is monitored to ensure it is going according to plan and actions can be taken if deviations occur. Basic tools support key testing activities, and the testing process is visible in the organization. Although organizations at this level begin to realize the important role of reviews in quality control, there is no formal review program and reviews do not as yet take place across the life cycle. A formal test measurement program has not yet been established to quantify a significant number of process and product attributes.

Level 4—Management and Measurement: (Goal 1: Establish an organizationwide review program; Goal 2: Establish a test measurement program; Goal 3: Software quality evaluation)

Testing at level 4 becomes a process that is measured and quantified. Reviews at all phases of the development process are now recognized as testing/quality control activities. They are a compliment to execution-based tests to detect defects and to evaluate and improve software quality. An extension of the V-model as shown in Figure 1.6 can be used to support the implementation of this goal [6,7]. Software products are tested for quality attributes such as reliability, usability, and maintainability. Test cases from all projects are collected and recorded in a test case database for the purpose of test case reuse and regression testing. Defects are logged and given a severity level. Some of the deficiencies occurring

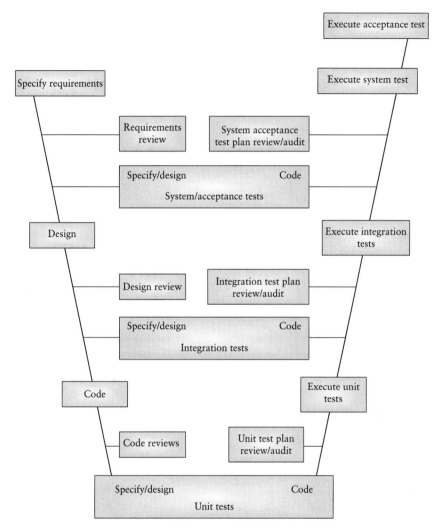

FIG. 1.6

The Extended/Modified V-model.

in the test process are due to the lack of a defect prevention philosophy, and the porosity of automated support for the collection, analysis, and dissemination of test-related metrics.

Level 5—Optimization/Defect Prevention/Quality Control: (Goal 1: Defect prevention; Goal 2: Quality control; Goal 3: Test process optimization)

Because of the infrastructure that is in place through achievement of the maturity goals at levels 1–4 of the TMM, the testing process is now said to be defined and managed; its cost and effectiveness can be monitored. At level 5, mechanisms are in place so that testing can be fine-tuned and continuously improved. Defect prevention and quality control are practiced. Statistical sampling, measurements of confidence levels, trustworthiness, and reliability drive the testing process. Automated tools totally support the running and rerunning of test cases. Tools also provide support for test case design, maintenance of test-related items, and defect collection and analysis. The collection and analysis of test-related metrics also has tool support. Process reuse is also a practice at TMM level 5 supported by a Process Asset Library (PAL).

KEY TERMS

Debugging
Process
Testing
Validation
Verification

EXERCISES

1. What are the differences between testing and debugging? What specific tasks are involved in each? Which groups should have responsibility for each of these processes?

2. What are the differences between verification and validation? How does your organization handle each of these activities?

3. Using the version of the V-model shown in Figure 1.6, describe the test-related activities that should be done, and why they should be done, during the following phases of the software development process: requirements specification, design, coding, installation.

4. Identify the members of the three critical groups in the testing process. How are they represented in the TMM structure?

5. Your organization has worked very hard to improve its testing process. The most recent test process assessment using the Testing Maturity Model showed that you are at TMM level 3. How would you describe your current testing process based on that assessment? What are the maturity goals that you have achieved at that TMM level?

REFERENCES

[1] D. Gotterbarn, K. Miller, S. Rogerson, "Computer Society and ACM Approve Software Engineering Code of Ethics," *IEEE Computer,* Vol. 32, No. 10, Oct., 1999, pp. 84–88.

[2] J. Speed. "What Do You Mean I Can't Call Myself a Software Engineer," *IEEE Software,* Nov./Dec., 1999, pp. 45–50.

[3] I. Burnstein, A. Homyen, T, Suwanassart, G. Saxena, R. Grom, "A Testing Maturity Model for Software Test Process Assessment and Improvement," *Software Quality Professional,* American Society for Quality, Vol. 1, No. 4, Sept. 1999, pp. 8–21.

[4] I. Burnstein, A. Homyen, T, Suwanassart, G. Saxena, R. Grom, "Using the Testing Maturity Model to Assess and Improve Your Software Testing Process," *Proc. of International Quality Week Conf. (QW'99),* San Jose, CA, May, 1999.

[5] I. Burnstein, A. Homyen, R. Grom, C. R. Carlson, "A Model for Assessing Testing Process Maturity," *CrossTalk: Journal of Department of Defense Software Engineering,* Vol. 11, No. 11, Nov., 1998, pp. 26–30.

[6] I. Burnstein, T. Suwanassart, C. R. Carlson, "Developing a Testing Maturity Model: Part I," *Cross-Talk: Journal of Defense Software Engineering,* Vol. 9, No. 8, Aug., 1996, pp. 21–24.

[7] I. Burnstein, T. Suwanassart, C. R. Carlson, "Developing a Testing Maturity Model: Part II," *Cross-Talk: Journal of Defense Software Engineering,* Vol. 9, No. 9, Sep., 1996, pp. 19–26.

[8] M. Paulk, C. Weber, B. Curtis, M. Chrissis, *The Capability Maturity Model,* Addison-Wesley, Reading MA, 1995.

[9] M. Paulk, M. Konrad, "An Overview of ISO's SPICE Project," *American Programmer,* Vol. 7, No. 2, Feb., 1994, pp. 16–20.

[10] L Osterweil, "Strategic Directions in Software Quality," *ACM Computing Surveys,* Vol. 28, No. 4, 1996, pp. 738–750.

[11] *IEEE Standard Glossary of Software Engineering Terminology* (Std610.12-1990). Copyright 1990 by IEEE. All rights reserved.

[12] D. Gelperin, B. Hetzel, "The Growth of Software Testing," *CACM,* Vol. 31, No. 6, 1988, pp. 687–695.

[13] B. Beizer, *Software Testing Techniques,* second edition, Van Nostrand Reinhold, New York, 1990.

[14] J. Durant, *Software Testing Practices Survey Report,* Software Practices Research Center, Technical Report, TR5-93, May 1993.

TESTING

FUNDAMENTALS

2.0 Initating a Study of Testing

The study of software testing in this text begins with a description of essential test-related vocabulary items. Knowledge of these basic terms is essential to insure that the discussions of testing concepts that follow are based on a common vocabulary that is widely accepted in academia and industry. A set of execution-based testing principles is also presented here to support test specialists. They provide a foundation for developing testing knowledge, acquiring testing skills, and developing an essential group of best practices. This introduction to the field of software testing concludes with a description of the role of the test specialist in a software development organization.

2.1 Basic Definitions

Below is a set of basic definitions for terms will be used in this text. Additional definitions appear in subsequent chapters to aid in concept understanding. Many of the definitions used in this text are based on the terms described in the *IEEE Standards Collection for Software Engineering* [1]. The standards collection includes the *IEEE Standard Glossary of Software Engineering Terminology,* which is a dictionary devoted to describing software engineering vocabulary [2]. It contains working definitions of terms that are in use in both the academic and industrial worlds. Where a definition has been directly adapted from an IEEE standards document a specific reference is given.

Errors

An error is a mistake, misconception, or misunderstanding on the part of a software developer.

In the category of developer we include software engineers, programmers, analysts, and testers. For example, a developer may misunderstand a design notation, or a programmer might type a variable name incorrectly.

Faults (Defects)

A fault (defect) is introduced into the software as the result of an error. It is an anomaly in the software that may cause it to behave incorrectly, and not according to its specification.

Faults or defects are sometimes called "bugs." Use of the latter term trivializes the impact faults have on software quality. Use of the term "defect" is also associated with software artifacts such as requirements and design documents. Defects occurring in these artifacts are also caused by errors and are usually detected in the review process.

Failures

A failure is the inability of a software system or component to perform its required functions within specified performance requirements [2].

During execution of a software component or system, a tester, developer, or user observes that it does not produce the expected results. In some cases a particular type of misbehavior indicates a certain type of fault is present. We can say that the type of misbehavior is a symptom of the fault. An experienced developer/tester will have a knowledge base of fault/symptoms/failure cases (fault models as described in Chapter 3) stored in memory.

Incorrect behavior can include producing incorrect values for output variables, an incorrect response on the part of a device, or an incorrect image on a screen. During development failures are usually observed by testers, and faults are located and repaired by developers. When the software is in operation, users may observe failures which are reported back to the development organization so repairs can be made.

A fault in the code does not always produce a failure. In fact, faulty software may operate over a long period of time without exhibiting any incorrect behavior. However when the proper conditions occur the fault will manifest itself as a failure. Voas [3] is among the researchers who discuss these conditions, which are as follows:

1. The input to the software must cause the faulty statement to be executed.
2. The faulty statement must produce a different result than the correct statement. This event produces an incorrect internal state for the software.
3. The incorrect internal state must propagate to the output, so that the result of the fault is observable.

Software that easily reveals its' faults as failures is said to be more testable. From the testers point-of-view this is a desirable software attribute. Testers need to work with designers to insure that software is testable. There are other meanings assigned to the terms "testable" and "testability" that will be described later on in this chapter.

Test Cases

The usual approach to detecting defects in a piece of software is for the tester to select a set of input data and then execute the software with the input data under a particular set of conditions. In order to decide whether the software has passed or failed the test, the tester also needs to know what are the proper outputs for the software, given the set of inputs and execution conditions. The tester bundles this information into an item called a test case.

> **A test case in a practical sense is a test-related item which contains the following information:**
>
> 1. *A set of test inputs.* **These are data items received from an external source by the code under test. The external source can be hardware, software, or human.**
> 2. *Execution conditions.* **These are conditions required for running the test, for example, a certain state of a database, or a configuration of a hardware device.**
> 3. *Expected outputs.* **These are the specified results to be produced by the code under test.**

The above description specifies the minimum information that should be found in a test case and is based on the IEEE description for this item [2]. An organization may decide that additional information should be included in a test case to increase its value as a reusable object, or to provide more detailed information to testers and developers. As an example, a test objective component could be included to express test goals such as to execute a particular group of code statements or check that a given requirement has been satisfied. Developers, testers, and/or software quality assurance staff should be involved in designing a test case specification that precisely describes the contents of each test case. The content and its format should appear in test documentation standards for the organization. Chapter 7 gives a more detailed description for a test case and other test-related items.

Test

> **A test is a group of related test cases, or a group of related test cases and test procedures (steps needed to carry out a test, as described in Chapter 7).**

A group of related tests is sometimes referred to as a test set. A group of related tests that are associated with a database, and are usually run together, is sometimes referred to as a test suite [4].

Test Oracle

> A test oracle is a document, or piece of software that allows testers to determine whether a test has been passed or failed.

A program, or a document that produces or specifies the expected outcome of a test, can serve as an oracle [5]. Examples include a specification (especially one that contains pre- and postconditions), a design document, and a set of requirements. Other sources are regression test suites. The suites usually contain components with correct results for previous versions of the software. If some of the functionality in the new version overlaps the old version, the appropriate oracle information can be extracted. A working trusted program can serve as its own oracle in a situation where it is being ported to a new environment. In this case its intended behavior should not change in the new environment [4].

Test Bed

> A test bed is an environment that contains all the hardware and software needed to test a software component or a software system.

This includes the entire testing environment, for example, simulators, emulators, memory checkers, hardware probes, software tools, and all other items needed to support execution of the tests.

Software Quality

Two concise definitions for quality are found in the *IEEE Standard Glossary of Software Engineering Terminology* [2]:

> 1. Quality relates to the degree to which a system, system component, or process meets specified requirements.
>
> 2. Quality relates to the degree to which a system, system component, or process meets customer or user needs, or expectations.

In order to determine whether a system, system component, or process is of high quality we use what are called quality attributes. These are characteristics that reflect quality. For software artifacts we can measure the degree to which they possess a given quality attribute with quality metrics.

> **A metric is a quantitative measure of the degree to which a system, system component, or process possesses a given attribute [2].**

There are product and process metrics. A very commonly used example of a software product metric is software size, usually measured in lines of code (LOC). Two examples of commonly used process metrics are costs and time required for a given task. Many other examples are found in Grady [6]. Appendix I gives additional references that discuss metrics in depth. Quality metrics are a special kind of metric.

> **A quality metric is a quantitative measurement of the degree to which an item possesses a given quality attribute [2].**

Many different quality attributes have been described for software, for example, in *IEEE Standards for Software Quality Metrics Methodology* and work by Schulmeyer and Grady [6–8]. Some examples of quality attributes with brief explanations are the following:

correctness–the degree to which the system performs its intended function

reliability–the degree to which the software is expected to perform its required functions under stated conditions for a stated period of time

usability–relates to the degree of effort needed to learn, operate, prepare input, and interpret output of the software

integrity–relates to the system's ability to withstand both intentional and accidental attacks

portability–relates to the ability of the software to be transferred from one environment to another

maintainability–the effort needed to make changes in the software

interoperability–the effort needed to link or couple one system to another.

Another quality attribute that should be mentioned here is testability. This attribute is of more interest to developers/testers than to clients. It can be expressed in the following two ways:

1. the amount of effort needed to test the software to ensure it performs according to specified requirements (relates to number of test cases needed),
2. the ability of the software to reveal defects under testing conditions (some software is designed in such a way that defects are well hidden during ordinary testing conditions).

Testers must work with analysts, designers and, developers throughout the software life system to ensure that testability issues are addressed.

Software Quality Assurance Group

The software quality assurance (SQA) group in an organization has ties to quality issues. The group serves as the customers' representative and advocate. Their responsibility is to look after the customers' interests.

> **The software quality assurance (SQA) group is a team of people with the necessary training and skills to ensure that all necessary actions are taken during the development process so hat the resulting software conforms to established technical requirements.**

They work with project managers and testers to develop quality-related policies and quality assurance plans for each project. The group is also involved in measurement collection and analysis, record keeping, and reporting. The SQA team members participate in reviews (see Chapter 10), and audits (special types of reviews that focus on adherence to standards, guidelines, and procedures), record and track problems, and verify that corrections have been made. They also play a role in software configuration management (see Chapter 10).

Reviews

In contrast to dynamic execution-based testing techniques that can be used to detect defects and evaluate software quality, reviews are a type of static testing technique that can be used to evaluate the quality of a software artifact such as a requirements document, a test plan, a design document, a code component. Reviews are also a tool that can be applied to revealing defects in these types of documents. A definition follows.

> A review is a group meeting whose purpose is to evaluate a software artifact or a set of software artifacts.

The composition of a review group may consist of managers, clients, developers, testers and other personnel depending on the type of artifact under review. A special type of review called an audit is usually conducted by a Software Quality Assurance group for the purpose of assessing compliance with specifications, and/or standards, and/or contractual agreements.

2.2 Software Testing Principles

Principles play an important role in all engineering disciplines and are usually introduced as part of an educational background in each branch of engineering. Figure 1.1 shows the role of basic principles in various engineering disciplines. Testing principles are important to test specialists/engineers because they provide the foundation for developing testing knowledge and acquiring testing skills. They also provide guidance for defining testing activities as performed in the practice of a test specialist. A principle can be defined as:

1. a general or fundamental, law, doctrine, or assumption;
2. a rule or code of conduct;
3. the laws or facts of nature underlying the working of an artificial device.

Extending these three definitions to the software engineering domain we can say that software engineering principles refer to laws, rules, or doctrines that relate to software systems, how to build them, and how they behave. In the software domain, principles may also refer to rules or codes of conduct relating to professionals who design, develop, test, and maintain software systems. Testing as a component of the software engineering discipline also has a specific set of principles that serve as guidelines for the tester. They guide testers in defining how to test software systems, and provide rules of conduct for testers as professionals. Glenford Myers has outlined such a set of *execution-based* testing principles in his pioneering book, *The Art of Software Testing* [9]. Some of these principles are described below. Principles 1–8, and 11 are derived directly from Myers' original set. The author has reworded these principles, and also has made modifications to the original set to reflect the evolution of testing from an art, to a quality-related process within the context of an engineering discipline. Note that the principles as stated below only relate to execution-based testing. Principles relating to reviews, proof of correctness, and certification as testing activities are not covered.

Principle 1. Testing is the process of exercising a software component using a selected set of test cases, with the intent of (i) revealing defects, and (ii) evaluating quality.

Software engineers have made great progress in developing methods to prevent and eliminate defects. However, defects do occur, and they have a negative impact on software quality. Testers need to detect these defects before the software becomes operational. This principle supports testing as an execution-based activity to detect defects. It also supports the separation of testing from debugging since the intent of the latter is to locate defects and repair the software. The term "software component" is used in this context to represent any unit of software ranging in size and complexity from an individual procedure or method, to an entire software system. The term "defects" as used in this and in subsequent principles represents any deviations in the software that have a negative impact on its functionality, performance, reliability, security, and/or any other of its specified quality attributes.

Bertolino, in the *Guide to the Software Engineering Body of Knowledge,* gives a view of testing as a "dynamic process that executes a program on valued inputs" [10]. This view, as well as the definition of testing given in Chapter 1, suggest that in addition to detecting defects, testing is also a process used to evaluate software quality. The purpose of the former has been described in the previous paragraph. In the case of the latter, the tester executes the software using test cases to evaluate properties such as reliability, usability, maintainability, and level of performance. Test results are used to compare the actual properties of the software to those specified in the requirements document as quality goals. Deviations or failure to achieve quality goals must be addressed.

The reader should keep in mind that testing can have a broader scope as described in test process improvement models such as the TMM and other quality models. Reviews and other static analysis techniques are included under the umbrella of testing in the models. These techniques, and how they relate to detecting defects and evaluating quality will be described in subsequent chapters of this text.

> **Principle 2.** When the test objective is to detect defects, then a good test case is one that has a high probability of revealing a yet-undetected defect(s).

Principle 2 supports careful test design and provides a criterion with which to evaluate test case design and the effectiveness of the testing effort when the objective is to detect defects. It requires the tester to consider the goal for each test case, that is, which specific type of defect is to be detected by the test case. In this way the tester approaches testing in the same way a scientist approaches an experiment. In the case of the scientist there is a hypothesis involved that he/she wants to prove or disprove by means of the experiment. In the case of the tester, the hypothesis is related to the suspected occurrence of specific types of defects. The goal for the test is to prove/disprove the hypothesis, that is, determine if the specific defect is present/absent. Based on the hypothesis, test inputs are selected, correct outputs are determined, and the test is run. Results are analyzed to prove/disprove the hypothesis. The reader should realize that many resources are invested in a test, resources for designing the test cases, running the tests, and recording and analyzing results. A tester can justify the expenditure of the resources by careful test design so that principle 2 is supported.

> **Principle 3.** Test results should be inspected meticulously.

Testers need to carefully inspect and interpret test results. Several erroneous and costly scenarios may occur if care is not taken. For example:

- A failure may be overlooked, and the test may be granted a "pass" status when in reality the software has failed the test. Testing may continue based on erroneous test results. The defect may be revealed at some later stage of testing, but in that case it may be more costly and difficult to locate and repair.

- A failure may be suspected when in reality none exists. In this case the test may be granted a "fail" status. Much time and effort may be spent on trying to find the defect that does not exist. A careful re-examination of the test results could finally indicate that no failure has occurred.

- The outcome of a quality test may be misunderstood, resulting in unnecessary rework, or oversight of a critical problem.

> **Principle 4.** A test case must contain the expected output or result.

It is often obvious to the novice tester that test inputs must be part of a test case. However, the test case is of no value unless there is an explicit statement of the expected outputs or results, for example, a specific variable value must be observed or a certain panel button that must light up. Expected outputs allow the tester to determine (i) whether a defect has been revealed, and (ii) pass/fail status for the test. It is very important to have a correct statement of the output so that needless time is not spent due to misconceptions about the outcome of a test. The specification of test inputs and outputs should be part of test design activities.

In the case of testing for quality evaluation, it is useful for quality goals to be expressed in quantitative terms in the requirements document if possible, so that testers are able to compare actual software attributes as determined by the tests with what was specified.

> **Principle 5.** Test cases should be developed for both valid and invalid input conditions.

A tester must not assume that the software under test will always be provided with valid inputs. Inputs may be incorrect for several reasons.

For example, software users may have misunderstandings, or lack information about the nature of the inputs. They often make typographical errors even when complete/correct information is available. Devices may also provide invalid inputs due to erroneous conditions and malfunctions. Use of test cases that are based on invalid inputs is very useful for revealing defects since they may exercise the code in unexpected ways and identify unexpected software behavior. Invalid inputs also help developers and testers evaluate the robustness of the software, that is, its ability to recover when unexpected events occur (in this case an erroneous input).

Principle 5 supports the need for the independent test group called for in Principle 7 for the following reason. The developer of a software component may be biased in the selection of test inputs for the component and specify only valid inputs in the test cases to demonstrate that the software works correctly. An independent tester is more apt to select invalid inputs as well.

> **Principle 6.** The probability of the existence of additional defects in a software component is proportional to the number of defects already detected in that component.

What this principle says is that the higher the number of defects already detected in a component, the more likely it is to have additional defects when it undergoes further testing. For example, if there are two components A and B, and testers have found 20 defects in A and 3 defects in B, then the probability of the existence of additional defects in A is higher than B. This empirical observation may be due to several causes. Defects often occur in clusters and often in code that has a high degree of complexity and is poorly designed. In the case of such components developers and testers need to decide whether to disregard the current version of the component and work on a redesign, or plan to expend additional testing resources on this component to insure it meets its requirements. This issue is especially important for components that implement mission or safety critical functions.

> **Principle 7.** Testing should be carried out by a group that is independent of the development group.

This principle holds true for psychological as well as practical reasons. It is difficult for a developer to admit or conceive that software he/she has created and developed can be faulty. Testers must realize that (i) developers have a great deal of pride in their work, and (ii) on a practical level it may be difficult for them to conceptualize where defects could be found. Even when tests fail, developers often have difficulty in locating the defects since their mental model of the code may overshadow their view of code as it exists in actuality. They may also have misconceptions or misunderstandings concerning the requirements and specifications relating to the software.

The requirement for an independent testing group can be interpreted by an organization in several ways. The testing group could be implemented as a completely separate functional entity in the organization. Alternatively, testers could be members of a Software Quality Assurance Group, or even be a specialized part of the development group, but in the latter case especially, they need the capability to be objective. Reporting to management that is separate from development can support their objectivity and independence. As a member of any of these groups, the principal duties and training of the testers should lie in testing rather than in development.

Finally, independence of the testing group does not call for an adversarial relationship between developers and testers. The testers should not play "gotcha" games with developers. The groups need to cooperate so that software of the highest quality is released to the customer.

Principle 8. Tests must be repeatable and reusable.

Principle 2 calls for a tester to view his/her work as similar to that of an experimental scientist. Principle 8 calls for experiments in the testing domain to require recording of the exact conditions of the test, any special events that occurred, equipment used, and a careful accounting of the results. This information is invaluable to the developers when the code is returned for debugging so that they can duplicate test conditions. It is also useful for tests that need to be repeated after defect repair. The repetition and reuse of tests is also necessary during regression test (the retesting of software that has been modified) in the case of a new release of the software. Scientists expect experiments to be repeatable by others, and testers should expect the same!

Principle 9. Testing should be planned.

Test plans should be developed for each level of testing, and objectives for each level should be described in the associated plan. The objectives should be stated as quantitatively as possible. Plans, with their precisely specified objectives, are necessary to ensure that adequate time and resources are allocated for testing tasks, and that testing can be monitored and managed.

Test planning activities should be carried out throughout the software life cycle (Principle 10). Test planning must be coordinated with project planning. The test manager and project manager must work together to coordinate activities. Testers cannot plan to test a component on a given date unless the developers have it available on that date. Test risks must be evaluated. For example, how probable are delays in delivery of software components, which components are likely to be complex and difficult to test, do the testers need extra training with new tools? A test plan template must be available to the test manager to guide development of the plan according to organizational policies and standards. Careful test planning avoids wasteful "throwaway" tests and unproductive and unplanned "test–patch–retest" cycles that often lead to poor-quality software and the inability to deliver software on time and within budget.

Principle 10. Testing activities should be integrated into the software life cycle.

It is no longer feasible to postpone testing activities until after the code has been written. Test planning activities as supported by Principle 10, should be integrated into the software life cycle starting as early as in the requirements analysis phase, and continue on throughout the software life cycle in parallel with development activities. In addition to test planning, some other types of testing activities such as usability testing can also be carried out early in the life cycle by using prototypes. These activities can continue on until the software is delivered to the users. Organizations can use process models like the V-model or any others that support the integration of test activities into the software life cycle [11].

Principle 11. Testing is a creative and challenging task [12].

Difficulties and challenges for the tester include the following:

- A tester needs to have comprehensive knowledge of the software engineering discipline.

- A tester needs to have knowledge from both experience and education as to how software is specified, designed, and developed.

- A tester needs to be able to manage many details.

- A tester needs to have knowledge of fault types and where faults of a certain type might occur in code constructs.

- A tester needs to reason like a scientist and propose hypotheses that relate to presence of specific types of defects.

- A tester needs to have a good grasp of the problem domain of the software that he/she is testing. Familiarly with a domain may come from educational, training, and work-related experiences.

- A tester needs to create and document test cases. To design the test cases the tester must select inputs often from a very wide domain. Those selected should have the highest probability of revealing a defect (Principle 2). Familiarly with the domain is essential.

- A tester needs to design and record test procedures for running the tests.

- A tester needs to plan for testing and allocate the proper resources.

- A tester needs to execute the tests and is responsible for recording results.

- A tester needs to analyze test results and decide on success or failure for a test. This involves understanding and keeping track of an enormous amount of detailed information. A tester may also be required to collect and analyze test-related measurements.

- A tester needs to learn to use tools and keep abreast of the newest test tool advances.

- A tester needs to work and cooperate with requirements engineers, designers, and developers, and often must establish a working relationship with clients and users.

- A tester needs to be educated and trained in this specialized area and often will be required to update his/her knowledge on a regular basis due to changing technologies.

2.3 The Tester's Role in a Software Development Organization

Testing is sometimes erroneously viewed as a destructive activity. The tester's job is to reveal defects, find weak points, inconsistent behavior, and circumstances where the software does not work as expected. As a tester you need to be comfortable with this role. Given the nature of the tester's tasks, you can see that it is difficult for developers to effectively test their own code (Principles 3 and 8). Developers view their own code as their creation, their "baby," and they think that nothing could possibly be wrong with it! This is not to say that testers and developers are adversaries. In fact, to be most effective as a tester requires extensive programming experience in order to understand how code is constructed, and where, and what kind of, defects are likely to occur. Your goal as a tester is to work with the developers to produce high-quality software that meets the customers' requirements. Teams of testers and developers are very common in industry, and projects should have an appropriate developer/tester ratio. The ratio will vary depending on available resources, type of project, and TMM level. For example, an embedded real-time system needs to have a lower developer/tester ratio (for example, 2/1) than a simple data base application (4/1 may be suitable). At higher TMM levels where there is a well-defined testing group, the developer/tester ratio would tend to be on the lower end (for example 2/1 versus 4/1) because of the availability of tester resources. Even in this case, the nature of the project and project scheduling issues would impact on the ratio.

In addition to cooperating with code developers, testers also need to work along side with requirements engineers to ensure that requirements are testable, and to plan for system and acceptance test (clients are also involved in the latter). Testers also need to work with designers to plan for integration and unit test. In addition, test managers will need to cooperate with project managers in order to develop reasonable test plans, and with upper management to provide input for the development and maintenance of organizational testing standards, polices, and goals. Finally, testers also need to cooperate with software quality assurance staff and software engineering process group members. In view of these requirements for multiple working relationships, communication and team-working skills are necessary for a successful career as a tester.

If you are employed by an organization that is assessed at TMM levels 1 or 2, you may find that there is no independent software test function in your organization. Testers in this case may be a part of the development group, but with special assignment to testing, or they may be part of the software quality assurance group. In fact, even at levels 3 and higher of the TMM the testers may not necessarily belong to a independent organizational entity, although that is the ideal case. However, testers should always have managerial independence from developers as described in Principle 8, and in the TMM at level 3. Testers are specialists, their main function is to plan, execute, record, and analyze tests. They do not debug software. When defects are detected during testing, software should be returned to the developers who locate the defect and repair the code. The developers have a detailed understanding of the code, and are the best qualified staff to perform debugging.

Finally, testers need the support of management. Developers, analysts, and marketing staff need to realize that testers add value to a software product in that they detect defects and evaluate quality as early as possible in the software life cycle. This ensures that developers release code with few or no defects, and that marketers can deliver software that satisfies the customers' requirements, and is reliable, usable, and correct. Low-defect software also has the benefit of reducing costs such as support calls, repairs to operational software, and ill will which may escalate into legal action due to customer dissatisfaction. In view of their essential role, testers need to have a positive view of their work. Management must support them in their efforts and recognize their contributions to the organization.

KEY TERMS

Error	Software quality
Failure	Software quality assurance group
Fault	Test
Metric	Test bed
Quality	Test case
metric	Test oracle
Review	

EXERCISES

1. Review the definitions of terms in this chapter. Be sure to understand the differences between errors, faults and, failures.

2. With respect to Principle 3–"test results should be meticulously inspected"– why do you think this is important to the tester? Discuss any experiences you have had where poor inspection of test results has led to delays in your testing efforts.

3. Give arguments for/against an independent testing group in an organization. Consider organizational size, resources, culture, and types of software systems developed as factors in your argument.

4. Given the many challenges facing a tester, what types of skills do you believe should be required of a person being hired as a test specialist. (You can compare skill list with the list presented in Chapter 8.)

5. Why, according to Principle 5, is it important to develop test cases for both valid and invalid input conditions?

REFERENCES

[1] *IEEE Standards Collection for Software Engineering,* 1994 edition, copyright 1994 by IEEE, all rights reserved.

[2] *IEEE Standard Glossary of Software Engineering Terminology* (Std 610.12-1990), copyright 1990 by IEEE, all rights reserved.

[3] J. Voas, "A Dynamic Failure Model for Propagation and Infection Analysis on Computer Programs," Ph.D. Thesis, College of William and Mary in Virginia, May 1990.

[4] B. Beizer, *Software Testing Techniques,* second edition, Van Nostrand Reinhold, New York, 1990.

[5] W. Howden, "A survey of dynamic analysis methods," In *Software Testing and Validation Techniques,* second edition, E. Miller, and W. Howden, eds., IEEE Computer Society Press, Los Alamitos, CA, 1981.

[6] R. Grady, *Practical Software Metrics for Project Management and Process Improvement,* Prentice Hall, Englewood Cliffs, NJ, 1992.

[7] *IEEE Standard for a Software Quality Metrics Methodology* (IEEE Std 1061-1992), copyright 1993, by IEEE, all rights reserved.

[8] G. Schulmeyer, "Software quality assurance metrics," in *Handbook of Software Quality Assurance,* G. Schulmeyer and J. McManus, eds., Van Nostrand Reinhold, New York, pp. 318–342.

[9] G. Myers, *The Art of Software Testing,* John Wiley, New York, 1979.

[10] A. Bertolino, "Software testing," in *Guide to the Software Engineering Body of Knowledge,* Trial version, A. Abran, J. Moore, P. Bourque, R. Dupuis, eds. IEEE Computer Society Press, Los Alamitos, CA, 2001.

[11] G. Daich, G. Price, B. Ragland, M. Dawood, *Software Test Technologies Report,* August 1994, Software Technology Support Center (STSC) Hill Air Force Base, UT, August 1994.

[12] J. Whittaker, "What is software testing? and why is it so hard?" *IEEE Software,* Jan./Feb. 2000, pp. 70–79.

DEFECTS, HYPOTHESES,

AND TESTS

3.0 Origins of Defects

The term *defect* and its relationship to the terms *error* and *failure* in the context of the software development domain has been discussed in Chapter 2. Defects have detrimental affects on software users, and software engineers work very hard to produce high-quality software with a low number of defects. But even under the best of development circumstances errors are made, resulting in defects being injected in the software during the phases of the software life cycle. Defects as shown in Figure 3.1 stem from the following sources [1,2]:

1. *Education:* The software engineer did not have the proper educational background to prepare the software artifact. She did not understand how to do something. For example, a software engineer who did not understand the precedence order of operators in a particular programming language could inject a defect in an equation that uses the operators for a calculation.

2. *Communication:* The software engineer was not informed about something by a colleague. For example, if engineer 1 and engineer 2

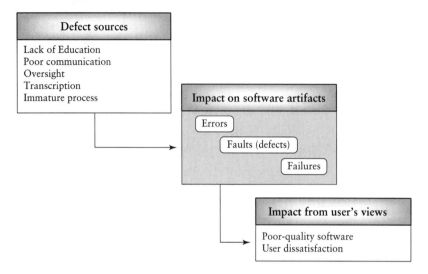

FIG. 3.1

Origins of defects.

are working on interfacing modules, and engineer 1 does not inform engineer 2 that a no error checking code will appear in the interfacing module he is developing, engineer 2 might make an incorrect assumption relating to the presence/absence of an error check, and a defect will result.

3. *Oversight:* The software engineer omitted to do something. For example, a software engineer might omit an initialization statement.
4. *Transcription:* The software engineer knows what to do, but makes a mistake in doing it. A simple example is a variable name being misspelled when entering the code.
5. *Process:* The process used by the software engineer misdirected her actions. For example, a development process that did not allow sufficient time for a detailed specification to be developed and reviewed could lead to specification defects.

When defects are present due to one or more of these circumstances, the software may fail, and the impact on the user ranges from a minor inconvenience to rendering the software unfit for use. Our goal as testers is to discover these defects preferably before the software is in operation. One of the ways we do this is by designing test cases that have a high probability of revealing defects. How do we develop these test cases? One approach is to think of software testing as an experimental activity. The results of the test experiment are analyzed to determine whether the software has behaved correctly. In this experimental scenario a tester develops hypotheses about possible defects (see Principles 2 and 9). Test cases are then designed based on the hypotheses. The tests are run and results analyzed to prove, or disprove, the hypotheses.

Myers has a similar approach to testing. He describes the successful test as one that reveals the presence of a (hypothesized) defect [3]. He compares the role of a tester to that of a doctor who is in the process of constructing a diagnosis for an ill patient. The doctor develops hypotheses about possible illnesses using her knowledge of possible diseases, and the patients' symptoms. Tests are made in order to make the correct diagnosis. A successful test will reveal the problem and the doctor can begin treatment. Completing the analogy of doctor and ill patient, one could view defective software as the ill patient. Testers as doctors need to have knowledge about possible defects (illnesses) in order to develop defect hypotheses. They use the hypotheses to:

- design test cases;

- design test procedures;

- assemble test sets;

- select the testing levels (unit, integration, etc.) appropriate for the tests;

- evaluate the results of the tests.

A successful testing experiment will prove the hypothesis is true—that is, the hypothesized defect was present. Then the software can be repaired (treated).

A very useful concept related to this discussion of defects, testing, and diagnosis is that of a fault model.

> A fault (defect) model can be described as a link between the error made (e.g., a missing requirement, a misunderstood design element, a typographical error), and the fault/defect in the software.

Digital system engineers describe similar models that link physical defects in digital components to electrical (logic) effects in the resulting digital system [4,5]. Physical defects in the digital world may be due to manufacturing errors, component wear-out, and/or environmental effects. The fault models are often used to generate a fault list or dictionary. From that dictionary faults can be selected, and test inputs developed for digital components. The effectiveness of a test can be evaluated in the context of the fault model, and is related to the number of faults as expressed in the model, and those actually revealed by the test. This view of test effectiveness (success) is similar to the view expressed by Myers stated above.

Although software engineers are not concerned with physical defects, and the relationships between software failures, software defects, and their origins are not easily mapped, we often use the fault model concept and fault lists accumulated in memory from years of experience to design tests and for diagnosis tasks during fault localization (debugging) activities. A simple example of a fault model a software engineer might have in memory is "an incorrect value for a variable was observed because the precedence order for the arithmetic operators used to calculate its value was incorrect." This could be called "an incorrect operator precedence order" fault. An error was made on the part of the programmer who did not understand the order in which the arithmetic operators would execute their operations. Some incorrect assumptions about the order were made. The defect (fault) surfaced in the incorrect value of the variable. The probable cause is a lack of education on the part of the programmer. Repairs include changing the order of the operators or proper use of parentheses. The tester with access to this fault model and the frequency of occurrence of this type of fault could use this information as the basis for generating fault hypotheses and test cases. This would ensure that adequate tests were performed to uncover such faults.

In the past, fault models and fault lists have often been used by developers/testers in an informal manner, since many organizations did not save or catalog defect-related information in an easily accessible form. To increase the effectiveness of their testing and debugging processes, software organizations need to initiate the creation of a defect database, or defect repository. The defect repository concept supports storage and retrieval of defect data from all projects in a centrally accessible location. A defect classification scheme is a necessary first step for developing the repository. The defect repository can be organized by projects and for all projects defects of each class are logged, along their frequency of occurrence, impact on operation, and any other useful comments. Defects found both during reviews and execution-based testing should be cataloged. Supplementary information can be added to the defect repository, for example, defect root causes (defect causal analysis is part of the recommended activities/tasks/responsibilities at higher levels of the TMM). Staff members can use this data for test planning, test design, and fault/defect diagnosis. The data can also be used for defect prevention and process improvement efforts at higher levels of testing process maturity.

For organizations that are initiating the development of a defect repository, there are many sources of information about defects, especially defect classes, which are useful for cataloging this type of information. For example, Beizer has an extensive discussion of defects types that he calls a taxonomy of bugs [6]. He describes many defect types, for example, requirements, structural, data, coding, interface, and test design defects. The *IEEE Standard Classification for Software Anomalies* has a collection of classes of anomalies from all life cycle phases [7]. Grady describes a defect classification scheme used at Hewlett-Packard [8]. Kaner et. al. also contains an extensive listing of what the authors call an "outline of common software errors" [9]. The defect categories described below use a combination of these schemes. The focus is mainly on describing those defect types that have an impact on the design and development of execution-based tests.

3.1 Defect Classes, the Defect Repository, and Test Design

Defects can be classified in many ways. It is important for an organization to adapt a single classification scheme and apply it to all projects. No matter which classification scheme is selected, some defects will fit into more than one class or category. Because of this problem, developers, testers, and SQA staff should try to be as consistent as possible when recording defect data. The defect types and frequency of occurrence should be used to guide test planning, and test design. Execution-based testing strategies should be selected that have the strongest possibility of detecting particular types of defects. It is important that tests for new and modified software be designed to detect the most frequently occurring defects. The reader should keep in mind that execution-based testing will detect a large number of the defects that will be described; however, software reviews as described in Chapter 10 are also an excellent testing tool for detection of many of the defect types that will be discussed in the following sections.

Defects, as described in this text, are assigned to four major classes reflecting their point of origin in the software life cycle—the development phase in which they were injected. These classes are: requirements/specifications, design, code, and testing defects as summarized in Figure 3.2. It should be noted that these defect classes and associated subclasses focus on defects that are the major focus of attention to execution-based testers. The list does not include other defects types that are best found in software reviews, for example, those defects related to conformance to styles and standards. The review checklists in Chapter 10 focus on many of these types of defects.

3.1.1 Requirements and Specification Defects

The beginning of the software life cycle is critical for ensuring high quality in the software being developed. Defects injected in early phases can persist and be very difficult to remove in later phases. Since many requirements documents are written using a natural language representation, there are very often occurrences of ambiguous, contradictory, unclear, redundant, and imprecise requirements. Specifications in many organizations are also developed using natural language representations, and these too are subject to the same types of problems as mentioned above. However, over the past several years many organizations have introduced the use of formal specification languages that, when accompanied by tools, help to prevent incorrect descriptions of system behavior. Some specific requirements/specification defects are:

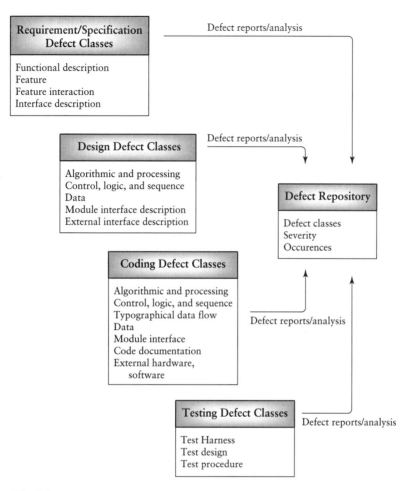

FIG. 3.2

Defect classes and the defect repository.

1. Functional Description Defects

The overall description of what the product does, and how it should behave (inputs/outputs), is incorrect, ambiguous, and/or incomplete.

2. Feature Defects

Features may be described as distinguishing characteristics of a software component or system.

Features refer to functional aspects of the software that map to functional requirements as described by the users and clients. Features also map to quality requirements such as performance and reliability. Feature defects are due to feature descriptions that are missing, incorrect, incomplete, or superfluous.

3. Feature Interaction Defects

These are due to an incorrect description of how the features should interact. For example, suppose one feature of a software system supports adding a new customer to a customer database. This feature interacts with another feature that categorizes the new customer. The classification feature impacts on where the storage algorithm places the new customer in the database, and also affects another feature that periodically supports sending advertising information to customers in a specific category. When testing we certainly want to focus on the interactions between these features.

4. Interface Description Defects

These are defects that occur in the description of how the target software is to interface with external software, hardware, and users.

For detecting many functional description defects, black box testing techniques, which are based on functional specifications of the software, offer the best approach. In Chapter 4 the reader will be introduced to several black box testing techniques such as equivalence class partitioning, boundary value analysis, state transition testing, and cause-and-effect graphing, which are useful for detecting functional types of detects. Random testing and error guessing are also useful for detecting these types of defects. The reader should note that many of these types of defects can be detected early in the life cycle by software reviews.

Black box–based tests can be planned at the unit, integration, system, and acceptance levels to detect requirements/specification defects. Many feature interaction and interfaces description defects are detected using black box–based test designs at the integration and system levels.

3.1.2 Design Defects

Design defects occur when system components, interactions between system components, interactions between the components and outside software/hardware, or users are incorrectly designed. This covers defects in the design of algorithms, control, logic, data elements, module interface descriptions, and external software/hardware/user interface descriptions. When describing these defects we assume that the detailed design description for the software modules is at the pseudo code level with processing steps, data structures, input/output parameters, and major control structures defined. If module design is not described in such detail then many of the defects types described here may be moved into the coding defects class.

1. Algorithmic and Processing Defects

These occur when the processing steps in the algorithm as described by the pseudo code are incorrect. For example, the pseudo code may contain a calculation that is incorrectly specified, or the processing steps in the algorithm written in the pseudo code language may not be in the correct order. In the latter case a step may be missing or a step may be duplicated. Another example of a defect in this subclass is the omission of error condition checks such as division by zero. In the case of algorithm reuse, a designer may have selected an inappropriate algorithm for this problem (it may not work for all cases).

2. Control, Logic, and Sequence Defects

Control defects occur when logic flow in the pseudo code is not correct. For example, branching to soon, branching to late, or use of an incorrect branching condition. Other examples in this subclass are unreachable pseudo code elements, improper nesting, improper procedure or function calls. Logic defects usually relate to incorrect use of logic operators, such as less than ($<$), greater than ($>$), etc. These may be used incorrectly in a Boolean expression controlling a branching instruction.

3. Data Defects

These are associated with incorrect design of data structures. For example, a record may be lacking a field, an incorrect type is assigned to a variable or a field in a record, an array may not have the proper number of elements assigned, or storage space may be allocated incorrectly. Software reviews and use of a data dictionary work well to reveal these types of defects.

4. Module Interface Description Defects

These are defects derived from, for example, using incorrect, and/or inconsistent parameter types, an incorrect number of parameters, or an incorrect ordering of parameters.

5. Functional Description Defects

The defects in this category include incorrect, missing, and/or unclear design elements. For example, the design may not properly describe the correct functionality of a module. These defects are best detected during a design review.

6. External Interface Description Defects

These are derived from incorrect design descriptions for interfaces with COTS components, external software systems, databases, and hardware devices (e.g., I/O devices). Other examples are user interface description defects where there are missing or improper commands, improper sequences of commands, lack of proper messages, and/or lack of feedback messages for the user.

3.1.3 Coding Defects

Coding defects are derived from errors in implementing the code. Coding defects classes are closely related to design defect classes especially if pseudo code has been used for detailed design. Some coding defects come from a failure to understand programming language constructs, and miscommunication with the designers. Others may have transcription or omission origins. At times it may be difficult to classify a defect as a design or as a coding defect. It is best to make a choice and be consistent when the same defect arises again.

1. Algorithmic and Processing Defects

Adding levels of programming detail to design, code-related algorithmic and processing defects would now include unchecked overflow and underflow conditions, comparing inappropriate data types, converting one data type to another, incorrect ordering of arithmetic operators (perhaps due to misunderstanding of the precedence of operators), misuse or omission of parentheses, precision loss, and incorrect use of signs.

2. Control, Logic and Sequence Defects

On the coding level these would include incorrect expression of case statements, incorrect iteration of loops (loop boundary problems), and missing paths.

3. Typographical Defects

These are principally syntax errors, for example, incorrect spelling of a variable name, that are usually detected by a compiler, self-reviews, or peer reviews.

4. Initialization Defects

These occur when initialization statements are omitted or are incorrect. This may occur because of misunderstandings or lack of communication between programmers, and/or programmers and designers, carelessness, or misunderstanding of the programming environment.

5. Data-Flow Defects

There are certain reasonable operational sequences that data should flow through. For example, a variable should be initialized, before it is used in a calculation or a condition. It should not be initialized twice before there is an intermediate use. A variable should not be disregarded before it is used. Occurrences of these suspicious variable uses in the code may, or may not, cause anomalous behavior. Therefore, in the strictest sense of the definition for the term "defect," they may not be considered as true instances of defects. However, their presence indicates an error has occurred and a problem exists that needs to be addressed.

6. Data Defects

These are indicated by incorrect implementation of data structures. For example, the programmer may omit a field in a record, an incorrect type or access is assigned to a file, an array may not be allocated the proper number of elements. Other data defects include flags, indices, and constants set incorrectly.

7. Module Interface Defects

As in the case of module design elements, interface defects in the code may be due to using incorrect or inconsistent parameter types, an incorrect number of parameters, or improper ordering of the parameters. In addition to defects due to improper design, and improper implementation of design, programmers may implement an incorrect sequence of calls or calls to nonexistent modules.

8. Code Documentation Defects

When the code documentation does not reflect what the program actually does, or is incomplete or ambiguous, this is called a code documentation defect. Incomplete, unclear, incorrect, and out-of-date code documentation affects testing efforts. Testers may be misled by documentation defects and thus reuse improper tests or design new tests that are not appropriate for the code. Code reviews are the best tools to detect these types of defects.

9. External Hardware, Software Interfaces Defects

These defects arise from problems related to system calls, links to databases, input/output sequences, memory usage, resource usage, interrupts and exception handling, data exchanges with hardware, protocols, formats, interfaces with build files, and timing sequences (race conditions may result).

Many initialization, data flow, control, and logic defects that occur in design and code are best addressed by white box testing techniques applied at the unit (single-module) level. For example, data flow testing is useful for revealing data flow defects, branch testing is useful for detecting control defects, and loop testing helps to reveal loop-related defects. White box testing approaches are dependent on knowledge of the internal structure of the software, in contrast to black box approaches, which are only dependent on behavioral specifications. The reader will be introduced to several white box–based techniques in Chapter 5. Many design and coding defects are also detected by using black box testing techniques. For example, application of decision tables is very useful for detecting errors in Boolean expressions. Black box tests as described in Chapter 4 applied at the integration and system levels help to reveal external hardware and software interface defects. The author will stress repeatedly throughout the text that a combination of both of these approaches is needed to reveal the many types of defects that are likely to be found in software.

3.1.4 Testing Defects

Defects are not confined to code and its related artifacts. Test plans, test cases, test harnesses, and test procedures can also contain defects. Defects in test plans are best detected using review techniques.

1. Test Harness Defects

In order to test software, especially at the unit and integration levels, auxiliary code must be developed. This is called the test harness or scaffolding code. Chapter 6 has a more detailed discussion of the need for this code. The test harness code should be carefully designed, implemented, and tested since it a work product and much of this code can be reused when new releases of the software are developed. Test harnesses are subject to the same types of code and design defects that can be found in all other types of software.

2. Test Case Design and Test Procedure Defects

These would encompass incorrect, incomplete, missing, inappropriate test cases, and test procedures. These defects are again best detected in test plan reviews as described in Chapter 10. Sometimes the defects are revealed during the testing process itself by means of a careful analysis of test conditions and test results. Repairs will then have to be made.

3.2 Defect Examples: The Coin Problem

The following examples illustrate some instances of the defect classes that were discussed in the previous sections. A simple specification, a detailed design description, and the resulting code are shown, and defects in each are described. Note that these defects could be injected via one or more of the five defect sources discussed at the beginning of this chapter. Also note that there may be more than one category that fits a given defect.

Figure 3.3 shown a sample informal specification for a simple program that calculates the total monetary value of a set of coins. The program could be a component of an interactive cash register system to support retail store clerks. This simple example shows requirements/specification defects, functional description defects, and interface description defects.

The functional description defects arise because the functional description is ambiguous and incomplete. It does not state that the input, number_of_coins, and the output, number_of_dollars and number_of_cents, should all have values of zero or greater. The number_of_coins cannot be negative, and the values in dollars and cents cannot be negative in the real-world domain. As a consequence of these ambiguities and specification incompleteness, a checking routine may be omitted from the design, allowing the final program to accept negative values for the input number_of_coins for each of the denominations, and consequently it may calculate an invalid value for the results.

A more formally stated set of preconditions and postconditions would be helpful here, and would address some of the problems with the specification. These are also useful for designing black box tests.

> **A precondition is a condition that must be true in order for a software component to operate properly.**

In this case a useful precondition would be one that states for example:

$$number\_of\_coins >= 0$$

> **A postcondition is a condition that must be true when a software component completes its operation properly.**

A useful postcondition would be:

$$number\_of\_dollars, number\_of\_cents >= 0.$$

In addition, the functional description is unclear about the largest number of coins of each denomination allowed, and the largest number of dollars and cents allowed as output values.

Specification for Program `calculate_coin_value`

This program calculates the total dollars and cents value for a set of coins. The user inputs the amount of pennies, nickels, dimes, quarters, half-dollars, and dollar coins held. There are six different denominations of coins. The program outputs the total dollar and cent values of the coins to the user.

Inputs: `number_of_coins` is an integer
Outputs: `number_of_dollars` is an integer
`number_of_cents` is an integer

FIG. 3.3

A sample specification with defects.

Interface description defects relate to the ambiguous and incomplete description of user–software interaction. It is not clear from the specification how the user interacts with the program to provide input, and how the output is to be reported. Because of ambiguities in the user interaction description the software may be difficult to use.

Likely origins for these types of specification defects lie in the nature of the development process, and lack of proper education and training. A poor-quality development process may not be allocating the proper time and resources to specification development and review. In addition, software engineers may not have the proper education and training to develop a quality specification. All of these specification defects, if not detected and repaired, will propagate to the design and coding phases. Black box testing techniques, which we will study in Chapter 4, will help to reveal many of these functional weaknesses.

Figure 3.4 shows the specification transformed in to a design description. There are numerous design defects, some due to the ambiguous and incomplete nature of the specification; others are newly introduced.

Design defects include the following:

Control, logic, and sequencing defects. The defect in this subclass arises from an incorrect "while" loop condition (should be less than or equal to six)

```
Design Description for Program calculate_coin_values

Program calculate_coin_values
number_of_coins is  integer
total_coin_value is integer
number_of_dollars is integer
number_of_cents is integer
coin_values is array of  six integers representing
each coin value in cents
initialized to: 1,5,10,25,25,100
begin

initialize total_coin_value to zero
initialize loop_counter to one
while loop_counter is less then six
begin
        output "enter number of coins"
        read (number_of_coins )
        total_coin_value = total_coin_value +
        number_of_coins * coin_value[loop_counter]
        increment loop_counter
end
number_dollars =  total_coin_value/100
number_of_cents = total_coin_value - 100 * number_of_dollars
output (number_of_dollars, number_of_cents)
end
```

FIG. 3.4

A sample design specification with defects.

Algorithmic, and processing defects. These arise from the lack of error checks for incorrect and/or invalid inputs, lack of a path where users can correct erroneous inputs, lack of a path for recovery from input errors. The lack of an error check could also be counted as a functional design defect since the design does not adequately describe the proper functionality for the program.

Data defects. This defect relates to an incorrect value for one of the elements of the integer array, coin_values, which should read 1,5,10,25,50,100.

External interface description defects. These are defects arising from the absence of input messages or prompts that introduce the program to the user and request inputs. The user has no way of knowing in which order the number of coins for each denomination must be input, and when to stop inputting values. There is an absence of help messages, and feedback for user if he wishes to change an input or learn the correct format and order for inputting the number of coins. The output description and output formatting is incomplete. There is no description of what the outputs means in terms of the problem domain. The user will note that two values are output, but has no clue as to their meaning.

The control and logic design defects are best addressed by white box–based tests, (condition/branch testing, loop testing). These other design defects will need a combination of white and black box testing techniques for detection.

Figure 3.5 shows the code for the coin problem in a "C-like" programming language. Without effective reviews the specification and design defects could propagate to the code. Here additional defects have been introduced in the coding phase.

Control, logic, and sequence defects. These include the loop variable increment step which is out of the scope of the loop. Note that incorrect loop condition $(i < 6)$ is carried over from design and should be counted as a design defect.

Algorithmic and processing defects. The division operator may cause problems if negative values are divided, although this problem could be eliminated with an input check.

Data Flow defects. The variable total_coin_value is not initialized. It is used before it is defined. (This might also be considered a data defect.)

Data Defects. The error in initializing the array coin_values is carried over from design and should be counted as a design defect.

External Hardware, Software Interface Defects. The call to the external function "scanf" is incorrect. The address of the variable must be provided (&number_of_coins).

Code Documentation Defects. The documentation that accompanies this code is incomplete and ambiguous. It reflects the deficiencies in the external interface description and other defects that occurred during speci-

```
/*******************************************************************
program calculate_coin_values  calculates the dollar and cents
value of a set of coins of different dominations input by the user
denominations are pennies, nickels, dimes, quarters, half dollars,
and dollars
*******************************************************************/
main ()
{
int total_coin_value;
int number_of_coins = 0;
int number_of_dollars = 0;
int number-of-cents = 0;
int coin_values = {1,5,10,25,25,100};
{
int  i = 1;
while ( i < 6)
{
      printf("input number of coins\n");
      scanf ("%d", number_of_coins);
      total_coin_value = total_coin_value +
      (number_of_coins * coin_value{i]);
}
i = i + 1;
number_of_dollars =  total_coin_value/100;
number_of_cents = total_coin_value - (100 * number_of_dollars);
printf("%d\n", number_of_dollars);
printf("%d\n", number-of-cents);
}

/*****************************************************************/
```

FIG. 3.5

A code example with defects.

fication and design. Vital information is missing for anyone who will need to repair, maintain or reuse this code.

The control, logic, and sequence, data flow defects found in this example could be detected by using a combination of white and black box testing techniques. Black box tests may work well to reveal the algorithmic and data defects. The code documentation defects require a code review for detection. The external software interface defect would probably be caught by a good compiler.

The poor quality of this small program is due to defects injected during several of the life cycle phases with probable causes ranging from lack of education, a poor process, to oversight on the part of the designers and developers. Even though it implements a simple function the program is unusable because of the nature of the defects it contains. Such software is not acceptable to users; as testers we must make use of all our static and dynamic testing tools as described in subsequent chapters to ensure that such poor-quality software is not delivered to our user/client group. We must work with analysts, designers and code developers to ensure that quality issues are addressed early the software life cycle. We must also catalog defects and try to eliminate them by improving education, training, communication, and process.

3.3 Developer/Tester Support for Developing a Defect Repository

The focus of this chapter is to show with examples some of the most common types of defects that occur during software development. It is important if you are a member of a test organization to illustrate to management and your colleagues the benefits of developing a defect repository to store defect information. As software engineers and test specialists we should follow the examples of engineers in other disciplines who have realized the usefulness of defect data. A requirement for repository development should be a part of testing and/or debugging policy statements. You begin with development of a defect classification scheme and then initiate the collection defect data from organizational projects. Forms and templates will need to be designed to collect the data. Examples are the test incident reports as described in Chapter 7, and defect fix reports as described in Chapter 4. You will need to be conscientious about recording each defect after testing, and also recording the frequency of occurrence for each of the defect types. Defect monitoring should continue for each on-going project. The distribution of defects will change as you make changes in your processes. The defect data is useful for test planning, a TMM level 2 maturity goal. It helps you to select applicable testing techniques, design (and reuse) the test cases you need, and allocate the amount of resources you will need to devote to detecting and removing these defects. This in turn will allow you to estimate testing schedules and costs. The defect data can support debugging activities as well. In fact, as Figure 3.6 shows, a defect repository can help to support achievement and continuous implementation of several TMM maturity goals including con-

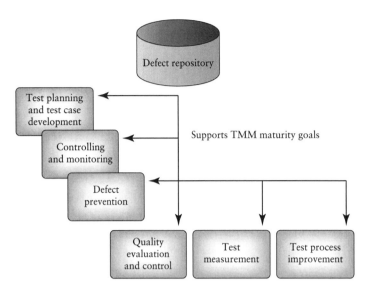

FIG. 3.6

The defect repository, and support for
TMM maturity goals.

trolling and monitoring of test, software quality evaluation and control, test measurement, and test process improvement. Chapter 13 will illustrate the application of this data to defect prevention activities and process improvement. Other chapters will describe the role of defect data in various testing activities.

KEY TERMS ▬▬▬▬▬▬▬▬▬▬▬▬▬▬▬▬▬▬▬▬▬▬▬▬▬▬▬▬▬▬▬▬▬▬

Fault model

Feature

Precondition

Postcondition

EXERCISES ▬▬▬▬▬▬▬▬▬▬▬▬▬▬▬▬▬▬▬▬▬▬▬▬▬▬▬▬▬▬▬▬▬▬

1. What are the typical origins of defects? From your own personal experiences what are the major sources of defects in the software artifacts that you have developed?

2. Programmer A and Programmer B are working on a group of interfacing modules. Programmer A tends to be a poor communicator and does not get along well with Programmer B. Due to this situation, what types of defects are likely to surface in these interfacing modules? What are the likely defect origins?

3. Suppose you are a member of a team that was designing a defect repository. What organizational approach would you suggest and why? What information do you think should be associated with each defect? Why is this information useful, and who would use it?

4. What type of defect classification scheme is used by your university or organization? How would you compare it to the classification scheme used in this text for clarity, learnability, and ease of use?

5. Suppose you were reviewing a requirements document and noted that a feature was described incompletely. How would you classify this defect? How would you insure that it was corrected?

6. Suppose you are testing a code component and you discover a defect: it calculates an output variable incorrectly. (a) How would you classify this defect? (b) What are the likely causes of this defect? (c) What steps could have been taken to prevent this type of defect from propagating to the code?

7. Suppose you are testing a code component and you find a mismatch in the order of parameters for two of the code procedures. Address the same three items that appear in question 6 for this scenario.

REFERENCES

[1] J. Gale, J. Tirso, C. Burchfiled, "Implementing the defect prevention process in the MVS interactive programming organization", *IBM Systems Journal,* Vol. 29, No. 1, 1990.

[2] W. Humphrey, *A Discipline for Software Engineering,* Addison-Wesley, Reading, MA, 1995.

[3] G. Myers, *The Art of Software Testing,* John Wiley, New York, 1979.

[4] M. Abramovici, M. Brever, A. Friedman, *Digital System Testing and Testable Design,* Computer Science Press, New York, 1990.

[5] B. Wilkins, *Principles of Testing in VSLI Circuits and Systems in Silicon,* A. Brown, ed., McGraw-Hill, New York, 1991, pp. 222–250.

[6] B. Beizer, *Software Testing Techniques,* second edition, Van Nostrand Reinhold, New York, 1990.

[7] *IEEE Standard Classification for Software Anomalies* (IEEE Std. 1044-1993), copyright 1994 by IEEE, all rights reserved.

[8] R. Grady, *Practical Software Metrics for Project Management and Process Improvement,* Prentice Hall, Englewoood Cliffs, NJ, 1992.

[9] C. Kaner, J. Falk, H. Nguyen, *Testing Computer Software,* second edition, Van Nostrand Reinhold, New York, 1993.

STRATEGIES AND METHODS FOR TEST CASE DESIGN I

4.0 Introduction to Testing Design Strategies

As a reader of this text, you have a goal to learn more about testing and how to become a good tester. You might be a student at a university who has completed some software engineering courses. Upon completing your education you would like to enter the profession of test specialist. Or you might be employed by an organization that has test process improvement as a company goal. On the other hand, you may be a consultant who wants to learn more about testing to advise your clients. It may be that you play several of these roles. You might be asking yourself, Where do I begin to learn more about testing? What areas of testing are important? Which topics need to be addressed first? The Testing Maturity Model provides some answers to these questions. It can serve as a learning tool, or framework, to learn about testing. Support for this usage of the TMM lies in its structure. It introduces both the technical and managerial aspects of testing in a manner that allows for a natural evolution of the testing process, both on the personal and organizational levels.

In this chapter we begin the study of testing concepts using the TMM as a learning framework. We begin the development of testing skills necessary to support achievement of the maturity goals at levels 2–3 of the Testing Maturity Model. TMM level 2 has three maturity goals, two of which are managerial in nature. These will be discussed in subsequent chapters. The technically oriented maturity goal at level 2 which calls for an organization to "institutionalize basic testing techniques and methods" addresses important and basic technical issues related to execution-based testing. Note that this goal is introduced at a low level of the TMM, indicating its importance as a basic building block upon which additional testing strengths can be built. In order to satisfy this maturity goal test specialists in an organization need to acquire technical knowledge basic to testing and apply it to organizational projects.

Chapters 4 and 5 introduce you to fundamental test-related technical concepts related to execution-based testing. The exercises at the end of the chapter help to prepare you for their application to real-world problems. Testing strategies and methods are discussed that are both basic and practical. Consistent application of these strategies, methods, and techniques by testers across the whole organization will support test process evolution to higher maturity levels, and can lead to improved software quality.

4.1 The Smart Tester

Software components have defects, no matter how well our defect prevention activities are implemented. Developers cannot prevent/eliminate all defects during development. Therefore, software must be tested before it is delivered to users. It is the responsibility of the testers to design tests that (i) reveal defects, and (ii) can be used to evaluate software performance, usabilty, and reliability. To achieve these goals, testers must select a finite number of test cases, often from a very large execution domain. Unfortunately, testing is usually performed under budget and time constraints. Testers often are subject to enormous pressures from management and marketing because testing is not well planned, and expectations are unrealistic. The smart tester must plan for testing, select the test cases, and monitor the process to insure that the resources and time allocated for the job are utilized effectively. These are formidable tasks, and to carry them out effectively testers need proper education and training and the ability to enlist management support.

Novice testers, taking their responsibilities seriously, might try to test a module or component using all possible inputs and exercise all possible software structures. Using this approach, they reason, will enable them to detect all defects. However an informed and educated tester knows that is not a realistic or economically feasible goal. Another approach might be for the tester to select test inputs at random, hoping that these tests will reveal critical defects. Some testing experts believe that randomly generated test inputs have a poor performance record [1]. Others disagree, for example, Duran [2]. Additional discussions are found in Chen [3], and Gutjahr [4].

The author believes that goal of the smart tester is to understand the functionality, input/output domain, and the environment of use for the code being tested. For certain types of testing, the tester must also understand in detail how the code is constructed. Finally, a smart tester needs to use knowledge of the types of defects that are commonly injected during development or maintenance of this type of software. Using this information, the smart tester must then intelligently select a subset of test inputs as well as combinations of test inputs that she believes have the greatest possibility of revealing defects within the conditions and constraints placed on the testing process. This takes time and effort, and the tester must chose carefully to maximize use of resources [1,3,5]. This chapter, as well as the next, describe strategies and practical methods to help you design test cases so that you can become a smart tester.

4.2 Test Case Design Strategies

A smart tester who wants to maximize use of time and resources knows that she needs to develop what we will call effective test cases for execution-based testing. By an effective test case we mean one that has a good possibility of revealing a defect (see Principle 2 in Chapter 2). The ability to develop effective test cases is important to an organization evolving toward a higher-quality testing process. It has many positive consequences. For example, if test cases are effective there is (i) a greater probability of detecting defects, (ii) a more efficient use of organizational resources, (iii) a higher probability for test reuse, (iv) closer adherence to testing and project schedules and budgets, and, (v) the possibility for delivery of a higher-quality software product. What are the approaches a tester should use to design effective test cases? To answer the question we must adopt the view that software is an engineered product. Given this view there are two basic strategies that can be used to design test cases. These are called the black box (sometimes called functional or specification) and white box (sometimes called clear or glassbox) test strategies. The approaches are summarized in Figure 4.1.

Using the black box approach, a tester considers the software-under-test to be an opaque box. There is no knowledge of its inner structure (i.e., how it works). The tester only has knowledge of what it does. The size of the software-under-test using this approach can vary from a simple module, member function, or object cluster to a subsystem or a complete software system. The description of behavior or functionality for the software-under-test may come from a formal specification, an Input/Process/Output Diagram (IPO), or a well-defined set of pre and post conditions. Another source for information is a requirements specification document that usually describes the functionality of the software-under-test and its inputs and expected outputs. The tester provides the specified inputs to the software-under-test, runs the test and then determines if the outputs produced are equivalent to those in the specification. Because the black box approach only considers software behavior and functionality, it is often called functional, or specification-based testing. This approach is especially useful for revealing requirements and specification defects.

The white box approach focuses on the inner structure of the software to be tested. To design test cases using this strategy the tester must have a knowledge of that structure. The code, or a suitable pseudo codelike representation must be available. The tester selects test cases to exercise specific internal structural elements to determine if they are working properly. For example, test cases are often designed to exercise all statements or true/false branches that occur in a module or member function. Since designing, executing, and analyzing the results of white box testing is very time consuming, this strategy is usually applied to smaller-sized pieces of software such as a module or member function. The reasons for the size

Test Strategy	Tester's View	Knowledge Sources	Methods
Black box	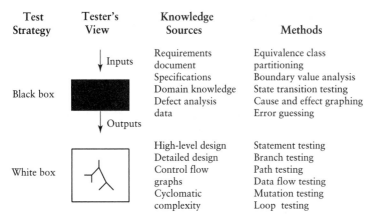	Requirements document Specifications Domain knowledge Defect analysis data	Equivalence class partitioning Boundary value analysis State transition testing Cause and effect graphing Error guessing
White box		High-level design Detailed design Control flow graphs Cyclomatic complexity	Statement testing Branch testing Path testing Data flow testing Mutation testing Loop testing

FIG. 4.1

The two basic testing strategies.

restriction will become more apparent in Chapter 5 where the white box strategy is described in more detail. White box testing methods are especially useful for revealing design and code-based control, logic and sequence defects, initialization defects, and data flow defects.

The smart tester knows that to achieve the goal of providing users with low-defect, high-quality software, *both* of these strategies should be used to design test cases. Both support the tester with the task of selecting the finite number of test cases that will be applied during test. Neither approach by itself is guaranteed to reveal all defects types we have studied in Chapter 3. The approaches complement each other; each may be useful for revealing certain types of defects. With a suite of test cases designed using both strategies the tester increases the chances of revealing the many different type of defects in the software-under-test. The tester will also have an effective set of reusable test cases for regression testing (re-test after changes), and for testing new releases of the software.

There is a great deal of material to introduce to the reader relating to both of these strategies. To facilitate the learning process, the material has been partitioned into two chapters. This chapter focuses on black box methods, and Chapter 5 will describe white box methods and how to apply them to design test cases.

4.3 Using the Black Box Approach to Test Case Design

Given the black box test strategy where we are considering only inputs and outputs as a basis for designing test cases, how do we choose a suitable set of inputs from the set of all possible valid and invalid inputs? Keep in mind that infinite time and resources are not available to exhaustively test all possible inputs. This is prohibitively expensive even if the target software is a simple software unit. As a example, suppose you tried to test a single procedure that calculates the square root of a number. If you were to exhaustively test it you would have to try all positive input values. This is daunting enough! But, what about all negative numbers, fractions? These are also possible inputs. The number of test cases would rise rapidly to the point of infeasibilty. The goal for the smart tester is to effectively use the resources available by developing a set of test cases that gives the maximum yield of defects for the time and effort spent. To help achieve this goal using the black box approach we can select from several methods. Very often combinations of the methods are used to detect different types of defects. Some methods have greater practicality than others.

4.4 Random Testing

Each software module or system has an input domain from which test input data is selected. If a tester randomly selects inputs from the domain, this is called random testing. For example, if the valid input domain for a module is all positive integers between 1 and 100, the tester using this approach would randomly, or unsystematically, select values from within that domain; for example, the values 55, 24, 3 might be chosen. Given this approach, some of the issues that remain open are the following:

- Are the three values adequate to show that the module meets its specification when the tests are run? Should additional or fewer values be used to make the most effective use of resources?

- Are there any input values, other than those selected, more likely to reveal defects? For example, should positive integers at the beginning or end of the domain be specifically selected as inputs?

- Should any values outside the valid domain be used as test inputs? For example, should test data include floating point values, negative values, or integer values greater than 100?

More structured approaches to black box test design address these issues.

Use of random test inputs may save some of the time and effort that more thoughtful test input selection methods require. However, the reader should keep in mind that according to many testing experts, selecting test inputs randomly has very little chance of producing an effective set of test data [1]. There has been much discussion in the testing world about whether such a statement is accurate. The relative effectiveness of random versus a more structured approach to generating test inputs has been the subject of many research papers. Readers should refer to references [2–4] for some of these discussions. The remainder of this chapter and the next will illustrate more structured approaches to test case design and selection of inputs. As a final note there are tools that generate random test data for stress tests. This type of testing can be very useful especially at the system level. Usually the tester specifies a range for the random value generator, or the test inputs are generated according to a statistical distribution associated with a pattern of usage.

4.5 Equivalence Class Partitioning

If a tester is viewing the software-under-test as a black box with well-defined inputs and outputs, a good approach to selecting test inputs is to use a method called equivalence class partitioning. Equivalence class partitioning results in a partitioning of the input domain of the software-under-test. The technique can also be used to partition the output domain, but this is not a common usage. The finite number of partitions or equivalence classes that result allow the tester to select a given member of an equivalence class as a representative of that class. It is assumed that all members of an equivalence class are processed in an equivalent way by the target software.

Using equivalence class partitioning a test value in a particular class is equivalent to a test value of any other member of that class. Therefore, if one test case in a particular equivalence class reveals a defect, all the other test cases based on that class would be expected to reveal the same defect. We can also say that if a test case in a given equivalence class did not detect a particular type of defect, then no other test case based on that class would detect the defect (unless a subset of the equivalence class falls into another equivalence class, since classes may overlap in some cases). A more formal discussion of equivalence class partitioning is given in Beizer [5].

Based on this discussion of equivalence class partitioning we can say that the partitioning of the input domain for the software-under-test using this technique has the following advantages:

1. It eliminates the need for exhaustive testing, which is not feasible.
2. It guides a tester in selecting a subset of test inputs with a high probability of detecting a defect.
3. It allows a tester to cover a larger domain of inputs/outputs with a smaller subset selected from an equivalence class.

Most equivalence class partitioning takes place for the input domain. How does the tester identify equivalence classes for the input domain? One approach is to use a set of what Glen Myers calls "interesting" input conditions [1]. The input conditions usually come from a description in the specification of the software to be tested. The tester uses the conditions to partition the input domain into equivalence classes and then develops a set of tests cases to cover (include) all the classes. Given that only the information in an input/output specification is needed, the tester can begin to develop black box tests for software early in the software life cycle in parallel with analysis activities (see Principle 11, Chapter 2). The tester and the analyst interact during the analysis phase to develop (i) a set of testable requirements, and (ii) a correct and complete input/output specification. From these the tester develops, (i) a high-level test plan, and (ii) a preliminary set of black box test cases for the system. Both the plan and the test cases undergo further development in subsequent life cycle phases. The V-Model as described in Chapter 8 supports this approach.

There are several important points related to equivalence class partitioning that should be made to complete this discussion.

1. The tester must consider both valid and invalid equivalence classes. Invalid classes represent erroneous or unexpected inputs.

2. Equivalence classes may also be selected for output conditions.

3. The derivation of input or outputs equivalence classes is a heuristic process. The conditions that are described in the following paragraphs only give the tester *guidelines* for identifying the partitions. There are no hard and fast rules. Given the same set of conditions, individual testers may make different choices of equivalence classes. As a tester gains experience he is more able to select equivalence classes with confidence.

4. In some cases it is difficult for the tester to identify equivalence classes. The conditions/boundaries that help to define classes may be absent, or obscure, or there may seem to be a very large or very small number of equivalence classes for the problem domain. These difficulties may arise from an ambiguous, contradictory, incorrect, or incomplete specification and/or requirements description. It is the duty of the tester to seek out the analysts and meet with them to clarify these documents. Additional contact with the user/client group may be required. A tester should also realize that for some software problem domains defining equivalence classes is inherently difficult, for example, software that needs to utilize the tax code.

Myers suggests the following conditions as guidelines for selecting input equivalence classes [1]. Note that a condition is usually associated with a particular variable. We treat each condition separately. Test cases, when developed, may cover multiple conditions and multiple variables.

List of Conditions

1. "If an input condition for the software-under-test is specified as a *range* of values, select one valid equivalence class that covers the allowed range and two invalid equivalence classes, one outside each end of the range."

   For example, suppose the specification for a module says that an input, the length of a widget in millimeters, lies in the range 1–499; then select one valid equivalence class that includes all values from 1 to 499. Select a second equivalence class that consists of all values less than 1, and a third equivalence class that consists of all values greater than 499.

2. "If an input condition for the software-under-test is specified as a *number* of values, then select one valid equivalence class that includes the allowed number of values and two invalid equivalence classes that are outside each end of the allowed number."

   For example, if the specification for a real estate-related module say that a house can have one to four owners, then we select one valid equivalence class that includes all the valid number of owners, and then two invalid equivalence classes for less than one owner and more than four owners.

3. "If an input condition for the software-under-test is specified as a *set* of valid input values, then select one valid equivalence class that contains all the members of the set and one invalid equivalence class for any value outside the set."

   For example, if the specification for a paint module states that the colors RED, BLUE, GREEN and YELLOW are allowed as inputs, then select one valid equivalence class that includes the set RED, BLUE, GREEN and YELLOW, and one invalid equivalence class for all other inputs.

4. "If an input condition for the software-under-test is specified as a *"must be"* condition, select one valid equivalence class to represent the "must be" condition and one invalid class that does not include the "must be" condition."

   For example, if the specification for a module states that the first character of a part identifier must be a letter, then select one valid equivalence class where the first character is a letter, and one invalid class where the first character is not a letter.

5. "If the input specification or any other information leads to the belief that an element in an equivalence class is not handled in an identical way by the software-under-test, then the class should be further partitioned into smaller equivalence classes."

To show how equivalence classes can be derived from a specification, consider an example in Figure 4.2. This is a specification for a module that calculates a square root.

The specification describes for the tester conditions relevant to the

```
Function square_root
   message (x:real)
      when x >= 0.0
         reply (y:real)
   where y >= 0.0 & approximately (y*y,x)
otherwise reply exception imaginary_square_root
            end function
```

FIG. 4.2

A specification of a square root function.

input/output variables x and y. The input conditions are that the variable x must be a real number and be equal to or greater than 0.0. The conditions for the output variable y are that it must be a real number equal to or greater than 0.0, whose square is approximately equal to x. If x is not equal to or greater than 0.0, then an exception is raised. From this information the tester can easily generate both invalid and valid equivalence classes and boundaries. For example, input equivalence classes for this module are the following:

EC1.   The input variable x is real, valid.

EC2.   The input variable x is not real, invalid.

EC3.   The value of x is greater than 0.0, valid.

EC4.   The value of x is less than 0.0, invalid.

Because many organizations now use some type of formal or semiformal specifications, testers have a reliable source for applying the input/output conditions described by Myers.

After the equivalence classes have been identified in this way, the next step in test case design is the development of the actual test cases. A good approach includes the following steps.

1.   Each equivalence class should be assigned a unique identifier. A simple integer is sufficient.
2.   Develop test cases for all valid equivalence classes until all have been covered by (included in) a test case. A given test case may cover more than one equivalence class.

3. Develop test cases for all invalid equivalence classes until all have been covered individually. This is to insure that one invalid case does not mask the effect of another or prevent the execution of another.

An example of applying equivalence class partitioning will be shown in the next section.

4.6 Boundary Value Analysis

Equivalence class partitioning gives the tester a useful tool with which to develop black box based-test cases for the software-under-test. The method requires that a tester has access to a specification of input/output behavior for the target software. The test cases developed based on equivalence class partitioning can be strengthened by use of an another technique called boundary value analysis. With experience, testers soon realize that many defects occur directly on, and above and below, the edges of equivalence classes. Test cases that consider these boundaries on both the input and output spaces as shown in Figure 4.3 are often valuable in revealing defects.

Whereas equivalence class partitioning directs the tester to select test cases from any element of an equivalence class, boundary value analysis requires that the tester select elements close to the edges, so that both the upper and lower edges of an equivalence class are covered by test cases. As in the case of equivalence class partitioning, the ability to develop high-quality test cases with the use of boundary values requires experience. The rules-of-thumb described below are useful for getting started with boundary value analysis.

1. If an input condition for the software-under-test is specified as a *range* of values, develop valid test cases for the ends of the range, and invalid test cases for possibilities just above and below the ends of the range.

   For example if a specification states that an input value for a module must lie in the range between -1.0 and $+1.0$, valid tests that include values for ends of the range, as well as invalid test cases for values just above and below the ends, should be included. This would result in input values of -1.0, -1.1, and 1.0, 1.1.

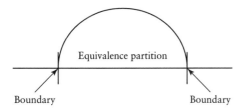

FIG. 4.3
Boundaries of an equivalence partition.

2. If an input condition for the software-under-test is specified as a *number* of values, develop valid test cases for the minimum and maximum numbers as well as invalid test cases that include one lesser and one greater than the maximum and minimum.

   For example, for the real-estate module mentioned previously that specified a house can have one to four owners, tests that include 0,1 owners and 4,5 owners would be developed.

   The following is an example of applying boundary value analysis to output equivalence classes. Suppose a table of 1 to 100 values is to be produced by a module. The tester should select input data to generate an output table of size 0,1, and 100 values, and if possible 101 values.

3. If the input or output of the software-under-test is an ordered set, such as a table or a linear list, develop tests that focus on the first and last elements of the set.

   It is important for the tester to keep in mind that equivalence class partitioning and boundary value analysis apply to testing both inputs and outputs of the software-under-test, and, most importantly, conditions are *not* combined for equivalence class partitioning or boundary value analysis. Each condition is considered separately, and test cases are developed to insure coverage of all the individual conditions. An example follows.

4.7 An Example of the Application of Equivalence Class Partitioning and Boundary Value Analysis

Suppose we are testing a module that allows a user to enter new widget identifiers into a widget data base. We will focus only on selecting equivalence classes and boundary values for the inputs. The input specification for the module states that a widget identifier should consist of 3–15 alphanumeric characters of which the first two must be letters. We have three separate conditions that apply to the input: (i) it must consist of alphanumeric characters, (ii) the range for the total number of characters is between 3 and 15, and, (iii) the first two characters must be letters.

Our approach to designing the test cases is as follows. First we will identify input equivalence classes and give them each an identifier. Then we will augment these with the results from boundary value analysis. Tables will be used to organize and record our findings. We will label the equivalence classes with an identifier ECxxx, where xxx is an integer whose value is one or greater. Each class will also be categorized as valid or invalid for the input domain.

First we consider condition 1, the requirement for alphanumeric characters. This is a "must be" condition. We derive two equivalence classes.

EC1.   Part name is alphanumeric, valid.

EC2.   Part name is not alphanumeric, invalid.

Then we treat condition 2, the range of allowed characters 3–15.

EC3.   The widget identifier has between 3 and 15 characters, valid.

EC4.   The widget identifier has less than 3 characters, invalid.

EC5.   The widget identifier has greater than 15 characters, invalid.

Finally we treat the "must be" case for the first two characters.

EC6.   The first 2 characters are letters, valid.

EC7.   The first 2 characters are not letters, invalid.

Note that each condition was considered separately. Conditions are *not* combined to select equivalence classes. The tester may find later on that a specific test case covers more than one equivalence class.

The equivalence classes selected may be recorded in the form of a table as shown in Table 4.1. By inspecting such a table the tester can

Condition	Valid equivalence classes	Invalid equivalence classes
1	EC1	EC2
2	EC3	EC4, EC5
3	EC6	EC7

TABLE 4.1

Example equivalence class reporting table.

confirm that all the conditions and associated valid and invalid equivalence classes have been considered.

Boundary value analysis is now used to refine the results of equivalence class partitioning. The boundaries to focus on are those in the allowed length for the widget identifier. An experienced tester knows that the module could have defects related to handling widget identifiers that are of length equal to, and directly adjacent to, the lower boundary of 3 and the upper boundary of 15. A simple set of abbreviations can be used to represent the bounds groups. For example:

BLB—a value just below the lower bound

LB—the value on the lower boundary

ALB—a value just above the lower boundary

BUB—a value just below the upper bound

UB—the value on the upper bound

AUB—a value just above the upper bound

For our example module the values for the bounds groups are:

BLB—2   **BUB**—14
LB—3   **UB**—15
ALB—4   **AUB**—16

Note that in this discussion of boundary value analysis, values just above the lower bound (ALB) and just below the upper bound (BUB) were selected. These are both valid cases and may be omitted if the tester does not believe they are necessary.

The next step in the test case design process is to select a set of actual input values that covers all the equivalence classes and the boundaries. Once again a table can be used to organize the results. Table 4.2 shows the inputs for the sample module. Note that the table has the module name, identifier, a date of creation for the test input data, and the author of the test cases.

Table 4.2 only describes the tests for the module in terms of inputs derived from equivalence classes and boundaries. Chapter 7 will describe the components required for a complete test case. These include test inputs as shown in Table 4.2, along with test conditions and expected outputs. Test logs are used to record the actual outputs and conditions when execution is complete. Actual outputs are compared to expected outputs to determine whether the module has passed or failed the test.

Note that by inspecting the completed table the tester can determine whether all the equivalence classes and boundaries have been covered by actual input test cases. For this example the tester has selected a total of nine test cases. The reader should also note then when selecting inputs based on equivalence classes, a representative value at the midpoint of the bounds of each relevant class should be included as a typical case. In this example, a test case was selected with 9 characters, the average of the range values of 3 and 15 (test case identifier 9). The set of test cases presented here is not unique: other sets are possible that will also cover all the equivalence classes and bounds.

Based on equivalence class partitioning and boundary value analysis these test cases should have a high possibility of revealing defects in the module as opposed to selecting test inputs at random from the input domain. In the latter case there is no way of estimating how productive the input choices would be. This approach is also a better alternative to exhaustive testing where many combinations of characters, both valid and invalid cases, would have to be used. Even for this simple module exhaustive testing would not be feasible.

4.8 Other Black Box Test Design Approaches

There are alternative methods to equivalence class partitioning/boundary value analysis that a tester can use to design test cases based on the func-

C1: Positive integer from 1 to 80

C2: Character to search for is in string

The output conditions, or effects are:

E1: Integer out of range

E2: Position of character in string

E3: Character not found

The rules or relationships can be described as follows:

> If C1 and C2, then E2.
> If C1 and not C2, then E3.
> If not C1, then E1.

Based on the causes, effects, and their relationships, a cause-and-effect graph to represent this information is shown in Figure 4.5.

The next step is to develop a decision table. The decision table reflects the rules and the graph and shows the effects for all possible combinations of causes. Columns list each combination of causes, and each column represents a test case. Given n causes this could lead to a decision table with $2n$ entries, thus indicating a possible need for many test cases. In this example, since we have only two causes, the size and complexity of the decision table is not a big problem. However, with specifications having large numbers of causes and effects the size of the decision table can be large. Environmental constraints and unlikely combinations may reduce the number of entries and subsequent test cases.

A decision table will have a row for each cause and each effect. The entries are a reflection of the rules and the entities in the cause and effect graph. Entries in the table can be represented by a "1" for a cause or effect that is present, a "0" represents the absence of a cause or effect, and a "—" indicates a "don't care" value. A decision table for our simple example is shown in Table 4.3 where C1, C2, C3 represent the causes, E1, E2, E3 the effects, and columns T1, T2, T3 the test cases.

The tester can use the decision table to consider combinations of inputs to generate the actual tests. In this example, three test cases are called for. If the existing string is "abcde," then possible tests are the following:

		Valid equivalence classes and bounds	Invalid equivalence classes and bounds
Test case identifier	Input values	covered	covered
1	abc1	EC1, EC3(ALB) EC6	
2	ab1	EC1, EC3(LB), EC6	
3	abcdef123456789	EC1, EC3 (UB) EC6	
4	abcde123456789	EC1, EC3 (BUB) EC6	
5	abc*	EC3(ALB), EC6	EC2
6	ab	EC1, EC6	EC4(BLB)
7	abcdefg123456789	EC1, EC6	EC5(AUB)
8	a123	EC1, EC3 (ALB)	EC7
9	abcdef123	EC1, EC3, EC6	
		(typical case)	

Module name: **Insert_Widget**
Module identifier: **AP62-Mod4**
Date: **January 31, 2000**
Tester: **Michelle Jordan**

TABLE 4.2

Summary of test inputs using equivalence class partitioning and boundary value analysis for sample module.

tional specification for the software to be tested. Among these are cause-and-effect graphing, state transition testing, and error guessing. Equivalence class partitioning combined with boundary value analysis is a practical approach to designing test cases for software written in both procedural and object-oriented languages since specifications are usually available for both member functions associated with an object and traditional procedures and functions to be written in procedural languages. However, it must be emphasized that use of equivalence class partitioning should be complimented by use of white box and, in many cases, other black box test design approaches. This is an important point for the tester to realize. By combining strategies and methods the tester can have more confidence that the test cases will reveal a high number of defects for the effort expended. White box approaches to test design will be described in the next chapter. We will use the remainder of this section to give a description of other black box techniques. Additional discussions are found in Beizer [5,7], Poston [6], Kit [7], and Roper [9]

4.8.1 Cause-and-Effect Graphing

A major weakness with equivalence class partitioning is that it does not allow testers to combine conditions. Combinations can be covered in some cases by test cases generated from the classes. Cause-and-effect graphing is a technique that can be used to combine conditions and derive an effective set of test cases that may disclose inconsistencies in a specification. However, the specification must be transformed into a graph that resembles a digital logic circuit. The tester is not required to have a background in electronics, but he should have knowledge of Boolean logic. The graph itself must be expressed in a graphical language [1].

Developing the graph, especially for a complex module with many combinations of inputs, is difficult and time consuming. The graph must be converted to a decision table that the tester uses to develop test cases. Tools are available for the latter process and allow the derivation of test cases to be more practical using this approach. The steps in developing test cases with a cause-and-effect graph are as follows [1]:

1. The tester must decompose the specification of a complex software component into lower-level units.
2. For each specification unit, the tester needs to identify causes and their effects. A cause is a distinct input condition or an equivalence class of input conditions. An effect is an output condition or a system transformation. Putting together a table of causes and effects helps the tester to record the necessary details. The logical relationships between the causes and effects should be determined. It is useful to express these in the form of a set of rules.
3. From the cause-and-effect information, a Boolean cause-and-effect graph is created. Nodes in the graph are causes and effects. Causes are placed on the left side of the graph and effects on the right. Logical relationships are expressed using standard logical operators such as

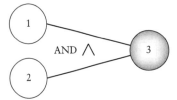

Effect 3 occurs if both causes 1 and 2 are present.

Effect 2 occurs if cause 1 occurs.

Effect 2 occurs if cause 1 does not occur.

FIG. 4.4
Samples of cause-and-effect graph notations.

AND, OR, and NOT, and are associated with arcs. An example of the notation is shown in Figure 4.4. Myers shows additional examples of graph notations [1].

4. The graph may be annotated with constraints that describe combinations of causes and/or effects that are not possible due to environmental or syntactic constraints.
5. The graph is then converted to a decision table.
6. The columns in the decision table are transformed into test cases.

The following example illustrates the application of this technique. Suppose we have a specification for a module that allows a user to perform a search for a character in an existing string. The specification state that the user must input the length of the string and the character to search for. If the string length is out-of-range an error message will appear. the character appears in the string, its position will be reported. If t character is not in the string the message "not found" will be output.

The input conditions, or causes are as follows:

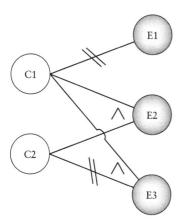

FIG. 4.5

Cause-and-effect graph for the character search example.

Inputs	Length	Character to search for	Outputs
T1	5	c	3
T2	5	w	Not found
T3	90		Integer out of range

One advantage of this method is that development of the rules and the graph from the specification allows a thorough inspection of the specification. Any omissions, inaccuracies, or inconsistencies are likely to be detected. Other advantages come from exercising combinations of test data that may not be considered using other black box testing techniques. The major problem is developing a graph and decision table when there are many causes and effects to consider. A possible solution to this is to decompose a complex specification into lower-level, simpler components and develop cause-and-effect graphs and decision tables for these.

Myers has a detailed description of this technique with examples [1]. Beizer [5] and Roper [9] also have discussions of this technique. Again, the possible complexity of the graphs and tables make it apparent that tool support is necessary for these time-consuming tasks. Although an effective set of test cases can be derived, some testers believe that equivalence class partitioning—if performed in a careful and systematic way—

	T1	T2	T3
C1	1	1	0
C2	1	0	—
E1	0	0	1
E2	1	0	0
E3	0	1	0

TABLE 4.3

Decision table for character search
example.

will generate a good set of test cases, and may make more effective use of a tester's time.

4.8.2 State Transition Testing

State transition testing is useful for both procedural and object-oriented development. It is based on the concepts of states and finite-state machines, and allows the tester to view the developing software in term of its states, transitions between states, and the inputs and events that trigger state changes. This view gives the tester an additional opportunity to develop test cases to detect defects that may not be revealed using the input/output condition as well as cause-and-effect views presented by equivalence class partitioning and cause-and-effect graphing. Some useful definitions related to state concepts are as follows:

> A state is an internal configuration of a system or component. It is defined in terms of the values assumed at a particular time for the variables that characterize the system or component.

> A finite-state machine is an abstract machine that can be represented by a state graph having a finite number of states and a finite number of transitions between states.

During the specification phase a state transition graph (STG) may be generated for the system as a whole and/or specific modules. In object-oriented development the graph may be called a state chart. STG/state charts are useful models of software (object) behavior. STG/state charts are commonly depicted by a set of nodes (circles, ovals, rounded rectangles) which represent states. These usually will have a name or number to identify the state. A set of arrows between nodes indicate what inputs or events will cause a transition or change between the two linked states. Outputs/actions occurring with a state transition are also depicted on a link or arrow. A simple state transition diagram is shown in Figure 4.6. S1 and S2 are the two states of interest. The black dot represents a pointer to the initial state from outside the machine. Many STGs also have "error" states and "done" states, the latter to indicate a final state for the system. The arrows display inputs/actions that cause the state transformations in the arrow directions. For example, the transition from S1 to S2 occurs with input, or event B. Action 3 occurs as part of this state transition. This is represented by the symbol "B/act3."

It is often useful to attach to the STG the system or component variables that are affected by state transitions. This is valuable information for the tester as we will see in subsequent paragraphs.

For large systems and system components, state transition graphs can become very complex. Developers can nest them to represent different levels of abstraction. This approach allows the STG developer to group a set of related states together to form an encapsulated state that can be represented as a single entity on the original STG. The STG developer must ensure that this new state has the proper connections to the unchanged states from the original STG. Another way to simplify the STG is to use a state table representation which may be more concise. A state table for the STG in Figure 4.6 is shown in Table 4.4.

The state table lists the inputs or events that cause state transitions. For each state and each input the next state and action taken are listed. Therefore, the tester can consider each entity as a representation of a state transition.

As testers we are interested in using an existing STG as an aid to designing effective tests. Therefore this text will not present a discussion of development and evaluation criteria for STGs. We will assume that the STGs have been prepared by developers or analysts as a part of the requirements specification. The STGs should be subject to a formal inspection when the requirement/specification is reviewed. This step is required for organization assessed at TMM level 3 and higher. It is essential that

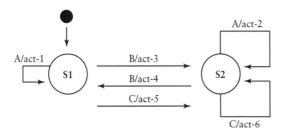

FIG. 4.6

Simple state transition graph.

testers be present at the reviews. From the tester's view point the review should ensure that (i) the proper number of states are represented, (ii) each state transition (input/output/action) is correct, (iii) equivalent states are identified, and (iv) unreachable and dead states are identified. Unreachable states are those that no input sequence will reach, and may indicate missing transitions. Dead states are those that once entered cannot be exited. In rare cases a dead state is legitimate, for example, in software that controls a destructible device.

After the STG has been reviewed formally the tester should plan appropriate test cases. An STG has similarities to a control flow graph in that it has paths, or successions of transitions, caused by a sequence of inputs. Coverage of all paths does not guarantee complete testing and may not be practical. A simple approach might be to develop tests that insure that all states are entered. A more practical and systematic approach suggested by Marik consists of testing every possible state transition [10]. For the simple state machine in Figure 4.6 and Table 4.4 the transitions to be tested are:

> Input A in S1
> Input A in S2
> Input B in S1
> Input B in S2
> Input C in S1
> Input C in S2

The transition sequence requires the tester to describe the exact inputs for each test as the next step. For example the inputs in the above tran-

	S1	S2
Inputs		
Input A	S1 (act-1)	S2 (act-2)
Input B	S2 (act-3)	S1 (act-4)
Input C	S2 (act-5)	S2 (act-6)

TABLE 4.4

A state table for the machine in Figure 4.6.

sitions might be a command, a menu item, a signal from a device or a button that is pushed. In each case an exact value is required, for example, the command might be "read," the signal might be "hot" or the button might be "off." The exact sequence of inputs must also be described, as well as the expected sequence of state changes, and actions. Providing these details makes state-based tests easier to execute, interpret, and maintain. In addition, it is best to design each test specification so that the test begins in the start state, covers intermediate states, and returns to the start state. Finally, while the tests are being executed it is very useful for the tester to have software probes that report the current state (defining a state variable may be necessary) and the incoming event. Making state-related variables visible during each transition is also useful. All of these probes allow the tester to monitor the tests and detect incorrect transitions and any discrepancies in intermediate results.

For some STGs it may be possible that a single test case specification sequence could use (exercise) all of the transitions. There is a difference of opinion as to whether this is a good approach [5,10]. In most cases it is advisable to develop a test case specification that exercises many transitions, especially those that look complex, may not have been tried before, or that look ambiguous or unreachable. In this way more defects in the software may be revealed. For further exploration of state-based testing the following references are suggested, [5,10,11].

4.8.3 Error Guessing

Designing test cases using the error guessing approach is based on the tester's/developer's past experience with code similar to the code-under-test, and their intuition as to where defects may lurk in the code. Code similarities may extend to the structure of the code, its domain, the design approach used, its complexity, and other factors. The tester/developer is sometimes able to make an educated "guess" as to which types of defects may be present and design test cases to reveal them. Some examples of obvious types of defects to test for are cases where there is a possible division by zero, where there are a number of pointers that are manipulated, or conditions around array boundaries. Error guessing is an ad hoc approach to test design in most cases. However, if defect data for similar code or past releases of the code has been carefully recorded, the defect types classified, and failure symptoms due to the defects carefully noted, this approach can have some structure and value. Such data would be available to testers in a TMM level 4 organization.

4.9 Black Box Testing and Commercial Off-the-Shelf (COTS) Components

As software development evolves into an engineering discipline, the reuse of software components will play an increasingly important role. Reuse of components means that developers need not reinvent the wheel; instead they can reuse an existing software component with the required functionality. The reusable component may come from a code reuse library within their organization or, as is most likely, from an outside vendor who specializes in the development of specific types of software components. Components produced by vendor organizations are known as commercial off-the-shelf, or COTS, components. The following data illustrate the growing usage of COTS components. In 1997, approximately 25% of the component portfolio of a typical corporation consisted of COTS components. Estimates for 1998 were about 28% and during the next several years the number may rise to 40% [12].

Using COTS components can save time and money. However, the COTS component must be evaluated before becoming a part of a developing system. This means that the functionality, correctness, and reliability of the component must be established. In addition, its suitability for the application must be determined, and any unwanted functionality must be identified and addressed by the developers. Testing is one process that is not eliminated when COTS components are used for development!

When a COTS component is purchased from a vendor it is basically a black box. It can range in size from a few lines of code, for example, a device driver, to thousands of lines of code, as in a telecommunication subsystem. It most cases, no source code is available, and if it is, it is very expensive to purchase. The buyer usually receives an executable version of the component, a description of its functionality, and perhaps a statement of how it was tested. In some cases if the component has been widely adapted, a statement of reliability will also be included. With this limited information, the developers and testers must make a decision on whether or not to use the component. Since the view is mainly as a black box, some of the techniques discussed in this chapter are applicable for testing the COTS components.

If the COTS component is small in size, and a specification of its inputs/outputs and functionality is available, then equivalence class partitioning and boundary value analysis may be useful for detecting defects and establishing component behavior. The tester should also use this approach for identifying any unwanted or unexpected functionality or side effects that could have a detrimental effect on the application. Assertions, which are logic statements that describe correct program behavior, are also useful for assessing COTS behavior [13]. They can be associated with program components, and monitored for violations using assertion support tools. Such support tools are discussed in Chapter 14.

Large-sized COTS components may be better served by using random or statistical testing guided by usage profiles.

> **Usage profiles are characterizations of the population of intended uses of the software in its intended environment [14].**

More information about usage profiles will be provided in Chapter 12. Other approaches to testing COTS components have been described, for example, by J. Voas [15]. These are not strictly black box in nature.

As in the testing of newly developing software, the testing of COTS components requires the development of test cases, test oracles, and auxiliary code called a test harness (described in Chapter 6). In the case of COTS components, additional code, called glue software, must be developed to bind the COTS component to other modules for smooth system functioning. This glue software must also be tested. All of these activities add to the costs of reuse and must be considered when project plans are developed. Researchers are continually working on issues related to testing and certification of COTS components.

| Certification refers to third-party assurance that a product (in our case a software product), process, or service meets a specific set of requirements.

Some articles on these topics can be found in References 13, 15, and 16.

4.10 Black Box Methods and TMM Level 2 Maturity Goals

Since the TMM is the guiding framework for this text, an association between chapter material and TMM levels will be a feature at the end of most of the book chapters. Activities, tasks, and responsibilities (ATRs) for the three critical groups (developers/testers, managers, users/clients) that bind the chapter material to a given set of maturity goals will be described.

In this chapter we are particularly interested in exploring the nature of the association between black box testing methods and the TMM level 2 maturity goal that reads as follows: "Institutionalize basic testing techniques and methods." The strong association of Chapter 4 material with this goal arises from the fact that black box testing methods are considered to be a part of this basic group of techniques and methods. The methods that were discussed in this chapter provide a systematic approach to test case design that (i) has roots in testing theory, (ii) supports a behavioral view of the software, (iii) is applicable to most levels of testing, (iv) provides sets of practical repeatable procedures for an organization to adapt and reuse, and (v) has associated notations that link testing with other development activities.

An organization that wishes to improve its testing process needs to adopt and consistently apply black box testing methods to software that is being developed and/or maintained. This needs to be accomplished early in the maturity level framework. However, not every black box (or white box) method needs to be used for every project. In fact, some black box methods require more in-depth training and sophisticated tools that the organization may not be ready for at TMM level 2. As the organization grows in maturity it can adapt those black box methods that meet both its needs and the needs of its clients.

Black box methods have ties to the other maturity goals at TMM level 2. For example, use of the methods must be prescribed in the testing goals/policy statements, applied in test plans, and included in training material. Use of black box methods also supports achievement of higher-level TMM maturity goals, for example, integration of testing into the life cycle, software quality evaluation, and quality control.

We now have determined that there are associations between black box testing methods and TMM maturity goals at level 2. Now we need to look at how the key players in the testing process, developers/testers, managers and users/clients can support achievement of this goal. For the remainder of this discussion the reader should keep in mind that at TMM level 2 there is no requirement for an independent test organization. Developers will often take on a dual role of both programmer and tester. As a consequence, note that the ATRs associated with this TMM level refer to a critical view called developer/tester.

As a *developer/tester,* you can play an important role in achieving satisfaction of maturity goals at TMM level 2. Your activities, tasks, and responsibilities include attending classes and training sessions, reading materials, acquiring tools, working with knowledgeable colleagues, and gaining hands-on experience in the application of the black box testing methods. After you master the black box methods in this chapter, you need to insure that a balance of these approaches is used for test design. The black box methods you select as a tester depend on the type of software being tested and the conditions and constraints on testing. For example, if the software-under-test is event or command-driven, then state-based testing should be one of your choices. Object-oriented systems also benefit from this technique. However individual methods in an object/class may also benefit from use of equivalence class partitioning and boundary value analysis. The latter also works well for standard processing systems that are procedural in nature and have well-defined input domains. Error guessing may be used to augment any of the other black box approaches. As a developer/tester you need to insure that white box testing methods are also applied especially for unit and integration test, and that both black and white-box based test cases are included with the test plan. White box testing methods will be described in the next chapter.

In addition to designing black/white-based test cases, you will also design test procedures. Both the test cases and test procedures will become part of the test plan as described in Chapter 7. The test procedures describe the necessary steps to carry out the tests. When the code is ready you will be responsible for setting up the necessary test environment, executing the tests, and observing the results. A part of your test execution responsibilities is to complete a test log, a detailed record of your observations during the test. If any anomalous behavior is observed you will also prepare a problem or test incident report (Chapter 7) which describes the conditions of the test and the anomalous behavior. In the report you should also describe how to reproduce the behavior that you have observed. This will help the person who must repair the code duplicate the conditions. Clues in the test incident report may help to isolate the defect. A defect/problem fix report is prepared when the code is repaired by a developer. The defect/problem fix report should contain the following information:

- project identifier

- the problem/defect identifier

- testing phase that uncovered the defect

- a classification for the defect found

- a description of the repairs that were done

- the identification number(s) of the associated tests

- the date of repair

- the name of the repairer.

The defects found as a result of the testing/debugging processes must be classified according to the organization's defect classification scheme and each should be stored, along with their frequency of occurrence in the defect repository as described in Chapter 3. Chapter 14 will described advanced tools that support these activities.

If a problem occurs while the software is in operation, a problem report issued by the user will be turned over to the development group.

The defect data again is recorded in the defect repository. Your responsibility as a developer/tester is to work with the users to understand the problem. Rerunning existing tests and designing an additional test set will provide supplementary information, and give clues to the location of the defect(s). When the problem/defect is isolated, the necessary repairs can be made and the modified software retested. The SQA group will keep track of the problem and fix reports to ensure that all problems are resolved. A more detailed description of test procedures, test logs, and test incident reports can be found in Chapter 7 under test documentation.

Managers provide support for achievement of TMM level 2 technical goals by insuring that developers/testers have the proper education and training to understand and apply the black box (and white box) methods to develop test cases. Developers/testers also need training to learn to prepare test procedures, test logs, and test incident reports.

Resources to support use of the black/white box methods such as tools and templates need to be supplied by management. Management should encourage cooperation between developer/testers and requirements analysts since the analysts supply the requirements documentation and specifications that are necessary for application of black box methods. Managers should also insure that organization policies and standards are designed to promote the institutionalization of black/white box methods. Test plans should include use of black/white box methods, and allocate adequate time and resources to design and execute the black/white box tests, and analyze the test results.

The *user/client* contribution to the application of black box methods is to give precise, accurate, and unambiguous descriptions of system requirements and specifications so that system behavior can be correctly modeled and used for black box test design.

KEY TERMS

Certification

Finite state machine

System state

Usage profile

EXERCISES

1. Describe the difference between the white box and black box testing strategies.

2. Suppose a tester believes a unit contains a specification defect. Which testing strategy would be best to uncover the defect and why?

3. Explain the differences between random testing and testing using error guessing.

4. Define the equivalence classes and develop a set of test cases to cover them for the following module description. The module accepts a color for a part. Color choices are {RED, BLUE, YELLOW, VIOLET}.

5. Define the equivalence classes and boundary values and develop a set of test cases to cover them for the following module description: The module is part of a public TV membership system. The module allows entry of a contribution from $0.01 to $99,999.99. It also enters a member status for the contributor that can be: regular, student/retiree, or studio club.

6. Develop black box test cases using equivalence class partitioning and boundary value analysis to test a module that is software component of an automated teller system. The module reads in the amount the user wishes to withdraw from his/her account. The amount must be a multiple of $5.00 and be less than or equal to $200.00. Be sure to list any assumptions you make and label equivalence classes and boundary values that you use.

7. Design a set of black box–based test cases using the coin problem specification as shown in Chapter 3. Use error guessing, random testing, equivalence class partitioning, and boundary value analysis to develop your test cases. List any assumptions you make. For each test case generated by equivalence class partitioning, specify the equivalence classes covered, input values, expected outputs, and test case identifiers. Show in tabular form that you have covered all the classes and boundaries. For the other black box testing methods show the test case identifiers, inputs, and expected outputs also in a tabular format. Implement the coin problem as shown in the specification in the language of your choice. Run the tests using your test cases, and record the actual outputs and the defects you found. Start with the original uncorrected version of the program for each black box technique you use. Save a copy of the original version for future use. Compare the methods with respect to their effectiveness in revealing defects. Were there any types of defects that were not detected by these methods?

8. Draw a state transition diagram for a simple stack machine. Assume the stack holds n data items where n is a small positive number. It has operations "push" and "pop" that cause the stack pointer to increment or decrement, respectively. The stack can enter states such as "full" if it contains n items and, "empty" if it contains no items. Popping an item from the empty stack, or pushing an item on the full stack cause a transition to an error state. Based on your state transition diagram, develop a set of black box test cases that cover the key state transitions. Be sure to describe the exact sequence of inputs, as well as the expected sequence of state changes and actions.

9. The following is a specification for a software unit.

   The unit computes the average of 25 floating point numbers that lie on or between bounding values which are positive values from 1.0 (lowest allowed boundary value) to 5000.0 (highest allowed boundary value). The bounding values and the numbers to average are inputs to the unit. The upper bound must be greater than the lower bound. If an invalid set of values is input for the boundaries an error message appears and the user is reprompted. If the boundary values are valid the unit computes the sum and the average of the numbers on and within the bounds. The average and sum are output by the unit, as well as the total number of inputs that lie within the boundaries.

   As in the previous problems, derive a set of equivalence classes for the averaging unit using the specification, and complement the classes using boundary value analysis. Be sure to identify valid and invalid classes. Design a set of test cases for the unit using your equivalence classes and boundary values. For each test case, specify the equivalence classes covered, input values, expected outputs, and test case identifier. Show in tabular form that you have covered all the classes and boundaries. Implement this module in the programming language of your choice. Run the module with your test cases and record the actual outputs. Save an uncorrected version of the program for future use. Provide a defect report containing all the defects you found using the test cases. The defects should have an identification number and a description. Classify the defects using the categories described in Chapter 3 and comment on the effectiveness of your test cases in finding the different types of defects.

10. For the specification in Problem 9, identify the input and output conditions and the rules that relate them. Tabularize your findings and draw a cause-and-effect graph. Develop a decision table and from that table a set of test cases. Run your original module developed for Problem 9 with these test cases and compare

the results to those obtained from equivalence class partitioning. Comment on your observations.

11. Suppose a program allowed a user to search for part name in a specific group of part records. The user inputs the record number that is believed to hold the part, and the part name to search for. The program will inform the user if the record number is within the legal range of allowed record numbers (1–1000). If it is not, then an error message will be issued—"record number is out of range." If the record number is within the range, and the part is found, the program will return "part found," else it will report "part not found." Identify the input and output conditions, i.e., causes and effects. Draw a "cause-and-effect" graph and a decision table for this specification. From the table generate a set of test inputs and expected outputs.

12. Describe the circumstances under which you would apply white box and black box testing techniques to evaluate a COTS component.

13. Suppose you were developing a simple assembler whose syntax can be described as follows :

    <statement> :: = <label field> <op code> <address>
    <label field> :: = "none" | <identifier> :
    <op code> :: = MOVE | JUMP
    <address> :: = <identifier> | <unsigned integer>

A stream of tokens is input to the assembler. The possible states for such an assember are:

S1, prelabel; S2, label; S3, valid op code; S4, valid address; S5, valid numeric address. Start, Error, and Done. A table that describes the inputs and actions for the assembler is as follows:

Inputs	Actions
no more tokens	A1: Put the label in the symbol table.
identifer	A2: Look up the op code and store its binary value in op code field.
MOVE, JUMP	A3: Look up symbol in symbol table and store its value in address field.
colon	A4: Convert number to binary, and store that value in address field.

integer   **A5: Place instruction in the object module, and print a line in the listing.**
A6: Print error message and put all zeroes in the instruction.

Using this information and any assumptions you need to make, develop a state transition diagram for the assembler. From the state transition diagram develop a set of test cases that will cover all of the state transitions. Be sure to describe the exact sequence of inputs as well as the expected sequence of state changes and actions.

14. Describe the role that managers play in institutionalizing basic testing techniques and methods, such as those described in this chapter.

REFERENCES

[1] G. Myers, *The Art of Software Testing;* John Wiley, New York, 1979.

[2] J. Duran, S. Ntafos, "An evaluation of random testing," *IEEE Trans. SW Engineering,* Vol. 10, 1984, pp. 438–444.

[3] T. Chen, Y. Yu, "On the expected number of failures detected by subdomain testing and random testing," *IEEE Trans. Software Engineering,* Vol. 22, 1996, pp. 109–119.

[4] W. Gutjahr, "Partition testing vs. random testing: the influence of uncertainty," *IEEE Trans. Software Engineering,* Vol. 25, No. 5, Sept./Oct. 1999, pp. 661–674.

[5] B. Beizer, *Software Testing Techniques,* second edition, Van Nostrand Reinhold, New York, 1990.

[6] R. Poston, *Automating Specification-Based Software Testing,* IEEE Computer Society Press, Los Alamitos, CA, 1996.

[7] B. Beizer, *Black Box Testing,* John Wiley, New York, 1995.

[8] E. Kit, *Software Testing in the Real World,* Addison-Wesley, Reading, MA, 1995.

[9] M. Roper, *Software Testing,* McGraw Hill, London, 1994.

[10] B. Marick, *The Craft of Software Testing,* Prentice Hall, Englewood Cliffs, NJ, 1995.

[11] D. Harel, "Statecharts: a visual formalism for complex systems," *Science of Computer Programming,* Vol. 8, pp. 231–274, 1987.

[12] J. Voas "Certification: reducing the hidden costs of poor quality," *IEEE Software,* July/August, 1999, pp. 22–25.

[13] B. Korel, I. Burnstein, R. Brevelle, "Post condition–based stress testing in certification of COTS components," *Proceedings of the First International Software Assurance Certification Conference,* Washington, D.C., March 1999.

[14] G. Walton, J. Poore, C. Trammell, "Statistical testing of software based on a usage model: software—practice and experience," Vol. 25, No. 1, 1995, pp. 97–108.

[15] J. Voas, "Certifying off-the-shelf software components," *IEEE Computer,* June 1998, pp. 53–59.

[16] S. Wakid, D. Kuhn, D. Wallace, "Toward credible IT testing and certification," *IEEE Software,* July/August, 1999, pp. 39–47.

STRATEGIES AND METHODS FOR TEST CASE DESIGN II

5.0 Using the White Box Approach to Test Case Design

In the previous chapter the reader was introduced to a test design approach that considers the software to be tested as a black box with a well-defined set of inputs and outputs that are described in a specification. In this chapter a complementary approach to test case design will be examined where the tester has knowledge of the internal logic structure of the software under test. The tester's goal is to determine if all the logical and data elements in the software unit are functioning properly. This is called the white box, or glass box, approach to test case design.

The knowledge needed for the white box test design approach often becomes available to the tester in the later phases of the software life cycle, specifically during the detailed design phase of development. This is in contrast to the earlier availability of the knowledge necessary for black box test design. As a consequence, white box test design follows black box design as the test efforts for a given project progress in time. Another point of contrast between the two approaches is that the black box test design strategy can be used for both small and large software components, whereas white box–based test design is most useful when testing small components. This is because the level of detail required for test design is very high, and the granularity of the items testers must consider when developing the test data is very small. These points will become more apparent as the discussion of the white box approach to test design continues.

5.1 Test Adequacy Criteria

The goal for white box testing is to ensure that the internal components of a program are working properly. A common focus is on structural elements such as statements and branches. The tester develops test cases that exercise these structural elements to determine if defects exist in the program structure. The term exercise is used in this context to indicate that the target structural elements are executed when the test cases are run. By exercising all of the selected structural elements the tester hopes to improve the chances for detecting defects.

Testers need a framework for deciding which structural elements to select as the focus of testing, for choosing the appropriate test data, and for deciding when the testing efforts are adequate enough to terminate the process with confidence that the software is working properly. Such a framework exists in the form of test adequacy criteria. Formally a test data adequacy criterion is a stopping rule [1,2]. Rules of this type can be used to determine whether or not sufficient testing has been carried out. The criteria can be viewed as representing minimal standards for testing a program. The application scope of adequacy criteria also includes:

(i) helping testers to select properties of a program to focus on during test;
(ii) helping testers to select a test data set for a program based on the selected properties;
(iii) supporting testers with the development of quantitative objectives for testing;
(iv) indicating to testers whether or not testing can be stopped for that program.

A program is said to be adequately tested with respect to a given criterion if all of the target structural elements have been exercised according to the selected criterion. Using the selected adequacy criterion a tester can terminate testing when he/she has exercised the target structures, and have some confidence that the software will function in manner acceptable to the user.

If a test data adequacy criterion focuses on the structural properties of a program it is said to be a program-based adequacy criterion. Program-based adequacy criteria are commonly applied in white box testing. They use either logic and control structures, data flow, program text, or faults as the focal point of an adequacy evaluation [1]. Other types of test data adequacy criteria focus on program specifications. These are called specification-based test data adequacy criteria. Finally, some test data adequacy criteria ignore both program structure and specification in the selection and evaluation of test data. An example is the random selection criterion [2].

Adequacy criteria are usually expressed as statements that depict the property, or feature of interest, and the conditions under which testing can be stopped (the criterion is satisfied). For example, an adequacy criterion that focuses on statement/branch properties is expressed as the following:

> **A test data set is statement, or branch, adequate if a test set T for program P causes all the statements, or branches, to be executed respectively.**

In addition to statement/branch adequacy criteria as shown above, other types of program-based test data adequacy criteria are in use; for example, those based on (i) exercising program paths from entry to exit, and (ii) execution of specific path segments derived from data flow combinations such as definitions and uses of variables (see Section 5.5). As we will see in later sections of this chapter, a hierarchy of test data adequacy criteria exists; some criteria presumably have better defect detecting abilities than others.

The concept of test data adequacy criteria, and the requirement that certain features or properties of the code are to be exercised by test cases, leads to an approach called "coverage analysis," which in practice is used to set testing goals and to develop and evaluate test data. In the context of coverage analysis, testers often refer to test adequacy criteria as "coverage criteria" [1]. For example, if a tester sets a goal for a unit specifying that the tests should be statement adequate, this goal is often expressed as a requirement for complete, or 100%, statement coverage. It follows from this requirement that the test cases developed must insure that all the statements in the unit are executed at least once. When a coverage-related testing goal is expressed as a percent, it is often called the "degree of coverage." The planned degree of coverage is specified in the test plan and then measured when the tests are actually executed by a coverage tool. The planned degree of coverage is usually specified as 100% if the tester wants to completely satisfy the commonly applied test adequacy, or coverage criteria. Under some circumstances, the planned degree of coverage may be less than 100% possibly due to the following:

- The nature of the unit

  —Some statements/branches may not be reachable.

  —The unit may be simple, and not mission, or safety, critical, and so complete coverage is thought to be unnecessary.

- The lack of resources

  —The time set aside for testing is not adequate to achieve 100% coverage.

  —There are not enough trained testers to achieve complete coverage for all of the units.

  —There is a lack of tools to support complete coverage.

- Other project-related issues such as timing, scheduling, and marketing constraints

The following scenario is used to illustrate the application of coverage analysis. Suppose that a tester specifies "branches" as a target property for a series of tests. A reasonable testing goal would be satisfaction of the branch adequacy criterion. This could be specified in the test plan as a requirement for 100% branch coverage for a software unit under test. In this case the tester must develop a set of test data that insures that all of the branches (true/false conditions) in the unit will be executed at least once by the test cases. When the planned test cases are executed under the control of a coverage tool, the actual degree of coverage is measured. If there are, for example, four branches in the software unit, and only two are executed by the planned set of test cases, then the degree of branch coverage is 50%. All four of the branches must be executed by a test set in order to achieve the planned testing goal. When a coverage goal is not met, as in this example, the tester develops additional test cases and re-executes the code. This cycle continues until the desired level of coverage is achieved. The greater the degree of coverage, the more adequate the test set. When the tester achieves 100% coverage according to the selected criterion, then the test data has satisfied that criterion; it is said to be adequate for that criterion. An implication of this process is that a higher degrees of coverage will lead to greater numbers of detected defects.

It should be mentioned that the concept of coverage is not only associated with white box testing. Coverage can also be applied to testing with usage profiles (see Chapter 12). In this case the testers want to ensure that all usage patterns have been covered by the tests. Testers also use coverage concepts to support black box testing. For example, a testing goal might be to exercise, or cover, all functional requirements, all equivalence classes, or all system features. In contrast to black box approaches, white box–based coverage goals have stronger theoretical and practical support.

5.2 Coverage and Control Flow Graphs

The application of coverage analysis is typically associated with the use of control and data flow models to represent program structural elements and data. The logic elements most commonly considered for coverage are based on the flow of control in a unit of code. For example,

(i) program statements;
(ii) decisions/branches (these influence the program flow of control);
(iii) conditions (expressions that evaluate to true/false, and do not contain any other true/false-valued expressions);

(**iv**) combinations of decisions and conditions;

(**v**) paths (node sequences in flow graphs).

These logical elements are rooted in the concept of a program prime. A program prime is an atomic programming unit. All structured programs can be built from three basic primes-sequential (e.g., assignment statements), decision (e.g., if/then/else statements), and iterative (e.g., while, for loops). Graphical representations for these three primes are shown in Figure 5.1.

Using the concept of a prime and the ability to use combinations of primes to develop structured code, a (control) flow diagram for the software unit under test can be developed. The flow graph can be used by the tester to evaluate the code with respect to its testability, as well as to develop white box test cases. This will be shown in subsequent sections of this chapter. A flow graph representation for the code example in Figure 5.2 is found in Figure 5.3. Note that in the flow graph the nodes represent sequential statements, as well as decision and looping predicates. For simplicity, sequential statements are often omitted or combined as a block that indicates that if the first statement in the block is executed, so are all the following statements in the block. Edges in the graph represent transfer of control. The direction of the transfer depends on the outcome of the condition in the predicate (true or false).

There are commercial tools that will generate control flow graphs from code and in some cases from pseudo code. The tester can use tool support for developing control flow graphs especially for complex pieces of code. A control flow representation for the software under test facilitates the design of white box–based test cases as it clearly shows the logic elements needed to design the test cases using the coverage criterion of choice.

Zhu has formally described a set of program-based coverage criteria in the context of test adequacy criteria and control/data flow models [1]. This chapter will presents control-flow, or logic-based, coverage concepts in a less formal but practical manner to aid the tester in developing test data sets, setting quantifiable testing goals, measuring results, and evaluating the adequacy of the test outcome. Examples based on the logic elements listed previously will be presented. Subsequent sections will describe data flow and fault-based coverage criteria.

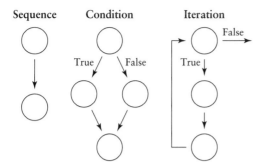

Sequence   Condition   Iteration

FIG. 5.1
Representation of program primes.

5.3 Covering Code Logic

Logic-based white box–based test design and use of test data adequacy/coverage concepts provide two major payoffs for the tester: (i) quantitative coverage goals can be proposed, and (ii) commercial tool support is readily available to facilitate the tester's work (see Chapter 14). As described in Section 5.1, testers can use these concepts and tools to decide on the target logic elements (properties or features of the code) and the degree of coverage that makes sense in terms of the type of software, its mission or safety criticalness, and time and resources available. For example, if the tester selects the logic element "program statements," this indicates that she will want to design tests that focus on the execution of program statements. If the goal is to satisfy the statement adequacy/coverage criterion, then the tester should develop a set of test cases so that when the module is executed, *all* (100%) of the statements in the module are executed at least once. In terms of a flow graph model of the code, satisfying this criterion requires that all the nodes in the graph are exercised at least once by the test cases. For the code in Figure 5.2 and its corresponding flow graph in Figure 5.3 a tester would have to develop test cases that exercise nodes 1–8 in the flow graph. If the tests achieve this goal, the test data would satisfy the statement adequacy criterion.

In addition to statements, the other logic structures are also associated with corresponding adequacy/coverage criteria. For example, to achieve complete (100%) decision (branch) coverage test cases must be designed

```
/* pos_sum finds the sum of all positive numbers (greater than zero) stored in an integer
array a. Input parameters are num_of_entries, an integer, and a, an array of integers with
        num_of_entries elements. The output parameter is the integer sume */
    1.    pos_sum(a, num_of_entries, sum)
    2.        sum = 0
    3.        inti = 1
    4.        while (i <= num_of_entries)
    5.            if a[i] > 0
    6.                    sum = sum + a[i]
                endif
    7.                i = i + 1
            end while
    8.    end pos_sum
```

FIG. 5.2

Code sample with branch and loop.

so that each decision element in the code (if-then, case, loop) executes with all possible outcomes at least once. In terms of the control flow model, this requires that all the edges in the corresponding flow graph must be exercised at least once. Complete decision coverage is considered to be a stronger coverage goal than statement coverage since its satisfaction results in satisfying statement coverage as well (covering all the edges in a flow graph will ensure coverage of the nodes). In fact, the statement coverage goal is so weak that it is not considered to be very useful for revealing defects. For example, if the defect is a missing statement it may remain undetected by tests satisfying complete statement coverage. The reader should be aware that in spite of the weakness, even this minimal coverage goal is not required in many test plans.

Decision (branch) coverage for the code example in Figure 5.2, requires test cases to be developed for the two decision statements, that is, the four true/false edges in the control flow graph of Figure 5.3. Input values must ensure execution the true/false possibilities for the decisions in line 4 (while loop) and line 5 (if statement). Note that the "if" statement has a "null else" component, that is, there is no "else" part. However, we include a test that covers both the true and false conditions for the statement.

A possible test case that satisfies 100% decision coverage is shown in Table 5.1. The reader should note that the test satisfies both the branch

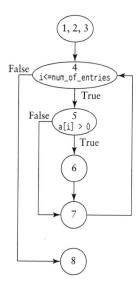

FIG. 5.3

*A control flow graph representation for
the code in Figure 5.2.*

adequacy criterion and the statement adequacy criterion, since all the
statements 1–8 would be executed by this test case. Also note that for this
code example, as well as any other code component, there may be several
sets of test cases that could satisfy a selected criterion.

This code example represents a special case in that it was feasible to
achieve both branch and statement coverage with one test case. Since one
of the inputs, "a," is an array, it was possible to assign both positive and
negative values to the elements of "a," thus allowing coverage of both
the true/false branches of the "if" statement. Since more than one iteration
of the "while" loop was also possible, both the true and false branches
of this loop could also be covered by one test case. Finally, note that the
code in the example does not contain any checks on the validity of the
input parameters. For simplicity it is assumed that the calling module does
the checking.

In Figure 5.2 we have simple predicates or conditions in the branch
and loop instructions. However, decision statements may contain multiple conditions, for example, the statement

Decision or branch	Value of variable i	Value of predicate	Test case: Value of a, num_of_entries
			a = 1, −45,3
			num_of_entries = 3
while	1	True	
	4	False	
if	1	True	
	2	False	

TABLE 5.1

A test case for the code in Figure 5.2 that satisfies the decision coverage criterion.

If $(x < \text{MIN}$ and $y > \text{MAX}$ and (not INT Z))

has three conditions in its predicate: (i) $x < \text{MIN}$, (ii) $y > \text{MAX}$, and (iii) not INT Z. Decision coverage only requires that we exercise at least once all the possible outcomes for the branch or loop predicates *as a whole,* not for each individual condition contained in a compound predicate. There are other coverage criteria requiring at least one execution of the all possible conditions and combinations of decisions/conditions. The names of the criteria reflect the extent of condition/decision coverage. For example, condition coverage requires that the tester insure that each individual condition in a compound predicate takes on all possible values at least once during execution of the test cases. More stringent coverage criteria also require exercising all possible combinations of decisions and conditions in the code. All of the coverage criterion described so far can be arranged in a hierarchy of strengths from weakest to strongest as follows: statement, decision, decision/condition. The implication for this approach to test design is that the stronger the criterion, the more defects will be revealed by the tests. Below is a simple example showing the test cases for a decision statement with a compound predicate.

```
if(age <65 and married = = true)
        do X
        do Y ........
else
        do Z
```

Condition 1: Age less than 65
Condition 2: Married is true

Test cases for simple decision coverage

Value for age	Value for married	Decision outcome (compound predicate as a whole)	Test case ID
30	True	True	1
75	True	False	2

Note that these tests would not exercise the possible outcome for married as false. A defect in the logical operator for condition 2, for example, may not be detected. Test cases 2 and 3 shown as follows would cover both possibilities.

Test cases for condition coverage

Value for age	Value for married	Condition 1 outcome	Condition 2 outcome	Test case ID
75	True	False	True	2
30	False	True	False	3

Note that the tests result in each condition in the compound predicate taking on a true/false outcome. However, all possible outcomes for the decision as a whole are not exercised so it would not satisfy decision/condition coverage criteria. Decision/condition coverage requires that every condition will be set to all possible outcomes and the decision as a whole will be set to all possible outcomes. A combination of test cases 1, 2, and 3 would satisfy this criterion.

Test cases for decision condition coverage

Value for age	Value for married	Condition 1 outcome	Condition 2 outcome	Decision outcome (compound predicate as a whole)	Test case ID
30	True	True	True	True	1
75	True	False	True	False	2
30	False	True	False	False	3

The criteria described above do not require the coverage of all the possible combinations of conditions. This is represented by yet another criterion called multiple condition coverage where all possible combinations of condition outcomes in each decision must occur at least once when the test cases are executed. That means the tester needs to satisfy the following combinations for the example decision statement:

Condition 1	Condition 2
True	True
True	False
False	True
False	False

In most cases the stronger the coverage criterion, the larger the number of test cases that must be developed to insure complete coverage. For code with multiple decisions and conditions the complexity of test case design increases with the strength of the coverage criterion. The tester must decide, based on the type of code, reliability requirements, and resources available which criterion to select, since the stronger the criterion selected the more resources are usually required to satisfy it.

5.4 Paths: Their Role in White Box–Based Test Design

In Section 5.2 the role of a control flow graph as an aid to white box test design was described. It was also mentioned that tools were available to generate control flow graphs. These tools typically calculate a value for a software attribute called McCabe's Cyclomatic Complexity $V(G)$ from a flow graph. The cyclomatic complexity attribute is very useful to a tester [3]. The complexity value is usually calculated from the control flow graph (G) by the formula

$$V(G) = E - N + 2 \qquad (1)$$

The value E is the number of edges in the control flow graph and N is the number of nodes. This formula can be applied to flow graphs where there are no disconnected components [4]. As an example, the cyclomatic complexity of the flow graph in Figure 5.3 is calculated as follows:

$$E = 7, N = 6$$
$$V(G) = 7 - 6 + 2 = 3$$

The cyclomatic complexity value of a module is useful to the tester in several ways. One of its uses is to provide an approximation of the number of test cases needed for branch coverage in a module of structured code. If the testability of a piece of software is defined in terms of the number of test cases required to adequately test it, then McCabes' cyclomatic complexity provides an approximation of the testability of a module. The tester can use the value of $V(G)$ along with past project data to approximate the testing time and resources required to test a software module. In addition, the cyclomatic complexity value and the control flow graph give the tester another tool for developing white box test cases using the concept of a path. A definition for this term is given below.

> **A path is a sequence of control flow nodes usually beginning from the entry node of a graph through to the exit node.**

A path may go through a given segment of the control flow graph one or more times. We usually designate a path by the sequence of nodes it encompasses. For example, one path from the graph in Figure 5.3 is

1-2-3-4-8

where the dashes represent edges between two nodes. For example, the sequence "4-8" represents the edge between nodes 4 and 8.

Cyclomatic complexity is a measure of the number of so-called "independent" paths in the graph. An independent path is a special kind of path in the flow graph. Deriving a set of independent paths using a flow graph can support a tester in identifying the control flow features in the code and in setting coverage goals. A tester identifies a set of independent paths for the software unit by starting out with one simple path in the flow graph and iteratively adding new paths to the set by adding new edges at each iteration until there are no more new edges to add. The independent paths are defined as any new path through the graph that introduces a new edge that has not be traversed before the path is defined.

A set of independent paths for a graph is sometimes called a basis set. For most software modules it may be possible to derive a number of basis sets. If we examine the flow graph in Figure 5.3, we can derive the following set of independent paths starting with the first path identified above.

(i)   1-2-3-4-8
(ii) 1-2-3-4-5-6-7-4-8
(iii) 1-2-3-4-5-7-4-8

The number of independent paths in a basis set is equal to the cyclomatic complexity of the graph. For this example they both have a value of 3. Recall that the cyclomatic complexity for a flow graph also gives us an approximation (usually an upper limit) of the number of tests needed to achieve branch (decision) coverage. If we prepare white box test cases so that the inputs cause the execution of all of these paths, we can be reasonably sure that we have achieved complete statement and decision coverage for the module. Testers should be aware that although identifying the independent paths and calculating cyclomatic complexity in a module of structured code provides useful support for achieving decision coverage goals, in some cases the number of independent paths in the basis set can lead to an overapproximation of the number of test cases needed for decision (branch) coverage. This is illustrated by the code example of Figure 5.2, and the test case as shown in Table 5.1.

To complete the discussion in this section, one additional logic-based testing criterion based on the path concept should be mentioned. It is the strongest program-based testing criterion, and it calls for complete path coverage; that is, every path (as distinguished from independent paths) in a module must be exercised by the test set at least once. This may not be a practical goal for a tester. For example, even in a small and simple unit of code there may be many paths between the entry and exit nodes. Adding even a few simple decision statements increases the number of paths. Every loop multiplies the number of paths based on the number of possible iterations of the loop since each iteration constitutes a different path through the code. Thus, complete path coverage for even a simple module may not be practical, and for large and complex modules it is not feasible.

In addition, some paths in a program may be unachievable, that is, they cannot be executed no matter what combinations of input data are used. The latter makes achieving complete path coverage an impossible task. The same condition of unachievability may also hold true for some branches or statements in a program. Under these circumstances coverage goals are best expressed in terms of the number of *feasible* or *achievable* paths, branches, or statements respectively.

As a final note, the reader should not confuse the coverage based on independent path testing as equivalent to the strongest coverage goal—complete path coverage. The basis set is a special set of paths and does not represent all the paths in a module; it serves as a tool to aid the tester in achieving decision coverage.

5.5 Additional White Box Test Design Approaches

In addition to methods that make use of software logic and control structures to guide test data generation and to evaluate test completeness there are alternative methods that focus on other characteristics of the code. One widely used approach is centered on the role of variables (data) in the code. Another is fault based. The latter focuses on making modifications to the software, testing the modified version, and comparing results. These will be described in the following sections of this chapter.

5.5.1 Data Flow and White Box Test Design

In order to discuss test data generation based on data flow information, some basic concepts that define the role of variables in a software component need to be introduced.

> **We say a variable is defined in a statement when its value is assigned or changed.**

For example in the statements

$$Y = 26 * X$$
$$\text{Read } (Y)$$

the variable *Y* is defined, that is, it is assigned a new value. In data flow notation this is indicated as a *def* for the variable *Y*.

> **We say a variable is used in a statement when its value is utilized in a statement. The value of the variable is not changed.**

A more detailed description of variable usage is given by Rapps and Weyuker [4]. They describe a predicate use (*p-use*) for a variable that indicates its role in a predicate. A computational use (*c-use*) indicates the variable's role as a part of a computation. In both cases the variable value is unchanged. For example, in the statement

$$Y = 26 * X$$

the variable *X* is used. Specifically it has a *c-use*. In the statement

$$\text{if } (X > 98)$$
$$Y = \text{max}$$

X has a predicate or *p-use*. There are other data flow roles for variables such as *undefined* or *dead,* but these are not relevant to the subsequent discussion. An analysis of data flow patterns for specific variables is often very useful for defect detection. For example, use of a variable without a definition occurring first indicates a defect in the code. The variable has not been initialized. Smart compilers will identify these types of defects. Testers and developers can utilize data flow tools that will identify and display variable role information. These should also be used prior to code reviews to facilitate the work of the reviewers.

Using their data flow descriptions, Rapps and Weyuker identified several data-flow based test adequacy criteria that map to corresponding coverage goals. These are based on test sets that exercise specific path segments, for example:

All def
All p-uses
All c-uses/some p-uses
All p-uses/some c-uses
All uses
All def-use paths

The strongest of these criteria is all def-use paths. This includes all p- and c-uses.

```
1       sum = 0                         sum, def
2       read (n),                       n, def
3       i = 1                           i, def
4       while (i <= n)                  i, n p-sue
5            read (number)              number, def
6.           sum = sum + number         sum, def, sum, number, c-use
7            i = i + 1                  i, def, c-use
8       end while
9       print (sum)                     sum, c-use
```

FIG. 5.4

Sample code with data flow
information.

▌ **We say a path from a variable definition to a use is called a def-use path.**

To satisfy the all def-use criterion the tester must identify and classify occurrences of all the variables in the software under test. A tabular summary is useful. Then for each variable, test data is generated so that all definitions and all uses for all of the variables are exercised during test. As an example we will work with the code in Figure 5.4 that calculates the sum of *n* numbers

The variables of interest are sum, *i, n,* and number. Since the goal is to satisfy the all def-use criteria we will need to tabulate the def-use occurrences for each of these variables. The data flow role for each variable in each statement of the example is shown beside the statement in italics. Tabulating the results for each variable we generate the following tables. On the table each def-use pair is assigned an identifier. Line numbers are used to show occurrence of the *def* or *use*. Note that in some statements a given variable is both defined and used.

Table for n

pair id	def	use
1	2	4

Table for number

pair id	def	use
1	5	6

Table for sum

pair id	def	use
1	1	6
2	1	9
3	6	6
4	6	9

Table for i

pair id	def	use
1	3	4
2	3	7
3	7	7
4	7	4

After completion of the tables, the tester then generates test data to exercise all of these def-use pairs In many cases a small set of test inputs will cover several or all def-use paths. For this example two sets of test data would cover all the def-use pairs for the variables:

Test data set 1: $n = 0$

Test data set 2: $n = 5$, number = 1,2,3,4,5

Set 1 covers pair 1 for n, pair 2 for sum, and pair 1 for i. Set 2 covers pair 1 for n, pair 1 for number, pairs 1,3,4 for sum, and pairs 1,2,3,4 for i. Note even for this small piece of code there are four tables and four def-use pairs for two of the variables.

As with most white box testing methods, the data flow approach is most effective at the unit level of testing. When code becomes more complex and there are more variables to consider it becomes more time consuming for the tester to analyze data flow roles, identify paths, and design the tests. Other problems with data flow oriented testing occur in the handling of dynamically bound variables such as pointers. Finally, there are no commercially available tools that provide strong support for data flow testing, such as those that support control-flow based testing. In the latter case, tools that determine the degree of coverage, and which portions of the code are yet uncovered, are of particular importance. These are not available for data flow methods. For examples of prototype tools and further discussion of data flow testing see Beizer [4], Laski [6], Rapps [5], Clarke [7], Horgan [8] and Ostrand [9].

5.5.2 Loop Testing

Loops are among the most frequently used control structures. Experienced software engineers realize that many defects are associated with loop constructs. These are often due to poor programming practices and lack of reviews. Therefore, special attention should be paid to loops during testing. Beizer has classified loops into four categories: simple, nested, concatenated, and unstructured [4]. He advises that if instances of unstructured loops are found in legacy code they should be redesigned to reflect structured programming techniques. Testers can then focus on the remaining categories of loops.

Loop testing strategies focus on detecting common defects associated with these structures. For example, in a simple loop that can have a range of zero to n iterations, test cases should be developed so that there are:

(i)   zero iterations of the loop, i.e., the loop is skipped in its entirely;
(ii)   one iteration of the loop;
(iii)   two iterations of the loop;
(iv) k iterations of the loop where $k < n;$
(v) $n - 1$ iterations of the loop;
(vi) $n + 1$ iterations of the loop (if possible).

If the loop has a nonzero minimum number of iterations, try one less than the minimum. Other cases to consider for loops are negative values for the loop control variable, and $n + 1$ iterations of the loop if that is possible. Zhu has described a historical loop count adequacy criterion that states that in the case of a loop having a maximum of n iterations, tests that execute the loop zero times, once, twice, and so on up to n times are required [1].

Beizer has some suggestions for testing nested loops where the outer loop control variables are set to minimum values and the innermost loop is exercised as above. The tester then moves up one loop level and finally tests all the loops simultaneously. This will limit the number of tests to perform; however, the number of test under these circumstances is still large and the tester may have to make trade-offs. Beizer also has suggestions for testing concatenated loops [4].

5.5.3 Mutation Testing

In Chapters 4 and 5 we have studied test data generation approaches that depend on code behavior and code structure. Mutation testing is another approach to test data generation that requires knowledge of code structure, but it is classified as a fault-based testing approach. It considers the possible faults that could occur in a software component as the basis for test data generation and evaluation of testing effectiveness.

Mutation testing makes two major assumptions:

1. *The competent programmer hypothesis.* This states that a competent programmer writes programs that are nearly correct. Therefore we can assume that there are no major construction errors in the program; the code is correct except for a simple error(s).
2. *The coupling effect.* This effect relates to questions a tester might have about how well mutation testing can detect complex errors since the changes made to the code are very simple. DeMillo has commented on that issue as far back as 1978 [10]. He states that test data that can distinguish all programs differing from a correct one only by simple errors are sensitive enough to distinguish it from programs with more complex errors.

Mutation testing starts with a code component, its associated test cases, and the test results. The original code component is modified in a simple way to provide a set of similar components that are called mutants. Each mutant contains a fault as a result of the modification. The original test data is then run with the mutants. If the test data reveals the fault in the mutant (the result of the modification) by producing a different output as a result of execution, then the mutant is said to be killed. If the mutants do not produce outputs that differ from the original with the test data, then the test data are not capable of revealing such defects. The tests cannot distinguish the original from the mutant. The tester then must develop additional test data to reveal the fault and kill the mutants.

A test data adequacy criterion that is applicable here is the following [11]:

> **A test set T is said to be mutation adequate for program *P* provided that for every inequivalent mutant *Pi* of *P* there is an element *t* in *T* such that *Pi(t)* is not equal to *P(t)*.**

The term T represents the test set, and t is a test case in the test set. For the test data to be adequate according to this criterion, a correct program must behave correctly and all incorrect programs behave incorrectly for the given test data.

Mutations are simple changes in the original code component, for example: constant replacement, arithmetic operator replacement, data statement alteration, statement deletion, and logical operator replacement. There are existing tools that will easily generate mutants. Tool users need only to select a change operator. To illustrate the types of changes made in mutation testing we can make use of the code in Figure 5.2. A first mutation could be to change line 7 from

$$i = i + 1 \quad \text{to} \quad i = i + 2.$$

If we rerun the tests used for branch coverage as in Table 5.1 this mutant will be killed, that is, the output will be different than for the original code. Another change we could make is in line 5, from

$$\text{if } a[i] > 0 \quad \text{to} \quad \text{if } a[i] < 0.$$

This mutant would also be killed by the original test data. Therefore, we can assume that our original tests would have caught this type of defect. However, if we made a change in line 5 to read

$$\text{if } a[i] > = 0,$$

this mutant would not be killed by our original test data in Table 5.1. Our inclination would be to augment the test data with a case that included a zero in the array elements, for example:

$$a = 0, 45, 3, \text{SIZE} = 3.$$

However, this test would not cause the mutant to be killed because adding a zero to the output variable sum does not change its final value. In this case it is not possible to kill the mutant. When this occurs, the mutant is said to be equivalent to the original program.

To measure the mutation adequacy of a test set T for a program P we can use what is called a mutation score (MS), which is calculated as follows [12]:

$$\text{MS } (P,T) = \frac{\text{\# of dead mutants}}{\text{\# total mutants } - \text{ \# of equivalent mutants}}$$

Equivalent mutants are discarded from the mutant set because they do not contribute to the adequacy of the test set.

Mutation testing is useful in that it can show that certain faults as represented in the mutants are not likely to be present since they would have been revealed by test data. It also helps the tester to generate hypotheses about the different types of possible faults in the code and to develop test cases to reveal them. As previously mentioned there are tools to support developers and testers with producing mutants. In fact, many hundreds of mutants can be produced easily. However, running the tests, analyzing results, and developing additional tests, if needed, to kill the mutants are all time consuming. For these reasons mutation testing is usually applied at the unit level. However, recent research in an area called interface mutation (the application of mutation testing to evaluate how well unit interfaces have been tested) has suggested that it can be applied effectively at the integration test level as well [12].

Mutation testing as described above is called strong mutation testing. There are variations that reduce the number of mutants produced. One of these is called weak mutation testing which focuses on specific code components and is described by Howden [13].

5.6 Evaluating Test Adequacy Criteria

Most of the white box testing approaches we have discussed so far are associated with application of an adequacy criterion. Testers are often faced with the decision of which criterion to apply to a given item under test given the nature of the item and the constraints of the test environment (time, costs, resources) One source of information the tester can use to select an appropriate criterion is the test adequacy criterion hierarchy as shown in Figure 5.5 which describes a subsumes relationship among the criteria. Satisfying an adequacy criterion at the higher levels of the hierarchy implies a greater thoroughness in testing [1,14–16]. The criteria at the top of the hierarchy are said to subsume those at the lower levels. For example, achieving all definition-use (def-use) path adequacy means the tester has also achieved both branch and statement adequacy. Note from the hierarchy that statement adequacy is the weakest of the test adequacy criteria. Unfortunately, in many organizations achieving a high level of statement coverage is not even included as a *minimal* testing goal.

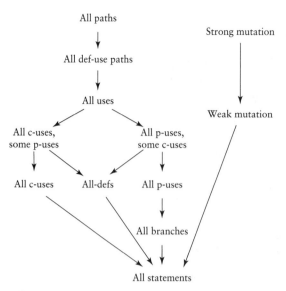

FIG. 5.5

A partial ordering for test adequacy criteria.

As a conscientious tester you might at first reason that your testing goal should be to develop tests that can satisfy the most stringent criterion. However, you should consider that each adequacy criterion has both strengths and weaknesses. Each, is effective in revealing certain types of defects. Application of the so-called "stronger" criteria usually requires more tester time and resources. This translates into higher testing costs. Testing conditions, and the nature of the software should guide your choice of a criterion.

Support for evaluating test adequacy criteria comes from a theoretical treatment developed by Weyuker [2]. She presents a set of axioms that allow testers to formalize properties which should be satisfied by any good program-based test data adequacy criterion. Testers can use the axioms to

* recognize both strong and weak adequacy criteria; a tester may decide to use a weak criterion, but should be aware of its weakness with respect to the properties described by the axioms;

- focus attention on the properties that an effective test data adequacy criterion should exhibit;

- select an appropriate criterion for the item under test;

- stimulate thought for the development of new criteria; the axioms are the framework with which to evaluate these new criteria.

The axioms are based on the following set of assumptions [2]:

(i)   programs are written in a structured programming language;
(ii) programs are SESE (single entry/single exit);
(iii) all input statements appear at the beginning of the program;
(iv) all output statements appear at the end of the program.

The axioms/properties described by Weyuker are the following [2]:

1. Applicability Property

"For every program there exists an adequate test set." What this axiom means is that for all programs we should be able to design an adequate test set that properly tests it. The test set may be very large so the tester will want to select representable points of the specification domain to test it. If we test on all representable points, that is called an exhaustive test set. The exhaustive test set will surely be adequate since there will be no other test data that we can generate. However, in past discussions we have ruled out exhaustive testing because in most cases it is too expensive, time consuming, and impractical.

2. Nonexhaustive Applicability Property

"For a program P and a test set T, P is adequately tested by the test set T, and T is not an exhaustive test set." To paraphrase, a tester does not need an exhaustive test set in order to adequately test a program.

3. Monotonicity Property

"If a test set T is adequate for program P, and if T is equal to, or a subset of T', then T' is adequate for program P."

4. Inadequate Empty Set

"An empty test set is not an adequate test for any program." If a program is not tested at all, a tester cannot claim it has been adequately tested!

Note that these first four axioms are very general and apply to all programs independent of programming language and equally apply to uses of both program- and specification-based testing. For some of the next group of axioms this is not true.

5. Antiextensionality Property

"There are programs P and Q such that P is equivalent to Q, and T is adequate for P, but T is not adequate for Q." We can interpret this axiom as saying that just because two programs are *semantically* equivalent (they may perform the same function) does not mean we should test them the same way. Their implementations (code structure) may be very different. The reader should note that if programs have equivalent specifications then their test sets may coincide using black box testing techniques, but this axiom applies to program-based testing and it is the differences that may occur in program code that make it necessary to test P and Q with different test sets.

6. General Multiple Change Property

"There are programs P and Q that have the same shape, and there is a test set T such that T is adequate for P, but is not adequate for Q." Here Weyuker introduces the concept of shape to express a syntactic equivalence. She states that two programs are the same shape if one can be transformed into the other by applying the set of rules shown below any number of times:

(i)   replace relational operator $r1$ in a predicate with relational operator $r2$;
(ii) replace constant $c1$ in a predicate of an assignment statement with constant $c2$;
(iii) replace arithmetic operator $a1$ in an assignment statement with arithmetic operator $a2$.

Axiom 5 says that *semantic* closeness is not sufficient to imply that two programs should be tested in the same way. Given this definition of shape, Axiom 6 says that even the *syntactic* closeness of two programs is not strong enough reason to imply they should be tested in the same way.

7. Antidecomposition Property

"There is a program P and a component Q such that T is adequate for P, T' is the set of vectors of values that variables can assume on entrance to Q for some t in T, and T' is not adequate for Q." This axiom states that although an encompassing program has been adequately tested, it does not follow that each of its components parts has been properly tested. Implications for this axiom are:

1. a routine that has been adequately tested in one environment may not have been adequately tested to work in another environment, the environment being the enclosing program.
2. although we may think of P, the enclosing program, as being more complex than Q it may not be. Q may be more semantically complex; it may lie on an unexecutable path of P, and thus would have the null set, as its test set, which would violate Axiom 4.

8. Anticomposition Property

"There are programs P and Q, and test set T, such that T is adequate for P, and the set of vectors of values that variables can assume on entrance to Q for inputs in T is adequate for Q, but T is not adequate for P; Q (the composition of P and Q)." Paraphrasing this axiom we can say that adequately testing each individual program component in isolation does not necessarily mean that we have adequately tested the entire program (the program as a whole). When we integrate two separate program components, there are interactions that cannot arise in the isolated components. Axioms 7 and 8 have special impact on the testing of object oriented code. These issues are covered in Chapter 6.

9. Renaming Property

"If P is a renaming of Q, then T is adequate for P only if T is adequate for Q. A program P is a renaming of Q if P is identical to Q expect for the fact that all instances of an identifier, let us say *a* in *Q* have been replaced in *P* by an identifier, let us say *b*, where "*b*" does not occur in *Q*, or if there is a set of such renamed identifiers." This axiom simply says that an inessential change in a program such as changing the names of the variables should not change the nature of the test data that are needed to adequately test the program.

10. Complexity Property

"For every *n*, there is a program *P* such that *P* is adequately tested by a size *n* test set, but not by any size *n* − 1 test set." This means that for every program, there are other programs that require more testing.

11. Statement Coverage Property

"If the test set *T* is adequate for *P*, then *T* causes every executable statement of *P* to be executed." Ensuring that their test set executed all statements in a program is a minimum coverage goal for a tester. A tester soon realizes that if some portion of the program has never been executed, then that portion could contain defects: it could be totally in error and be working improperly. Testing would not be able to detect any defects in this portion of the code. However, this axiom implies that a tester needs to be able to determine which statements of a program are executable. It is possible that not all of program statements are executable. Unfortunately, there is no algorithm to support the tester in the latter task, but Weyuker believes that developers/testers are quite good at determining whether or not code is, or is not, executable [2]. Issues relating to infeasible (unexecutable) paths, statements, and branches have been discussed in Section 5.4.

The first eight axioms as described by Weyuker exposed weaknesses in several well-known program-based adequacy criteria. For example, both statement and branch adequacy criteria were found to fail in satisfying several of the axioms including the applicability axiom. Some data flow adequacy criteria also failed to satisfy the applicability axiom. An additional three axioms/properties (shown here as 9–11) were added to the original set to provide an even stronger framework for evaluating test adequacy criteria. Weyuker meant for these axioms to be used as a tool by testers to understand the strengths and weaknesses of the criteria they select. Note that each criterion has a place on the "subsumes" hierarchy as shown in Figure 5.5. A summary showing several criteria and eight of the axioms they satisfy, and fail to satisfy, is shown in Table 5.2 [11].

Weyuker's goal for the research community is to eventually develop criteria that satisfy all of the axioms. Using these new criteria, testers will be able to have greater confidence that the code under test has been adequately tested. Until then testers will need to continue to use exiting criteria such as branch- and statement-based criteria. However, they should be aware of inherent weaknesses of each, and use combinations of criteria and different testing techniques to adequately test a program.

As a note to the reader, there are existing studies that discuss issues relating to when to apply specific test adequacy criteria, and whether satisfaction of stronger criteria does in fact reveal more defects than weaker criteria. The effectiveness of tests based on the criteria relative to those derived from the random test data generation approach is also discussed. The studies are both theoretical and empirical in nature. The key researchers in this area include Frankl, Weyuker, Zhu, Parrish, and Gutjahr [1,2,11,13–17].

5.7 White Box Testing Methods and the TMM

In the previous chapter we discussed various black box–based testing methods and established a connection between these methods and TMM level 2 maturity goals. A similar argument can be made for the important role of white box methods in the evolution of test process maturity and for their association with TMM maturity goals. As in the case of black box–based test design, white box methods also provide a systematic way of developing test cases. However, white box methods have a stronger theoretical foundation and are supported by test adequacy criteria that guide the development of test data and allow evaluation of testing goals when tests are subsequently executed. In addition, white box methods have adequate tool support, and they depend on the use of notations that allow a connection to other development activities, for example, design. Use of black box as well as white box methods needs to be specified in the organizational testing goals/policy statement, and both need to be

	Statement	Branch	Mutation
Axiom 1	No	No	Yes
Axiom 2	Yes	Yes	Yes
Axiom 3	Yes	Yes	Yes
Axiom 4	Yes	Yes	Yes
Axiom 5	Yes	Yes	Yes
Axiom 6	Yes	Yes	Yes
Axiom 7	No	No	Yes
Axiom 8	No	No	Yes

TABLE 5.2

Sample test data adequacy criteria and axiom satisfaction [11].

applied in test plans. Managers should ensure that testers are trained in the use of both for consistent application to all organizational projects as described in the TMM. The Activities/Tasks/Responsibilities (ATR's) associated with adapting and implementing black box methods also apply to white box methods as well.

Several white box testing techniques were discussed in this chapter, and once again the role of smart developer/tester is to choose among them. In addition to the selection of properties to test based on test adequacy criteria, the developer/tester must also decide on the degree of coverage that is appropriate in each case. When making a choice among white box testing methods the tester must consider the nature of the software to be tested, resources available, and testing constraints and conditions. For example, a tester might choose to develop test designs using elements of control flow such as branches. In this same example, to insure coverage of compound conditions the tester may decide that multiple decision coverage is a wise testing goal. However, if the code is not complex, and is not mission, safety, or business critical, then simple branch coverage might be sufficient. The tester must also apply this reasoning to selection of a degree of coverage. For example, for a simple nonmission critical module, 85% branch coverage may prove to be a sufficient goal for the module if testing resources are tight. Remember that the higher up on the ordering hierarchy you climb, and the greater the degree of coverage you specify, the more testing resources are likely to be required to achieve testing goals.

In all cases the tester should select a combination of strategies to develop test cases that includes both black box and white box approaches. No one test design approach is guaranteed to reveal all defects, no matter what its proponents declare! Use of different testing strategies and methods has the following benefits:

1. The tester is encouraged to view the developing software from several different views to generate the test data. The views include control flow, data flow, input/output behavior, loop behavior, and states/state changes. The combination of views, and the test cases developed from their application, is more likely to reveal a wide variety of defects, even those that are difficult to detect. This results in a higher degree of software quality.

2. The tester must interact with other development personnel such as requirements analysts and designers to review their representations of the software. Representations include input/output specifications, pseudo code, state diagrams, and control flow graphs which are rich sources for test case development. As a result of the interaction, testers are equipped with a better understanding of the nature of the developing software, can evaluate its testability, give intelligent input during reviews, generate hypotheses about possible defects, and develop an effective set of tests.

3. The tester is better equipped to evaluate the quality of the testing effort (there are more tools and approaches available from the combination of strategies). The testers are also more able to evaluate the quality of the software itself, and establish a high degree of confidence that the software is operating occurring to the specifications. This higher confidence is a result of having examined software behavior and structural integrity in several independent ways.

4. The tester is better able to contribute to organizational test process improvement efforts based on his/her knowledge of a variety of testing strategies. With a solid grasp of both black and white box test design strategies, testers can have a very strong influence on the development and maintenance of test policies, test plans, and test prac-

tices. Testers are also better equipped to fulfill the requirements for the Activities, Tasks, and Responsibilities called for at TMM level 2 (see Section 3.12 and Appendix III). With their knowledge they can promote best practices, technology transfer, and ensure organization-wide adaptation of a variety of test design strategies and techniques.

KEY TERMS

Branch/statement adequate
Defined variable
Def-use path
Mutation adequate
Path
Used variable

EXERCISES

1. What is a control flow graph? How is it used in white box test design?

2. Draw a flow graph for the code in Figure 5.4. Calculate its cyclomatic complexity. Why is this value useful to the tester?

3. You are developing a module whose logic impacts on data acquisition for a flight control system. Your test manager has given you limited time and budget to test the module. The module is fairly complex; it has many loops, conditional statements, and nesting levels. You are going to unit test the module using white box testing approaches. Describe three test adequacy criteria you would consider applying to develop test cases for this module. What are the pros and cons for each. Which will have the highest strength?

4. Suppose you have developed a module with the following conditional statement:

```
if (value < 100 and found = = true)
    call (enter_data (value))
else
    print ("data cannot be entered")
```

Create tables as shown in the text containing test data that will enable you to achieve (i) simple decision coverage, (ii) condition coverage, and (iii) decision/condition coverage.

5. The following is a pseudocode fragment that has no redeeming features except for the purpose of this question. Draw a control flow graph for the example and clearly label each node so that it is linked to its corresponding statement. Calculate its cyclomatic complexity. How can you use this value as a measure of testability? Describe how a tester could use the cyclomatic complexity and the control flow graph to design a set of white box tests for this module that would at least cover all its branches.

```
module nonsense()
/* a[] and b[] are global variables */
begin
    int i,x
    i = 1
    read (x)
    while (i < x) do begin
    a[i] = b[i] * x
    if a[i] > 50 then
        print ("array a is over the limit")
    else
        print ("ok")
    i = i + 1
    end
    print ("end of nonsense")
end
```

6. The following is a unit that implements a binary search. It decides if a particular value of x occurs in the sorted integer array v. The elements of v are sorted in increasing order. The unit returns the position (a value between 0 and $n - 1$ if x occurs in v, and -1 if not. Draw a control flow graph for the example, and clearly label each node to show its correspondence to a statement. Calculate its cyclomatic complexity. How many test cases are needed to adequately cover the code with respect to its branches? Develop the necessary test cases using sample values for x, n, and v as needed and show how they cover the branches.

```
int binsearch (int x,int v[], int n)
{
  int low, high, mid;
  low = 0;
  high = n-1;
  while (low <= high) {
    mid = (low+high)/2
    if (x < v[mid]
      high = mid&ndash;1;
    else if (x > v[mid])
      low = mid+ 1;
    else /* found match*/
      return mid;
  }
  return-1;/* no match*/
}
```

7. Using your original (untested) version of the coin program (Problem 7, Chapter 4), design a set of test cases based on the branch adequacy criterion. Be sure to develop tables that identify each branch and the test cases that are assigned to execute it. Run the tests on the original code. Be sure that your tests actual execute all the branches; your goal is 100% coverage. If your original set is not adequate, add more tests to the set. Compare the defects you detected using the branch adequacy criterion in terms of number and type to results from each of the black box testing techniques you used in Chapter 4. What differences were apparent? Comment on these.

8. Use the same approach as in Problem 7 above with the original code developed for Problem 9 in Chapter 4. Again compare the results you observed using the branch adequacy criterion as compared to the black box techniques. Are there any particular classes of defects more effectively detected by the white or black box techniques? Compare the number of test cases needed for all the approaches and the number of defects detected of each type. Are there major differences? What would you recommend in terms of using combinations of these techniques?

9. For the code in Figure 5.2 identify the data flow information for each variable in each statement. Construct tables for each variable identifying their def-use paths. From the tables generate test data to exercise as many def-use paths as you can making any necessary assumptions needed.

10. For following looping construct, describe the set of tests you would develop based on the number of loop iterations in accordance with the loop testing criteria described in this chapter.

```
for (i = 0; i < 50; i++)
}
    text_box[i] = value[i];
    full = full-1;
}
```

11. A programmer using a mutation analysis tool finds that a total of 35 mutants have been generated for a program module A. Using a test set she has developed she finds after running the tests the number of dead mutants is 29 and the number of equivalent mutants is 2. What is the mutation score (MS) for module A. Is her test set for module A mutation adequate? Should she develop additional test cases. Why?

12. Given the test adequacy criteria hierarchy of Figure 5.5, and the observation that for many organizations statement adequacy at *best* is likely to be planned for, evaluate the strength of their testing approach. Make suggestions for improvement based on what you have learned in this chapter and your own testing experiences.

13. From your understanding of Weyuker's axioms and the information on Table 5.2 explain why statement adequacy does/does not satisfy Axioms 1, 7, and 8.

14. From your own testing experiences and what you have learned from this text, why do you think it is important for a tester to use both white and black box-based testing techniques to evaluate a given software module?

REFERENCES

[1] H. Zhu, P. Hall, J. May, "Software unit test coverage and adequacy," *ACM Computing Surveys,* Vol. 29, No. 4, 1997, pp. 366–427.

[2] E. Weyuker, "The evaluation of program-based software test adequacy criteria," *CACM,* Vol. 31, No. 6, 1988, pp. 668–675.

[3] T. McCabe, C. Butler, "Design complexity measurement and testing," *CACM,* Vol. 32, No. 12, 1989. pp. 1415–1425.

[4] B. Beizer, *Software Testing Techniques,* second edition, Van Nostrand Reinhold, New York, 1990.

[5] S. Rapps, E. Weyuker, "Selecting software test data using data flow information," *IEEE Trans. Software Engineering,* Vol. 11, No. 4, 1985, pp. 367–375.

[6] J. Laski, B. Korel, "A data flow oriented testing strategy," *IEEE Trans. Software Engineering,* Vol. 9, No. 3, 1983, pp. 347–354.

[7] L. Clarke, A. Podgurski, A. Richardson, S. Zeil, "A comparison of data flow path selection criteria," *Proc. Eighth International Conf. on SW Engineering*, August 1985, pp. 244–251.

[8] J. Horgan, S. London, "Data flow coverage and the C language," *Proc. ACM SIGSOFT Symposium on Testing, Analysis, and Verification*, Oct. 1991, pp. 87–97.

[9] T. Ostrand, E. Weyuker, "Data flow–based test adequacy analysis for languages with pointers," *Proc. ACM SIGSOFT Symposium on Testing, Analysis, and Verification*, Oct. 1991, pp. 74–86.

[10] R. DeMillo, R. Lipton, F. Sayward, "Hints on test data selection: help for the practicing programmer," *Computer*, Vol. 11, No. 4, 1978, pp. 34–41.

[11] E. Weyuker, "Axiomatizing software test data adequacy," *IEEE Trans. Software Engineering*, Vol. 12, No. 12, 1986, pp. 1128–1138.

[12] M. Delamaro, J. Maldonado, A. Mathur, "Interface mutation: an approach for integration testing," *IEEE Transactions on Software Engineering*, Vol. 27, No. 3, March 2001, pp. 228–247.

[13] W. Howden, "Weak mutation testing and completeness of test sets," *IEEE Trans. Software Engineering*, Vol. 8, No. 4. 1982, pp. 371–379.

[14] P. Frankl, E. Weyuker, "A formal analysis of the fault-detecting ability of testing methods," *IEEE Trans. Software Engineering*, Vol. 19, No. 3, 1993, pp. 202–213.

[15] P. Frankl, E. Weyuker, "Provable improvements on branch testing," *IEEE Trans. Software Engineering*, Vol. 19, No. 10, Oct. 1993, pp. 962–975.

[16] A. Parrish, S. Zweben, "Analysis and refinement of software test data adequacy properties," *IEEE Trans. Software Engineering*, Vol. 17, No. 7, 1991, pp. 565–581.

[17] W. Gutjahr, "Partition testing vs. random testing: the influence of uncertainty," *IEEE Trans. Software Engineering*, Vol. 25, No. 5., Sept./Oct. 1999, pp. 661–674.

LEVELS

OF TESTING

6.0 The Need for Levels of Testing

Execution-based software testing, especially for large systems, is usually carried out at different levels. In most cases there will be 3–4 levels, or major phases of testing: unit test, integration test, system test, and some type of acceptance test as shown in Figure 6.1. Each of these may consist of one or more sublevels or phases. At each level there are specific testing goals. For example, at unit test a single component is tested. A principal goal is to detect functional and structural defects in the unit. At the integration level several components are tested as a group, and the tester investigates component interactions. At the system level the system as a whole is tested and a principle goal is to evaluate attributes such as usability, reliability, and performance.

An orderly progression of testing levels is described in this chapter for both object-oriented and procedural-based software systems. The major testing levels for both types of system are similar. However, the nature of the code that results from each developmental approach demands dif-

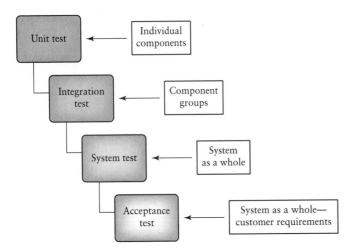

FIG. 6.1

Levels of testing.

ferent testing strategies, for example, to identify individual components, and to assemble them into subsystems. The issues involved are described in Sections 6.0.1, 6.1, and 6.2.3 of this chapter. For both types of systems the testing process begins with the smallest units or components to identify functional and structural defects. Both white and black box test strategies as discussed in Chapters 4 and 5 can be used for test case design at this level. After the individual components have been tested, and any necessary repairs made, they are integrated to build subsystems and clusters. Testers check for defects and adherence to specifications. Proper interaction at the component interfaces is of special interest at the integration level. In most cases black box design predominates, but often white box tests are used to reveal defects in control and data flow between the integrated modules.

System test begins when all of the components have been integrated successfully. It usually requires the bulk of testing resources. Laboratory equipment, special software, or special hardware may be necessary, especially for real-time, embedded, or distributed systems. At the system level the tester looks for defects, but the focus is on evaluating performance, usability, reliability, and other quality-related requirements.

If the system is being custom made for an individual client then the next step following system test is acceptance test. This is a very important testing stage for the developers. During acceptance test the development organization must show that the software meets all of the client's requirements. Very often final payments for system development depend on the quality of the software as observed during the acceptance test. A successful acceptance test provides a good opportunity for developers to request recommendation letters from the client. Software developed for the mass market (i.e., shrink-wrapped software) often goes through a series of tests called alpha and beta tests. Alpha tests bring potential users to the developer's site to use the software. Developers note any problems. Beta tests send the software out to potential users who use it under real-world conditions and report defects to the developing organization.

Implementing all of these levels of testing require a large investment in time and organizational resources. Organizations with poor testing processes tend to skimp on resources, ignore test planning until code is close to completion, and omit one or more testing phases. This seldom works to the advantage of the organization or its customers. The software released under these circumstances is often of poor quality, and the additional costs of repairing defects in the field, and of customer dissatisfaction are usually under estimated.

6.0.1 Levels of Testing and Software Development Paradigms

The approach used to design and develop a software system has an impact on how testers plan and design suitable tests. There are two major approaches to system development—bottom-up, and top-down. These approaches are supported by two major types of programming languages—procedure-oriented and object-oriented. This chapter considers testing at different levels for systems developed with both approaches using either traditional procedural programming languages or object-oriented programming languages. The different nature of the code produced requires testers to use different strategies to identify and test components and component groups. Systems developed with procedural languages are generally viewed as being composed of passive data and active procedures. When test cases are developed the focus is on generating input data to pass to the procedures (or functions) in order to reveal defects. Object-oriented systems are viewed as being composed of active data along with allowed operations on that data, all encapsulated within a unit similar to an abstract data type. The operations on the data may not be called upon in any specific order. Testing this type of software means designing an order of calls to the operations using various parameter values in order to reveal defects. Issues related to inheritance of operations also impact on testing.

Levels of abstraction for the two types of systems are also somewhat different. In traditional procedural systems, the lowest level of abstraction is described as a function or a procedure that performs some simple task. The next higher level of abstraction is a group of procedures (or functions) that call one another and implement a major system requirement. These are called subsystems. Combining subsystems finally produces the system as a whole, which is the highest level of abstraction. In object-oriented systems the lowest level is viewed by some researchers as the method or member function [1–3]. The next highest level is viewed as the class that encapsulates data and methods that operate on the data [4]. To move up one more level in an object-oriented system some researchers use the concept of the cluster, which is a group of cooperating or related classes [3,5]. Finally, there is the system level, which is a combination of all the clusters and any auxiliary code needed to run the system [3]. Not all researchers in object-oriented development have the same view of the abstraction levels, for example, Jorgensen describes the thread as a highest level of abstraction [1]. Differences of opinion will be described in other sections of this chapter.

While approaches for testing and assembling traditional procedural type systems are well established, those for object-oriented systems are still the subject of ongoing research efforts. There are different views on how unit, integration, and system tests are best accomplished in object-oriented systems. When object-oriented development was introduced key beneficial features were encapsulation, inheritance, and polymorphism. It was said that these features would simplify design and development and encourage reuse. However, testing of object-oriented systems is not straightforward due to these same features. For example, encapsulation can hide details from testers, and that can lead to uncovered code. Inheritance also presents many testing challenges, among those the retesting of inherited methods when they are used by a subclass in a different context.

It is also difficult to define a unit for object-oriented code. Some researchers argue for the method (member function) as the unit since it is procedurelike. However, some methods are very small in size, and developing test harnesses to test each individually requires a large overhead. Should a single class be a unit? If so, then the tester need to consider the complexity of the test harness needed to test the unit since in many cases, a particular class depends on other classes for its operation. Also, object-oriented code is characterized by use of messages, dynamic binding, state changes, and nonhierarchical calling relationships. This also makes testing more complex. The reader should understand that many of these issues are yet to be resolved. Subsequent sections in this chapter will discuss several of these issues using appropriate examples. References 1–9 represent some of the current research views in this area.

6.1 Unit Test: Functions, Procedures, Classes, and Methods as Units

A workable definition for a software unit is as follows:

▌ **A unit is the smallest possible testable software component.**

It can be characterized in several ways. For example, a unit in a typical procedure-oriented software system:

- performs a single cohesive function;
- can be compiled separately;
- is a task in a work breakdown structure (from the manager's point of view);
- contains code that can fit on a single page or screen.

A unit is traditionally viewed as a function or procedure implemented in a procedural (imperative) programming language. In object-oriented systems both the method and the class/object have been suggested by researchers as the choice for a unit [1–5]. The relative merits of each of these as the selected component for unit test are described in sections that follow. A unit may also be a small-sized COTS component purchased from an outside vendor that is undergoing evaluation by the purchaser,

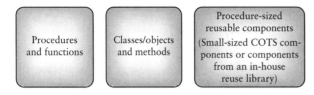

Fig. 6.2

Some components suitable for unit test.

or a simple module retrieved from an in-house reuse library. These unit types are shown in Figure 6.2.

No matter which type of component is selected as the smallest testable component, unit test is a vital testing level. Since the software component being tested is relatively small in size and simple in function, it is easier to design, execute, record, and analyze test results. If a defect is revealed by the tests it is easier to locate and repair since only the one unit is under consideration.

6.2 Unit Test: The Need for Preparation

The principal goal for unit testing is insure that each individual software unit is functioning according to its specification. Good testing practice calls for unit tests that are planned and public. Planning includes designing tests to reveal defects such as functional description defects, algorithmic defects, data defects, and control logic and sequence defects. Resources should be allocated, and test cases should be developed, using both white and black box test design strategies. The unit should be tested by an independent tester (someone other than the developer) and the test results and defects found should be recorded as a part of the unit history (made public). Each unit should also be reviewed by a team of reviewers, preferably before the unit test.

Unfortunately, unit test in many cases is performed informally by the unit developer soon after the module is completed, and it compiles cleanly. Some developers also perform an informal review of the unit. Under these circumstances the review and testing approach may be ad hoc. Defects found are often not recorded by the developer; they are private (not public), and do not become a part of the history of the unit. This is poor practice, especially if the unit performs mission or safely critical tasks, or is intended for reuse.

To implement best practices it is important to plan for, and allocate resources to test each unit. If defects escape detection in unit test because of poor unit testing practices, they are likely to show up during integration, system, or acceptance test where they are much more costly to locate and repair. In the worst-case scenario they will cause failures during operation requiring the development organization to repair the software at the clients' site. This can be very costly.

To prepare for unit test the developer/tester must perform several tasks. These are:

(i) plan the general approach to unit testing;
(ii) design the test cases, and test procedures (these will be attached to the test plan);
(iii) define relationships between the tests;
(iv) prepare the auxiliary code necessary for unit test.

The text sections that follow describe these tasks in detail.

6.3 Unit Test Planning

A general unit test plan should be prepared. It may be prepared as a component of the master test plan or as a stand-alone plan. It should be developed in conjunction with the master test plan and the project plan for each project. Documents that provide inputs for the unit test plan are the project plan, as well the requirements, specification, and design documents that describe the target units. Components of a unit test plan are described in detail the *IEEE Standard for Software Unit Testing* [10]. This standard is rich in information and is an excellent guide for the test planner. A brief description of a set of development phases for unit test planning is found below. In each phase a set of activities is assigned based on those found in the IEEE unit test standard [10]. The phases allow a steady evolution of the unit test plan as more information becomes available. The reader will note that the unit test plan contains many of the same components as the master test plan that will be described in Chapter 7. Also note that a unit test plan is developed to cover all the units within a software project; however, each unit will have its own associated set of tests.

Phase 1: Describe Unit Test Approach and Risks

In this phase of unit testing planning the general approach to unit testing is outlined. The test planner:

(i)   identifies test risks;
(ii) describes techniques to be used for designing the test cases for the units;
(iii) describes techniques to be used for data validation and recording of test results;
(iv) describes the requirements for test harnesses and other software that interfaces with the units to be tested, for example, any special objects needed for testing object-oriented units.

During this phase the planner also identifies completeness requirements—what will be covered by the unit test and to what degree (states, functionality, control, and data flow patterns). The planner also identifies termination conditions for the unit tests. This includes coverage requirements, and special cases. Special cases may result in abnormal termination of unit test (e.g., a major design flaw). Strategies for handling these special cases need to be documented. Finally, the planner estimates resources needed for unit test, such as hardware, software, and staff, and develops a tentative schedule under the constraints identified at that time.

Phase 2: Identify Unit Features to be Tested

This phase requires information from the unit specification and detailed design description. The planner determines which features of each unit will be tested, for example: functions, performance requirements, states, and state transitions, control structures, messages, and data flow patterns. If some features will not be covered by the tests, they should be mentioned and the risks of not testing them be assessed. Input/output characteristics associated with each unit should also be identified, such as variables with an allowed ranges of values and performance at a certain level.

Phase 3: Add Levels of Detail to the Plan

In this phase the planner refines the plan as produced in the previous two phases. The planner adds new details to the approach, resource, and scheduling portions of the unit test plan. As an example, existing test cases that can be reused for this project can be identified in this phase. Unit availability and integration scheduling information should be included in the revised version of the test plan. The planner must be sure to include a description of how test results will be recorded. Test-related documents that will be required for this task, for example, test logs, and test incident reports, should be described, and references to standards for these documents provided. Any special tools required for the tests are also described.

The next steps in unit testing consist of designing the set of test cases, developing the auxiliary code needed for testing, executing the tests, and recording and analyzing the results. These topics will be discussed in Sections 6.4–6.6.

6.4 Designing the Unit Tests

Part of the preparation work for unit test involves unit test design. It is important to specify (i) the test cases (including input data, and expected outputs for each test case), and, (ii) the test procedures (steps required run the tests). These items are described in more detail in Chapter 7. Test case data should be tabularized for ease of use, and reuse. Suitable tabular formats for test cases are found in Chapters 4 and 5. To specifically support object-oriented test design and the organization of test data, Berard has described a test case specification notation [8]. He arranges the components of a test case into a semantic network with parts, Object_ID, Test_Case_ID, Purpose, and List_of_Test_Case_Steps. Each of these items has component parts. In the test design specification Berard also includes lists of relevant states, messages (calls to methods), exceptions, and interrupts.

As part of the unit test design process, developers/testers should also describe the relationships between the tests. Test suites can be defined that bind related tests together as a group. All of this test design information is attached to the unit test plan. Test cases, test procedures, and test suites may be reused from past projects if the organization has been careful to store them so that they are easily retrievable and reusable.

Test case design at the unit level can be based on use of the black and white box test design strategies described in Chapters 4 and 5. Both of these approaches are useful for designing test cases for functions and procedures. They are also useful for designing tests for the individual methods (member functions) contained in a class. Considering the relatively small size of a unit, it makes sense to focus on white box test design for procedures/functions and the methods in a class. This approach gives the tester the opportunity to exercise logic structures and/or data flow sequences, or to use mutation analysis, all with the goal of evaluating the structural integrity of the unit. Some black box–based testing is also done at unit level; however, the bulk of black box testing is usually done at the integration and system levels and beyond. In the case of a smaller-sized COTS component selected for unit testing, a black box test design approach may be the only option. It should be mentioned that for units that perform mission/safely/business critical functions, it is often useful and prudent to design stress, security, and performance tests at the unit level if possible. (These types of tests are discussed in latter sections of this chapter.) This approach may prevent larger scale failures at higher levels of test.

6.5 The Class as a Testable Unit: Special Considerations

If an organization is using the object-oriented paradigm to develop software systems it will need to select the component to be considered for unit test. As described in Section 6.1, the choices consist of either the individual method as a unit or the class as a whole. Each of these choices requires special consideration on the part of the testers when designing and running the unit tests, and when retesting needs to be done. For example, in the case of the method as the selected unit to test, it may call other methods within its own class to support its functionality. Additional code, in the form of a test harness, must be built to represent the called methods within the class. Building such a test harness for each individual method often requires developing code equivalent to that already existing in the class itself (all of its other methods). This is costly; however, the tester needs to consider that testing each individual method in this way helps to ensure that all statements/branches have been executed at least once, and that the basic functionality of the method is correct. This is especially important for mission or safety critical methods.

In spite of the potential advantages of testing each method individually, many developers/testers consider the class to be the component of choice for unit testing. The process of testing classes as units is sometimes called component test [11]. A class encapsulates multiple interacting methods operating on common data, so what we are testing is the intra-class interaction of the methods. When testing on the class level we are able detect not only traditional types of defects, for example, those due to control or data flow errors, but also defects due to the nature of object-oriented systems, for example, defects due to encapsulation, inheritance, and polymorphism errors. We begin to also look for what Chen calls object management faults, for example, those associated with the instantiation, storage, and retrieval of objects [12].

This brief discussion points out some of the basic trade-offs in selecting the component to be considered for a unit test in object-oriented systems. If the class is the selected component, testers may need to address special issues related to the testing and retesting of these components. Some of these issues are raised in the paragraphs that follow.

Issue 1: Adequately Testing Classes

The potentially high costs for testing each individual method in a class have been described. These high costs will be particularly apparent when there are many methods in a class; the numbers can reach as high as 20 to 30. If the class is selected as the unit to test, it is possible to reduce these costs since in many cases the methods in a single class serve as drivers and stubs for one another. This has the effect of lowering the complexity of the test harness that needs to be developed. However, in some cases driver classes that represent outside classes using the methods of the class under test will have to be developed.

Stack Class
Data for Stack ⋮

Member functions
for Stack
`create(s, size)`
`push(s, item)`
`pop(s, item)`
`full(s)`
`empty(s)`
`show_top(s)`

Fig. 6.3
Sample stack class with multiple methods.

In addition, if it is decided that the class is the smallest component to test, testers must decide if they are able to adequately cover all necessary features of each method in class testing. Some researchers believe that coverage objectives and test data need to be developed for each of the methods, for example, the *create, pop, push, empty, full,* and *show_top* methods associated with the stack class shown in Figure 6.3. Other researchers believe that a class can be adequately tested as a whole by observation of method interactions using a sequence of calls to the member functions with appropriate parameters.

Again, referring to the stack class shown in Figure 6.3, the methods *push, pop, full, empty,* and *show_top* will either read or modify the state of the stack. When testers unit (or component) test this class what they will need to focus on is the operation of each of the methods in the class and the interactions between them. Testers will want to determine, for example, if *push* places an item in the correct position at the top of the stack. However, a call to the method *full* may have to be made first to determine if the stack is already full. Testers will also want to determine if *push* and *pop* work together properly so that the stack pointer is in the correct position after a sequence of calls to these methods. To properly test this class, a sequence of calls to the methods needs to be specified as part of component test design. For example, a test sequence for a stack that can hold three items might be:

create(s,3), empty(s), push(s,item-1), push(s,item-2), push(s,item-3), full(s), show_top(s), pop(s,item), pop(s,item), pop(s,item), empty(s), . . .

The reader will note that many different sequences and combination of calls are possible even for this simple class. Exhaustively testing every possible sequence is usually not practical. The tester must select those sequences she believes will reveal the most defects in the class. Finally, a tester might use a combination of approaches, testing some of the critical methods on an individual basis as units, and then testing the class as a whole.

Issue 2: Observation of Object States and State Changes

Methods may not return a specific value to a caller. They may instead change the state of an object. The state of an object is represented by a specific set of values for its attributes or state variables. State-based testing as described in Chapter 4 is very useful for testing objects. Methods will often modify the state of an object, and the tester must ensure that each state transition is proper. The test designer can prepare a state table (using state diagrams developed for the requirements specification) that specifies states the object can assume, and then in the table indicate sequence of messages and parameters that will cause the object to enter each state. When the tests are run the tester can enter results in this same type of table. For example, the first call to the method *push* in the stack class of Figure 6.3, changes the state of the stack so that *empty* is no longer true. It also changes the value of the stack pointer variable, *top*. To determine if the method *push* is working properly the value of the variable *top* must be visible both before and after the invocation of this method. In this case the method *show_top* within the class may be called to perform this task. The methods *full* and *empty* also probe the state of the stack. A sample augmented sequence of calls to check the value of *top* and the *full/empty* state of the three-item stack is:

empty(s), push(s,item-1), show_top(s), push(s,item-2),
show_top(s), push(s,item-3), full(s), show_top(s), pop(s,item),
show_top(s), pop(s,item), show_top(s), empty(s), . . .

Test sequences also need to be designed to try to push an item on a full stack and pop an item from an empty stack. This could be done by adding first an extra *push* to the sequence of pushes, and in a separate test adding an extra *pop* to the sequence of pops.

In the case of the stack class, the class itself contains methods that can provide information about state changes. If this is not the case then additional classes/methods may have to be created to show changes of state. These would be part of the test harness. Another option is to include in each class methods that allows state changes to be observable. Testers should have the option of going back to the designers and requesting changes that make a class more testable. In any case, test planners should insure that code is available to display state variables, Test plans should provide resources for developing this type of code.

Issue 3: The Retesting of Classes—I

One of the most beneficial features of object-oriented development is encapsulation. This is a technique that can be used to hide information. A program unit, in this case a class, can be built with a well-defined public interface that proclaims its services (available methods) to client classes. The implementation of the services is private. Clients who use the services are unaware of implementation details. As long as the interface is unchanged, making changes to the implementation should not affect the client classes. A tester of object-oriented code would therefore conclude that only the class with implementation changes to its methods needs to be retested. Client classes using unchanged interfaces need not be retested. This is not necessarily correct, as Perry and Kaiser explain in their paper on adequate testing for object-oriented systems [13]. In an object-oriented system, if a developer changes a class implementation that class needs to be retested as well as all the classes that depend on it. If a superclass, for example, is changed, then it is necessary to retest all of its subclasses. In addition, when a new subclass is added (or modified), we must also retest the methods inherited from each of its ancestor superclasses. The new (or changed) subclass introduces an unexpected form of dependency because there now exists a new context for the inherited components. This is a consequence of the antidecomposition testing axiom as described in Chapter 5 [13].

Issue 4: The Retesting of Classes—II

Classes are usually a part of a class hierarchy where there are existing inheritance relationships. Subclasses inherit methods from their superclasses. Very often a tester may assume that once a method in a superclass has been tested, it does not need retested in a subclass that inherits it. However, in some cases the method is used in a different context by the subclass and will need to be retested.

In addition, there may be an overriding of methods where a subclass may replace an inherited method with a locally defined method. Not only will the new locally defined method have to be retested, but designing a new set of test cases may be necessary. This is because the two methods (inherited and new) may be structurally different. The antiextentionality axiom as discussed in Chapter 5 expresses this need [13].

The following is an example of such as case using the shape class in Figure 6.4. Suppose the shape superclass has a subclass, triangle, and triangle has a subclass, equilateral triangle. Also suppose that the method *display* in shape needs to call the method *color* for its operation. Equilateral triangle could have a local definition for the method *display*. That method could in turn use a local definition for *color* which has been defined in triangle. This local definition of the *color* method in triangle has been tested to work with the inherited *display* method in shape, but not with the locally defined *display* in equilateral triangle. This is a new context that must be retested. A set of new test cases should be developed. The tester must carefully examine all the relationships between members of a class to detect such occurrences.

Many authors have written about class testing and object-oriented testing in general. Some have already been referenced in this chapter. Others include Desouza, Perry, and Rangaraajan who discuss the issue of when the retesting of methods within classes and subclasses is necessary [2,13,14]. Smith, Wilde, Doong, McGregor, and Tsai describe frameworks and tools to assist with class test design [3,6,7,11,15]. Harrold and co-authors have written several papers that describe the application of data flow testing to object-oriented systems [16,17]. The authors use data flow techniques to test individual member functions and also to test interactions among member functions. Outside of class interactions are also covered by their approach. Finally, Kung has edited a book that contains

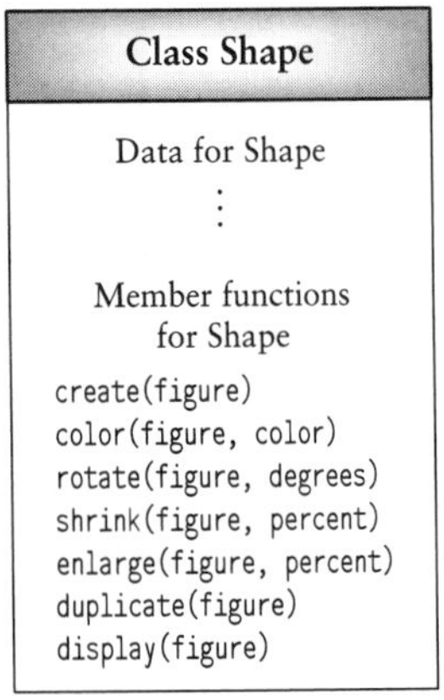

```
┌─────────────────────────────────┐
│       Class Shape               │
├─────────────────────────────────┤
│       Data for Shape            │
│              ⋮                   │
│                                 │
│       Member functions          │
│          for Shape              │
│    create(figure)               │
│    color(figure, color)         │
│    rotate(figure, degrees)      │
│    shrink(figure, percent)      │
│    enlarge(figure, percent)     │
│    duplicate(figure)            │
│    display(figure)              │
└─────────────────────────────────┘
```

Fig. 6.4

Sample shape class.

key papers devoted to object-oriented testing. The papers discuss many of the above issues in detail [18].

6.6 The Test Harness

In addition to developing the test cases, supporting code must be developed to exercise each unit and to connect it to the outside world. Since the tester is considering a stand-alone function/procedure/class, rather than a complete system, code will be needed to call the target unit, and also to represent modules that are called by the target unit. This code called the test harness, is developed especially for test and is in addition to the code that composes the system under development. The role is of the test harness is shown in Figure 6.5 and it is defined as follows:

> **The auxiliary code developed to support testing of units and components is called a test harness. The harness consists of drivers that call the target code and stubs that represent modules it calls.**

The development of drivers and stubs requires testing resources. The drivers and stubs must be tested themselves to insure they are working prop-

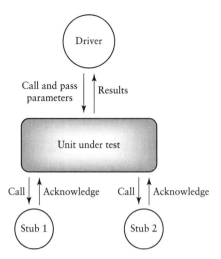

Fig. 6.5

The test harness.

erly and that they are reusable for subsequent releases of the software. Drivers and stubs can be developed at several levels of functionality. For example, a driver could have the following options and combinations of options:

(i)   call the target unit;
(ii) do 1, and pass inputs parameters from a table;
(iii) do 1, 2, and display parameters;
(iv) do 1, 2, 3 and display results (output parameters).

The stubs could also exhibit different levels of functionality. For example a stub could:

(i)   display a message that it has been called by the target unit;
(ii) do 1, and display any input parameters passed from the target unit;
(iii) do 1, 2, and pass back a result from a table;
(iv) do 1, 2, 3, and display result from table.

Drivers and stubs as shown in Figure 6.5 are developed as procedures and functions for traditional imperative-language based systems. For object-oriented systems, developing drivers and stubs often means the design and implementation of special classes to perform the required testing tasks. The test harness itself may be a hierarchy of classes. For example, in Figure 6.5 the driver for a procedural system may be designed as a single procedure or main module to call the unit under test; however, in an object-oriented system it may consist of several test classes to emulate all the classes that call for services in the class under test. Researchers such as Rangaraajan and Chen have developed tools that generate test cases using several different approaches, and classes of test harness objects to test object-oriented code [12,14].

The test planner must realize that, the higher the degree of functionally for the harness, the more resources it will require to design, implement, and test. Developers/testers will have to decide depending on the nature of the code under test, just how complex the test harness needs to be. Test harnesses for individual classes tend to be more complex than those needed for individual procedures and functions since the items being tested are more complex and there are more interactions to consider.

6.7 Running the Unit Tests and Recording Results

Unit tests can begin when (i) the units becomes available from the developers (an estimation of availability is part of the test plan), (ii) the test cases have been designed and reviewed, and (iii) the test harness, and any other supplemental supporting tools, are available. The testers then proceed to run the tests and record results. Chapter 7 will describe documents called test logs that can be used to record the results of specific tests. The status of the test efforts for a unit, and a summary of the test results, could be recorded in a simple format such as shown in Table 6.1. These forms can be included in the test summary report, and are of value at the weekly status meetings that are often used to monitor test progress.

It is very important for the tester at any level of testing to carefully record, review, and check test results. The tester must determine from the results whether the unit has passed or failed the test. If the test is failed, the nature of the problem should be recorded in what is sometimes called

Unit Test Worksheet			
Unit Name: _____			
Unit Identifier: _____			
Tester: _____			
Date: _____			
Test case ID	Status (run/not run)	Summary of results	Pass/fail

TABLE 6.1

Summary work sheet for unit test results.

a test incident report (see Chapter 7). Differences from expected behavior should be described in detail. This gives clues to the developers to help them locate any faults. During testing the tester may determine that additional tests are required. For example, a tester may observe that a particular coverage goal has not been achieved. The test set will have to be augmented and the test plan documents should reflect these changes.

When a unit fails a test there may be several reasons for the failure. The most likely reason for the failure is a fault in the unit implementation (the code). Other likely causes that need to be carefully investigated by the tester are the following:

- a fault in the test case specification (the input or the output was not specified correctly);

- a fault in test procedure execution (the test should be rerun);

- a fault in the test environment (perhaps a database was not set up properly);

- a fault in the unit design (the code correctly adheres to the design specification, but the latter is incorrect).

The causes of the failure should be recorded in a test summary report, which is a summary of testing activities for all the units covered by the unit test plan.

Ideally, when a unit has been completely tested and finally passes all of the required tests it is ready for integration. Under some circumstances a unit may be given a conditional acceptance for integration test. This may occur when the unit fails some tests, but the impact of the failure is not significant with respect to its ability to function in a subsystem, and the availability of a unit is critical for integration test to proceed on schedule. This a risky procedure and testers should evaluate the risks involved. Units with a conditional pass must eventually be repaired.

When testing of the units is complete, a test summary report should be prepared. This is a valuable document for the groups responsible for integration and system tests. It is also a valuable component of the project history. Its value lies in the useful data it provides for test process improvement and defect prevention. Finally, the tester should insure that the test cases, test procedures, and test harnesses are preserved for future reuse.

6.8 Integration Test: Goals

Integration test for procedural code has two major goals:

(i) to detect defects that occur on the interfaces of units;
(ii) to assemble the individual units into working subsystems and finally a complete system that is ready for system test.

In unit test the testers attempt to detect defects that are related to the functionality and structure of the unit. There is some simple testing of unit interfaces when the units interact with drivers and stubs. However, the interfaces are more adequately tested during integration test when each unit is finally connected to a full and working implementation of those units it calls, and those that call it. As a consequence of this assembly or integration process, software subsystems and finally a completed system is put together during the integration test. The completed system is then ready for system testing.

With a few minor exceptions, integration test should only be performed on units that have been reviewed and have successfully passed unit testing. A tester might believe erroneously that since a unit has already been tested during a unit test with a driver and stubs, it does not need to be retested in combination with other units during integration test. However, a unit tested in isolation may not have been tested adequately for the situation where it is combined with other modules. This is also a consequences of one of the testing axioms found in Chapter 4 called anticomposition [13].

Integration testing works best as an iterative process in procedural-oriented system. One unit at a time is integrated into a set of previously integrated modules which have passed a set of integration tests. The interfaces and functionally of the new unit in combination with the previously integrated units is tested. When a subsystem is built from units integrated in this stepwise manner, then performance, security, and stress tests can be performed on this subsystem.

Integrating one unit at a time helps the testers in several ways. It keeps the number of new interfaces to be examined small, so tests can focus on these interfaces only. Experienced testers know that many defects occur at module interfaces. Another advantage is that the massive failures that often occur when multiple units are integrated at once is avoided. This approach also helps the developers; it allows defect search and repair to be confined to a small known number of components and interfaces. Independent subsystems can be integrated in parallel as long as the required units are available.

The integration process in object-oriented systems is driven by assembly of the classes into cooperating groups. The cooperating groups of classes are tested as a whole and then combined into higher-level groups. Usually the simpler groups are tested first, and then combined to form higher-level groups until the system is assembled. This process will be described in the next sections of this chapter.

6.9 Integration Strategies for Procedures and Functions

For conventional procedural/functional-oriented systems there are two major integration strategies—top-down and bottom-up. In both of these strategies only one module at a time is added to the growing subsystem. To plan the order of integration of the modules in such system a structure chart such as shown in Figure 6.6 is used.

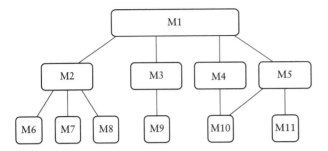

Fig. 6.6

Simple structure chart for integration
test examples.

Structure charts, or call graphs as they are otherwise known, are used to guide integration. These charts show hierarchical calling relationships between modules. Each node, or rectangle in a structure chart, represents a module or unit, and the edges or lines between them represent calls between the units. In the simple chart in Figure 6.6 the rectangles M1–M11 represent all the system modules. Again, a line or edge from an upper-level module to one below it indicates that the upper level module calls the lower module. Some annotated versions of structure charts show the parameters passed between the caller and called modules. Conditional calls and iterative calls may also be represented.

Bottom-up integration of the modules begins with testing the lowest-level modules, those at the bottom of the structure chart. These are modules that do not call other modules. In the structure chart example these are modules M6, M7, M8, M9, M10, M11. Drivers are needed to test these modules. The next step is to integrate modules on the next upper level of the structure chart whose subordinate modules have already been tested. For example, if we have tested M6, M7, and M8, then we can select M2 and integrate it with M6, M7, and M8. The actual M2 replaces the drivers for these modules.

In the process for bottom-up integration after a module has been tested, its driver can be replaced by an actual module (the next one to be integrated). This next module to be integrated may also need a driver, and this will be the case until we reach the highest level of the structure chart. Accordingly we can integrate M9 with M3 when M9 is tested, and

M4 with M10 when M10 is tested, and finally M5 with M11 and M10 when they are both tested. Integration of the M2 and M3 subsystems can be done in parallel by two testers. The M4 and M5 subsystems have overlapping dependencies on M10. To complete the subsystem represented by M5, both M10 and M11 will have to be tested and integrated. M4 is only dependent on M10. A third tester could work on the M4 and M5 subsystems.

After this level of integration is completed, we can then move up a level and integrate the subsystem M2, M6, M7, and M8 with M1 when M2 has been completed tested with its subordinates, and driver. The same conditions hold for integrating the subsystems represented by M3, M9, M4, M10, and M5, M10, M11 with M1. In that way the system is finally integrated as a whole. In this example a particular sequence of integration has been selected. There are no firm rules for selecting which module to integrate next. However, a rule of thumb for bottom-up integration says that to be eligible for selection as the next candidate for integration, all of a module's subordinate modules (modules it calls) must have been tested previously. Issues such as the complexity, mission, or safety criticalness of a module also impact on the choices for the integration sequence.

Bottom-up integration has the advantage that the lower-level modules are usually well tested early in the integration process. This is important if these modules are candidates for reuse. However, the upper-level modules are tested later in the integration process and consequently may not be as well tested. If they are critical decision-makers or handle critical functions, this could be risky. In addition, with bottom-up integration the system as a whole does not exist until the last module, in our example, M1, is integrated. It is possible to assemble small subsystems, and when they are shown to work properly the development team often experiences a boost in morale and a sense of achievement.

Top-down integration starts at the top of the module hierarchy. The rule of thumb for selecting candidates for the integration sequence says that when choosing a candidate module to be integrated next, at least one of the module's superordinate (calling) modules must have been previously tested. In our case, M1 is the highest-level module and we start the sequence by developing stubs to test it. In order to get a good upward flow of data into the system, the stubs may have to be fairly complex (see

Section 6.2.3). The next modules to be integrated are those for whom their superordinate modules has been tested. The way to proceed is to replace one-by-one each of the stubs of the superordinate module with a subordinate module. For our example in Figure 6.6, we begin top-down integration with module M1. We create four stubs to represent M2, M3, M4, and M5. When the tests are passed, then we replace the four stubs by the actual modules one at a time. The actual modules M2–M5 when they are integrated will have stubs of their own. Figure 6.7 shows the set up for the integration of M1 with M2.

When we have integrated the modules M2–M5, then we can integrate the lowest-level modules. For example, when, M2 has been integrated with M1 we can replace its stubs for M6, M7, and M8 with the actual modules, one at a time, and so on for M3, M4, and M5. One can traverse the structure chart and integrate the modules in a depth or breadth-first manner. For example, the order of integration for a depth-first approach would be M1, M2, M6, M7, M8, M3, M9, M4, M10, M5, M11. Breadth-first would proceed as M1, M2, M3, M4, M5, M6, M7, M8, M9, M10, M11. Note that using the depth-first approach gradually forms subsystems as the integration progresses. In many cases these subsystems can be assembled and tested in parallel. For example, when the testing of M1 is completed, there could be parallel integration testing of subsystems M2 and M3. A third tester could work in parallel with these testers on the subsystems M4 and M5. The test planner should look for these opportunities when scheduling testing tasks.

Top-down integration ensures that the upper-level modules are tested early in integration. If they are complex and need to be redesigned there will be more time to do so. This is not the case with bottom-up integration. Top-down integration requires the development of complex stubs to drive significant data upward, but bottom-up integration requires drivers so there is not a clear-cut advantage with respect to developing test harnesses. In many cases a combination of approaches will be used. One approach is known as sandwich, where the higher-level modules are integrated top-down and the lower-level modules integrated bottom-up.

No matter which integration strategy is selected, testers should consider applying relevant coverage criteria to the integration process. Linnenkugel and Mullerburg have suggested several interprocedural control and data flow–based criteria [19]. Example control flow criteria include:

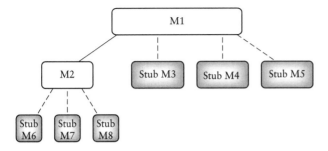

Fig. 6.7

Top-down integration of modules M1 and M2.

all modules in the graph or chart should be executed at least once (all nodes covered), all calls should be executed at least once (all edges covered), and all descending sequences of calls should be executed at least once (all paths covered).

The smart test planner takes into account risk factors associated with each of the modules, and plans the order of integration accordingly. Some modules and subsystems may be handling mission/safety/business critical functions; some might be complex. The test planner will want to be sure that these are assembled and tested early in the integration process to insure they are tested adequately. For example, in the sample structure chart shown in Figure 6.6, if modules M6 and M10 are complex and/or safety critical modules, a tester would consider bottom-up integration as a good choice since these modules would be integrated and tested early in the integration process.

Another area of concern for the planner is the availability of the modules. The test planner should consult the project plan to determine availability dates. Availability may also be affected during the testing process depending on the number and nature of the defects found in each module. A subsystem may be assembled earlier/later then planned depending in the amount of time it takes to test/repair its component modules. For example, we may be planning to integrate branch M2 before branch M3; however, M2 and its components may contain more defects then M3 and its components, so there will be a delay for repairs to be made.

6.10 Integration Strategies for Classes

For object-oriented systems the concept of a structure chart and hierarchical calling relationships are not applicable. Therefore, integration needs to proceed in a manner different from described previously. A good approach to integration of an object-oriented system is to make use of the concept of object clusters. Clusters are somewhat analogous to small subsystems in procedural-oriented systems.

> **A cluster consists of classes that are related, for example, they may work together (cooperate) to support a required functionality for the complete system.**

Figure 6.8 shows a generic cluster that consists of four classes/objects interacting with one another, calling each others methods. For purposes of illustration we assume that they cooperate to perform functions whose result (Out message) is exported to the outside world. As another illustration of the cluster concept we can use the notion of an object-oriented system that manages a state vehicle licensing bureau. A high-level cluster of objects may be concerned with functions related to vehicle owners, while another cluster is concerned with functions relating to the vehicles themselves. Coad and Yourdon in their text on object-oriented analysis give examples of partitioning the objects in a system into what they call subject layers that are similar in concept to clusters. The partitioning is based on using problem area subdomains [20]. Subject layers can be identified during analysis and design and help to formulate plans for integration of the component classes.

To integrate an object-oriented system using the cluster approach a tester could select clusters of classes that work together to support simple functions as the first to be integrated. Then these are combined to form higher-level, or more complex, clusters that perform multiple related functions, until the system as a whole is assembled.

An alternative integration approach for object-oriented systems consists of first selecting classes for integration that send very few messages and/or request few, or no, services from other classes. After these lower-level classes are integrated, then a layer of classes that use them can be selected for integration, and so on until the successive selection of layers of classes leads to complete integration.

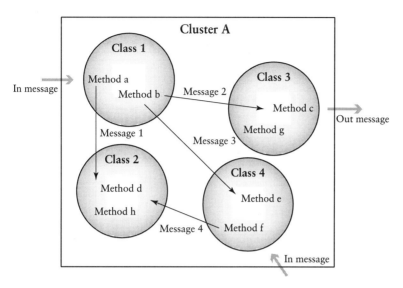

Fig. 6.8

An generic class cluster.

6.11 Designing Integration Tests

Integration tests for procedural software can be designed using a black or white box approach. Both are recommended. Some unit tests can be reused. Since many errors occur at module interfaces, test designers need to focus on exercising all input/output parameter pairs, and all calling relationships. The tester needs to insure the parameters are of the correct type and in the correct order. The author has had the personal experience of spending many hours trying to locate a fault that was due to an incorrect ordering of parameters in the calling routine. The tester must also insure that once the parameters are passed to a routine they are used correctly. For example, in Figure 6.9, Procedure_b is being integrated with Procedure_a. Procedure_a calls Procedure_b with two input parameters in3, in4. Procedure_b uses those parameters and then returns a value for the output parameter out1. Terms such as *lhs* and *rhs* could be any variable or expression. The reader should interpret the use of the variables in the broadest sense. The parameters could be involved in a number of *def* and/or *use* data flow patterns. The actual usage patterns of the parameters

Other modules

```
Procedure_a(in1,in2,out2)

...
in3 =  rhs
in4 =  rhs
...
call Procedure_b(in3,in4,out1)
...
lhs = out1
...
out2 = rhs
```

in3
in4   out1

```
Procedure_b(in3,in4,out1)

...
if( in3 ...)
...
end if

lhs = in4
...
out1 = rhs
```

Other modules

Fig. 6.9

Example integration of two procedures.

must be checked at integration time. Data flow–based (def-use paths) and control flow (branch coverage) test data generation methods are useful here to insure that the input parameters, in3, in4, are used properly in Procedure_b. Again data flow methods (def-use pairs) could also be used to check that the proper sequence of data flow operations is being carried out to generate the correct value for out1 that flows back to Procedure_a. Black box tests are useful in this example for checking the behavior of the pair of procedures. For this example test input values for the input parameters in1 and in2 should be provided, and the outcome in out2 should be examined for correctness.

For conventional systems, input/output parameters and calling relationships will appear in a structure chart built during detailed design.

Testers must insure that test cases are designed so that all modules in the structure chart are called at least once, and all called modules are called by every caller. The reader can visualize these as coverage criteria for integration test. Coverage requirements for the internal logic of each of the integrated units should be achieved during unit tests.

Some black box tests used for module integration may be reusable from unit testing. However, when units are integrated and subsystems are to be tested as a whole, new tests will have to be designed to cover their functionality and adherence to performance and other requirements (see example above). Sources for development of black box or functional tests at the integration level are the requirements documents and the user manual. Testers need to work with requirements analysts to insure that the requirements are testable, accurate, and complete. Black box tests should be developed to insure proper functionally and ability to handle subsystem stress. For example, in a transaction-based subsystem the testers want to determine the limits in number of transactions that can be handled. The tester also wants to observe subsystem actions when excessive amounts of transactions are generated. Performance issues such as the time requirements for a transaction should also be subjected to test. These will be repeated when the software is assembled as a whole and is undergoing system test.

Integration testing of clusters of classes also involves building test harnesses which in this case are special classes of objects built especially for testing. Whereas in class testing we evaluated intraclass method interactions, at the cluster level we test interclass method interaction as well. We want to insure that messages are being passed properly to interfacing objects, object state transitions are correct when specific events occur, and that the clusters are performing their required functions. Unlike procedural-oriented systems, integration for object-oriented systems usually does not occur one unit at a time. A group of cooperating classes is selected for test as a cluster. If developers have used the Coad and Yourdon's approach, then a subject layer could be used to represent a cluster. Jorgenson et al. have reported on a notation for a cluster that helps to formalize object-oriented integration [1]. In their object-oriented testing framework the method is the entity selected for unit test. The methods and the classes they belong to are connected into clusters of classes that are represented by a directed graph that has two special types of entities. These are method-message paths, and atomic systems functions that represent input port events. A method-message path is described as a sequence of method executions linked by messages. An atomic system function is an input port event (start event) followed by a set of method-messages paths and terminated by an output port event (system response). Murphy et al. define clusters as classes that are closely coupled and work together to provide a unified behavior [5]. Some examples of clusters are groups of classes that produce a report, or monitor and control a device. Scenarios of operation from the design document associated with a cluster are used to develop test cases. Murphy and his co-authors have developed a tool that can be used for class and cluster testing.

6.12 Integration Test Planing

Integration test must be planned. Planning can begin when high-level design is complete so that the system architecture is defined. Other documents relevant to integration test planning are the requirements document, the user manual, and usage scenarios. These documents contain structure charts, state charts, data dictionaries, cross-reference tables, module interface descriptions, data flow descriptions, messages and event descriptions, all necessary to plan integration tests. The strategy for integration should be defined. For procedural-oriented system the order of integration of the units of the units should be defined. This depends on the strategy selected. Consider the fact that the testing objectives are to assemble components into subsystems and to demonstrate that the subsystem functions properly with the integration test cases. For object-oriented systems a working definition of a cluster or similar construct must be described, and relevant test cases must be specified. In addition, testing resources and schedules for integration should be included in the test plan.

For readers integrating object-oriented systems Murphy et al. has a detailed description of a Cluster Test Plan [5]. The plan includes the following items:

(i) clusters this cluster is dependent on;
(ii) a natural language description of the functionality of the cluster to be tested;
(iii) list of classes in the cluster;
(iv) a set of cluster test cases.

As stated earlier in this section, one of the goals of integration test is to build working subsystems, and then combine these into the system as a whole. When planning for integration test the planner selects subsystems to build based upon the requirements and user needs. Very often subsystems selected for integration are prioritized. Those that represent key features, critical features, and/or user-oriented functions may be given the highest priority. Developers may want to show clients that certain key subsystems have been assembled and are minimally functional. Hetzel has an outline for integration test planning that takes these requirements into consideration [21].

6.13 System Test: The Different Types

When integration tests are completed, a software system has been assembled and its major subsystems have been tested. At this point the developers/testers begin to test it as a whole. System test planning should begin at the requirements phase with the development of a master test plan and requirements-based (black box) tests. System test planning is a complicated task. There are many components of the plan that need to be prepared such as test approaches, costs, schedules, test cases, and test procedures. All of these are examined and discussed in Chapter 7.

System testing itself requires a large amount of resources. The goal is to ensure that the system performs according to its requirements. System test evaluates both functional behavior and quality requirements such as reliability, usability, performance and security. This phase of testing is especially useful for detecting external hardware and software interface defects, for example, those causing race conditions, deadlocks, problems with interrupts and exception handling, and ineffective memory usage. After system test the software will be turned over to users for evaluation during acceptance test or alpha/beta test. The organization will want to be sure that the quality of the software has been measured and evaluated before users/clients are invited to use the system. In fact system test serves as a good rehearsal scenario for acceptance test.

Because system test often requires many resources, special laboratory equipment, and long test times, it is usually performed by a team of testers. The best scenario is for the team to be part of an independent testing group. The team must do their best to find any weak areas in the software; therefore, it is best that no developers are directly involved.

There are several types of system tests as shown on Figure 6.10. The types are as follows:

- Functional testing

- Performance testing

- Stress testing

- Configuration testing

- Security testing

- Recovery testing

Two other types of system testing called reliability and usability testing will be discussed in Chapter 12. The TMM recommends that these be formally integrated into the testing process by organizations at higher levels of testing maturity since at that time they have the needed expertise and infrastructure to properly conduct the tests and analyze the results.

Not all software systems need to undergo all the types of system testing. Test planners need to decide on the type of tests applicable to a particular software system. Decisions depend on the characteristics of the system and the available test resources. For example, if multiple device configurations are not a requirement for your system, then the need for configuration test is not significant. Test resources can be used for other types of system tests. Figure 6.10 also shows some of the documents useful for system test design, such as the requirements document, usage profile, and user manuals. For both procedural- and object-oriented systems, use cases, if available, are also helpful for system test design.

As the system has been assembled from its component parts, many of these types of tests have been implemented on the component parts and subsystems. However, during system test the testers can repeat these tests and design additional tests for the system as a whole. The repeated tests can in some cases be considered regression tests since there most probably have been changes made to the requirements and to the system itself since the initiation of the project. A conscientious effort at system test is essential for high software quality. Properly planned and executed system tests are excellent preparation for acceptance test. The following

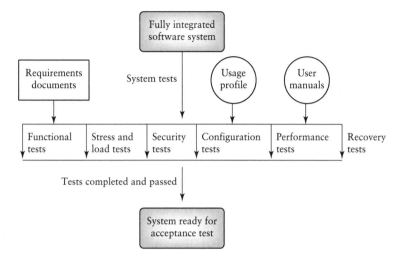

Fig. 6.10

Types of system tests.

sections will describe the types of system test. Beizer provides additional material on the different types of system tests [22].

Paper and on-line forms are helpful for system test. Some are used to insure coverage of all the requirements, for example, the Requirements Traceability Matrix, which is discussed in Chapter 7. Others, like test logs, also discussed in Chapter 7, support record keeping for test results. These forms should be fully described in the organization's standards documents.

An important tool for implementing system tests is a load generator. A load generator is essential for testing quality requirements such as performance and stress.

▌ **A load is a series of inputs that simulates a group of transactions.**

A transaction is a unit of work seen from the system user's view [19]. A transaction consists of a set of operations that may be performed by a person, software system, or a device that is outside the system. A use case can be used to describe a transaction. If you were system testing a telecommunication system you would need a load that simulated a series of phone calls (transactions) of particular types and lengths arriving from different locations. A load can be a real load, that is, you could put the system under test to real usage by having actual telephone users connected to it. Loads can also be produced by tools called load generators. They will generate test input data for system test. Load generators can be simple tools that output a fixed set of predetermined transactions. They can be complex tools that use statistical patterns to generate input data or simulate complex environments. Users of the load generators can usually set various parameters. For example, in our telecommunication system load generator users can set parameters for the mean arrival rate of the calls, the call durations, the number of wrong numbers and misdials, and the call destinations. Usage profiles, and sets of use cases can be used to set up loads for use in performance, stress, security and other types of system test.

6.13.1 Functional Testing

System functional tests have a great deal of overlap with acceptance tests. Very often the same test sets can apply to both. Both are demonstrations of the system's functionality. Functional tests at the system level are used to ensure that the behavior of the system adheres to the requirements specification. All functional requirements for the system must be achievable by the system. For example, if a personal finance system is required to allow users to set up accounts, add, modify, and delete entries in the accounts, and print reports, the function-based system and acceptance tests must ensure that the system can perform these tasks. Clients and users will expect this at acceptance test time.

Functional tests are black box in nature. The focus is on the inputs and proper outputs for each function. Improper and illegal inputs must also be handled by the system. System behavior under the latter circumstances tests must be observed. All functions must be tested.

Many of the system-level tests including functional tests should be designed at requirements time, and be included in the master and system test plans (see Chapter 7). However, there will be some requirements changes, and the tests and the test plan need to reflect those changes. Since functional tests are black box in nature, equivalence class partitioning and boundary-value analysis as described in Chapter 4 are useful methods that can be used to generate test cases. State-based tests are also valuable. In fact, the tests should focus on the following goals.

- All types or classes of legal inputs must be accepted by the software.

- All classes of illegal inputs must be rejected (however, the system should remain available).

- All possible classes of system output must exercised and examined.

- All effective system states and state transitions must be exercised and examined.

- All functions must be exercised.

As mentioned previously, a defined and documented form should be used for recording test results from functional and all other system tests. If a failure is observed, a formal test incident report should be completed and returned with the test log to the developer for code repair. Managers keep track of these forms and reports for quality assurance purposes, and to track the progress of the testing process. Readers will learn more about these documents and their importance in Chapter 7.

6.13.2 Performance Testing

An examination of a requirements document shows that there are two major types of requirements:

1. *Functional requirements*. Users describe what functions the software should perform. We test for compliance of these requirements at the system level with the functional-based system tests.
2. *Quality requirements*. There are nonfunctional in nature but describe quality levels expected for the software. One example of a quality requirement is performance level. The users may have objectives for the software system in terms of memory use, response time, through-put, and delays.

The goal of system performance tests is to see if the software meets the performance requirements. Testers also learn from performance test whether there are any hardware or software factors that impact on the system's performance. Performance testing allows testers to tune the system; that is, to optimize the allocation of system resources. For example, testers may find that they need to reallocate memory pools, or to modify the priority level of certain system operations. Testers may also be able to project the system's future performance levels. This is useful for planning subsequent releases.

Performance objectives must be articulated clearly by the users/clients in the requirements documents, and be stated clearly in the system test plan. The objectives must be quantified. For example, a requirement that the system return a response to a query in "a reasonable amount of time" is not an acceptable requirement; the time requirement must be specified in quantitative way. Results of performance tests are quantifiable. At the end of the tests the tester will know, for example, the number of CPU cycles used, the actual response time in seconds (minutes, etc.), the actual number of transactions processed per time period. These can be evaluated with respect to requirements objectives.

Resources for performance testing must be allocated in the system test plan. Examples of such resources are shown in Figure 6.11. Among the resources are:

- A source of transactions to drive the experiments. For example if you were performance testing an operating system you need a stream of data that represents typical user interactions. Typically the source of transaction for many systems is a load generator (as described in the previous section).

- An experimental testbed that includes hardware and software the system-under-test interacts with. The testbed requirements sometimes include special laboratory equipment and space that must be reserved for the tests.

- Instrumentation or probes that help to collect the performance data. Probes may be hardware or software in nature. Some probe tasks are event counting and event duration measurement. For example, if you are investigating memory requirements for your software you could use a hardware probe that collected information on memory usage (blocks allocated, blocks deallocated for different types of memory per unit time) as the system executes. The tester must keep

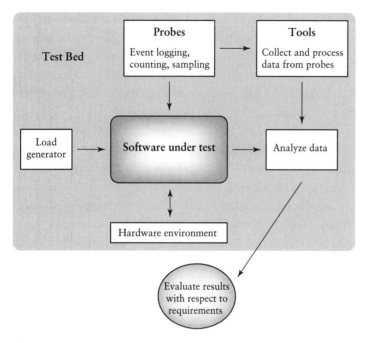

Fig. 6.11
Examples of special resources needed for a performance test.

in mind that the probes themselves may have an impact on system performance.

- A set of tools to collect, store, process, and interpret the data. Very often, large volumes of data are collected, and without tools the testers may have difficulty in processing and analyzing the data in order to evaluate true performance levels.

Test managers should ascertain the availability of these resources, and allocate the necessary time for training in the test plan. Usage requirements for these resources need to be described as part of the test plan.

6.13.3 Stress Testing

When a system is tested with a load that causes it to allocate its resources in maximum amounts, this is called stress testing. For example, if an operating system is required to handle 10 interrupts/second and the load causes 20 interrupts/second, the system is being stressed. The goal of stress test is to try to break the system; find the circumstances under which it will crash. This is sometimes called "breaking the system." An everyday analogy can be found in the case where a suitcase being tested for strength and endurance is stomped on by a multiton elephant!

Stress testing is important because it can reveal defects in real-time and other types of systems, as well as weak areas where poor design could cause unavailability of service. For example, system prioritization orders may not be correct, transaction processing may be poorly designed and waste memory space, and timing sequences may not be appropriate for the required tasks. This is particularly important for real-time systems where unpredictable events may occur resulting in input loads that exceed those described in the requirements documents. Stress testing often uncovers race conditions, deadlocks, depletion of resources in unusual or unplanned patterns, and upsets in normal operation of the software system. System limits and threshold values are exercised. Hardware and software interactions are stretched to the limit. All of these conditions are likely to reveal defects and design flaws which may not be revealed under normal testing conditions.

Stress testing is supported by many of the resources used for performance test as shown in Figure 6.11. This includes the load generator. The testers set the load generator parameters so that load levels cause stress to the system. For example, in our example of a telecommunication system, the arrival rate of calls, the length of the calls, the number of misdials, as well as other system parameters should all be at stress levels. As in the case of performance test, special equipment and laboratory space may be needed for the stress tests. Examples are hardware or software probes and event loggers. The tests may need to run for several days. Planners must insure resources are available for the long time periods required. The reader should note that stress tests should also be conducted at the integration, and if applicable at the unit level, to detect stress-related defects as early as possible in the testing process. This is especially critical in cases where redesign is needed.

Stress testing is important from the user/client point of view. When system operate correctly under conditions of stress then clients have confidence that the software can perform as required. Beizer suggests that devices used for monitoring stress situations provide users/clients with visible and tangible evidence that the system is being stressed [22].

6.13.4 Configuration Testing

Typical software systems interact with hardware devices such as disc drives, tape drives, and printers. Many software systems also interact with multiple CPUs, some of which are redundant. Software that controls real-time processes, or embedded software also interfaces with devices, but these are very specialized hardware items such as missile launchers, and nuclear power device sensors. In many cases, users require that devices be interchangeable, removable, or reconfigurable. For example, a printer of type X should be substitutable for a printer of type Y, CPU A should be removable from a system composed of several other CPUs, sensor A should be replaceable with sensor B. Very often the software will have a set of commands, or menus, that allows users to make these configuration changes. Configuration testing allows developers/testers to evaluate system performance and availability when hardware exchanges and reconfigurations occur. Configuration testing also requires many resources including the multiple hardware devices used for the tests. If a system does not have specific requirements for device configuration changes then large-scale configuration testing is not essential.

According to Beizer configuration testing has the following objectives [22]:

- Show that all the configuration changing commands and menus work properly.

- Show that all interchangeable devices are really interchangeable, and that they each enter the proper states for the specified conditions.

- Show that the systems' performance level is maintained when devices are interchanged, or when they fail.

Several types of operations should be performed during configuration test. Some sample operations for testers are [22]:

(i) rotate and permutate the positions of devices to ensure physical/logical device permutations work for each device (e.g., if there are two printers A and B, exchange their positions);

(ii) induce malfunctions in each device, to see if the system properly handles the malfunction;

(iii) induce multiple device malfunctions to see how the system reacts.

These operations will help to reveal problems (defects) relating to hardware/software interactions when hardware exchanges, and reconfigurations occur. Testers observe the consequences of these operations and determine whether the system can recover gracefully particularly in the case of a malfunction.

6.13.5 Security Testing

Designing and testing software systems to insure that they are safe and secure is a big issue facing software developers and test specialists. Recently, safety and security issues have taken on additional importance due to the proliferation of commercial applications for use on the Internet. If Internet users believe that their personal information is not secure and is available to those with intent to do harm, the future of e-commerce is in peril! Security testing evaluates system characteristics that relate to the availability, integrity, and confidentially of system data and services. Users/clients should be encouraged to make sure their security needs are clearly known at requirements time, so that security issues can be addressed by designers and testers.

Computer software and data can be compromised by:

(i) criminals intent on doing damage, stealing data and information, causing denial of service, invading privacy;

(ii) errors on the part of honest developers/maintainers who modify, destroy, or compromise data because of misinformation, misunderstandings, and/or lack of knowledge.

Both criminal behavior and errors that do damage can be perpetuated by those inside and outside of an organization. Attacks can be random or systematic. Damage can be done through various means such as:

(i)   viruses;

(ii) trojan horses;

(iii) trap doors;

(iv) illicit channels.

The effects of security breaches could be extensive and can cause:

(i)   loss of information;

(ii) corruption of information;

(iii) misinformation;

(iv) privacy violations;

(v) denial of service.

Physical, psychological, and economic harm to persons or property can result from security breaches. Developers try to ensure the security of their systems through use of protection mechanisms such as passwords, encryption, virus checkers, and the detection and elimination of trap doors. Developers should realize that protection from unwanted entry and other security-oriented matters must be addressed at design time. A simple case in point relates to the characteristics of a password. Designers need answers to the following: What is the minimum and maximum allowed length for the password? Can it be pure alphabetical or must it be a mixture of alphabetical and other characters? Can it be a dictionary word? Is the password permanent, or does it expire periodically? Users can specify their needs in this area in the requirements document. A password checker can enforce any rules the designers deem necessary to meet security requirements.

Password checking and examples of other areas to focus on during security testing are described below.

Password Checking—Test the password checker to insure that users will select a password that meets the conditions described in the password checker specification. Equivalence class partitioning and boundary value analysis based on the rules and conditions that specify a valid password can be used to design the tests.

Legal and Illegal Entry with Passwords—Test for legal and illegal system/data access via legal and illegal passwords.

Password Expiration—If it is decided that passwords will expire after a certain time period, tests should be designed to insure the expiration period is properly supported and that users can enter a new and appropriate password.

Encryption—Design test cases to evaluate the correctness of both encryption and decryption algorithms for systems where data/messages are encoded.

Browsing—Evaluate browsing privileges to insure that unauthorized browsing does not occur. Testers should attempt to browse illegally and observe system responses. They should determine what types of private information can be inferred by both legal and illegal browsing.

Trap Doors—Identify any unprotected entries into the system that may allow access through unexpected channels (trap doors). Design tests that attempt to gain illegal entry and observe results. Testers will need the support of designers and developers for this task. In many cases an external "tiger team" as described below is hired to attempt such a break into the system.

Viruses—Design tests to insure that system virus checkers prevent or curtail entry of viruses into the system. Testers may attempt to infect the system with various viruses and observe the system response. If a virus does penetrate the system, testers will want to determine what has been damaged and to what extent.

Even with the backing of the best intents of the designers, developers/testers can never be sure that a software system is totally secure even after extensive security testing. If security is an especially important issue, as in the case of network software, then the best approach if resources permit, is to hire a so-called "tiger team" which is an outside group of penetration experts who attempt to breach the system security. Although a testing group in the organization can be involved in testing for security breaches, the tiger team can attack the problem from a different point of view. Before the tiger team starts its work the system should be thoroughly tested at all levels. The testing team should also try to identify any trap doors and other vulnerable points. Even with the use of a tiger team there is never any guarantee that the software is totally secure.

6.13.6 Recovery Testing

Recovery testing subjects a system to losses of resources in order to determine if it can recover properly from these losses. This type of testing is especially important for transaction systems, for example, on-line banking software. A test scenario might be to emulate loss of a device during a transaction. Tests would determine if the system could return to a well-known state, and that no transactions have been compromised. Systems with automated recovery are designed for this purpose. They usually have multiple CPUs and/or multiple instances of devices, and mechanisms to detect the failure of a device. They also have a so-called "checkpoint" system that meticulously records transactions and system states periodically so that these are preserved in case of failure. This information allows the system to return to a known state after the failure. The recovery testers must ensure that the device monitoring system and the checkpoint software are working properly.

Beizer advises that testers focus on the following areas during recovery testing [22]:

1. *Restart.* The current system state and transaction states are discarded. The most recent checkpoint record is retrieved and the system initialized to the states in the checkpoint record. Testers must insure that all transactions have been reconstructed correctly and that all devices are in the proper state. The system should then be able to begin to process new transactions.
2. *Switchover.* The ability of the system to switch to a new processor must be tested. Switchover is the result of a command or a detection of a faulty processor by a monitor.

In each of these testing situations all transactions and processes must be carefully examined to detect:

(i) loss of transactions;
(ii) merging of transactions;

(iii) incorrect transactions;

(iv) an unnecessary duplication of a transaction.

A good way to expose such problems is to perform recovery testing under a stressful load. Transaction inaccuracies and system crashes are likely to occur with the result that defects and design flaws will be revealed.

6.14 Regression Testing

Regression testing is not a level of testing, but it is the *retesting* of software that occurs when changes are made to ensure that the new version of the software has retained the capabilities of the old version and that no new defects have been introduced due to the changes. Regression testing can occur at any level of test, for example, when unit tests are run the unit may pass a number of these tests until one of the tests does reveal a defect. The unit is repaired and then retested with all the old test cases to ensure that the changes have not affected its functionality. Regression tests are especially important when multiple software releases are developed. Users want new capabilities in the latest releases, but still expect the older capabilities to remain in place. This is where regression testing plays a role. Test cases, test procedures, and other test-related items from previous releases should be available so that these tests can be run with the new versions of the software. Automated testing tools support testers with this very time-consuming task. Later chapters will describe the role of these testing tools.

6.15 Alpha, Beta, and Acceptance Tests

In the various testing activities that have been described so far, users have played a supporting role for the most part. They have been involved in requirements analysis and reviews, and have played a role in test planning. This is especially true for acceptance test planning if the software is being custom made for an organization. The clients along with test planners design the actual test cases that will be run during acceptance test.

Users/clients may also have participated in prototype evaluation, usage profile development, and in the various stages of usability testing (see Chapter 12). After the software has passed all the system tests and defect repairs have been made, the users take a more active role in the testing process. Developers/testers must keep in mind that the software is being developed to satisfy the users requirements, and no matter how elegant its design it will not be accepted by the users unless it helps them to achieve their goals as specified in the requirements. Alpha, beta, and acceptance tests allow users to evaluate the software in terms of their expectations and goals.

When software is being developed for a specific client, acceptance tests are carried out after system testing. The acceptance tests must be planned carefully with input from the client/users. Acceptance test cases are based on requirements. The user manual is an additional source for test cases. System test cases may be reused. The software must run under real-world conditions on operational hardware and software. The software-under-test should be stressed. For continuous systems the software should be run at least through a 25-hour test cycle. Conditions should be typical for a working day. Typical inputs and illegal inputs should be used and all major functions should be exercised. If the entire suite of tests cannot be run for any reason, then the full set of tests needs to be rerun from the start.

Acceptance tests are a very important milestone for the developers. At this time the clients will determine if the software meets their requirements. Contractual obligations can be satisfied if the client is satisfied with the software. Development organizations will often receive their final payment when acceptance tests have been passed.

Acceptance tests must be rehearsed by the developers/testers. There should be no signs of unprofessional behavior or lack of preparation. Clients do not appreciate surprises. Clients should be received in the development organization as respected guests. They should be provided with documents and other material to help them participate in the acceptance testing process, and to evaluate the results. After acceptance testing the client will point out to the developers which requirement have/have not been satisfied. Some requirements may be deleted, modified, or added due to changing needs. If the client has been involved in prototype evaluations then the changes may be less extensive.

If the client is satisfied that the software is usable and reliable, and they give their approval, then the next step is to install the system at the client's site. If the client's site conditions are different from that of the developers, the developers must set up the system so that it can interface with client software and hardware. Retesting may have to be done to insure that the software works as required in the client's environment. This is called installation test.

If the software has been developed for the mass market (shrink-wrapped software), then testing it for individual clients/users is not practical or even possible in most cases. Very often this type of software undergoes two stages of acceptance test. The first is called alpha test. This test takes place at the developer's site. A cross-section of potential users and members of the developer's organization are invited to use the software. Developers observe the users and note problems. Beta test sends the software to a cross-section of users who install it and use it under real-world working conditions. The users send records of problems with the software to the development organization where the defects are repaired sometimes in time for the current release. In many cases the repairs are delayed until the next release.

6.16 Summary Statement on Testing Levels

In this chapter we have studied the testing of software at different levels of abstraction as summarized in Figure 6.1. The reader should note that each testing level:

- focuses on a specific level of abstraction of the software;

- has a set of specific goals;

- is useful for revealing different types of defects (problems);

- uses a specific set of documents as guides for designing tests;

- is useful for evaluating certain functional and quality attributes of the software;

- is associated with a level-oriented test plan (described in Chapter 7).

The study of the material in this chapter gives the reader an appreciation of the size and complexity of the entire testing effort. To achieve testing goals and to perform testing in an effective manner, testers must be motivated, have good technical and communication skills, and be good planners and managers. It is the goal of the testing group working along with developers and other software professionals to release a software system to the customer that meets all requirements.

6.17 The Special Role of Use Cases

The importance of software models as aids to the tester has been described throughout this book. For example, the role of state models, data flow, and control flow models in designing black and white box test cases is described in Chapters 4 and 5. In this chapter, another important model is introduced called the "use case." A description of a use case is as follows.

> **A use case is a pattern, scenario, or exemplar of usage. It describes a typical interaction between the software system under development and a user.**

A use case scenario begins with some user of the system (human, hardware device, an interfacing software system) initiating a transaction or a sequence of events. The interaction is often depicted as a diagram or graphical drawing showing the entities involved. In addition, a textual description of the interaction often accompanies the graphic representation. The text describes the sequence of events that occurs when such a transaction is initiated. All the events that occur and the system's responses to the events are part of the textural description (scenario script). The design of use cases typically begins in the requirements phase. User interactions with respect to primary system functions are collected and analyzed. Each of the scenarios/interactions in the collection are modeled in the form of a use case. As development continues the use cases can be refined to include, for example, exception conditions. Scenarios for interactions involving secondary system functions can be added. The entire collection of use cases gives a complete description of system use by users. The use cases are usually reviewed with testers as participants in the review process. Customers also review the use cases.

The development of use cases is often associated with object-oriented development. They are used frequently to describe object responsibilities and/or to model object interactions. Current uses include application to both object-oriented and procedure-oriented systems to model user–system interactions. Use cases are especially of value to testers, and are useful for designing tests at the integration or system level for both types of systems. For example, a given use case may model a thread or transaction implemented by a subsystem or a class cluster. A set of use cases can also serve as a model for transactions involving the software system as whole. Use cases are also very useful for designing acceptance tests with customer participation. A reasonable testing goal would be to test uses of the system through coverage of all of the use cases. Each thread of functionality should be covered by a test.

Jacobson et al. briefly describe how use cases support integration and system test in object-oriented systems [23]. They suggest tests that cause the software to follow the expected flow of events, as well as tests that trigger odd or unexpected cases of the use case—a flow of events different than expected. An example use case associated with an automated payment system is shown in Figure 6.12. The customer initiates the transaction by inserting a card and a PIN. The steps following describe the interaction between the customer and the system in detail for a particular type of transaction—the automated payment. For our use case example we could develop a set of test inputs during integration or system test so that a typical interaction for the automated payment system would follow the flow of steps. The set of inputs for the test includes:

Valid user PIN: IB-1234

Selection option: Automated payment

Valid account number of the recipient: GWB-6789

Selection payment schedule: Weekly

Selection of day of the month: 15

```
┌─────────────────────────────────────────────────────────────┐
│               Automated Payment Sequence                      │
│             ATM Machine Software System                        │
├─────────────────────────────────────────────────────────────┤
```

1. Customer inserts card in machine slot and enters PIN.
2. The card and PIN are verified and the main menu is shown.
3. Customer selects the "transaction services" menu, the menu is then displayed by the ATM.
4. Customer selects the "automated payment" service from the menu.
5. Customer is prompted for the account number of the recipient of the payment.
6. Customer enters the recipient's account number.
7. Recipient's account number is verified, and "payment schedule" menu is displayed.
8. Customer selects monthly payment schedule from menu. Choices include: weekly, monthly, yearly, etc. Secondary menu displays choices to refine payment schedule.
9. Customer inputs day-of-month for periodic payments.
10. Secondary menu displays options to set fixed and maximum amount.
11. Customer selects the maximum amount option (e.g., a $60 value). A menu for start date is displayed. On this date the payment is due.
12. Customer selects today's date as the start date.
13. The transaction is verified, and the main menu is displayed.

Fig. 6.12

Example text-based use case.

Maximum payment option value: $50

Start date: 3-15-01

In our example, use of an invalid recipient account number as input would alter the flow of events described and could constitute one odd use of the case. Other exceptions could include a payment entered that is larger than the customer's current account holding.

6.18 Levels of Testing and the TMM

The material covered in this chapter is associated with the TMM level 2 maturity goal, "institutionalize basic testing techniques and methods," which addresses important technical issues related to execution-based testing. The focus is on the different levels of testing that must occur when a complex software system is being developed. An organization at TMM level 2 must work hard to plan, support, and implement these levels of testing so that it can instill confidence in the quality of its software and the proficiency of its testing process. This is why the maturity goal to "institutionalize basic testing techniques and methods," which encompasses multilevel testing, appears at lower levels of the maturity goal hierarchy (TMM level 2). In Chapter 7 you will learn how these testing levels are supported by test planning. Later chapters will describe the tools to support these levels of testing.

Readers can see that testing at different levels requires many resources. Very often when budgets and schedules are tight, these levels are sacrificed and the organization often reverts to previous immature practices such as "big bang" integration and multiple test, debug, patch, and repair cycles. This will occur unless there are concerted efforts by the developers, quality personnel, and especially management to put these levels of testing into place as part of a concerted TMM-based test process improvement effort. Otherwise the organization's reputation for consistently releasing quality products will not be maintainable.

The three maturity goals at TMM level 2 are interrelated and support areas from the three critical groups overlap. In Chapters 4 and 5 you learned how the members of the three critical groups support the adaptation and application of white and black box testing methods. Chapter 7 will describe how critical group members support test planning and policy making. Below is a brief description of how critical group members support multilevel testing. Again, you will notice some overlap with the group responsibilities described in Chapters 4, 5, and 7.

Managers can support multilevel testing by:

- ensuring that the testing policy requires multilevel testing;

- ensuring that test plans are prepared for the multiple levels;

- providing the resources needed for multilevel testing;

- adjusting project schedules so that multilevel testing can be adequately performed;

- supporting the education and training of staff in testing methods and techniques needed to implement multilevel testing.

Developers/testers give their support by:

- attending classes and training sessions to master the knowledge needed to plan and implement multilevel testing;

- supporting management to ensure multilevel testing is a part of organizational policy, is incorporated into test plans, and is applied throughout the organization;

- working with project managers (and test managers at TMM level 3 and higher) to ensure there is time and resources to test at all levels;

- mentoring colleagues who wish to acquire the necessary background and experience to perform multilevel testing;

- work with users/clients to develop the use cases, usage profiles, and acceptance criteria necessary for the multilevel tests;

- implement the tests at all levels which involves:
    —planning the tests
    —designing the test cases
    —gathering the necessary resources
    —executing unit, integration, system, and acceptance tests
    —collecting test results
    —collecting test-related metrics
    —analyzing test results
    —interacting with developers, SQA staff, and user/clients to resolve problems

The *user/clients* play an essential role in the implementation of multilevel testing. They give support by:

- providing liaison staff to interact with the development organization testing staff;

- working with analysts so that system requirements are complete and clear and testable;

- providing input for system and acceptance test;

- providing input for the development of use cases and/or a usage profile to support system and acceptance testing;

- participating in acceptance and/or alpha and beta tests;

- providing feedback and problem reports promptly so that problems can be addressed after the system is in operation.

LIST OF KEY TERMS

Cluster
Load
Test harness
Unit
Use case

EXERCISES

1. How would you define a software unit? In terms of your definition, what constitutes a unit for procedural code; for object-oriented code?

2. Summarize the issues that arise in class testing.

3. The text gives example sequences of inputs and calls to test the stack class as shown in Figure 6.3. Develop sequences for testing the stack that try to push an item on a full stack, and to pop an item from an empty stack.

4. Why is it so important to design a test harness for reusability?

5. Suppose you were developing a stub that emulates a module that passes back a hash value when passed a name. What are the levels of functionality you could implement for this stub? What factors could influence your choice of levels?

6. What are the key differences in integrating procedural-oriented systems as compared to object-oriented systems?

7. From your knowledge of defect types in Chapter 3 of this text, what defect types are most likely to be detected during integration test of a software system? Describe your choices in terms of both the nature of integration test and the nature of the defect types you select.

8. Using the structure chart shown below, show the order of module integration for the top-down (depth and breadth first), and bottom-up integration approaches. Estimate the number of drivers and stubs needed for each approach. Specify integration testing activities that can be done in parallel, assuming you have a maximum of three testers. Based on resource needs and the ability to carry out parallel testing activities, which approach would you select for this system and why?

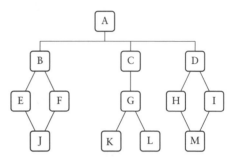

9. This chapter describe several types of system tests. Select from these types those you would perform for the software described below. For each category you choose (i) specify the test objectives, and (ii) give a general description of the tests you would develop and tools you would need. You may make any assumptions related to system characteristics that are needed to support your answers.

An on-line fast food restaurant system. The system reads customer orders, relays orders to the kitchen, calculates the customer's bill, and gives change. It also maintains inventory information. Each wait-person has a terminal. Only authorized wait-persons and a system administrator can access the system.

10. An air-traffic control system can have one or many users. It interfaces with many hardware devices such as displays, radar detectors, and communications devices. This system can occur in a variety of configurations. Describe how you would carry out configuration tests on this system.

11. As in Problem 9, describe the types of system tests you would select for the following software. The project is a real-time control system for a new type of laser that will be used for cancer therapy. Some of the code will be used to control hardware devices. Only qualified technicians can access the system.

12. Discuss the importance of regression testing when developing a new software release. What items from previous release would be useful to the regression tester?

13. **From your experience with online and/or catalog shopping, develop a use case to describe a user purchase of a television set with a credit card from a online vendor using web-based software. With the aid of your use case, design a set of tests you could use during system test to evaluate the software.**

14. **Describe the Activities/Tasks and Responsibilities for developer/testers in support of multilevel testing.**

REFERENCES

[1] P. Jorgensen, C. Erikson, "Object-oriented integration Test," *CACM,* Vol. 37, No. 9, 1994, pp. 30–38.

[2] R. D'Souza, R. LeBlanc, "Class testing by examining pointers," *J. Object Oriented Programming,* July–August, 1994, pp. 33–39.

[3] M. Smith, D. Robson, "A framework for testing object-oriented programs," *J. Object Oriented Programming,* June 1992, pp. 45–53.

[4] S. Fiedler, "Object-oriented unit testing," *Hewlett-Packard Journal,* April, 1989, pp. 69–74.

[5] G. Murphy, P. Townsend, P. Wong, "Experiences with cluster and class testing," *CACM,* Vol. 37, No. 9, 1994, pp. 39–47.

[6] N. Wilde, "Testing your objects," *The C Users Journal,* May 1993, pp. 25–32.

[7] R. Doong, P. Frankl, "The ASTOOT approach to testing object-oriented programs," *ACM Transactions of Software Engineering and Methodology,* Vol. 3, No., 1994, pp 101–130.

[8] E. Berard, *Essays on Object-Oriented Software Engineering,* Volume 1, Prentice Hall, Englewood Cliffs, NJ, 1993.

[9] B. Marick, *The Craft of Software Testing,* Prentice Hall, Englewood Cliffs, NJ, 1995.

[10] IEEE/ANSI Std 1008-1987 (Reaff 1993), Standard for Software Unit Testing, Institute of Electrical and Electronics Engineers, Inc., 1987.

[11] J. McGregor, A. Kare, "Parallel architecture for component testing of object-oriented software," *Proc. Ninth International Quality Week Conf.,* May 1996.

[12] M. Chen, M. Kao, "Investigating test effectiveness on object-oriented software: a case study," *Proc. Twelfth International Quality Week Conf.,* May 1999.

[13] D. Perry. G. Kaiser, "Adequate testing and object-oriented programming," *J. Object Oriented Programming,* Vol. 2, No. 5, 1990, pp. 13–19.

[14] K Rangaraajan, P. Eswar, T. Ashok, "Retesting C++ classes," *Proc. Ninth International Quality Week Conf.,* May 1996.

[15] B. Tsai, S. Stobart, N. Parrington, I. Mitchell, "A state-based testing approach providing data flow coverage in object-oriented class testing," *Proc. Twelfth International Quality Week Conf.,* May 1999.

[16] M Harrold, J. McGregor, K. Fitzpatrick, "Incremental testing of object-oriented class structures," *Proc. 14th International Conf. on Software Engineering,* May 1992, pp. 68–80.

[17] M. Harrold, G. Rothermel, "Performing data flow testing on classes," *Proc. Second ACM SIGSOFT Symposium on Foundations of Software Engineering,* Dec. 1994, pp. 154–163.

[18] D. Kung, P. Hsia, J. Gao, *Testing Object-Oriented Software,* IEEE Computer Society Press, Los Alamitos, CA, 1998.

[19] U. Linnenkugel, M. Mullerburg, "Test data selection criteria for (software) integration testing," *Proc. First International Conf. Systems Integration,* April 1990, pp. 709–717.

[20] P. Coad, E. Yourdon, *Object-Oriented Analysis,* second edition, Yourdon Press, Englewood Cliffs, NJ, 1991.

[21] B. Hetzel *The Complete Guide to Software Testing,* second edition, QED Information Sciences, Inc., Wellesley, MA. 1988.

[22] B. Beizer, *Software Testing and Quality Assurance,* Von Nostrand Reinhold, New York, 1984.

[23] I. Jacobson, M. Christerson, P. Jonsson, G. Overgaard, *Object-Oriented Software Engineering: A Use Case Driven Approach,* Addison-Wesley, Reading, MA, 1992.

TESTING GOALS, POLICIES, PLANS AND DOCUMENTATION

7.0 Introductory Concepts

This chapter focuses on preparing the reader to address two fundamental maturity goals at level 2 of the TMM: (i) developing organizational goals/policies relating to testing and debugging, and (ii) test planning. These maturity goals are managerial in nature. They are essential to support testing as a managed process. According to R. Thayer, a managed process is one that is planned, monitored, directed, staffed, and organized [1]. At TMM level 2 the planning component of a managed process is instituted. At TMM levels 3 and 4 the remaining managerial components are integrated into the process. By instituting all of the managerial components described by Thayer in an incremental manner, an organization is able to establish the high-quality testing process described at higher levels of the TMM. The test specialist has a key role in developing and implementing these managerial components. In this chapter concepts and tools are introduced to build test management skills, thus supporting the reader in his/her development as a test specialist.

The development, documentation, and institutionalization of goals and related policies is important to an organization. The goals/policies may be business-related, technical, or political in nature. They are the basis for decision making; therefore setting goals and policies requires the participation and support of upper management. Technical staff and other interested parties also participate in goal and policy development. Simple examples of the three types of goals mentioned are shown below.

1. *Business goal:* to increase market share 10% in the next 2 years in the area of financial software.

2. *Technical goal:* to reduce defects by 2% per year over the next 3 years.

3. *Business/technical goal:* to reduce hotline calls by 5% over the next 2 years.

4. *Political goal:* to increase the number of women and minorities in high management positions by 15% in the next 3 years.

Planning is guided by policy, supports goal achievement, and is a vital part of all engineering activities. In the software domain, plans to achieve goals associated with a specific project are usually developed by a project manager. In the testing domain, test plans support achieving testing goals for a project, and are either developed by the project manager as part of the overall project plan, or by a test or quality specialist in conjunction with the project planner. Test planning requires the planner to articulate the testing goals for a given project, to select tools and techniques needed to achieve the goals, and to estimate time and resources needed for testing tasks so that testing is effective, on time, within budget, and consistent with project goals. The first sections of this chapter will provide insight into the nature of test-related goals and policies. In latter sections the reader will learn how to organize and develop test plans and other test-related documents.

7.1 Testing and Debugging Goals and Policies

> A goal can be described as (i) a statement of intent, or (ii) a statement of a accomplishment that an individual or an organization wants to achieve.

A goal statement relates to an area where an individual, group, or organization wants to make improvements. Goals project future states of an organization, a group, or an individual.

In an organization there is often a hierarchy of goals. At the top level are general organizational goals. There are intermediate-level goals that may be associated with a particular organizational functional unit. Individual projects have specific goals. These usually reflect organizational goals. There are personal-level goals as well. Each individual in an organization has a set of goals for self-improvement so that he or she can more effectively contribute to the project, functional unit, and organization as a whole.

Goal statements can express expectations in quantitative terms or be more general in nature. For the testing goals below, goals 1 and 2 express what is to be achieved in a more quantitative manner than goals 3 and 4.

1. One-hundred percent of testing activities are planned.
2. The degree of automation for regression testing is increased from 50% to 80% over the next 3 years.
3. Testing activities are performed by a dedicated testing group.
4. Testing group members have at least a bachelor-level degree and have taken a formal course in software testing.

In general, quantitative goals are more useful. These are measurable goals, and give an organization, group, or individual the means to evaluate progress toward achieving the goal.

In the testing domain, goal statements should provide a high-level vision of what testing is to accomplish in the organization with respect to quality of process and product. In addition to general testing goal statements, lower-level goal statements should be developed for all levels of testing. Goals for the education and training of testing personnel should also be included with testing goal statements. Test plans should express testing goals for each project. These reflect overall organizational testing goals as well as specific goals for the project.

The TMM itself is built on a hierarchy of high-level testing maturity goals and subgoals which support the growth of an effective software testing process and promote high software quality. The TMM can be used by decision-makers in an organization to develop both long- and short-term testing goals based on the TMM goal hierarchy.

> **A policy can be defined as a high-level statement of principle or course of action that is used to govern a set of activities in an organization.**

Because a policy provides the vision and framework for decision making, it is important to have the policy formally adopted by the organization, documented, and available for all interested parties. An intraorganizational web site is suggested as a location for policy statements. This would allow for updates and visibility within the organization. A policy statement should be formulated by a team or task force consisting of upper management, executive personnel, and technical staff. In the case of testing, a testing policy statement is used to guide the course of testing activities and test process evolution. It should be agreed upon as workable by all concerned.

Testing policy statements reflect, integrate, and support achievement of testing goals. These goals in turn often target increasing software quality and improving customer satisfaction. Test policies also provide high-level guidance as to how testing is to be done in the organization, how its effectiveness will be evaluated, who will be responsible, and what choices of resources are possible. They should be explicit enough to guide decisions on all important testing issues, for example, how to test, what to test, and who will test. Policies are not written in stone, and as an organization grows in maturity its policies will change and mature. The task force should establish documented procedures for policy change.

A brief outline of a sample testing policy statement appropriate for a TMM level 2 organization follows.

Testing Policy: Organization X

Our organization, the X Corporation, realizes that testing is an important component of the software development process and has a high impact on software quality and the degree of customer satisfaction. To ensure that our testing process is effective and that our software products meet the client's requirements we have developed and adopted the following testing policy statement.

1. Delivering software of the highest quality is our company goal. The presence of defects has a negative impact on software quality. Defects affect the correctness, reliability, and usability of a software product, thus rendering it unsatisfactory to the client. We define a testing activity as a set of tasks whose purpose is to reveal functional and quality-related defects in a software deliverable. Testing activities include traditional execution of the developing software, as well as reviews of the software deliverables produced at all stages of the life cycle. The aggregation of all testing activities performed in a systematic manner supported by organizational policies, procedures, and standards constitutes the testing process.

2. A set of testing standards must be available to all interested parties on an intraorganizational web site. The standards contain descriptions of all test-related documents, prescribed templates, and the methods, tools, and procedures to be used for testing. The standards must specify the types of projects that each of these items is to be associated with.

3. In our organization the following apply to all software development/maintenance projects:

- Execution-based tests must be performed at several levels such as unit, integration, system, and acceptance tests as appropriate for each software product.

- Systematic approaches to test design must be employed that include application of both white and black box testing methods.

- Reviews of all major product deliverables such as requirements and design documents, code, and test plans are required.

- Testing must be planned for all projects. Plans must be developed for all levels of execution-based testing as well as for reviews of deliverables. Test plan templates must be included in organizational standards documents and implemented online. A test plan for a project must be compatible with the project plan for that project. Test plans must be approved by the project manager and technical staff. Acceptance test plans must also be approved by the client.

- Testing activities must be monitored using measurements and milestones to ensure that they are proceeding according to plan.

- Testing activities must be integrated into the software life cycle and carried out in parallel with other development activities. The extended modified V-model as shown in the testing standards document has been adopted to support this goal.

- Defects uncovered during each test must be classified and recorded.

- There must be a training program to ensure that the best testing practices are employed by the testing staff.

4. Because testing is an activity that requires special training and an impartial view of the software, it must be carried out by an independent testing group. Communication lines must be established to support cooperation between testers and developers to ensure that the software is reliable, safe, and meets client requirements.

5. Testing must be supported by tools, and, test-related measurements must be collected and used to evaluate and improve the testing process and the software product.

6. Resources must be provided for continuos test process improvement.

7. Clients/developer/tester communication is important, and clients must be involved in acceptance test planning, operational profile development, and usage testing when applicable to the project. Clients must sign off on the acceptance test plan and give approval for all changes in the acceptance test plan.

8. A permanent committee consisting of managerial and technical staff must be appointed to be responsible for distribution and maintenance of organizational test policy statements.

Whatever the nature of the test policy statement, it should have strong support and continual commitment from management. After the policy statement has been developed, approved, and distributed, a subset of the task force should be appointed to permanently oversee policy implementation and change.

Note that the TMM maturity goals at level 2 call for separate organizational goals (and policies) for testing and debugging. This is important for several reasons. First, at TMM level 2 testing becomes a planned activity and can therefore be managed. Debugging is difficult to manage because predictions about the types of defects present in the software are usually not accurate. At higher levels of the TMM where data relating to defects from past releases and projects are available, the project manager may have some success in this area. In addition, testing and debugging have different goals and psychologies. Each requires different techniques, methods, and tools. Because of the differing psychologies involved they should be performed by different groups having different training. Policies for both of these processes should describe these differences. It should be clear what the goals for both of these processes are. In this way managers will better be able to allocate resources, decide on proper training, apply appropriate tools, and keep track of the costs for each. A sample debugging policy statement is shown below. This debugging policy is applicable to organizations at TMM level 2. At higher levels of the TMM, organizations will want to modify the policy statements to include support for activities such as defect prevention. At TMM levels 3 and higher there is separate testing group. The duties of the testers and developers will be separate and responsibilities will be transferred from developers to testers and vice versa. It will be the software developers who will have primary responsibilities for debugging efforts.

Debugging Policy: Organization X

Our organization, the X Corporation, is committed to delivering high-quality software to our customers. Effective testing and debugging processes are essential to support this goal. It is our policy to separate testing and debugging, and we consider them as two separate processes. Each has different psychologies, goals, and requirements. The resources, training, and tools needed are different for both. To support the separation of these two processes we have developed individual testing and debugging policies. Our debugging policy is founded on our quality goal to remove all defects from our software that impact on our customers' ability to use our software effectively, safely, and economically. To achieve this goal we have developed the following debugging policy statement.

1. Testing and debugging are two separate processes. Testing is the process used to detect (reveal) defects. Debugging is the process dedicated to locating the defects, repairing the code, and retesting the software. Defects are anomalies that impact on software functionality as well as on quality attributes such as performance, security, ease of use, correctness, and reliability.

2. Since debugging is a timely activity, all project schedules must allow for adequate time to make repairs, and retest the repaired software.

3. Debugging tools, and the training necessary to use the tools, must be available to developers to support debugging activities and tasks.

4. Developers/testers and SQA staff must define and document a set of defect classes and defect severity levels. These must be must be available to all interested parties on an intraorganizational web site, and applied to all projects.

5. When failures are observed during testing or in operational software they are documented. A problem, or test incident, report is completed by the developer/tester at testing time and by the users when a failure/problem is observed in operational software. The problem report is forwarded to the development group. Both testers/developers and SQA staff must communicate and work with users to gain an understanding of the problem. A fix report must be completed by the developer when the defect is repaired and code retested. Standard problem and fix report forms must be available to all interested parties on an intraorganizational web site, and applied to all projects.

7. All defects identified for each project must be cataloged according to class and severity level and stored as a part of the project history.

8. Measurement such as total number of defects, total number of defects/KLOC, and time to repair a defect are saved for each project.

9. A permanent committee consisting of managerial and technical staff must be appointed to be responsible for distribution and maintenance of organizational debugging policy statements.

7.2 Test Planning

A plan can be defined in the following way.

> **A plan is a document that provides a framework or approach for achieving a set of goals.**

In the software domain, plans can be strictly business oriented, for example, long-term plans to support the economic growth of an organization, or they can be more technical in nature, for example, a plan to develop a specific software product. Test plans tend to be more technically oriented. However, a software project plan that may contain a test plan as well will often refer to business goals. In this chapter we focus on planning for execution-based software testing (validation testing). In Chapter 10, where reviews are discussed, planning for verification activities is described.

Test planning is an essential practice for any organization that wishes to develop a test process that is repeatable and manageable. Pursuing the maturity goals embedded in the TMM structure is not a necessary precondition for initiating a test-planning process. However, a test process improvement effort does provide a good framework for adopting this essential practice. Test planning should begin early in the software life cycle, although for many organizations whose test processes are immature this practice is not yet in place. Models such as the V-model, or the Extended/Modified V-model (Figure 1.5), help to support test planning activities that begin in the requirements phase, and continue on into successive software development phases [2,3].

In order to meet a set of goals, a plan describes what specific tasks must be accomplished, who is responsible for each task, what tools, procedures, and techniques must be used, how much time and effort is needed, and what resources are essential. A plan also contains milestones.

> **Milestones are tangible events that are expected to occur at a certain time in the project's lifetime. Managers use them to determine project status.**

Tracking the actual occurrence of the milestone events allows a manager to determine if the project is progressing as planned. Finally, a plan should assess the risks involved in carrying out the project.

Test plans for software projects are very complex and detailed documents. The planner usually includes the following essential high-level items.

1. *Overall test objectives.* As testers, why are we testing, what is to be achieved by the tests, and what are the risks associated with testing this product?
2. *What to test (scope of the tests).* What items, features, procedures, functions, objects, clusters, and subsystems will be tested?
3. *Who will test.* Who are the personnel responsible for the tests?
4. *How to test.* What strategies, methods, hardware, software tools, and techniques are going to be applied? What test documents and deliverable should be produced?
5. *When to test.* What are the schedules for tests? What items need to be available?
6. *When to stop testing.* It is not economically feasible or practical to plan to test until all defects have been revealed. This is a goal that testers can never be sure they have reached. Because of budgets, scheduling, and customer deadlines, specific conditions must be outlined in the test plan that allow testers/managers to decide when testing is considered to be complete.

Test plans can be organized in several ways depending on organizational policy. There is often a hierarchy of plans that includes several levels of quality assurance and test plans. The complexity of the hierarchy depends on the type, size, risk-proneness, and the mission/safety criticality of software system being developed. All of the quality and testing plans should also be coordinated with the overall software project plan. A sample plan hierarchy is shown in Figure 7.1.

At the top of the plan hierarchy there may be a software quality assurance plan. This plan gives an overview of all verification and validation activities for the project, as well as details related to other quality issues such as audits, standards, configuration control, and supplier control. Below that in the plan hierarchy there may be a master test plan that includes an overall description of all execution-based testing for the software system. A master verification plan for reviews inspections/walkthroughs would also fit in at this level. The master test plan itself may be a component of the overall project plan or exist as a separate

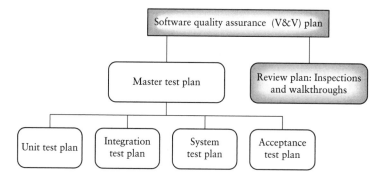

FIG. 7.1

A hierarchy of test plans.

document. Depending on organizational policy, another level of the hierarchy could contain a separate test plan for unit, integration, system, and acceptance tests. In some organizations these are part of the master test plan. The level-based plans give a more detailed view of testing appropriate to that level. The *IEEE Software Engineering Standards Collection* has useful descriptions for many of these plans and other test and quality-related documents such as verification and validation plans [4–7].

The persons responsible for developing test plans depend on the type of plan under development. Usually staff from one or more groups cooperates in test plan development. For example, the master test plan for execution-based testing may be developed by the project manager, especially if there is no separate testing group. It can also be developed by a tester or software quality assurance manager, but always requires cooperation and input from the project manager. It is essential that development and testing activities be coordinated to allow the project to progress smoothly. The type and organization of the test plan, the test plan hierarchy, and who is responsible for development should be specified in organizational standards or software quality assurance documents.

The remainder of this chapter focuses on the development of a general-purpose execution-based test plan that will be referred to as a "test plan." The description of the test plan contents is based on a discussion of recommended test plan components appearing in the *IEEE Standard for Software Test Documentation: IEEE/ANSI Std 829-1983* [5]. This standard also contains examples of other test-related documents described in this chapter. The reader should note that the IEEE test plan description serves as a guideline to test planners. The actual templates and documents developed by test planners should be tailored to meet organizational needs and conform to organizational goals and policies. An abbreviated example of a test plan appears in Appendix II.

7.3 Test Plan Components

This section of the text will discuss the basic test plan components as described in IEEE Std 829-1983 [5]. They are shown in Figure 7.2. These components should appear in the master test plan and in each of the level-based test plans (unit, integration, etc.) with the appropriate amount of detail. The reader should note that some items in a test plan may appear in other related documents, for example, the project plan. References to such documents should be included in the test plan, or a copy of the appropriate section of the document should be attached to the test plan.

1. Test Plan Identifier

Each test plan should have a unique identifier so that it can be associated with a specific project and become a part of the project history. The project history and all project-related items should be stored in a project database or come under the control of a configuration management system. Organizational standards should describe the format for the test plan identifier and how to specify versions, since the test plan, like all other software items, is not written in stone and is subject to change. A mention was made of a configuration management system. This is a tool that supports change management. It is essential for any software project and allows for orderly change control. If a configuration management system is used, the test plan identifier can serve to identify it as a configuration item (see Chapter 9).

2. Introduction

In this section the test planner gives an overall description of the project, the software system being developed or maintained, and the soft-

Test Plan Components
1. Test plan identifier
2. Introduction
3. Items to be tested
4. Features to be tested
5. Approach
6. Pass/fail criteria
7. Suspension and resumption criteria
8. Test deliverables
9. Testing Tasks
10. Test environment
11. Responsibilities
12. Staffing and training needs
13. Scheduling
14. Risks and contingencies
15. Testing costs
16. Approvals

FIG. 7.2

Components of a test plan.

ware items and/or features to be tested. It is useful to include a high-level description of testing goals and the testing approaches to be used. References to related or supporting documents should also be included in this section, for example, organizational policies and standards documents, the project plan, quality assurance plan, and software configuration plan. If test plans are developed as multilevel documents, that is, separate documents for unit, integration, system, and acceptance test, then each plan must reference the next higher level plan for consistency and compatibility reasons.

3. Items to Be Tested

This is a listing of the entities to be tested and should include names, identifiers, and version/revision numbers for each entity. The items listed could include procedures, classes, modules, libraries, subsystems, and systems. References to the appropriate documents where these items and their behaviors are described such as requirements and design documents, and the user manual should be included in this component of the test plan. These references support the tester with traceability tasks. The focus of traceability tasks is to ensure that each requirement has been covered with an appropriate number of test cases. In this test plan component also refer to the transmittal media where the items are stored if appropriate; for example, on disk, CD, tape. The test planner should also include items that will *not* be included in the test effort.

4. Features to Be Tested

In this component of the test plan the tester gives another view of the entities to be tested by describing them in terms of the features they encompass. Chapter 3 has this definition for a feature.

> **Features may be described as distinguishing characteristics of a software component or system.**

They are closely related to the way we describe software in terms of its functional and quality requirements [4]. Example features relate to performance, reliability, portability, and functionality requirements for the software being tested. Features that will *not* be tested should be identified and reasons for their exclusion from test should be included.

In this component of the test plan references to test design specifications for each feature and each combination of features are identified to establish the associations with actual test cases. The test design specifications, test procedures, and test case specifications appear in other sections of the test plan.

5. Approach

This section of the test plan provides broad coverage of the issues to be addressed when testing the target software. Testing activities are described. The level of descriptive detail should be sufficient so that the major testing tasks and task durations can be identified. More details will appear in the accompanying test design specifications.

The planner should also include for each feature or combination of features, the approach that will be taken to ensure that each is adequately tested. Tools and techniques necessary for the tests should be included. Expectations for test completeness and how the degree of completeness will be determined should be described. For example, the planner should specify degree of coverage expected for white box tests. This can be expressed in terms of the percentage of statement coverage, branch coverage, and so on expected. Techniques that will be used to trace requirements to test should be covered.

Constraints on testing should be also be included in this section, such as time and budget limitations. The planner should also describe how the testing process will be monitored to insure it is going according to plans. Criteria to be used for making decisions on when to stop testing must also be included. These should be well thought out. Unfortunately, testing usually stops when time and money run out. This is the least desirable scenario. It is often useful to specify stop-test criteria based on percentage of coverage for each coverage category and/or the rate of error detection and/or the detection of a specific amount of defects based on a statistical analysis of errors found in previous releases. A reasonable stop test decision statement is: "System testing is completed when the number of defects found per week (X) that cause failures of a certain severity level (Y) falls below a given value (Z)." The number of defects X, the severity level Y and the given value Z, all must be quantified. The concept of severity (sometimes called criticality) introduced here is a useful one that can be applied to errors, defects, and failures. A brief discussion of severity is given in item 6 below. Sample severity levels that can be utilized for rating defects and failures are described in Chapter 9. Other approaches to use to for a stop test decision are found in Chapter 12.

6. Item Pass/Fail Criteria

Given a test item and a test case, the tester must have a set of criteria to decide on whether the test has been passed or failed upon execution. The master test plan should provide a general description of these criteria. In the test design specification section more specific details are given for each item or group of items under test with that specification.

A definition for the term "failure" was given in Chapter 2. Another way of describing the term is to state that a failure occurs when the actual output produced by the software does not agree with what was expected, under the conditions specified by the test. The differences in output behavior (the failure) are caused by one or more defects. The impact of the defect can be expressed using an approach based on establishing severity levels. Using this approach, scales are used to rate failures/defects with respect to their impact on the customer/user (note their previous use for stop-test decision making in the preceding section). For example, on a scale with values from 1 to 4, a level 4 defect/failure may have a minimal impact on the customer/user, but one at level 1 will make the system unusable.

As an example of the application of severity levels, let us suppose we are testing the report-generation capability of a personal accounting software system. Results may show that it prints a required report with correct data, but with a slightly different spacing then was specified. This failure would be rated at a low severity level (3–4) since the software is still usable by the customer. A high-level failure (level 1) for this software might be assigned to a system crash when a report is requested by the user. This renders the system unusable and unacceptable.

The test planner can use this technique to specify an acceptable severity level for the failures revealed by each test. This is done in detail in the test design specification. Upon execution, a failure occurring with a severity rating above the acceptable level indicates the software has failed the test. Usually a failure rated below the acceptable severity level will still allow the software to conditionally pass the test. Testing can continue and the defect causing the failure can be repaired later on.

7. Suspension and Resumption Criteria

In this section of the test plan, criteria to suspend and resume testing are described. In the simplest of cases testing is suspended at the end of a working day and resumed the following morning. For some test items this condition may not apply and additional details need to be provided by the test planner. The test plan should also specify conditions to suspend testing based on the effects or criticality level of the failures/defects observed. Conditions for resuming the test after there has been a suspension should also be specified. For some test items resumption may require certain tests to be repeated.

8. Test Deliverables

Execution-based testing has a set of deliverables that includes the test plan along with its associated test design specifications, test procedures, and test cases. The latter describe the actual test inputs and expected outputs. Deliverables may also include other documents that result from testing such as test logs, test transmittal reports, test incident reports, and a test summary report. These documents are described in subsequent sections of this chapter. Preparing and storing these documents requires considerable resources. Each organization should decide which of these documents is required for a given project.

Another test deliverable is the test harness. This is supplementary code that is written specifically to support the test efforts, for example, module drivers and stubs. Drivers and stubs are necessary for unit and integration test. Very often these amount to a substantial amount of code. They should be well designed and stored for reuse in testing subsequent releases of the software. Other support code, for example, testing tools that will be developed especially for this project, should also be described in this section of the test plan.

9. Testing Tasks

In this section the test planner should identify all testing-related tasks and their dependencies. Using a Work Breakdown Structure (WBS) is useful here.

> A Work Breakdown Structure is a hierarchical or treelike representation of all the tasks that are required to complete a project.

High-level tasks sit at the top of the hierarchical task tree. Leaves are detailed tasks sometimes called work packages that can be done by 1–2 people in a short time period, typically 3–5 days. The WBS is used by project managers for defining the tasks and work packages needed for project planning. The test planner can use the same hierarchical task model but focus only on defining testing tasks. Rakos gives a good description of the WBS and other models and tools useful for both project and test management [8].

10. The Testing Environment

Here the test planner describes the software and hardware needs for the testing effort. For example, any special equipment or hardware needed such as emulators, telecommunication equipment, or other devices should be noted. The planner must also indicate any laboratory space containing the equipment that needs to be reserved.

The planner also needs to specify any special software needs such as coverage tools, databases, and test data generators. Security requirements for the testing environment may also need to be described.

11. Responsibilities

The staff who will be responsible for test-related tasks should be identified. This includes personnel who will be:

- transmitting the software-under-test;

- developing test design specifications, and test cases;

- executing the tests and recording results;

- tracking and monitoring the test efforts;

- checking results;

- interacting with developers;

- managing and providing equipment;

- developing the test harnesses;

- interacting with the users/customers.

This group may include developers, testers, software quality assurance staff, systems analysts, and customers/users.

12. Staffing and Training Needs

The test planner should describe the staff and the skill levels needed to carry out test-related responsibilities such as those listed in the section above. Any special training required to perform a task should be noted.

13. Scheduling

Task durations should be established and recorded with the aid of a task networking tool. Test milestones should be established, recorded, and scheduled. These milestones usually appear in the project plan as well as the test plan. They are necessary for tracking testing efforts to ensure that actual testing is proceeding as planned. Schedules for use of staff, tools, equipment, and laboratory space should also be specified. A tester will find that PERT and Gantt charts are very useful tools for these assignments [8].

14. Risks and Contingencies

Every testing effort has risks associated with it. Testing software with a high degree of criticality, complexity, or a tight delivery deadline all impose risks that may have negative impacts on project goals. These risks should be: (i) identified, (ii) evaluated in terms of their probability of occurrence, (iii) prioritized, and (iv) contingency plans should be developed that can be activated if the risk occurs. Barry Bohem has a very useful method for risk management using these types of activities. A test planner can apply them to develop the "risk and contingencies" component of a test plan [9].

An example of a risk-related test scenario is as follows. A test planner, lets say Mary Jones, has made assumptions about the availability of the software under test. A particular date was selected to transmit the test item to the testers based on completion date information for that item in the project plan. Ms. Jones has identified a risk: she realizes that the item may not be delivered on time to the testers. This delay may occur for several reasons. For example, the item is complex and/or the developers are inexperienced and/or the item implements a new algorithm and/or it needs redesign. Due to these conditions there is a high probability that this risk could occur. A contingency plan should be in place if this risk occurs. For example, Ms. Jones could build some flexibility in resource allocations into the test plan so that testers and equipment can operate beyond normal working hours. Or an additional group of testers could be made available to work with the original group when the software is ready to test. In this way the schedule for testing can continue as planned, and deadlines can be met.

It is important for the test planner to identify test-related risks, analyze them in terms of their probability of occurrence, and be ready with a contingency plan when any high-priority risk-related event occurs. Experienced planners realize the importance of risk management.

15. Testing Costs

The IEEE standard for test plan documentation does not include a separate cost component in its specification of a test plan. This is the usual case for many test plans since very often test costs are allocated in the overall project management plan. The project manager in consultation with developers and testers estimates the costs of testing. If the test plan is an independent document prepared by the testing group and has a cost component, the test planner will need tools and techniques to help estimate test costs. Test costs that should included in the plan are:

- costs of planning and designing the tests;

- costs of acquiring the hardware and software necessary for the tests (includes development of the test harnesses);

- costs to support the test environment;

- costs of executing the tests;

- costs of recording and analyzing test results;

- tear-down costs to restore the environment.

Other costs related to testing that may be spread among several projects are the costs of training the testers and the costs of maintaining the test database. Costs for reviews should appear in a separate review plan.

When estimating testing costs, the test planner should consider organizational, project, and staff characteristics that impact on the cost of testing. Several key characteristics that we will call "test cost impact items" are briefly described below.

The nature of the organization; its testing maturity level, and general maturity. This will determine the degree of test planning, the types of testing methods applied, the types of tests that are designed and implemented, the quality of the staff, the nature of the testing tasks, the availability of testing tools, and the ability to manage the testing effort. It will also determine the degree of support given to the testers by the project manager and upper management.

The nature of the software product being developed. The tester must understand the nature of the system to be tested. For example, is it a real-time, embedded, mission-critical system, or a business application? In general, the testing scope for a business application will be smaller than one for a mission or safely critical system, since in case of the latter there is a strong possibility that software defects and/or poor software quality could result in loss of life or property. Mission- and safety-critical software systems usually require extensive unit and integration tests as well as many types of system tests (refer to Chapter 6). The level of reliability required for these systems is usually much higher than for ordinary applications. For these reasons, the number of test cases, test procedures, and test scripts will most likely be higher for this type of software as compared to an average application. Tool and resource needs will be greater as well.

The scope of the test requirements. This includes the types of tests required, integration, performance, reliability, usability, etc. This characteristic directly relates to the nature of the software product. As described above, mission/safety-critical systems, and real-time embedded systems usually require more extensive system tests for functionality, reliability, performance, configuration, and stress than a simple application. These test requirements will impact on the number of tests and test procedures required, the quantity and complexity of the testing tasks, and the hardware and software needs for testing.

The level of tester ability. The education, training, and experience levels of the testers will impact on their ability to design, develop, execute, and analyze test results in a timely and effective manner. It will also impact of the types of testing tasks they are able to carry out.

Knowledge of the project problem domain. It is not always possible for testers to have detailed knowledge of the problem domain of the software they are testing. If the level of knowledge is poor, outside experts or consultants may need to be hired to assist with the testing efforts, thus impacting on costs.

The level of tool support. Testing tools can assist with designing, and executing tests, as well as collecting and analyzing test data. Automated support for these tasks could have a positive impact on the productivity of the testers; thus it has the potential to reduce test costs. Tools and hardware environments are necessary to drive certain types of system tests, and if the product requires these types of tests, the cost should be folded in.

Training requirements. State-of-the-art tools and techniques do help improve tester productivity but often training is required for testers so that they have the capability to use these tools and techniques properly and effectively. Depending on the organization, these training efforts may be included in the costs of testing. These costs, as well as tool costs, could be spread over several projects.

Project planners have cost estimation models, for example, the COCOMO model, which they use to estimate overall project costs [10,11]. At this time models of this type have not been designed specifically for test cost estimation. However, test planners often borrow cost estimation techniques and models from project planners and apply them to testing. Several of these are shown in Figure 7.3. To support the application of these approaches, the test planner should have access to a historical record of past projects that includes test-related data. Items such as the size and cost of the project as a whole, size and cost of the test effort, number of designed test cases, number of test procedures, durations of testing tasks, equipment, and tool costs are all useful for test cost estimations as applied to the current project. The utility of these data items will be demonstrated in the following paragraphs which describe approaches to test cost estimation based on:

(i) the COCOMO model and heuristics;
(ii) use of test cost drivers;
(iii) test tasks;
(iv) tester/developer ratios;
(v) expert judgment (Delphi).

One approach to test cost estimation makes use of the COCOMO model in an indirect way. The test planner can use the COCOMO model to estimate total project costs, and then allocate a fraction of those costs for test. Application of the COCOMO model is based on a group of project constants that depend on the nature of the project and items known as cost drivers.

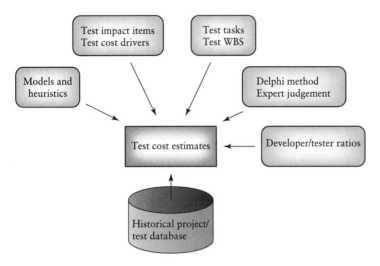

FIG. 7.3

Some approaches to test cost estimation.

> **A cost driver can be described as a process or product factor that has an impact on overall project costs.**

To be more precise, a cost driver should have a positive coefficient of correlation with project costs. In the testing domain cost drivers are factors that contribute to testing costs. There should be a correlation between the factors and testing costs and also some causal connection between them.

Project constants and cost drivers are available for overall project development efforts. To use the COCOMO model a project manager must first estimate the size of the new project and identify its type. This is facilitated by the availability of historical project data. The simple COCOMO equation used for an initial estimate is

$$E = a \text{ (size in KLOC)}^b \tag{1}$$

where E is estimated effort in man-months, and a and b are constants that can be determined from tables provided by Boehm or by the organization itself based on its own historical data [10]. Selection of values from the table depend on project types. The intermediate COCOMO model, used when more project details are known, incorporates project cost drivers and uses a slightly more complex set of calculations. Cost drivers for project the include:

- product attributes such as the required level of reliability;

- hardware attributes such as memory constraints;

- personnel attributes such as experience level;

- project attributes such as use of tools and methods.

The project cost drivers are rated on an ordinate scale and folded into what Boehm calls an effort adjustment factor (EAF). The results from equation (1) can be multiplied by the EAF to give a revised estimate. Note the test cost impact items previously described are similar in nature to these project cost drivers. Unfortunately, no work has been done at this time to formalize them into a COCOMO-like model for testing.

After the total project costs have been estimated with COCOMO, the test planner can then use a heuristic that estimates testing costs for a new project as some fraction of total project costs. The appropriate fraction can be determined by using historical data containing project costs and test costs for similar projects. Roper suggests a fractional value of about 50% of total project costs as shown in equation (2) [12].

$$\text{Testing costs} = 0.5 \times \text{total project costs} \qquad (2)$$

Another approach to test cost estimation involves the use of singular cost drivers that have been suggested for the testing domain. Many of the test cost drivers are size-related, for example [12]:

- number of test procedures;

- number of requirements;

- number of modules.

The reader will note that these are covered in the test cost impact items descriptions previously discussed. The test cost impact items could be the source of additional drivers in the future.

In many cases testers use the drivers listed to estimate testing costs using historical data. However, they need to cautious and understand the nature of the relationship between the drivers and test costs. For example, using the number of requirements to estimate test efforts and costs may be tricky unless the test planner realizes that all requirements are not alike in their need for test resources. For example, a requirement that a submarine-positioning device display a position with a stated precision and accuracy will need more test resources to show compliance then a requirement for the system to display the opening welcome message. To apply the number of requirements to a test effort/cost estimate, testers must develop categories of requirements with respect to resource needs. Each requirement in the new product should be classified in a category before being included in the cost estimation calculation [12].

Using the number of modules to estimate test effort/costs may be useful for unit and integration tests, where there appears to be a strong linear relationship between the number of modules and tests costs. But this driver does not work well for estimating system test costs since the number of modules may not be related to the number of system functions. In addition, quality evaluation for attributes such as reliability, performance, and usability may not be correlated with the number of modules.

The estimated number of test procedures for a project can be used to estimate test effort/costs. Again, an organization will need a historical database with information on software size (in lines of code, function points, number of objects), number of test procedures, and man-hours of effort. There should be projects in the database that are similar in character to the new project. A relationship between software size and the number of test procedures required should be established. This allows the test planner to estimate the number of test procedures needed for the new project given the software size estimate. The historical database is also used to establish an adjustment factor relating the number of test procedures and the man-hours of effort needed. Given the estimated number of test procedures and the adjustment factor, the test effort for the new project can be estimated. For example, if the test planner estimates the number of test procedures for a new project to be 650 based on past project data, and the ratio of hours/test procedures was established as 5.5, then the test hours of effort needed for the new product is 650 $\times$

5.5 = 3575. This number of hours needs to be distributed over the allocated test period.

An alternative test cost estimation method uses a bottom-up, testing-task–oriented approach. This approach will work well if the testing tasks, task durations, and resources (such as hardware and software tools) for similar projects are well defined and documented in the historical database. Testing tasks can be represented in the database as a test-oriented Work Breakdown Structure (WBS), which is a hierarchical representation of all test-related tasks. High-level components of a test WBS are shown in Table 7.1. These represent high-level testing tasks. Each of these is broken down into lower-level tasks. Table 7.2 shows a breakdown for the higher-level "test planning" task. The historical record should also contain values for the time and manpower needed to perform each task in the testing WBS. The new project is compared to those in the database in terms of size and complexity. The most similar project provides the best support for the cost estimation. Reuse of existing tests, regression tests and test harnesses should be folded into the estimating process. When tasks, and durations of the tasks have been calculated for the new project, the test planner can use the sum of the time estimated for all the tasks, adjusted to account for differences between the completed and new projects, to estimate total test time and expenses.

Dustin et. al. suggest an additional approach to test effort estimation. This approach is based on the estimated number of developers and a selected developer/tester ratio [13]. Using this approach the size of the test team for a new project is estimated by first estimating the number of developers needed for the project, and then using an appropriate developer/tester ratio for the project to calculate the estimated number of testers. The developer/tester ratio will vary with the type of project. For example, for a mission-critical system a ratio of 1 tester to 2 developers may be required; for a business application a ratio of 1 tester to 4 developers may be indicated. The size of the test team and the duration of the testing effort give a handle on the estimated costs for test.

Finally, test planners can use the Delphi method for estimating test costs. This technique, which involves a group of cost estimation experts lead by a moderator, is often used to estimate the size/costs of an entire project. It can be applied to estimate test costs as well. The group members

1. Project startup
2. Management coordination
3. Tool selection
4. Test planning
5. Test design
6. Test development
7. Test execution
8. Test measurement, and monitoring
9. Test analysis and reporting
10. Test process improvement

TABLE 7.1

Example WBS elements for testing.

are given appropriate documentation relating to the project before the estimation meeting. The group comes together in the meeting and may have a discussion about the project and its characteristics. In the testing domain, test-related issues would be discussed. After the discussion each group member gives an anonymous estimate to the moderator. The moderator calculates an average and mean of the estimates and distributes the values to the group. Each group member can determine where his/her individual estimate falls with respect to the group, and reestimate based on this information and additional discussion. The group may have several cycles of "discussion, estimate, and analysis," until consensus on the estimate is reached.

As in the case of cost estimates for a software project, more than one approach should be used to estimate test costs to allow for biases. Consultation with the project manager in all cases is essential. As a final note, if both the estimated and actual values for the test-related effort/costs are included in the historical database, the test planner can make further adjustments to the new estimate to compensate for over/under estimates. For example, if the test planner observes that the estimated task durations are usually 10% lower than the actual durations, the planner can fold this factor into the new estimate.

4.0 Test Planning

4.1   Meet with project manager. Discuss test requirements.

4.2   Meet with SQA group, client group. Discuss quality goals and plans.

4.3   Identify constraints and risks of testing.

4.4   Develop goals and objectives for testing. Define scope.

4.5   Select test team.

4.6   Decide on training required.

4.7   Meet with test team to discuss test strategies, test approach, test monitoring, and controlling mechanisms.

4.8   Develop the test plan document.

4.9   Develop test plan attachments (test cases, test procedures, test scripts).

4.10 Assign roles and responsibilities.

4.11 Meet with SQA, project manager, test team, and clients to review test plan.

TABLE 7.2

A breakdown of testing planning element from table 7.1.

16. Approvals

The test plan(s) for a project should be reviewed by those designated by the organization. All parties who review the plan and approve it should sign the document. A place for signatures and dates should be provided.

7.4 Test Plan Attachments

The previous components of the test plan were principally managerial in nature: tasks, schedules, risks, and so on. A general discussion of technical issues such as test designs and test cases for the items under test appears in Section 5 of the test plan, "Approach." The reader may be puzzled as to where in the test plan are the details needed for organizing and executing the tests. For example, what are the required inputs, outputs, and procedural steps for each test; where will the tests be stored for each item or feature; will it be tested using a black box, white box, or functional approach? The following components of the test plan contain this detailed information. These documents are generally attached to the test plan.

Requirement identifier	Requirement description	Priority (scale 1–10)	Review status	Test ID
SR-25-13.5	Displays opening screens	8	Yes	TC-25-2 TC-25-5
SR-25-52.2	Checks the validity of user password	9	Yes	TC-25-18 TC-25-23

TABLE 7.3

Example of entries in a requirements traceability matrix.

7.4.1 Test Design Specifications

The IEEE standard for software test documentation describes a test design specification as a test deliverable that specifies the requirements of the test approach [5]. It is used to identity the features covered by this design and associated tests for the features. The test design specification also has links to the associated test cases and test procedures needed to test the features, and also describes in detail pass/fail criteria for the features [5]. The test design specification helps to organize the tests and provides the connection to the actual test inputs/outputs and test steps.

To develop test design specifications many documents such as the requirements, design documents, and user manual are useful. For requirements-based test, developing a requirements traceability matrix is valuable. This helps to insure all requirements are covered by tests, and connects the requirements to the tests. Examples of entries in such a matrix are shown in Table 7.3. Tools called requirements tracers can help to automate traceability tasks [2]. These will be described in Chapter 14.

A test design specification should have the following components according to the IEEE standard [5]. They are listed in the order in which the IEEE recommends they appear in the document. The test planner should be sure to list any related documents that may also contain some of this material.

Test Design Specification Identifier
Give each test design specification a unique identifier and a reference to its associated test plan.

Features to Be Tested

Test items, features, and combination of features covered by this test design specification are listed. References to the items in the requirements and/or design document should be included.

Approach Refinements

In the test plan a general description of the approach to be used to test each item was described. In this document the necessary details are added. For example, the specific test techniques to be used to generate test cases are described, and the rational is given for the choices. The test planner also describes how test results will be analyzed. For example, will an automated comparator be used to compare actual and expected results? The relationships among the associated test cases are discussed. This includes any shared constraints and procedural requirements.

Test Case Identification

Each test design specification is associated with a set of test cases and a set of set procedures. The test cases contain input/output information, and the test procedures contain the steps necessary to execute the tests. A test case may be associated with more than one test design specification.

Pass/Fail Criteria

In this section the specific criteria to be used for determining whether the item has passed/failed a test is given.

7.4.2 Test Case Specifications

This series of documents attached to the test plan defines the test cases required to execute the test items named in the associated test design specification. There are several components in this document. IEEE standards require the components to appear in the order shown here, and references should be provided if some of the contents of the test case specification appear in other documents [5].

Much attention should be placed on developing a quality set of test case specifications. Strategies and techniques, as described in Chapters 4 and 5 of this text, should be applied to accomplish this task. Each test case must be specified correctly so that time is not wasted in analyzing the results of an erroneous test. In addition, the development of test software and test documentation represent a considerable investment of resources for an organization. They should be considered organizational assets and stored in a test repository. Ideally, the test-related deliverables may be recovered from the test repository and reused by different groups for testing and regression testing in subsequent releases of a particular product or for related products. Careful design and referencing to the appropriate test design specification is important to support testing in the current project and for reuse in future projects.

Test Case Specification Identifier
Each test case specification should be assigned a unique identifier.

Test Items
This component names the test items and features to be tested by this test case specification. References to related documents that describe the items and features, and how they are used should be listed: for example the requirements, and design documents, the user manual.

Input Specifications
This component of the test design specification contains the actual inputs needed to execute the test. Inputs may be described as specific values, or as file names, tables, databases, parameters passed by the operating system, and so on. Any special relationships between the inputs should be identified.

Output Specifications
All outputs expected from the test should be identified. If an output is to be a specific value it should be stated. If the output is a specific feature such as a level of performance it also should be stated. The output specifications are necessary to determine whether the item has passed/failed the test.

Special Environmental Needs
Any specific hardware and specific hardware configurations needed to execute this test case should be identified. Special software required to execute the test such as compilers, simulators, and test coverage tools should be described, as well as needed laboratory space and equipment.

Special Procedural Requirements
Describe any special conditions or constraints that apply to the test procedures associated with this test.

Intercase Dependencies
In this section the test planner should describe any relationships between this test case and others, and the nature of the relationship. The test case identifiers of all related tests should be given.

7.4.3 Test Procedure Specifications

> A procedure in general is a sequence of steps required to carry out a specific task.

In this attachment to the test plan the planner specifies the steps required to execute a set of test cases. Another way of describing the test procedure specification is that it specifies the steps necessary to analyze a software item in order to evaluate a set of features. The test procedure specification has several subcomponents that the IEEE recommends being included in the order shown below [5]. As noted previously, reference to documents where parts of these components are described must be provided.

Test Procedure Specification Identifier
Each test procedure specification should be assigned a unique identifier.

Purpose
Describe the purpose of this test procedure and reference any test cases it executes.

Specific Requirements
List any special requirements for this procedure, like software, hardware, and special training.

Procedure Steps
Here the actual steps of the procedure are described. Include methods, documents for recording (logging) results, and recording incidents. These will have associations with the test logs and test incident reports that result from a test run. A test incident report is only required when an unexpected output is observed. Steps include [5]:

(i) setup: to prepare for execution of the procedure;
(ii) start: to begin execution of the procedure;

(iii) proceed: to continue the execution of the procedure;

(iv) measure: to describe how test measurements related to outputs will be made;

(v) shut down: to describe actions needed to suspend the test when unexpected events occur;

(vi) restart: to describe restart points and actions needed to restart the procedure from these points;

(vii) stop: to describe actions needed to bring the procedure to an orderly halt;

(viii) wrap up: to describe actions necessary to restore the environment;

(ix) contingencies: plans for handling anomalous events if they occur during execution of this procedure.

7.5 Locating Test Items: The Test Item Transmittal Report

Suppose a tester is ready to run tests on an item on the date described in the test plan. She needs to be able to locate the item and have knowledge of its current status. This is the function of the Test Item Transmittal Report. This document is not a component of the test plan, but is necessary to locate and track the items that are submitted for test. Each Test Item Transmittal Report has a unique identifier. It should contain the following information for each item that is tracked [5].

(i) version/revision number of the item;

(ii) location of the item;

(iii) persons responsible for the item (e.g., the developer);

(iv) references to item documentation and the test plan it is related to;

(v) status of the item;

(vi) approvals—space for signatures of staff who approve the transmittal.

7.6 Reporting Test Results

The test plan and its attachments are test-related documents that are prepared *prior* to test execution. There are additional documents related to testing that are prepared during and after execution of the tests. The *IEEE Standard for Software Test Documentation* describes the following documents [5].

Test Log

The test log should be prepared by the person executing the tests. It is a diary of the events that take place during the test. It supports the concept of a test as a repeatable experiment [14]. In the experimental world of engineers and scientists detailed logs are kept when carrying out experimental work. Software engineers and testing specialists must follow this example to allow others to duplicate their work.

The test log is invaluable for use in defect repair. It gives the developer a snapshot of the events associated with a failure. The test log, in combination with the test incident report which should be generated in case of anomalous behavior, gives valuable clues to the developer whose task it is to locate the source of the problem. The combination of documents helps to prevent incorrect decisions based on incomplete or erroneous test results that often lead to repeated, but ineffective, test-patch-test cycles.

Retest that follows defect repair is also supported by the test log. In addition, the test log is valuable for (i) regression testing that takes place in the development of future releases of a software product, and (ii) circumstances where code from a reuse library is to be reused. In all these cases it is important that the exact conditions of a test run are clearly documented so that it can be repeated with accuracy.

The test log can have many formats. An organization can design its own format or adopt IEEE recommendations. The IEEE Standard for Software Test Documentation describes the test log as a chronological record of all details relating to the execution of its associated tests. It has the following sections [5]:

Test Log Identifier
Each test log should have a unique identifier.

Description
In the description section the tester should identify the items being tested, their version/revision number, and their associated Test Item/Transmittal Report. The environment in which the test is conducted should be described including hardware and operating system details.

Activity and Event Entries

The tester should provide dates and names of test log authors for each event and activity. This section should also contain:

1. *Execution description:* Provide a test procedure identifier and also the names and functions of personnel involved in the test.
2. *Procedure results:* For each execution, record the results and the location of the output. Also report pass/fail status.
3. *Environmental information:* Provide any environmental conditions specific to this test.
4. *Anomalous events:* Any events occurring before/after an unexpected event should be recorded. If a tester is unable to start or compete a test procedure, details relating to these happenings should be recorded (e.g., a power failure or operating system crash).
5. *Incident report identifiers:* Record the identifiers of incident reports generated while the test is being executed.

There are other formats for test logs. A useful example of what is called a "Test Report Template" is found in Humphrey [15]. While not as detailed as the analogous IEEE standard document test log description, it can provide much valued information from the execution of tests and is a good guide for designing an individual or organizational standard.

Test Incident Report

The tester should record in a test incident report (sometimes called a problem report) any event that occurs during the execution of the tests that is unexpected, unexplainable, and that requires a follow-up investigation. The *IEEE Standard for Software Test Documentation* recommends the following sections in the report [5]:

1. *Test Incident Report identifier:* to uniquely identify this report.
2. *Summary:* to identify the test items involved, the test procedures, test cases, and test log associated with this report.
3. *Incident description:* this should describe time and date, testers, observers, environment, inputs, expected outputs, actual outputs, anomalies, procedure step, environment, and attempts to repeat. Any other information useful for the developers who will repair the code should be included.

4. *Impact:* what impact will this incident have on the testing effort, the test plans, the test procedures, and the test cases? A severity rating should be inserted here.

Test Summary Report

This report is prepared when testing is complete. It is a summary of the results of the testing efforts. It also becomes a part of the project's historical database and provides a basis for lessons learned as applied to future projects. When a project postmortem is conducted, the Test Summary Report can help managers, testers, developers, and SQA staff to evaluate the effectiveness of the testing efforts. The IEEE test documentation standard describes the following sections for the Test Summary Report [5]:

1. *Test Summary Report identifier:* to uniquely identify this report.
2. *Variances:* these are descriptions of any variances of the test items from their original design. Deviations and reasons for the deviation from the test plan, test procedures, and test designs are discussed.
3. *Comprehensiveness assessment:* the document author discusses the comprehensiveness of the test effort as compared to test objectives and test completeness criteria as described in the test plan. Any features or combination of features that were not as fully tested as was planned should be identified.
4. *Summary of results:* the document author summarizes the testing results. All resolved incidents and their solutions should be described. Unresolved incidents should be recorded.
5. *Evaluation:* in this section the author evaluates each test item based on test results. Did it pass/fail the tests? If it failed, what was the level of severity of the failure?
6. *Summary of activities:* all testing activities and events are summarized. Resource consumption, actual task durations, and hardware and software tool usage should be recorded.
7. *Approvals:* the names of all persons who are needed to approve this document are listed with space for signatures and dates.

Figure 7.4 shows the relationships between all the test-related documents we have discussed in this chapter as described in the IEEE standards

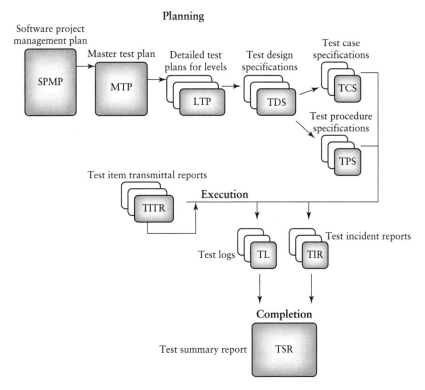

Planning

FIG. 7.4

Test-related documents as
recommended by IEEE [5].

document [5]. In the figure it is assumed that an overall Master Test Plan (MTP) is developed at first, and this is followed by more detailed test plans for the different levels of testing, unit, integration, system, acceptance, and so on. From the figure and the discussion in this chapter, it is apparent that the preparation of a complete set of test documents that fully conform to IEEE standards requires many resources and an investment of a great deal of time and effort. Not all organizations require such an extensive set of test-related documents. Each organization should describe, as part of its testing or quality standards, which test-related documents should be prepared. The content and format for each document should be included in the standards. Very often, a subset of the IEEE-recommended documents is satisfactory, especially if the organization is small and there is no separate testing group.

7.7 The Role of the Three Critical Groups in Testing Planning and Test Policy Development

Recall that in the TMM framework three groups were identified as critical players in the testing process. They all work together toward the evolution of a quality testing process. These groups were managers, developers/testers, and users/clients. In TMM terminology they are called the three critical views (CV). Each group views the testing process from a different perspective that is related to their particular goals, needs, and requirements. The manager's view involves commitment and support for those activities and tasks related to improving testing process quality. The developer/tester's view encompasses the technical activities and tasks that when applied, constitute best testing practices. The user/client view is defined as a cooperating or supporting view. The developers/testers work with client/user groups on quality-related activities and tasks that concern user-oriented needs. The focus is on soliciting client/user support, consensus, and participation in activities such as requirements analysis, usability testing, and acceptance test planning. At each TMM level the three groups play specific roles in support of the maturity goals at that level.

Chapters 3–5 of this text discussed testing concepts of a technical nature that support the TMM level 2 maturity goals. The concluding sections of these chapters described the roles of the three critical groups, and how they help to achieve these goals. The careful reader will understand how mastery of the concepts in Chapters 3–5 supports these roles. Of particular relevance to the material in these chapters is the maturity goal, "Institutionalize Basic Testing Techniques and Methods." The remaining two maturity goals at TMM level 2, "Develop Testing and Debugging Goals" and "Initiate a Testing Planning Process," are more managerial in nature. In the following paragraphs contributions to achievement of the managerial-oriented maturity goals by the three critical views is discussed. Critical group participation for all three TMM level 2 maturity goals is summarized in Figure 7.5.

For the TMM maturity goal, "Develop Testing and Debugging Goals," the TMM recommends that *project* and *upper management*:

- Provide access to existing organizational goal/policy statements and sample testing policies such as shown in this text, in Hetzel [16], and

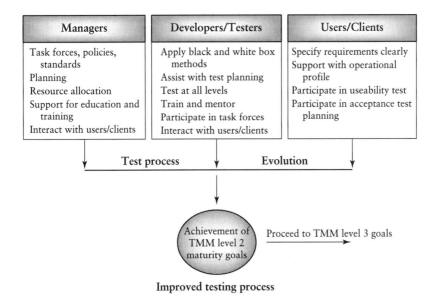

Managers	Developers/Testers	Users/Clients
Task forces, policies, standards Planning Resource allocation Support for education and training Interact with users/clients	Apply black and white box methods Assist with test planning Test at all levels Train and mentor Participate in task forces Interact with users/clients	Specify requirements clearly Support with operational profile Participate in useability test Participate in acceptance test planning

Test process   Evolution

Achievement of TMM level 2 maturity goals   Proceed to TMM level 3 goals

Improved testing process

FIG. 7.5

Reaching TMM level 2: summary of critical group roles.

from other sources. These serve as policy models for the testing and debugging domains.

- Provide adequate resources and funding to form the committees (team or task force) on testing and debugging. Committee makeup is managerial, with technical staff serving as comembers.

- Support the recommendations and policies of the committee by:

  —distributing testing/debugging goal/policy documents to project managers, developers, and other interested staff,

  —appointing a permanent team to oversee compliance and policy changemaking.

- Ensure that the necessary training, education, and tools to carry out defined testing/debugging goals is made available.

- Assign responsibilities for testing and debugging.

Developers have an important role in the development of testing goals and policies. (Recall that at TMM level 2 there is no requirement for a dedicated testing group.) They serve as members of the goal/policy development teams. As representatives of the technical staff they must ensure that the policies reflect best testing practices, are implementable, receive management support, and support among technical personnel. The activities, tasks, and responsibilities for the developers/testers include:

- Working with management to develop testing and debugging policies and goals.

- Participating in the teams that oversee policy compliance and change management.

- Familiarizing themselves with the approved set of testing/debugging goals and policies, keeping up-to-date with revisions, and making suggestions for changes when appropriate.

- When developing test plans, setting testing goals for each project at each level of test that reflect organizational testing goals and policies.

- Carrying out testing activities that are in compliance with organizational policies.

Users and clients play an indirect role in the formation of an organization's testing goals and polices since these goals and policies reflect the organizations efforts to ensure customer/client/user satisfaction. Feedback from these groups and from the marketplace in general has an influence on the nature of organizational testing goals and policies. Successful organizations are sensitive to customer/client/user needs. Their policies reflect their desire to insure that their software products meet the customer's requirements. This allows them to maintain, and eventually increase, their market share of business.

"Initiate a Test Planning Process," the second management-oriented maturity goal at TMM level 2, also requires input from the three critical groups.

Upper management supports this goal by:

- Establishing an organizationwide test planning committee with funding.

- Ensuring that the testing policy statement and quality standards support test planning with commitment of resources, tools, templates, and training.

- Ensuring that the testing policy statement contains a formal mechanism for user input to the test planning process, especially for acceptance and usability testing.

- Ensuring that all projects are in compliance with the test planning policy.

- Ensuring that all developers/testers complete all the necessary posttest documents such as test logs and test incident reports.

Project managers support the test planning maturity goal by preparing the test plans for each project with inputs and support from developers. At TMM level 3 this task will be assigned to a test specialist or test manager. Managers can use the organizational test plan template as a guide for preparing the test plan.

Developers who are experienced in testing support this maturity goal by participating in test planning. They assist the project manager in determining test goals, selecting test methods, procedures and tools, and developing the test case specifications, test procedure specifications, and other test-related documents as described in this chapter. (At TMM level 3 the testing group leaders have this role.) Developers are also responsible for ensuring that testability issues are addressed during the requirements and design phases of development to support test planning and test design.

From the *user/client* point of view support for test planning is in the form of articulating their requirements clearly, and supplying input to the acceptance test plan. The required functional and performance-related attributes that are expected by the client/users must be specified. Users/clients may also participate in the development of an operational profile which may be used to guide system and acceptance tests. They can also participate in usability test planning as it is applied throughout the development life cycle, and in use case development.

7.8 Process and the Engineering Disciplines: The Role of the Individual as a Process Facilitator

What we are now witnessing is the evolution of software development from a craft to an engineering discipline. Computer science students are now being introduced to the fundamentals of software engineering. As the field matures, they will be able to obtain a degree and be certified in the area of software engineering As members of this emerging profession we must realize that one of our major focuses as engineers is on designing, implementing, managing, and improving the processes related to software development. Testing is such a process. If you are a member of a TMM level 1 organization, there is a great opportunity for you become involved in process issues. You can serve as the change agent, using your education in the area of testing to form a process group or to join an existing one. You can initiate the implementation of a defined testing process by working with management and users/clients toward achievement of the technical and managerial-oriented maturity goals at TMM level 2. Minimally you can set an example on a personal level by planning your own testing activities. If the project manager receives effective personal test plans from each developer or test specialist, then the quality of the overall test plan will be improved. You can also encourage management in your organization to develop testing goals and policies, you can participate in the committees involved, and you can help to develop test planning standards that can be applied organizationwide. Finally, you can become proficient in, and consistently apply, black and white box testing techniques, and promote testing at the unit, integration, and system levels. You need to demonstrate the positive impact of these practices on software quality, encourage their adaptation in the organization, and mentor your colleagues, helping them to appreciate, master, and apply these practices.

KEY TERMS

Cost driver	Plan
Feature	Policy
Goal	Procedure
Milestone	Work breakdown structure

EXERCISES

1. Using the policy model in the text, sketch out a testing policy statement for a small-sized software development organization (30 employees) assessed to be at TMM level 3.

2. Why is testing planning so important for developing a repeatable and managed testing process?

3. Test-related documents are developed and used before, during, and after execution-based testing. The test plan is a test-related document that is prepared before execution-based testing takes place. (a) What are some of the essential items a tester should include in a test plan? (b) Describe the test-related documents that are developed during, and after execution-based testing. Include in the description how these documents are used by managers, developers, and testers.

4. Suppose you were developing an online system for a specific vendor of electronic equipment. Suggest a set of test deliverables appropriate for the project that should be specified in the test plan Which of these items would be internal, and which would you deliver to the client?

5. Suggest some suspend/resume criteria that are applicable for system testing the software of Problem 4.

6. A project manager estimates that the total costs of a project as $375,000. The project is a business application. There are security, performance, and configuration requirements (the latter due to devices that will interface with the software system). The testers are experienced and have tool support and training. The number of test procedures is estimated at 670, with a ratio of 5.9 hours/test procedure from the historical database of similar projects. Assume that the salary of the testers is $37/hour. Estimate the costs of test for this project in as many ways as you can using the information given. Compare the results of the estimates. Which result do you have more confidence in?

7. What is the purpose of the test transmittal report, the test log?

8. A mission-critical system fails, there are injuries, and lives and expensive equipment are lost. When the case is investigated, the investigating committee finds that the test plan did not include tests for the scenarios that caused the software to fail. Think about this situation carefully. Who do you think is responsible for the loss of life and property—the test manager who developed the plan, the testers who carried out the tests, the project manager who did not check the plan carefully enough, or the clients who did not call for the appropriate types of tests during acceptance test?

9. What do you think are the advantages/disadvantages of having separate unit, integration, and system test plans as opposed to an inclusive test plan that contains all three in the same document?

10. Suppose you are a member of upper management and your company is interested in improving it's testing process. One of its first objectives is to satisfy the test planning maturity goal at level 2 of the TMM. In what specific ways could you support achievement of this maturity goal?

11. What role do users/clients play in the development of test plans for a project? Should they be present at any of the test plan reviews. If so, which ones, and why?

12. Acquire a requirements specification document associated with a project at work, or from your instructor, and create a system test plan appropriate for that project (see Appendix II for a sample test plan).

REFERENCES

[1] R. Thayer, ed. *Software Engineering Project Management,* second edition, IEEE Computer Society Press, Los Alamitos, CA, 1997.

[2] G. Daich, G. Price, B. Ragland, M. Dawood, *Software Test Technologies Report,* August 1994, Software Technology Support Center (STSC), Hill Air Force Base, UT.

[3] I. Burnstein, T. Suwanassart, C. R. Carlson, "Developing a testing maturity model: part II," *CrossTalk,*

Journal of Defense Software Engineering, Vol. 9, No. 9, Sept. 1996, pp. 19–26.

[4] *IEEE Standard Glossary of Software Engineering Terminology* (IEEE Std 610.12-1990), copyright 1990 by IEEE, all rights reserved.

[5] *IEEE Standard for Software Test Documentation* (IEEE Std 829–1983), copyright 1983 by IEEE, all rights reserved.

[6] *IEEE Standard for Software Unit Testing* (IEEE Std 1008–1987), copyright 1986 by IEEE, all rights reserved.

[7] *IEEE Standard for Software Verification and Validation Plans* (IEEE Std 1012–1986), copyright 1986 by IEEE, all rights reserved.

[8] J. Rakos, *Software Project Management for Small- to Medium-Sized Projects,* Prentice Hall, Englewood Cliffs, NJ, 1990.

[9] B. Boehm, "Software risk management: principles and practices," *IEEE Software,* Jan. 1991, pp. 32–41.

[10] B. Boehm, *Software Engineering Economics,* Prentice Hall, Englewood Cliffs, NJ, 1981.

[11] D. Legg, "Synopsis of COCOMO," *Software Engineering Project Management,* second edition, R. Thayer, ed., IEEE Computer Society Press, Los Alamitos, CA, 1997, pp. 230–245.

[12] T. Roper, *Software Testing Management: Life on the Critical Path,* Prentice Hall, Englewood Cliffs, NJ, 1993.

[13] E. Dustin, J. Rashka, J. Paul, *Automated Software Testing,* Addison-Wesley, Reading, MA, 1999

[14] G. Myers, *The Art of Software Testing,* John Wiley, New York, 1979.

[15] W. Humphrey, *A Discipline for Software Engineering,* Addison-Wesley, Reading, MA. 1995.

[16] B. Hetzel, *The Complete Guide to Software Testing,* second edition, QED Information Sciences, Inc., Wellesley, MA. 1988.

THE TEST

ORGANIZATION

8.0 Introducing the Test Specialist

When an organization has reached TMM level 2 it has accomplished a great deal. Fundamental testing maturity goals have been achieved. There are testing and debugging policies in place, which are available for all project personnel to access. There is management support for these policies. Management ensures they are applied to all projects. Testing for each project is planned. The test plan is prepared in conjunction with the project plan so that project goals can be achieved. The organization has institutionalized basic black and white box methods and applies them to design, and execute tests on software that is being developed, acquired, and maintained. The organization tests its software at several levels (unit, integration, system, etc.) Moving up to TMM level 3 requires further investment of organizational resources in the testing process. One of the maturity goals at TMM level 3 calls for the "Establishment of a test organization." This is an important step for a software organization. It implies a commitment to better testing and higher-quality software. This commitment requires that testing specialists be hired, space be given to house the testing group, resources be allocated to the group, and career paths for testers be established. It also implies that the functional and managerial hierarchy of the organization be redesigned, changes in the reporting structure be made, as well as changes be made to the organizational culture. Although there are many costs to establishing a testing group, there are also many benefits. By supporting a test group an organization acquires *leadership* in areas that relate to testing and quality issues. For example, there will be staff with the necessary skills and motivation to be responsible for:

- maintenance and application of test policies;

- development and application of test-related standards;

- participating in requirements, design, and code reviews;

- test planning;

- test design;

- test execution;

- test measurement;

- test monitoring (tasks, schedules, and costs);

- defect tracking, and maintaining the defect repository;

- acquisition of test tools and equipment;

- identifying and applying new testing techniques, tools, and methodologies;

- mentoring and training of new test personnel;

- test reporting.

The staff members of such a group are called test specialists or test engineers. Their primary responsibly is to ensure that testing is effective and productive, and that quality issues are addressed. Testers are not developers, or analysts, although background in these areas is very helpful and necessary. Testers don't repair code. However, they add value to a software product in terms of higher quality and customer satisfaction.

They are not destructive; they are constructive. The organizational culture needs to reflect this view.

Test specialists need to be educated and trained in testing and quality issues. Over the last several years the body of knowledge required to educate test specialists has been emerging, and courses at the graduate level have been developed to address the educational needs of such a group. This text was designed to support such a course and help you develop skills as a test specialist. If your organization does not have a testing function you can be the agent for change. With your newly acquired technical and managerial knowledge you are more able to convince the management of your company of the important role of such a group.

8.1 Skills Needed by a Test Specialist

Given the nature of technical and managerial responsibilities assigned to the tester that are listed in Section 8.0, many managerial and personal skills are necessary for success in the area of work. On the *personal* and *managerial* level a test specialist must have:

- organizational, and planning skills;

- the ability to keep track of, and pay attention to, details;

- the determination to discover and solve problems;

- the ability to work with others and be able to resolve conflicts;

- the ability to mentor and train others;

- the ability to work with users and clients;

- strong written and oral communication skills;

- the ability to work in a variety of environments;

- the ability to think creatively

The first three skills are necessary because testing is detail and problem oriented. In addition, testing involves policymaking, a knowledge of different types of application areas, planning, and the ability to organize and monitor information, tasks, and people. Testing also requires interactions with many other engineering professionals such as project managers, developers, analysts, process personal, and software quality assurance staff. Test professionals often interact with clients to prepare certain types of tests, for example acceptance tests. Testers also have to prepare test-related documents and make presentations. Training and mentoring of new hires to the testing group is also a part of the tester's job. In addition, test specialists must be creative, imaginative, and experiment-oriented. They need to be able to visualize the many ways that a software item should be tested, and make hypotheses about the different types of defects that could occur and the different ways the software could fail.

On the *technical* level testers need to have:

- an education that includes an understanding of general software engineering principles, practices, and methodologies;

- strong coding skills and an understanding of code structure and behavior;

- a good understanding of testing principles and practices;

- a good understanding of basic testing strategies, methods, and techniques;

- the ability and experience to plan, design, and execute test cases and test procedures on multiple levels (unit, integration, etc.);

- a knowledge of process issues;

- knowledge of how networks, databases, and operating systems are organized and how they work;

- a knowledge of configuration management;

- a knowledge of test-related documents and the role each documents plays in the testing process;

- the ability to define, collect, and analyze test-related measurements;

- the ability, training, and motivation to work with testing tools and equipment;

- a knowledge of quality issues.

All of these skills are summarized in Figure 8.1

Tester Requirements   The Tester

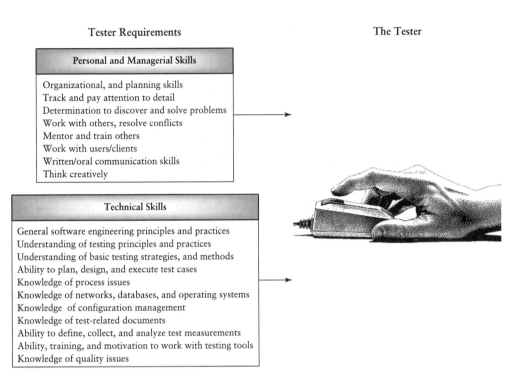

Personal and Managerial Skills

Organizational, and planning skills
Track and pay attention to detail
Determination to discover and solve problems
Work with others, resolve conflicts
Mentor and train others
Work with users/clients
Written/oral communication skills
Think creatively

Technical Skills

General software engineering principles and practices
Understanding of testing principles and practices
Understanding of basic testing strategies, and methods
Ability to plan, design, and execute test cases
Knowledge of process issues
Knowledge of networks, databases, and operating systems
Knowledge of configuration management
Knowledge of test-related documents
Ability to define, collect, and analyze test measurements
Ability, training, and motivation to work with testing tools
Knowledge of quality issues

FIG. 8.1

Test specialist skills.

In order to carry out testing tasks testers need to have knowledge of how requirements, specifications, and designs are developed and how different methodologies can be applied. They should understand how errors and defects are introduced into the software artifacts even at early stages of the life cycle. Testers should have strong programming backgrounds to help them visualize how code works, how it behaves, and the possible defects it could contain. They also need coding experience to support the development of the test harnesses which often involve a considerable coding effort in themselves.

Testers must have a knowledge of both white and black box techniques and methods and the ability to use them to design test cases. Organizations need to realize that this knowledge is a necessary prerequisite for tool use and test automation. Testers need to understand the need for multilevel tests and approaches used for testing at each level. It is important that testers understand the role of test-related documents in the testing process, so that they are willing to spend the time needed to prepare, present, and preserve these items. Testers need to understand process issues; how to evaluate a process, and the importance of measuring, defining, and improving a process. Testers also need to understand quality measures such as reliability, maintainability, usability, and how to test for them. In addition to all of these requirements, it is very important for testers to be willing and able to work with testing tools and configuration management systems. They need to have an awareness of new technical and tools, be able to evaluate them, and apply them in the organization. These skills will promote technology transfer. Finally, testers should have some knowledge of the problem domain for which the software has been written. This knowledge, for example, can help them to understand the domain vocabulary, domain operations, and domain requirements and constraints.

The list of skills and knowledge requirements needed to be a successful test specialist is long and complex. Acquiring these skills takes education, training, experience, and motivation. Organizations must be willing to support such staff since they play a valuable role in the organizational structure and have a high impact on the quality of the software delivered. If your organization is building a testing group it will have to recruit people with these skills and offer appropriate benefits. Competition is keen since there is a scarcity of people that meet all of these qualifications.

8.2 Building a Testing Group

In Chapter 7, it was mentioned that organizing, staffing, and directing were major activities required to manage a project and a process [1]. These apply to managing the testing process as well. Staffing activities include filling positions, assimilating new personnel, education and training, and staff evaluation [1]. Directing includes providing leadership, building teams, facilitating communication, motivating personnel, resolving conflicts, and delegating authority. Organizing includes selecting organizational structures, creating positions, defining responsibilities, and delegating authority. Hiring staff for the testing group, organizing the testing staff members into teams, motivating the team members, and integrating the team into the overall organizational structure are organizing, staffing, and directing activities your organization will need to perform to build a managed testing process.

Establishing a specialized testing group is a major decision for an organization. The steps in the process are summarized in Figure 8.2. To initiate the process, upper management must support the decision to establish a test group and commit resources to the group. Decisions must be made on how the testing group will be organized, what career paths are available, and how the group fits into the organizational structure (see Section 8.3). When hiring staff to fill test specialist positions, management should have a clear idea of the educational and skill levels required for each testing position and develop formal job descriptions to fill the test group slots. Dustin describes a typical job requisition for a test specialist [2]. Included on this requisition are the job title, full time/part time, location, salary, location, qualifications that are required (the applicant must have these), qualifications that are desired (the recruiter is flexible on these), and a description of the duties. When the job description has been approved and distributed, the interviewing process takes place.

Interviews should be structured and of a problem-solving nature. The interviewer should prepare an extensive list of questions to determine the interviewee's technical background as well as his or her personal skills and motivation. Zawacki has developed a general guide for selecting technical staff members that can be used by test managers [3]. Dustin describes the kinds of questions that an interviewer should ask when selecting a test specialist [2]. When the team has been selected and is up and working on projects, the team manager is responsible for keeping the test team positions filled (there are always attrition problems). He must continually evaluate team member performance. Bartol and Martin have written a paper that contains guidelines for evaluation of employees that can be applied to any type of team and organization [4]. They describe four categories for employees based on their performance: (i) retain, (ii) likely to retain, (iii) likely to release, (iv) and release. For each category, appropriate actions need to be taken by the manager to help employee and employer. The reader should note that the papers by Zawacki and

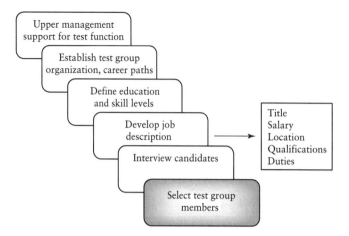

FIG. 8.2

Steps in forming a test group.

Bartol and many more useful papers related to software project management appear in Thayer [1]. The papers are relevant to managing testing efforts as well.

8.3 The Structure of the Test Group

It is important for a software organization to have an independent testing group. The group should have a formalized position in the organizational hierarchy. A reporting structure should be established and resources allocated to the group. The group should be staffed by people who have the skills and motivation as described in Section 8.1 to be good testers. They should be dedicated to establishing awareness of, and achieving, existing software quality goals, and also to strengthening quality goals for the future software products. They are quality leaders—the test and quality policy makers. They measure quality, and have responsibilities for ensuring the software meets the customers' requirements. The term independence was used, and each organization must develop its own interpretation and implementation of independence. In the TMM sense, independence for the testing group means that testers are recognized as engineering specialists. Testers are not considered to be developers, and most importantly they report to management independent of development. Testers are assigned and control their own budgets and resources. They have different responsibilities, and because of the differences in responsibilities they evaluated in ways different from developers. This allows testers to be objective and impartial, and unhindered by development managerial pressures. To support this independence ideally the test group should be a separate organizational entity or function. However, that is not always possible or practical given the size of an organization and the resources available.

In TMM level 1 and 2 organizations there is usually not a separate testing function. This is true for many organizations. Testing is done by developers; it is part of their responsibilities. Developers design test cases, execute the tests and also perform fault localization duties which consist of locating the faults, repairing the code, and retesting it. There are no staff persons whose full-time responsibilities are concerned with testing. In some cases there may be a decentralized nonpermanent group of staff persons called testers who are associated with specific projects. Test planning is done by the project manager who hires and supervises the testers. They are not independent, and are not part of a permanent testing group. When a project is completed they may be terminated or become associated with a different project. For these staff members there is no well-defined career path to follow. Turnover rates may be high.

When an organization is reaching toward TMM level 3 it has a keen awareness of the importance of testing and must make a commitment to support a testing organization. It has policies, practices, and planning capabilities in place to support a test organization. The test organization could be a component of a software quality assurance organization that is given testing responsibilities. Under those circumstances, the testers would be supervised by an SQA manager. Organizations at higher levels of the TMM, where reviews are a part of the testing process, may include a function called the Independent Validation and Verification Group (IV&V). This group sometimes exists as an internal entity or as independent subcontractor. The group is responsible for conducting inspections and walkthroughs as well as execution-based testing activities. They may also do quality assurance work such as develop standards and conduct audits.

An organization that wants to grow in testing strength and capability will eventually need to upgrade their testing function to the best case scenario which is a permanent centralized group of dedicated testers with the skills described earlier in this chapter. This group is solely responsible for testing work. The group members are assigned to projects throughout the organization where they do their testing work. When the project is completed they return to the test organization for reassignment. They report to a test manager or test director, not a project manager. In such an organization testers are viewed as assets. They have defined career paths to follow which contributes to long-term job satisfaction. Since they can be assigned to a project at its initiation, they can give testing support throughout the software life cycle. Because of the permanent nature of the test organization there is a test infrastructure that endures. There is a test knowledge base of test processes, test procedures, test tools, and test histories (lessons learned). Dedicated staff is responsible for maintaining a test case and test harness library.

A test organization is expensive, it is a strategic commitment. Given the complex nature of the software being built, and its impact on society, organizations must realize that a test organization is necessary and that it has many benefits. By investing in a test organization a company has access to a group of specialists who have the responsibilities and motivation to:

- maintain testing policy statements;

- plan the testing efforts;

- monitor and track testing efforts so that they are on time and within budget;

- measure process and product attributes;

- provide management with independent product and process quality information;

- design and execute tests with no duplication of effort;

- automate testing;

- participate in reviews to insure quality;

- work with analysts, designers, coders, and clients to ensure quality goals are meet;
- maintain a repository of test-related information;
- give greater visibility to quality issues organization wide;
- support process improvement efforts.

The problem with evaluating test cost/benefit ratios for most organizations is that they don't know the actual costs of testing, and they also do not realize the costs of inadequate testing! Very often the costs that occur after coding is complete are counted as testing costs. This includes the costs of training, fault localization, fault repair, and analysis meetings. To help support the ability to account for true testing costs and resource use, the TMM calls for testing and debugging policies to be developed by an organization at TMM level 2.

Hetzel estimates in most cases, direct testing costs are about 25% of total development costs [5]. He also estimates that the costs of poor testing may be much higher. At TMM level 2 testing costs except for those associated with reviews can be calculated by test planners. This will give management a baseline figure. At higher TMM levels the costs of reviews and other testing activities can be folded in. Mangers can compare these costs to the costs of poor testing that include: ineffective tests; duplicated tests; repetitive and unproductive tests; repetitive debug, patch code, and retest cycles; customer hot line expenses; failures in the field; repairs to operational software; analysis/action meetings; and customer dissatisfaction. In the worst case the latter can lead to expensive legal actions, all of which could have been avoided with effective testing! (A good source for anecdotal information related to poor development and testing practices is the book called *The Day the Phones Stopped* [6].)

Given a formal testing function in an organization, with test specialists available to perform the testing activities associated with software projects, the question becomes how to effectively organize the testers as specialized teams that are allocated to different software projects. There are many different possibilities for team structures. These apply to any type of team. They range from a democratic, or egoless, team with little or no internal structure to the hierarchical team that has a definite head and a formal reporting structure [7]. Industry specialists often recommend a more hierarchical structure for the testing team. At the top of the hierarchy is a test manger. (In some organizations there may also be a test director who is the managerial head of the test organization.) A typical testing team assigned to a project will consist of 3–4 or more test specialists with a test team leader at the head of each team. If the project is very large the number of testers rises and could go as high as 20–30. There is some debate on what is a good tester/developer ratio. Ratios of 1/2, 2/3, or 1/4 are common [2]. This will depend on the nature of the software under development. The test team usually consists of a test lead as the head of the team. That person has the strongest testing background and experience. Other team members are the test engineers and the junior test engineers as shown in Figure 8.3. At higher levels of the TMM test team members can also include usability engineers who work with users throughout the software life cycle to ensure that usability requirements are meet (see Chapter 12).

The duties of the team members may vary in individual organizations. The following gives a brief description of the duties for each tester that are common to most organizations.

The Test Manager

In most organizations with a testing function, the test manager (or test director) is the central person concerned with all aspects of testing and quality issues. The test manager is usually responsible for test policy making, customer interaction, test planning, test documentation, controlling and monitoring of tests, training, test tool acquisition, participation in inspections and walkthroughs, reviewing test work, the test repository, and staffing issues such as hiring, firing, and evaluation of the test team members. He or she is also the liaison with upper management, project management, and the quality assurance and marketing staffs.

The Test Lead

The test lead assists the test manager and works with a team of test engineers on individual projects. He or she may be responsible for duties such as test planning, staff supervision, and status reporting. The test lead also participates in test design, test execution and reporting, technical reviews, customer interaction, and tool training.

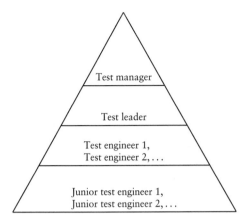

FIG. 8.3

The test team hierarchy.

The Test Engineer

The test engineers design, develop, and execute tests, develop test harnesses, and set up test laboratories and environments. They also give input to test planning and support maintenance of the test and defect repositories.

The Junior Test Engineer

The junior test engineers are usually new hires. They gain experience by participating in test design, test execution, and test harness development. They may also be asked to review user manuals and user help facilities defect and maintain the test and defect repositories.

8.4 The Technical Training Program

Establishing a test organization is a key maturity goal at TMM level 3. Another maturity goal at level 3 is to establish a technical training program. The two goals are closely related and interdependent. One of the principal objectives of a technical training program is to support the test organization and the training of test specialists. A quality training program ensures that members of the test organization continue to improve their testing skills, and continually update their knowledge of technical and process issues related to testing. A training program as interpreted by the TMM includes in-house courses and training sessions, college/university courses, a college/university degree program, or courses taken at a external commercial training center.

Establishing a training program is an additional commitment on the part of an organization to support a high-quality testing staff and to promote continuous test process improvement. An organization can structure its training program to suit its own development, acquisition, testing and quality policies and goals. Because the training program covers a wide variety of technical and managerial issues, many different topics are likely to be the subject of in-house courses, training sessions, and university classes. An organization can include under the umbrella of technical training sessions that cover topics such as:

- quality issues;

- measurement identification, collection, and analysis;

- testing techniques and methodologies;

- design techniques;

- tool usage (for all life cycle phases);

- configuration management;

- planning;

- process evaluation and improvement;

- policy development;

- technical review skills;

- software acquisition;

- project management skills;

- business skills

- communication skills.

Our greatest training concerns as testers are related to training in test case design, measurement, tools for automated testing, planning, and process issues. At higher levels of the TMM our training requirements will focus on technical review skills and statistical testing as well as other advanced test-related topics. The training group should keep abreast of new testing techniques, methods, and tools. They should be prepare courses and materials to instruct the testers in these new areas and they should also give their support to technology transfer.

The TMM does not prescribe a particular format for the training program. Each organization should develop its own guidelines and materials for training. It is important that members of the training team have:

- experience and education in the field of software engineering;

- good oral and written communication skills;

- strong technical skills;

- an enthusiasm for tool use and evaluation;

- willingness to serve as mentors;

- ability to support technology transfer.

From the viewpoint of the test organization, the training group needs to support test planning, test measurement, test documentation, test techniques, and tool usage. As the organization moves up the TMM levels the knowledge required for testers grows in complexity. The training program should help testers to acquire the knowledge and expertise they need to improve their testing skills. To accomplish this goal training plans need to be developed by teams of mangers and developers, testers, SQA, and the training staff. There could be a master training plan and then a set of subordinate plans for training members of specific teams. These can be prepared as separate documents. In the training plans the following items should be included:

- staffing requirements for the training team;

- identification of areas that have specific training needs;

- goals for the training courses/sessions should be set;

- a time frame (schedule) for the training courses should be set;

- funding sources for the training programs need to be identified (a funding mechanism to compensate staff for outside university courses and commercial sessions needs to be set up);

- the materials, facilities, and tools needed should be identified;

- staff members who will receive the training should be identified;

- training evaluation criteria should be specified so that the effectiveness of the training program can be measured.

Training programs represent a commitment of funds and resources. An organization can decide to support an internal training group or outsource technical training to specialized groups external to the organization. Sources for technical training include educational institutions, and commercial technical training centers. Appendix I has a listing of web sites and other sources that are useful for identifying training programs for testers.

8.5 Career Paths for Testers: An Industry Example

When an organization makes a commitment to establish a testing group, one of the major issues of concern is how to keep highly skilled testers in the group for the long term. In the past testers have been selected from the ranks of the inexperienced and poorly trained. If the test group is to attract and retain highly qualified staff, there must be established career paths for the test group members so that they can view themselves as valuable professionals and can improve the nature of their status and rewards. Weyuker and co-authors describe such a career path for testers at AT&T [8]. The researchers have identified a group of general engineering skills that testers require such as a knowledge of computers, information systems, system architectures, software development methods, and operating and database systems. Testers also need good communication skills and technical skills, for example in, test planning, test design, test tool usage, and test execution. The need for these skills has been described earlier in this chapter.

Weyuker and co-authors also describe the phases in a tester's career path in their organization, AT&T [8]. These phases or levels in a tester's career path are shown in Figure 8.4 and are described below. They have a rough correspondence with the tester hierarchy described in Section 8.3. The junior test engineer roughly corresponds to the apprentice level as described below. The test engineer has a correspondence to the mastery level. The test leader overlaps with the specialization level, and the test manger overlaps with the leader level. The top level in the AT&T career path would correspond to a test division manager. Readers should note that the AT&T approach is one of many possible approaches to test career path definition. Each organization will need to establish its own career path and responsibility levels for testers. These should be reflected in the organizational test policy. (Note that test policy modification is usually required as an organization's test process evolves and moves up the levels of the TMM.)

"Apprenticeship": A new staff member at AT&T enters the testing group with a position called "software tester." That person spends time attending courses, seminars, and conferences to learn best testing practices and core competency skills as performed both within and outside of the organization. They are mentored by more experienced test group members.

"Mastery": After mastering core areas, testers assume more responsibility. They hold the position of "software test engineers" and participate in test planning, test management, and test execution. They continue to take courses and be mentored by upper-level testers.

"Specialization": The next level of competency for a tester at AT&T is to become a specialist in one or more areas of testing. The tester then advances to the position of a "test specialist." According to the AT&T career description, test specialists should exhibit expertise in one or more of the following areas: testing tools and automation, test environment architecture, test equipment, architecture verification (involves performance modeling, software reliability engineering, and security standards), operations readiness testing (testers build test suites to determine whether a software system is ready for production), and end-to-end testing (testing products that span multiple applications, or business units).

"Leadership": When a tester becomes a specialist in the one or more specialization areas, then he or she becomes eligible to advance to "lead software test specialist." Testers in this position often need to coordinate many testers working on complex projects. For this level, testers need

FIG. 8.4

The AT&T tester career path [8].

technical testing expertise as well as negotiation skills, process and project management skills, and good oral and written communication skills.

"Top Level Tester": The highest level in the tester hierarchy is that of an "enterprise software tester." This is a highly skilled individual with breadth and depth of knowledge of software testing. The enterprise software tester must have expertise in at least four of the specialization areas including architecture verification. This person will work with top management, provide strategic direction for software testing, and advise the organization on emerging software testing technologies. The enterprise software tester serves as a mentor and speaker giving presentations at both internal and external test training courses and conferences.

8.6 Tester Certification

Most mature engineering professions address the issue of certification which insures a level of competency for all practicing members of the profession. In Chapter 1 it was mentioned that certification activities have begun for the profession of software engineering in some states [9]. The IEEE/ACM task forces on software engineering and the deliverables produced by these task forces support the emerging profession of software engineer and a certification process. Certification is currently available to testers. Note that the AT&T tester is encouraged, but not required, to be certified in order to advance in his or her career. However, AT&T does recognize certification as a technical accomplishment and an indicator of a tester's expertise and professional standing.

Certification for testers in the United States is available from two organizations, the American Society for Quality (ASQ) and the Quality Assurance Institute (QAI). Neither of these are licensing boards and if a tester is certified by either organization this has no legal significance. Both organizations require an examination and experience for certification. The ASQ has compiled a body of knowledge based on the work of software quality assurance professionals and a survey of ASQ members. Candidates for certification must show knowledge in areas that include:

- ethics;
- quality management;
- process knowledge;
- project management;
- measurement;
- testing;
- V&V (includes inspections);
- audits;
- configuration management.

Readers can get more information about these certification processes from the organizational web sites: www.qaiusa.com and www.asq.org. The British Computer Society also offers tester certification (www.bcs.org.uk). It is hoped that in the future the IEEE and ACM will also offer this service. Certification for testers is not yet required, but it probably will be in the future along with certification for software engineers, especially in situations where the software is mission or safety critical.

8.7 Integrating Testing Activities into the Software Life Cycle

Organizations with ad hoc testing processes soon realize that addressing testing issues at the end of the software life cycle does not consistently produce quality software that is on time and within budget. They learn through experience and through guidance from models like the TMM and the V-model that testing activities need to begin as early as possible in the life cycle. They also learn that testing is not only an execution-based activity. There are a variety of testing activities that need be performed before the end of the coding phase. These activities should be carried out *in parallel* with development activities, and testers need to work with developers and analysts so they can perform these activities and tasks and produce a set of test deliverables. When a formal test organization has been established and testers are well educated and have full responsibility for testing, then the full integration of testing activities into the software life cycle becomes a much more realizable goal. The availability of test specialists means that at each life cycle phase there are personnel that are trained, motivated, and responsible for carrying out test-related tasks. The V-model is a model that illustrates how testing activities can be integrated into each phase of the standard software life cycle. A version of the V-model is shown in Figure 8.5.

Individual organizations may interpret the V-model in different ways since each block of the model is abstract enough to represent a variety of tasks. However, specific activities assigned to each block should be compatible with organizational testing policies and the overall model philosophy. Using the V-model as a framework we will look at test-related activities in each life cycle phase, and the deliverables that result. Below is an example for the distribution of activities.

Requirements Phase

Testers use requirements documents and interactions with users/clients to develop the initial versions of system and acceptance tests based on functional requirements, quality requirements, and the specification of system behavior. Testers also work with users/clients to develop a usage profile to provide support for system and acceptance tests. Black box testing methods are used for test design. Discussions with requirements staff helps to ensure that all requirements are testable. Testers, with the cooperation of project managers, also initiate development of the master test plan that describes the overall testing approach for the project. Items 1–15 for the master test plan as described in Chapter 7 can be sketched out with the information at hand. Testing requirements and testing goals are specified in the plan. Testing schedules and costs can be estimated.

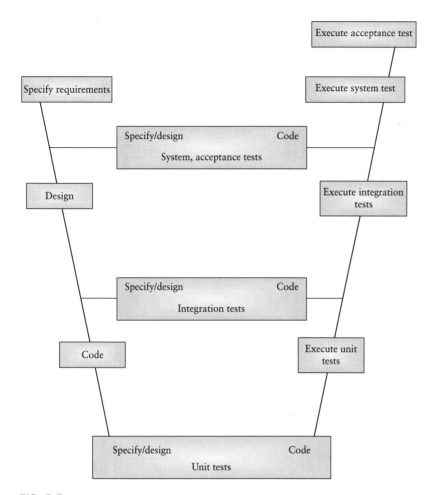

FIG. 8.5
The V-model.

Deliverables are (i) the initial version of the master test plan, (ii) initial versions of system and acceptance tests, and (iii) an initial version of the system test plan and acceptance test plan with the preliminary system and acceptance tests attached (these may be a component of the master test plan depending on organizational policy).

Design Phase

When design is complete, the system architecture has been described and the structure of the system components is usually known for both procedure- and object-oriented systems. Testers can interact with designers to address any testability issues. The design documents can then be used to develop integration tests and an integration test plan (if a separate plan is specified). The master test plan can be reviewed and augmented with new information as needed. If detailed design is complete enough, then designs for unit test can also begin.

Deliverables are (i) a revised master/and or system test plan, (ii) an integration test plan if specified, (iii) integration test plan attachments, and (iv) test milestone reports (address progress in testing).

Coding Phase

Testers can complete unit test designs if this activity has already begun at the end of the design phase. If not, they can carry out the necessary unit test design tasks at this time. All other test plans can modified as needed based on the detailed knowledge of the software available at the coding phase. According to the V-model, work begins on the test harness code for unit test. If the design details for the units are well known at design time, work on the test harnesses can begin at the end of that phase and continue on in parallel with the coding phase.

Deliverables are (i) revised master/system/integration test plans with attached tests, (ii) unit test plan, with unit tests attached, (iii) test milestone reports, and (iv) code for the unit test harnesses.

Test Execution

With guidance from the V-model, an organization has performed a great deal of the testing work by the time that coding is complete, and they are now well-prepared to execute the planned tests at the unit, integration, and system levels. According to the model, coding the test harness for unit and integration test is a task that is carried out before execution of these tests. However, these tasks can also be done by testers in parallel with the coding phase as mentioned previously.

Although the V-model itself does not formally call for test plan reviews, organizations may do so before each level of testing execution commences. The Extended/Modified V-model described in Chapters 1 and 10 allows for this. Finally, the V-model does not formally address the need for developing additional tests that often occurs as testing progresses. Testers are often required to develop new and unplanned tests because of conditions that arise, for example, to achieve coverage goals. Existing tests may also have to be modified. These tasks can be carried out as needed during the execution-based testing phases without disrupting the testing efforts, since the bulk of all the test planning and coding work has already been accomplished. Therein lies the beauty of the V-model, and the philosophy of integrating testing activities into the earlier software life cycle phases.

Deliverables from this testing phase are (i) the tested code, (ii) test logs and test incident reports, (iii) test milestone reports, (iv) test measurement data, and (v) a test summary report.

8.8 The Test Organization, Technical Training Program, and Test Integration: Support from the Three Critical Views

TMM level 3 has four maturity goals. Controlling and monitoring of test is discussed in Chapter 9, and the supporting roles of the three critical group members for that goal is discussed in that chapter. In this chapter the other three level 3 maturity goals—establishing a test organization, establishing a training program, and integration of testing into software life cycle—are discussed. This section describes how managers, testers, and users/clients can support the achievement and continuous implementation of these maturity goals. The maturity goals are highly interrelated and responsibilities assigned to the three critical groups with respect to these goals may overlap.

Provision for a test organization is a major financial and managerial commitment for a software company. It implies strong interest in the testing process, a recognition of its important role in software, development acquisition, and maintenance. It represents a commitment to test process evaluation and improvement. This investment also indicates to the internal world of the organization, and to the external world of users/clients, a commitment to greater software quality. It is a great morale booster for members of the testing teams, and gives recognition to the value-added nature of the testing process. Contributions from each of the three TMM critical groups are necessary to support this level 3 maturity goal and to a achieve a good return on this investment. Roles for each of the three critical groups in supporting a test organization are described below.

Managers play a very important role in supporting the test organization. They need to:

- ensure that the role and responsibilities of the test organization are stated in the testing policy statement;

- make needed changes in the organizational reporting structure;

- establish standards, requirements, and career paths for the test group staff;

- support cultural changes;

- provide resources, staff, and funding for the test organization;

- encourage cooperation between development, test, and SQA organizations;

- recruit and hire test specialists;

- evaluate and supervise testing personnel;

- periodically assess the maturity, effectiveness, and performance of the test organization;

- support education and training of test group members;

- monitor the performance of the test group;

- propose and support test organization growth and test process improvement efforts.

Testers are the backbone of the test organization. Their major responsibilities have been described earlier in this chapter, and are reviewed here. The role of a tester in a test organization is to:

- work with analysts, developers, and SQA staff to develop quality software products;

- work with project managers and test managers on test planning and monitoring;

- design test cases, test procedures, execute tests;

- prepare test documents;

- collect, analyze, and apply test-related measurements;

- contribute to test policy making;

- maintain the test and defect repositories;

- recruit new staff members;

- mentor new test staff members;

- establish product and process standards;

- evaluate and apply new testing techniques and tools;

- participate in technical reviews;

- contribute to test process evaluation and improvement

Users/clients do have interactions with the test organization and SQA group to voice their requirements and to participate in acceptance and usability test development. They make major contributions to the development of operational or usage profiles and use cases. They may also give feedback to management on the quality of user/client–tester interactions.

The integration of test activities into the software life cycle is an indication of a growing level of test process quality and a dedication to software quality. The integration process as we have discussed is supported by the V-model and its extensions or any other model that supports this integration goal. The following paragraphs describe the roles of the three critical groups in the support for test integration activities.

Management supports integration of testing into the software life cycle by:

- reviewing, approving, and adopting a test integration model such as the V-model;

- ensuring that integration of testing activities is a part of the testing policy and standards documents;

- ensuring that the integration of testing activities is applied throughout the organization for all projects, and giving support for integration;

- ensuring that all testers are trained to carry out integrated testing activities;

- monitoring the integrated testing activities and deliverables, evaluating them, and proposing improvements if needed.

Testers support test integration maturity goal by:

- working with management to review, approve, and institute a test activities integration model;

- performing the required test activities throughout the software life cycle as described in the test model, the organizations' policy, and standards documents;

- preparing all test deliverables that result from each of the integrated testing activities.

Users/clients play their supporting roles in some the integrated testing activities such as acceptance test planning and usage profile development during the requirements and specifications phases.

A technical training program needs the support of management as it requires an investment of organizational staff and resources. It also requires cultural changes in the organization. Managers and staff need to recognize the need for such a training program and the benefits it will bring.

Management supports the training program by:

- ensuring that the training program is supported by organizational policy;

- providing funding for the program, including staff, resources, training materials, tools, and laboratories;

- recruiting and hiring qualified staff for the training organization;

- ensuring that training plans are developed;

- monitoring the training program and evaluating its effectiveness.

Testers support the training program by:

- requesting training and advanced education to improve their testing skills and capabilities;

- participating in training classes, doing homework, applying their newly acquired knowledge and skills to organizational projects.

Users/clients are usually not involved in organizational training programs. However, in some cases they could be invited by the development organization to participate in technical review, usability testing, and acceptance testing training sessions.

EXERCISES

1. You are a test manager for a mid-sized software development organization. Your company develops software in the telecommunication domain. You want to hire a new tester for your team. Prepare a job description for the test engineer position that you could use to screen applicants for the job. What type of interviews would you conduct? What are some of the questions you would ask a candidate?

2. Discuss the advantages and disadvantages of having an independent test group, that is, one that is a separate organizational entity with its own reporting structure.

3. Suppose you are working for a very large software development organization. Your company is often involved in developing very large and complex mission-critical software for customers affiliated with the defense industry. Suggest approaches to organize a test group for your company, keeping in mind the size of the company and the type of software developed. Give reasons for your choice.

4. For the organization described in Problem 1, prepare a job description for hiring members of a technical training team.

5. Develop a training plan outline for instruction on test planning for the test group in your organization.

6. Why is it so important to integrate testing activities into the software life cycle?

7. Using a version of the V-model, describe the test-related activities that should be done and why they should be done during the following phases of the software life cycle: project initiation, requirements specification, design, and coding.

8. What role does management play in support of a technical training program?

9. What role do managers play in support of a test group?

10. What role do testers play in support of the integration of testing activities into the software life cycle?

REFERENCES

[1] R. Thayer, ed. *Software Engineering Project Management,* second edition, IEEE Computer Society Press, Los Alamitos, CA, 1997.

[2] E. Dustin, J. Rashka, J. Paul, *Automated Software Testing,* Addison-Wesley, Reading, MA, 1999.

[3] R. Zawacki, "How to pick Eagles," *Datamation Magazine,* Sept. 1995, pp. 115–16.

[4] K. Bartol, D. Martin, "Managing the consequences of the DP turnover: a human resources planning perspective," *Proc. 20th ACM Computer Personnel Research Conf.,* 1983, pp. 79–86.

[5] B. Hetzel, *The Complete Guide to Software Testing,* second edition, QED Information Sciences, Inc., Wellesley, MA, 1988.

[6] L. Lee, *The Day the Phones Stopped,* Primus, New York, 1992.

[7] M. Mantei, "The effect of programming team structures on programming tasks," *CACM,* Vol. 24, No. 3, 1981, pp. 106–113.

[8] E. Weyuker, T. Ostrand, J. Brophy, R. Prasad, "Clearing a career path for software testers," *IEEE Software,* Vol. 17, No. 2, March/April 2000, pp. 76–82.

[9] J. Speed. "What do you mean I can't call myself a software engineer," *IEEE Software,* Nov./Dec. 1999, pp. 45–50.

CONTROLLING AND MONITORING THE TESTING PROCESS

9.0 Defining Terms

In Chapter 1, software testing was described as a process. As is true for all processes, the testing process has components that are the methods, practices, standards, policies, and procedures associated with it. Processes are instantiated by individual projects that use its associated practices, methods, procedures, and so on, to achieve project goals. Goals include assembling, developing, or evaluating a product. Engineers monitor and control the processes that drive each engineering project. In order to do so the project must first be planned by a engineering project manager using the underlying process components as the planning framework. As the project progresses it is monitored (tracked) and controlled with respect to the plan. Monitoring and controlling are engineering management activities, and should be practiced by software engineers as a part of their professional engineering duties. The TMM supports controlling and monitoring of testing with a maturity goal at level 3. A description of these two activities follows.

> Project monitoring (or tracking) refers to the activities and tasks managers engage in to periodically check the status of each project. Reports are prepared that compare the actual work done to the work that was planned.

Monitoring requires a set of tools, forms, techniques, and measures. A precondition for monitoring a project is the existence of a project plan.

> Project controlling consists of developing and applying a set of corrective actions to get a project on track when monitoring shows a deviation from what was planned.

If monitoring results show deviations from the plan have occurred, controlling mechanisms must be put into place to direct the project back on its proper track. Controlling a project is an important activity which is done to ensure that the project goals will be achieved occurring to the plan. Many managerial experts group the two activities into one called "controlling" [1]. This author believes that separating the two activities gives greater insight into the resources and skills required to carry them both out effectively.

In the domain of software engineering, project managers monitor and control the development process for each project. Plans for monitoring and controlling are part of the overall project plan. Test managers, as engineering specialists, need to apply these management activities to the testing process for each individual project. In fact, a monitoring and controlling component for the testing efforts in each project is strongly recommended as part of a test plan at TMM level 3 and above.

Thayer partitions what he calls "project controlling" into six major tasks [1]. The following is a modified description of the tasks suggested by Thayer. The description has been augmented by the author to include supplemental tasks that provide additional support for the controlling and monitoring functions.

1. *Develop standards of performance.* These set the stage for defining goals that will be achieved when project tasks are correctly accomplished.
2. *Plan each project.* The plan must contain measurable goals, milestones, deliverables, and well-defined budgets and schedules that take into consideration project types, conditions, and constraints.

3. *Establish a monitoring and reporting system.* In the monitoring and reporting system description the organization must describe the measures to be used, how/when they will be collected, what questions they will answer, who will receive the measurement reports, and how these will be used to control the project. Each project plan must describe the monitoring and reporting mechanisms that will be applied to it. If status meetings are required, then their frequency, attendees, and resulting documents must be described.

4. *Measure and analyze results.* Measurements for monitoring and controlling must be collected, organized, and analyzed. They are then used to compare the actual achievements with standards, goals, and plans.

5. *Initiate corrective actions for projects that are off track.* These actions may require changes in the project requirements and the project plan.

6. *Reward and discipline.* Reward those staff who have shown themselves to be good performers, and discipline, retrain, relocate those that have consistently performed poorly.

7. *Document the monitoring and controlling mechanisms.* All the methods, forms, measures, and tools that are used in the monitoring and controlling process must be documented in organization standards and be described in policy statements.

8. *Utilize a configuration management system.* A configuration management system is needed to manage versions, releases, and revisions of documents, code, plans, and reports.

It was Thayer's intent that these activities and actions be applied to monitor and control software development projects. However, these activities/actions can be applied to monitor and control testing efforts as well. The reader should note that several of these items have been covered with respect to the testing process in previous sections of this text. Test planning and testing goals have been discussed in Chapter 7. Chapter 8 discusses test staffing issues. In this chapter we will cover topics in measurement, monitoring, reporting, and taking corrective actions. We will briefly cover configuration management. Many of the activities/actions described in items 1–8 are also covered by papers appearing in Thayer [1]. The author recommends that readers who do not have a strong project management background refer to this material.

9.1 Measurements and Milestones for Monitoring and Controlling

All processes should have measurements (metrics) associated with them. The measurements help to answer questions about status and quality of the process, as well as the products that result from its implementation. Measurements in the testing domain can help to track test progress, evaluate the quality of the software product, manage risks, classify and prevent defects, evaluate test effectiveness, and determine when to stop testing. Level 4 of the TMM calls for a formal test measurement program. However, to establish a baseline process, to put a monitoring program into place, and to evaluate improvement efforts, an organization needs to define, collect, and use measurements starting at the lower levels of the TMM.

To begin the collection of meaningful measurements each organization should answer the following questions:

- Which measures should we collect?

- What is their purpose (what kinds of questions can they answer)?

- Who will collect them?

- Which forms and tools will be used to collect the data?

- Who will analyze the data?

- Who to have access to reports?

When these question have been addressed, an organization can start to collect simple measurements beginning at TMM level 1 and continue to add measurements as their test process evolves to support test process evaluation and improvement and process and product quality growth. In this chapter we are mainly concerned with monitoring and controlling of the testing process as defined in Section 9.0, so we will confine ourselves to discussing measurements that are useful for this purpose. Chapter 11 will provide an in-depth discussion of how to develop a full-scale measurement program applicable to testing. Readers will learn how measurements support test process improvement and product quality goals.

The following sections describe a collection of measurements that support monitoring of test over time. Each measurement is shown in italics to highlight it. It is recommended that measurements followed by an asterisk (*) be collected by all organizations, even those at TMM level 1. The reader should note that it is not suggested that all of the measurements listed be collected by an organization. The TMM level, and the testing goals that an organization is targeting, affect the appropriateness of these measures. As a simple example, if a certain degree of branch coverage is not a testing objective for a organization at this time, then this type of measurement is not relevant. However, the organization should strive to include such goals in their test polices and plans in the future.

Readers familiar with software metrics concepts should note that most of the measures listed in this chapter are mainly process measures; a few are product measures. Other categories for the measures listed here are (i) explicit, those that are measured directly from the process or product itself, and (ii) derived, those that are a result of the combination of explicit and/or other derived measures. Note that the ratios described are derived measures.

Now we will address the question of how a testing process can be monitored for each project. A test manager needs to start with a test plan. What the manager wants to measure and evaluate is the actual work that was done and compare it to work that was planned. To help support this goal, the test plan must contain testing milestones as described in Chapter 7.

> **Milestones are tangible events that are expected to occur at a certain time in the project's lifetime. Managers use them to determine project status.**

Test milestones can be used to monitor the progress of the testing efforts associated with a software project. They serve as guideposts or goals that need to be meet. A test manger uses current testing effort data to determine how close the testing team is to achieving the milestone of interest. Milestones usually appear in the scheduling component of the test plan (see Chapter 7). Each level of testing will have its own specific milestones. Some examples of testing milestones are:

- completion of the master test plan;

- completion of branch coverage for all units (unit test);

- implementation and testing of test harnesses for needed integration of major subsystems;

- execution of all planned system tests;

- completion of the test summary report.

Each of these events will be scheduled for completion during a certain time period in the test plan. Usually a group of test team members is responsible for achieving the milestone on time and within budget. Note that the determination of whether a milestone has been reached depends on availability of measurement data. For example, to make the above milestones useful and meaningful testers would need to have measurements in place such as:

- degree of branch coverage accomplished so far;

- number of planned system tests currently available;

- number of executed system tests at this date.

Test planners need to be sure that milestones selected are meaningful for the project, and that completion conditions for milestone tasks are not too ambiguous. For example, a milestone that states "unit test is completed when all the units are ready for integration" is too vague to use for monitoring progress. How can a test manager evaluate the condition, "ready"? Because of this ambiguous completion condition, a test manager will have difficulty determining whether the milestone has been reached.

During the monitoring process measurements are collected that relates to the status of testing tasks (as described in the test plan), and milestones. Graphs using test process data are developed to show trends over a selected time period. The time period can be days, weeks, or months depending on the activity being monitored. The graphs can be in

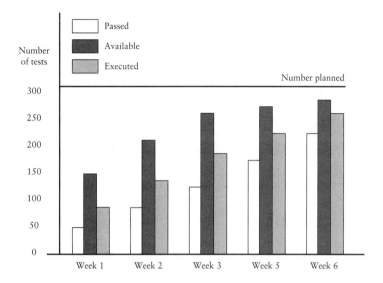

FIG. 9.1

Graph showing trends in test execution.

the form of a bar graph as shown in Figure 9.1 which illustrates trends for test execution over a 6-week period. They can also be presented in the form of x,y plots where the y-axis would be the number of tests and the x-axis would be the weeks elapsed from the start of the testing process for the project. These graphs, based on current measurements, are presented at the weekly status meetings and/or at milestone reviews that are used to discuss progress.

At the status meetings, project and test leaders present up-to-date measurements, graphs and plots showing the status of testing efforts. Testing milestones met/not met and problems that have occurred are discussed. Test logs, test incident reports, and other test-related documents may be examined as needed. Managers will have questions about the progress of the test effort. Mostly, they will want to know if testing is proceeding according to schedules and budgets, and if not, what are the barriers. Some of the typical questions a manager might ask at a status meeting are:

- Have all the test cases been developed that were planned for this date?

- What percent of the requirements/features have been tested so far?

- How far have we proceeded on achieving coverage goals: Are we ahead or behind what we scheduled?

- How many defects/KLOC have been detected at this time? How many repaired? How many are of high severity?

- What is the earned value so far? Is it close to what was planned (see Section 9.1.3)?

- How many available test cases have been executed? How many of these were passed?

- How much of the allocated testing budget has been spent so far? Is it more or less than we estimated?

- How productive is tester X? How many test cases has she developed? How many has she run? Was she over, or under, the planned amount?

The measurement data collected helps to answer these questions. In fact, links between measurements and question are described in the Goals/Questions/Metrics (GQM) paradigm reported by Basili [2]. In the case of testing, a major *goal* is to monitor and control testing efforts (a maturity goal at TMM level 3). An organizational team (developers/testers, SQA staff, project/test managers) constructs a set of likely *questions* that test/project managers are likely to ask in order to monitor and control the testing process. The sample set of questions previously described is a good starting point. Finally, the team needs to identify a set of *measurements* that can help to answer these questions. A sample set of measures is provided in the following sections. Any organizational team can use them as a starting point for selecting measures that help to answer test-related monitoring and controlling questions.

Four key items are recommended to test managers for monitoring and controlling the test efforts for a project. These are:

(i) testing status;
(ii) tester productivity;

(iii) testing costs;

(iv) errors, faults, and failures.

In the next sections we will examine the measurements required to track these items. Keep in mind that for most of these measurements the test planner should specify a planned value for the measure in the test plan. During test the actual value will be measured during a specific time period, and the two then compared.

9.1.1 Measurements for Monitoring Testing Status

Monitoring testing status means identifying the current state of the testing process. The manager needs to determine if the testing tasks are being completed on time and within budget. Given the current state of the testing effort some of the questions under consideration by a project or test manager would be the following:

- Which tasks are on time?

- Which have been completed earlier then scheduled, and by how much?

- Which are behind schedule, and by how much?

- Have the scheduled milestones for this date been meet?

- Which milestones are behind schedule, and by how much?

The following set of measures will help to answer these questions. The test status measures are partitioned into four categories as shown in Figure 9.2. A test plan must be in place that describes, for example, planned coverage goals, the number of planned test cases, the number of requirements to be tested, and so on, to allow the manager to compare actual measured values to those expected for a given time period.

1. Coverage Measures

As test efforts progress, the test manager will want to determine how much coverage has been actually achieved during execution of the

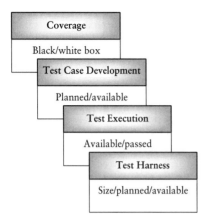

FIG. 9.2

Types of testing status measurements.

tests, and how does it compare to planned coverage. Depending on coverage goals for white box testing, a combination of the following are recommended.

> *Degree of statement, branch, data flow, basis path, etc., coverage (planned, actual)**

Tools can support the gathering of this data. Testers can also use ratios such as:

> *Actual degree of coverage/planned degree of coverage*

to monitor coverage to date.

For black box coverage the following measures can be useful:

> *Number of requirements or features to be tested**
> *Number of equivalence classes identified*
> *Number of equivalence classes actually covered*
> *Number or degree of requirements or features actually covered**

Testers can also set up ratios during testing such as:

> *Number of features actually covered/total number of features**

This will give indication of the work completed to this date and the work that still needs to be done.

2. Test Case Development

The following measures are useful to monitor the progress of test case development, and can be applied to all levels of testing. Note that some are explicit and some are derived. The number of estimated test cases described in the master test plan is:

Number of planned test cases

The number of test cases that are complete and are ready for execution is:

Number of available test cases

In many cases new test cases may have to be developed in addition to those that are planned. For example, when coverage goals are not meet by the current tests, additional tests will have to be designed. If mutation testing is used, then results of this type of testing may require additional tests to kill the mutants. Changes in requirements could add new test cases to those that were planned. The measure relevant here is:

Number of unplanned test cases

In place of, or in addition to, test cases, a measure of the number planned, available, and unplanned test procedures is often used by many organizations to monitor test status.

3. Test Execution

As testers carry out test executions, the test manager will want to determine if the execution process is going occurring to plan. This next group of measures is appropriate.

Number of available test cases executed*
Number of available tests cases executed and passed*
Number of unplanned test cases executed
Number of unplanned test cases executed and passed.

For a new release where there is going to be regression testing then these are useful:

Number of planned regression tests executed
Number of planned regression tests executed and passed

Testers can also set up ratios to help with monitoring test execution. For example:

Number of available test cases executed/number of available test cases
Number of available test cases executed/number of available test cases executed and passed

These would be derived measures.

4. Test Harness Development

It is important for the test manager to monitor the progress of the development of the test harness code needed for unit and integration test so that these progress in a timely manner according to the test schedule. Some useful measurements are:

Lines of Code (LOC) for the test harnesses (planned, available)*

Size is a measure that is usually applied by managers to help estimate the amount of effort needed to develop a software system. Size is measured in many different ways, for example, lines of code, function points, and feature points. Whatever the size measure an organization uses to measure its code, it can be also be applied to measure the size of the test harness, and to estimate the effort required to develop it. We use lines of code in the measurements listed above as it is the most common size metric and can be easily applied to estimating the size of a test harness. Ratios such as:

Available LOC for the test harness code/planned LOC for the test harnesses

are useful to monitor the test harness development effort over time.

9.1.2 Measurements to Monitor Tester Productivity

Managers have an interest in learning about the productivity of their staff, and how it changes as the project progresses. Measuring productivity in the software development domain is a difficult task since developers are involved in many activities, many of which are complex, and not all are readily measured. In the past the measure LOC/hour has been used to evaluate productivity for developers. But since most developers engage in a variety of activities, the use of this measure for productivity is often not credible. Productivity measures for testers have been sparsely reported. The following represent some useful and basic measures to collect for support in test planning and monitoring the activities of testers throughout the project. They can help a test manger learn how a tester distributes his time over various testing activities. For each developer/tester, where relevant, we measure both planned and actual:

Time spent in test planning
Time spent in test case design*
Time spent in test execution*
Time spent in test reporting
Number of test cases developed*
Number of test cases executed*

Productivity for a tester could be estimated by a combination of:

Number of test cases developed/unit time*
Number of tests executed/unit time*
Number of LOC test harness developed/unit time*
Number of defects detected in testing/unit time

The last item could be viewed as an indication of testing efficiency. This measure could be partitioned for defects found/hour in each of the testing phases to enable a manager to evaluate the efficiency of defect detection for each tester in each of these activities. For example:

Number of defects detected in unit test/hour
Number of defects detected in integration test/hour, etc.

The relative effectiveness of a tester in each of these testing activities could be determined by using ratios of these measurements. Marks suggests as a tester productivity measure [3]:

Number of test cases produced/week

All of the above could be monitored over the duration of the testing effort for each tester. Managers should use these values with caution because a good measure of testing productivity has yet to be identified. Two other comments about these measures are:

1. Testers perform a variety of tasks in addition to designing and running test cases and developing test harnesses. Other activities such as test planning, completing documents, working on quality and process issues also consume their time, and those must be taken into account when productivity is being considered.

2. Testers should be aware that measurements are being gathered based on their work, and they should know what the measurements will be used for. This is one of the cardinal issues in implementing a measurement program. All involved parties must understand the purpose of collecting the data and its ultimate use.

9.1.3 Measurements for Monitoring Testing Costs

Besides tracking project schedules, recall that managers also monitor costs to see if they are being held within budget. One good technique that project managers use for budget and resource monitoring is called earned value tracking. This technique can also be applied to monitor the use of resources in testing. Test planners must first estimate the total number of hours or budget dollar amount to be devoted to testing. Each testing task is then assigned a value based on its estimated percentage of the total time or budgeted dollars. This gives a relative value to each testing task, with respect to the entire testing effort. That value is credited only when the task is completed. For example, if the testing effort is estimated to require 200 hours, a 20-hour testing task is given a value of 20/200*100 or 10%. When that task is completed it contributes 10% to the cumulative earned value of the total testing effort. Partially completed tasks are not given any credit. Earned values are usual presented in a tabular format or as a graph. An example will be given in the next section of this chapter. The graphs and tables are useful to present at weekly test status meetings. Detailed discussions of earned value tracking can be found in Humphey

[4], Rakos [5], and Hurst [6]. To calculate planned earned values we need the following measurement data:

Total estimated time or budget for the overall testing effort
Estimated time or budget for each testing task

Earned values can be calculated separately for each level of testing. This would facilitate monitoring the budget/resource usage for each individual testing phase (unit, integration, etc.). We want to compare the above measures to:

Actual cost/time for each testing task*

We also want to calculate:

Earned value for testing tasks to date

and compare that to the planned earned value for a specific date. Section 9.2 shows an earned value tracking form and contains a discussion of how to apply earned values to test tracking.

Other measures useful for monitoring costs such as the number of planned/actual test procedures (test cases) are also useful for tracking costs if the planner has a good handle on the relationship between these numbers and costs (see Chapter 7).

Finally, the ratio of:

Estimated costs for testing/Actual costs for testing

can be applied to a series of releases or related projects to evaluate and promote more accurate test cost estimation and higher test cost effectiveness through test process improvement.

9.1.4 Measurements for Monitoring Errors, Faults, and Failures

Monitoring errors, faults, and failures is very useful for:

- evaluating product quality;

- evaluating testing effectiveness;

- making stop-test decisions;

- defect casual analysis;

- defect prevention;

- test process improvement;

- development process improvement.

Test logs, test incident reports, and problem reports provide test managers with some of the raw data for this type of tracking. Test managers usually want to track defects discovered as the testing process continues over time to address the second and third items above. The other items are useful to SQA staff, process engineers, and project managers. At higher levels of the TMM where defect data has been carefully stored and classified, mangers can use past defect records from similar projects or past releases to compare the current project defect discovery rate with those of the past. This is useful information for a stop-test decision (see Section 9.3). To strengthen the value of defect/failure information, defects should be classified by type, and severity levels should be established depending on the impact of the defect/failure on the user. If a failure makes a system inoperable it has a higher level of severity than one that is just annoying. A example of a severity level rating hierarchy is shown in Figure 9.3.

Some useful measures for defect tracking are:

Total number of incident reports (for a unit, subsystem, system)*
*Number of incident reports resolved/unresolved (for all levels of test)**
*Number of defects found of each given type**
Number of defects causing failures of severity level greater than X found (where X is an appropriate integer value)
*Number of defects/KLOC (This is called the defect volume. The division by KLOC normalizes the defect count)**
*Number of failures**
Number of failures over severity level Y (where Y is an appropriate integer value)
*Number of defects repaired**
Estimated number of defects (from historical data)

1. **Catastrophic:** a failure that could cause loss of life or property and/or loss of a system.
2. **Critical:** a failure that could cause major harm or major injury to life or property and/or cause major damage to a software system.
3. **Marginal:** a failure that could cause minor harm or minor injury to life, or cause a software system to perform poorly or reduce its availability.
4. **Minor or Annoying:** a failure that does not cause any significant harm or injury to life, property or a software system, but does require repair.

FIG. 9.3

A sample severity level hierarchy.

Other failure-related data that are useful for tracking product reliability will be discussed in later chapters.

9.1.5 Monitoring Test Effectiveness

To complete the discussion of test controlling and monitoring and the role of test measurements we need to address what is called test effectiveness. Test effectiveness measurements will allow managers to determine if test resources have been used wisely and productively to remove defects and evaluate product quality. Test effectiveness evaluations allow managers to learn which testing activities are or are not productive. For those areas that need improvement, responsible staff should be assigned to implement and monitor the changes. At higher levels of the TMM members of a process improvement group can play this role. The goal is to make process changes that result in improvements to the weak areas. There are several different views of test effectiveness. One of these views is based on use of the number of defects detected. For example, we can say that our testing process was effective if we have successfully revealed all defects that have a major impact on the users. We can make such an evaluation in several ways, both before and after release.

1. *Before release.* Compare the numbers of defects found in testing for this software product to the number expected from historical data. The ratio is:

Number of defects found during test/number of defects estimated

This will give some measure of how well we have done in testing the current software as compared to previous similar products. Did we find more or fewer errors given the test resources and time period? This is not the best measure of effectiveness since we can never be sure that the current release contains the same types and distribution of defects as the historical example.

2. *After release.* Continue to collect defect data after the software has been released in the field. In this case the users will prepare problem reports that can be monitored. Marks suggests we use measures such as "field fault density" as a measure of test effectiveness. This is equal to:

> *Number of defects found/thousand lines of new and changed code* [3].

This measure is applied to new releases of the software.

Another measure suggested is a ratio of:

> *Pre-ship fault density/Post-ship fault density* [3].

This ratio, sometimes called the "defect removal efficiency," gives an indication of how many defects remain in the software when it is released. As the testing process becomes more effective, the number of predelivery defects found should increase and postdelivery defects found should fall. The value of the postship fault density (number of faults/KLOC) is calculated from the problem reports returned to the development organization, so testers need to wait until after shipment to calculate this ratio. Testers must examine the problem reports in detail when using the data. There may be duplicate reports especially if the software is released to several customers. Some problem reports are due to misunderstandings; others may be requests for changes not covered in the requirements. All of these should be eliminated from the count.

Other measurements for test effectiveness have been proposed. For example, a measurement suggested by Graham is [7]:

> *Number of defects detected in a given test phase/total number of defects found in testing.*

For example, if unit test revealed 35 defects and the entire testing effort revealed 100 defects, then it could be said that unit testing was 35% effective. If this same software was sent out to the customer and 25 additional defects were detected, then the effectiveness of unit test would then be 25/125, or 20%. Testers can also use this measure to evaluate test effectiveness in terms of the severity of the failures caused by the defects. In the unit test example, perhaps it was only 20% effective in finding defects that caused severe failures.

The fault seeding technique as described in Section 9.3 could also be applied to evaluate test effectiveness. If you know the number of seeded faults injected and the number of seeded faults you have already found, you can use the ratio to estimate how effective you have been in using your test resources to date. Another useful measure, called the "detect removal leverage (DRL)" described in Chapter 10 as a review measurement, can be applied to measure the relative effectiveness of: reviews versus test phases, and test phases with respect to one another. The DRL sets up ratios of defects found. The ratio denominator is the base line for comparison. For example, one can compare:

$$\text{DRL (integration/unit test)} \quad = \quad \frac{\text{Number of defects found}}{\text{Number of defects found}}$$
$$\frac{\text{integration test}}{\text{in unit test}}$$

Section 10.7 gives more details on the application of this metric. The costs of each testing phase relative to its defect detecting ability can be expressed as:

$$\frac{\text{Number of defects detected in testing phase X}}{\text{Costs of testing in testing phase X}}$$

Instead of actual dollar amounts, tester hours, or any other indicator of test resource units could also be used in the denominator. These ratios could calculated for all test phases to compare their relative effectiveness. Comparisons could lead to test process changes and improvements.

An additional approach to measuring testing effectiveness is described by Chernak [8]. The main objectives of Chernak's research are (i) to show how to determine if a set of test cases (a test suite) is sufficiently effective in revealing defects, and (ii) to show how effectiveness measures can lead to process changes and improvements. The effectiveness metric called the TCE is defined as follows:

$$\text{TCE} = \frac{\text{Number of defects found by the test cases}}{\text{Total number of defects} \times 100}$$

The total number of defects in this equation is the sum of the defects found by the test cases, plus the defects found by what Chernak calls side effects. Side effect are based on so-called "test-escapes." These are software defects that a test suite does not detect but are found by chance in the testing cycle.

Test escapes occur because of deficiencies in the testing process. They are identified when testers find defects by executing some steps or conditions that are not described in a test case specification. This happens by accident or because the tester gets a new idea while performing the assigned testing tasks. Under these conditions a tester may find additional defects which are the test-escapes. These need to be recorded, and a casual analysis needs to be done to develop corrective actions.

The use of Chernak's metric depends on finding and recording these types of defects. Not all types of projects are candidates for this type of analysis. From his experience, Chernak suggests that client–server business applications may be appropriate projects. He also suggests that a baseline value be selected for the TCE and be assigned for each project. When the TCE value is at or above the baseline then the conclusion is that the test cases have been effective for this test cycle, and the testers can have some confidence that the product will satisfy the uses needs. All test case escapes, especially in the case of a TCE below the specified baseline, should be studied using Pareto analysis and Fishbone diagram techniques (described in Chapter 13), so that test design can be improved, and test process deficiencies be removed. Chernak illustrates his method with a case study (a client–server application) using the baseline TCE to evaluate test effectiveness and make test process improvements. When the TCE in the study was found to be below the baseline value (< 75 for this case), the organization analyzed all the test-escapes, classified them by cause, and built a Pareto diagram to describe the distribution of causes. Incomplete test design and incomplete functional specifications were found to be the main causes of test-escapes. The test group then addressed these process issues, adding both reviews to their process and sets of more "negative" test cases to improve the defect-detecting ability of their test suites.

The TMM level number determined for an organization is also a metric that can be used to monitor the testing process. It can be viewed as a high-level measure of test process effectiveness, proficiency, and overall maturity. A mature, testing process is one that is effective.

The TMM level number that results from a TMM assessment is a measurement that gives an organization information about the state of its testing process. A lower score on the TMM level number scale indicates a less mature, less proficient, less effective testing process state then a higher-level score. The usefulness of the TMM level number as a measurement of testing process strength, proficiency, and effectiveness is derived not only from its relative value on the TMM maturity scale, but also from the process profile that accompanies the level number showing strong and weak testing areas. In addition, the maturity goals hierarchy give structure and direction to improvement efforts so that the test process can become more effective. Chapters 11, 15, and 16 will provide the reader with more details.

9.2 Status Meetings, Reports, and Control Issues

Roughly forty measurements have been listed here that are useful for monitoring testing efforts. Organizations should decide which are of the most value in terms of their current TMM level, and the monitoring and controlling goals they want to achieve. The measurement selection process should begin with these goals, and compilation of a set of questions most likely to be asked by management relating to monitoring and controlling of the test process. The measurements that are selected should help to answer the questions (see brief discussion of the Goal/Question/Metric paradigm in Section 9.1). A sample set of questions is provided at the beginning of this chapter. Measurement-related data, and other useful test-related information such as test documents and problem reports, should be collected and organized by the testing staff. The test manager can then use these items for presentation and discussion at the periodic meetings used for project monitoring and controlling. These are called project status meetings.

Test-specific status meetings can also serve to monitor testing efforts, to report test progress, and to identify any test-related problems. Testers can meet separately and use test measurement data and related documents to specifically discuss test status. Following this meeting they can then participate in the overall project status meeting, or they can attend the project meetings as an integral part of the project team and present and discuss test-oriented status data at that time. Each organization should decide how to organize and partition the meetings. Some deciding factors may be the size of the test and development teams, the nature of the project, and the scope of the testing effort.

Another type of project-monitoring meeting is the milestone meeting that occurs when a milestone has been met. A milestone meeting is an important event; it is a mechanism for the project team to communicate with upper management and in some cases user/client groups. Major testing milestones should also precipitate such meetings to discuss accomplishments and problems that have occurred in meeting each test milestone, and to review activities for the next milestone phase. Testing staff, project managers, SQA staff, and upper managers should attend. In some cases process improvement group and client attendance is also useful.

Milestone meetings have a definite order of occurrence; they are held when each milestone is completed. How often the regular statues meetings are held depends on the type of project and the urgency to discuss issues. Rakos recommends a weekly schedule as best for small- to medium-sized projects [5]. Typical test milestone meeting attendees are shown in Figure 9.4. It is important that all test-related information be available at the meeting, for example, measurement data, test designs, test logs, test incident reports, and the test plan itself.

Status meetings usually result in some type of status report published by the project manager that is distributed to upper management. Test managers should produce similar reports to inform management of test progress. Rakos recommends that the reports be brief and contain the following items [5]:

- *Activities and accomplishments during the reporting period.* All tasks that were attended to should be listed, as well as which are complete. The latter can be credited with earned value amounts. Progress made since the last reporting period should also be described.

- *Problems encountered since the last meeting period.* The report should include a discussion of the types of new problems that have occurred, their probable causes, and how they impact on the project. Problem solutions should be described.

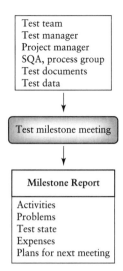

FIG. 9.4

Test milestone meetings, participants,
inputs, and outputs.

- *Problems solved.* At previous reporting periods problems were reported that have now been solved. Those should be listed, as well as the solutions and the impact on the project.

- *Outstanding problems.* These have been reported previously, but have not been solved to date. Report on any progress.

- *Current project (testing) state versus plan.* This is where graphs using process measurement data play an important role. Examples will be described below. These plots show the current state of the project (testing) and trends over time.

- *Expenses versus budget.* Plots and graphs are used to show budgeted versus actual expenses. Earned value charts and plots are especially useful here.

- *Plans for the next time period.* List all the activities planned for the next time period as well as the milestones.

Preparing and examining graphs and plots using the measurement data we have discussed helps managers to see trends over time as the test effort progresses. They can be prepared for presentation at meetings and included in the status report. An example bar graph for monitoring purposes is shown in Figure 9.1. The bar graph shows the numbers for tests that were planned, available, executed, and passed during the first 6 weeks of the testing effort. Note the trends. The number of tests executed and the number passed has gone up over the 6 weeks, The number passed is approaching the number executed. The graph indicates to the manager that the number of executed tests is approaching the number of tests available, and that the number of tests passed is also approaching the number available, but not quite as quickly. All are approaching the number planned. If one extrapolates, the numbers should eventually converge at some point in time. The bar graph, or a plot, allows the manager to identify the time frame in which this will occur. Managers can also compare the number of test cases executed each week with the amount that were planned for execution.

Figure 9.5 shows another graph based on defect data. The total number of faults found is plotted against weeks of testing effort. In this plot the number tapers off after several weeks of testing. The number of defects repaired is also plotted. It lags behind defect detection since the code must be returned to the developers who locate the defects and repair the code. In many cases this be a very time-consuming process. Managers can also include on a plot such as Figure 9.5 the expected rate of defect detection using data from similar past projects. However, even if the past data are typical there is no guarantee that the current software will behave in a similar way. Other ways of estimating the number of potential defects use rules of thumb (heuristics) such as "0.5–1% of the total lines of code" [8]. These are at best guesses, and give managers a way to estimate the number of defects remaining in the code, and as a consequence how long the testing effort needs to continue. However, this heuristic gives no indication of the severity level of the defects.

Hetzel gives additional examples of the types of plots that are useful for monitoring testing efforts [9]. These include plots of number of requirements tested versus weeks of effort and the number of statements not yet exercised over time. Other graphs especially useful for monitoring testing costs are those that plot staff hours versus time, both actual and planned. Earned value tables and graphs are also useful. Table 9.1 is an example [4].

Note that the earned value table shown in Table 9.1 has two parti-

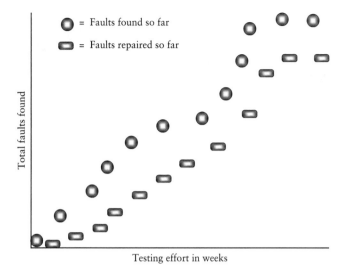

FIG. 9.5

Sample plot for monitoring fault detection durings test.

tions, one for planned values and one for actual values. Each testing task should be listed, as well as its estimated hours for completion. The total hours for all the tasks is determined and the estimated earned value for each task is then calculated based on its estimated percentage of the total time as described previously. This gives a relative value to each testing task with respect to the entire testing effort. The estimated earned values are accumulated in the next column. When the testing effort is in progress, the date and actual earned value for each task is listed, as well as the actual accumulated earned values. In status report graphs, earned value is usually plotted against time, and on the same graph budgeted expenses and actual expenses may also be plotted against time for comparison. Although actual expenses may be more than budget, if earned value is higher than expected, then progress may be considered satisfactory [4,5].

The agenda for a status meeting on testing includes a discussion of the work in progress since the last meeting period. Measurement data is presented, graphs are produced, and progress is evaluated. Test logs and incident reports may be examined to get a handle on the problems occurring. If there are problem areas that need attention, they are discussed

Testing task	Estimated hours	Planned			Date	Actual	
		Estimated earned value	Cummulative earned value			Actual earned value	Cummulative earned value

TABLE 9.1

Sample earned value table [4].

and solutions are suggested to get the testing effort back on track (control it). Problems currently occurring may be closely associated with risks identified by the test manager through the risk analysis done in test planning. Recall that part of the planner's job is identify and prioritize risks, and to develop contingency plans to handle the risk-prone events if they occur. If the test manager has done a careful job, these contingency plans may be applied to the problem at hand. Suggested and agreed-upon solutions should appear in the status report. The corrective actions should be put in place, their effect on testing monitored, and their success/failure discussed at the next status meeting.

As testing progresses, status meeting attendees have to make decisions about whether to stop testing or to continue on with the testing efforts, perhaps developing additional tests as part of the continuation process. They need to evaluate the status of the current testing efforts as compared to the expected state specified in the test plan. In order to make a decision about whether testing is complete the test team should refer to the stop-test criteria included in the test plan (see the next section for a discussion on stop-test criteria). If they decide that the stop-test criteria have been met, then the final status report for testing, the test summary report, should be prepared. This is a summary of the testing efforts, and becomes a part of the project's historical database. At project postmortems the test summary report can be used to discuss successes and failures that occurred during testing. It is a good source for test lessons learned for each project. The test summary report is described in more detail in Chapter 7.

9.3 Criteria for Test Completion

In the test plan the test manager describes the items to be tested, test cases, tools needed, scheduled activities, and assigned responsibilities. As the testing effort progresses many factors impact on planned testing schedules and tasks in both positive and negative ways. For example, although a certain number of test cases were specified, additional tests may be required. This may be due to changes in requirements, failure to achieve coverage goals, and unexpected high numbers of defects in critical modules. Other unplanned events that impact on test schedules are, for example, laboratories that were supposed to be available are not (perhaps because of equipment failures) or testers who were assigned responsibilities are absent (perhaps because of illness or assignments to other higher-priority projects). Given these events and uncertainties, test progress does not often follow plan. Tester managers and staff should do their best to take actions to get the testing effort on track. In any event, whether progress is smooth or bumpy, at some point every project and test manager has to make the decision on when to stop testing.

Since it is not possible to determine with certainty that all defects have been identified, the decision to stop testing always carries risks. If we stop testing now, we do save resources and are able to deliver the software to our clients. However, there may be remaining defects that will cause catastrophic failures, so if we stop now we will not find them. As a consequence, clients may be unhappy with our software and may not want to do business with us in the future. Even worse there is the risk that they may take legal action against us for damages. On the other hand, if we continue to test, perhaps there are no defects that cause failures of a high severity level. Therefore, we are wasting resources and risking our position in the market place. Part of the task of monitoring and controlling the testing effort is making this decision about when testing is complete under conditions of uncertainly and risk. Managers should not have to use guesswork to make this critical decision. The test plan should have a set of quantifiable stop-test criteria to support decision making.

The weakest stop test decision criterion is to stop testing when the project runs out of time and resources. TMM level 1 organizations often operate this way and risk client dissatisfaction for many projects. TMM level 2 organizations plan for testing and include stop-test criteria in the test plan. They have very basic measurements in place to support management when they need to make this decision. Shown in Figure 9.6 and described below are five stop-test criteria that are based on a more quantitative approach. No one criteria is recommended. In fact, managers should use a combination of criteria and cross-checking for better results.

The stop-test criteria are as follows.

1. All the Planned Tests That Were Developed Have Been Executed and Passed.

This may be the weakest criterion. It does not take into account the actual dynamics of the testing effort, for example, the types of defects found and their level of severity. Clues from analysis of the test cases and defects found may indicate that there are more defects in the code that the planned test cases have not uncovered. These may be ignored by the testers if this stop-test criteria is used in isolation.

2. All Specified Coverage Goals Have Been Met.

An organization can stop testing when it meets its coverage goals as specified in the test plan. For example, using white box coverage goals we can say that we have completed unit test when we have reached 100% branch coverage for all units. Using another coverage category, we can say we have completed system testing when all the requirements have been covered by our tests. The graphs prepared for the weekly status meetings can be applied here to show progress and to extrapolate to a completion date. The graphs will show the growth of degree of coverage over the time.

3. The Detection of a Specific Number of Defects Has Been Accomplished.

This approach requires defect data from past releases or similar projects. The defect distribution and total defects is known for these projects, and is applied to make estimates of the number and types of defects for the current project. Using this type of data is very risky, since it assumes the current software will be built, tested, and behave like the past projects. This is not always true. Many projects and their development environments are not as similar as believed, and making this assumption could

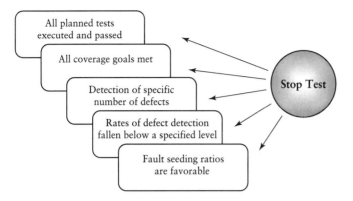

FIG. 9.6

Some possible stop-test criteria.

be disastrous. Therefore, using this stop-criterion on its own carries high risks.

4. The Rates of Defect Detection for a Certain Time Period Have Fallen Below a Specified Level.

The manager can use graphs that plot the number of defects detected per unit time. A graph such as Figure 9.5, augmented with the severity level of the defects found, is useful. When the rate of detection of defects of a severity rating under some specified threshold value falls below that rate threshold, testing can be stopped. For example, a stop-test criterion could be stated as: "We stop testing when we find 5 defects or less, with impact equal to, or below severity level 3, per week." Selecting a defect detection rate threshold can be based on data from past projects.

5. Fault Seeding Ratios Are Favorable.

Fault (defect) seeding is an interesting technique first proposed by Mills [10]. The technique is based on intentionally inserting a known set of defects into a program. This provides support for a stop-test decision. It is assumed that the inserted set of defects are typical defects; that is, they are of the same type, occur at the same frequency, and have the same impact as the actual defects in the code. One way of selecting such a set of defects is to use historical defect data from past releases or similar projects.

The technique works as follow. Several members of the test team insert (or seed) the code under test with a known set of defects. The other members of the team test the code to try to reveal as many of the defects as possible. The number of undetected seeded defects gives an indication of the number of total defects remaining in the code (seeded plus actual). A ratio can be set up as follows:

$$\frac{\text{Detected seeded defects}}{\text{Total seeded defects}} = \frac{\text{Detected actual defects}}{\text{Total actual defects}}$$

Using this ratio we can say, for example, if the code was seeded with 100 defects and 50 have been found by the test team, it is likely that 50% of the actual defects still remain and the testing effort should continue. When all the seeded defects are found the manager has some confidence that the test efforts have been completed.

There are other stop-test criteria that can be used by organizations at the higher levels of the TMM, for example, those based on reliability and confidence levels. Those will be discussed in Chapter 12.

9.4 Software Configuration Management

Software systems are constantly undergoing change during development and maintenance. By software systems we include all software artifacts such as requirements and design documents, test plans, user manuals, code, and test cases. Different versions, variations, builds, and releases exist for these artifacts. Organizations need staff, tools, and techniques to help them track and manage these artifacts and changes to the artifacts that occur during development and maintenance. The Capability Maturity Model includes configuration management as a Key Process Area at level 2. This is an indication of its fundamental role in support of repeatable, controlled, and managed processes. To control and monitor the testing process, testers and test mangers also need access to configuration management tools and staff.

There are four major activities associated with configuration management. These are:

1. Identification of the Configuration Items

The items that will be under configuration control must be selected, and the relationships between them must be formalized. An example relationship is "part-of" which is relevant to composite items. Relationships are often expressed in a module interconnection language (MIL). Figure 9.7 shows four configuration items, a design specification, a test specification, an object code module, and source code module as they could exist in a configuration management system (CMS) repository (see item 2 below for a brief description of a CMS). The arrows indicate links or relationships between them. Note in this example that the configuration management system is aware that these four items are related only to one another and not to other versions of these items in the repository.

In addition to identification of configuration items, procedures for establishment of baseline versions for each item must be in place.

> Baselines are formally reviewed and agreed upon versions of software artifacts, from which all changes are measured. They serve as the basis for further development and can be changed only through formal change procedures.

> Baselines plus approved changes from those baselines constitute the correct configuration identification for the item. [11].

2. Change Control

There are two aspects of change control—one is tool-based, the other team-based. The team involved is called a configuration control board. This group oversees changes in the software system. The members of the board should be selected from SQA staff, test specialists, developers, and analysts. It is this team that oversees, gives approval for, and follows up on changes. They develop change procedures and the formats for change request forms. To make a change, a change request form must be prepared by the requester and submitted to the board. It then reviews and approves/disapproves. Only approved changes can take place. The board also participates in configuration reporting and audits as described further on in this section.

In addition to the configuration control board, control of configuration items requires a configuration management system (CMS) that will

Configuration Management Tool Repository

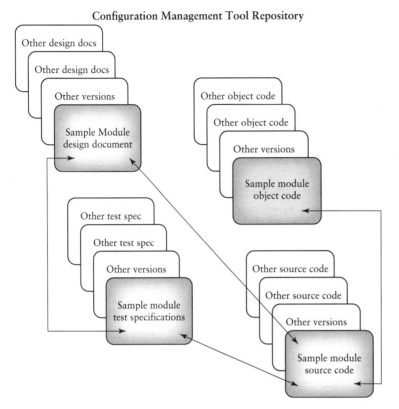

FIG. 9.7

Sample configuration items.

store the configuration items in a repository (or project database) and maintain control and access to those items. The CMS will manage the versions and variations of the items. It will keep track of the items and their relationships with one another. For example, developers and testers need to know which set of test cases is associated with which design item, and which version of object code is associated with which version of source code? The CMS will provide the information needed to answer these questions by supporting relationships as shown in Figure 9.7. It also supports baseline versions for each configuration item, and it only allows designated engineers to make changes to a configuration item after formal approval by the change control board. The software engineer must checkout the item undergoing change from the CMS. A copy of it is made in her work station. When the changes are complete, and they are reviewed, the new version is "checked in" to the CMS, and the version control mechanism in the CMS creates the newest version in its repository. Relationships to existing configuration items are updated. The CMS controls change-making by ensuring that an engineer has the proper access rights to the configuration item. It also synchronizes the change-making process so that parallel changes made by different software engineers do not overwrite each other. The CMS also allows software engineers to create builds of the system consisting of different versions and variations of object and source code.

3. Configuration status reporting

These reports help to monitor changes made to configuration items. They contain a history of all the changes and change information for each configuration item. Each time an approved change is made to a configuration item, a configuration status report entry is made. These reports are kept in the CMS database and can be accessed by project personnel so that all can be aware of changes that are made. The reports can answer questions such as:

- who made the change;

- what was the reason for the change;

- what is the date of the change;

- what is affected by the change.

Reports for configuration items can be disturbed to project members and discussed at status meetings.

4. Configuration audits

After changes are made to a configuration item, how do software engineers follow up to ensure the changes have been done properly? One way to do this through a technical review, another through a configuration audit. The audit is usually conducted by the SQA group or members of the configuration control board. They focuses on issues that are not covered in a technical review. A checklist of items to cover can serve as the agenda for the audit. For each configuration item the audit should cover the following:

(i) *Compliance with software engineering standards.* For example, for the source code modules, have the standards for indentation, white space, and comments been followed?

(ii) *The configuration change procedure.* Has it been followed correctly?

(iii) *Related configuration items.* Have they been updated?

(iv) *Reviews.* Has the configuration item been reviewed?

Why is configuration management of interest to testers? Configuration management will ensure that test plans and other test-related documents are being prepared, updated, and maintained properly. To support these objectives, Ayer has suggested a test documentation checklist to be used for configuration audits to verify the accuracy and completeness of test documentation [12]. Configuration management also allows the tester to determine if the proper tests are associated with the proper source code, requirements, and design document versions, and that the correct version of the item is being tested. It also tells testers who is responsible for a given item, if any changes have been made to it, and if it has been reviewed before it is scheduled for test.

Configuration management is a complex set of activities. To support configuration management, organizational policy should require each project to have an associated configuration management plan that describes the staff, tools, policies, and resources required. Organizations can get started using the information found in IEEE standards documents [13,14]. Readers who want additional information can consult papers by Tichy and the text by Ayer [12,15]

9.5 Controlling and Monitoring: Three Critical Views

Controlling and monitoring of the testing process is a maturity goal at TMM level 3. Establishing a test organization and a test training program are also maturity goals at this level. The goals are mutually supportive. Controlling and monitoring is best carried out by a group of test specialists who have the focus, training, and expertise to do the job. They are the staff persons responsible for test planning, test design, test execution, and test reporting and are therefore in the best position to control and monitor testing (review Chapter 8). When describing the three critical views with respect to the controlling and monitoring maturity goal we can now assume that test specialists and test managers will carry out this role, since a test organization is now established and training is available. Developers may not be heavily involved.

From the *manager's view,* support for the controlling and monitoring of testing includes the following commitments.

- Testing policy statements are updated with the participation and approval of management. The updated policy statements dictate a role for controlling and monitoring of testing efforts. Mechanisms to accomplish controlling and monitoring of test are outlined in the test policy statement and described in detail in SQA and standards documents. Management ensures that controlling and monitoring activities are part of each test plan.

- Adequate funding, training, and resources are given to support controlling and monitoring activities including measurement collection.

- Managers assign responsibilities for controlling and monitoring.

- Managers participate in status and audit meetings, contribute to problem-solving sessions, and support follow-up for corrective actions.

Since there is now a test group we will consider the *test manager's view* for controlling and monitoring as well. We add the following activities, tasks, and responsibilities.

- Working with upper management/project management to develop controlling and monitoring policies for testing.

- Working with SQA to develop standards for test-related artifacts and standards for quality-related procedures.

- Developing test plans with appropriate resources set aside for controlling and monitoring.

- Selecting appropriate measurements to guide controlling and monitoring of test.

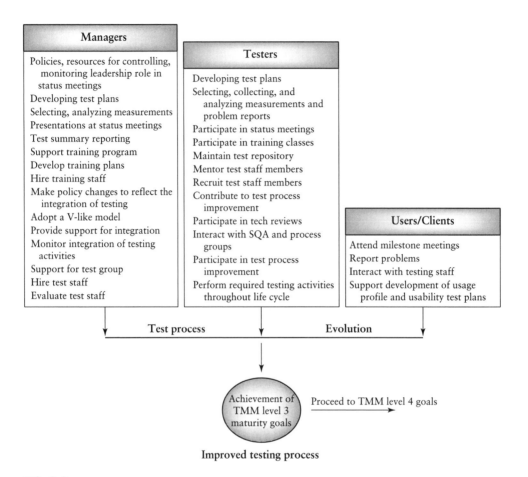

FIG. 9.8
*Contributions of three critical groups
to TMM level 3 maturity goals.*

- Ensuring all appropriate test documents are prepared such as test logs and test incident reports.

- Collecting, analyzing, and presenting test-related measurements and data to interested management and staff.

- Setting up periodic test status meetings, leading discussions, and presenting all relevant material at test status meetings.

- Initiating and following-up corrective actions when problems occur during testing.

- Preparing and presenting the test summary report.

- Assigning responsibilities to testers for corrective actions that address test-related problems.

- Following up and reporting on corrective actions taken.

- Supporting the installation of a CMS and playing a role on the configuration control board.

The *tester's* role in controlling and monitoring is as follows:

- Collecting and analyzing test measurements.

- Participation in test status meetings.

- Training in tools and methods for test process monitoring and controlling, including configuration management.

- Serving as members of the change control board.

- Completing follow-up activities for corrective actions.

- Preparing test-related documents such as test logs and test incident reports.

- Contributing to test summary report.

The *users/client* role in controlling and monitoring of test is limited. These are examples of user/client impact in this area of testing.

- Attendance at special test milestone meetings. If the software is being developed for a specific client, the development organization may invite a user/client group to attend a test milestone meeting to show progress.

- Stop-test criteria for acceptance test. In the case of software custom-built for a specific client, the client should be asked to give input on stop-test criteria that indicate the completeness of acceptance test.

- Test effectiveness. If an organization is measuring test-effectiveness using postrelease problem reports, the users/client will play an important role in reporting problems and insuring they are returned to the proper personnel in the development organization.

As a final note, this chapter and Chapter 8 provide background material to support individuals and organizations working toward achieving the maturity goals described in level 3 of the TMM. For review, a summary of the contributions of the three critical groups to TMM level 3 maturity goals is shown in Figure 9.8.

KEY TERMS

Baseline
Milestone
Project controlling
Project monitoring

EXERCISES

1. Suppose you are a test manager. What are the milestones you would select for a unit test plan, an integration test plan, and a system test plan?

2. What measurements would you suggest for monitoring test status during system test for a large application with no mission- or safety-critical features?

3. For the system in Problem 2, suggest appropriate measurements for monitoring tester productivity.

4. For the system in Problem 2, suggest appropriate measurements for monitoring testing costs.

5. For the system in Problem 2, suggest appropriate measurements for monitoring defects/faults and failures.

6. Some of your customers have suggested that the number of defects found in the software that was delivered to them is unacceptable in future releases. You are concerned that your test effectiveness is poor. What measurements could you

use to evaluate your current test effectiveness and any changes in effectiveness due to improvements in your process? How could you evaluate the relative effectiveness of each of your testing phases?

7. For a given small-sized software system the test group found 7 defects in design review, 24 defects in unit test, and 13 in integration test. What is the defect removal leverage of reviews and integration test with respect to unit test?

8. Figure 9.1 shows a plot that illustrates trends in test execution using number of tests versus weeks of testing. What other test-related measures could you plot to show testing trends for a test status meeting?

9. Suppose a test group was testing a mission-critical software system. The group has found 85 out of the 100 seeded defects. If you were the test manager, would you stop testing at this point? Explain your decision. If in addition you found 70 actual nonseeded defects, what would be your decision and why?

10. What should be included in a milestone report for testing? Who should prepare the report, and who should be included on the distribution list?

11. Which groups do you think should contribute to membership of a configuration control board and why?

12. A test plan has as a goal 100% branch coverage for all units. The test effort is running behind schedule and current status of coverage for all units is 87%. The manager is under pressure and is thinking of stopping unit test at this point. The project is a straightforward business application. The development group has implemented similar applications in the past. Advise the manager about this decision. What types of data will be useful to support a decision?

13. Your team is developing a patient record system for a medical group that will contain vital patient information as well as billing data for the medical practice. This is the first time your company is developing software for this domain. The test manger is developing the test plan and is deciding on appropriate stop test criteria for this project. Which of the stop test criteria described in this chapter do you believe is appropriate for this project? Give reasons for your choice(s).

14. What is the role of the tester in supporting the monitoring and controlling of testing?

REFERENCES

[1] R. Thayer, ed. *Software Engineering Project Management,* second edition, IEEE Computer Society Press, Los Alamitos, CA, 1997.

[2] V. Basili, D. Weiss, "A methodology for collecting valid software engineering data," *IEEE Transactions on Software Engineering,* Vol. SE-10, No. 6, 1984, pp. 728–738.

[3] D. Marks, *Testing Very Big Systems,* McGraw-Hill, New York, 1992.

[4] W. Humphrey, *A Discipline for Software Engineering,* Addison-Wesley, Reading, MA, 1995.

[5] J. Rakos, *Software Project Management for Small-to Medium-Sized Projects,* Prentice Hall, Englewood Cliffs, NJ, 1990.

[6] P Hurst, "Software project management: threads of control," in *Software Engineering Project Management,* second edition, R. Thayer, ed., IEEE Computer Society Press, Los Alamitos, CA, 1997, pp. 410–422.

[7] D. Graham, "Measuring the effectiveness and efficiency of testing," *Proc. Software Testing,* Paris, France, June 1996.

[8] Y. Chernak, "Validating and improving test-case effectiveness," *IEEE Software,* Vol. 16, No. 1, 2001, pp. 81–86.

[9] B. Hetzel, *The Complete Guide to Software Testing,* second edition, QED Information Sciences, Inc., Wellesley, MA. 1988.

[10] H. Mills, *On the Statistical Validation of Computer Programs,* Technical Report FSC-72-6015, IBM Federal Systems Division, Gaithersburg, MD, 1972.

[11] *IEEE Standard Glossary of Software Engineering Terminology* (IEEE Std 610.12-1990), copyright 1990 by IEEE, all rights reserved.

[12] S. Ayer, F. Patrinostro, *Software Configuration Management,* McGraw-Hill, Inc., New York, 1992.

[13] *IEEE Guide to Software Configuration Management* (ANSI/IEEE Std 1042-1987), copyright 1988 by IEEE, all rights reserved.

[14] *IEEE Standard for Software Configuration Management Plans* (IEEE Std. 828-1990), copyright 1990 by IEEE, all rights reserved.

[15] W. Tichy, "Design, implementation, and evaluation of a revision control system," *Proc. Sixth International Conf. Software Engineering,* 1982, pp. 58–67.

REVIEWS AS A
TESTING ACTIVITY

10.0 Expanding the Testing Activity Umbrella

In Chapter 1 several software engineering terms related to testing were presented. The terms *validation* and *verification* were defined and two definitions for testing were given. The latter are repeated here as a means for initiating a discussion of two major types of testing for software. Other descriptions of the term "testing" are found in IEEE software engineering standards documents and guides [1]. The term "software" here is used in the broadest sense to mean source code and all of its associated artifacts, for example, requirements and design documents, test plans, and user manuals.

> Testing is generally described as a group of procedures carried out to evaluate some aspect of a piece of software.

> Testing can be described as a process used for revealing defects in software and for establishing that the software has attained a specified degree of quality with respect to selected attributes.

The definitions for testing outline analysis objectives that relate to evaluation, (revealing) defects, and quality. We can use two approaches to achieve these objectives:

(i)   static analysis methods where the software artifact is examined manually, or with a set of tools, but not executed;

(ii) dynamic analysis methods where the software artifact is executed using a set of input values, and its output behavior is then examined and compared to what is expected.

Dynamic execution can only be applied to the software code. We use dynamic execution as a tool to detect defects and to evaluate quality attributes of the code. This testing option is not applicable for the majority of the other software artifacts. Among the questions that arise are: How can we evaluate or analyze a requirements document, a design document, a test plan, or a user manual? How can we effectively preexamine the source code before execution? One powerful tool that we can use is a manual static testing technique that is generally known as the technical review. Most software deliverables can be tested using review techniques as shown in Figure 10.1.

The technical review involves a group of people who meet to evaluate a software-related item. A general definition for a review is given in Chapter 2 and repeated below.

> **A review is a group meeting whose purpose is to evaluate a software artifact or a set of software artifacts.**

The general goals for the reviewers are to:

*   identify problem components or components in the software artifact that need improvement;

*   identify components of the software artifact that do not need improvement;

*   identify specific errors or defects in the software artifact (defect detection);

*   ensure that the artifact conforms to organizational standards.

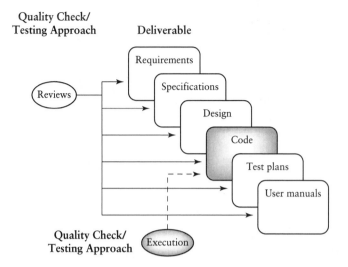

Quality Check/
Testing Approach   Deliverable

Reviews

Requirements

Specifications

Design

Code

Test plans

User manuals

Quality Check/
Testing Approach   Execution

FIG. 10.1

*Role of reviews in testing software
deliverables.*

Other review goals are informational, communicational, and educational, whereby review participants learn about the contents of the developing software artifacts to help them understand the role of their own work and to plan for future stages of development. Reviews often represent project milestones and support the establishment of a baseline for a software artifact. Thus, they also have a role in project management, project monitoring, and control. Review data can also have an influence on test planning. The types and quantity of defects found during review can help test planners select effective classes of tests, and may also have an influence testing goals. In some cases clients/users attend the review meetings and give feedback to the development team, so reviews are also a means for client communication. To summarize, the many benefits of a review program are:

- higher-quality software;

- increased productivity (shorter rework time);

- closer adherence to project schedules (improved process control);

- increased awareness of quality issues;

- teaching tool for junior staff;

- opportunity to identify reusable software artifacts;

- reduced maintenance costs;

- higher customer satisfaction;

- more effective test planning;

- a more professional attitude on the part of the development staff.

Not all test educators, practitioners, and researchers consider technical reviews to be a testing activity. Some prefer to consider them in a special category called verification testing; others believe they should be associated with software quality assurance activities. The author, as well as many others, for example, Hetzel [2], hold the position that testing activities should cover both validation and verification, and include both static and dynamic analyses. The TMM structure supports this view. If one adheres to this broader view of testing, then the author argues the following:

(i) Reviews as a verification and static analysis technique should be considered a testing activity.

(ii) Testers should be involved in review activities.

Also, if you consider the following:

(i) a software system is more than the code; it is a set of related artifacts;

(ii) these artifacts may contain defects or problem areas that should be reworked, or removed; and

(iii) quality-related attributes of these artifacts should be evaluated;

then the technical review is one of the most important tools we can use to accomplish these goals. In addition, reviews are the means for testing these artifacts early in the software life cycle. It gives us an early focus on quality issues, helps us to build quality into the system from the beginning, and, allows us to detect and eliminate errors/defects *early* in the software life cycle as close as possible to their point of origin. If we detect defects early in the life cycle, then:

- they are easier to detect;

- they are less costly to repair;

- overall rework time is reduced;

- productivity is improved;

- they have less impact on the customer.

Use of the review as a tool for increasing software quality and developer productivity began in the 1970s. Fagen [3] and Myers [4] wrote pioneering papers that described the review process and its benefits. This chapter will discuss two types of technical reviews, inspections, and walk-throughs. It will show you how they are run, who should attend, what the typical activities and outputs are, and what are the benefits. Having a review program requires a commitment of organizational time and resources. It is the author's goal to convince you of the benefits of reviews, their important role in the testing process, their cost effectiveness as a quality tool, and why you as a tester should be involved in the review process.

10.1 Types of Reviews

Reviews can be formal or informal. They can be technical or managerial. Managerial reviews usually focus on project management and project status. The role of project status meetings is discussed in Chapter 9. In this chapter we will focus on technical reviews. These are used to:

- verify that a software artifact meets its specification;

- to detect defects; and

- check for compliance to standards.

Readers may not realize that informal technical reviews take place very frequently. For example, each time one software engineer asks another to evaluate a piece of work whether in the office, at lunch, or over a beer, a review takes place. By review it is meant that one or more peers have inspected/evaluated a software artifact. The colleague requesting the review receives feedback about one or more attributes of the reviewed software artifact. Informal reviews are an important way for colleagues to communicate and get peer input with respect to their work. There are two major types of technical reviews—inspections and walkthroughs—which are more formal in nature and occur in a meeting-like setting. Formal reviews require written reports that summarize findings, and in the case of one type of review called an inspection, a statement of responsibility for the results by the reviewers is also required. The two most widely used types of reviews will be described in the next several paragraphs.

10.1.1 Inspections as a Type of Technical Review

Inspections are a type of review that is formal in nature and requires prereview preparation on the part of the review team. Several steps are involved in the inspection process as outlined in Figure 10.2. The responsibility for initiating and carrying through the steps belongs to the inspection leader (or moderator) who is usually a member of the technical staff or the software quality assurance team. Myers suggests that the inspection leader be a member of a group from an unrelated project to preserve objectivity [4].

The inspection leader plans for the inspection, sets the date, invites the participants, distributes the required documents, runs the inspection meeting, appoints a recorder to record results, and monitors the follow-up period after the review. The key item that the inspection leader prepares is the checklist of items that serves as the agenda for the review. The checklist varies with the software artifact being inspected (examples are provided later in this chapter). It contains items that inspection participants should focus their attention on, check, and evaluate. The inspection participants address each item on the checklist. The recorder records any discrepancies, misunderstandings, errors, and ambiguities; in general, any problems associated with an item. The completed checklist is part of the review summary document.

The inspection process begins when inspection preconditions are met as specified in the inspection policies, procedures, and plans. The inspec-

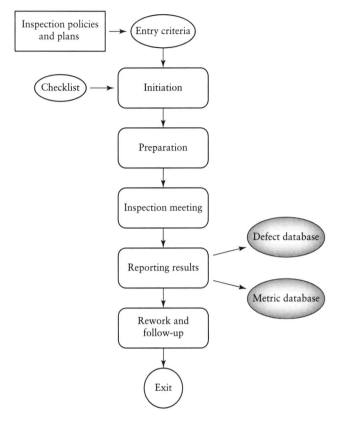

FIG. 10.2

Steps in the inspection process.

tion leader announces the inspection meeting and distributes the items to be inspected, the checklist, and any other auxiliary material to the participants usually a day or two before the scheduled meeting. Participants must do their homework and study the items and the checklist. A personal preinspection should be performed carefully by each team member [3,5]. Errors, problems, and items for discussion should be noted by each individual for each item on the list. When the actual meeting takes place the document under review is presented by a reader, and is discussed as it read. Attention is paid to issues related to quality, adherence to standards, testability, traceability, and satisfaction of the users/clients requirements. All the items on the checklist are addressed by the group as a whole, and the problems are recorded. Inspection metrics are also recorded (see Section 10.7). The recorder documents all the findings and the measurements.

When the inspection meeting has been completed (all agenda items covered) the inspectors are usually asked to sign a written document that is sometimes called a summary report that will be described in Section 10.4.6. The inspection process requires a formal follow-up process. Rework sessions should be scheduled as needed and monitored to ensure that all problems identified at the inspection meeting have been addressed and resolved. This is the responsibility of the inspection leader. Only when all problems have been resolved and the item is either reinspected by the group or the moderator (this is specified in the summary report) is the inspection process completed.

10.1.2 Walkthroughs as a Type of Technical Review

Walkthroughs are a type of technical review where the producer of the reviewed material serves as the review leader and actually guides the progression of the review [6]. Walkthroughs have traditionally been applied to design and code. In the case of detailed design or code walkthroughs, test inputs may be selected and review participants then literally walk through the design or code with the set of inputs in a line-by-line manner. The reader can compare this process to a manual execution of the code. The whole group "plays computer" to step through an execution lead by a reader or presenter. This is a good opportunity to "pretest" the design or code. If the presenter gives a skilled presentation of the material, the walkthrough participants are able to build a comprehensive mental (internal) model of the detailed design or code and are able to both evaluate its quality and detect defects. Walkthroughs may be used for material other than code, for example, data descriptions, reference manuals, or even specifications [6].

Some researchers and practitioners believe walkthroughs are efficient because the preparer leads the meeting and is very familiar with the item under review. Because of these conditions a larger amount of material can be processed by the group. However, many of the steps that are mandatory for an inspection are not mandatory for a walkthrough. Comparing inspections and walkthroughs one can eliminate the checklist and the preparation step (this may prove to be a disadvantage to the review team) for the walkthrough. In addition, for the walkthrough there usually no mandatory requirement for a formal review report and a defect list. There is also no formal requirement for a follow-up step. In some cases the walkthrough is used as a preinspection tool to familiarize the team with the code or any other item to be reviewed.

There are other types of technical reviews, for example, the round-robin review where there is a cycling through the review team members so that everyone gets to participate in an equal manner. For example, in some forms of the round-robin review everyone would have the opportunity to play the role of leader. In another instance, every reviewer in a code walkthrough would lead the group in inspecting a specific line or a section of the code [6]. In this way inexperienced or more reluctant reviewers have a chance to learn more about the review process. In subsequent sections of this chapter the general term review will be used in the main to represent the inspection process, which is the review type most formal in nature. Where specific details are relevant for other types of reviews, such as round-robin or walkthroughs, these will be mentioned in the discussion.

10.2 Developing a Review Program

Reviews are an effective tool used along with execution-based testing to support defect detection, increased software quality, and customer satisfaction. Reviews should be used for evaluating newly developing products as well as new releases or versions of existing software. If reviews are conducted on the software artifacts as they are developed throughout the software life cycle, they serve as filters for each artifact. A multiple set of filters allows an organization to separate out and eliminate defects, inconsistencies, ambiguities, and low-quality components early in the software life cycle. If we compare the process of defect detection during reviews and execution-based testing/debugging we can see that the review process may be more efficient for detecting, locating, and repairing these defects, especially in the code, for the following reasons:

1. When testing software, unexpected behavior is observed because of a defect(s) in the code. The symptomatic information is what the de-

veloper works with to find and repair (fix) the defect. In most cases, in order to locate the defect, the developer must build a mental (internal) model of the code to determine what it does and how it works. The developer looks for discrepancies in the code that render it different from what is expected. A casual relationship must be established between a found discrepancy in the code, and the unexpected behavior in order to make a repair. These complex cognitive processes take place in a separate context from testing (observation of the failure). This is true even if the developer and tester are the same person. In addition, model building during testing is often done in haste and under deadline pressures. The many details involved are not recorded properly, making the likelihood of incorrect or incomplete fixes higher than during a review.

In contrast reviews are a more orderly process. They concentrate on stepping through the reviewed item focusing on specific areas. During a review there is a systematic process in place for building a real-time mental model of the software item. The reviewers step through this model-building process as a group. If something unexpected appears it can be processed in the context of the real-time mental model. There is a direct link to the incorrect, missing, superfluous item and a line/page/figure that is of current interest in the inspection. Reviewers know exactly where they are focused in the document or code and where the problem has surfaced. *They can basically carry out defect detection and defect localization tasks at the same time.* Compare the review process to execution-based testing and debugging (fault localization), which are two separate processes. Testing reveals the defect, but its location is usually unknown. Because of the circumstances that occur during a review it is much easier fix problems/defects properly in the rework/ follow-up period. The defect location task, which is sometimes the most difficult and time-consuming task associated with debugging, has already been done. In addition, the fixes are more likely to be correct after a review session that a testing session because of the better quality of the mental models developed, and also because there is less pressure for a quick fix (the ship date for the software is further in the future during review time).

2. Reviews also have the advantage of a two-pass approach for defect detection. Pass 1 has individuals first reading the reviewed item and pass 2 has the item read by the group as a whole. If one individual reviewer

did not identify a defect or a problem, others in the group are likely to find it. The group evaluation also makes false identification of defects/problems less likely. Individual testers/ developers usually work alone, and only after spending many fruitless hours trying to locate a defect will they ask a colleague for help.

3. Inspectors have the advantage of the checklist which calls their attention to specific areas that are defect prone. These are important clues. Testers/developers may not have such information available.

10.3 The Need for Review Policies

TMM level 4 calls for establishment of a formal organizational review program, although it is recommended that at lower TMM levels reviews of selected items such as the code take place. The formal review program may begin initially with plans to train a limited number of review leaders and formally review one or two key project deliverables. The program can gradually increase in scope to cover all major life cycle deliverables. The incremental introduction of reviews allows for cultural adaptation and for a gradual realization of the benefits of the review program [7]. The implementation of a review program represents a large investment of organizational resources and changes in organizational polices and culture. However, in the long run an organization will realize the many benefits of such a program. This section of the chapter addresses some of the issues that arise when developing a review program.

Since reviews require many changes in organization processes and culture, a set of review-related policies must be developed and supported by management. At TMM level 4 there is an infrastructure in place to support the review program and its policies. For example, the following are present:

(i) testing policies with an emphasis on defect detection and quality, and measurements for controlling and monitoring;

(ii) a test organization with staff devoted to defect detection and quality issues;

(iii) policies and standards that define requirements, design, test plan, and other documents;

(iv) organizational culture with a focus on quality products and quality processes.

All of these are needed for the review program to be successful

Review policies should specify when reviews should take place, what is to be reviewed, types of reviews that will take place, who is responsible, what training is required and what the review deliverables are. Review procedures should define the steps and phases for each type of review. Policies should ensure that each project has an associated project plan, test plan, configuration management plan, and a review plan, and/or a software quality assurance plan. Project plans and the review plans should ensure that adequate time and resources are available for reviews and that cycle time is set aside for reviews. Managers need to follow-up and enforce the stated policies. This becomes very difficult when projects are behind schedule and over budget. Only strong managerial commitment will lead to a successful review program.

10.4 Components of Review Plans

Reviews are development and maintenance activities that require time and resources. They should be planned so that there is a place for them in the project schedule. An organization should develop a review plan template that can be applied to all software projects. The template should specify the following items for inclusion in the review plan.

- review goals;

- items being reviewed;

- preconditions for the review;

- roles, team size, participants;

- training requirements;

- review steps;

- checklists and other related documents to be disturbed to participants;

- time requirements;

- the nature of the review log and summary report;

- rework and follow-up.

We will now explore each of these items in more detail.

10.4.1 Review Goals

As in the test plan or any other type of plan, the review planner should specify the goals to be accomplished by the review. Some general review goals have been stated in Section 9.0 and include (i) identification of problem components or components in the software artifact that need improvement, (ii) identification of specific errors or defects in the software artifact, (iii) ensuring that the artifact conforms to organizational standards, and (iv) communication to the staff about the nature of the product being developed. Additional goals might be to establish traceability with other project documents, and familiarization with the item being reviewed. Goals for inspections and walkthroughs are usually different; those of walkthroughs are more limited in scope and are usually confined to identification of defects.

10.4.2 Preconditions and Items to Be Reviewed

Given the principal goals of a technical review—early defect detection, identification of problem areas, and familiarization with software artifacts—many software items are candidates for review. In many organizations the items selected for review include:

- requirements documents;

- design documents;

- code;

- test plans (for the multiple levels);

- user manuals;

- training manuals;

- standards documents.

Note that many of these items represent a deliverable of a major life cycle phase. In fact, many represent project milestones and the review serves as a progress marker for project progress. Before each of these items are reviewed certain preconditions usually have to be met. For example, before a code review is held, the code may have to undergo a successful compile. The preconditions need to be described in the review policy statement and specified in the review plan for an item. General preconditions for a review are:

(i)   the review of an item(s) is a required activity in the project plan. (Unplanned reviews are also possible at the request of management, SQA or software engineers. Review policy statements should include the conditions for holding an unplanned review.)
(ii) a statement of objectives for the review has been developed;
(iii) the individuals responsible for developing the reviewed item indicate readiness for the review;
(iv) the review leader believes that the item to be reviewed is sufficiently complete for the review to be useful [8].

The review planner must also keep in mind that a given item to be reviewed may be too large and complex for a single review meeting. The smart planner partitions the review item into components that are of a size and complexity that allows them to be reviewed in 1–2 hours. This is the time range in which most reviewers have maximum effectiveness. For example, the design document for a procedure-oriented system may be reviewed in parts that encompass:

(i)   the overall architectural design;
(ii) data items and module interface design;
(iii) component design.

If the architectural design is complex and/or the number of components is large, then multiple design review sessions should be scheduled for each. The project plan should have time allocated for this.

10.4.3 Roles, Participants, Team Size, and Time Requirements

Two major roles that need filling for a successful review are (i) a leader or moderator, and (ii) a recorder. These are shown in Figure 10.3. Some of the responsibilities of the moderator have been described. These include planning the reviews, managing the review meeting, and issuing the review report. Because of these responsibilities the moderator plays an important role; the success of the review depends on the experience and expertise of the moderator. Reviewing a software item is a tedious process and requires great attention to details. The moderator needs to be sure that all are prepared for the review and that the review meeting stays on track. Reviewers often tire and become less effective at detecting errors if the review time period is too long and the item is too complex for a single review meeting. The moderator/planner must ensure that a time period is selected that is appropriate for the size and complexity of the item under review. There is no set value for a review time period, but a rule of thumb advises that a review session should not be longer than 2 hours [3]. Review sessions can be scheduled over 2-hour time periods separated by breaks. The time allocated for a review should be adequate enough to ensure that the material under review can be adequately covered.

The review recorder has the responsibility for documenting defects, and recording review findings and recommendations, Other roles may include a reader who reads or presents the item under review. Readers are usually the authors or preparers of the item under review. The author(s) is responsible for performing any rework on the reviewed item. In a walkthrough type of review, the author may serve as the moderator, but this is not true for an inspection. All reviewers should be trained in the review process.

The size of the review team will vary depending type, size, and complexity of the item under review. Again, as with time, there is no fixed size for a review team. In most cases a size between 3 and 7 is a rule of thumb, but that depends on the items under review and the experience level of the review team. Of special importance is the experience of the review moderator who is responsible for ensuring the material is covered, the review meeting stays on track, and review outputs are produced. The minimal team size of 3 ensures that the review will be public [6].

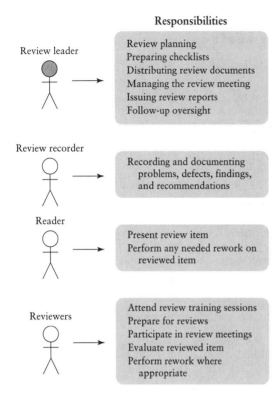

Responsibilities

Review leader
- Review planning
- Preparing checklists
- Distributing review documents
- Managing the review meeting
- Issuing review reports
- Follow-up oversight

Review recorder
- Recording and documenting problems, defects, findings, and recommendations

Reader
- Present review item
- Perform any needed rework on reviewed item

Reviewers
- Attend review training sessions
- Prepare for reviews
- Participate in review meetings
- Evaluate reviewed item
- Perform rework where appropriate

FIG. 10.3
Review roles.

Organizational policies guide selection of review team members. Membership may vary with the type of review. As shown in Figure 10.4 the review team can consist of software quality assurance staff members, testers, and developers (analysts, designers, programmers). In some cases the size of the review team will be increased to include a specialist in a particular area related to the reviewed item; in other cases "outsiders" may be invited to a review to get a more unbiased evaluation of the item. These outside members may include users/clients. Users/clients should certainly be present at requirements, user manual, and acceptance test plan reviews. Some recommend that users also be present at design and even code reviews. Organizational policy should refer to this issue, keeping in mind the limited technical knowledge of most users/clients.

In many cases it is wise to invite review team members from groups

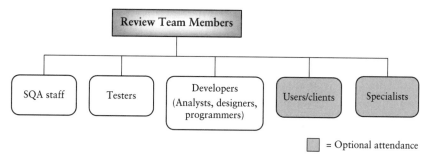

FIG. 10.4

Review team membership constituency.

that were involved in the preceding and succeeding phases of the life cycle document being reviewed. These participants could be considered to be outsiders. For example, if a design document is under review, it would be useful to invite a requirements team representative and a coding team member to be a review participant since correctness, consistency, implementability, and traceability are important issues for this review. In addition, these attendees can offer insights and perspectives that differ from the group members that were involved in preparing the current document under review. It is the author's option that testers take part in all major milestone reviews to ensure:

- effective test planning;

- traceability between tests, requirements, design and code elements;

- discussion, and support of testability issues;

- support for software product quality issues;

- the collection and storage of review defect data;

- support for adequate testing of "trouble-prone" areas.

Testers need to especially interact with designers on the issue of testability. A more testable design is the goal. For example, in an object-oriented system a tester may request during a design review that additional methods be included in a class to display its state variables. In this case and others, it may appear on the surface that this type of design is more expensive to develop and implement. However, consider that in the long run if the software is more testable there will be two major positive effects:

(i) the testing effort is likely to be decreased, thus lowering expenses, and
(ii) the software is likely to be of higher quality, thus increasing customer satisfaction.

10.4.4 Review Procedures

For each type of review that an organization wishes to implement, there should be a set of standardized steps that define the given review procedure. For example, the steps for an inspection are shown in Figure 10.2. These are initiation, preparation, inspection meeting, reporting results, and rework and follow-up. For each step in the procedure the activities and tasks for all the reviewer participants should be defined. The review plan should refer to the standardized procedures where applicable.

10.4.5 Review Training

Review participants need training to be effective. Responsibility for reviewer training classes usually belongs to the internal technical training staff. Alternatively, an organization may decide to send its review trainees to external training courses run by commercial institutions. Review participants, and especially those who will be review leaders, need the training. Test specialists should also receive review training. Suggested topics for a training program are shown in Figure 10.5 and described below. Some of the topics can be covered very briefly since it is assumed that the reviewers (expect for possible users/clients) are all technically proficient.

1. Review of Process Concepts.

Reviewers should understand basic process concepts, the value of process improvement, and the role of reviews as a product and process improvement tool.

```
┌─────────────────────────────────────────────┐
│             Review Training Topics            │
├─────────────────────────────────────────────┤
│                                               │
│ Topic1.                                       │
│    Basic concepts                             │
│ Topic 2.                                      │
│    Review of quality issues                   │
│ Topic 3.                                      │
│    Review of standards                        │
│ Topic 4.                                      │
│    Understanding the material to be reviewed  │
│ Topic 5.                                      │
│    Defect and problem types                   │
│ Topic 6.                                      │
│    Communication and meeting management skills│
│ Topic 7.                                      │
│    Review documentation and record keeping    │
│ Topic 8.                                      │
│    Special instructions                       │
│ Topic 9.                                      │
│    Practice review sessions                   │
│                                               │
└─────────────────────────────────────────────┘
```

FIG. 10.5

Topics for review training sessions.

2. Review of Quality Issues.

Reviewers should be made familiar with quality attributes such as correctness, testability, maintainability, usability, security, portability, and so on, and how can these be evaluated in a review.

3. Review of Organizational Standards for Software Artifacts.

Reviewers should be familiar with organizational standards for software artifacts. For example, what items must be included in a software document; what is the correct order and degree of coverage of topics expected; what types of notations are permitted. Good sources for this material are IEEE standards and guides [1,9,10].

4. Understanding the Material to Be Reviewed.

Concepts of understanding and how to build mental models during comprehension of code and software-related documents should be covered.

A critical issue is how fast a reviewed document should be read/checked by an individual and by the group as a whole. This applies to requirements, design, test plans and other documents, as well as source code. A rate of 5–10 pages/hour or 125–150 LOC/hour for a review group has been quoted as favorable [7]. Reading rates that are too slow will make review meetings ineffective with respect to the number of defects found per unit time. Readings that are too fast will allow defects and problems to go undetected.

5. Defect and Problem Types.

Review trainees need to become aware of the most frequently occurring types of problems or errors that are likely to occur during development. They need to be aware what their causes are, how they are transformed into defects, and where they are likely to show up in the individual deliverables. The trainees should become familiar with the defect type categories, severity levels, and numbers and types of defects found in past deliverables of similar systems. Review trainees should also be made aware of certain indicators or clues that a certain type of defect or problem has occurred [3]. The definitions of defects categories, and maintenance of a defect data base are the responsibilities of the testers and SQA staff.

6. Communication and Meeting Management Skills.

These topics are especially important for review leaders. It is their responsibility to communicate with the review team, the preparers of the reviewed document, management, and in some cases clients/user group members. Review leaders need to have strong oral and written communication skills and also learn how to conduct a review meeting. During a review meeting there are interactions and expression of opinion from a group of technically qualified people who often want to be heard. The review leader must ensure that all are prepared, that the meeting stays on track, that all get a chance to express their opinions, that the proper page/code document checking rate is achieved, and that results are recorded. Review leaders also must trained so that they can ensure that authors of the document or artifact being reviewed are not under the impression that they themselves are being evaluated. The review leader needs to uphold the organizational view that the purpose of the review is to support the authors in improving the quality of the item they have developed. Policy statements to this effect need to be written and explained to review trainees, especially those who will be review leaders.

Skills in conflict resolution are very useful, since very often reviewers will have strong opinions and arguments can dominate a review session unless there is intervention by the leader. There are also issues of power and control over deliverables and aspects of deliverables and other hidden agenda that surface during a review meeting that must be handled by the review leader. In this case people and management skills are necessary, and sometime these cannot be taught. They come through experience.

7. Review Documentation and Record Keeping.

Review leaders need to learn how to prepare checklists, agendas, and logs for review meetings. Examples will be provided for some of these documents later in this chapter. Other examples can be found in Freedman and Weinberg [6], Myers [11], and Kit [12]. Checklists for inspections should be appropriate for the item being inspected. Checklists in general should focus on the following issues:

- most frequent errors;

- completeness of the document;

- correctness of the document;

- adherence to standards.

Section 10.4.5 has a more detailed discussion of checklists.

8. Special Instructions.

During review training there may be some topics that need to be covered with the review participants. For example, there may be interfaces with hardware that involve the reviewed item, and reviewers may need some additional background discussion to be able to evaluate those interfaces.

9. Practice Review Sessions.

Review trainees should participate in practice review sessions. There are very instructive and essential. One option is for instructors to use existing documents that have been reviewed in the past and have the trainees do a practice review of these documents. Results can be compared to those of experienced reviewers, and useful lessons can be learned from problems identified by the trainees and those that were not. Instructors can discuss so-called "false positives" which are not true defects but are identified as such. Trainees can also attend review sessions with experienced reviewers as observers, to learn review lessons.

In general, training material for review trainees should have adequate examples, graphics, and homework exercises. Instructors should be provided with the media equipment needed to properly carry out instruction. Material can be of the self-paced type, or for group course work.

10.4.6 Review Checklists

Inspections formally require the use of a checklist of items that serves as the focal point for review examinations and discussions on both the individual and group levels. As a precondition for checklist development an organization should identify the typical types of defects made in past projects, develop a classification scheme for those defects, and decide on impact or severity categories for the defects. If no such defect data is available, staff members need to search the literature, industrial reports, or the organizational archives to retrieve this type of information.

Checklists are very important for inspectors. They provide structure and an agenda for the review meeting. They guide the review activities, identify focus areas for discussion and evaluation, ensure all relevant items are covered, and help to frame review record keeping and measurement. Reviews are really a two-step process: (i) reviews by individuals, and (ii) reviews by the group. The checklist plays its important role in both steps. The first step involves the individual reviewer and the review material. Prior to the review meeting each individual must be provided with the materials to review and the checklist of items. It is his responsibility to do his homework and individually inspect that document using the checklist as a guide, and to document any problems he encounters. When they attend the group meeting which is the second review step, each reviewer should bring his or her individual list of defect/problems, and as each item on the checklist is discussed they should comment. Finally, the reviewers need to come to a consensus on what needs to be fixed and what remains unchanged.

Each item that undergoes a review requires a different checklist that addresses the special issues associated with quality evaluation for that item. However each checklist should have components similar to those shown in Table 10.1. The first column lists all the defect types or potential problem areas that may occur in the item under review. Sources for these defect types are usually data from past projects. Abbreviations for detect/problem types can be developed to simplify the checklist forms. Status refers to coverage during the review meeting—has the item been discussed? If so, a check mark is placed in the column. Major or minor are the two severity or impact levels shown here. Each organization needs to decide on the severity levels that work for them. Using this simple severity scale, a defect or problem that is classified as major has a large impact on product quality; it can cause failure or deviation from specification. A minor problem has a small impact on these; in general, it would affect a nonfunctional aspect of the software. The letters M, I, and S indicate whether a checklist item is missing (M), incorrect (I), or superfluous (S).

In this section we will look at several sample checklists. These are shown in Tables 10.2–10.5. One example is the general checklist shown in Table 10.2, which is applicable to almost all software documents. The checklist is used is to ensure that all documents are complete, correct, consistent, clear, and concise. Table 10.2 only shows the problem/defect types component (column) for simplicity's sake. All the components as found in Table 10.1 should be present on each checklist form. That also holds true for the checklists illustrated in Tables 10.3–10.5.

The recorder is responsible for completing the group copy of the checklist form during the review meeting (as opposed to the individual checklist form completed during review preparation by each individual reviewer). The recorder should also keep track of each defect and where in the document it occurs (line, page, etc.). The group checklist can appear on a wallboard so that all can see what has been entered. Each individual should bring to the review meeting his or her own version of the checklist completed prior to the review meeting.

In addition to using the widely applicable problem/defect types shown in Table 10.2 each item undergoing review has specific attributes that

Problem/defect type	Status	Major	Minor	M	I	S

TABLE 10.1

Example components for an inspection checklist.

should be addressed on a checklist form. Some examples will be given in the following pages of checklist items appropriate for reviewing different types of software artifacts.

Requirements Reviews

In addition to covering the items on the general document checklist as shown in Table 10.2, the following items should be included in the checklist for a requirements review.

- completeness (have all functional and quality requirements described in the problem statement been included?);

- correctness (do the requirements reflect the user's needs? are they stated without error?);

- consistency (do any requirements contradict each other?);

- clarity (it is very important to identify and clarify any ambiguous requirements);

- relevance (is the requirement pertinent to the problem area? requirements should not be superfluous);

- redundancy (a requirement may be repeated; if it is a duplicate it should be combined with an equivalent one);

- testability (can each requirement be covered successfully with one or more test cases? can tests determine if the requirement has been satisfied?);

Problem/Defect Type: General Checklist

Coverage and completeness
Are all essential items completed?
Have all irrelevant items been omitted?
Is the technical level of each topic addressed properly for this document?
Is there a clear statement of goals for this document? Are the goals consistent with policy?

Correctness
Are there any incorrect items?
Are there any contradictions?
Are there any ambiguities?

Clarity and Consistency
Are the material and statements in the document clear?
Are the examples clear, useful, relevant, correct?
Are the diagrams, graphs, illustrations clear, correct, use the proper notation, effective, in the proper place?
Is the terminology clear, and correct?
Is there a glossary of technical terms that is complete and correct?
Is the writing style clear (nonambiguous)?

References and Aids to Document Comprehension
Is there an abstract or introduction?
Is there a well-placed table of contents?
Are the topics or items broken down in a manner that is easy to follow and is understandable?
Is there a bibliography that is clear, complete and correct?
Is there an index that is clear, complete and correct?
Is the page and figure numbering correct and consistent?

TABLE 10.2

A sample general review checklist for software documents.

- feasibility (are requirements implementable given the conditions under which the project will progress?).

Users/clients or their representatives should be present at a requirements review to ensure that the requirements truly reflect their needs, and that the requirements are expressed clearly and completely. It is also very important for testers to be present at the requirements review. One of their major responsibilities it to ensure that the requirements are testable. Very often the master or early versions of the system and acceptance test plans are included in the requirements review. Here the reviewers/testers can use a traceability matrix to ensure that each requirement can be covered by one or more tests. If requirements are not clear, proposing test cases can be of help in focusing attention on these areas, quantifying imprecise requirements, and providing general information to help resolve problems.

Although not on the list above, requirements reviews should also ensure that the requirements are free of design detail. Requirements focus on what the system should do, not on how to implement it.

Design Reviews

Designs are often reviewed in one or more stages. It is useful to review the high level architectural design at first and later review the detailed design. At each level of design it is important to check that the design is consistent with the requirements and that it covers all the requirements. Again the general checklist is applicable with respect to clarity, completeness, correctness and so on. Some specific items that should be checked for at a design review are:

- a description of the design technique used;

- an explanation of the design notation used;

- evaluation of design alternatives (it is important to establish that design alternatives have been evaluated, and to determine why this particular approach was selected);

- quality of the high-level architectural model (all modules and their relationships should be defined; this includes newly developed modules, revised modules, COTS components, and any other reused modules; module coupling and cohesion should be evaluated.);

- description of module interfaces;

- quality of the user interface;

- quality of the user help facilities;

- identification of execution criteria and operational sequences;

- clear description of interfaces between this system and other software and hardware systems;

- coverage of all functional requirements by design elements;

- coverage of all quality requirements, for example, ease of use, portability, maintainability, security, readability, adaptability, performance requirements (storage, response time) by design elements;

- reusability of design components;

- testability (how will the modules, and their interfaces be tested? how will they be integrated and tested as a complete system?).

For reviewing detailed design the following focus areas should also be revisited:

- encapsulation, information hiding and inheritance;

- module cohesion and coupling;

- quality of module interface description;

- module reuse.

Both levels of design reviews should cover testability issues as described above. In addition, measures that are now available such as module complexity, which gives an indication of testing effort, can be used to estimate the extent of the testing effort. Reviewers should also check traceability from tests to design elements and to requirements. Some organizations may re-examine system and integration test plans in the context of the design elements under review. Preliminary unit test plans can also be examined along with the design documents to ensure traceability, consistency, and complete coverage. Other issues to be discussed include language issues and the appropriateness of the proposed language to implement the design.

Code Reviews

Code reviews are useful tools for detecting defects and for evaluating code quality. Some organizations require a clean compile as a precondition for a code review. The argument is that it is more effective to use an automated tool to identify syntax errors than to use human experts to perform this task. Other organizations will argue that a clean compile makes reviewers complacent. Under these circumstances reviewers may not be as diligent in checking for defects since they will assume the compiler has detected many of them.

Code review checklists can have both general and language-specific components. The general code review checklist can be used to review code written in any programming language. There are common quality features that should be checked no matter what implementation language is selected. Table 10.3 shows a list of items that should be included in a general code checklist.

The general checklist is followed by a sample checklist that can be used for a code review for programs written in the C programming language. The problem/defect types are shown in Table 10.4. When developing your own checklist documents be sure to include the other columns as shown in Table 10.1. The reader should note that since the language-specific checklist addresses programming-language-specific issues, a different checklist is required for each language used in the organization.

Test Plan Reviews

Test plans are also items that can be reviewed. Some organizations will review them along with other related documents. For example, a master test plan and an acceptance test plan could be reviewed with the requirements document, the integration and system test plans reviewed with the design documents, and unit test plans reviewed with detailed design documents [2]. Other organizations, for example, those that use the Extended/Modified V-model, may have separate review meetings for each of the test plans. In Chapter 7 the components of a test plan were discussed, and the review should insure that all these components are present and that they are correct, clear, and complete. The general document checklist can be applied to test plans, and a more specific checklist can be developed for test-specific issues. An example test plan checklist is shown in Table 10.4. The test plan checklist is applicable to all levels of test plans.

Other testing products such as test design specifications, test procedures, and test cases can also be reviewed. These reviews can be held in conjunction with reviews of other test-related items or other software

Problems/Defect Types: General Code Checklist

Design Issues
Does each unit implement a single function?
Are there instances where the unit should be partitioned?
Is code consistent with detailed design?
Does the code cover detailed design?

Data Items
Is there an input validity check?
Arrays—check array dimensions, boundaries, indices.
Variables—are they all defined, initiated? have correct types and scopes been checked?
Are all variables used?

Computations
Are there computations using variables with inconsistent data types?
Are there mixed-mode computations?
Is the target value of an assignment smaller than the right-hand expression?
Is over- or underflow a possibility (division by zero)?
Are there invalid uses of integers or floating point arithmetic?
Are there comparisons between floating point numbers?
Are there assumptions about the evaluation order in Boolean expressions?
Are the comparison operators correct?

Control Flow Issues
Will the program, module or, unit eventually terminate?
Is there a possibility of an infinite loop, a loop with a premature exit, a loop that never executes?

Interface Issues
Do the number and attributes of the parameters used by a caller match those of the called routine? Is the order of parameters also correct and consistent in caller and callee?
Does a function or procedure alter a parameter that is only meant as an input parameter?
If there are global variables, do they have corresponding definitions and attributes in all the modules that use them?

Input/output Issues
Have all files been opened for use?
Are all files properly closed at termination?
If files are declared are their attributes correct?
Are EOF or I/O errors conditions handed correctly?
Is I/O buffer size and record size compatible?

Portability Issues
Is there an assumed character set, and integer or floating point representation?
Are their service calls that may need to be modified?

Error Messages
Have all warnings and informational messages been checked and used appropriately?

Comments/Code Documentation
Has the code been properly documented? are there global, procedure, and line comments where appropriate?
Is the documentation clear, and correct, and does it support understanding?

Code Layout and White Space
Has white space and indentation been used to support understanding of code logic and code intent?

Maintenance
Does each module have a single exit point?
Are the modules easy to change (low coupling and high cohesion)?

TABLE 10.3

A sample general code review checklist.

Problems/Defect Types C Programming Language Checklist

Data Items
Are all variables lowercase?
Are all variables initialized?
Are variable names consistent, and do they reflect usage?
Are all declarations documented (except for those that are very simple to understand)?
Is each name used for a singe function (except for loop variable names)?
Is the scope of the variable as intended?

Constants
Are all constants in uppercase?
Are all constants defined with a "#define"?
Are all constants used in multiple files defined in an INCLUDE header file?

Pointers
Are pointers declared properly as pointers?
Are the pointers initialized properly?

Control
Are if/then, else, and switch statements used clearly and properly?

Strings
Strings should have proper pointers.
Strings should end with a NULL.

Brackets
All curly brackets should have appropriate indentations and be matched.

Logic Operators
Do all initializations use an " = " and not an " = = "?
Check to see that all logic operators are correct, for example, use of $=/==$, and ‖.

Computations
Are parentheses used in complex expressions and are they used properly for specifying precedences?
Are shifts used properly?

TABLE 10.4

A sample code review checklist for C programs.

items. For example, Hetzel suggests that test specifications be reviewed with the detailed design document, and that test cases and test procedures be evaluated at a code review [2].

Additional examples of checklists for reviewing software artifacts can be found in Hetzel [2], Myers [4,11], Kit [12] and Humphrey [13]. The IEEE standards for document descriptions also contain helpful information for reviewers [9,10]. It is recommended that each organization create its own checklists that reflect organizational policies and quality goals.

Problems/Defect Types: Test Plan Review

Test Items
Are all items to be tested included in the test plan?
Has each requirement, feature and, design element been covered in the test plan?
Has the testing approach been clearly described?
Have pass/fail criteria been clearly described?
Have suspension and resumption criteria been clearly described?
Have all the test deliverables been included?

Staffing Scheduling and Responsibilities
Have the testing tasks been defined, allocated, and scheduled?
Are the schedules and responsibilities compatible with the overall project schedule?
Have training needs been addressed and provided for in the schedule?

The Test Environment
Has the test environment been described clearly, and does it include hardware and software needs, laboratory space, data bases, etc.?
Has time for setting up and tearing down the environment been allocated?

Testing Risks
Have all the risks associated with testing the software product been identified and analyzed in the test plan?

Testing Costs
Does the plan account for testing costs?
Are testing costs compatible to those specified in the project plan?

Test Plan Attachments
Have all the test design specifications been completed?
Are they in conformance with organizational standards?
Has a traceability matrix been developed to insure all requirements, features, and design elements have been covered in the tests?
Have the test cases been specified? are they correct, and complete?
Has there been a description of the design approach for the test cases?
Are the proper links between test cases, test procedures, and test design specifications established?
Have black and white box testing methods been applied properly and appropriately?
Are the tests adequate for each item?
For integration test, has the approach to integration been included, explained, and documented?
Have the test procedures been documented? are they complete and according to standards?
Have posttest documentation requirements been specified?
Have the users been given ample opportunity to give inputs to acceptance test?

TABLE 10.5

A sample checklist for a test plan review.

10.5 Reporting Review Results

Several information-rich items result from technical reviews. These items are listed below. The items can be bundled together in a single report or distributed over several distinct reports. Review polices should indicate the formats of the reports required. The review reports should contain the following information.

1. *For inspections*—the group checklist with all items covered and comments relating to each item.
2. *For inspections*—a status, or summary, report (described below) signed by all participants.
3. A list of defects found, and classified by type and frequency. Each defect should be cross-referenced to the line, pages, or figure in the reviewed document where it occurs.
4. Review metric data (see Section 10.7 for a discussion).

The inspection report on the reviewed item is a document signed by all the reviewers. It may contain a summary of defects and problems found and a list of review attendees, and some review measures such as the time period for the review and the total number of major/minor defects. The reviewers are responsible for the quality of the information in the written report [6]. There are several status options available to the review participants on this report. These are:

1. *Accept:* The reviewed item is accepted in its present form or with minor rework required that does not need further verification.
2. *Conditional accept:* The reviewed item needs rework and will be accepted after the moderator has checked and verified the rework.
3. *Reinspect:* Considerable rework must be done to the reviewed item. The inspection needs to be repeated when the rework is done.

Before signing their name to such a inspection report reviewers need to be sure that all checklist items have been addressed, all defects recorded, and all quality issues discussed. This is important for several reasons. Very often when a document has passed an inspection it is viewed as a baseline item for configuration management, and any changes from this baseline item need approval from the configuration management board. In addition, the successful passing of a review usually indicates a project milestone has been passed, a certain level of quality has been achieved, and the project has made progress toward meeting its objectives.

A milestone meeting is usually held, and clients are notified of the completion of the milestone.

If the software item is given a conditional accept or a reinspect, a follow-up period occurs where the authors must address all the items on the problem/defect list. The moderator reviews the rework in the case of a conditional accept. Another inspection meeting is required to reverify the items in the case of a "reinspect" decision.

For an inspection type of review, one completeness or exit criterion requires that all identified problems be resolved. Other criteria may be required by the organization. In addition to the summary report, other outputs of an inspection include a defect report and an inspection report. These reports are vital for collecting and organizing review measurement data. The defect report contains a description of the defects, the defect type, severity level, and the location of each defect. On the report the defects can be organized so that their type and occurrence rate is easy to determine. IEEE standards suggest that the inspection report contain vital data such as [8]:

(i)   number of participants in the review;
(ii) the duration of the meeting;
(iii) size of the item being reviewed (usually LOC or number of pages);
(iv) total preparation time for the inspection team;
(v)   status of the reviewed item;
(vi) estimate of rework effort and the estimated date for completion of the rework.

This data will help an organization to evaluate the effectiveness of the review process and to make improvements.

The IEEE has recommendations for defect classes [8]. The classes are based on the reviewed software items' conformance to:

• standards;

• capability;

• procedures;

• interface;

• description.

A defect class may describe an item as missing, incorrect, or superfluous as shown in Table 10.1. Other defect classes could describe an item as ambiguous or inconsistent [8]. Defects should also be ranked in severity, for example:

(i) major (these would cause the software to fail or deviate from its specification);
(ii) minor (affects nonfunctional aspects of the software).

A ranking scale for defects can be developed in conjunction with a failure severity scale as described in Section 9.1.4.

A walkthrough review is considered complete when the entire document has been covered or walked through, all defects and suggestions for improvement have been recorded, and the walkthrough report has been completed. The walkthrough report lists all the defects and deficiencies, and contains data such as [8]:

- the walkthrough team members;
- the name of the item being examined;
- the walkthrough objectives;
- list of defects and deficiencies;
- recommendations on how to dispose of, or resolve the deficiencies.

Note that the walkthrough report/completion criteria are not as formal as those for an inspection. There is no requirement for a signed status report, and no required follow-up for resolution of deficiencies, although that could be recommended in the walkthrough report.

A final important item to note: The purpose of a review is to evaluate a software artifact, *not* the developer or author of the artifact. Reviews should not be used to evaluate the performance of a software analyst, developer, designer, or tester [3]. This important point should be well established in the review policy. It is essential to adhere to this policy for the review process to work. If authors of software artifacts believe they are being evaluated as individuals, the objective and impartial nature of the review will change, and its effectiveness in revealing problems will be minimized [3].

10.6 Review, Rework and Follow-Up

If problems/defects have been identified in the reviewed items there must be a rework period so that all of these are resolved by the authors of the reviewed item. This is especially true for inspections where the rework follow-up period is mandatory. The rework/follow-up periods embody a set of tasks similar to those associated with fault localization when applied to code. The problems/defects have been detected and localized during the review meeting. During rework and follow-up the defects/problems are repaired and then the item is retested by the review moderator or the review group as a whole. One scenario that may occur during rework is that a decision to disregard or redesign an extremely problem prone item has to be made. This may be costly and time consuming, but may in the long run be the best choice.

In the review follow-up period it is the responsibility of the review moderator to insure that all the proper rework has been done. The review summary should specify if the item needs to be reinspected by the moderator, or subject to a rereview by the entire review team when the rework is completed.

10.7 Review Metrics

It is important to collect measurement data related to the review process so that the review process can be evaluated, made visible as a testing tool, and improved (made more effective). The defect data collected from a review is also very useful for predicting product quality, analyzing the development process, performing defect casual analysis, and establishing defect prevention activities. The two latter activities are associated with the higher levels of the TMM and are discussed in Chapter 13.

Some basic measurements that can be collected from any type of review are as follows:

1. *Size of the item reviewed.* For a code review, size can be measured in lines of code. For detailed design, lines of pseudo code can be counted. For other documents, the number of pages can be used as a size measure. If test cases or test procedures are being reviewed, then the actual number of these can be counted.

2. *The review time.* This is usually the time for the group review meeting in hours.

3. *The number of defects found.* This can be expressed in many ways. For example, the total number of defects (major/minor), number of defects sorted by category, and frequency of occurrence. The defect categories may be different for the different items that are reviewed.

4. *The number of defects that have escaped and were found in later review and testing activities, and finally in operation by the user.* This will tell you how good your review filtering process was.

These four items can be directly measured. There are other measures that can be derived from combinations of these measures such as:

5. *The number of defects found per hour of review time.*

6. *The number of defects found per page or per LOC.*

7. *The LOC or pages of document that were reviewed per hour.*

Humphrey describe two additional useful review measures [13]:

8. *Defect removal leverage (DRL).* This a ratio of the defect detection rates from two review or test phases and can be expressed as:

$$\text{DRL} = \frac{\text{Defects/hour (review or test phase X)}}{\text{Defects/hour (review or test phase Y)}}$$

Suppose you wanted to compare the relative rates of defect detection between code review and unit test. You could express this as:

$$\text{DRL} = \frac{\text{Defects/hour in code review}}{\text{Defects/hour in unit test}}$$

The DRL is a simple calculation that provides a great deal of information about the relative effectiveness of various defect filtering or testing activities. Another useful measure described by Humphrey is called the phase yield [13]. This is calculated as:

$$\text{Phase yield} = 100 * \frac{\text{Defects removed in review or test phase X}}{\text{Defects removed in phase X} + \text{net escapes from review or test phase X}}$$

You may not be able to calculate the phase yield until the software is being used by the clients to determine the actual number of net escapes. If you limit escapes to include those found through the execution-based testing phases, then you can estimate the phase yield before the software goes to the client.

Spensor has used some of these measurements to show the growth of a software inspection program at Applicon [7]. The program was introduced over a 2-year period in that organization. Among the first year's activities were the creation of a toolkit of checklists and handouts, introduction of a 2-day course for inspection leaders, creation of an inspection database in Excel, support for inspection of software project documents and code, and the collection and reporting of inspection data monthly to the engineering staff. In the second year the planned activities included inspection overview presentations to senior management and project mangers, mandatory inspection of requirements and specifications for all major projects, and a requirement that at least 20% of the people in each project group have inspection leadership training. The inspection measurements and the actual data collected over the 2-year period can be summarized as follows [7]:

Inspection measurement	Data from 2-year period
Number of document inspections	Increased from 39 to 100
Number of code inspections	Increased from 9 to 63
Average time to find and fix a major problem	Went from 0.8 hours to 0.9 hours
Average effectiveness (documents)	Increased from 2.3 problems/page to 2.5 problems/pages
Average effectiveness (code)	Went from 28.7 major problems/KLOC to 53.3 major problems/KLOC
Average checking rates	9.9 pages/hour (docs), 300 LOC/hour (code) to 9.1 pages/hour (docs), 200 LOC/hour (code)
Number staff completing inspection leader training	Increased from 48 to 70
Certified leaders	Increased from 8 to 28

Note that the checking rates did slow down in the second year; however, the number of problems identified increased, indicating the slower rate had a positive impact on the detection of problems. The time to find a major problem also increased, but the number of problems found increased at a greater rate, again indicating a more effective inspection process. The inspection program was declared a success. Many managers now require inspections of more than the two mandatory documents. The inspection leader's role also acquired a great deal of status among the staff, and emphasis on, and attention to, quality issues has increased. Collecting, analyzing, and applying review measurements are among the keys to success reported in the article. The author believes that measurements are important to give added visibility to the benefits of inspections, and that they are useful for improving and optimizing the inspection process.

10.8 Support from the Extended/Modified V-Model

A TMM level 4 maturity goal recommends that an organization establish a review program and apply the review process to major life cycle deliverables. The Extended/Modified V-model as shown in Chapter 1 and again reproduced here in Figure 10.6 can be used as a framework to introduce review activities into the development or maintenance process. According to the model, reviews begin at requirements time and continue through development at the conclusion of each major life cycle phase. During execution-based testing phases reviews are conducted at each level of testing for the associated test plans. Use of the Extended/Modified V-model is optional, and each organization should establish its own policy for review scheduling, keeping in mind that it is beneficial to remove problems as close as possible to their point of origin. Readers should note that other options for scheduling of test plan reviews are discussed in Section 10.4.6.

10.9 The Self-Check or Personal Review

Inspections and walkthroughs are activities where peer groups meet to evaluate and improve a software artifact. Their introduction goes back

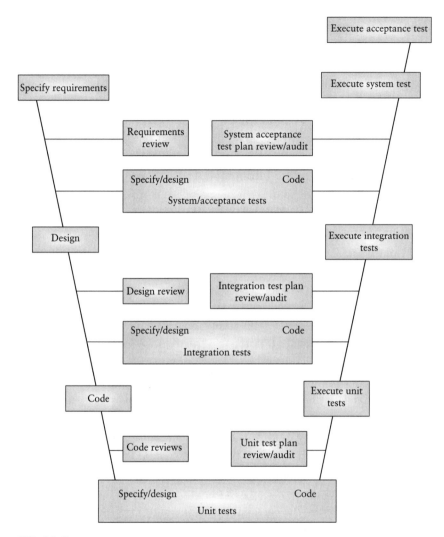

FIG. 10.6
The Extended/Modified V-model.

to early history of programming. One other type of review that has been used since the origins of programming is the self-check, sometimes called the desk-check. It was primarily applied to code. Before the advent of interactive tools, the desk-check was used by programmers to detect defects in order to improve code quality and productivity. The typical development scenario in the early days of programming was as follows. A developer would submit a program for processing (usually on a set of punch cards) to the computer operator. The program was placed on a batch-processing queue, and over a period of several hours the program would be submitted first to the to the compiler, then to a linker, and finally a loader. After loading, run time software would provide the necessary environment for executing the program in the language it was written in. If there were any compile, link, or run-time errors the program was removed from the batch-processing queue and returned to the developer. With very little aid from tools, the developer had to identify the source of the problem. In the case of compile and link errors the developer would proceed to identify and repair them and resubmit the code. If there were additional compile or link errors, the program was returned again over a period of hours. This cycle would be repeated until all compile/link errors were removed.

When all the compile and link errors were removed, then the program could be run provided the loader could allocate the needed amount of memory. If there were run-item errors then the submit, wait, return, repair, and resubmit cycle was repeated to remove logic and other programming errors until the program ran correctly. Even for the relatively noncomplex programs that were developed in the 1960s and 1970s, this process was very time consuming. The best tool a developer could use to avoid these multiple cycles was a self- or desk-check of the code. Each individual developer would read their code carefully, and play computer (walk through it with test cases) to detect syntax, link, and logic-based defects. The process was very cost effective and still is!

Unfortunately, with the advent of interactive tools, the self-check has been eliminated from the personal development process for most software engineers. From her own personal experience and that of others, the author recommends this practice to every software engineer for any work product being developed. In fact, Watts Humphrey includes a personal design and code review as part of the Personal Software Process (PSP) he has developed [13]. Humphrey recommends that each software engineer have personal review goals, define a personal review process, collect individual review measurements, and use defined checklists for their personal design and code reviews. He gives a strong argument for the personal review as being an effective tool for defect detection. On the

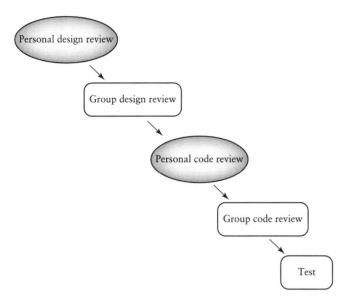

FIG. 10.7

A role for the personal review.

personal level, review data can also be used for personal process improvement, and for defect analysis and prevention [13]. Figure 10.7 shows the role of the personal review in a series of quality evaluation steps. Both on the group and personal levels, reviews are an effective testing activity: they are cost effective and have many benefits.

10.10 Reviews and the TMM Critical Views

The many benefits of reviews have been reported in the literature and in software engineering texts. The arguments for use of reviews are strong enough to convince organizations that they should use reviews as a quality- and productivity-enhancing tool. One of the maturity goals that must be satisfied to reach level 4 of the TMM is to establish a review program. This implies that a formal review program needs to be put in place, supported by policies, resources, training, and requirements for mandatory reviews of software artifacts. The artifacts selected for mandatory review should be identified in the review policy statement, and should include major life cycle deliverables such as requirements documents, design documents, code, test plans, and user manuals. The three critical groups play the following roles in achieving this maturity goal.

Managers ensure that a review policy is developed, documented, and made available for all interested parties. The policy should describe what will be reviewed, the type of reviews that are held, which are mandatory, what are the conditions to hold an unplanned review, what are review pre- and postconditions, what are review steps, who will attend the review meeting, what kind of training is necessary for the reviewers, and who receives the review summary reports. Management should ensure that the policy supports the impartially of reviews; only an item is being reviewed, not its authors! Management must also enforce these policies.

A review plan template should be developed for each type of review. For inspections, checklists should be developed, as well as templates for summary reports. Problem types need to be classified for data collection purposes. Problem data should be stored as a part of the project history and used for execution-based testing planning and later on for defect prevention activities. Managers need to enforce the mandatory review requirements for the selected software items. Upper management needs to work with project managers to ensure that project plans provide time and resources for reviewing project deliverables. Managers also should support the review process by providing training, and resources for the review process.

Testers support the review program by working with management and software engineers to develop review polices and plans. They serve as review leaders, review instructors, and review participants as prescribed in the review policy statements. Testers also attend review training sessions as needed. As review meeting participants, testers give input on quality issues and are responsible for ensuring that testability requirements are addressed. There must be a focus on quality attributes (including testability) early in the software life cycle. Testers have responsibilities for review follow-up work as described in the testing policy, review policy and review plans. Another important responsibility of the testers is to work with SQA staff to (i) identify classes and severity levels for review defects, (ii) analyze and store review defect data, and (iii) develop checklists for the reviewed items.

Testers should use current and past review defect data to help them in test planning and test design. This is an important point, not emphasized enough when test planning is discussed. The reason is that many organizations have immature testing processes; they do have regular reviews; do not classify, collect and adequately store the defect data collected from reviews; and in many cases testers do not attend critical document reviews meetings. At TMM level 4 there is a framework in place to collect, store, analyze, and apply this important data.

Problem and defect data gathered during reviews has the potential to guide testers in the development of test plans. For example, in a design review, high complexity modules are identified, as well as areas of high coupling and low cohesion. Faulty data and control structures, and faulty module interfaces, are also identified. These are areas where a tester can invest testing resources and plan appropriate tests to ensure that these problems have not been carried over into the program code. Another review-related scenario that testers may be involved in is the case where reviewed code is still found to be extremely faulty during testing. A repeated inspection may be called for. Decisions will also have to be made on the wisdom of continuing the testing effort for this item or disregarding/redesigning the faulty item.

Users and clients support the review process by participating in review training and attending review sessions as indicated in the review policy. For example, attendance at requirements, acceptance test plan, and user manual reviews are vital to ensure software quality and satisfaction of user needs and requirements. Communication between clients and developers, testers, and analysts is greatly fostered during review activities.

KEY TERMS

Review

Testing

EXERCISES

1. Which software artifacts are candidates for review, and why?

2. A software engineering group is developing a mission-critical software system that guides a commercial rocket to its proper destination. This is a new product; the group and its parent organization have never built such a product before. There is a debate among the group as to whether an inspection or walkthrough is the best way to evaluate the quality of the code. The company standards are ambiguous as to which review type should be used here. Which would you recommend and why?

3. What size of a review team would you recommend for the project in Problem 2, and why? What are the different roles for members of the review team? Which groups should send representatives to participate in the review?

4. Suppose you were a member of a technical training team. Describe the topics that you would include for discussion in training sessions for review leaders.

5. Describe the special role of the review recorder.

6. Discuss the importance of review follow-ups and rework.

7. Based on knowledge of your own coding process and the types of defects that typically appear in your code, design a personal code checklist. Apply it in conjunction with your next programming project, and record your observations. Record your conclusions as to its usefulness for reducing the number of defects in your code.

8. Arrange a practice code inspection session with your classmates or colleagues. Use a personal checklist, or one developed by your organization. If there are training materials, your inspection team and you should familiarize yourselves with them. Review code you have developed or code developed by a team member. Appoint a leader and recorder, and note the time to inspect the code, the number of lines inspected, and the number and types of defects found. Analyze your findings and write a review report describing the strengths and weaknesses of your inspection procedure.

9. Your organization has just begun a review program. What are some of the metrics you would recommend for collection to evaluate the effectiveness of the program?

10. There is some debate as to whether code should be compiled and then reviewed, or vice versa. Based on your own experiences give an opinion on this matter.

11. **Suppose a group of testers has found 10 defects in unit test and 5 in integration test. What is the DRL for these test phases with unit test as the base for comparison? For the same piece of code, under review prior to test, 35 defects were detected. Compute the DRL for the review versus unit test. Based only on this information, which defect-filtering activity was most effective, and why? If we consider the defects found in unit and integration tests to be code review phase escapes, what is the phase yield for the code review? What does the phase yield measurement tell us about the relative effectiveness of a particular testing/review activity?**

12. **How can adaptation of a model such as the Extended/Modified V-model help support a review program?**

13. **How can review data from past projects be used to aid testers working on current projects?**

REFERENCES

[1] *IEEE Standards Collection for Software Engineering,* 1994 edition, Institute of Electrical and Electronics Engineers, Inc., New York, 1994.

[2] B. Hetzel, *The Complete Guide to Software Testing,* second edition, QED Information Sciences, Inc., Wesley, MA. 1988.

[3] M. Fagen, "Design and code inspections to reduce errors in program development," *IBM Systems Journal,* Vol. 15, No. 3, 1976, pp. 182–211.

[4] G. Myers, "A controlled experiment in program testing and code walkthroughs/inspections," *CACM,* 1978, pp. 760–768.

[5] C. Sauer, D. Jeffery, L. Land, P. Yetton, "The effectiveness of software development technical reviews: a behaviorally motivated program of research," *IEEE Transactions on Software Engineering,* Vol. 26, No. 1, 2000, pp. 1–14.

[6] P. Freedman, G. Weinberg, *Handbook of Walkthroughs, Inspections, and Technical Reviews,* Dorest House Publishing, New York, 1990.

[7] B. Spencer, "Software inspections at Applicon," *CrossTalk, Journal of Defense Software Engineering,* Vol. 7, No. 10. Oct., 1994, pp. 11–17.

[8] *IEEE Standard for Software Reviews and Audits* (IEEE Std 1028-1988), copyright 1989 by IEEE, all rights reserved.

[9] *IEEE Recommended Practices for Software Design Descriptions* (ANSI/IEEE Std 1016–1987), copyright 1987 by IEEE, all rights reserved.

[10] *IEEE Recommended Practices for Software Requirements Specification* (IEEE Std 830–1993). Copyright 1994 by IEEE, all rights reserved.

[11] G. Myers, *The Art of Software Testing,* John Wiley, New York, 1979. E. Kit

[12] E. Kit, *Software Testing in the Real World,* Addison-Wesley, Reading, MA, 1995.

[13] W. Humphrey, *A Discipline for Software Engineering,* Addison-Wesley, Reading, MA, 1995.

A MEASUREMENT PROGRAM

TO SUPPORT PRODUCT

AND PROCESS QUALITY

11.0 The Need for a Formal Test Measurement Program

In preceding chapters of this text procedures and practices have been presented that support increasing levels of testing process proficiency, as well as improved software product quality. These procedures and practices have been discussed within the framework of TMM maturity levels and goals. In order to implement these goals, management and staff have worked together to:

- develop testing and debugging policies;

- develop training programs;

- assemble teams of qualified staff;

- define, collect, and apply simple test-related measurements for controlling and monitoring of tests;

- implement test planning;

- institutionalize basic testing techniques and methods;

- develop a technical review program;

- implement a simple defect repository.

Achieving these goals has had the benefit of putting into place a technical, managerial, and staffing infrastructure capable of continuous support for testing process improvements. With this infrastructure in place, a formal test measurement program can be established to encourage further growth and accomplishment. Such a program is essential for engineering both product and process. Indeed, if we consider ourselves to be members of an engineering profession then measurements and a measurement program must assume a central role in our practice. In our field, measurements are essential for achieving engineering goals such as:

- quantitative management of the testing process;

- evaluating the quality and effectiveness of the testing process;

- assessing the productivity of the testing personnel;

- estimating and tracking testing costs;

- monitoring test process improvement efforts;

- developing quantitative quality goals for software work products;

- supporting software quality evaluation;

- test process optimization;

- defect prevention;

- software quality control.

Note that a formal test measurement program in the context of these goals has two focal areas: it supports both *process* and *product* quality evaluation and improvement.

A formal test measurement program must be carefully planned and managed. Measurements to be collected should be identified, and decisions made on how they should be organized, stored, and used, and by whom. Intelligent tools should support data collection and analysis so that software engineers do not feel burdened by the measurement process and can give it their fullest support.

This text has covered measurement topics in previous chapters. For example, Chapter 9 introduced measurements in the context of the TMM level 3 maturity goal, "controlling and monitoring of the testing process." Chapter 9 also suggested that an organization should begin to collect data related to the testing process starting at TMM level 1. Some initial measurements that have been suggested include:

Size of the software product (KLOC)
Number of requirements or features to be tested
Number of incident reports
Number of defects/KLOC
Number of test cases developed
Costs for each testing task
Number of test cases executed

These measurements, and others as described in Chapter 9, are both process and product related. For example, measurements in the categories of monitoring test status, tester productivity, and testing costs are useful for understanding the current testing process state, showing project trends, and monitoring improvement efforts. Measurements relating to errors, faults (defects), and failures as described in Chapter 9 can help testers to evaluate product quality. Additional defect-related measures are described in Chapter 3. In that chapter it was recommended that an organization at the lower TMM levels begin to assemble defect-related measurements in the context of a simple defect repository. The recommended practice was that defects found in each project should be catalogued with respect to attributes such as defect type, phase injected, phase detected, and impact on the users. Other defect-related data such as frequency of occurrence and time to repair were also recommended for inclusion.

Realizing the need for measurement, and collecting and applying a simple group of measurements, are first steps for developing a measurement program in an organization. Organizations at TMM levels 1 through 3 usually find themselves at this stage of measurement practice. When the first steps have been taken, an organization needs to evolve further in its measurement practices. In fact, a hierarchy of metrics acceptance and practice has been described by Grady [1] derived from his experiences at Hewlett-Packard (HP). He observed that a measurement (metrics) program evolves and passes through the following phases:

(i) acceptance of the need for measurement;
(ii) project trend data available;
(iii) common terminology; data comparisons;
(iv) experiments validating best practices with data;
(v) data collection automated; analysis with expert system support.

These phases imply that (i) an organization should realize that measurement can support improvement in process and product quality, (ii) measurements should be used to track project direction and for guidance in future related projects, (iii) measurements should be defined for the overall organization so data can be compared over many projects (so you aren't comparing apples and oranges), (iv) measurements should be used to evaluate and then validate best practices, and (v) automated tools (with intelligent components) should be available to support software engineers in collecting and analyzing data.

In order to achieve quantitative quality control of both process and product, measurements additional to those suggested in Chapters 3 and 9 are needed. Moving toward TMM level 4, an organization will realize the need for these additional measures to achieve greater levels of test process maturity. Anticipating these needs the TMM calls for a formal test measurement program as a maturity goal to be achieved at level 4.

For most organizations it may be practical to implement such a test measurement program as a supplement to a general measurement program. A general measurement program can support overall process improvement. This is illustrated in the Capability Maturity Model which has associated with each Key Process Area (KPA) a common feature called "measurement and analysis" [2]. Implicit in the CMM structure is the importance of measurement for process evaluation and improvement and for achieving higher levels of software quality. In the TMM the need for a test measurement program is more explicit as reflected in the measurement-related maturity goal at TMM level 4. Implicit support for measurement comes from recommendations for measurement collection and application at TMM levels 3 and below.

11.1 Some Measurement-Related Definitions

Before we begin the discussion of steps to initiate a measurement program, some basic definitions need to be presented. Two of these definitions appear in Chapter 2 and will be repeated here for review. Relevant definitions also appear in IEEE standards documents, and in a metrics text and a paper by Fenton. [3–6].

Measure

A measure is an empirical objective assignment of a number (or symbol) to an entity to characterize a particular attribute.

Measurement

Measurement is the act of measuring.

Metric

(A similar definition can be applied to the term "software quality metric.")

A metric is a quantitative measure of the degree to which a system, system component, or process possesses a given attribute [4].

Quality attribute

A characteristic of software or a genetic term that is applied to quality factor, subfactor, or metric value [3].

Quality factor

A management-oriented attribute of a piece of software that contributes to its quality [3].

Quality subfactor

A decomposition of a quality factor or subfactor into its technical components [3].

Quality requirement

A requirement that a software attribute be present in the software to satisfy a contract, standard, specification, or any other formal or binding document [3].

11.2 Initiating a Measurement Program

How does one begin to implement a formal measurement program? A first step would be to form a measurement committee, team, or task force to plan for the program and oversee its implementation. This team could have members from management, development, testing, process, and software quality assurance groups. The work of Grady and Caswell as described in their text entitled *Software Metrics: Establishing a Companywide Program* is a useful guide to initiate such a effort. Their work is based on experiences with a very successful measurement program initiated at Hewlett-Packard (HP) [7]. They describe the key role of a team called the "Metrics Council" which was responsible for implementing the program.

The major steps useful for putting a general measurement program into place are described in the Grady and Caswell text [7]. These steps, adapted from the text, are shown in Figure 11.1, and are described here with permission from Pearson Education. The following discussion of the steps is augmented with comments relating to a test measurement component. Keep in mind that the measurement program phases described below can be implemented as:

- a general measurement program with a test measurement program as a component;

- a stand-alone test measurement program.

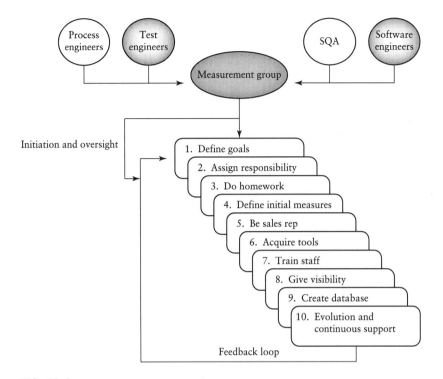

FIG. 11.1

Phases in establishing and maintaining a measurement program from Software Metrics: Establishing a Companywide Program *by Grady and Caswell. Adapted with permission from Pearson Education, Upper Saddle River, NJ [7].*

The latter could work well in an organization that lacks a general measurement program, and is working on achieving TMM maturity goals. In this case the organization may wish to begin with the implementation of a specialized test-oriented measurement program that will eventually evolve into a general measurement program. Under these circumstances, where there are limited resources, this approach may be very attractive.

The measurement program steps as described by Grady and Caswell are as follows [7]:

1. Define Company/Project Goals with Respect to the Measurement Program.

An organization should have some clear indication of goals to be achieved with respect to the measurement program. The goal statement should answer questions such as the purpose of the program, what the measurements will be used for, who will use them, how much the organization is willing to invest in the program, what are the benefits/risks of a program, which levels of management support the program, and what is the priority level of the program?

For the testing domain, testing measurement program goals should be established. These can supplement a test or SQA policy statement.

2. Assign Responsibility.

The organization should decide who will be responsible for implementing and overseeing the measurement program. This decision indicates the functional organization/group and specific members of that organization/group responsible for carrying out measurement goals and policies. The constituency of a measurement program team could include members from development, test, process improvement, and/or a software quality assurance group. The extent of the group depends on the size of the organization, its structure, the resources it is willing to expend, and the scope of the measurement program.

Responsible staff should assemble a measurement program plan that outlines the goals, procedures, resources, staff, tasks, and costs involved. Assigning responsibilities helps to give visibility to the measurement program, and supports the cultural changes it invokes. The group responsible for measurement will also be the change agents and will support the adaptation of the metrics program throughout the organization. Grady and Caswell compare the role of the measurement program team to that of a team of sale representatives (see item 5), in light of their responsibility to sell the usefulness of the program to managers, developers, testers, and other technical personnel.

A good approach to developing a stand-alone test measurement program is to have it fall under the umbrella of the testing organization, possibly in conjunction with SQA staff. This group should define the measures to collect, design forms to collect the measures, select tools for assistance in collection and analysis, and contact the technical training group to provide proper training as described in phase 7 below. Specific personnel who will collect, analyze, and apply the measurements should be identified. As part of their measurement program responsibilities, test personal should be involved in collecting defect data, and they should take part in establishing and maintaining the defect repository.

3. Gather Background Material.

To support the developing measurement program, measurement group members and responsible staff should search the literature to identify useful measurements and the procedures and practices required to support the specific objectives of their organization. Measures that support process and product quality evaluation allow for the observation of trends and support estimations using data from past projects are particularity useful. For guidance in this area, books by Grady [1] and by Grady and Caswell [7] are very helpful. These books have an extensive bibliography with many sources and references. For testers, a useful source is Chapter 9 of this text and sections at the end of this chapter which provide an ample collection of measurements. Additional references are found in the appendices of this text. Perry also has a list of test measurements [8].

In terms of homework to be done, it is also useful for the measurement group to consult the IEEE standards document, *Software Quality Metrics Methodology,* which describes an approach to establishing quality requirements and identifying quality metrics [3]. In this context, the standards document contains a framework for defining quality factors, subfactors, and metrics that can be applied to measuring the quality of a software system. Finally, the measurement team may also want to consult the IEEE standard for *Software Productivity Metrics* as an additional information source [9].

4. Define the Initial Metrics to Collect.

Given that background information has been collected, goals for the program have been set, and responsibilities assigned, the measurement group will next need to identify and define an initial set of measurements. These should be simple, easy to collect and use, and cost effective. The group needs to be sure that the selected metrics are valid, that is, that each measure is a proper numerical characteristic of the claimed attribute [5]. For example, a valid measure of the attribute program length must really be a measure of that characteristic; it should not contradict an intuitive notion of what length is. Fenton has a discussion of how validation has been performed for existing metrics [5].

Metrics related to software size, number of defects, and effort are recommended by Grady and Caswell to initiate the measurement program. In the test measurement domain these can be mapped to measures such as the size of test harness (lines of test harness code), number of test cases developed, number of test cases executed/unit time, number of defects/lines of code, and costs of testing tasks.

The metrics need to be standardized for overall organizational use. For example, if software engineers are collecting measurements on software size the measurement group will need to decide on units for size. If a line of code is used as a unit, then the group must define what is meant by a line of code, and how to count a line of code. Line-counting tools that are based on coding and counting standards will greatly facilitate the collection of size measures.

In addition to the standards, the measurement group will also need to design forms for collecting the data that can be applied organization-wide. At Hewlett-Packard the forms defined a common terminology for the organization. These were filled out and sent to the designated group or team which incorporated the data into a database. An example form for collecting size data is found in Figure 11.2.

5. Be a Sales Representative.

This is the measurement program development phase where the team takes on a salesman's role. They will need to convince the members of the technical staff of the usefulness of the measures, starting with the initial set. If the measurement team is convincing, then the staff will be motivated and later commit to implementing a more extensive set of measurements. Project managers/test managers should also be convinced of measurement benefits so that they will allocate resources for measurement collection and analysis, and apply the measurements to evaluate and improve process and product quality.

```
┌─────────────────────────────────────────────────────────────┐
│                                                               │
│                    The X Corporation                          │
│                  Size Measurement Form                        │
│                                                               │
│   Product Identifier _____   Programming Language _____ │
│   Name _____         Date _____  │
│   Release Number _____       Line Counting Tool _____ │
│                                                               │
│                                                               │
│   Number of compiler directives                               │
│                                                               │
│   Number of data declarations                                 │
│                                                               │
│   Number of executable lines                                  │
│                                                               │
│   Number of noncommented source lines (subtotal)              │
│                                                               │
│   Number of comment lines                                     │
│                                                               │
│   Number of blank lines                                       │
│                                                               │
│   Total lines                                                 │
│                                                               │
│   Lines of documentation                                      │
│                                                               │
│                                                               │
└─────────────────────────────────────────────────────────────┘
```

FIG. 11.2

Sample measurement collection form.

6. Acquire Tools for Automated Collection and Analysis.

To ease the burden that measurement imposes on the technical staff, tools should be acquired or developed in-house to facilitate the data collection/analysis process. The tools can simplify data collection, increase the accuracy of the data, reduce time expended, and support consistency and completeness. For the testing domain tools such as coverage analyzers (see Chapter 14) can greatly facilitate measurement of the degree of coverage during testing. Tools that perform statistical analysis, draw plots, and output trend reports are also very useful.

7. Train the Staff.

At TMM level 3 a technical training program is in place to support this measurement program requirement. The presence of a training program in the context of the TMM introduces the staff to quality issues, and facilitates preparing developers/testers for the collection and analysis of measurement data and the use of measurement tools (see Chapter 8). The CMM also calls for a training program as one of its Key Process Areas (KPA) at CMM level 3 [2]. This program should support metrics training. If an organization does not have a training program, one should be established that includes full coverage of quality and measurement concepts.

Training gives visibility to the measurement program, and supports the accurate and consistent collection and analysis of the data. With proper training staff members will gain an appreciation of the benefits of the measurement program. Training also helps to ensure that the measurement program will be applied across the organization.

Another issue that needs to be addressed here is a human or cultural issue—people do not like to be measured. Initially they may have a very negative view of the measurement program. Properly trained staff and management need to ensure that goals for all measurements are specified and that anonymity of individuals is retained where possible. In order to get the full cooperation of all concerned staff members they need to be assured that the measures collected will not be used against them. Management and trained staff should set up the proper cultural environment to support the measurement program. A major task of the measurement program sales representatives as described in phase 5 is to insure that all of these concerns are addressed.

8. Give Visibility to Measurement Program Successes, and Promote the Exchange of Ideas.

Successful application of measurements should be made visible within the organization. This promotes motivation and pride in the program for the participants and attracts other interested parties. A newsletter, and/or a series of internal presentations, can be used to promote the exchange of ideas. Outside publication of books and papers also promotes this goal.

9. Create Measurement Databases.

Data is an organizational asset! Therefore the measurements collected should be stored in one or more databases so the information is available for use in current and future projects. Storing the measurement data systematically using a database system will promote standardized data definitions and data usage throughout the organization for purposes such as:

- process analysis and improvement efforts;

- defect prevention activities;

- trend analysis;

- software quality evaluation and improvement;

- planning/cost/effort estimation.

The measurement team must ensure that the measurements are validated before being stored and used for decision making. A discussion of measurement validation is beyond the scope of this book. Good sources of material on this subject include books by Grady and Caswell, Fenton, and IEEE standards documents [3,5,7].

Many different kinds of measurements may be collected and utilized by an organization, and this may result in the need for more that one database system to store and retrieve the measurement information. For example, there may be a project database, a test database, a review database, and a detect database (repository). A test database is a good place to store test measurements from all projects, for example, measurements such as:

Degree of statement, branch, data flow, basis path, etc., coverage—planned/actual

Number or degree of requirements or features covered—planned/actual

Number of planned test cases

Number of planned tests cases executed and passed

Size of the test harness (LOC)

Estimated time and/or budget for each testing task

Actual time/and or budget for each testing task

Number of test cases developed/unit time

Many other test-related measurements are useful and could be included in such a database. Section 11.4 describes a more complete set of test-related measurements that are appropriate for each of the TMM levels.

As part of the discussion of measurement databases we return to the defect repository, which is essentially a database for storing and retrieving defect-related measurements. The benefits of having this information available were described in Chapter 3. The presence of a test organization and training and review programs as described for TMM level 3 supports the development and maintenance of the defect repository. The existence of the formal measurement program called for at TMM level 4 also gives strong support for the evolution of such a repository. An organization at TMM level 4 is in the position of having dedicated and trained testing staff, and in the context of the measurement program these staff members can (i) refine an existing classification taxonomy for the defects developed at lower TMM levels; and (ii) develop standards that specify the information to be stored with each unit of defect data. Figure 11.3 shows the contents of an example defect record suitable for a defect database organized by project. Additional information can be added to a defect record when the practice of defect causal analysis is introduced at TMM level 5 (see discussion of defect prevention in Chapter 13).

In addition to defect, review, and test data, there are many other types of measurements that can be associated with organizational projects. As stated in phase 4 of the measurement program description, an organization must decide on which measurements are most useful to achieve its goals. The costs and benefits of collecting these measurements, and maintaining the measurement databases, should be evaluated. After a measurement is deemed to be beneficial, decisions should be made on how the measurement will be validated, stored, and utilized.

10. Provide Continuous Support for the Measurement Program.

A measurement program is not a static entity. For a measurement program to contribute to organizational efforts for product and process improvement on a continual basis it needs a permanent group of overseers who will carry out phases 1–9 in response to the continuous evolution of organizational polices and goals. New measures may be introduced, and existing measures and measurement standards may be modified or retired. Hewlett-Packard (HP) has a Metrics Council which initiated, and contin-

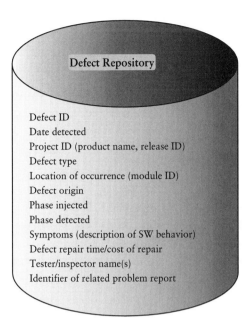

Defect Repository

Defect ID
Date detected
Project ID (product name, release ID)
Defect type
Location of occurrence (module ID)
Defect origin
Phase injected
Phase detected
Symptoms (description of SW behavior)
Defect repair time/cost of repair
Tester/inspector name(s)
Identifier of related problem report

FIG. 11.3
Sample defect record contents.

ues to oversee, its measurement program [7]. The council has about 20 members selected from various HP divisions representing developers and quality assurance groups. Since the measurement program was put in place the council has continued to meet about twice a year, one time for a major meeting that lasts over several days and features workshops and speakers. A minor meeting is also scheduled principally for information exchange and recognition of current measurement efforts. The council sees its principal missions as:

- being responsible for measurement standards change and approval;

- keeping abreast of research efforts;

- performing measurement-related experiments and reporting results;

- publication of metrics information and results internally;

- keeping the measurement program visible throughout the organization;

- providing motivation and enthusiasm to staff;

- being actively involved in software process improvement efforts.

In addition to the Metrics Council at HP, a body called the Software Engineering Lab (SEL) continually supports the measurement program. It works with members of the council, resolving critical issues and monitoring action items that surface during the council meetings. The SEL also provides references/papers from the literature to the council in support of phase 3 activities.

Each organization needs to decide on a group/team structure that will provide continuous support for its measurement program. The structure should be a good fit in terms of the organizational units, and available resources and goals for the program. A variety of staff should be selected for membership in the group; for example, developers, testers, process engineers, and software quality assurance group members as shown in Figure 11.1. There are major costs associated with setting up such a program, but the benefits are well documented [1,2,7].

11.3 Software Quality Evaluation

Developing a test measurement program is one of the maturity goals to be achieved at TMM level 4. Another related maturity goal at level 4 calls for software quality evaluation to ensure that the software meets its requirements and that the customer is satisfied with the product. One of the purposes of software quality evaluation at this level of the TMM is to relate software quality issues to the adequacy of the testing process. Software quality evaluation involves defining quality attributes, quality metrics, and measurable quality goals for evaluating software work products. Quality goals are tied to testing process adequacy since a mature testing process must lead to software that is at least correct, reliable, usable, maintainable, portable, and secure.

Software quality evaluation is supported by having a dedicated testing group, technical training, a review program, and a measurement program in place. Addressing the maturity goals at each level of the TMM will ensure that the necessary staff and programs are part of the organizational infrastructure.

Each software product will have different quality requirements. Therefore, test and quality plans should include a specification of tests (both static and dynamic) that will ensure that the quality requirements are met. Quality requirements are often expressed in terms of quality factors such as reliability, functionality, maintainability, and usability. Some of these may not directly measurable, and so they need to be decomposed further into quality subfactors and finally into a set of metrics. This type of decomposition hierarchy is shown in Figure 11.4. It is adapted from material discussed in the *IEEE Standard for a Software Quality Metrics Methodology* [3].

To examine the nature of a decomposition we will use the quality factor "maintainability" as our first example. Maintainability is defined in IEEE standards as "an attribute that relates to the amount of effort needed to make changes in the software" [3]. Maintainability, according to the standard, can be partitioned into the quality subfactors: testability, correctability, and expandability.

Testability is usually described as an indication of the degree of testing effort required.

Correctability is described as the degree of effort required to correct errors in the software and to handle user complaints.

Expandability is the degree of effort required to improve or modify the efficiency or functions of the software.

Each of these subfactors have measures associated with them such as time to close a problem report, number of test cases required to achieve branch coverage, change count, and change size [3].

Another decomposition example is the quality factor *functionality* which is described as "an attribute that relates to the existence of certain properties and functions that satisfy stated or implied user needs." It can be decomposed into the subfactors [3]:

Completeness: The degree to which the software possesses the necessary and sufficient functions to satisfy the users needs.

Correctness: The degree to which the software performs its required functions.

Security: The degree to which the software can detect and prevent information leak, information loss, illegal use, and system resource destruction.

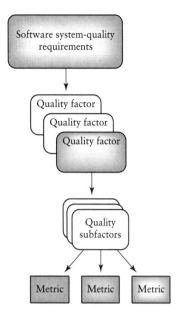

FIG. 11.4

A quality requirement decomposition scheme [3].

Compatibility: The degree to which new software can be installed without changing environments and conditions that were prepared for the replaced software.

Interoperability: The degree to which the software can be connected easily with other systems and operated.

These subfactors also have measures associated with them that can be collected for software quality evaluation. For example, *completeness* can be estimated using the ratio of number of completed documents or software components to the total number of planned documents or software components.

In addition to *maintainability* and *functionality*, the IEEE standard document for Software Quality Metrics Methodology also has examples of other quality factors such as efficiency, portability, reliability, and usability [3]. The document also describes the subfactors associated with these factors. For each of these selected there will be a group of measurements that can be defined for them in the context of a measurement program (an iteration of phase 4). The standards document also describes a five-step methodology that guides an organization in establishing quality requirements, applying software metrics that relate to these requirements, and analyzing and validating the results. These steps can be applied by an organization that is addressing the TMM level 4 maturity goal of "software quality evaluation." The steps support the development of quality requirements as specified in the TMM. In this context the TMM recommends that:

- resources be allocated in project, test, and quality plans so that quality requirements can be achieved;

- client input for the development of the requirements is essential, and should be solicited;

- acceptance test(s) be the setting in which the user/client group can assess whether the quality requirements have been met.

The five steps in the IEEE-recommended methodology are shown in Figure 11.5 and are described below [3]. As the reader proceeds through the steps the importance of, and interdependencies between, a measurement program, a training program, and dedicated testing staff will become apparent.

1. Establish Software Quality Requirements.

This requires a list of quality factors to be selected, prioritized, and quantified at the start of product development or when changes are being made to an existing product. The quality requirements should be represented in the form of direct or predictive values, for example, reliability as "mean-time-to-failure," which can be measured directly or "number of design and code defects," which may be an indicator or predictor of reliability.

The requirements are used to guide and monitor product development. Clients should be part of the team that establishes the requirements. The requirements should be prioritized and their feasibility analyzed. Conflicting requirements should be identified and the conflicts resolved. Clients should also actively participate in acceptance testing where the

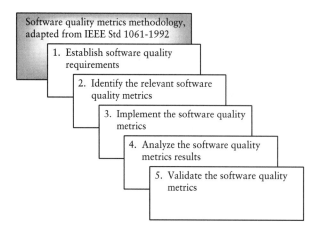

FIG. 11.5

Steps in Software Quality Metrics Methodology adapted from IEEE Std 1061–1992 [5].

final evaluation with respect to quality requirements will be made. During the software development life cycle testers should be part of the team that determines whether the evolving software is meeting the quality requirements.

2. Identify the Relevant Software Quality Metrics.

A decomposition as shown in Figure 11.3 is applied to each requirement (factor) to identify quality subfactors and metrics. The metrics selected should be validated metrics. For each metric selected assign a target value, a critical value, and a range that should be achieved during development. These may be called planned, best, and worst values as prescribed by Gilb's work and discussed below. The framework and the target values for the metrics should be viewed by clients, managers, and technical staff. This step also supports a cost–benefit analysis for implementation of the metrics.

3. Implement the Software Quality Metrics.

The data to be collected should be described. A procedure for collection should be established. Pilot projects can be selected to test the measurement procedures. As a project progresses the data is collected. Part of the testing effort would be to collect quality-related data such as degree of coverage, complexity, test plan completeness, and so on. Time and tools should be allocated in the project and test plans for collecting data.

4. Analyze the Metrics Results.

The measurement results are analyzed and reported to help monitor the project and to evaluate the evolving software. Metrics that indicate low quality for software components should be subject to further scrutiny. Further scrutiny may lead to alternative conclusions, for example:

(i)   the software should be redesigned;
(ii) the software should be discarded;
(iii) the software should be left unchanged.

Actions based on such evaluations should be cautious since measurements are not infallible and poor evaluations may not necessarily mean the software will perform poorly in operation.

5. Validate the Software Quality Metrics.

The purpose of metrics validation is to identify process and product metrics that can predict specified quality factor values. Quality factors, as we have learned, are quantitative representations of quality requirements. If the metrics we have selected are to be useful to us, they need to indicate accurately whether the quality requirements have been achieved or are likely to be achieved in the future. If predictive metrics have been used they need to be validated to determine if they accurately measure their associated factors. To consider a metric valid it must demonstrate a high degree of association with the quality factor it represents. Criteria for validity evaluation are given in the IEEE standards document [3]. Finally, it should be noted that in many cases, if a predictive metric is used in a different environment it may need revalidation.

In addition to the IEEE standards documents, support for software quality evaluation also comes from the work of Gilb [10]. Among his contributions is a template called an "attribute specification format template" that can be used to clearly describe measurable system attributes. These templates can be very useful for documenting quality requirements for a given project (as described in step 2 in the software quality metrics methodology).

Among the template components described by Gilb are [10]:

Scale: describes the scale (measurement units) that will be used for the measurement; for example, time in minutes to do a simple repair.

Test: This describes the required practical tests and measurement tools needed to collect the measurement data.

Plan: This is the value or level an organization plans to achieve for this quality metric. It should be of a nature that will satisfy the users/clients. (An example would be a planned system response time of 5 seconds.)

Best: This is the best level that can be achieved; it may be state-of-the-art, an engineering limit for this particular development environment, but is not an expected level to be reached in this project. (An example would be a best system response time of 3.5 seconds.)

Worst: This indicates the minimal level on the measurement scale for acceptance by the users/clients. Any level worse than this level indicates total system failure, no matter how good the other system attributes are. (An example would be a system response time of 6 seconds.)

Now: This is the current level for this attribute in an existing system. It can be used for comparison with planned and worst levels for this project.

See: This template component provides references to more detailed or related documents.

It should be noted the "Test" component of the template can be specified for testing activities that occur in different phases of software development, for example,

Test (design phase)	Fagen inspection
Test (unit test)	Standard unit test procedures
Test (system test)	Performance and stress

Some examples of product- and process-related measurement descriptions that can be collected by testers are shown below. Product-related measures may be associated with quality goals for the project. Descriptive remarks are also included to support data collection.

Suppose a quality goal is to reach a specified level of performance. It is appropriate for testers to collect data during system test relating to:

Response time. Record time in seconds for processing and responding to a user request. (Descriptive remarks for data collection: An average value for the response time should be derived from not less than 75 representative requests, both under normal load and under stress conditions.)

Memory usage. Record number of bytes used by the application and for overhead. (Descriptive remarks for data collection: Data should be collected for normal and heavy stress and volume.)

To address quality goals such as testability, the following can be collected by the testers:

Cyclomatic complexity. (Descriptive remarks for data collection: McCabes' cyclomatic complexity should be calculated using tool support. Collect during detailed design and/or code. If value of complexity is greater than 10, review, and seriously consider redesign.)

Number of test cases required to achieve a specified coverage goal. Count for code structures such as statement or branch. (Descriptive remarks for data collection: Testers initially estimate number based on structure of pseudo code during detailed design. Revise during coding and make proper modifications to test plan attachments.)

Testing effort-unit test. Record cumulative time in hours for testers to execute unit tests for an application. (Descriptive remarks for data collection: Collect data from daily time logs of qualified testers. Convert time into costs using compensation data.)

For addressing goals with respect to maintainability, the following measurements are appropriate for testers to collect:

Number of changes to the software. (Descriptive remarks for data collection: Count number of problem reports)

Mean time to make a change or repair. Record mean-time-to-repair (MTTR) in time units of minutes. (Descriptive remarks for data collection: Use daily repair logs from actual defects repaired or conduct tests with artificially injected defects of typical types for this project. Consult defect repository for examples. The log sample should contain logs from at least four qualified maintainers. Total time includes time for finding, correcting, and retesting a change/repair. Time can be converted to costs using compensation data)

For additional sources of information on software quality evaluation, testers and SQA staff can refer to the work of Grady and Caswell who describe the Hewlett-Packard approach to defining and measuring quality attributes [7]. These researchers have a quality attribute model called FURPS, whose high-level components include functionality (F), usability (U), reliability (R), performance (P), and supportability (S). FURPS are decomposable into lower level and measurable quality attributes. Other sources for quality attribute hierarchies have been reported; for example, in the work of McCall [11] and Boehm [12]. The International Organization for Standards also has a collection of key quality attributes— ISO/IECIS 9126 [13].

11.4 Measurements and TMM Levels

Although the TMM does not call for a formal measurement program until level 4, it is important for organizations at all TMM levels to collect measurements to help define a baseline process, to aid in process understanding, and to provide support for achievement of testing maturity goals. Measurement also benefit organizations in the following areas:

• identification of testing strengths and weaknesses;

• providing insights into the current state of the testing process;

• evaluating testing risks;

• benchmarking;

• improving planning;

• improving testing effectiveness;

- evaluating and improving product quality;

- measuring productivity;

- determining level of customer involvement and satisfaction;

- supporting controlling and monitoring of the testing process;

- comparing processes and products with those both inside and outside the organization.

Previous discussions in this text have advised that an organization should begin a measurement effort with a simple set of measures and expand the set as it reaches for higher levels of the TMM. Measurements selected should provide support for achieving and maintaining testing goals and best testing practices. Managers should keep in mind that adding measurement responsibilities to those already assigned to developers and testers results in an increase in their work load. Simple tools should be made available to each software engineer to support data collection. Examples of recommended tools are:

- spreadsheet programs;

- database programs;

- personal digital assistant;

- laptop computer.

More sophisticated tools to collect and record data, and to issue reports, are introduced at higher TMM levels as described in Chapter 14.

The next several subsections in this chapter describe a set of measurements that are applicable at each of the TMM levels. These measurements are recommended and *not* mandatory. Organizations can select a small number of initial measurements and build on these as their test process matures.

11.4.1 Measurements for TMM Level 1

TMM level 1 has no maturity goals. However, it is important for organizations to begin to collect basic measurements at this level. In this way an organization begins to build a historical database of project data that is invaluable for achieving higher levels of test process proficiency and general process maturity. The basic measurements suggested for TMM 1 are aimed at establishing a baseline process and preparing the organization for addressing TMM level 2 maturity goals. Some examples of initial measurements to collect at TMM level 1 are listed below. Support for these choices comes from the work of Grady and Caswell who recommend these classes of measurements to initiate a measurement program [7].

The suggested measurements for TMM level 1 are:

- Size measurements

   Size of the software product (KLOC)
   Size of the test harness
   Number of requirements or features to be tested
   Number of test cases developed
   Number of test cases executed

- Defect measurements

   Number of incident reports
   Number of defects/KLOC

- Cost/Effort

   Costs for the project as a whole
   Hours spent in testing tasks
   Costs of the testing efforts.

Size is an important measurement used for project and test planning, cost/effort estimations, risk evaluation, productivity measures, and for normalization of other product and process attributes. A normalization example is defect density which is total number of defects/KLOC. Size in the testing domain can be represented in several ways. For example, the size of the test harness, the number of requirements or features to be tested, the number of test cases developed, and executed, all give an indication of the volume of the testing effort and can be useful for the test planner. Automated line counters can be used to count lines of code and will work to produce consistent counts for all projects if they are based on a line counting standard and adherence to a coding standard [14].

In addition to size, defect data should be collected by an organization at lower levels of the TMM so that there is a documented record of the actual number found in its software products. The overall defect count can later be partitioned by test phases and identification of "phase injected" and "phase found" for each defect (see measurements for TMM level 2). The defect data will help to evaluate software quality, support improvements in the development and testing processes, and provide the basis for initiating a defect repository.

The cost measurements listed above will assist with test cost estimation when test planning is formally initiated at TMM level 2. By collecting the cost/effort measurements an organization begins to assemble a historical cost database that is invaluable for estimating these items in future projects.

11.4.2 Measurements for TMM Level 2

At TMM level 2 an organization should select measurements that continue to support baselining the testing process and also achievement and sustainment of level 2 maturity goals. There are three maturity goals at this level: "Establishing a test planning process," "Developing testing and debugging goals and policies," and "Institutionalizing basic testing techniques and methods." To support test planing, the size and cost/effort metrics previously suggested for TMM level 1 are useful. In addition, measures of the distribution of time/effort in the various testing phases should be collected to support and evaluate the effectiveness of multilevel testing activities. For example:

> *Time/effort spent in test planning (this can be distributed over the hierarchy of test plans)*
> *Time/effort spent in unit testing*
> *Time/effort spent in integration testing*
> *Time/effort spent in system testing*
> *Time/effort spent in regression testing*
> *Total time/effort spent in testing*

For finer granularity the above can be decomposed into lower-level measurements for each testing phase. For example:

Time spent in test design for unit (integration, system, etc.) testing
Time spent in test execution for unit (integration, system, etc.) testing

Other measurements that are useful for initiating, evaluating, and improving test planning are:

Number of planned test cases
Number of unplanned test cases
Cost performance index(CPI)
Planned/actual degree of statement/branch coverage

The cost performance index is the ratio of planned testing time and actual testing time [14]. This is a simple measure that provides information about the quality of test plans. Ideally, the ratio should be close to one. If it is less than 1.0, the organization is spending more time then planned on testing. If it is much greater than 1.0, planning is too conservative. The first two measurements of this group can also be partitioned by testing level, for example, number of planned test cases for unit test, and so on.

The measure of time spent in fixing/repairing defects (by testing level) should also be recorded so that an organization is able to understand and evaluate the cost and impact of fixing defects. If the costs are recorded by level found, an organization should discover the increased costs of repairing defects as they propagate into later testing phases (and finally into operational software). The organization can compare the defect repair costs to the costs of quality activities that reduce defects. An appreciation of the cost effectiveness of the latter should result. This measurement will also help to distinguish testing from debugging activities, and allow test and project planners to identify distinct testing and debugging tasks, develop policy statements, and allocate appropriate resources.

To support achievement of the maturity goals at TMM level 2, the continued collection of other defect-related measurements is also important. The number of defects is counted as in TMM level 1 but is now distributed over the testing levels. The frequency of occurrence for defects of each type should also be recorded. Recommended measurements are:

Number of defects injected in each life cycle phase
Number defects found in each testing phase (levels)
Number of each type of defect found (a defect classification scheme
as described in Chapter 3 should be developed)

Additional defect attributes as shown in Figure 11.3 can be added to the defect data set as an organization matures and builds a comprehensive defect repository. At TMM level 4, building a comprehensive defect repository is a recommend practice.

The measurements described here provide support for evaluating the relative effectiveness of each level of testing, and they also help an organization to evaluate the impact of changes to the testing process. At higher levels of the TMM data of the latter type will support defect prevention activities, test effectiveness, and evaluation. By initiating the collection of detailed defect-related data and associating defects with specific projects, a foundation is being laid for:

- defect prevention activities;

- setting quality goals for future projects;

- risk management for subsequent releases.

11.4.3 Measurements for TMM Level 3

The maturity goals at TMM level 3 include "Controlling and monitoring the testing process," "Integrating testing into the software life cycle," "Establishing a technical training program," and "Establishing a test organization." At TMM level 3 a test group is established, and this group should be prepared through the training program to collect, store, analyze, and apply measurements for improvement of processes and products. The training program should also include modules that focus on evaluation and use of testing and measurement tools. At TMM level 3 tool support should be available to support the collection of data. Defect trackers and coverage analyzers are examples of useful tools in this area (see Chapter 14). Since there is a training program and a dedicated testing group, an organization at TMM level 3 may decide it is useful and cost effective to develop an internal set of forms and tools for collecting and analyzing test data.

Chapter 9 of this text is a good source for appropriate measures to collect at TMM level 3 in the context of the "controlling and monitoring" maturity goal. The set in Chapter 9 includes measurements for controlling and monitoring testing status, tester productivity, testing costs, and errors, faults, and failures. Measurements are also suggested for evaluating test process effectiveness and to make stop-test decisions. For review, some example measurements from Chapter 9 are:

Degree of statement, branch, data flow, coverage achieved to date
Number of features covered to date
Number of planned test cases executed and passed
Number of test cases produced/week (for each tester)
Planned earned value for testing tasks
Defect removal leverage (DRL)
Fault seeding ratios
Number of defects detected/unit time period/severity level (a defect tracking tool can support collection and recording of this data)

At TMM level 3 an organization is also developing a technical training program. Some measurements useful for evaluating and improving the program would be:

Size of the training staff
Costs of the training program (total and per training module)
Time to master a training module
Time allocated for training sessions per tester

To evaluate the cost effectiveness of tools, an organization may also want to measure:

Costs of tool evaluation
Costs of tool training
Cost of tool acquisition
Cost of tool update and maintenance (especially if tools are developed in-house)

The organization can apply some of these cost measurements to evaluate the impact of training and tools using ratios such as:

Cost/efforts of performing testing tasks before and after training
Cost/efforts of performing testing tasks before and after tool support

The organization should also monitor the number of defects detected both before and after the introduction of training and tools.

Another useful measure that can support the maturity goal of "establishing a test organization" by giving visibility to testers is:

Tester/developer ratio

This measure can also be used to assist in test planning. The ratio indicates the number of dedicated testers relative to the number of developers for each project. At lower levels of the TMM there is no dedicated testing group; however, some development staff may be designated as testers. As an organization matures and designates more resources to software testing, a specific role is defined for the tester. Training and tool support become available, and therefore it is meaningful to measure the ratio of testers to developers for different types of projects. Ratios may range from 1/4 to 1/2 depending on the nature of the project. Ratios from past projects are useful in estimating testing resources and costs for testing planning when the characteristics of the new project are a good match with those in the historical project data base (see section on testing cost estimation in Chapter 7).

Since there is a test organization at TMM level 3, and members of that organization interact with users/clients, a useful measure of user/client involvement with testers is user/client hours spent providing inputs for acceptance test plans and/or use cases. At higher TMM levels a measurement of the time spent supporting the development of operational profiles may also be useful for the organization.

At TMM level 3 organization should also be collecting data relating to help or hot-line calls and the number of problem reports submitted when the software is in operation. This data will shed light on the number of defects that have escaped from the testing process, and allows for a more complete assessment of software quality. The measures could also be used to assess the impact of process changes on software quality. Appropriate measures are:

Number of help or hot-line calls (for a particular software product)

Number of customer complaints
Number of problem reports when the software is in operation
Number of field faults

At TMM level 3 an organization practices regression testing in addition to multilevel testing. Reuse of test cases for this purpose is a necessary part of this practice. Some useful measurements to monitor the practice are:

- *number of test cases reused;*

- *number of test cases added to a test database or tool repository (e.g., in a capture replay tool);*

- *number of test cases rerun when changes are made to the software.*

Integration of testing activities into the software life cycle is another maturity goal at TMM level 3 that needs to be supported by measurements. To achieve this goal, an organization should ensure that test planning occurs early in the life cycle, test risks are identified, and that there is preliminary development of test plans and test cases based on information from the requirements, specifications, and design documents. Some measures to evaluate progress in this area are:

Cyclomatic complexity of the units (pseudo code or code)
Halstead's metrics
Number of hours spent in test planning during requirements phase
Number of hours spent in test planning during specification
Number of hours spent in test planning during design
Number of test cases/test scenarios developed from requirement-related information
Number of test cases/test scenarios developed from specification-related information
Number of test cases developed from design information
Number of hours spent in development of a requirements traceability matrix

11.4.4 Measurements for TMM Level 4

At TMM level 4 an organization puts into place a formal test measurement program. It also establishes a process for software quality evaluation and a review program, all of which are specified as maturity goals at this level. By progressing up the levels of the TMM, an organization has an infrastructure in place to support these goals. For example, the organization now has dedicated and trained testing personnel, testing and debugging policies, testing standards, and a defined test planning, tracking, and monitoring process. At TMM level 4 an organization collects measurements for continuous support of previously achieved test process maturity goals and for support of the current maturity goals at this level. The scope of the measurements collected is broadened, and an organization is now better able to learn about the costs of quality and the cost of lack of quality, the degree of customer involvement, in the development process, and the degree of customer satisfaction. Emphasis at this level is placed on product-related measurements to support the maturity goal of software quality evaluation. Review measurements are also added so that the effectiveness of the review process can be evaluated and improvements made. Finally, a defect repository is formally established and a full complement of defect attributes as shown in Figure 11.3 is included in each defect record.

For measurements specific to the review process the reader is urged to consult Chapter 10 where review topics are described in detail. The role of measurements in evaluating and improving the review process is discussed there and several measurements are suggested such as:

> *Size of the item reviewed*
> *Time for the review meetings*
> *Number of defects found per hour of review time*
> *LOC or pages of a document reviewed per hour*
> *Defect removal leverage*
> *Phase yield (for each review phase)*

Since a formal test measurement program is initiated at TMM level 4, an organization should also collect measurements relevant to this program to assess its strengths and weaknesses. For example:

Costs of measurement training
Costs of measurement tools
Costs of maintaining the measurement databases (and defect repository)

It should be noted that an organization may decide to include the costs of the measurement program in the "cost of quality" as described in Chapter 12. An organization may also want to have an indicator of the growth and access to the measurement databases. It will want to determine if the software engineers are adding to the corporate knowledge bases over time, and using the data to make decisions and plan actions. Useful measures that can be used for monitoring are:

Size of the historical databases
Number of references to historical data (in the project databases)

As part of the discussion of appropriate measurements at TMM level 4, the important role of software quality evaluation in the hierarchy of maturity goals must be emphasized. Recall that testing principle 1 states that we test to detect defects and to evaluate software quality (Chapter 2). To evaluate software quality, a number of software quality attributes can be evaluated by an organization reaching TMM level 4. Those appropriate for each project are selected, suitable measurements defined, and described in the quality plan for the project. Quality measurements are extensively discussed in this book. Some examples of quality measurements for software products are described below. In addition, Section 11.3 has examples of quality-related measurements and how testers should collect them. Chapter 12 describes quality attributes such as reliability and usability. Chapter 13 discusses defect-related measurements, and Chapters 9 and 15 focus on process-related measurements. For supplementary material readers can consult Pressman, Grady, and Caswell who also provide discussions of quality measurements [1,7,15].

Sample software quality attributes and related measurements are:

Correctness. This is the degree to which the software performs its required functions. A common measure is defect density (number of defects/KLOC).

Efficiency. This is an attribute that is used to evaluate the ability of a software system to perform its specified functions under stated or implied conditions within appropriate time frames. One useful measure is response time—the time it takes for the system to respond to a user request.

Testability. This attribute is related to the effort needed to test a software system to ensure it performs its intended functions A quantification of testability could be the number of test cases required to adequately test a system, or the cyclomatic complexity of an individual module.

Maintainability. The effort required to make a change. Sometimes defined in terms of the mean-time-to-repair (MTTR) which reflects the time it takes to analyze a change request, design a modification, implement the change, test it, and distribute it.

Portability. This relates to the effort (time) required to transfer a software system from one hardware/software environment to another.

Reusability. This attribute refers to the potential for the newly developed code to be reused in future products. One measurement that reflects reusability is the number of lines of new code that has been inserted into a reuse library as a result of the current development effort [14].

In order to evaluate the quality of its software, an organization should define these attributes and associated measurements and decide on how the test team will determine the degree to which the software possesses each attribute. Scales, units, and recording forms must be defined. Finally, as part of the work in achieving test process maturity, an organization must craft its testing process so that it is used to evaluate these quality attributes. Adoption of TMM practices supports this goal. As previously described, project, test, and/or quality plans for each product should contain measurable quality goals relating to these attributes.

11.4.5 Measurements for TMM Level 5

TMM level 5 is the highest level of test process maturity. There are three maturity goals to achieve at this level: "Defect prevention," "Quality control," and "Test process optimization." There is an emphasis on measurements for:

- defect classification, detection, analysis, and prevention activities; the latter through process change;

- quantitative product and process control;

- continuous process improvement and optimization.

Chapters 12, 13, and 15 cover topics related to these goals.

Measurements to support defect prevention are in the main defect-related. An organization engaged in defect-prevention activities must have a defect repository for support. Figure 11.3 shows an example of a defect record in such a repository. Of particular importance is the defect type and number of occurrences. Section 13.2 has suggestions for further information to add to the record including:

- close date (date when defect is repaired);

- author of fix;

- causal category;

- description of associated actions for prevention;

- requirement or business rule with which it is associated;

- status (e.g., open, under repair, repair completed, closed).

After actions are taken through action plans to prevent the defects from reoccurring, then defect-related measures as described for TMM levels 2 and 3, product-related measurements as described for TMM level 4, and general process-related measurements such as those described in the CMM common features, are appropriate to monitor and evaluate the change [2]. Test process changes that result from defect prevention actions can be tracked using the monitoring and controlling measures described for TMM level 3. Organizations may also want to collect measurements related to defect casual analysis meetings to evaluate their costs and effectiveness; for example;

> *Time/effort spent in defect causal analysis*
> *Number of actions suggested*
> *Effort/costs for the action planning team (most of the team works part-time on action planning)*
> *Efforts/costs of the action plans (process changes)*

An organization may consider some of these costs as part of the costs of process improvement. These costs should be weighed against appraisal costs such as testing and reviewing, and failure costs such as rework and complaint resolution. Chapter 13 gives more details.

At TMM level 4 an organization is involved in software quality evaluation, and testing is used to detect defects and evaluate software quality. At TMM level 5 a more quantitative approach to evaluating software quality is used. A major practice at this level is the use of statistical testing based on operational profiles to evaluate software reliability. A simple measure for reliability is mean time between failures (MTBF). Chapter 12 discusses reliability measurement and statistical testing in detail.

To evaluate the costs versus benefits of statistical testing, an organization will want to measure the resources required to develop the operational profile, build reliability models, and perform the statistical testing. Some useful measurements are:

> *Tester time/effort needed to develop and maintain an operational profile*
> *User/client effort to support development of an operational profile*
> *Costs of tester training for profile development, reliability modeling, and statistical testing*
> *Costs of statistical testing*

Measurements of reliability, number of field faults, number of problem reports, and customer satisfaction should be collected both before, and after operational profiles and statistical testing are applied to the testing process to evaluate the impact of this change.

At TMM level 5, organizations put into place a mechanism for quantitative process control. In order to support the practice of testing process control many of the process measurements already suggested for the lower TMM levels are useful, for example, data relating to problem reports, time, and effort to accomplish testing tasks and size of items under review. Usually a software engineering process group (SEPG) is responsible for the activities associated with this practice as described in Chapter 15. To monitor this practice some additional measurements that are useful are:

> *Effort/costs of training the SEPG team in process control*
> *Effort/costs of quantitative process analysis (this can be decomposed*

into lower-level costs such as data collection, data analysis, reporting, etc., as described in Chapter 15)
Effort/costs of process adjustments (process changes)

An organization may decide to combine some of these efforts and costs into one category such as:

Effort/costs of maintaining an SEPG
Costs of test process improvement and optimization

The costs of technology transfer can also be folded into the latter.

Usability testing is also carried out at TMM level 5 and many measurements are associated with this type of testing. Chapter 12 describes many of these which include:

Time to complete a task with the software
Time to access information in the user manual
Time to access information from on-line help
Number of errors made
Number and percentage of tasks completed correctly

Finally, at TMM level 5 test process reuse becomes a practice because of the high quality and effectiveness of the testing process and its component subprocesses. As described in Chapter 15 there is a process asset library where process templates are stored for application and reuse throughout the organization. Some simple measurements that can be used to monitor this practice are:

Training costs for process reuse
Costs to maintain the process asset library
Size of the process asset library
Number of processes reused
Costs/efforts associated with reuse of a process (such as instantiating a process from a template object)

11.5 A Test Measurement Program, Software Quality Evaluation, and the Three Critical Views

The discussion of topics related to TMM level 4 maturity goals began in Chapter 10 and is concluded in this chapter. The maturity goals of interest

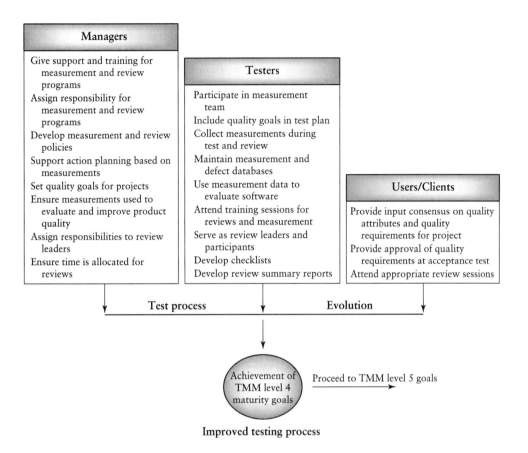

FIG. 11.6

Support by three critical groups for
TMM level 4 maturity goals.

are "Software quality evaluation," "Establish a test measurement program," and, "Establish an organization wide review program." As in the case of the previous maturity goals already discussed, the three critical groups play an important role in goal satisfaction. The major responsibilities of the three critical groups for TMM level 4 maturity goals are summarized in Figure 11.6. This section also gives details on the activities, tasks, and responsibilities assigned to the group members in support of a test measurement program and software quality evaluation.

A test measurement program has impact on both product and process. It provides useful information that management can use to evaluate the quality of the testing process to assess productivity of personnel who are responsible for testing, and to monitor improvements. A test measurement program also supports evaluation of test work products, controlling and monitoring of testing activities, and predictions relating to test performance and costs. With respect to product quality, the presence of a measurement program allows an organization to implement a software quality evaluation process by defining quality factors, quality attributes, and quality metrics. These in turn support the identification and quantification of quality requirements and goals and the collection and analysis of quality-related data. Testing, supported by the measurement program, is one of the key processes through which an organization determines if the software it produces meets specified quality goals.

Test measurement and software quality evaluation programs must be carefully planned and managed. To carry out the many complex tasks involved, contributions in the form of ATRs from the three critical groups are essential. These are described below.

To support a test measurement program *managers* will need to establish goals, polices, and plans for the program, and provide adequate training, tools, resources, and funding. Responsibilities need to be assigned by managers for defining, collecting, storing, analyzing, and applying the measurement data. When and where the data are to be applied, and by whom, must also be decided by management. When the program is in place, test managers should use the measurement data to oversee the testing process and provide appropriate actions when measurements (and supporting assessments) indicate the testing process needs to be changed and improved.

Test mangers and project managers should also use measurements collected during test to evaluate and improve product quality. Managers need to ensure that each project sets quality goals, and that test plans include appropriate measurement and testing activities so that the testing process can support achievement of quality goals for the product.

Testers are essential members of a measurement team. They assist in measurement program planning, help select tools and methods, help define quality attributes, and undergo training to support these responsibilities. Testers develop and maintain the test measurement database; they also support development and maintenance of the defect repository. After the decision has been made on what test-related data needed to be collected, responsibilities are assigned for collecting this data, participating in analysis and application of results. Responsibility may be distributed so that testers will be working with other groups such as developers and software quality assurance staff to carry out measurement-related tasks. Testers should ensure that the appropriate measures are used for test process evaluation, and improvement, and for ensuring that quality goals for each project are meet.

Testing activities need to directed so that each software product can be evaluated with respect to quality requirements. Test plans should provide adequate time and resources for this. During test, testers should collect data related to the quality attributes of the software. For example, if appropriate for the product, during the system test, stress, performance, configuration, recovery, and security tests should be performed by the test group. Using the resulting data, testers and SQA staff should be able to determine if specific quality goals in those areas have been met.

Users/clients should supply consensus on quality attributes and should also provide input and approval for the quality requirements that are important to them with respect to the software being developed. These goals should appear in the requirements document for the project. Observations/evaluations and inputs from the user/client group during an acceptance test will determine if the quality requirements have been met.

LIST OF KEY TERMS

Measure
Measurement
Metric
Quality attribute
Quality factor
Quality requirement

EXERCISES

1. What are some of the costs and benefits of adopting a test measurement program?

2. Describe the steps in the Grady/Caswell model for establishing a measurement program.

3. In view of the Grady/Caswell steps, why is it important to have a trained staff? How does achieving TMM maturity goals support this need?

4. Suppose your organization selected you to establish a team to develop a test measurement program. You can select members of your team from any organizational group. Which groups do you think would provide qualified members for your team? What are the qualifications you would use to select members of your measurement team?

5. If you were a member of higher management, what type of a group would you assemble to provide continuous support for a measurement program? Who would you select as members of this group?

6. What types of databases would you select to store measurement data (relational, object-oriented, etc.)? Give reasons for your selection in terms of requirement for the collection, storage, retrieval of data, and report-generating capabilities. Consider the different types of data you will collect, and the different uses. Can you suggest commercial database systems that fulfill your requirements?

7. Suppose you are a test manager and your testing process is assessed at TMM level 2. Your group has been collecting and applying measurements such as size of the product, size of the test harness, number of problem reports, and time spent in test. What additional measurements might you select to add to the set, and why?

8. Using Gilb's "Attribute Specification Format Template," design a specification for response time for a real-time theater reservation system. Use values you believe appropriate for this type of system.

9. Why is it important to begin a measurement program with measures of size, defects, and costs? How does the knowledge gained from collecting/analyzing these measurements support process evolution?

10. What measurements could be useful for evaluating widely used software quality attributes such as correctness, testability, maintainability, and reusability?

11. Describe a set of measurements that can be used to evaluate the measurement program itself.

12. What activities, tasks and responsibilities can be assigned to testers to support a test measurement program?

REFERENCES

[1] R. Grady, *Practical Software Metrics for Project Management and Process Improvement*, Prentice Hall, Englewood Cliff, NJ, 1992.

[2] M. Paulk, C. Weber, B. Curtis, M. Chrissis, *The Capability Maturity Model*, Addison-Wesley, Reading, MA, 1995.

[3] *IEEE Standard for a Software Quality Metrics Methodology* (IEEE Std 1061-1992), copyright 1993 by IEEE, all rights reserved.

[4] *IEEE Standard Glossary of Software Engineering Terminology* (IEEE Std 610.12-1990), copyright 1990 by IEEE, all rights reserved.

[5] N. Fenton, *Software Metrics: A Rigorous Approach*, Chapman & Hall, London, 1991.

[6] N. Fenton, "Software measurement: a necessary scientific Basis," *IEEE Transactions on Software Engineering*, Vol. SE-20, No. 3, pp. 199–206, 1994.

[7] R. Grady, D. Caswell, *Software Metrics: Establishing a Companywide Program*, Prentice Hall, Englewood Cliff, NJ, 1987.

[8] W. Perry, *Effective Methods for Software Testing*, John Wiley and Sons, New York, 1995.

[9] *IEEE Standard for Software Productivity Metrics* (IEEE Std 1045-1992), copyright 1993 by IEEE, all rights reserved.

[10] T. Gilb, *Principles of Software Engineering Management*, Addison-Wesley, Reading, MA, 1988.

[11] J. McCall, P. Richards, G. Walters, *Factors in Software Quality*, Technical Report 77CIS 02, General Electric, Command and Information Systems, Sunnyvale, CA, 1977.

[12] B. Boehm, J. Brown, M. Lipow, "Quantitative evaluation of software quality," *IEEE 2nd International Conf. on Software Engineering*, San Francisco, CA, pp. 592–605, Oct., 1976.

[13] International Organization for Standards, *Information technology: Software Product Evaluation: Quality Characteristics and Guidelines for Their Use*, ISO/IEC IS 9126, ISO, Geneva, 1991.

[14] W. Humphrey, *A Discipline for Software Engineering*, Addison-Wesley, Reading, MA, 1995.

[15] R. Pressman, *Software Engineering: A Practitioner's Approach*, fifth edition, McGraw-Hill, New York, 2001.

EVALUATING SOFTWARE QUALITY: A QUANTITATIVE APPROACH

12.0 Review of Quality Concepts

Our role as software testers involves participation in activities where we evaluate the quality of an evolving software product. To engage in these activities in an effective way we need to understand what quality means, and how to quantify and measure it. We need to be able to detect the weaknesses and defects in our products that impact on quality, and do this in an efficient and effective way. Finally, we need to understand the nature of the development and testing processes and how these processes impact on software quality. Practices in our processes that have a negative effect on quality should be eliminated, and those that have a positive effect should be promoted. The TMM assessment process is designed to support the latter goals.

To promote understanding of quality concepts this text has addressed quality issues in several of the preceding chapters. For example, in Chapter 2 definitions for software quality from the *IEEE Standard Glossary of Software Engineering Terminology* were given and are repeated for readers to review [1].

> 1. Quality relates to the degree to which a system, system component, or process meets specified requirements.
>
> 2. Quality relates to the degree to which a system, system component, or process, meets customer, or user, needs or expectations.

Chapter 2 also gave a description of the role of a quality assurance group that is repeated here for review.

> The software quality assurance (SQA) group is a team of people with the necessary training and skills to ensure that all necessary actions are taken during the development process so that the resulting software conforms to established technical requirements.

For completeness, a managerial view of SQA should also be added to the above description. Pressman gives such a view in his discussion of quality issues. He states that a major function of the SQA team is to provide management with information relevant to product quality [2]. To support this role, Pressman and others advise that a SQA team prepare an SQA plan for each project that describes the audits and reviews to be performed, the standards that are relevant to the project, the procedures for error reporting and tracking, and documents they will produce. The team should also describe the nature of the communication links between themselves, the development group, and the testing group.

If the SQA team identifies problems that impact on product quality and then reports these to management, then management must address the problems and provide resources to resolve them so that quality is improved. A detailed discussion of SQA activities is beyond the scope of this text. Readers can consult the *IEEE Standard for Software Quality Assurance Plans* and the *Standard for Software Reviews and Audits,* which are good sources for detailed discussions of SQA activities [3,4].

Coverage of quality issues is a major goal for this text. For example, Chapter 9 describes a set of measurements that support test process controlling and monitoring. Use of these measures enables us to track testing progress and address quality issues. Chapter 10 discusses software reviews, which are essential to support quality evaluation and achievement of quality goals. Additional discussion of quality issues appears in Chapter 11 where the focus is on measurements, measurement programs, and software quality attributes. The relationship between quality factors, subfactors, and metrics is described there, as well as a software quality metrics methodology. An active role in software quality evaluation for testers is also discussed. In the current chapter we expand our view of quality. We bind testers, software quality assurance staff, developers, and managers into an organizationwide team that works together to address quality issues with respect to software products. The structure of the TMM promotes this binding through achievement of its maturity goals, supported by the three critical views. An organizational infrastructure is built that supports cooperation of all relevant groups so they can address quality issues and implement quality evaluation and control.

This chapter will introduce the concepts and practices related to quality control as applied to software. Quality control is a maturity goal at TMM level 5 and is achievable within the framework of an effective software testing process. This chapter also introduces two additional quality factors—usability and reliability. We will learn how to test for usability and reliability, and discover how reliability relates to statistical testing and quality control. Additional coverage of quality issues is also given in Chapter 13, which discusses defect prevention, and in Chapter 15, which describes process quality control.

12.1 Quality Costs

Readers should be aware that quality evaluation and control have economic as well as technical aspects. Implementation of these quality-related procedures and practices is expensive; however, most organizations realize that the benefits greatly outweigh the costs. Unfortunately, many organizations do not realize what quality, and particularly the lack of quality, really costs. A TMM level 5 organization has a handle on both of these costs.

According to Pressman [2] and Humphrey [5], the costs of quality can be decomposed into three major areas: (i) prevention, (ii) appraisal, and (iii) failure. The costs to find and fix a defect increase rapidly as we proceed through prevention, detection, and failure phases. Prevention costs are associated with activities that identify the causes of defects and those actions that are taken to prevent them. Pressman includes as part of prevention costs:

- quality planning;

- test and laboratory equipment;

- training;

- formal technical reviews.

The author would also include in this group activities related to defect casual analysis/prevention as described in Chapter 13.

Appraisal costs involve the costs of evaluating the software product to determine its level of quality. According to Pressman these include:

- testing;

- equipment calibration and maintenance;

- in-process and interprocess inspections.

The author would place reviews in this category.

Failure costs are those costs that would not exist if the software had no defects; that is, if it met all of the user's requirements. Pressman partitions failure costs into internal and external categories. Internal failure costs occur when a defect is detected in the software prior to shipment. These costs include:

- diagnosis, or failure mode analysis;

- repair and regression testing;

- rework.

External failure costs occur when defects are found in the software after it has been shipped to the client. These include:

- complaint resolution;

- return of the software and replacement;

- help line support;

- warranty work.

"Lack of quality" costs include these failure costs. This author would also add to "lack of quality" costs the cost of liability, which may occur if the software causes damage, or loss of life or property. Other costs associated with lack of quality are customer dissatisfaction and loss of market share. The TMM maturity goal structure supports implementation of prevention and appraisal activities so that we can reduce these "lack of quality" costs.

12.2 What Is Quality Control?

Quality control can be described in several ways. It has origins in modern manufacturing processes where random sampling techniques, testing, measurements, inspections, defect casual analysis, and acceptance sampling were among the techniques used to ensure the manufacture of quality products [6]. One description of quality control follows:

> Quality control consists of the procedures and practices employed to ensure that a work product or deliverable conforms to standards or requirements.

The IEEE Standard Glossary of Software Engineering Terminology gives what it calls a nonstandard description of the term [1]:

> Quality control is the set of activities designed to evaluate the quality of developed or manufactured products.

The glossary entry also calls quality control a synonym for quality assurance; however, a definition for quality assurance also includes activities that are used to evaluate processes as well as products. The discussion in this text is based a broad view of quality control, and includes control of products and processes as well. This view is supported by Pressman who states that quality control encompasses a feedback loop to the process that created the product [2]. An organization can use this feedback, as well as process assessments and associated process measurements, to evaluate their processes. The organization can fine-tune and improve the processes when products cannot meet their specifications.

What procedures, practices, and resources are needed to promote the implementation of quality control in its broadest sense? Given the above descriptions for quality control, such a list would include:

- policies and standards;

- review and audit procedures;

- a training program;

- dedicated, trained, and motivated staff (for testing and quality assurance);

- a measurement program;

- a planning process (for test and quality assurance);

- effective testing techniques, statistical techniques, and tools;

- process monitoring and controlling systems;

- a test process assessment system (TMM-AM);

- a configuration management system.

As we move up the levels of the TMM [1–4], and achieve the maturity goals associated with each level we build an infrastructure that encompasses the above items and supports the implementation of software product, and test process quality control. At TMM level 5 two maturity goals give additional support for quality control. Achieving the "defect prevention" maturity goal puts into place practices such as defect casual analysis and action planning to prevent defects from reoccurring. The process changes often lead to better process control. The "quality control" maturity goal at level 5 builds on the product quality evaluation maturity goal at TMM level 4. However, it is broader in scope: it focuses on control of both process and product. In particular, in the product area it calls for development of operational profiles for software products, and use of statistical testing based on these profiles to promote evaluation of software reliability and the achievement of reliability goals. In addition, at TMM level 5 an organization is also able to evaluate software usability and achieve usability goals. Finally, it is able to make estimations of confidence levels and software trustworthiness.

With respect to the process side of quality control, the infrastructure and all the associated capabilities at TMM level 5 can be focused on quality control of the testing process. These capabilities, coupled with application of the TMM Assessment Model, action planning, and process control procedures, promote testing process quality evaluation and continuous test process improvement. In this chapter we focus on quality control of software. Test process quality control and continuous test process improvement will be discussed in detail in Chapter 15.

12.3 The Role of Operational Profiles and Usage Models in Quality Control

As previously described, quality control in manufacturing involves acceptance sampling and the application of statistical methods to evaluate the manufactured product. In the software domain we can apply conceptually similar techniques to quality control. For example, we can use operational profiles and perform statistical testing. The operational profiles allow us to sample the input space according to usage patterns. Given the operational profile we can then perform statistical testing. An operational profile can be described as follows:

> **1. An operational profile is a quantitative characterization of how a software system will be used in its intended environment [7].**
>
> **2. An operational profile is a specification of classes of inputs and the probability of their occurrence.**

The usefulness of an operational profile is that it is the population from which a statistically correct sample of test cases can be developed. An operational profile is essential for evaluation of software reliably, an quality factor of great importance especially for mission- and safety-critical systems. Usage models capture information similar to what is found in operation profiles [8–10]. Both operational profiles and usage models may have different representations, for example, graphs, tables, or matrices. In subsequent discussions the term "operational profile" will be used, but either term would be appropriate.

Controlling the quality of a software product and predicting and measuring its reliability requires a model of expected operational use of the software, a test environment that simulates the operational environment, and a way of analyzing the test data and making statistically valid inferences about reliability [8]. The use of an operational profile helps a test manager to allocate testing resources properly. A manager can concentrate testing resources on the most-used operations, and have some confidence that these operations have been the target of a large fraction of the testing efforts. The reliability level of the software will then be the highest that is practical to achieve given the time and resources available for testing [7].

An operational profile is based on a functional specification for a software system and requires user/client participation for its development. This group need to express very clearly the operations it believes will be most heavily used. Other partners in operational profile development include analysts, testers, designers, software quality assurance staff, and, in many cases, representatives from marketing. An operational profile can be prepared early in the software life cycle. Planning for statistical testing based on the profile can also be done in parallel with other development activities. An operational profile has many uses besides estimation of reliability. These include validation of requirements, resource and scheduling estimations for testing, and test management. Developing an operational profile requires the investment of organizational resources, but it is cost effective and has many benefits in terms of its impact on software quality. It may be possible to reuse an operational profile over several releases with updates as required to minimize costs.

A goal for testers is to ensure that the software they are evaluating is reliable, especially with respect to the most frequently requested operations users will want to carry out. The operational profile reflects this frequency of use and can be developed in some cases by using historical data from past releases of the software to uncover the different classes of inputs used and the probability of their occurrence. In some problem domains such as telecommunication switching systems, there is industry-generated knowledge about typical usage patterns. However, in this domain and in most others, user/client participation is required, especially for the development of an operational profile for a new system or a new release. In many cases developing an accurate profile is difficult because of the lack of detailed information. The resulting profile may be inaccu-

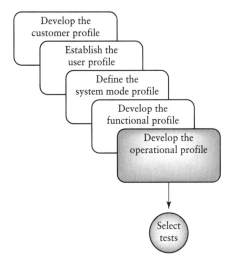

FIG. 12.1

Steps to develop an operational profile [7].

rate since users may not be firm on how they will use a system, and/or the profile may require change as the system is used. Developing an operational profile often requires a great deal of organizational commitment, but the benefits usually outweigh the costs.

Musa describes a 5-step methodology for creating an operational profile [7]. The steps are shown in Figure 12.1 and are briefly described below. You begin the process at a high level of abstraction—the customer level—and add more details to the operational model by focusing on users, system modes, functions, and then on operations, runs, and inputs. The reader should note that not all the steps are needed to develop a profile for every application.

1. Develop the Customer Profile.

Musa describes a customer, as the person, group, or institution that is acquiring the software being developed. A customer group is the set of customers that will be using the software in the same way. The customer profile is the complete set of customer groups and their associated occurrence probabilities. The best measure of customer group probability is the proportion of use it represents. If such information is not available you may have to make some assumptions based on the proportions of each group you expect in your customer base. For example, consider an automated tax preparation system. It is reasonable to assume there are three major customer groups, professional accounting firms, individual professional accountants, and ordinary taxpayers who will be using your software. Assume that 40% of customers will be accounting firms, 35% will be individual accountants, and 25% ordinary taxpayers, then the customer profile is 0.45 for professional accounting firms, 0.35 for individual accountants, and 0.25 for non-professional ordinary taxpayers.

2. Establish the User Profile.

Users and customers are not necessarily the same groups. For example a physicians group might provide funding to acquire an automated medical office management system, but the predominant users will be nurses, technicians, and medical office clerks. A user then is an individual, group or institution that actually uses a given software system. A user group is a set of users who will engage the system in the same way. The user profile is the set of user groups and their occurrence probability. For example, if the medical office has a staff of 10, with 5 nurses, 3 technicians, and 2 office clerks, then the nurses user group has a probability of 0.5, technicians, 0.3, and office clerks 0.2, as shown in Table 12.1.

You can derive a user profile from a customer profile by studying each customer group and identifying the user groups within it. Musa suggests that the best way to establish the occurrence probability of a user group within a customer group is to use the proportion of the customer group's usage it represents. If there are multiple customer groups, a profile developer can calculate the overall probability for each user group by multiplying each user group's probability by its customer group's probability, If user groups are combined across customer groups, their overall user group probabilities should be added to yield the total user group probability.

3. Develop the System Mode Profile.

Musa describes a system mode as a set of functions or operations that you group for convenience in order to analyze execution behavior. Hence

Medical office system	
User mode	**Occurrence probability**
Nurses	0.50
Technicians	0.30
Clerks	0.20

TABLE 12.1

Sample user profile.

a given system mode may map to several functions or operations. A system mode profile is the set of system modes and their associated occurrence probabilities. Some example modes for the automated medical office management system are system administrator mode, nurse/technician mode, and clerk mode. For each system mode, you need to develop an operational and perhaps a functional profile.

4. Develop the Functional Profile.

Functional profiles are usually developed in the requirements phase. In case of requirements changes they should be updated. To develop a functional profile you need to break down each system mode into the functions needed to support it. You create a function list and determine each function's occurrence probability. The functional profile provides a quantitative view of the relative use of each of the different system functions.

An initial function list is developed that focuses on features. These are functional aspects of the system that are of interest and significance to users. These should be clearly visible from the requirements document. User input is essential for developing this list. As a part of this step Musa also prescribes that a set of what he calls environmental input variables be identified. These variables describe the conditions that affect the way the system runs, that is, the control paths it takes and the data it uses. They might cause the software to respond in different ways; however, they do not relate directly to features. In a telecommunication system an input variable in this context would be the type of telephone used by a customer—digital, or analog.

The final function list is the product of the number of functions in the initial function list and the number of environmental variables, each with its own set of values. You eliminate those combinations of initial functions and environmental variable values that do not occur. The last task in this phase is to determine occurrence probabilities. The best source of data for this task is usage measurements taken from:

- the latest release of this software;

- a similar system;

- studies of the manual function that you are automating.

Most systems under development will be a mixture of previously released functions for which you will have data, and new functions for which you will have to estimate use.

5. Develop the Operational Profile.

An operation, according to Musa, represents a task being accomplished by a software system as viewed by the staff who will run the system. It is not the same as a function; there may not be a straightforward mapping between the two. A function may be composed of one or more operations, or a set of functions may be rearranged into a different set of operations. Operations are less abstract than functions; they represent a specific task, with specific input variable values or ranges of values. In general, there may be more operations than functions associated with a system. As a simple example, a function to modify a record could evolve into two operations: (i) delete old record and (ii) add new record. Testers focus on testing operations.

Musa describes a series of steps for developing the final operational profile using information from the profiles already developed. These include

(i) dividing the execution into runs;
(ii) identifying the input space;
(iii) partitioning the input space into operations;
(iv) determining the occurrence probabilities for operations.

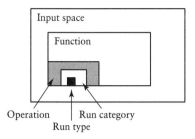

FIG. 12.2

General relationship between functions, operations, and runs [7].

Operations are associated with runs. A run, according to Musa, "is a logical entity that can be described as a segment of a program's execution time." The segment is usually based on accomplishing a user-oriented task in a particular environment. Operations may comprise many run types. Each run type has an associated input state or set of input variable values that are external to the run, and are used by or affect it. The general relationships between functions, operations, and runs according to Musa is shown in Figure 12.2 [7].

An airline reservation system is a good illustration of these types of entities. In such a system different run types would exist for single-leg flights. The input variables would be different; for example, there would be differences in customer names, flights numbers, originating and terminating cities. A reservation transaction for a single-leg versus a two-leg flight represents two different operations since each has a different set of input variables. Common variables for both would be customer name, flight number, and originating and terminating city. However the two-leg flight reservation has additional variables such as a second flight number and a connecting city, so it should be considered as a distinct operation according to Musa.

An important aspect of this final step is to understand the nature of the program's input space. A program's input space is the set of input states that can occur during its operations. This can be large for a real-world application. The most important issue here, according to Musa, is to develop a comprehensive list of input variables. You proceed to partition the input space to reduce the number of profile elements you may have to handle. Portions of the input space will correspond to an operation; these are called domains. The run types you group together should have the same input variables, so you can develop a set of common and efficient test procedures for the domain. After these partitions or operations have been identified, you determine their occurrence probabilities. Refinement of functional profiles can help with this task; you can refine and map functions to operations and to runs. Musa represents the final operational profile as a table similar in format to Table 12.1, where there are listings of operations and their occurrence probability.

Along with the tasks of preparing the different profiles, testers also need to develop, or acquire, tools that will instrument and monitor the software under test. The tool needs to extract ample data relating to input variables so that the operations being executed can be identified to ensure coverage.

The operational profile is then used by testers to select operations and test inputs (through run types and categories) according to their occurrence probabilities. As stated by Musa, the nature of an operational profile dictates that tests selected using the profile identify failures on average, in the order of how often they occur. Testing in this way and repairing the faults causing the observed failures increases reliability because the failures that occur more frequently are caused by the faulty operations used most frequently. Testers may use more than one operational profile to represent the variations in system use that can occur.

There are other approaches to developing models of typical usage patterns. Walton et al. describe such as approach that results in what they call a usage model [8]. Expected groups of users, uses, and environments are identified. A representation of the usage model is constructed as a graph (nodes are usage states and arcs are stimuli that cause transitions between usage states), a formal grammar, or using a Markov usage chain. The next step is to assign probabilities to each transition in the usage representation structure. The set of transition probabilities defines a probability distribution which is the usage distribution over the input domain. A simple example of such a graph is shown in Figure 12.3. There are four states represented in the graph. The values in parentheses over each arc or arrow represent stimulus probability pairs. For example, the item (Stim2, 0.2) indicates a stimulus "Stim2" and a 0.2 probability. The prob-

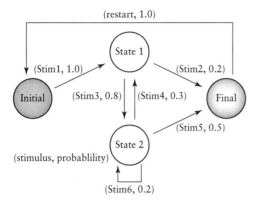

(restart, 1.0)

State 1

(Stim1, 1.0)

(Stim2, 0.2)

Initial

(Stim3, 0.8)

(Stim4, 0.3)

Final

(Stim5, 0.5)

State 2

(stimulus, probablility)

(Stim6, 0.2)

FIG. 12.3

A simple example of a usage model representation.

ability represents the likelihood that a given arc will be selected for a transition from that state. When the model is developed it is verified using available information about intended usage of the software. The model can then be used to generate test cases. To perform this task, a tester traverses the model from the initial to the final state, and randomly selects stimuli based on the transaction probabilities. Sequences of stimuli selected in this way are the basis for test cases. As previously mentioned, models of this type and those developed with Musa's approach can both be used to drive statistical testing and reliability evaluation as described in subsequent sections of this chapter.

12.4 Support for Quality Control: Statistical Testing

A statistical approach to software testing was developed by Mills et al. [11] at IBM in the context of Cleanroom Software Engineering and by Musa [7] at AT&T. Both of these research groups based their efforts on approaches to testing and quality control in other engineering disciplines. A similar approach for quality control in manufacturing processes is described by Cho [6]. Cho describes the traditional approach to quality control and certification which consists of:

- selecting random samples of the product;

- developing and executing tests that are characteristic of the operational use of the product;

- analyzing or making statistical inferences from test results;

- certifying for use products meeting a standard.

In the application of statistical testing to software, we do not select random samples of the product to test, but we do select samples of its usage. We actually select for test a subset of all possible usages of the software as represented by the usage model or operational profile, and test results are the basis for conclusions about its general operational performance. In other words, the sample, as represented in the operational profile or usage model, is used to develop conclusions about the so-called "population" of all uses. What is being expressed through this approach is that it is not possible to exhaustively test any reasonably sized piece of software with all usage scenarios. Application of an operational profile and statistical testing allows us to be "smart testers" and select a representative sample of uses and inputs.

After a usage model, or operational profile, is developed for a software system, testers generate test cases (inputs) using samples of the uses or operations. In the case of usage models that are in graphical form, test cases can be generated as described in the previous section by traversing the usage states of the model, guided by the transition probabilities. Traversals result in an accumulation of successive stimuli that represent a test case [9]. When test cases are generated from a usage model, they are generated to reflect probabilities in the usage model. During the actual test period testers must ensure that the test experience is representative of actual usage. The randomly generated test cases cause an accumulation of usage events in proportion to usage probabilities. As testing progresses, testers use can use tools and measurements such as a discriminant to determine if testing is a representation of actual use.

> **A discriminant is a measure of the degree to which the actual testing experience has become a good representation of expected usage [9].**

A discriminant tends the change in value as the testing effort proceeds according to the usage model. When tests are run with the test cases, testers observe the value of the discriminant as it changes and the actual behavior of the software. The latter is compared to specified behavior. Results are recorded, including any failures. The test results are analyzed with respect to a reliability model (as discussed in the next section of this chapter) to provide a basis for statistical inference of reliability during operational use. In addition, when testers are satisfied that the tests are sufficient to simulate expected performance in the field (i.e., the discriminant has converged on a certain value that indicates that the testing scenario is sufficiently similar to expected usage), they can use this information along with other data, to help make stop test decisions. It should be noted that conclusions drawn from statistical testing apply only to the particular release or software version under test, under the specified conditions. New versions or new releases usually result in different usage patterns, and the usage models applied to test them need to reflect the new patterns of use.

Statistical testing very often results in large volumes of test data to examine, and analysis of results may require large amounts of testers' time and expertise. Therefore, use of statistical testing techniques requires testers that are trained and motivated; they need to have a good understanding of software specifications and statistical techniques. Organizations assessed at TMM 5 have the staff with the necessary skills to carry our these types of tests.

Statistical testing has several major benefits which include:

(i) concentrating testing resources on the parts of the system mostly likely to be used; this should result in a more reliable system from the users viewpoint;
(ii) supporting estimations or predications of reliability which should be accurate from the user's viewpoint;
(iii) providing quantitative criteria for decisions on the completeness of testing and system release.

Statistical testing is a large part of the certification process for software in Cleanroom Software Engineering [9–11]. Certification goals are developed for the software which includes expectations for reliability, confidence, and reliability growth rates. The application of usage models, statistical testing, as well as traditional testing techniques, allows Cleanroom certifiers to determine if the software is fit for use with respect to the certification goals.

12.5 Software Reliability

In previous chapters this text has described several software quality attributes and their role in defining and evaluating software quality. The text has also introduced concepts related to quality control of software. As software plays a more critical role in society, demands for its proper functioning with an absence of failures over long periods of time increase. Users/clients require software products that produce consistent and expected results over long periods of use. Deviations from expected behavior that result in software failures are costly, and may have impact on medical, commercial, military, and social aspects of our society. Hence the drive in our profession to understand, model, evaluate, and control a critically important software quality attribute we call reliability. As part of our quality control activities at higher levels of the TMM we measure and strive to improve software reliability.

A definition for software reliability is as follows:

> **Software reliability is the ability of a system or component to perform its required functions under stated conditions for a specified period of time [1].**

Another definition that expresses reliability in terms of probability is:

> **Software reliability is the probability that a software system will operate without failure under given conditions for a given time interval.**

Note that reliability focuses on behavior of the software over a period of time. We usually express reliability using a scale from 0 to 1. Software that has a reliability measure close to 1 is highly reliable. We also expect crucial software to be available to us when it is needed to support us with our tasks. Availability is a concept related to reliability but has a different meaning.

> **Availability is the degree to which a system or component is operational and accessible when required for use [1].**

An alternative definition of availability in terms of probability is:

▌ **Availability is the probability that a software system will be available for use [12].**

Availability is also measured on a scale from 0 to 1. A system that is up and running has availability of 1. One that is unusable has an availability of 0. We measure availability in clock time, not execution time as in the case of reliability. As an example of the differences between reliability and availability, let us examine the case of a household appliance such as an oven that has only been seen by the repairman twice in 15 years (two failures). It is highly reliable. But if it is not working on the day it is needed to prepare dinner for a family party, then it is not available. In this section we focus on reliability issues.

Another related term that should be mentioned here is trustworthiness.

▌ **Trustworthiness is the probability that there are no errors in the software that will cause the system to fail catastrophically [12].**

Appropriate and quantitative quality goals should be set with respect to these attributes for all projects. This is essential, especially for critical software systems, and is supported in the *IEEE Standard for Recommended Practices for Software Requirements Specification,* which includes a description of reliability requirements that should appear in a requirements document [13].

Testers play an important role in evaluating and ensuring the reliability, availability, and trustworthiness of a software system. This is part of their responsibility in support of software quality control. However, testers should not bear the sole responsibility for releasing highly reliable and trustworthy software. The quality (maturity) of the development/ testing processes, the types of design approaches used, the level of education and expertise of developers, software engineers, systems analysts, and software quality assurance staff are among the factors that have a high impact on the reliability and trustworthiness of a software system.

An initial approach to addressing reliability issues in software systems might be to adapt techniques that have been applied successfully in the hardware domain. However, a study of the issues reveals that there are fundamental differences between achieving hardware and software reliability goals. Thus, the approach taken to addressing the software and hardware reliability problem will be different. If we begin with a surface view of hardware and software systems, it is obvious that the two reliability problems are not the same, since software does not consist of physical components that wear out or exhibit manufacturing faults. Given its physical nature, a hardware system, unlike a software system, could fail if a component wears out (gets corroded or oxidized) or its manufacture was faulty. In these cases, the faulty component can be repaired or replaced, and the system restored to its running state. Its reliability is maintained when the repair is complete. Software is a set of instructions for the computer to carry out. It cannot wear out, but it can be wrong, that is, defective.

Defects/faults introduced in the software can be latent and manifest themselves only when a particular set of conditions occurs. It is under these circumstances that a failure is observed. The defect/fault must be isolated and the software repaired. Software engineers have the expectation that the repair will increase the reliability of the software; unfortunately, this is not always true. During the process of repair new defects may be introduced.

In addition to physical differences, the abstraction level of the components that hardware and software engineers are concerned with also differ. Hardware engineers are concerned mainly with discrete components such as resistors and capacitors and integrated chips. Software engineers are also concerned with so-called "primitives," such as instructions, procedures, and modules. However, they are also concerned with higher-level components such as packages, subprograms, libraries, and finally large programs [14].

Given the differences between the hardware and software reliability problem, the question becomes, how should we, as software engineers, approach reliability issues in our own domain? First, we need to decide how we will measure reliability, and then we need to develop the models and techniques needed to evaluate and improve reliability. Hamlet suggests that two kinds of models are useful in the software engineering domain—reliability growth models and reliability models [15]. Reliability growth models are applied mainly during a system test, where cycles of run tests, observe failures, repair, and continue testing are repeated. Test managers observe changes in the failure rate over time and use these to make a decision about when to stop testing. Reliability growth models rely on observational data and use of accurate usage models. Reliability models are predictive models that are applied after the software has been tested. Testers can use them to predict the mean time to failure—the probability of failure-free operation of the software. They are based on use of statistics and probability.

12.5.1 Measurements for Software Reliability

Several time-related measurements are associated with reliability and availability in the software domain. Using these we can express reliability, and its associated attribute availability, as values between 0 and 1 as previously described. A value of zero for these items indicates that a system is unreliable or unavailable, and a value of 1 indicates that it is completely reliable and always available. In order to discuss these measurements we need to describe the role of the tester and the necessity for collecting failure data. As we test the software and move through the levels of testing we observe failures and try to remove defects. Our attempts to remove defects are sometimes successful, and sometimes when making changes we introduce new defects or create conditions that allow other defects to cause failures. As this process progresses we collect the failure data especially during a system test. It is essential that during system test we use test data that reflects actual usage patterns. As testing continues we monitor the system as it executes. Ideally, we hope to observe that the incidence of failures is decreasing, that is, we have longer and longer time periods where the software is executing and no failures are observed. Sometimes this is true and sometime it is not, at least over the short term. In any case let us assume that we have observed $i-1$ failures. We can record the interfailure times or the times elapsed between each of the $i-1$ failures, $t_1, t_2, t_3, \ldots, t_{i-1}$. The average of those observed values is what we call the mean time to failure, MTTF. The computation of the MTTF is dependent on accurately recording the elapsed time between the observed failures. Time units need to be precise. CPU execution time is in most cases more appropriate than wall clock time [16].

After a failure has been observed, software engineers must repair the code. We can calculate the average time it takes to repair a defect in the code and calculate this time as the mean time to repair, MTTR.

We use both of these measures to calculate a value called the mean time between failure, MTBF.

$$\text{MTBF} = \text{MTTF} + \text{MTTR}$$

Some researchers use the measure of mean time between failures as a estimate of a system's reliability. Other suggested measures for reliability (R) have been suggested by Shooman [17]:

$$R = \frac{MTBF}{1 + MTBF}$$

Shooman also proposes a definition for availability (A) as:

$$A = \frac{MTBF}{MTBF + MTTR}$$

A measure for maintainability, another quality attribute of interest to us is also derived from Shooman's work. One definition for maintainability is:

> **The ease with which a software system or component can be modified to correct faults, improve performance or other attributes, or adapt to a changing environment [1].**

From Shooman's work maintainability (M) is calculated solely as a function of the mean time to repair:

$$M = \frac{1}{1 + MTTR}$$

There are other approaches that try to capture the essence of reliability, availability, and maintainability in a practical way. For example, some organizations use the values of fault density (i.e., number of faults/KLOC) as a measure of software reliability. Using fault density as a measure of reliability is not as useful as mean time to failure from a client/user point of view since each error in the software may not have the same failure rate. Organizations using fault density as a measure of reliability are likely to be organizations operating on lower levels of the TMM where fault and failure data are not routinely recorded and available, and the development of accurate usage profiles and use of statistical testing is not a common practice.

12.6 Reliability, Quality Control, and Stop-Test Decisions

Addressing software reliability issues requires a great deal of expertise, for example, expertise in defect prevention, process evaluation, predictive modeling, usage modeling, statistics, testing, and measurement. Specialists called reliability engineers have the education and training needed to become leaders in this area of reliability management [12]. Reliability engineering practitioners and researchers in this area have developed reliability models of many types, for example, Markov, Bayesian, and unified, error seeding, curve fitting, and the nonhomogeneous Poisson process [12]. Reliability growth models that will help to determine when to stop testing include types such as logistic growth curve, Duane growth, Weibull growth, and Gompertz growth curves [12]. A detailed discussion of these models is beyond the scope of this book; however, readers can get a good start by studying books and papers by leaders in the field, for example, Musa [7,18], Pham [12], Shooman [17], and Musa and Ackerman [19]. Another good source of information is the July 1992 issue of *IEEE Software* which is dedicated to reliability measurement articles.

For testers and test managers a key issue is the determination of when the software is reliable enough to release, that is, when can testing be stopped? Figure 12.4 shows some of the consequences of making this decision too early or too late in the testing process. Timely stop-test decisions are critical since testing too much may be wasteful of resources, delay time-to-market, and increase costs. However, stopping testing too soon, before the software is reliable, could allow high-severity defects to remain in the shipped software, resulting in loss of life and property as a worst-case scenario. Customer dissatisfaction, high costs of repair to operational software, and increased hot line calls are also consequences of a premature stop-test decision. Stop-test decisions can be supported by use of operation profiles, statistical testing, and reliability growth models which will be described later in this section. In addition, reliability goals must be defined for the software under test. Life cycle activities associated with use of reliability measurement to support a stop-test decision include:

(i) setting reliability goals in the requirements document (a reliability specification is the result);

(ii) providing adequate time and resources in the test plan to allow for developing/modifying the usage profile, running the tests, and collecting, cataloging, and analyzing the reliability data;

(iii) developing a usage or operational profile that accurately models usage patterns;

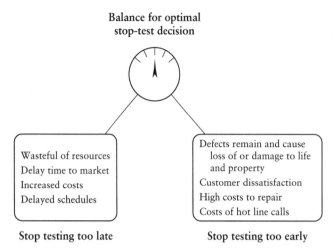

Balance for optimal
stop-test decision

Wasteful of resources
Delay time to market
Increased costs
Delayed schedules

Defects remain and cause
loss of or damage to life
and property
Customer dissatisfaction
High costs to repair
Costs of hot line calls

Stop testing too late   Stop testing too early

FIG. 12.4

Consequences of untimely stop-test
decisions.

(iv) establishing levels of severity for failures;

(v) selecting a reliability growth model suitable for the project;

(vi) carrying out statistical testing based on the operational profile.

Of these six items, items (i)–(iv) could be placed under the umbrella of what might be called reliability knowledge development [20]. This knowledge is gathered throughout the software life cycle. The usage or operational profile mentioned in items (ii) and (iii) and described in Section 12.3, is very important for reliability measurement. It allows a representative sample of actual inputs to be supplied during testing. Statistical testing mentioned in item (vi) and described in Section 12.4 is a type of testing where the emphasis is on measuring the reliability of the software rather than on detecting specific defects. It is used in conjunction with reliability growth models to make stop-test decisions. To monitor reliability growth testers select test data representing typical patterns of usage. The software is executed, and the amount of execution time between each failure is recorded. CPU time is one of the time units that can be used. Other time units include the number of transactions, or calendar time if the system is in continuous operation. After a statistically significant number of failures have been observed by the testers, the number of failures detected and the time between those failures, is used to compute a reliability measure.

With respect to item (iv), it is important for the reliability testing team to identify different classes or levels of failure and consider how they should be treated in the reliability specification. Since highly reliable software is very expensive, if the software is very large the team may decide to set separate reliability goals for each of its subsystems.

To develop the reliability specification the reliability testing team should:

(i) identify the types of system failures and their impact on the system. Impact is the basis for developing a severity level hierarchy as was described in Section 9.1.4 and shown in Figure 9.3.
(ii) Establish a reliability requirement for each failure level—for a failure of severity level "X" the reliability metric for MTBF is "Y," where "X" is one of the numbered severity levels and "Y" is an appropriate time duration that depends on the severity level.

The emphasis in testing should be on handling the most severe failures; these are of the greatest interest. We want to be sure that our testing process has eliminated them to the best of our ability. Reliability goals may be stated with respect to failures of particular severity levels that have a high impact on system usage and customer satisfaction.

12.6.1 Applying Reliability Models

Testers can use reliability models to help them predict how software reliability should grow or improve over time as the software is executed, faults are located, and repairs are made. The models can predict when, or if, a particular level of reliability is likely to be obtained within the constraints associated with the project and the testing effort. Testers can also use these models to assess how quickly software quality is improving over time. The test scenario is as follows. The software is run using the operational profile and a statistical testing approach as described previously. Its reliability is measured over time. When a number of reliability measurements have been made they are compared with a selected growth model and reliability predictions are made. Musa and Ackerman have a good discussion of this process [19]. They describe three useful reliability growth model types—static, basic, and logarithmic Poisson. The static model is best applied to unchanging software with an unchanging operational profile, for example, a terminal program that is usually permanently installed in a terminal as firmware. The basic model is useful for modeling failure occurrence for software being tested and continuously debugged. In this case, the software is run with test cases, failures are observed and recorded, and faults are constantly being repaired. Ideally, the failure intensity (failures/CPU hour) should decrease as testing proceeds and the code is repaired. This model works best if the faults in the software are equally likely to cause failures so that the average failure intensity improves by the same amount whenever a correction is made. This model also works well for the case where the operational profile remains unchanged, but where an action to correct a fault is taken whenever a failure is observed. Corrections need not be perfect.

If you assume that some faults are more likely to cause failures, and that on the average the improvement in failure intensity with each correction decreases exponentially as the corrections are made, then Musa and Ackerman recommend use of the logarithmic Poisson execution-time model [19]. Like the basic model, this model also works for cases where the operational profile remains unchanged, and where corrections (perfect or imperfect) are made when a failure is observed.

Data from these reliability studies can be collected and tabularized as shown on Table 12.2. Plots can be made of the observed cumulative number of failures versus execution time. Figure 12.5 gives the reader a rough idea of what such a plot for the basic model might look like. Musa and Ackerman [19], Sheldon et al. [20], Fenton [21], and Lyu and Nikora [22] show some actual plots. Reliability measurement tools can be used to help testers analyze the data collected. Several types of reliability models can be handled by the tools. The tools will perform statistical analysis and provide summary reports of data collected. Most importantly, they can give an estimate of the CPU time needed to reach reliability objectives. CPU time can be converted to calendar days and completion time for system test. The test manager can use this information to adjust schedules

Failure number	CPU sections since last failure
1	2
2	28
3	85
4	116
5	65
6	155
. . .	. . .
. . .	. . .
89	2004
90	2123
. . .	. . .

TABLE 12.2

A sample table for collecting failure data.

and resources. The outputs of the tools may also indicate to the manager that some renegotiation with the user/client group is necessary to reach the reliability goals [19].

There are uncertainties in using many of the reliability growth models. Testers and developers can never be certain that in repairing a defect that another defect is not injected, or that the repair initiates some condition that activates other failures. They also cannot be sure what contribution removal of a particular defect will make to increased reliability. This is the reason that testers may not observe interfailure times always increasing when a defect is repaired. In addition, testers cannot be sure exactly how the software will actually be used in operation. The exact set of inputs, or the order in which they will be submitted to the system, is not known since in many cases accurate and stable operational profiles are not available to testers. In a practical sense, test managers and clients also need to be aware of the costs of reaching a certain level of reliability. Given the higher costs of reaching higher levels of reliability, customers will need to make appropriate choices under existing cost constraints.

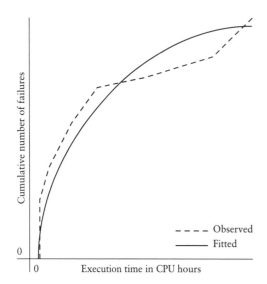

FIG. 12.5

A rough sample plot of cumulative number of failures versus execution time in CPU hours, both observed and fitted.

Other approaches to reaching a stop-test decision using reliability-type models have been reported in the literature. One of these is discussed in a paper by Ehrlich and co-authors [23]. The authors describe an interesting approach that uses software reliability engineering, and an economic model to support a decision on an optimal release time. They applied their model to a network management system that receives data from a telemetry network. The steps in their process were as follows.

1. Identification of a model to quantify the economic consequences of terminating test at a reliability achievable with a given number of units of test program execution.
2. Collection of data on failures and program execution time during system test.
3. Analysis of reliability data by selecting a reliability growth model and fitting the model to this data at several points during system test.
4. Combining reliability and economic knowledge by applying the re-

liability model's estimated values to the economic model to determine the optimal time for system release.

The economic model that the authors used was adapted from the work of Dalal and Mallows [24]. The model quantifies the economic consequences involved in a stop-test decision at a reliability level achievable with given units of execution time. There were several parameters associated with the economic model. These include (i) the cost of testing activities, (ii) the cost of resolving failures, (iii) the total expected number of faults, (iv) the software failure intensity rate, (v) the expected program execution time of the software release per field site, (vi) the number of field sites, and (vii) the cost to customer operations of a failure in the field. An operation profile for the system was available for this work, and failure data was collected from system test and beta-test sites.

The authors collected and analyzed reliability data, and chose to try three reliability growth models to apply to their data. An exponential model was selected based on its ability to gave the best fit to the data. The economic model was applied to determine the benefit-to-cost ratio associated with identifying the optimal time to release the software. For these experiments, costs included those associated with testing and reliability engineering, such as developing the operational profile and collecting and analyzing reliability measurements. The cost savings, or benefits, indicate the gain from having knowledge of the optimal time to release the software, and this is calculated from the author's model by using the available reliability and economic knowledge. The benefit-to-cost ratio associated with determining the optimal time to release is then calculated easily from this information. This approach gives testers information about the savings gained for the project as a result of stopping testing at the optimal time.

Another reliability-related approach to support stop-test decision making was reported by Brettschnieder at Motorola [25]. The author uses a simple model called the "zero-failure testing" model. It assumes that the problem rate $p(t)$ can be expressed as follows.

$$p(t) = a^* \, e(\exp(-b(t))$$

where a and b are constants and t is time. The model can be used to determine how many hours the system must be tested in order to meet a reliability goal. Three inputs are required: (i) the target projected number of customer failures, (ii) the number of test failures observed so far, and (iii). the total number of test execution hours up to the last failure. The equation to use for calculating zero-failure test hours is:

$$\frac{\ln \text{ (customer problems)}/(0.5 + \text{customer problems})}{\ln \text{ (0.5 + customer problems)}/(\text{test + customer problems})}$$

$$\times \text{ Test hours to last problem}$$

The author gives the following example of use of this equation. Suppose you are testing a 33,000-line program, and to date 15 repairable failures have been detected over an execution time of 500 hours. No failures have been observed in the last 50 hours of testing. Management want to know how much more testing is needed to ensure that the customers observe no more than a projected average of 0.03 failures per KLOC. In this case for the 33,000 lines that would indicate one customer failure should be observed. Using the equation shown above you calculate:

$$\frac{\ln \text{ (1/1.5)}}{\ln(1.5/16)} \times 450 = 77 \text{ zero failure test hours}$$

The value of 16 problems is the sum of the 15 problems observed so far, and the one problem (failures) allowed. The 450 is the result of 500 test hours minus the 50 failure-free hours already accomplished. The value of 1.5 is derived from the sum of 0.5 and the 1 allowed customer failure. Since you have already tested for 50 hours you need only test for $(77 - 50) = 27$ hours more. However, if there is a failure during the 27 additional hours, you will need to continue to test, recalculate, and restart your testing clock.

12.7 Confidence Levels and Quality Control

As a part of their quality control activities, testers at TMM level 5 can make estimations relating to the confidence level of the software. Confidence, usually expressed as a percent, gives testers information as to the likelihood that software is fault free. If a statement is made that a system is fault free with a 95% level of confidence, this means that the probability that the software has no faults is 0.95. Confidence levels are derived using fault seeding, a technique that was discussed in Chapter 9. To demonstrate how this technique is applicable let us suppose that the following situation exists: We have planted S faults in a program, and we believe the program has N actual faults. We then test the program until we find the S seeded faults. If n is the number of unseeded faults found during testing then the confidence level can be calculated as

$$C \begin{cases} = 1, & \text{if } n > N \\ = S/(S - N + 1), & \text{if } n \leqslant N \end{cases}$$

As an example of how testers can use this equation, let us suppose that we have a program and we claim it has no faults, that is, $N = 0$. If we seed this program with 15 faults, and we test and find all 15 without encountering any other faults, we can calculate the confidence level with $S = 10$ and $N = 0$ of

$$15 \ (15 - 0 + 1) = 15/16 \text{ or } 94\%$$

If our customer requires a 98% confidence level, then we would need to seed with

$$S/S - (0 + 1) = 0.98$$

or 49 seeded faults. To achieve this confidence level, we must continue testing until we find all of these seeded faults and no other unseeded faults. Note that this approach depends on finding all of the seeded faults to make an estimate of the confidence levels. A change to the above equation can be made to enable testers to estimate confidence levels using the number of detected seeded faults. This estimate of confidence can be calculated using the equation shown below where s is the number of detected seeded faults. This approach assumes that all faults have an equal probability of being detected which may not be true [26].

$$C \begin{cases} = 1, & \text{if } n > N \\ = \left(\dfrac{S}{S - 1} \right) \Big/ \left(\dfrac{S + N + 1}{N + s} \right), & \text{if } n \leqslant N \end{cases}$$

12.8 Usability Testing, and Quality Control

The descriptions and definitions for quality control focus on evaluation of the quality of a software system in terms of user requirements. For this reason quality control activities should certainly include a usability evaluation, usability being a software quality factor directly related to a user's view of a software system. Usability can be described in the following way.

> Usability is a quality factor that is related to the effort needed to learn, operate, prepare input, and interpret the output of a computer program.

Usability is a complex quality factor and can be decomposed according to IEEE standards into the subfactors [27]:

Understandability: The amount of effort required to understand the software.

Ease of learning: The degree to which user effort required to understand the software is minimized.

Operability: The degree to which the operation of the software matches the purpose, environment, and physiological characteristics of users; this includes ergonomic factors such as color, shape, sound, font size, etc.

Communicativeness: The degree to which the software is designed in accordance with the psychological characteristics of the users.

In the past it was believed that simple measurements such as the number of help screens and menu options could be used to measure usability. However, human factors groups in many large software organizations began to work with developers, designers, and analysts to:

(i) conduct experiments and empirical studies to identify improved usability-related attributes;

(ii) earn how to address usability issues in design;

(iii) learn how to engineer the development process so that usability concerns were addressed; and

(iv) learn how to test to ensure that usability goals were met.

Much was learned through this process, and over the past several years a new branch of testing has evolved called usability testing. A new profession of usability engineer has also emerged. A usability engineer should have education and training in the areas of human factors, software design, software quality, and usability testing. Usability engineers learn how to plan, design, set up, conduct, analyze, and report the results of usability tests. They need to ensure that results of usability test are used to improve the quality of the evolving software. Usability engineers need resources such as laboratory space to conduct the tests, training programs for new hires, and tools to collect and analyze data. In many organizations positions for usability engineers do not yet exist. In such cases usability testing, particularity in the latter portion of the software life cycle, could be carried out through a collaboration between human factors staff, software developers/testers, and software quality assurance staff. These groups will need to work with representatives of the target population who will be using the software to ensure that the software product meets the usability goals that were specified in the requirements. Rubin has written a book that is an excellent guide to this branch of testing [28]. Other papers and texts of interest in this field include references 29–33. Rubin has a detailed bibliography of such references. In the remainder of this section, usability, and a brief overview of usability testing using Rubin's approach will be presented to introduce the reader to this area of testing.

12.9 An Approach to Usability Testing

Rubin's approach to usability testing employs techniques to collect empirical data while observing a representative group of end users using the software product to perform a set of tasks that are representative of the proposed usage. Rubin emphasizes that participants in the usability tests must be selected carefully and be representative of the target group of users. He describes four types of tests: (i) exploratory, (ii) assessment, (iii) validation, and (iv) comparison. These are shown in Figure 12.6 and described in the following sections. The four test types comprise the whole of usability testing and occur throughout the software life cycle [28].

Types of usability tests　　　Life cycle phase applied

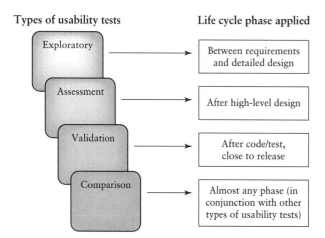

FIG. 12.6

Types of usability tests [28].

It is important to describe the basic elements of usability testing to show how they are related to designer, developer, and tester interests. The elements are (i) the development of a test objective (designers, testers), (ii) use of a representative sample of end users (testers), (iii) an environment for the test that represents the actual work environment (designers, testers), (iv) observations of the users who either review or use a representation of the product (the latter could be a prototype) (developers, testers), (v) the collection, analysis, and summarization of qualitative and quantitative performance and preference measurement data (designers, developers, and testers), and (vi) recommendations for improvement of the software product (designers, developers)

12.9.1 Exploratory Usability Testing

As previously mentioned, usability testing spans the entire life cycle of the software product. Exploratory tests are carried out early in the life cycle between requirements and detailed design. A user profile and usage model should be developed in parallel with this activity. The objective of exploratory usability testing is to examine a high-level representation of the user interface to see if it characterizes the user's mental model of the software. The results of these types of tests are of particular importance to designers who get early feedback on the appropriateness of the preliminary user interface design. More than one design approach can be presented via paper screens, early versions of the user manual, and/or prototypes with limited functionality.

Users may be asked to attempt to perform some simple tasks, or if it is too early in the prototying or development process, then the users can "walkthrough" or review the product and answer questions about it in the presence of a tester. The users and testers interact. They may explore the product together; the user may be asked to "think aloud" about the product. Users are usually asked for their input on how weak, unclear, and confusing areas can be improved. The data collected in this phase is more qualitative then quantitative.

12.9.2 Assessment Usability Testing

Assessment tests are usually conducted after a high-level design for the software has been developed. Findings from the exploratory tests are expanded upon; details are filled in. For these types of tests a functioning prototype should be available, and testers should be able to evaluate how well a user is able to actually perform realistic tasks. More quantitative data is collected in this phase of testing then in the previous phase. Examples of useful quantitative data that can be collected are:

(i)   number of tasks corrected completed/unit time;
(ii) number of help references/unit time;
(iii) number of errors (and error type);
(iv) error recovery time.

Using this type of data, as well as questionnaire responses from the users, testers and designers gain insights into how well the usability goals as specified in the requirements have been addressed. The data can be used to identify weak areas in the design, and help designers to correct problems before major portions of the system are implemented.

12.9.3 Validation Usability Testing

This type of usability testing usually occurs later in the software life cycle, close to release time, and is intended to certify the software's usability

[28]. A principal objective of validation usability testing is to evaluate how the product compares to some predetermined usability standard or benchmark. Testers want to determine whether the software meets the standards prior to release; if it does not, the reasons for this need to be established.

Having a standard is a precondition for usability validation testing. The usability standards may come from internal sources. These are usually based on usability experiences with previous products. External standards may come from competitors' products. Usability requirements should be set for each project, and these may be based on precious products, marketing surveys, and/or interviews with potential users. Usability requirements are usually expressed in quantitative terms as performance criteria. The performance criteria usually relate to how well, and how fast, a user can perform tasks using the software. Measurements taken during usability testing as described in the next section relate to usability subfactors similar to those described in Section 12.8.

Other objectives of validation usability testing include:

1. *Initiating usability standards.* The test results themselves can be used to set standards for future releases. For example, if in the first release we find during usability testing that a user can set up the system satisfactorily in 10 minutes with only one error occurring, that can be the standard for future releases.

2. *Evaluating how well user-oriented components of a software system work together.* This may be the first opportunity to test the interaction between online help, user manuals, documentation, software, and hardware from the user's point of view. In many cases these are developed by independent teams and are not tested together as an integral system until this time.

3. *Ensuring that any show-stoppers or fatal defects are not present.* If the software is new and such a defect is revealed by the tests, the development organization may decide to delay the release of the software. If the organization decides to market the software in spite of the defect, at least its nature is known and the organization can prepare for releasing a fix, training a support team, and/or public relations responses.

12.9.4 Comparison Test

Comparison tests may be conducted in any phase of the software life cycle in conjunction with other types of usability tests. This type of test uses a side-by-side approach, and can be used to compare two or more alternative interface designs, interface styles, and user manual designs. Early in the software life cycle comparison test is very useful for comparing various user interface design approaches to determine which will work best for the user population. Later it can be used at a more fine-grained level, for example, to determine which color combinations work best for interface components. Finally, comparison test can be used to evaluate how the organization's software product compares to that of a competing system on the market.

12.9.5 Usability Testing: Resource Requirements

To carry out usability testing requires organizational commitment in the form of:

1. *A usability testing laboratory.* This does not have to be an elaborate set-up, but should minimally consist of a private area that includes a user workstation, a sitting area for a tester (and other observers), and a video camera. More elaborate set-ups include multiple video cameras and separate observation rooms for multiple observers.
2. *Trained personnel.* Full-scale usability testing should involve staff trained as usability testers, In many organizations much of the work in usability testing may be carried out by human factors staff. SQA staff and software test specialists may also participate. Developers who are familiar with the technical aspects of the software play an auxiliary role during these tests. They need to be present to ensure that the software is functioning during the tests, and to restore or restart the system in case of crashes or other technical problems. The tasks and responsibilities for the usability testing staff include:

   - selecting the user participants;

   - designing, administering, and monitoring of the tests;

- developing forms needed to collect relevant data from user participants;

- analyzing, organizing, and distributing data and results to relevant parties;

- making recommendations to development staff and management.

3. *Usability test planning.* Like all other tests, usability tests need to be planned. Test objectives, staff, and resources needed, user profiles, task lists, test methodologies, evaluation measures (data to be collected), and types of test reports are among the items that should be included in the usability test plan. In his text, Rubin shows an example of a usability test plan [28].

   Initializing a usability test program is best done with pilot projects. Successes with the pilot projects provide a foundation for including additional projects that can be added incrementally to the program. Usability testers, with support from management, and successes from pilot projects, should inform and educate others within the organization to the benefits of a usability testing program. Potential benefits that should be mentioned include higher customer satisfaction, larger market share, fewer hot-line calls, and fewer repairs to operational software,

12.9.6 Usability Tests and Measurements

Tests designed to measure usability are in some ways more complex than those required for traditional software testing. With regard to usability tests, there are no simple inputs/output combinations that are of concern to the traditional tester. The approach to test design calls for the tester to present the user with a set of tasks to be performed. Therefore, knowledge of typical usage patterns (use cases can be helpful) for the software is necessary to plan the tests. Tasks that constitute a series of usability tests should be prioritized by frequency, criticality, and vulnerability (those tasks suspected before testing to be difficult, or poorly designed) [28]. For example a usability test for a word processing program might consist of tasks such as:

(i)   open an existing document;
(ii)   add text to the document;
(iii) modify the old text;
(iv)   change the margins in selected sections;
(v)   change the font size in selected sections;
(vi)   print the document;
(vii) save the document.

As the user performs these tasks she will be observed by the testers and video cameras. Time periods for task completion and the performance of the system will be observed and recorded. Any errors made by the user will be noted. Time to recover from errors will be noted. Users' comments as they work may be solicited and recorded. In addition, the video cameras can be used to record facial expressions and spoken comments, which may be very useful for evaluating the system. These observations, comments, and recordings are the outputs/results of the usability tests.

Many of the usability test results will recorded as subjective evaluations of the software. Users will be asked to complete questionnaires that state preferences and ranking with respect to features such as:

(i)   usefulness of the software;
(ii)   how well it met expectations;
(iii) ease of use;
(iv)   ease of learning;
(v)   usefulness and availability of help facilities.

In comparison testing, participants may also be asked to rank:

(i)   one prototype over another;
(ii)   the current software system versus a competitor's;
(iii) a new version of the software over the previous versions.

Usability testers also collect quantitative measures. For example:

(i)   time to complete each task;
(ii)   time to access information in the user manual;
(iii) time to access information from on-line help;

(iv) number and percentage of tasks completed correctly;

(v) number or percentage of tasks completed incorrectly;

(vi) time spent in communicating with help desk.

Testers can also count the number of:

(i) errors made;

(ii) incorrect menu choices;

(iii) user manual accesses;

(iv) help accesses;

(v) time units spent in using help;

(vi) incorrect selections;

(vii) negative comments or gestures (captured by video).

These measures in conjunction with subjective data from user question-naires, can be used to evaluate the software with respect to the four us-ability subfactors: understandability, ease of learning, operability, and communicativeness, as described in Section 12.8. For example, time to complete a each task, number of user manual accesses, and time to access information in the user manual can be used to evaluate the subfactors, understandability, and ease of learning. The number of incorrect selec-tions, and the number of negative comments or gestures can be used to evaluate the operability and communicativeness of the software.

The raw data should be summarized and then analyzed [28]. For performance data, such as task timings, common descriptive statistics should be calculated, for example, average, median, and standard devi-ation values. Usability testers should identify and focus on those tasks that did not meet usability goals and those that presented difficulties to users. Problem areas should be prioritized so that the development team can first work on those deemed the most critical.

As a result of the usability tests, all the analyzed data should be used to make recommendations for actions. In this phase of usability testing designers with a knowledge of user-centered design, and human factors staff with knowledge of human–computer interaction can work as part of the recommendation team. A final report should be developed and distributed to management and the technical staff who are involved in the project. In some cases the usability testing team may also make a presentation. When the project is complete, and the usability requirements are satisfied, the usability data should be stored and used as benchmark data for subsequent releases and similar projects.

Usability testing is an important aspect of quality control. It is one of the procedures we can use as testers to evaluate our product to ensure that it meets user requirements on a fundamental level. Setting up a usability program to implement all the types of the types of usability tests as described by Rubin is costly. To support usability testing an organization must also be committed to include usability requirements in the requirements specification which is not always the case. There are other approaches to usability evaluation that are less expensive, such as preparing simple prototypes and questionnaires early in the life cycle for volunteer users, and instrumenting source code to collect usage information. Finally, each software product can be annotated with a "complaint" facility that allows users to give feedback to developers about problems that occur. None of these approaches work as well as full usability testing; in many cases the data is collected after the software has been in operation and it is not possible to make changes or improve quality. Hopefully subsequent releases of the software will benefit from the feedback.

12.10 Software Quality Control and the Three Critical Views

By satisfying maturity goals at TMM levels 2 and 3, an organization builds an improved, and more effective testing process. Thus, it is equipped to carry out quality evaluation activities at TMM level 4 where testing focuses on measuring quality-related attributes such as correctness, security, portability, interoperability, and maintainability. At level 5 the testing infrastructure is solid enough to address quality control issues. Development of operational profiles, their application to statistical testing, and reliability evaluation is feasible given the level of staffing knowledge and training, and the commitment of organizational resources. At TMM level 5 testers have the expertise, training, and resources available to measure confidence levels, and evaluate trustworthiness, usability, and reliability as part of the testing process. The testing group and the software quality assurance group are quality leaders at TMM level 5. They work closely with managers, software designers, and implementors to incorporate techniques and tools to reduce defects and to control software quality. Client/user input is also needed to support these goals. The following paragraphs give examples of the activities, tasks, and responsibilities assigned to the three critical groups at TMM level 5 in support of quality control practices as applied to an evolving software system.

Managers Role

Managers have a strong supporting role for quality control. They should ensure that testing and SQA policies and plans include references to quality control issues. Managers should also make sure that resources and training are dedicated to quality control activities, and that adequate time is allocated in the project and test plans for quality control practices. Managers should monitor all testing activities (this includes activities such as reviews and execution-based test) to ensure that quality goals are being achieved. Feedback from quality evaluation activities such as reviews, and reliability/usability testing should be applied to improve the quality of the software.

In the case of testing for reliability and usability goals, managers again should be sure that these goals have been adequately described in the requirements document, and that proper hardware, software, and staffing resources are being allocated to support the appropriate teams. Managers should also ensure that operational profiles and typical usage scenarios for the software are defined and applied to reliability and usability testing. To promote the important role of quality control, and related reliability/usability engineering activities, managers should make sure that the involved staff are trained, rewarded, and have career paths available to them.

Testers Role

Testers continue their role as quality evaluators that began at lower levels of the TMM. Testers, along with managers, should ensure that quality goals are clearly expressed in requirements documents. Testers should attend necessary training/education courses to gain to knowledge necessary to:

- develop and maintain operational profiles;

- develop a hierarchy of severity levels;

- carry out statistical testing and analyze results;

- understand and apply reliability models;

- collect and store quality-related measurements, for example, from reliability and usability tests;

- design and execute tests to measure attributes such as correctness, portability, reliability, usability, confidence, availability, and trust-worthiness;

- develop usability test plans;

- identity user groups for usability testing;

- design usability tests;

- support set up of usability testing laboratories;

- monitor, analyze, and report the results of usability tests.

Users/Clients Role

Users and clients have a responsibility to establish quality requirements for the projects they are involved in. They should give strong support to testers and reliability engineers engaged in the process of developing an operational profile. Users and clients should also help to set reliability goals for their projects. Users should help develop typical usage scenarios, and participate in usability testing by using the evolving software to carry out typical tasks and giving feedback to the testing team. It is important for users to state their opinions regarding the strengths and weaknesses of the developing software system.

KEY TERMS

Availability
Confidence
Discriminant
Maintainability
Operational profile
Quality

Quality control
Software quality assurance
Software reliability
Trustworthiness
Usability

EXERCISES

1. Categorize in your own terms the costs related to software quality activities.

2. Some organizations use the measure of defect density (number of defects/ KLOC), as an indication of the reliability of their software. Comment on the usefulness of this measurement from the user's point of view of reliability.

3. What is an operational profile, and what is the user/client role in its development?

4. Describe the steps in the Musa methodology for developing an operational profile.

5. How does the Walton model represent usage states and transition probabilities?

6. Suppose you were a test manager and you were organizing a team to develop an operational profile/usage model for an automated airline reservation system that was being developed by your company. From which organizational, and non-organizational groups would you select members for the team? Give your reasons in terms of the qualifications needed. What approach could you use to verify the profile/model?

7. How does development of an operational/usage profile support statistical testing?

8. What is the difference between software reliability and availability from the viewpoint of a software user?

9. Suppose you were testing a 45,000-line program and to date 17 repairable failures have been detected over an execution time of 550 hours. No failures have

been observed in the last 68 hours of test. Your manager wants to know how much more testing is needed to ensure that the customers observe no more than a projected average of 0.04 failures per KLOC. Use Brettschnieder's equations to calculate the remaining hours of test you will need to meet the customer's requirement.

10. How can reliability growth models be applied to make stop-test decisions? Compare the costs of using these models to make stop-test decisions as opposed to the stop-test criteria discussed in Section 9.3 of this text. If you were testing a safety-critical application, which approach would you take, provided you had adequate funding for any of the choices?

11. Discuss the types of usability tests suggested by Rubin.

12. What are the resources requirements for usability testing, and how do the TMM maturity goals support the acquisition of these resources?

13. Describe the stages of usability testing you would recommend for an automated hotel reservation system. What critical measurements would you collect and analyze to help determine the level of usability?

14. What roles and responsibilities do the user/client groups have in software quality control?

REFERENCES

[1] *IEEE Standard Glossary of Software Engineering Terminology* (IEEE Std 610.12-1990), copyright 1990 by IEEE, all rights reserved.

[2] R. Pressman, *Software Engineering: A Practitioner's Approach,* fifth edition, McGraw-Hill, New York 2000.

[3] *IEEE Standard for Software Reviews and Audits* (IEEE Std 1028-1988), copyright 1989 by IEEE, all rights reserved.

[4] *IEEE Standard for Software Quality Assurance Plans* (IEEE Std 730-1989), copyright 1989 by IEEE, all rights reserved.

[5] W. Humphrey, *A Discipline for Software Engineering,* Addison-Wesley, Reading, MA, 1995.

[6] C. Cho, "Statistical methods applied to software quality control," in *Handbook of Software Quality Assurance,* second edition, G. Schulmeyer, J McManus, eds., Van Nostrand, Reinhold, New York, 1992.

[7] J. Musa, "Operational profiles in software reliability engineering," *IEEE Software,* Vol. 10, No. 3, pp. 14–32, 1993.

[8] G. Walton, J. Poore, C. Trammell, "Statistical testing of software based on a usage model," *Software: Practice and Experience,* Vol. 25, No. 1, pp. 97–108, 1995.

[9] S. Prowell, C. Trammell, R. Linger, J. Poore, *Cleanroom Software Engineering*, Addison-Wesley, Reading, MA, 1999.

[10] R. Cobb, H. Mills, "Engineering software under statistical quality control," *IEEE Software*, Vol. 7, No. 5. pp. 44–54, 1990.

[11] H. Mills, M. Dyer, R. Linger, "Cleanroom software engineering," *IEEE Software*, Vol. 4, No. 5, pp. 19–24, 1987.

[12] H. Pham, *Software Reliability and Testing*, IEEE Computer Society Press, Los Alamitos, CA, 1995.

[13] *IEEE Recommended Practice for Software Requirements Specifications* (IEEE Std 830-1993), copyright 1994 by IEEE, all rights reserved.

[14] D. Zeitler, "Realistic assumptions for software reliably models," *Proc. International Symp. Software Reliability Eng.*, IEEE Press, Los Alamitos, Ca, pp. 67–74, 1991.

[15] D. Hamlet, "Are we testing for true reliability?" *IEEE Software*, Vol. 9, No. 4, pp. 21–27, 1992.

[16] *IEEE Guide for the Use of IEEE Standard Dictionary of Measures to Produce Reliable Software* (IEEE Std 982.2-1988), copyright 1989 by IEEE, all rights reserved.

[17] M. Shooman, *Software Engineering: Design, Reliability, and Management*, McGraw-Hill, New York, 1983.

[18] J. Musa, A Iannino, K. Olomoto, *Software Reliability: Measurement, Prediction, and Application*, McGraw-Hill, New York, 1987.

[19] J. Musa, A. Ackerman, "Quantifying software validation: when to stop testing," *IEEE Software*, Vol. 6, No. 3, May 1989.

[20] F. Sheldon, K. Kavi, R. Tausworthe, J. Yu, R. Brettschneider, W. Everett, "Reliability measurement: from theory to practice," *IEEE Software*, Vol. 9, No. 4, pp. 13–20, July 1992.

[21] N. Fenton, *Software Metrics: A Rigorous Approach*, Chapman & Hall, London, 1991.

[22] M. Lyu, A. Nikora, "Applying reliability models more effectively," *IEEE Software*, Vol. 9, No. 4, pp. 43–52, 1992.

[23] W. Ehrlich, B. Prasanna, J. Stampfel, J. Wu, "Determining the cost of a stop-test decision," *IEEE Software*, Vol. 10, No. 2, pp. 33–42, 1993.

[24] S. Dalal, C. Mallows, "When should one stop testing software?" *J. American Statistical Assoc.*, Vol. 81, No. 403, pp. 872–879, 1988.

[25] R. Brettschneider, "Is your software ready for release?" *IEEE Software*, Vol. 6, No. 4, pp. 100–108, 1989.

[26] F. Richards, *Computer Software: Testing, Reliability Models, and Quality Assurance*, Technical Report, NPS-55RH74071A, Naval Postgraduate School, Monterey, CA, 1974.

[27] *IEEE Standard for a Software Quality Metrics Methodology* (IEEE Std 1061-1992), copyright 1993 by IEEE, all rights reserved.

[28] J. Rubin, *Handbook of Usability Testing*, John Wiley & Sons, New York, 1994.

[29] P. Booth, *An Introduction to Human–Computer Interaction*, Lawrence Erlbaum Associates, London, 1989.

[30] M. Dieli, "A problem-solving approach to usability test planning," *Proc. International Professional Communication Conf.*, Seattle, pp. 265–267, 1988.

[31] C. Mills, "Usability testing in the real world," *SIGCHI Bulletin*, Vol. 19, No. 1, pp. 43–46, 1987.

[32] P. Sullivan, "Beyond a narrow conception of usability testing," *IEEE Transactions on Professional Communications*, Vol. 32, No. 4, pp. 256–264, 1989.

[33] D. Schell, "Overview of a typical usability test," *Proc. International Professional Communications Conf.*, Winnipeg, pp. 117–125, 1987.

DEFECT ANALYSIS AND PREVENTION

13.0 Processes and Defects

Various classes of software defects have been described in previous chapters. This knowledge is important to us as testers. We use our understanding of defect classes to develop defect hypotheses. We also use our understanding of both static and dynamic testing techniques to develop test cases based on these hypotheses for defect detection. In addition to our work in defect detection, we as testers have an additional set of defect-related goals. These goals are to:

- analyze defects to find their root causes;

- take actions and make changes

    —in our overall development processes;

    —in our testing process;

- prevent defects from reoccurring.

The TMM maturity goals support us with these objectives. When we do the work to achieve the maturity goals at TMM levels 2–5 we acquire the necessary policies, tools, plans, training, and techniques that allow us to prevent defects from reoccurring in our software deliverables, both internal and external. Internal deliverables include, for example, design documents and test-related items such as test plans, test cases, and test procedures. External deliverables include the code, system, and user manuals that are delivered to the client.

Defect analysis and defect prevention are activities that are of increasing importance as the software we develop becomes more complex and has greater and greater impact on our safely, health, and financial well-being. We as testers need to be involved in defect prevention activities since we have expertise and motivation to carry out the necessary tasks. We want to apply these activities to our testing process as defects can be injected during this phase of development. We also want to apply them to the overall development process to prevent defects from reoccurring in other life cycle phases. As a result of our efforts in both of these directions, we will be able to improve the quality of our final software product. The TMM provides a framework for defining tester responsibility in support of these efforts.

The goal of defect prevention is not entirely new, nor is it strictly limited to the software industry as the reader will note in the next section. An interesting point that should be made here is that carrying out the goal of defect prevention to its limit, in theory, could lead to defect-free software. Some argue that the latter is a feasible goal for software engineers [1]. However, given the case that software is designed, developed, and tested by humans who under the best of circumstances may introduce defects, a more practical objective would be to improve our processes so that we can develop software with a very low defect content. The emphasis should be on process because the nature of the development/test process, the tools and techniques used, the quality of the staff—all have a great impact on the defect content. Given these circumstances, we should carefully note that testers alone are not able to produce, nor are they solely responsible for producing, very low defect software.

What we can do as testers is to concentrate on defect classification, detection, removal, and prevention activities. We can have a high impact in these areas. We can, and should, offer our input and expertise to improve development/test process areas so that high-quality software is the result. As far as our own testing process is concerned, we should aim for identification of weaknesses that allow:

- defects to be injected into our test work products;
- defects to escape from our defect-filtering activities and propagate into the software product.

We need to use our process knowledge and also our knowledge of defect types, defect occurrences, defect analysis techniques, dynamic, and static testing techniques to prevent defects from occurring, and to ensure that those that do occur are detected by our testing activities.

It is very expensive to remove defects. Defect removal in many cases accounts for a high fraction of the costs of software development (see Section 12.1) [2]. The longer the defect exists in our software product the more expensive it is to remove. If a defect exists in the software we develop that causes harm or damage to life and/or property, the costs and social consequences due to that defect may be disastrous. If we prevent defects from being injected and/or propagated into subsequent software development phases, we benefit in the economic, legal, and social arenas.

As we move up the levels of the TMM we build a more proficient testing process. It becomes defined, measured, staffed, managed, and more predictable. It supports production of high-quality, low-defect software. We understand its strengths and weaknesses through repeated cycles of TMM assessments. We build an infrastructure that enables us make further progress in optimizing our testing process. In this chapter we will examine defect analysis and prevention techniques associated with TMM level 5 maturity goals. We examine these techniques in a general way and apply them to improve our development process and our testing process as well. By applying these techniques we are more able to learn from our past mistakes, and take actions to prevent them from reoccurring. In the framework of the TMM we are able to strengthen our testing process, and make it more effective, and predictive.

13.1 History of Defect Analysis and Prevention

In this chapter we will study two highly interrelated processes. These are (i) defect analysis, and (ii) defect prevention. Why are these two process so important to us as testers and software engineers? Humphrey and Mays give the following arguments [2,3]. These are summarized in Figure 13.1.

1. Defect analysis/prevention processes help to reduce the costs of developing and maintaining software by reducing the number of defects that require our attention in both review and execution-based testing activities. Defect localization and repair are in the main unplanned activities. When they occur they make our process less predictable. Fewer defects means that we are better able to meet our budget requirements, and our overall process is likelier to be more on time and within budget.

2. Defect analysis/prevention processes help to improve software quality. If we identity the cause of a class of defects and change our process so that it does not reoccur, our software should be less defective with respect to that class of defects and more able to meet the customer's requirements.

3. If our software contains fewer defects, this reduces the total number of problems we must look for; the sheer volume of problems we need to address may be significantly smaller. If we can eliminate noncritical (trivial) defects, then we as testers are in a better position to apply our time and expertise to detecting the fewer, but perhaps more serious, defects. This, in turn, could increase the effectiveness of our testing process.

4. Defect analysis/prevention processes provide a framework for overall process improvement activities. They can serve as drivers for process improvement. When we know the cause of a defect, we identify a specific area of our process that needs work. Improvements made in this area usually produce readily visible benefits. Defect analysis/ prevention activities not only help to fine-tune an organizations' current process and practices, but also support the identification and implementation of new methods and tools so that current process continues to evolve and comes closer to being optimized. In the case of an organization using the TMM for process assessment and improvement, there is a strong relationship and mutually supporting roles for defect prevention and overall test process improvement.

5. Defect analysis/prevention activities encourage interaction between a

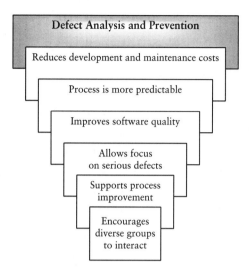

FIG. 13.1

Benefits of defect analyses and prevention processes.

diverse number of staff members, for example, project managers, developers, testers, and SQA staff, The close interrelationships between specialized group activities and the quality of internal and external deliverables becomes more apparent. The success of a defect prevention program depends on cooperation between, and the participation of, members of these groups.

Time and resources are required to implement the defect analyses/ prevention processes, and it is essential that management be committed to providing the necessary support. There must also be an infrastructure in place that includes trained and motivated staff, measurement and review programs, and a monitoring and controlling system. In addition, the existence of a defect repository as described in Chapter 3 is a necessary precondition for the implementation of both defect analysis and defect prevention activities.

The term defect analysis is applied to the process of identifying the root causes of defects. We have already laid the groundwork for discussion of this process with the material that is presented in Chapter 3 where we examined the root causes (origins) of defects in the general sense.

Recall in that discussion that defect origins were attributed to lack of communication, oversight, lack of education, poor transcription, and a poor or immature process. For a particular type of defect, defect causal analysis carefully focuses in on an exact cause which must be described in detail. For example, if we find that a lack of initialization of variables is a reoccurring defect, we need to be specific about its cause. If we determine in the general sense that it originates from lack of education, we must identify the educational area that should be addressed. For example, it may occur because of (i) poor programming language education, (ii) lack of training in use of static analysis tools, or (iii) a poor design education. We want to pinpoint the exact cause so that we can take action to make improvements.

Defect prevention describes the process that allows an organization to devise actions to prevent defects from reoccurring knowing their root cause. Actions must be tracked and monitored. Feedback must be provided from the actions implemented. As a result of successful actions, processes will undergo changes to eliminate the causes, and these changes must be measured and monitored to determine if all the goals have been meet. This is a continuous process. Defect prevention activities include action planning. action tracking, feedback, and process change.

Defect analysis and prevention are important aspects of quality control and have roots in the fields of quality management and quality control. Pioneers in these fields were, for example, Crosby [4], Deming [5], and Juran [6–7]. Related work in this area was described in Chapter 12 of this text. Recall that quality control activities as described by Cho were said to include random sampling, testing, measurements, inspections, defect causal analysis, and defect prevention [8]. We have covered several of these topics in previous chapters. In this chapter the focus is on defect analysis and prevention which are coupled together in what we will call in this text a defect prevention program. Such a program is embedded in the TMM level 5 maturity goal, "defect prevention."

13.2 Necessary Support for a Defect Prevention Program

When an organization decides to implement a defect prevention program it needs to have attained a certain level of process maturity in the sense that there should be an infrastructure in place consisting of polices, goals, staff, methods, tools, measurements, and organizational structures to support the program. Note that like the TMM, the CMM has a Key Process Area called "defect prevention," which is at its highest maturity level [9]. Placing this goal at the highest maturity levels of the models ensures that the infrastructure described above is in place, and that gives the program the necessary support to become a success.

In addition to a process infrastructure, an organization also must have managerial commitment to successfully implement a defect prevention program. Management must provide leadership, resources, and support cultural changes. An additional precondition is the existence of a defect repository and a defect (problem) reporting system. You cannot prevent defects if you do not consistently classify, count, and record them as they occur. In this way you know they exist, where, and when they occur, and their frequency of occurrence. Chapter 3 of this text discusses the importance of a defect repository and Figure 3.6 shows how the repository can support several of the TMM maturity goals including defect prevention. The defect repository can be organized in a manner to suit the organization. Some useful items that can be associated with each defect to support defect prevention activities were described in Chapter 11. A sample defect record was shown in Figure 11.3. Fields in the record included:

- defect identifier;

- product identifier;

- defect type;

- where found (module ID, give a line number for code);

- phase injected;

- phase detected;

- date of detection;

- tester/inspector names.

At TMM level 5 we can add additional fields to a defect record, for example, a status field (open, under repair, closed). Given the activities associated with defect prevention, when the defect has been closed, and subject to causal analysis then we can add:

- close date;

- author of fix;

- causal category (education, transcription, process, etc.);

- comments and discussion of cause;

- description of associated actions for prevention.

Finally, we can add a severity rating for each defect, and a priority level based on impact.

There are several other essential elements necessary to implement a defect prevention program. These are:

1. A training program to prepare staff members for defect analysis and defect prevention activities (supported by TMM level 3 maturity goal). This includes training in defect causal analysis techniques and use of statistical analysis tools.
2. A defect causal analysis process where defects from all projects are analyzed using the techniques described in the next section. Process goals are to identify the mechanisms by which each particular defect is injected into a software deliverable. When the cause is identified, preventive actions (process changes) can be suggested.
3. Action teams to implement and oversee the suggested process changes as applied to pilot projects.
4. A tracking system to monitor the process changes, and provide feedback on the usefulness of the changes, and their impact on software quality.
5. A technology transfer, or process improvement group, that will ensure that defect prevention becomes a standard set of practices and that process changes to support defect prevention are implemented throughout the organization (supported by the TMM level 5 maturity goal, "Test process optimization").

13.3 Techniques for Defect Analysis

One of the most useful techniques we can apply to analyzing defects is based on the Pareto principle as described by Juran, and discussed by McCabe and Schulmeyer [1,6,7,10,11]. Juran stated the principle very simply as "concentrate on the vital few and not the trivial many" [6,7]. An alternative expression of the principle is to state that 80% of the problems can be fixed with 20% of the effort. With respect to software defects, the principle can be applied to guide us in the allocation of our efforts and resources. We concentrate them on exploring those defects that occur most frequently and have the most negative impact on the quality of our software. The collection and classification of defect data, along with the application of Pareto analysis techniques, can give us a good indication of which defects we need to examine and address. These are the ones we must try to prevent, and we must make changes in our process to prevent them. The results of Pareto analysis give our quality improvement effects a definite direction.

As an example, suppose we have data on classes of code defects and frequencies of occurrence for a hypothetical software system as shown in Table 13.1. The technique we apply is to plot this data on a Pareto diagram as shown in Figure 13.2. The figure shows a true Pareto diagram which is a bar graph showing the frequency of occurrence of focus items with the most frequent ones appearing first [11]. Note that the Pareto diagram in Figure 13.2 guides us in identifying the defects, and sequences the defects in order of their frequency of occurrence. From the diagram we can immediately identify the vital few—those defects that have occurred in the greatest number during the development of our hypothetical software system. Defects of the data flow and initialization types dominate in their occurrences. Our greatest attention should be focused on determining their causes and developing action plans to prevent their reoccurrence. The Pareto diagram helps us to decide where to invest resources for quality improvement efforts.

Readers should note that use of Pareto diagrams is not restricted to identifying and analyzing code defects. Defects found in reviews and other software evaluation activities can also be analyzed in this way to drive defect prevention programs. Pareto diagrams can also be used to analyze defect occurrences by code modules (plot defect frequency for each mod-

Defect type	Number occurrences	Percent of total
1. Control and logic	21	10.5
2. Algorithmic	9	4.5
3. Typographical	19	9.5
4. Initialization	55	27.5
5. Data flow	73	36.5
6. Module interface	15	7.5
7. External hardware–software interface	8	4.0
TOTAL	200	

TABLE 13.1

Sample defect data.

ule) or by development phase (plot defect frequency for each phase) This information can help identity the most error-prone modules or development phases and provides useful information for future releases and for process improvement efforts [9]. An additional use for Pareto diagrams is to analyze defect causes. Once the basic causes of defects have been established these can be plotted as a function of frequency of occurrence (causal frequency instead of defect frequency) so that action plans for process changes can be developed to address the most frequent causes of defects [10].

There are many discussions that show Pareto analysis is a useful tool for addressing quality issues and making decisions on process changes. Some general guidelines for applying Pareto analysis are to:

(i)   collect data relevant to problem area;
(ii) develop appropriate Pareto diagrams;
(iii) use the diagrams to identity the vital few as issues that should be dealt with on an individual basis;
(iv) use the diagrams to identity the trivial many as issues that should be dealt with as classes.

Using the Pareto technique we can identify our problem areas, quantify their impact, and plan for changes. We can also prioritize the changes that need to be made to improve quality. Pareto analysis is simple; it

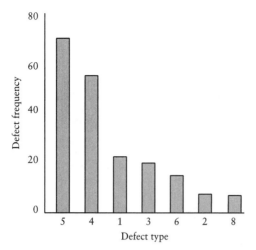

FIG. 13.2

Pareto diagram for defect distribution shown in Table 13.1.

does not require any expensive tools or extensive training, but it is very powerful.

Another technique that is very useful for defect causal analysis makes use of what is called an Ishikawa or "fishbone" diagram. Use of the Ishikawa diagram began with the introduction of Quality Circles (QC). These were small groups that met voluntarily to perform quality control in a workshop. The QC was originally used for manufacturing processes, but can be applied to software production as well. The diagrams were used to identify what were called influential factors that impact on a problem area. In our domain we can use these diagrams to identify probable causes for a particular effect. A generic version of a fishbone diagram is shown in Figure 13.3. The major horizontal arrow points to an effect. The diagonal arrowed lines are probable causes. Originally each major cause was related to what was called a major control point. Major control points were categorized as the "4M"—manpower, machines, methods and materials. The smaller horizontal lines intersecting the diagonal arrows are individual causes within a major 4M category. The group in the QC would prepare the fishbone diagram and circle the most likely causes, which would then receive appropriate attention [11]. When applied to

Causes

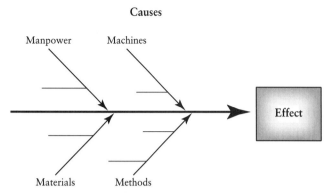

FIG. 13.3
A generic fishbone diagram.

identifying causes for software defects the 4Ms are not entirely appropriate and other categories can be defined by an organization.

13.4 Defect Causal Analysis

Defect causal analysis is a component of what we call a defect prevention program. Action planning, action implementation, tracking, and feedback, as well as process evolution, are the other components of this program. A team or task force should be established to initiate and oversee a defect prevention program. The team members should be trained and motivated. Testers, developers, project managers, SQA staff, and process improvement group members are good candidates to carry out the tasks and responsibilities essential for initiation of the program. The team is responsible for developing policies and goals that relate to defect analysis and prevention. These policies/goals should be documented and made available to appropriate parties. Defect causal categories should be established as part of the policy statement. Sources for such categories are, for example, Chapter 3 in this book, or those reported by Endres [12] and Grady and Caswell [13].

Practically speaking there are two separate groups that are actually involved in implementing a defect prevention program. These are (i) the causal analysis group, and (ii) the action planning/tracking team as shown in Figure 13.4. In this section the work of the defect causal group will be described. The next section will describe the work of the action planning, implementation, and tracking group.

The mechanism for implementing defect causal analysis is usually a meeting. Attendees, need to bring all necessary items such as problem reports, test logs, defect fix reports, defect repository reports, and specially requested designer/developer reports. The make-up of the causal analysis group will vary. For example, if defects from requirements and design stages are being analyzed, attendees should of course include analysts and designers. If test defects are the focus of attention, then the test group should make up a large portion of the attendees. If coding defects are being analyzed then developers should comprise a large number of the attendees. It is also useful to have members of SQA and process improvement groups present at these meetings.

The agenda for the meetings should allow for discussions that focus on (i) finding a defect cause or origin for each type of defect, (ii) exploring and developing process change suggestions, or actions, for preventing the reoccurrence of each defect type in future projects, and (iii) establishing priorities for the actions that are proposed.

Appropriate times to hold defect causal analysis meeting vary. Some organizations call for such meetings after a significant number of defects have been detected. Others call for meetings after each life cycle phase. Humphrey suggests that causal analysis meetings should be held at various times both before and after the release of the software. He suggests the following time periods as shown in Figure 13.5 [2]:

(i)   shortly after the detailed design stage is complete for all system modules (analyze problems/defects found by reviews);

(ii) shortly after each module has completed a test phase or level of testing (analyze defects found at that level of test);

(iii) after release of the software, and there are a reasonable number of problems or defects reported in operation;

(iv) on an annual basis after the software has been released even if the number of problems/defect reported is relatively low.

Humphrey also suggests keeping the number of meeting participants between 5 and 8, and that a leader and recorder should be appointed

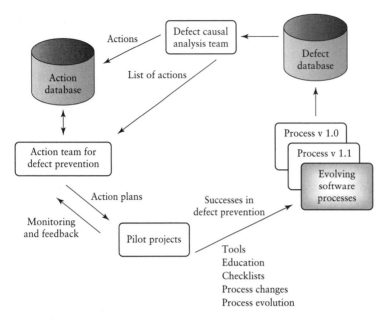

FIG. 13.4

The defect prevention process.

for the meeting. They have roles similar to those played in an inspection meeting.

The tone of a causal analysis meeting should be constructive and positive. The purpose is not to lay blame for the defects, but to find root causes and to take action to prevent them. The format of the meeting may vary, but usually there is a review of information available for each defect. Participants may suggest causes for defects that will be discussed by all. Fishbone diagrams can be prepared and/or discussed for each defect. The team as a whole then can propose actions/process changes to prevent the defect from reoccurring. Other process-related issues may also be discussed, for example, use of new tools, techniques, and management issues.

In a typical meeting about 10–15 defects detected through reviews or by testing undergo analysis [3]. Usually these will result in 15–25 suggested actions. The suggested actions relate to the causes and may focus on, for example, improving education, communication, review and/or management practices. The recommended actions need to be described in detail so that the action team is able to implement them on pilot projects.

Prerelease meeting times
for defect causal analysis

Postrelease meeting times
for defect causal analysis

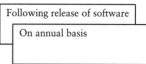

Following detailed design
Following unit test
Following integration test
Following system test
Following acceptance test

Following release of software
On annual basis

FIG. 13.5

*Suggested meeting times for defect
causal analysis [2].*

The actions can also be classified into related groups and should be prioritized based on the impact of the defects on software quality, the costs of process changes, and overall organizational quality goals, Deliverables from the causal analysis meetings may include Pareto and Ishikawa diagrams, a record of each defect, its cause and recommended actions for prevention. An example of two defect records from a causal analysis meeting after the coding phase is shown in Table 13.2. Cause categories were selected from those described in Chapter 3.

As testers we can participate in defect causal analysis meetings on two levels:

1. *Defect analysis on the general process level.* We can participate as members of a causal analysis team with an interest in identifying defect causes for all types of defects found in all phases the development process. We are ideally suited to assist in this process since we are actively engaged in detecting, logging, and classifying defects during execution-based testing and as members of review teams.

2. *Defect analysis for defects confined to the testing process.* We are particularly interested in identifying, finding causes for, and preventing defects that occur during testing. We can initiate causal analysis meetings for the purpose of analyzing defects that occur during testing, that is, they are particular to testing. In this case we apply defect analysis techniques to finding the causes of defects that originate in testing, for example, in test documents, practices and procedures. An example deliverable from

Defect description	Cause category	Cause description	Phase injected	Suggested action
Dangling pointers	Oversight	Developer fails to deallocate pointer when memory location is no longer in use; was aware that this should be done.	Code	1. Add to checklist for design/code review. 2. Add to coding standard.
Parameter mismatches	Communcation	Documentation from design is inadequate; no detailed parameter descriptions.		1. Modify design standards. 2. Coders attend design reviews. 3. Add to design checklist. 4. Institute commu-nication meetings between designers and coders.

TABLE 13.2

Example causal analysis report for design/code defects.

such a meeting is a fishbone diagram such as the one shown in Figure 13.6, which was developed to identify causes of branch test case design defects.

13.5 The Action Team: Making Process Changes

When the defect causal analysis team has completed its work, the action team now initiates the preventative actions. The actions can include

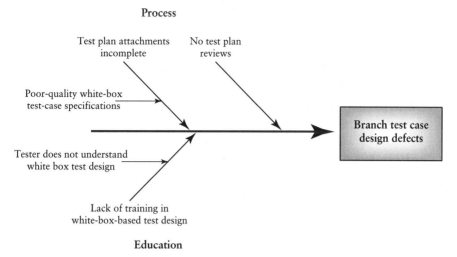

Process

Test plan attachments incomplete

No test plan reviews

Poor-quality white-box test-case specifications

Branch test case design defects

Tester does not understand white box test design

Lack of training in white-box-based test design

Education

FIG. 13.6

An example of a fishbone diagram for test defects.

changes in practices, adding tools and training, application of new methods, and improvements in communications. The action team should be organized so there is a manager or leader. This person is often a member of a process improvement team, and plays a leadership role on that team. If the causal analysis team has been focusing on test defects, then an experienced test manager should play a leading role on the action team since it is likely there will be changes in the testing process. Keep in mind that the action team leader must have the expertise and authority to make changes in organizational processes. He will have to negotiate time for others in the organization to work on actions, suggest project/test management improvements and request resources for making the changes. As mentioned previously other team members could be selected from development, test, and SQA staff. It is important to include developers and testers on an action planning team since the process changes are likely to have high impact on tasks that they perform. In this way they are included in the decision-making process, and there will be less resistance to the changes on their part.

In many organizations there is a hierarchy of action teams. Some of the teams are engaged in short-term process changes/improvements, others in long-term efforts. In the case of an organization using the TMM assessment process, there will be action teams put into place to achieve TMM maturity goals. That team is likely have a longer duration and a higher place in the action team hierarchy than perhaps an team working to eliminate defects that require simple process changes. In fact, the teams in the hierarchy need to cooperate in many efforts since their goals may overlap.

The action team members need specialized skills. Using these skills, team members fulfill roles such as:

- *Tool expert:* Team member who can develop tools, or is familiar with procedures to evaluate and acquire tools from outside the organization.

- *Education coordinator:* Member of the training group who can educate/train staff with respect to aspects of the new process.

- *Technical writer/communicator:* Person who can prepare the necessary documentation for the newly changed process, prepare reports for managers, develop articles for the organizational newsletter on action-related topics, and make presentations to ensure (a) visibility for the implemented actions in the organization and (b) that all key staff contributing staff are recognized.

- *Planner:* Team member who can develop plans for the actions to be implemented.

- *Measurement expert:* Team member who can select appropriate measurements for monitoring the changed process, and who can apply measurement results to evaluate the changes.

The members of the defect prevention/action team usually work part-time in this area, spending roughly 10–15% of their time on implementing, tracking, and reporting on actions [3]. Team membership will usually rotate, especially with respect to developers/testers as defect analysis focuses on different types of projects and processes.

The action team has many responsibilities that include prioritization of action items, planning and assigning responsibilities for implementation of the highest priority actions, tracking action implementations, coordinating their activities with other action planning teams, and reporting results to management and to the organization in general.

The action team should meet weekly or biweekly. During the meeting period the team should discuss progress-to-date on actions that are being currently implemented, discuss results of current causal analysis meetings, plan new actions, and analyze and report results of current actions to management.

13.6 Monitoring Actions and Process Changes

Ideally all actions should be entered in an action database that is updated continuously as data is collected for actions that are implemented. Its role in the defect prevention process is shown in Figure 13.4. A suggested list of items for an entry in an action database is shown in Table 13.3. Other items in the entry that can be filled in when the action plan is complete are, for example:

- actual costs;

- actual completion date;

- comments.

The establishment of an action database allows the action team to enter new actions, assign priority and status (open, closed) to actions, as well as target dates, costs, and effectiveness.

The action team needs to identify measurements that are essential for tracking each implemented action. These should be identified in the action plan. The most important item the action team needs to monitor is the number of reoccurrences of a target defect type after the process has been changed. For example, if a lack of education is the cause of a particular type of defects, and a training program is put into place to address this, the number of these defects that occur in some designated time period (6 or 12 months [3]) after the education program has been in place should be measured to determine if this change has been effective in preventing these defects from reoccurring. If the number of reoccurrences is still high, further actions may need to be taken. Other measurements of importance

Item	Description
Action name, identifier	Unique identifier for this action
Action developer	person(s) creating the action
Date created	mon/day/yr
Products	Products/projects to which actions are applied
Impact area	Tools, education, communication, process, etc.
Action descriptor	Textual-based description of the action
Priority of the action	A value on action team priority scale
Status	Open/closed/under investigation
Cost	Estimated cost to implement
Completion date	Planned date for completion
Associated defects	Which defect is this action designated to prevent?

TABLE 13.3

Suggested entry in action database.

include the costs of defect prevention activities, time needed to complete tasks, and number of action items and their status (proposed, open, completed).

Action plans are usually applied to pilot projects. The action team should select projects that have motivated and committed project/test managers and staff. At the start of a project the action team members should attend the staff meetings, describe and explain the changes to the process and the need for cooperation and commitment. Sufficient resources should be committed to the pilot project especially if project members will be required to perform additional tasks. The action team can use available controlling and monitoring mechanisms to track progress of the pilot projects. Reports on the status of actions should be issued periodically to upper management. A report could contain information such as (i) how much as been invested in the program, (ii) time spent in causal analysis, action planning, education, and training, and (iii) number of open and closed actions during a specific time period. The action database should support the preparation of such status reports. There should also be feedback on the progress of the action plans. Results should be distributed to developers, testers, and other involved in product development.

If the pilot projects show success, and the changes in the process are not extensive, then the process changes should be considered for organizationwide implementation. If this is approved then process-related documents and standards should be updated to reflect the changes. If process changes are substantial then it may be wise to continue to use the new process in additional pilots before widespread changes are made.

Finally, knowledge of common defects, their causes, actions to prevent them, and results of related process changes should be distributed throughout the organization to make all staff aware, and to keep them informed in this important area of process work. A useful time to make this knowledge available to project teams is at the "kick-off" meetings that begin each project phase [2,3].

13.7 Benefits of a Defect Prevention Program

A defect prevention program provides a nucleus for process changes. It can be represented as a series of reoccurring cycles as shown in Figure 13.4 that support continuous process improvement. Defect prevention involves many diverse staff members who have the opportunity to provide input for the process changes. It can be applied to any process in any organization, hence its prominent role in the TMM at level 5. In the context of the TMM, defect prevention is one responsibility of a tester, and, as previously mentioned, testers can be involved in the application of the program to improve the general development process and also to reduce defects injected into the test process itself. As an example of the latter, we could have a case where errors occur frequently in specific types of test cases or test procedures. The test organization could then initiate a causal analysis group to analyze these defects, and develop action plans that call for changes in the testing process to address the problem. At higher levels of the TMM this certainly is a viable approach since there is support in the form of a test organization, education and training, and process feedback and optimization capabilities.

Defect prevention programs do have associated costs. These include costs of defect analysis and costs of the action plans as applied to projects. However, finding and repairing defects usually has larger costs. Recall that in the discussion of the costs of quality in Chapter 12 we listed the cost categories, prevention, appraisal, and failure. Appraisal costs—which include testing, reviewing, and inspecting—and failure costs—which include rework, complaint resolution, and warranty work—usually cost much more than defect prevention activities. Defect prevention activities should lower appraisal and failure costs. Beside the benefits of possible cost reductions in the appraisal and failure areas of quality there are also other benefits for a defection prevention program which include:

- a more aware and motivated staff;

- a more satisfied customer;

- a more reliable, manageable and predictable process;

- cultural changes that bring quality issues in focus;

- a nucleus for continuous process improvement.

13.8 Defect Prevention and the Three Critical Views

In this section we will examine the roles of the three critical groups in defect prevention as applied in the most general sense, that is, preventing defects in all software deliverables, for example: code, design, and test deliverables. Process improvement is applied to the overall development process and the test process as well.

Managers Role

To ensure the success of a defect prevention program managers must provide strong support. This support is in the form of planning, supplying resources, training, and tools. Management must also establish supporting policies and encourage necessary cultural changes. Managers should ensure that a defect prevention team is well staffed, and has appropriate resources and organizational support. When pilot projects indicate positive results, managers should promote visibility for the successes and support appropriate process changes throughout the organization. Managers participate and serve as leaders in defect prevention activities such as action planning and monitoring. They are the leaders in project kick-off meetings. Managers should promote discussion and distribute lists of common defects and process change information to project team members. They should also promote the inclusion of defect prevention activities as part of the project/test plans, and follow-up to ensure that all approved process changes are reflected in process documents and standards.

Testers Role

The tester's role includes the collection of defect data and entry of the data into the defect database. Testers serve along with developers and SQA staff as members of causal analysis teams that address software defects. Defect data records must be updated as a result of the meeting and action plans. Testers also form causal analysis teams that specially address test-related defects. Where appropriate, testers go to training classes to learn causal analysis and defect prevention techniques such as the preparation of Pareto and fishbone diagrams. They are especially responsible for planning and implementing actions that make changes in the test process. They monitor the changes to the test process as applied to pilot projects, and report results. They serve as ambassadors for cultural changes.

Users/Clients Role

Users/clients have a limited role in a defect prevention program. Their role is confined to reporting defects and problems in operating software so these can be entered into the defect database for causal analysis.

EXERCISES ▬▬▬▬▬▬▬▬▬▬▬▬▬▬▬▬▬▬▬▬

1. Summarize the benefits of putting a defect-prevention program in place.

2. What are some of the elements necessary to implement a defect-prevention program?

3. The implementation of a defect-prevention program is a maturity goal at TMM level 5. However, an organization on a lower level of the TMM, for example, on level 2, may decide to try to implement such a program. Do you think that this is a wise decision? What types of problems is the organization likely to encounter as it tries to implement the program? Given the limited capabilities of an organization at TMM level 2, what are some of the first steps they could take to set up a foundation for such a program?

4. Suppose you are a test manager and you observe that many defects appear in the test procedures developed by your testing team. You decide to apply defect causal analysis techniques to try to prevent these defects from reoccurring. Your test team consists of many new hires. They have attended a few training sessions; most do not have advanced degrees. Some of the team members have had extensive development experience; others have not. Develop a fishbone diagram to trace the causes of these defects based on the above scenario. You may need to make some assumptions about the testing environment to supplement the information given. It also helps to review the origins of defects in Chapter 3 to develop the diagram.

5. A test engineer has just started to record defect data for her process. She spends the bulk of her time developing test harness code. The following defect data was collected from 10 recent projects she has worked on. The defect types are: 10, documentation; 20, syntax; 30, build; 40, assignment; 50, interface; 60, checking; 70, data; 80, function; 90, system; 100, environment.

Defect type	Number of occurrences
10	5
20	40
30	5
40	22
50	14
60	9

Defect type	Number of occurrences
70	11
80	38
90	2
100	1

Draw a Pareto distribution for this data set. From this diagram discuss the areas where you think this engineer should focus her defect-detection and defect-prevention activities. What actions do you suggest?

6. Describe the role of action teams in the defect-prevention process.

7. Design a format for entries in an action database to be used for defect prevention.

8. How does the availability of a defect database support defect-prevention activities?

9. Suggest meeting times for defect causal analysis groups before and after release of the software. What would be the items to focus on during the course of these meetings?

10. What is management's role in support of a defect-prevention program?

REFERENCES

[1] G. Schulmeyer, "The move to zero defect software," in *Handbook of Software Quality Assurance,* second edition, G. Schulmeyer, J. McManus, eds., Van Nostrand Reinhold, New York, 1992.

[2] W. Humphrey, *Managing the Software Process,* Addison-Wesley, Reading, MA, 1990.

[3] R. Mays, "Defect prevention and total quality management," in *Total Quality Management for Software,* G. Schulmeyer, J. McManus, eds., Van Nostrand Reinhold, New York, 1992.

[4] P. Crosby. *Quality Is Free: The Art of Making Quality Certain,* Mentor/New American Library, New York, 1979.

[5] W. Deming, *Out of the Crisis,* MIT Center for Advanced Engineering Study, Cambridge, MA, 1986.

[6] J. Juran, *Managerial Breakthrough,* McGraw-Hill, New York, 1964.

[7] J. Juran, M. Gryna, M. Frank Jr., R. Bingham Jr., eds., *Quality Control Handbook,* third edition, McGraw-Hill, New York, 1979.

[8] C. Cho, "Statistical methods applied to software quality control," in *Handbook of Software Quality Assurance,* second edition, G. Schulmeyer, J. McManus, eds., Van Nostrand Reinhold, New York, 1992.

[9] M. Paulk, C. Weber, B. Curtis, M. Chrissis, *The Capability Maturity Model: Guidelines for Improving the Software Process,* Addison-Wesley, Reading, MA, 1995.

[10] T. McCabe, G. Schulmeyer, "The Pareto principle applied to software quality assurance," in *Handbook*

of Software Quality Assurance, second edition, G. Schulmeyer, J. McManus, eds., Van Nostrand Reinhold, New York, 1992.

[11] G. Schulmeyer, "Software quality lessons from the quality experts," in *Handbook of Software Quality Assurance,* second edition, G. Schulmeyer, J. McManus, eds., Van Nostrand Reinhold, New York, 1992.

[12] A. Endres, "An analysis of errors and causes in system programs," *IEEE Transactions on Software Engineering,* Vol. SE-1, No. 2, 1975.

[13] R. Grady, D. Caswell, *Software Metrics: Establishing a Companywide Program,* Prentice-Hall, Englewood Cliff, NJ, 1987.

14

THE TESTERS'
WORKBENCH

14.0 Goals for the Testers' Workbench

Throughout this book testing has been described as an intellectually challenging activity. It requires many skills, including the ability to plan the testing efforts, generate hypotheses about defects, design test cases and test procedures, collect and analyze measurements, set up the test environments, run the tests, and log and analyze test results. Software testers, like testers in other fields need tools to help them with their tasks. For example, digital test engineers regularly use tools such as simulators and test pattern generators to support their testing efforts. There are tools available to software testers, but there is a need to learn how to integrate them in a more effective manner into the testing process.

Tool usage requires organizational investments in time and dollars. Testers and their organizations need to understand that benefits from investing in testing tools will only be realized when:

- testers have the proper education and training to use them;

- the organizational culture supports tool evaluation, tool use, and technology transfer;

- the tools are introduced into the process incrementally;

- the tools are appropriate for the testing process maturity level and the skill level of the testers;

- the tools support incremental testing process growth and improvement.

The use of automated tools for software testing has the potential to increase productivity, shorten cycle time, reduce risks, and improve both product and process quality. Unfortunately, organizations do not have adequate guidelines as to which tools will be useful given their current goals, the abilities of their testing staff, and the current state of their testing process. The TMM provides a valuable framework for selecting appropriate tools and integrating these tools into the testing process. This chapter will describe a set of testing tools called the Testers' Workbench. The choice of tools for the workbench is guided by TMM maturity goals. In the set of testing tools suggested for the workbench the author includes those that support a wide variety of quality and test-related activities such as test planning, configuration management, test design, and reviews, in addition to traditional tools that support test case execution. The proposed Testers' Workbench should fulfill the following requirements.

1. The Testers' Workbench contains a generic set of tools that support automation of testing tasks. Only broad categories of tools are described. They are classified principally by tool function. TMM users will need to collect information on specific commercially available tools they wish to acquire. Some tools could be built in-house.

2. The Testers' Workbench is built in steps, beginning at level 1 of the TMM. Tools are added as the organization moves up the TMM levels. At the highest level of the TMM testing activities should be fully supported by tools.

3. Each tool supports the achievement of one or more maturity goals at the level of the TMM where it is introduced, and may support additional maturity goals at other TMM levels.

4. The Testers' Workbench is updatable as new tools are introduced commercially or in-house.

Members of the three critical groups use the tools to accomplish the activities, tasks, and responsibilities assigned to them. Criteria for tool association with a TMM level is as follows:

- the tool supports achievement of the maturity goals at a given level (and possibly a lower level);

- the tools helps some (all) members of the three critical groups to carry out their activities, tasks, and responsibilities;

- the organization has the infrastructure in place in terms of staff expertise, managerial commitment, and technical training, so that the tool can be fully utilized.

14.1 Evaluating Testing Tools for the Workbench

Testing tools should be introduced at a maturity level appropriate for their use. Each tool purchase should be evaluated individually. Firth and co-authors have proposed a set of six criteria useful for the acquisition of any type of software engineering tool [1]. These criteria, plus two additional criteria suggested by this author, are shown in Figure 14.1 and are summarized below. The summary includes appropriate questions to ask when evaluating a tool according to each criterion.

1. *Ease of Use.* Is the tool easy to learn? Is its behavior predictable? Is there meaningful feedback for the user? Does it have adequate error-handling capabilities? Is the interface compatible with other tools already existing in the organization?

2. *Power.* Does it have many useful features? Do the commands allow the user to achieve their goals? Does it "understand" the objects it

Tool Evaluation Checklist

1. Ease of use ✓
2. Power ___
3. Robustness ✓
4. Functionality ___
5. Ease of insertion ___
6. Quality of support ✓
7. Cost ___
8. Organizational fit ✓

FIG. 14.1

Tool evaluation criteria.

manipulates? Does the tool operate at different levels of abstraction? Does it perform validation checks on objects or structures?

3. *Robustness.* Is the tool reliable? Does it recover from failures without major loss of information? Can the tool evolve and retain compatibility between old and new versions?

4. *Functionality.* What functional category does the tool fit (e.g., test planning, test execution, test management)? Does it perform the task it is designed to perform? Does it support the methodologies used by the organization? Can new methodologies be integrated? Does it produce correct outputs?

5. *Ease of Insertion.* How easy will it be to incorporate the tool into the organizational environment? Will users have the proper background to use it? Is the time required to learn to use the tool acceptable? Are results available to the user without a long set-up process? Does the tool run on the operating system used by the organization? Can data be exchanged between this tool and others already in use? Can the tool be supported in a cost effective manner?

6. *Quality of Support.* What is the tool's track record (it is very useful to contact other organizations already using the tool)? What is the vendor history? What type of contract, licensing, or rental agreement is involved? Who does maintenance, installation, and training? What is the nature of the documentation? Will the vendor supply lists of previous purchasers? Will they provide a demonstration model?

The author of this text would add two additional criteria to this list of considerations.

7. *Cost of the Tool.* Organizations have budgets that must be adhered to. Considerations for tool purchases should include a cost factor. A cost/benefit analysis is very useful. If a tool looks very promising, and budgets are tight, purchase in the next fiscal period should be considered.

8. *Fit with Organizational Policies and Goals.* The need for testing and debugging policies and goals has already been discussed. Tool purchases should be aligned with these policies and goals as stated. For example, if the testing policy/goal statement does not provide for coverage goals then purchasing a coverage tool at this time may not a sensible choice. If an organization is engaged in test process improvement, and is working on addressing TMM goals, the tools selected should support these goals as well.

Poston has written several papers on the acquisition of testing tools [2–4]. Many of the evaluation criteria he suggests overlap with those of Firth. He also has developed forms that are useful for test tool evaluation based on the criteria listed above. Other authors who have written about test tool use and evaluation are Kemerer [5], Mosely [6], Kit [7], and Daich and Price [8].

It is important for an organization to decide on a standard set of evaluation criteria for test tool acquisition. Forms can be developed from the criteria selected. Each criterion can be assigned a weight according to how important it is in the decision process. For example, if "ease of use" is more important to the organization than "ease of insertion," then "ease of use" should carry a higher weight or greater influence in the decision process. Each tool should be evaluated and the form completed. Comparisons can be made on the overall ratings for each tool. Test managers and members of the testing group should carefully evaluate each tool before purchase. The loan of a demonstration model or a trial usage period for the actual product is useful for evaluating the tool in your environment. If none of these can be arranged by the tool vendor, you probably should look elsewhere for a comparable tool. Vendors should also be able to supply a list of organizations/users who have already purchased their tool. Their feedback should be solicited. Surveys and case studies regarding specific tools may be found on the web, in trade magazines, or from the vendors.

When the selected tool is purchased it should have trial use in pilot projects and then reevaluated to determine if the tool performed as was expected. If results are satisfactory it can be integrated into the organizational environment. When the tool is in use, measurements should be used to determine the impact of the tool on software and process quality. At TMM level 5 a technology transfer process is in place to support these activities (see Section 15.5).

14.2 Tool Categories

Testing tools are sometimes referred to CAST tools—Computer-Aided Software Testing Tools. There are several ways to classify testing tools. One is by their functionality, that is, what they do. For example, a test coverage tool monitors test execution and measures the degree of code coverage for the tests; a capture/reply tool captures test inputs and outputs and replays the test upon request; a defect tracking tool logs and keeps track of defects and their status. Another broader classification scheme uses the testing phase or testing activity in which the tool is employed to classify it, for example, tools to support development of test requirements, test design, test execution, test preparation, and test resource management tools [8]. Some tools have multiple functionality and also can be used in more than one development phase, so they can be classified in more than one way.

In this text we describe tools in two ways: (i) by their functionality, and (ii) by the testing maturity level they support. For example, tools are placed in the "phase definition" category if they support maturity goals at TMM level 2 that help to establish testing as a distinct development/maintenance phase that is supported by policies, plans, and basic techniques. There are many possible tools that can be introduced at each TMM maturity level. An organization can select tools of each type; however, it is not necessary to obtain every type of tool recommended for the Testers' Workbench. Organizations must make decisions based on a variety of criteria, for example: organization size, TMM level, budgetary allowance, scope of process improvement efforts, staff education, level and training available, and types of products being developed.

Tools are introduced at a TMM level where it is believed that an organization will most benefit from its use. TMM level is an important consideration for tool acquisition. Many organizations make major investments in testing tool purchases with the goals of improving productivity and software quality. In many cases the investments have no benefits—the organizations fail to achieve their goals because they lack the infrastructure and maturity level necessary to support tool usage.

For some tools a simpler version or a more restricted usage is recommended at lower TMM levels since the organization may not be ready to make full use of all capabilities. An upgraded version of the tool with more features/functions may be suggested for a higher TMM level. Many of the tools are components of packages that integrate them within a common interface. At a lower level of the TMM only some of the features may be used, and others made use of as an organization's testing process becomes more mature. In the context of the TMM, specific brand names of tools are not recommended. The reader should consult Refs. 1–3, 8, and 9 for evaluation criteria of commercially available specific testing tools. For lists of commercially available tools, some sources are Daitch and Price [8] and Dustin and Cashka [10], proceedings from test- and quality-related conferences such as International Quality Week, and web sites such as:

www.stlabs.com/marik/faqs/tools/html
www.soft.com/Partners/Aonix
www.methods-tools.com/tools/testing.html
    (from Software Research–TestWorks)
www.revlabs.com
www.sqe.com
www.ovum.com

The goal for developing the Testers' Workbench was to include the most widely used functional types of tools. Some of the tools may not be considered strictly as testing tools, but they do support the testing effort in a direct or indirect manner, and they do support maturity goals for a particular TMM level.

The discussion in the subsequent sections of this chapter is organized in the following way. Each TMM level is listed and its maturity goals are discussed briefly. The suggested tools to support achievement of the maturity goals are then listed. The rational for the selection of the tools is presented, and usage and application for each is described.

14.2.1 Maturity Goals and Tools for TMM Level 1: Initial

At TMM level 1, testing is a chaotic process. It is ill-defined and not distinguished from debugging. Tests are developed in an ad hoc way after coding is done. Testing and debugging are interleaved to get the bugs out of the software. The objective of testing is to show the software works. Software products are often released without quality assurance. There is a lack of resources, tools, and properly trained staff. There are no maturity goals at TMM level 1 [11–13].

14.2.2 Tools for TMM Level 1

Although there are no maturity goals at this level, an organization can begin to assemble components for the Testers' Workbench. The goal is to provide a minimum set of basic tools for each developer. These tools do not require advanced training and should be available to all developers. Access to the tools is through a personal computer or workstation at each person's desk. The PC or workstation for each developer should be equipped with (i) a word processing program, (ii) a spreadsheet program, (iii) a file comparison utility that indicates if two files are the same or different, (iv) an emailer to ensure adequate communication, and (v) a screen capture program that allows the contents of a screen to be sent to a file or to a printer. A laptop computer is also useful for simple measurement collection (see Chapter 11). Supported by a PC, laptop, or workstation platform, the Testers' Workbench can be initiated with a minimal set of tools that will introduce developers to benefits of tool usage, and support simple measurement collection. The following tools as shown in Figure 14.2 are suggested.

1. *Interactive Debuggers.* These tools assist developers in code comprehension and locating defects. They should have trace back and breakpoint capabilities to enable developers to understand the dynamics of program execution and to identify suspect areas of the code. Debugging tools set the stage for the separation of the testing and debugging

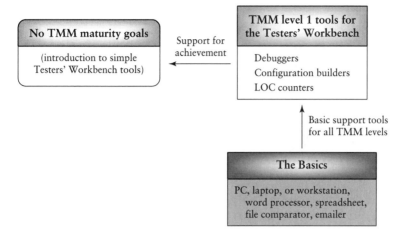

FIG. 14.2

Basic Testers' Workbench tools for
TMM level 1.

processes by illustrating the different skills, models, and psychologies required for both of these processes.

2. *Configuration Building tools.* These tools (e.g., the UNIX "MAKE" utility) allow construction of software system configurations in a controlled environment. They support an orderly, manageable, and repeatable system construction process for developers and testers. These will be supplemented by configuration management tools when the organization is ready at TMM level 3.

3. *Line of Code (LOC) counters.* Software size measurement has many useful applications. A tool that automatically measures size will result in consistently repeatable size measures that are useful for many purposes including cost estimations essential for project and test managers, calculations of defect volume (number of defects/KLOC), and measures of productivity (LOC produced/unit time). The LOC counter may require the development or adaptation of a line-counting standard and coding standards that will need to be followed [14].

The reader should note that spreadsheets were listed above as a basic necessity for all software engineering staff. The role of the spreadsheet at

TMM level 1 should be explained in more detail. Spreadsheets are very useful to record simple measurements such as actual time spent in testing activities, LOC measures for each project, and the number of defects of each type found for each project. The data collected in this way will help an organization to develop a measurable baseline for its testing process and later will supply data to support the defect repository. Spreadsheets can also support the development of a validation cross-reference matrix for testing. Eventually the spreadsheet is replaced by more advanced tools at higher levels of the TMM where the testing staff is well educated and trained.

14.2.3 TMM Level 2: Maturity Goals for Phase Definition

At level 2 of the TMM testing is separated from debugging and is defined as a phase that follows coding. It is a planned activity; however, test planning at level 2 may occur after coding for reasons related to the immaturity of the testing process. Basic testing techniques and methods are in place; for example, use of black box and white box testing strategies, and a validation cross-reference matrix. Many quality problems at this TMM level occur because test planning occurs late in the life cycle. In addition, defects are propagated from the requirements and design phases into the code. There are no review programs as yet to address this important issue. Postcode, execution-based testing is still considered the primary testing activity. The maturity goals at this level are [11–13]:

Develop Testing and Debugging Goals

An organization must clearly distinguish between the processes of testing and debugging. The goals, tasks, activities, and tools for each must be identified. Responsibilities for each must be assigned. Plans and policies must be made by management to accommodate and institutionalize both of these processes. The separation of these two processes is essential for testing maturity growth since they are different in goals, methods, and psychology. Testing at this level is now a well-planned activity and therefore it can be managed. Management of debugging is much more difficult due to the unpredictability of defect occurrences, and the time and resources required to locate and repair them.

Initiate a Test Planning Process

Planning is essential for a process that is to be repeatable, defined, and managed. Test planning involves stating objectives, analyzing risks, outlining strategies, and developing test design specifications and test cases. In addition, the test plan must address the allocation of resources and the responsibilities for testing on the unit, integration, system, and acceptance levels.

Institutionalize Basic Testing Techniques and Methods

To improve test process capability, basic testing techniques, methods, and practices must be applied across the organization. How and when these techniques and methods are to be applied, and any basic tool support for them, should be clearly specified. Examples of basic techniques, methods, and practices are black-box and white-box-based testing methods, use of a requirements validation matrix, and the division of execution-based testing into subphases such as unit, integration, system, and acceptance testing.

14.2.4 Tools for Phase Definition

AT TMM level 2 an organization establishes a distinct testing phase as part of its development life cycle. The testing phase is supported by policies, plans, techniques, and practices. Policymaking requires people-oriented resources. Tools for supporting this goal consist mainly of word processors to record the policies. An intraorganizational set of web pages containing the policy help to promote its availability and distribution throughout the organization.

Planning tools at TMM level 2 are especially needed to support the test planning maturity goal since planning is essential for a defined and managed testing process. Tools are also needed to support basic testing techniques, and to denote the different tasks and activities associated with testing and debugging. The tools introduced at TMM level 2 should be simple and easily mastered by developers since there is no dedicated software testing group and no formal technical training program as yet. Tools should support improved planning, increased productivity, and software quality. Positive results from tool usage should be made clearly visible so as to provide a strong incentive for peer adaptation and for management support.

The tools selected here and shown in Figure 14.3 mainly support the front end of testing (planning) and the back end (execution). The latter automate tasks that are familiar to developers and so there is little cultural bias to their introduction and a clear incentive to use them. Since a formal test planning process is new for the organization, planning support tools can ease the integration and adaptation of this activity into the testing process with strong management support. Introduction of the planning tools not only supports the building of a defined, managed and optimizable test process, but also has the added feature of helping to distinguish testing from debugging. That planning can become well-defined and useful for effective testing will become apparent as the organization adopts and implements a test planning process. In contrast, organizations will learn that planning for debugging is difficult even at the highest levels of process maturity. The other tools introduced at TMM levels 1 and 2 also serve to separate the two activities. For example, several of the tools introduced at TMM level 2 focus on testing as an activity whose purpose is to reveal defects. The debugging tool introduced at TMM level 1 focuses attention on locating the defects.

In addition to introducing test planning tools, error checkers, and a cross-reference tool at TMM level 2, some simple tools for test data generation are introduced to support the maturity goal that calls for the application of basic testing techniques and methods. The tools support the white and black box testing strategies that are part of the basic level 2 technical practices. A white-box-based coverage tool is also introduced to help the organization to set test goals, develop improved test plans, and produce higher-quality software.

1. *Project Planners and Test Planners.* These tools are necessary to automate and standardize the process of test planning in the organization. The tools will support the specification and recording of items necessary for a high-quality test plan. Example items include testing goals, test resources required, costs, schedules, techniques to be used, test designs, and the assignment of staff responsible for testing tasks. Since very few planning tools specific for the testing process are commercially available, an organization may decide to develop its own

test plan templates and support tools and make them available to all internal groups. Guidelines for components that should be included in test plans can be found in Chapter 7, and are also described in IEEE standards documents [15]. Project planning tools could augment the in-house test templates and be used to develop and record schedules, costs, task lists, and so on. At TMM level 2 organizations should be testing at the unit, integration, and system levels. Tools that support test planning can aid in the differentiation of these testing subphases, and individual plans can be developed for each subphase.

2. *Run-Time Error Checkers.* These tools are also known as bounds checkers, memory testers, and leak detectors. They detect memory problems, array boundary under- or overflows, memory allocated and not freed, and the use of unitialized memory locations. This group of tools will aid in revealing defects and usually supply detailed error messages that help users to track defects.

3. *Test Preparation Support Tools (Beginning Level).* Since there is no dedicated testing group at TMM level 2, and developers are just beginning to use basic testing techniques and strategies, it is best to introduce simple test preparation support tools that aid in the development of black-box- and white box-based test cases.

   One of the tools recommended is one that generates black box test data using algorithmic methods. For example, tools that require a cause-and-effect graph, or an input of equivalence classes and boundary values. Use of these tools will give developers additional incentives to master the testing concepts and strengthen their use organizationally. Tools that support white box testing at TMM level 2 are control flow analyzers that generate control flow graphs, and data flow analyzers that produce data flow information. These tools can be introduced to help developers identify branches, basis paths, and variable usages. Using this information developers can design test cases that satisfy coverage goals (see the discussion of coverage analyzers below). More advanced test data generation tools will be recommended at higher TMM levels.

4. *Coverage Analyzers.* Adaptation of coverage analyzers assists with white box testing. The tools support the development of measurable test completion goals for test plans and ensure that the goals are met.

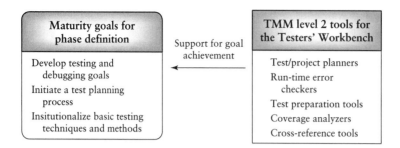

┌─────────────────────────────┐   ┌─────────────────────────────┐
│ **Maturity goals for**   │   │ **TMM level 2 tools for** │
│ **phase definition**   │ Support for goal │ **the Testers' Workbench** │
│   │ achievement │   │
│ Develop testing and   │ ◄────────── │ Test/project planners   │
│   debugging goals   │   │ Run-time error   │
│ Initiate a test planning   │   │   checkers   │
│   process   │   │ Test preparation tools   │
│ Insitutionalize basic testing │   │ Coverage analyzers   │
│   techniques and methods   │   │ Cross-reference tools   │
└─────────────────────────────┘   └─────────────────────────────┘

FIG. 14.3

Testers' Workbench tools for TMM
level 2.

Executing the target code under the control of a coverage tool gives the developer a measure of the degree of statement and/or branch coverage and indicates which program structures(paths) have been, or have not been, exercised by a given set of test cases. If coverage goals are not met with the current set of test cases, the developer can design additional test cases and rerun the code under the control of the tool to determine if the coverage goals have now been met.

5. *Cross-Reference Tools.* These are simple tools that allow users to trace occurrences of items as they appear in different software artifacts. Cross-reference tools are helpful for building mental models of software for the purpose of making changes, developing tests, and rerunning tests. For example, a developer or tester may want to determine where a specific variable appears in all source code listings so that tests centered on the variable will be complete. Other items that can be traced or referenced are labels, literals, parameters, and subroutine calls.

14.2.5 TMM Level 3: Maturity Goals for Integration

This is a critical maturity level. Its maturity goals center on addressing testing and quality issues early in the software life cycle. The testing phase is no longer just a phase that follows coding. Instead it is expanded into a set of well-defined activities that are integrated into the software life cycle. All of the life cycle phases have testing activities associated with them. Support for integration is provided by institutionalization of some variation of the V-model which associates testing activities with life cycle phases such as requirements and design. At this level management supports the formation and training of a software test group. These are specialists who are responsible for testing. This group serves as a liaison with the users/clients to insure their participation in the testing process. At TMM level 3 basic testing tools support institutionalized test techniques and methods. Both technical and managerial staff are beginning to realize the value of review activities as a tool for defect detection and quality assurance [11–13]. Maturity goals for TMM level 3 are as follows:

Establish a Software Test Organization

The purpose of establishing a software test organization is to identify a group of people that is responsible for testing. Since testing in its fullest sense has a great influence on product quality and consists of complex activities that are usually done under tight schedules and high pressure, management realizes that it is necessary to have a well-trained and dedicated group of specialists in charge of this process. Among the responsibilities of the test group are test planning, test execution and recording, test-related standards, test metrics, the test database, the defect repository, and, test tracking and evaluation.

Establish a Technical Training Program

A technical training program will insure that a skilled staff is available to the testing group. Testers must be properly trained so they can do their jobs both efficiently and effectively. At level 3 of the TMM, the testing staff is trained in test planning, testing methods, standards, and tools. At the higher levels of the TMM the training program will prepare testers for identifying, collecting, analyzing and applying test-related metrics. The training program also will prepare the staff for the review process, and provide instruction for review leaders. It will provide training for process control and defect prevention activities. Training includes in-house courses, self-study, mentoring programs, and support for attendance at academic institutions.

Integrate Testing into the Software Life Cycle

Management and technical staff now realize that carrying out testing activities in parallel with all life cycle phases is critical for test process maturity and software product quality. Test planning is now initiated early in the life cycle. A variation of the V-model or any other model that supports this integration is used by the testers and developers. User input to the testing process is solicited through established channels for several of the testing phases.

Control and Monitor the Testing Process

According to Thayer, management consists of five principal activities: (i) planning, (ii) directing, (iii) staffing, (iv) controlling, and (v) organizing [16]. Level 2 of the TMM introduces planning capability to the testing process. In addition to staffing, directing, and organizing capabilities, level 3 introduces controlling and monitoring activities. The purpose of controlling and monitoring in the testing process is to provide visibility to its associated activities and to ensure that the testing process proceeds according to plan. When actual activities deviate from the test plans, management can take effective action to correct the deviations in order to accomplish the goals in the test plan on time and within budget. Test progress is determined by comparing the actual test work products, test effort, costs, and schedule to the test plan. Support for controlling and monitoring comes from developing the following: standards for test products, test milestones, test logs, test-related contingency plans, and test metrics that can be used to evaluate test progress and test effectiveness.

14.2.6 Tools for Integration

At TMM level 3 an organization will have a group dedicated to testing as well as a technical training program. Testing tools can be introduced, and it can be expected that the test specialists will have the resources and skills to evaluate, purchase, use, integrate, and institutionalize the tools. Unlike less mature organizations, those at TMM level 3 should exhibit a high rate of tool usage when all the maturity goals through this level are achieved.

The tools recommended for TMM level 3 as shown in Figure 14.4, are diverse in nature and were selected to support level 3 maturity goals and to:

- improve software quality;

- control and monitor testing;

- improve tester/developer productivity;

- integrate testing throughout the life cycle;

- give visibility to the testing organization;

- illustrate the benefits of having both a dedicated test organization and technical training program.

The tools provide continuing support for test planning, test design, and automated execution. Support for controlling, monitoring, and tracking the testing process is also provided. Note there is a very strong emphasis on tools related to requirements gathering and tracing to test. These serve to support integration of testing activities with other life cycle activities, a maturity goal at TMM level 3. Use of these tools allows integration to begin early in the software life cycle. They also allow for role definition in the testing process for users/clients.

1. Configuration Management Tools. These are complex tools that are essential to ensure change-making that is monitored and controlled for all project-related artifacts. Artifacts, called configuration items, under control of these tools include code versions, change requests, as well as test related items such as test plans, test procedures, and test cases (see Chapter 11). For successful operation of these tools organizational structures such as a change control board are essential. Test specialists should be among the members of this board.

A configuration management tool will support two of the maturity goals at TMM level 3, "integration of testing activities into the software life cycle" and, "controlling and monitoring of testing." Support for these

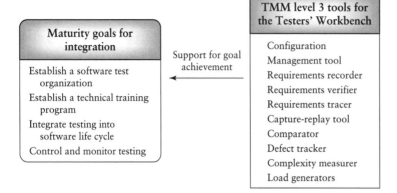

FIG. 14.4

Testers' Workbench tools for TMM level 3.

goals is in the form of managing, coordinating, and maintaining the dependencies and relationships between all software artifacts. For example, the relationships between requirements and test cases, and design elements and test cases, can be established and made available using a configuration management tool. The tools also have controlling and coordinating functions for overseeing all changes made to configuration items. They also support assess privileges to configuration items for all developers/testers. The tool also provides visibility to the testing process in the organization, and helps to establish the need for a group of test specialists to develop the test-related work products.

2. *Requirements Recorders (Use Case Recorders)*. At TMM level 3 a primary goal is the early introduction of testing activities into the software life cycle. Good testing practices call for an organization to begin to develop a high-level test plan in the requirements phase. Testers need to be sure that requirements represent a testable product. Many organizations record requirements in a natural language format using a text processor. Others use requirements modeling tools, and record information in a graphical format such as data flow diagrams. These requirements representations may not provide adequate support for testers. There are requirements modeling tools now available that will give stronger support

to testers. Of special interest are the use case recorders that assist with the development of use cases as described in Section 6.17 of this text. Some of these tools will also generate test cases based on the use cases.

3. Requirements Verifiers. Requirements verifiers have the ability to check requirements for ambiguity, consistency, and statement completeness. However, they are not a substitute for a requirements review, which, among other things, will check for the completeness and correctness of the requirements specification.

4. Requirements-to-Test Tracers. These will provide automated assistance for use of a requirements traceablity matrix as introduced at TMM level 2. At TMM level 2 it was suggested that use of the matrix could be supported in a simple way using a spreadsheet. Requirements-to-test tracers tools add more functionality and capability. They provide links between requirements, design, source code, and test cases. What formally was a tedious time-consuming task is now automated with these tools [8]. The tools also play a role in monitoring the testing process as they indicate which requirements have/have not been covered by a test case.

5. Capture-Replay Tools. These tools are essential for automating the execution and reexecution of tests. They have a positive impact on tester productivity. The tools usually are combined with a comparator. A tester executes the target program under the control of the capture-replay tool. The tool records all input and output information and in replay mode it will play back whatever has been recorded. The tools will capture mouse movements, keyboard strokes, and screen images. After a software change, recorded tests can easily be rerun (regression testing). The tool can play back the recorded tests and validate the results for the changed software by comparing them to the previously saved baseline from the previous version. Many different types of reports can be issued by the tools, for example:

(i) a time report that list the execution time for each test;
(ii) a failed report that lists the tests that have been failed;
(iii) a regression report that lists only those tests whose outcomes have changed since the previous test activation;
(iv) a cumulative report that lists current and past test results for every test executed.

Most of these tools assist testers in developing test scripts in a scripting language that will describe all the steps necessary to run/repeat/rerun a particular test. The test scripts have a set of commands each of which will carry out a user request. Some example commands are:

mouse()   will send a mouse event to an application

log()   will write text to the script log file

real_time   will set a real time mode on/off

screen_shot will capture a screen image and place it in the playback image file

delay()   will delay the playback of the next line in the script by a specified length of time

The scripting languages also have programming-language-like constructs such as for/next loops that will repeat a single or block of script statements a given number of times, and a call statement that will call a test subscript.

Capture-replay tools can be categorized as native where the tool and the software being tested reside on the same system. Nonnative tools require an additional hardware system for the tool. The latter are very useful when testing embedded systems.

Capture-replay tools will automate the execution of tests so that testers will not have to repeatedly rerun them manually. The tests can run unattended for long periods of time. The many capabilities of capture-replay tools make them a very useful addition to the Testers' Workbench. But they should be introduced when the organization has the infrastructure in place to support their use. Investment in the tools is often costly. To obtain benefits, testers need management support to ensure they have the proper education, training, software, and hardware to take advantage of the many capabilities the tools have to offer. This is most likely to occur at TMM level 3 where the achievement of the associated maturity goals builds an infrastructure that supports their adaptation.

6. *Comparators.* These tools compare actual test outputs to expected outputs and flag the differences. They have more complex capabilities than the simple file comparators recommended as a basic tool at TMM level 1. The software under test will pass if the actual and expected outputs are the same within allowed tolerances. A simple comparator like the "diff" facility in UNIX system compares text files for equality. More

sophisticated tools may exhibit better performance and have the ability to compare other types of output for equality; for example, screens and graphical data. In many cases a comparator may be a component in a tool package such as a capture/replay tool as described above.

7. *Defect Trackers.* These tools are also called problem managers. To support controlling and monitoring of the testing process this type of tool is essential. The tools if properly used have the added benefits of improving customer satisfaction, improving productivity, increasing software quality, and improving morale [17]. At TMM level 3 a staff of trained testing specialists is available to take advantage of the capabilities of such a tool. Previously at levels 2 and 3 of the TMM spreadsheets have been suggested as a way to record defect data, but they do not have the functionalities needed for the more advanced applications that mature organizations need. Defect trackers allow testers and developers to record, track, and manage defects throughout the life cycle. In order for the tool to be effective, a defect tracking process must be in place and that requires the support of a test organization and training for the testing and development staff. After a defect has been detected, it must be logged into the defect database supported by the tool. A defect tracking tool allows users to build a more sophisticated defect repository than possible with a simple spreadsheet program. Testers should be able to record extensive defect information as described in Sections 11.2 and 13.2 using the tracking tool.

Resolution of the problem follows the recording of available information about the defect. The order of resolution may depend on the impact of the defect and an assigned priority. As defect repair continues, the status of each defect is updated to reflect its current state of resolution. Code with a repaired defect is subject to retest by the testing team. Once approved, a defect fix report should be issued and the status of the defect updated in the defect tracker record. These defect processing steps are shown in Figure 14.5.

Having a defect resolution process supported by the capabilities of a defect tracker allows continuous monitoring of defects, and helps to ensure they are all resolved. More sophisticated defect trackers support communication between developers and testers to promote defect resolution, and integration of testing activities throughout the life cycle. Defect trackers can also issue (i) defect reports that track resolution efforts, and (ii) summary reports that include types of defects, their frequency of occur-

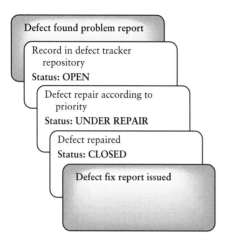

FIG. 14.5

Steps in defect resolution.

rence, and age. Plots can be developed as described in Chapter 9 to help control and monitor the testing and defect resolution processes. Defect trackers also support maturity goals at higher TMM levels such as the development of qualitative testing goals and defect prevention activities.

Defect tracking systems introduce many changes into an organization. There must be support particularly from a test group that has the proper education, training, and attitude to make proper use of the tools. From the testers' viewpoint, the adaptation of defect tracker tools serves to increase their visibility in the organization and highlights their role in improving software quality. Beginning at TMM level 1 with a simple spreadsheet to record defects, building up to TMM level 2 with its emphasis on testing/debugging policies and defect classifications, then on to TMM level 3 with a focus on the test group, training, and controlling and monitoring mechanisms, an organization can prepare itself for the introduction and integration of these important tools. The defect tracking and handling process should be enhanced at TMM level 4 to include defects detected from reviews as well as execution-based test. Finally, at TMM level 5 the capabilities of defect tracking tools should be applied to the defect prevention process, and to the process of continuous test process improvement.

8. Complexity Measurers. These tools are sometimes called metrics reporters. They will measure cyclomatic complexity and will often be integrated with other tools such as a size measurer (line-of-code counter), a data flow analyzer, and/or a control flow analyzer. Some of these tools will measure complexity at the detailed design stage if a module is written in a structured and standardized pseudo code language. Others will also generate Software Science Metrics (Halstead's metrics) which are related to complexity. Examples of such metrics are number of unique operators, number of unique operands, and total number of operands. At TMM level 3 the complexity of a module can play an important role in testing. The level of complexity of a module gives an indication of how risk prone the module is in terms of the likelihood of defects [18], and the number of test cases needed to adequately test it. Organizations should set limits on the level of complexity allowed, and modules displaying values over the limit should be considered for redesign.

9. Load Generators. Now that a trained and dedicated testing group is in place, and testing is carried out at all levels (unit, integration, system), it is appropriate to introduce load-generating tools into the Testers' Workbench. As described in Section 6.13 these tools will generate the large volumes of data needed for system tests such as stress and performance tests. Load generators can be used to produce a stream of transactions. For example, if you were system testing a telecommunication system you would need a load that simulated a series of transactions in the form of phone calls of particular types and lengths, arriving from different locations. Since a very large volume of data is produced when load generators are used, tools to collect and analyze the data should be available to testers.

14.2.7 TMM Level 4: Maturity Goals for Management and Measurement

The principal focus at level 4 of the TMM is on broadening the definition of what a testing activity is and extensive measurement of the testing process. Controlling and monitoring functions can now be fully supported by a test measurement program that is put into place. Staffing activities are supported by a training program. The definition of what is a testing activity is expanded to include reviews/inspections and/or walkthroughs at *all* phases of the life cycle, and is applied to both software work products and test-related work products such as test plans, test designs, and test procedures. This expanded definition of testing covers activities typically categorized as verification and validation activities. A major goal for this broadened set of testing operations is to uncover defects occurring in all phases of the life cycle, and to uncover them as early as possible. Defects uncovered by reviews as well as execution-based tests are saved as a part of project history, and deposited in the defect repository. Test cases and test procedures are stored for reuse and regression testing [11,13]. The Extended/Modified V-Model illustrates the integration of these activities and provides support for several TMM level 4 maturity goals [19,20]. Testing at TMM level 4 is also applied to the evaluation of software quality. Quality requirements for the software are established at project initiation, and testing is used to determine if the requirements have been met. TMM level 4 has the following maturity goals:

Establish an Organizationwide Review Program

At TMM level 3 an organization integrates testing activities into the software life cycle. At level 4 this integration is augmented by the establishment of a review program. Reviews are conducted at all phases of the life cycle to identify, catalog, and remove defects from software work products and test work products early and effectively. Reviewers are trained and review metrics are used to evaluate and improve the review process.

Establish a Test Measurement Program

Although simple test measurements have been recommended for collection at lowering TMM levels to establish a baseline process, and for the controlling and monitoring of testing, no formal test measurement program has yet been put into place. At TMM level 4 an organization is mature enough to support a formal test measurement program. Such a program is essential for the following:

- evaluating the quality of the testing process;
- evaluating software quality;
- assessing customer satisfaction;

- assessing the productivity of the testing personnel;

- evaluating the effectiveness of the testing process;

- supporting of test process improvement.

A test measurement program must be carefully planned and managed. At TMM level 4 there is trained staff available to take responsibility for this program. Staff must identify the test data to be collected, and decisions must be made on how the data is to be used and by whom. Measurements include those related to test progress, test costs, data on errors and defects, and product measures such as software reliability. Measurement data related to client/user satisfaction should also be collected and analyzed.

Software Quality Evaluation

One of the purposes of software quality evaluation at this level of the TMM is to relate software quality issues to the adequacy of the testing process. Software quality evaluation involves defining measurable quality attributes, and defining quality goals for evaluating software work products. Quality goals are tied to testing process adequacy since a mature testing process must lead to software that is at least correct, usable, maintainable, portable, and secure.

14.2.8 Tools for Management and Measurement

At TMM level 4 the definition of a testing activity is extended to include reviews, and this is expressed as a maturity goal. Measurements and software quality evaluation are also important goals. For this level suggested tools are shown in Figure 14.6. Some of the tools support reviews as a defect-detecting activity. Reviews are personnel-intense activities and have very little automated support, but there is a group of tools that can assist reviewers in understanding the software and detecting defects in software-related artifacts. The review support tools usually perform some type of static analysis on the artifact under review. For example, we have introduced a requirements recorder and a complexity measurer at lower levels of the TMM to support maturity goals at those levels. Continued

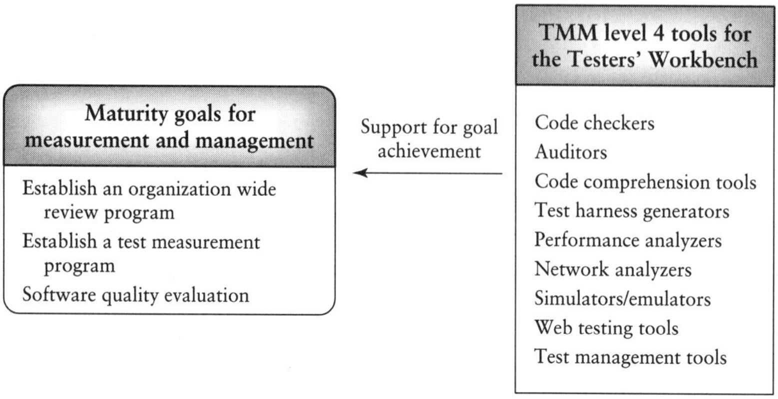

FIG. 14.6

Tester's Workbench tools for TMM level 4.

use of these tools will support the implementation of requirements and design reviews. At TMM level 4 tools that perform static analysis of the code are introduced. These can be used either pre- or postreview to detect defects before actual execution of the code. These tools detect certain types of defects—for example, data flow anomalies—and should be used in conjunction with the review activities. Other types of tools called program understanders are also useful to code reviewers and testers to help build mental models of the code for program understanding tasks. Examples of the these types of tools are:

1. *Code Checkers.* Sometimes called static analyzers, these tools search for misplaced pointers, uninitialized variables, and other data flow anomalies. Some are able to identify unreachable code.

2. *Auditors.* These tools will scan the code to identify violations of established coding standards and/or coding formats.

3. *Code Comprehension Tools.* Some of the features of these tools may be duplicated by code checkers. However, many other useful code properties may be revealed through use of these tools. For example, some perform forward and backward program slicing, and provide detailed data and control flow information. More sophisticated versions of these tools have artificial intelligence components and contain special knowl-

edge bases of programs plans (stereotypical code patterns). They attempt to perform reverse engineering tasks and match code to plans for concept recognition [21–23]. Unfortunately, not many of examples of the latter type of tool are commercially available at this time.

To support the TMM level 4 maturity goal of software quality evaluation the tools listed below are suggested to help automate large-scale system testing and allow the collection of data related to software quality attributes. Tools introduced at lower TMM levels also support this goal, for example, capture-replay tools, complexity measures, defect trackers, line of code counters, and requirements tracers.

4. Test Harness Generators. To carry out unit, integration, and system testing, auxiliary code must be written that is in addition to the code developed for the system-under-test. This extra code, often called the test harness, may include drivers, stubs, interfaces to an operating system, and interfaces to a database system. The test harness may be very large in size, represent considerable effort, and is often specially built for testing a given application. Recent advances in the development of interface standards and standard approaches to describing application interfaces has enabled the introduction of commercial tools to assist with test harness preparation [4]. These tools can be very useful; they reduce time and effort in testing, and produce reusable test harnesses.

5. Performance Testing Tools. These tools monitor timing characteristics of software components. They support load and stress testing, and are essential for supporting the testing of real-time systems in order to evaluate performance quality. The availability of these tools can help to determine if performance goals have been met.

6. Network Analyzers. These are useful tools for testing network systems such as software that runs on client/server systems, web environments, and multitier systems. The tools have the ability to analyze network traffic and identify problem areas and conditions. Many of the network testing tools allow a tester to monitor and diagnose performance across a network.

7. Simulators and Emulators. These tools may be used to replace software or hardware components that are missing, currently unavailable, or too expensive to replace. Both tools types are used for economic or safely reasons. Examples are terminal emulators, and emulators or simulators to substitute for components in nuclear power plants. The tools may be bundled with performance analyzers and/or load generators. The latter will generate large volumes of test data to test, for example, transaction-based, operating, and telecommunication systems.

8. Web Testing Tools. These are specialized tools that support the testing of web-based applications. Many are similar in nature to simulators and emulators in that they simulate real-world web traffic patterns that allow testers to evaluate the performance capabilities of a web application. Measuring performance allows developers to tune a web-based application so that it operates in an effective manner. Some of the web-based testing tools also have capabilities that allow users to validate web links.

9. Test Management Tools. Several measurements have be suggested for collection at lower levels of the TMM. Forms and templates to facilitate this collection should be formalized at TMM level 4. Responsibilities for data analysis and the dissemination of information should be assigned. Tools such as spreadsheets and databases can be used to organize and store some of the data for eventual analysis and application to test process improvement. Defect trackers complement these tools to store, manage, and analyze defect data. Another more sophisticated tool that is useful for collecting and retrieving test-related data is a test management tool. A database of test cases is part of the tool repository. Ideally this tool should be a component of a capture-replay system, or have a seamless interface with a capture-replay system. A fully functioning tool of this type provides some very valuable capabilities such as:

- a user interface that assists users in managing tests;

- ability to organize tests, and to facilitate retrieval and maintenance;

- ability to manage test execution for tests the user selects;

- ability to generate test reports, for example, on test status, and number of test cases executed over a specified time period.

14.2.9 TMM Level 5: Maturity Goals for Optimization/Defect Prevention/ Quality Control

Because of the infrastructure that is in place through achievement of the maturity goals at levels 1–4 of the TMM, the testing process is now said to be defined and managed; its cost and effectiveness can be monitored. At TMM level 5 mechanisms are in place that allow testing to be fine-tuned and continuously improved. Quality control techniques are applied to the testing process so that it can become more predictable and tunable. Defect prevention and quality control are practiced. Statistical sampling, measurements of confidence levels, trustworthiness, and reliability drive the testing process. There is an established procedure for selecting and evaluating testing tools. Automated tools totally support the running and rerunning of test cases. Tools also provide support for test case design, maintenance of test-related items, and defect collection and analysis. The collection, and analysis of test-related metrics also has tool support. [11–13] At TMM level 5 reliability growth models use test and defect data to follow the improvement of reliability through the testing and debugging processes. Tools such as defect trackers, load generators, network analyzers, and performance tools supply and collect the necessary data for reliability evaluation [24]. Maturity goals associated with TMM level 5 are as follows:

Defect Prevention

Mature organizations are able to learn from their past history. Following this philosophy, organizations at the highest level of the TMM record defects, analyze defect patterns, and identify root causes of errors. Actions plans are developed, actions are taken to prevent their recurrence, and there is a mechanism for tracking action progress. At TMM level 5, defect prevention is applied across all projects and across the organization. There is a defect prevention team that is responsible for defect prevention activities. They interact with developers to apply defect prevention activities throughout the life cycle.

Quality Control

At level 4 of the TMM organizations focus on testing for a group of quality-related attributes such as correctness, security, portability, interoperability, performance, and maintainability. At level 5 of the TMM, organizations use statistical sampling, measurements of confidence levels, trustworthiness, and reliability goals to drive the testing process. The testing group and the software quality assurance group are quality leaders;

they work with software designers and developers to incorporate techniques and tools to reduce defects and improve software quality. Automated tools support the running and rerunning of test cases and defect collection and analysis. Usage modeling is used to perform statistical testing. Usability testing supports customer satisfaction. The cost of achieving quality goals is measured relative to the cost of not testing for quantitative quality goals.

Test Process Optimization

At the highest level of the TMM the testing process is subject to continuous improvement across projects and across the organization. The test process is controlled and quantified. It can be fine-tuned so that capability growth is an on-going process. At TMM level 5, organizations realize that high-quality optimizable processes are an asset. A library of process component templates is put into place that allows managers throughout the organization to instantiate an instance of a process or subprocess for use within a specific project. An organizational infrastructure exists to support this continual growth and reuse. This infrastructure, consisting of policies, standards, training, facilities, tools and organizational structures has been put in place through the goal achievement processes that constitute the TMM hierarchy.

14.2.10 Tools for Optimization/Defect Prevention/Quality Control

By moving up the levels of the TMM and assembling a customized Testers' Workbench, an organization has put into place a set of automated tools that support all the phases of the testing life cycle, and provide continuing support for the maturity goals that are already in place. Management is aware of the benefits of these tools and test-related measurements.

At TMM level 5, an organization can select additional tools as shown in Figure 14.7 that assist in defect prevention activities, ensure high-quality software products, and provide continuous support for test process improvement. At this level of the TMM many very mature testing subprocesses are in place and can be stored in a Process Asset Library for

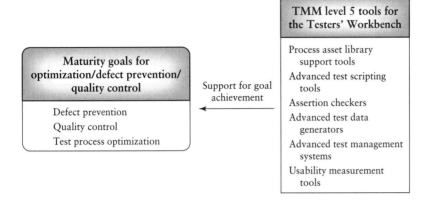

FIG. 14.7

Testers' Workbench tools for TMM level 5.

tailoring and subsequent reuse [25]. Tools can also be used to support this activity.

    1. Process Asset Library (PAL) Support Tools. Currently there are no commercial tools designed specifically to support test process component reuse. Organizations can use conventional tools for this task such as database management systems or configuration management systems to store and retrieve test process components. Another alternative is for an organization to develop its own tool for this purpose.

    2. Advanced Test Scripting Tools. Many capture-replay systems include a test scripting language. This language enables the tester to fully automate the execution of tests. At TMM level 5 all of the capabilities of the language should be used by the testing organization, since the test team is now highly trained, motivated, and has the required expertise to use the broad power of the language.

    3. Assertion Checkers. Assertions are logical statements about program conditions that evaluate to "true" or "false." They describe correct program behavior. A specialized language is often associated with these tools to allow users to input the assertions. Test-related information such as equivalence classes and pre- and postconditions provide useful information for designing the assertions [26]. The code-under-test is run under control of the assertion checker and if an assertion is violated the user is notified. The information is useful for evaluating the code, and locating defects.

4. Advanced Test Data Generators. Many requirements management tools such as those described for TMM level 3 have advanced capabilities. They can be coupled with a test data generator; the requirements information is used to create test cases by statistical, algorithmic, or heuristic methods. Using statistical (or random) methods the tool generates test data based on input structures and values to form a statistically random distribution. With the algorithmic approach, the tool uses a set of rules or procedures to generate test data. Equivalence class partitioning, boundary value analysis and cause-and-effect graphing can be used to drive the test data generation algorithms. Heuristic, or failure-based test generation methods require the tools to have a specialized knowledge base. The knowledge base contain records of failures frequently discovered in the past as input by a user. The tool uses this information to generate test data.

5. Advanced Test Management Systems. At TMM level 4 a test management tool was described that managed test cases, test execution, and generated test reports. There are more advanced test management systems that provide a centralized, sharable location for all test-related items including test harnesses and test outputs. These could be very important support tools for test process optimization, quality control, and defect prevention. Features of such a system should include [27]:

- links to other application packages such as email, project management tools, spreadsheets, and reporting tools;

- ability to define, track, and modify requirements and link them to tests for traceability capabilities;

- ability to track builds and components of the software being developed;

- ability to define test harnesses at different levels of detail (unit, integration test, etc.);

- ability to track test execution with links to test automation tools;

- full capability for defect tracking, including follow-ups;

- ability to develop, store, and track test plans and other test documents;

- integrated measurement capabilities to facilitate collecting, storing, and retrieving metrics related to testing activities.

Research versions of this type of tool have been described in the literature [27]. Commercial tools with all of these capabilities may not be currently available; however, as the testing maturity level of organizations increases, the demand will make advanced tool development more attractive for commercial vendors. An organization could use a combination of existing tools to implement all of these capabilities. There have been proposals for open architectures that would allow related tools to be integrated, but these plug-in architectures have not yet become widely available.

In addition to the features listed above for the advanced test management tool another benefit of its use is to provide a central site where all development team members could assess test-related information. This capability would greatly accelerate discussion and resolution of quality issues related both to process and product. An advanced test management tool of this type could also be developed to run on a corporate network. It could provide all of the capabilities described above, as well as support for distributed development and testing on a global basis.

6. Usability Measurement Tools. At TMM level 5 an organization has the capability to perform usability testing as an activity to support software quality control (see Chapter 12 for discussion). There is a training program, a motivated staff, policies, measurements, and an organizational quality culture in place to support this type of testing. Simple tools to support usability testing are video and audio recorders which help usability testers to record user sessions and play them back for analysis. Other automated tools are available that will make usability factors more visible to developers and testers. Tools of this type can automatically log user actions, log observers notes, identify operational difficulties, solicit user intentions, analyze decisionmaking, and generate reports [10].

14.3 The Testers' Workbench and the Three Critical Views

A large number of test-related tools recommended for inclusion in a Testers' Workbench has been described in this chapter. The order in which they have been integrated into the Testers' Workbench is related to their support for achieving TMM maturity goals. Many of the tools support the achievement and continuous implementation of more than one maturity goal. For example, a complexity measurer supports test planning, controlling and monitoring of testing, test measurement, integration of testing into the software life cycle and software quality evaluation. A defect tracker supports test planning, controlling and monitoring of testing, test measurement, defect prevention, test process improvement, and quality control. The tools are introduced at a TMM level that ensures there will be cultural, managerial, and policy support, as well as staff with the proper training, education, and motivation to benefit from tool support.

An organization need not adapt all of the tools described for the Testers' Workbench. It is best for an organization to build its own customized Testers' Workbench selecting from among the tools described here those that satisfy organizational goals and policies, and those that will fit the organizational culture and environment. The workbench should be built incrementally, with the tools introduced at the recommended TMM levels. When selecting tools, if possible, choose those that complement one another in functionality, for example, a capture-replay tool and a comparator. Pilot projects using the selected tools should be used for tool evaluation. Measured success in several pilots supports organizationwide adaptation of the tools.

Tool adaptation is not a maturity goal at any of the TMM levels. However, tools can support the achievement of TMM maturity goals as we have seen in this chapter. The selection, integration, and continued use of testing tools are responsibilities assigned to members of several different organizational groups. Tool-related responsibilities will vary at the different TMM levels. For example, at TMM levels 1 and 2 there is no testing group, and therefore there is little support for the systematic evaluation and acquisition of testing tools. In addition, the technology transfer knowledge is lacking to smoothly integrate the tools into the organizational process. At these levels developers and project managers are most likely to be assigned responsibilities for testing tool acquisition and usage. As an organization's TMM level increases, the tasks and responsibilities relating to testing tools will shift from developers (D) and project managers (PM) to test managers (TM) and testers (T). Upper management (UM) should be involved at all levels. The shift in responsibilities is likely to occur when a test organization is formed at TMM level 3. It is recommended that at this level tool evaluation criteria, procedures, and processes be established, since there is now an infrastructure in place to support this. The suggested ATRs for developing the Testers' Workbench and the responsible parties are listed below. The reader should keep in mind that many of these are recommended for the higher TMM levels (3–5) where the proper infrastructure is in place.

- Policies for tool evaluation, tool usage, tool integration should be established (PM, TM, UM).

- Goals for the tools should be established (PM, TM).

- Tasks to be automated and/or supported by the tools should be identified (PM, TM, D, T).

- Sources of funding, resources, and training to support the tools should be provided (PM, TM, UM).

- Candidate tools should be identified; current technologies should be researched to identify tool candidates (primarily TM, T).

- A set of tool evaluation criteria should be developed (TM, T).

- Forms for tool evaluation based on the evaluation criteria should be developed (TM, T).

- A tool evaluation procedure should be developed (TM).

- Relevant measurements to monitor tool usage should be selected (TM, T).

- Policies for selecting pilot projects should be developed (PM, TM).

- Managers should develop action plans and procedures for integrating the selected tools into the testing process (PM, TM, UM).

- Technology transfer issues should be discussed and resolved (UM, PM, TM).

- Developers and testers should attend training sessions to learn how to use selected tools (D,T).

- Developers and testers should apply the selected tools in each project to support test-related tasks (D,T).

- Developers and testers should collect measurements related to tool usage to evaluate their effectiveness (D,T).

Users/clients are not usually involved in selecting and using testing tools. In the case of requirements-based and usability measurement tools, they may have a role in using the tools.

A final comment on tool acquisition should be made here. Some organizations prefer to develop their own in-house versions of testing tools. This often occurs when they cannot find a commercial tool that is suitable to their needs. However, given the growing tool market and the availability of so many tools, some of which may be customizable or have open architectures, it may be more cost-effective to purchase a commercial tool than develop and maintain an in-house version.

EXERCISES

1. Select a set of testing tool evaluation criteria that would be appropriate for your organization. Based on these criteria, design a form for testing tool evaluation and acquisition.

2. Why is a "line of code counter" an important tool for any organization to put in place?

3. Your organization is assessed to be at TMM level 2. Your project manager is reluctant to provide resources to purchase testing tools. Give an argument to convince him or her of the usefulness of test tool support. Which tools would you recommend for your organization at this stage of test process maturity?

4. How do requirements recorders and requirements-to-test tracers support early integration of testing activities into the software life cycle?

5. How do capture/replay tools support testing and retesting of software?

6. What role does a complexity measurer play in test planning and in controlling and monitoring of test?

7. Give your opinion on the use of a code checker before or after a code review.

8. How do simulators and emulators support effective testing?

9. Develop a conceputal design for a test management tool that would faciltiate test management, test execution, and test montioring.

10. Are there any other test-related tools you would recommend for the Testers' Workbench that have not been described in this chapter? Which TMM level would you recommend for their introduction? Which maturity goals do you think they would support?

11. What are the benefits of having a PAL (Process Assst Library) support tool?

12. What role do managers play in the development of a Testers' Workbench?

REFERENCES

[1] R. Firth, V. Mosley, R. Pethia, L. Roberts, W. Wood, "A guide to the classification and assessment of software engineering tools," Technical Report CMU/SEI-87-TR-10, ESD-TR-87-11, Software Engineering Institute, Carneagie Mellon, 1987.

[2] R. Poston, M. Sexton, "Evaluating and selecting testing tools," *IEEE Software,* pp. 33–42, May 1992.

[3] R. Poston, "Testing tools combine best of new and old," *IEEE Software,* pp. 122–126, March 1995.

[4] R. Poston, *Automating Specification-Based Software Testing,* IEEE Computer Society Press, Los Alamitos, CA, 1996.

[5] C. Kemerer, "How the learning curve affects CASE tool adaptation," *IEEE Software,* pp. 23–28, May 1993.

[6] V. Moseley, "How to assess tools efficiently and quantitatively," *IEEE Software,* pp. 29–32, May 1993.

[7] E. Kit, *Software Testing in the Real World,* Addison-Wesley, Reading, MA, 1995.

[8] G. Daich, G. Price, B. Ragland, M. Dawood, *Software Test Technologies Report,* August 1994, Software Technology Support Center (STSC) Hill Air Force Base, UT, August 1994.

[9] *IEEE Recommended Practice for the Evaluation and Selection of CASE Tools* (IEEE Std 1209-1992), copyright 1993 by IEEE, all rights reserved.

[10] E. Dustin, J. Cashka, J. Paul, *Automated Software Testing,* Addison-Wesley, Reading, MA, 1999.

[11] I. Burnstein, A. Homyen, T. Suwanassart, G. Saxena, R. Grom, "A testing maturity model for software test process assessment and improvement," *Software Quality Professional* (American Society for Quality), Vol. 1, No. 4 Sept. 1999, pp 8–21.

[12] I. Burnstein, A. Homyen, T. Suwanassart, G. Saxena, R. Grom, "Using the testing maturity model to assess and improve your software testing process," *Proc. of International Quality Week Conf.* (QW '99), San Jose, CA, May 1999.

[13] I. Burnstein, T. Suwanassart, C. R. Carlson, "Developing a testing maturity model for software test process evaluation," *IEEE International Test Conference '96*, Washington, DC, Oct. 1996, pp. 581–589.

[14] W. Humphrey, *A Discipline for Software Engineering*, Addison-Wesley, Reading, MA, 1995.

[15] *IEEE Standard for Software Test Documentation* (IEEE Std 829-1983), copyright 1983 by IEEE, all rights reserved.

[16] R. Thayer, ed. *Software Engineering Project Management*, second edition, IEEE Computer Society Press, Los Alamitos, CA, 1997.

[17] B. Subramaniam, "Effective software defect tracking, reducing project costs, and enhancing quality," *CrossTalk: The Journal of Defense Software Engineering*, Vol. 12, No. 4, April 1999, pp. 3–9.

[18] T. Khoshgoftarr, J. Munson, "Predicting software development errors using software complexity metrics," *IEEE J. Selected Areas in Comm.*, Vol. 8, No. 2, Feb. 1990, pp. 252–261.

[19] I. Burnstein, T. Suwanassart, C. R. Carlson, "Developing a testing maturity model: part I," *CrossTalk: Journal of Defense Software Engineering*, Vol. 9, No. 8, August 1996, pp. 21–24.

[20] I. Burnstein, T. Suwanassart, C. R. Carlson, "Developing a testing maturity model: part II," *CrossTalk: Journal of Defense Software Engineering*, Vol. 9, No. 9, Sept. 1996, pp. 19–26.

[21] I. Burnstein, F. Saner, "Fuzzy reasoning to support automated program understanding," *International Journal of Software Engineering and Knowledge Engineering*, Vol. 10, No. 1, Feb. 2000, pp. 115–137.

[22] W. Kozaczynski, J. Ning, "Automated program recognition by concept recognition," *Automated Software Engineering*, Vol. 1, 1994, pp. 61–78.

[23] A. Quilici, "A memory-based approach to recognizing program plans," *CACM*, Vol. 37, No. 5, 1994, pp. 84–93.

[24] H. Pham, *Software Reliability and Testing*, IEEE Computer Society Press, Los Alamitos, CA, 1995.

[25] M. Kellner, R. Phillip, "Practical technology for process assets," *Proc. 8th International Software Process Workshop: State of the Practice in Process Technology*, Warden, Germany, March 1993, pp. 107–112.

[26] B. Korel, I. Burnstein, R. Brevelle, "Postcondition based stress testing in certification of COTS components," *Proceedings of the First International Software Assurance Certification Conference*, Washington, DC, March 1999.

[27] J. Hearns, S. Garcia, "Automated test team management—it works!!", *Proc. 10th Software Engineering Process Group Conference (SEPG'98)*, Chicago, IL, March 1998.

[28] J. Rubin, *Handbook of Usability Testing*, John Wiley & Sons, New York, 1994.

PROCESS CONTROL

AND OPTIMIZATION

15.0 TMM Maturity Goals: Support for a Quality Testing Process

As an organization moves up the levels of the Testing Maturity Model and achieves the TMM testing maturity goals, it makes significant improvements in the quality of its testing process. The overall testing process becomes defined, managed, and measured. It is more stable and predictable. As a consequence of test process improvement there is also the potential for positive gains in the quality of the software that the organization produces. At TMM level 5 the focus on process quality continues, and mechanisms are put in place so that testing can be controlled, finetuned, and continuously improved. The maturity goals of "Defect prevention," "Quality control," and "Process optimization" all give support to continuous process improvement. In the context of the TMM, process optimization means a testing process that can support:

- automation of testing tasks;

- measurements and mechanisms for process change;

- control and fine tuning of process steps;

- technology transfer;

- reuse of process components.

These three TMM maturity goals are mutually supportive. For example, a defect prevention program supports product/process quality control. Quality control contributes to process optimization, and process optimization activities will support both defect prevention and quality control. All of these maturity goals are, in turn, supported by the continued implementation of practices acquired through achievement of the lower-level maturity goals.

Previous chapters in this book have covered topics that relate to TMM level 5 maturity goals. For example, software quality control issues are discussed in Chapter 12. In Chapter 13, the process of defect prevention was described. We have learned about tools for the automation of test in Chapter 14. Chapters 9 and 11 gave us an understanding of the role of measurements, and examples of measurements that can be used for monitoring and controlling the test process. In this chapter we will focus on test process quality control, and test process optimization issues. We will learn how the measurements, monitoring system, training program, staff, and tools that we have put into place by moving up the TMM levels supports the following objectives:

(i) development of a standardized baseline for our testing process;

(ii) identification of upper and lower limits for the operation of our testing process;

(iii) application of techniques to tune our testing process so that it stays within acceptable limits;

(iv) development of systems to continuously improve our testing process;

(v) development of a set of process assets.

15.1 Process Engineering and Quality Control

In Chapter 1, arguments were made to support software development as an emerging engineering discipline. Software testing was presented as a subdiscipline within the domain of software engineering. The important role of process as an element of an engineering discipline was also described. (It is helpful for the reader to review Section 1.1.) If we consider ourselves to be test specialists and engineers, then test process engineering and its component activity of test process control are among our responsibilities. Process engineering, like all engineering activities, involves the development and maintenance of artifacts using appropriate principles, practices, and procedures. Process artifacts, like software artifacts, should be planned, measured, evaluated, and reused. Hollenbach and Kellner are among the researchers who have done work in this area. [1–3]

To support the engineering of processes a process life cycle is needed. Phases analogous to those described for the software life cycle are useful in this context. These phases support the development of high-quality software processes that are engineered, and are candidates for reuse in future projects. A process life cycle is described below.

1. *Requirements Phase.* The goals and requirements for the process are defined. The domain and conditions under which this process will operate are outlined. Users/customers for the process are described. Process developers may examine existing processes that are relevant to help develop the requirements and design for this new process. The process requirements are reviewed.

2. *Design Phase.* The process is designed. Process inputs/outputs are defined, as well as quality indicators, and entry and exit criteria (these are necessary for process reuse). Interfaces to other processes are described in terms of an overall process architecture. This will support the integration of this process with others it must interact with. In the detailed design phase the process steps are described, as well as methods, procedures, roles, and feedback and control mechanisms. The design is reviewed.

3. *Implementation and Testing Phase.* The process is implemented (executed) and evaluated. It can be evaluated on its own, analogous to a unit test, or it can be integrated with other interfacing processes and evaluated as a part of an entire process context. In both cases, process execution is monitored, measured, and analyzed for effectiveness and for adherence to standards. An assessment team, or Software Engineering Process Group (SEPG), should be involved in the testing

phases. If the process looks promising with respect to fulfilling requirements and goals, it could receive approval by the assessment team for widespread adaptation and reuse.

4. *Operation/Maintenance and/or Evolutionary Phase.* The process is maintained and continually improved. Related documentation is updated to reflect any changes. In mature organizations a process undergoes assessment, change, and evolution to higher maturity states. It may also undergo tailoring for reuse.

In addition to support from a process life cycle, test process engineering is also supported by putting into place TMM practices, and progressing through TMM assessment/improvement cycles. A discipline called process control is also an important support tool for process engineering and is part of the TMM goal framework. Process control encompasses a set of procedures, and practices that seek to determine if a process is behaving as expected. A controlled process is desirable since it is stable and predictable. Process control and quality control are related concepts. Chapter 12 describes the nature of quality control as applied to software products. A general definition for quality control was given and is repeated below for review.

> **Quality control consists of the procedures and practices employed to ensure that a work product or deliverable conforms to standards or requirements.**

As practioners in an engineering discipline, we can apply quality control procedures and practices to our processes as well as to our products. This is a reasonable and practical approach for us because we are now aware of the direct impact of process on the quality of our products. We are also more aware of the role of quality attributes and quality measurements. We now realize that process artifacts can be considered as work products and organizational assets. When our process is engineered in a disciplined way, and it is controlled, it becomes stable and predictable. We can, under these conditions, use its past performance to predict future performance. We can also be more confident that it can be depended upon to give us high-quality deliverables on time and within budget. Support for process control as a high-level process goal comes from other process improvement models, for example, the Capability Maturity

Model [4]. A Key Process Area (KPA) that supports process control is described at CMM level 4, and is called "quantitative process management." This KPA addresses many of the same concerns as the TMM maturity goals, "Quality control" (for process) and "Process optimization."

Chapter 12 described several process characteristics that were needed to support quality control for software products. Many of these apply to quality control of the test process itself. There are additional characteristics that should be added to the description for completeness. Figure 15.1 shows a fuller set of programs, practices, and procedures necessary for quantitative quality control of the testing process. These are also listed below:

- test process policies, goals, and standards;

- test process documentation;

- a training program;

- dedicated, trained, and motivated staff;

- a measurement program;

- a planning process;

- use of statistical process control techniques and tools;

- use of testing tools such as coverage tools and defect trackers;

- test process monitoring and controlling systems;

- a test process assessment system (TMM-AM);

- a defect repository;

- a defect prevention program with action planning and feedback;

- a software engineering or test process group.

Many groups must work together to achieve the goal of test process quality control. A Software Engineering Process Group (SEPG) is suggested as the umbrella organization for putting the process control team

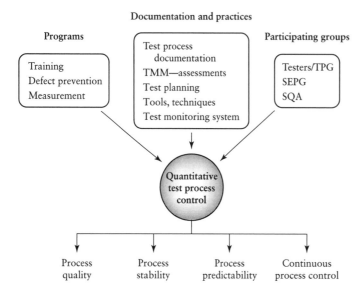

FIG. 15.1

Quantitative test process control—
supporting items.

together. Team participants may be selected from diverse functional units, for example, development, test, and SQA. Both management and staff should participate. Each team member will have different responsibilities. For example, some group members will set and document quantitative performance goals and limits for the test process. Others will measure its actual performance when applied to software projects. Group members will also analyze the measurement results and make adjustments (control the process) to ensure that the process performs within the acceptable limits. The role and organization of an SEPG is discussed in more detail in Section 15.5.

The SEPG alone cannot achieve control of any process without co-operation from management and staff persons working on the diverse projects sponsored by the organization. This implies a cultural awareness and support for process control goals, practices, and measurements within an organization. Management must ensure that team work and common goals are emphasized, and that the benefits of process control and optimization are visible throughout the organization.

15.2 Fundamentals of Quantitative Process Control

Quantitative process control is supported by statistical process control techniques and methodologies. Statistical process control (SPC) is a discipline based on measurements and statistics [5–8]. Decisions are made and plans developed based on the actual collection and evaluation of measurement data rather than on intuition and past experience [5]. The basis for SPC is a view of the development (or testing) process as a series of steps, each of which is a process in itself with a set of inputs and outputs. This view is shown in Figure 15.2. Ideally the output of each step is determined by rules/procedures/standards that prescribe how it is to be executed. Practically speaking the outcome of a step may be different then expected. The differences are caused by variations. Variations may be due to, for example, human error, influences outside of the process, and/or unpredictable events such as hardware/software malfunctions. If there are many unforeseen variations impacting on the process steps, then the process will be unstable, unpredictable, and out of control. When a process is unpredictable then we cannot rely upon it to give us quality results.

Implementing statistical process control depends on having trained and motivated staff who take pride in their work. The staff members must be flexible and willing and able to make process changes to improve the quality of their work. SPC also depends on the realization that every process has variations, and that if the same task is done repeatedly by the same person, the results/outputs may not always be the same, even if the same rules and procedures apply. It is important to realize that the magnitude of the variation is an issue. In a defined, managed, and measured process, variations will be smaller and have smaller impacts on the final process deliverables. Another issue to consider is the type of variation. There are two types of variations that are described within the context of SPC. These are (i) common cause, and (ii) assignable (or special) cause variations. The total number of variations in a process can be expressed as the sum of these types of variations:

$$\text{Total variations} = \text{common cause variations} + \text{assignable cause variations}$$

Common cause variations are those caused by so-called "normal" variations that occur where there are normal interactions between people,

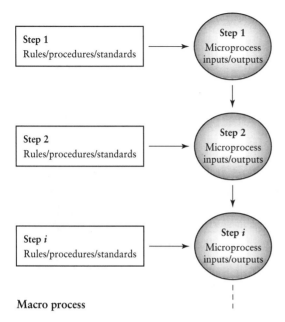

Macro process

FIG. 15.2
Process view for support of quality control.

machines (hardware), methods, techniques, and environments. These are the cause of noise in the process. Assignable variations come from events that are not part of the normal process. These show up as highs and lows in process data. For example, in week 2 the number of test cases executed in a system test for a product may be low and the next week (week 3) the value may be high. Such a variation could be due to a failure in system test support tools that occurred in week 2. The assignable variations are said to be the signals in process data.

One of the tasks of an SEPG is to determine if a process variation is caused by special circumstances (an assignable cause) which may be linked to a specific time or location, or by the variations inherent in the nature of the process itself (common cause). Identifying the causes of variation is a key task for the SEPG engaged in SPC activities. The action necessary to control the process and the choice of staff responsible for the action are related to the type and nature of the cause. An analogous situation occurs in the area of defect prevention, where developing preventative actions is dependent on the origins or causes of the defects.

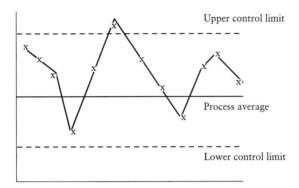

FIG. 15.3
Generic control chart.

A technique that is useful for monitoring processes and determining causes is based on the development of what is called a control chart. Affourtit describes the control chart as a decision support tool that helps to develop actions; these actions will lead to control of the process [5]. Control charts are useful for identifying special or assignable causes when they appear. They also provide information about process performance over time, and give an indication of process stability and predictability. Finally, control charts give us quantitative insights into the behavior of our processes. An example of a generic control chart is shown in Figure 15.3.

A control chart is basically a plot of process-related items. On the chart there is a depiction of an upper, lower, and average control limit for a process. The limits are determined by the SEPG by using data collected over many projects. Very often the mean and standard deviations are calculated for the process data items, and charts such as R charts (a graph of the range, or difference between the largest and smallest measurement in each sample set over time) and Xbar charts (a graph of the average of each sample set taken over time) are plotted to help determine these limits [4–6].

Some data items that can be plotted on a control chart are the number of users completing a task versus task number (usability test process), cycle time, versus test task sequence number (test planning process), source lines of code inspected per hour, versus inspection sequence number (inspection process), and problem rate, versus week (test process) [5,7,8]. Note that many different processes can be evaluated using a variety of data items.

The upper control limits (UCL) and lower control limits (LCL) as depicted on a control chart help the SEPG to separate the signals from the noise. The limits can be calculated from process data as described in research work done by Florac [7], Weller [8], and Putman [9]. The variation of data points inside the control limits is due to noise in the process (common cause, or normal variations). The points outside the control limits probably represent assignable causes, that is, these variations are caused by events outside of the process's normal operations. If a process is judged to be out of control from the process data, the SEPG needs to take a careful look at the points outside of the limits and try find assignable causes for them (e.g., the point outside the UCL in Figure 15.3). The group must then identify ways to eliminate these causes in future executions of the process. It should also be noted that a process may be judged to be stable (under control) in the sense that its average and upper/lower control limits are predictable. However, if a process stabilizes at an unacceptable level of performance, then further changes to the process will be needed to make improvements. A control chart would then help to show the impact of the changes on process performance. Incremental changes supported by the TMM maturity goals can guide the improvement efforts.

15.3 Activities for Quantitative Test Process Control

Quantitative management of the testing process can be accomplished by adapting the tools, methods, and procedures used for general process control in the software engineering domain. It is useful to initially select test subprocesses as targets for control since their scope is smaller and therefore easier to manage. Some example test subprocesses that are suggested are inspections, system test, and unit test.

As a precondition to quantitative control, the target testing process, or subprocess must be documented and its steps well defined. Measurements must be standardized, and expected ranges for the measurements must also be documented. The measurements are the basic elements of quality control. They need to be collected and analyzed. Adjustments are then made to the process based on the analyses so that it becomes stable and more predictable.

An organization involved in implementing test process quality control should have a defined and documented test process. At TMM level 5 where quality control is a maturity goal, these requirements are met easily. The organization should also define activities/tasks and responsibilities to operate the control system. A procedure for process control should be developed and documented. Key procedure steps and activities are summarized in Figure 15.4 and are briefly described below. Note the feedback loop in Figure 15.4 for the last several steps. The steps described here are very general in the sense that they can be applied to most development processes. Testers can apply them specifically to the testing process and test subprocesses.

1. Organize a Process Control Team to Oversee the System.

A team is organized to oversee the process control system. The team should include developers, testers, and SQA staff. If an organization has a Software Process Engineering Group (SEPG), then that group and/or some of its members can serve on the process control team.

2. Develop Policies, Goals, and Plans.

Overall policies, goals, and plans for process control are developed by the team. Each project may have its own process control plan and process performance goals. The plans should be reviewed by the process control team.

3. Allocate Funds and Resources.

Resources and funding are allocated to the process control team. Support tools such as statistical analysis packages, problem trackers, and databases should be available to the team.

4. Training.

The process team and key project staff members are trained in process control tools and techniques. (The training program as described in Chapter 8 supports this step.)

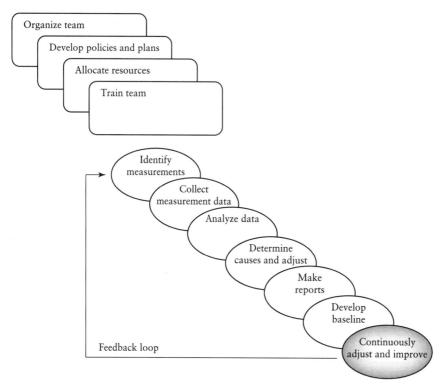

FIG. 15.4

General steps for process control.

5. Identify Measurements.

Based on goals and plans, the team identifies the measurements to be collected for process control. These measurements should reflect key properties of the process. For test, several of the measurements described in Chapters 9 and 11 are useful in this context. The team also decides on strategies and procedures for data collection and analysis.

6. Collect and Validate Data.

The process control team reviews process control activities with each project (test) manager. The team collects and validates process data from projects across the organization according to the selected procedures and plans. The data is stored in a measurement database. (The measurement program as described in Chapter 11 supports this step as well as step 5.)

7. Analyze Data.

Analysis of the data is carried out using appropriately selected tools as in the control plan. Control charts as described previously are very useful, and can be developed from the appropriate data for each project to analyze target processes. A baseline, and acceptable levels for process performance in terms of the measurements collected, should result for each project (upper and lower control limits). Other useful information for process control can be derived from plots, Pareto, and scatter diagrams that are prepared from the project data.

8. Determine Causes, and Make Adjustments.

The control charts are used to determine common cause variations and assignable cause variations. Process adjustments reflecting these causes are made to align the process's performance to within acceptable limits.

9. Compose and Distribute Reports.

Reports of process control activities from all projects are developed and disturbed to upper management and other interested parties, for example, the SQA group.

10. Develop and Document a Standardized Baseline Process for the Organization.

Process performance data is stored for each project in a process database. From the accumulation of process control data from the organizational projects, a baseline for the overall organizational process is developed, documented, and established as the standard.

11. Continuously Adjust Baseline and Standards.

This serves as a process maintenance step. Any changes that result from the monitoring of new projects (those that are substantially different from projects developed in the past) and/or applying process adjustments should be reflected as changes in the organizational process baseline and in standards adjustments. For example, results of TMM assessments and subsequent process changes require adjustments. A feedback loop to step 5 can help to organize the updates and adjustments.

It should be noted that the achievement of process control most often leads to process changes so that a process becomes both effective and quantitatively controlled. There are other activities that also lead to process change, for example, those involving defect prevention and process assessment. Several teams may be involved in these process improvement activities, and they will need to cooperate and coordinate their activities. They should:

- coordinate their actions;

- share data;

- share resources and personnel;

- support cultural changes;

- support technology transfer.

In earlier sections of this chapter it was suggested that an SEPG serve as the umbrella organization to coordinate process improvement goals and activities. Section 15.5 discusses the role of such a team in more detail.

15.4 Examples of the Application of Statistical Process Control

Readers interested in current applications of statistical process control (SPC) in the software domain can refer to several papers in this area. Florac and his group have reported on their work in SPC as applied to the Space Shuttle Onboard Software Project [7]. The purpose of their study was to determine if using SPC on certain key development processes could further increase the reliability of the space shuttle's software. A key process selected for the study was the software inspection process. It was

selected because it was a commonly used process that was well documented, cost effective, and small in scope. The latter factor is important
in starting up an SPC program since initiating SPC systems for large and
complex processes often causes frustration with application of the techniques involved. Another supporting factor for the selection of the inspection process was the fact that the researchers also had a database of
inspection process attribute values readily available to them.

The group used inspection data to develop control charts for inspections performed on six key software components [7]. Most often, control
charts plotted source lines of code per inspection hour versus inspection
sequence number. Upper and lower control limits were determined. The
charts were successfully used to (i) understand the inspection process and
causes of variations, (ii) set baselines for process performance, and
(iii) identity issues requiring actions for process improvement.

Weller also reports on the application of SPC techniques in the software domain [8]. In his study at Bull HN Information Systems, SPC was
applied to analyze inspection and test data. Results of the study helped
to understand and predict release quality, and to understand the process
that controls quality. Control charts developed from inspection data were
used to identify causes for variations in the inspection process, and to
determine when the inspection process was under control.

Weller also applied SPC to testing phases. For example, during system
testing SPC was used to help make stop-test decisions. Control charts
similar to the generic example shown in Figure 15.3 were developed plot-
ting problem arrival rates (which indicate defects) versus weeks of testing.
Upper and lower control limits were calculated and indicated on the
charts. SPC techniques supported by control charts were then used by
Weller and his group to determine when the system test process was under
control. Using the charts the researchers were also able to establish a
predicted "weekly problem arrival rate." An "end of test" point could be
estimated if certain conditions were observed. For example, if the control
chart showed a downward trend of problem arrival over a specific period
of time with points dropping below the LCL this observation was per-
ceived to be an indication of a stop test point. One condition for making
the stop-test decision using this information was that the downward trend
indicate an assignable cause for the variation, and the cause be product-
related. Weller concluded that there were additional costs related to using

SPC, but these were not high and were offset by the benefits of process understanding, support for decision making, and the ability to establish quality goals.

An article by Affourtit is an additional source for discussion of SPC as applied to the software domain [5]. A good general discussion of SPC is provided in this article, as well as suggestions for application of SPC to the design, coding, testing, and maintenance phases of development. For the testing process use of SPC is suggested to support stop-test decisions; however, not many experimental details are given. Affourtit also suggests use of control charts that plot "faults encountered per module" to help identify defect-prone modules.

15.5 Test Process Optimization: The Role of a Process Improvement Group

The characteristics of an optimizing testing process are briefly described in Section 15.0. In this section the set of characteristics is augmented, and an optimizing testing process is said to be one that is:

- defined;

- measured;

- managed;

- well staffed;

- quantitatively controlled;

- predictable;

- effective;

- supported by automation;

- able to support technology transfer;

- able to support process component reuse;

- focused on defect prevention;

- focused on process change, continuous improvement.

The optimized testing process is monitored, supports software quality control, and increased tester productivity. It is periodically assessed to give feedback to management on its status, and to ensure that it is controlled, predictable, and effective. It is also assessed to determine its strengths and weaknesses (see Chapter 16 for further details on TMM assessments). Weaknesses are focus areas for process improvement goals that lead to increased process quality. Strengths suggest areas for process asset extraction. The optimized testing process makes effective use of available resources, and is able to incorporate new techniques and technologies that will result in further improvement gains. It supports a process asset library that contains reusable test process components (assets) applicable throughout the organization.

Application of the TMM supports an organization in achieving an optimizing level for its test process by raising process performance goals in a structured and incremental manner. The incremental increase in capability is supported by a framework of maturity levels, associated maturity goals, and TMM assessments. The latter reveal weak areas in a testing process that may prevent an organization from reaching high levels of process performance. Moving up the levels of the TMM builds an infrastructure of practices, policies, tools, techniques, trained staff, and organizational groups/structures/teams that can support optimization and continuous improvement.

To support the growth of a strong test process infrastructure, and to plan and implement process improvement efforts, a process improvement group should be founded and be staffed by members who have the motivation and training required for success in these areas. In many organizations this group is called the Software Engineering Process Group (SEPG). This group can support overall process assessment and improvement using models such as the CMM, as well as test process assessment and improvement with the TMM. A separate Test Process Group (TPG) that cooperates with the general SEPG or functions as a stand-alone group is also a possible staffing approach. In subsequent discussions this text will use the term SEPG in a general sense to cover any of these possible arrangements. No matter how it is organized, a process improvement group should focus on process-related activities such as process definition, analysis and assessment, action planning, and evaluation. The group should also be involved in identifying reusable process components, and making these available throughout the organization. Note that such a group was described in Section 15.1 as the umbrella organization for other process-related activities that include process control, defect prevention, and technology transfer.

It is best if a SEPG is a permanent entity in the organization, not one that is temporality assembled when an assessment is scheduled to take place. A charter or policy statement relating to the group should be developed and distributed. This statement should describe group goals, membership, roles, associations, and responsibilities. Membership in the SEPG should include personnel from projects in place throughout the organization such as test managers, project managers, SQA managers, and lead engineers. It is important to include personnel who are practitioners, that is, staff involved in a "hand-on" manner with the development and testing of software. They supply valuable input with respect to the nature of the current process, and are able to provide the cultural support and motivation needed for successful process change [10].

With respect to test process improvement, support for a process-centered group begins formally at TMM level 3 where a test organization is established, and a training program is in place to increase the level of skills and knowledge required for the success of this team. It is therefore appropriate to initiate a Test, or Software Engineering Process Group (TPG/SEPG) at this TMM level. In addition, at TMM level 3 and higher, an organization fully understands the value of process change and improvement and is more willing to provide the group with adequate resources and funding. Such an organization is also more willing to assign development and test team members process responsibilities, and these team members can serve as interfaces or members of a TPG/SEPG. At TMM levels 4 and 5, the responsibilities of the TPG/SEPG can grow as more higher level practices are introduced. For example, an organization at TMM level 5 recognizes that high-quality processes are corporate assets and would be more willing to provide support for a process asset library. The TPG/SEPG would then have the responsibility for identifying reusable process assets and developing and maintaining the process asset library (PAL). The relationships between TMM levels and the responsibilities for an SEPG/TPG working on test process improvement are shown in Figure 15.5.

There are reports in the literature that focus on experiences with an

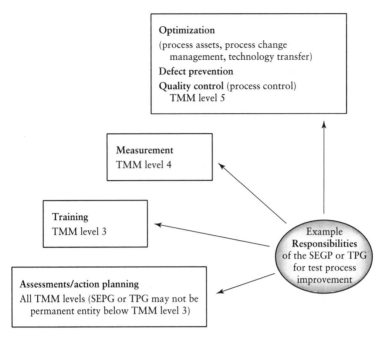

Optimization
(process assets, process change
    management, technology transfer)
Defect prevention
Quality control (process control)
    TMM level 5

Measurement
TMM level 4

Training
TMM level 3

Example
Responsibilities
of the SEGP or TPG
for test process
improvement

Assessments/action planning
All TMM levels (SEPG or TPG may not be
    permanent entity below TMM level 3)

FIG. 15.5

Responsibilities for a SEPG/TPG for
test process improvement.

SEPG. For example, Wigle and Yamamura describe the tasks performed
and the challenges that must be met by an SEPG as a result of their experiences at Boeing [10]. Challenges include people issues such as changing the organizational culture, and obtaining sponsorship from the different management levels. Process challenges include formation of the
SEPG itself, developing process assets and understanding process improvement model practices. Asset challenges include making process assets available to users, and compliance of process assets to company or
industry standards. Readers should be aware of these challenges when
instituting a SEPG or TPG. Wigle and Yamamura also describe the responsibilities of the SEPG group in their organization. These responsibilities include:

Process Definition: The SEPG documents the organizational software process. This documentation can be in the form of software standards doc-

uments, project guidelines, or software process procedures. The group reviews the documents. They propose and review changes (improvements), and they ensure that undocumented procedures are recorded. Process documents produced at lower maturity levels are revised and updated by this team to reflect higher level practices.

Process Change Management: The SEPG encourages improvement proposals from process owners/users and reviews them. The group also manages the change process using appropriate forms and reports (these are analogous to software changes/problem reports). A history of changes is maintained.

Technology Insertion: The SEPG reviews and selects proposed technological changes that may originate from multiple sources. Changes may result from the introduction of new tools, methods, training procedures, and techniques. After a change is selected, the SEPG oversees technology transfer issues. For example, pilot projects are initiated, monitored, and results evaluated. The SEPG group prepares plans for technology insertion if pilot projects indicate applicability and success.

Process Evaluation: The SEPG team is involved in process control. The team reviews and analyzes performance measurements that support process control. The group oversees the establishment of a process baseline and also through quantitative analysis and process assessment, identifies areas for improvement.

Training: Wigle and Yamamura report that in their organization the SEPG supports staff training. The group is responsible for training planning, maintaining training records, and preparing training materials.

Process Asset Support: The SEPG establishes and maintains a set of (i) process assets including a process asset library (PAL), (ii) process measurements, and (iii) lessons learned.

Process Assessment: When an assessment is to be carried out the SEPG has the responsibility for assessment preparation. The assessments can be internal self-assessments or performed by an outside group of assessors. In either of these cases the SEPG supports the necessary preparation activities such as data gathering, interviewing, review of documents, and presentations. When the assessment is complete, the SEPG team is involved in action planning and action implementation and evaluation.

Wigle and Yamamura also indicate that in large organizations a hierarchy of SEPG teams may be necessary because of the large number of projects and staff, and the increased level of process complexity. In the context of the TMM and test process improvement efforts, several different organizations for a process improvement group have been suggested. They are summarized below.

- an independent Test Process Group (TPG) that specifically addresses test process issues using TMM guidelines;

- a combination SEPG/TPG; the SEPG component covers general process issues related to CMM goals, and the TPG focuses on testing issues guided by the TMM;

- a single umbrella SEPG that covers all process improvement activities guided by one or more process improvement models;

- a hierarchical umbrella SEPG for general process improvement; the TPG can be one part of the hierarchical structure; the umbrella could also cover the work done by process control and defect prevention teams.

Each organization should decide on an appropriate process improvement team structure depending on size, process goals, culture, and resources available.

15.6 Technology Transfer

At TMM level 5 an organization has in place a high-quality and effective testing process. A characteristic of such a high-level process is the ability to identify, evaluate, and integrate new technologies into the organizational processes in a smooth and effective way. This ability supports test process optimization. The CMM indicates the importance of such a group of abilities by specifying it in a Key Process Area called "technology change management" at CMM level 5. In the context of the TMM this group of abilities is called technology transfer and is a component of the "test process optimization" maturity goal.

Technology transfer involves several steps or phases. Responsibility for the implementation of the steps is appropriately assigned to SEPG or TPG members. The group selected must ensure that there is a policy for technology change management, there is support for these changes by upper management, there is a measurement program that will support evaluation of technological changes, and there is a training program to introduce new technologies into the organization. These requirements suggest that a mature testing process is necessary, thus, the reason for including technology transfer as a component of a TMM level 5 maturity goal.

The phases required for successful technology transfer are shown in Figure 15.6, described by Daich [11], and discussed below.

1. *Awareness.* Members of the SEPG/TPG should request suggestions for new test technology from practitioners, managers and other informed staff members. SEPG/TPG team members should attend test-related conferences, search the literature, the internet, organizational publications, and trade publication for new technologies. The groups need to learn how these technologies have been applied and which have had successful application in industry. They should be aware of areas in the process where new technologies could support improvement, and should keep project and test managers informed with respect to these new technologies and how they could support improvement goals.

2. *Understanding.* After a new technology is identified and there is and interest in adoption, the SEPG/TPG should evaluate and thoroughly understand the new technology. They should obtain available data and documentation relating to the new technology, and solicit reports on usage, weaknesses, and strengths. Criteria such as those described in Chapter 14 for test tool evaluation can be used in this context. Report forms for evaluation of tools and technologies based on a documented set of evaluation criteria, should be developed and be available for application and distribution.

Technology transfer support

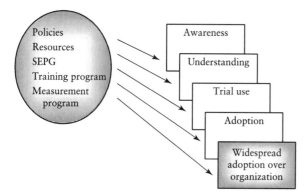

FIG. 15.6

Steps in the technology transfer process.

3. *Trial Use (Pilots)* When the SEPG/TPG team identifies a promising new technology, plans for applying that technology to a select number of pilot projects should be made. As in other process improvement trials, appropriate pilots should be selected with trained and motivated staff. The SEPG should support pilot project staff, and ensure that all necessary resources are provided. Data based on the incorporation of the new technology is collected as the project progresses, and upon completion, the feasibility, economics, and effectiveness of the new technology is evaluated. Benefits of more widespread use are discussed. The SEPG/TPG then decides whether to abandon this technology, continue with pilot studies, or work toward broader adoption.

4. *Adoption.* When results from pilot projects indicate that a new technology is promising and suitable for adoption on a larger scale then the new technology should be applied in a wider variety of projects across the organization. That is, the scope of application should be broader then in the case of the pilot projects. As in the case of trial use in pilots, support by the SEPG/TPG group for managers and practitioners is important in this phase. Application on this larger scale gives management and the SEPG/TPG additional opportunities to

evaluate the technology. Projects should be selected, personnel trained, and results evaluated through documented procedures.

5. *Organizational Adaptation.* When results from broader-scale application indicate that the new technology has a positive impact on the test process, then it can integrated and applied across the organization according to a documented procedure. The documents describing the organizational test process and policy should be updated to reflect the new technology. Training in the new technology should be widespread over the organization to ensure all effected personnel understand how to use and apply it.

As the reader will note, technology transfer requires a good deal of effort and coordination by diverse groups in the organization. A time frame of many months from initial identification of a new technology to its organizational adoption is not unusual. Technology transfer is a necessary aspect of test process optimization efforts and should be strongly supported by upper management and key organizational players.

15.7 Process Reuse

Organizations are now beginning to realize that processes are corporate assets and those of high quality should be documented and stored in a process repository in a templatelike form that is modifiable for reuse in future projects. Such a process repository is often called a process asset library (PAL). Process reuse must be supported by a process life cycle, a process reuse policy, and a process repository or library [1–3]. Management must give support for reuse, and training to develop reusable processes must be available. A process measurement program, and a group such as SEPG must be in place. An organization undergoing regular process assessments has additional support for process reuse since this practice provides a mechanism for identifying and evaluating potentially reusable processes. Procedures, policies, and practices that support general process reuse apply to test process reuse as well. Organizations on TMM level 5 have the capabilities to implement test process reuse with support from management, the test group, and an SEPG.

Process reuse in the context of the current discussion means the use of one process description to create another process description. It does not mean multiple executions of the same process on a given project [1]. For process reuse to succeed, an organization should view process components as reusable objects in the same context as reusable design and code objects. Ideally, a reusable process should be stored in the process repository in a format that allows application to appropriate organizational projects. There are many potential benefits of process reuse, for example, Refs. 1–3:

- transfer of process knowledge between projects;

- transfer of expertise between projects;

- reduction of training costs;

- support for process improvement over the organization;

- improved project planning;

- increased product quality;

- increased process quality;

- increased productivity;

- reduced cycle time.

One way to identify reusable test processes is through TMM assessment and improvement efforts. From an assessment, an overall process profile is developed that indicates the strengths and weakness of a testing process. Areas of strength are indicators of test subprocesses that are candidates for reuse, especially at the highest levels of the TMM. These may represent so-called "core-processes" which are vital for operation and considered to be organizational assets. After identifying the areas of strength, further work will need to be done to make the candidate processes suitable for inclusion in a process reuse library. For example a suitable process definition and associated process measurements must be available, and a template for the process developed (see next section on reusable process templates). Reuse candidates can also be a product of

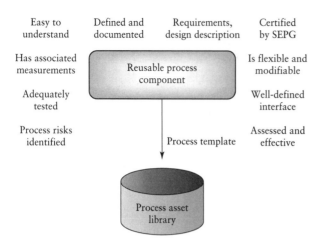

FIG. 15.7

Characteristics of a reusable process.

process improvement and optimization efforts where new processes are designed to strengthen a weak area of an existing process. Figure 15.7 shows the process characteristics needed to select candidate process components for reuse. They are also described below. Note that these characteristics are similar to those required for successful reuse of software components.

1. The process should be defined and documented according to organizational standards. That includes having a requirements and design description for the process. Entrance and exit conditions for the process should be documented. An input and output specification should also be available. Applicable domains and the implementation environment should also be identified.

2. The process should be easy to understand and implement. Its implementation steps and associated procedures should be clear and unambiguous.

3. The process should have associated measurements available, for example, costs of implementation, time requirements for process steps, and levels of expertise needed. These can serve as quality indicators for outputs of the process and for the process itself.

Process Reuse Template

Process name
General process information
Customer description
Interface description
Procedural description
Context description
Measurement description

FIG. 15.8
Example template for reusable process [1].

4. The process should have been carefully reviewed and successfully applied to several projects to ensure that it has been adequately tested in the field. The projects should represent a variety of organizational projects to demonstrate the various application domains for the process.
5. Process-related risks should be evaluated and documented.
6. The process should have a well-defined interface to other related processes.
7. The process should be flexible and modifiable so that it can be applied to different projects.
8. The process should be certified by the SEPG and/or an assessment team as a candidate for reuse.

15.7.1 Templates for Reusable Processes

Process reuse has been reported in the literature by researchers such as Hollenbach and Frakes [1], Kellner and Phillip [2], and Kellner and Briand [3]. To support process reuse, each candidate process object meeting the reuse criteria should represented by a process template. The template should contain information that allows the process components to be tailored for specific projects. Hollenbach and Frakes describe such a template in their work [1]. Homyen expands on this work and gives an instantiation of a template for an action planning process [12]. A useful process template specification should allow both common and variant elements of a process to be described so that the process can be applied in a variety of situations. The template can be partitioned into major and minor components. Some example template components are shown in Figure 15.8. A brief description from Hollenbach for each component is given below [1].

General Information

- Unique process identifier and a version number.
- A description of the purpose of the process.
- Standards applicable to the process and the products it produces.
- Related processes—processes that interface with this process.

Customer Description

A description of the potential customers, both internal and external, that may receive products and services from the outputs of this process.

Interface Description

Entrance Criteria: conditions that must be satisfied before the process steps can be initiated. A discussion of process inputs and outputs.

Exit Criteria: conditions that must be satisfied to consider the process complete.

Procedural Description

A description of the groups that participate in the process, and their responsibilities for carrying out the process steps.

A description of the tasks that need to be accomplished during the process execution.

Tools and resources: describe any tools needed to enact the process.

Context Description

Domain: In this section the application domains to which this process is applicable are described. All necessary domain knowledge needed for the execution of the process is also described. A description of how the process has been used for past projects is included. Appropriate metrics and process results should also be included.

Organization: The description should include the organization size appropriate for this process and the size limits. This template component should also contain a description of the specific organizational groups or functions that need to be in place to carry out the process steps.

Project: An appropriate project length for this process should be described as well as an appropriate level of software size and complexity.

Communications: This template component should describe how the group will communicate, and whether a local or distributed group can carry out the process.

Management: A description of the costs and benefits of this process and the risks associated with its execution is also included.

Measurement Description

Tracking, evaluation, and quality indicators: This process template component should contain the measures that can be used to track the process and evaluate its outcome. Performance evaluation should be tied to customer products and services that result. These are quality indicators. Measurements that will be collected during process execution at critical points also need to be described. These will be used to evaluate the process itself.

15.7.2 Procedures for Process Reuse

Hollenbach and Frakes describe what they call a context for defining and tailoring reusable processes [1]. Their goal was to use the context to create reusable processes that project (and test) managers can cost-effectively tailor to their project requirements. There are three major phases in this context: a defining phase, a tailoring phase, and an implementation phase. Within each of these phases there are several sub phases. These are shown in Figure 15.9 and described in the paragraphs below.

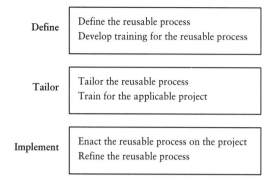

FIG. 15.9

Tailoring a reusable process [1].

Define the Reusable Process

In this step a process description is developed along with guidelines on how to tailor the process, and a description of output work products. The process definition can be in the form of a process manual, handbook, or a set of process procedures. The candidate process must be tested to ensure it is fit for (re)use.

Develop Training for the Reusable Process

A training package for the process should be developed. At TMM levels 3 and higher there is a training program and staff in place to develop such a package.

Tailor the Reusable Process to the Project

Tailoring consists of retrieving a suitable process (as a template from a PAL) and applying it in a new context, that is, a new project. The project (or test) manager instantiates the process for this project. Changes may be needed to meet the requirements and environment of the new project. Tailoring should begin with a plan for tailoring efforts, followed by the selection of a reusable process by the process team. A project-specific process description results in a document suitable for use by project (or test) managers and software engineers.

Tailoring the Reusable Process Training to the Tailored Project Process

The generic training package is tailored to meet project-specific needs. The training package is used to instruct project staff.

Enact the Process on the Project

The tailored process is implemented (executed) for the project. It is monitored and controlled using appropriate mechanisms. An SQA or SEPG team follows the project to ensure the process is properly executed. Measurements are taken during process execution.

Refine the Process

Using the measurements taken during process execution, the process is evaluated. The SEPG group determines whether the process is stable (they can use SPC techniques), and effective. If there are failures, the process is analyzed to determine why and where it is weak. Appropriate changes are made to the process definition, staff is retrained, and the process re-executed.

In summary, the practice of process reuse is relatively new, but research in this area is accelerating. Resulting applications of the research ideas look promising. Organizations on level 5 of the TMM have the required infrastructure to successfully implement this practice. The potential benefits of process reuse are great, and include higher-quality processes and products, cost reductions, and a shorter time to market.

15.8 Activities, Tasks, and Responsibilities for Test Process Control and Optimization

Test process control and test process optimization require much support and effort on the part of two of the critical groups, managers, and testers. Users/clients do not play any significant role in support of these maturity goals. Some examples of major ATRs are described in the paragraphs below.

Achieving the maturity goals of test process control and optimization require that *managers:*

- provide resources and funding for these activities;

- assist in developing appropriate polices, plans, and supporting documents;

- support and charter teams such as the SEPG/TPG;

- provide resources for training for involved personnel;

- assist in selecting and providing support for pilot projects that are involved in process control implementation and trial technology;

- be aware of current tools and technology to support optimization;

- provide support for technology transfer;

- support cultural changes necessary for process control, technology transfer, and process change management;

- support training for process control, optimization, and reuse;

- support periodic process assessments with the TMM;

- support development and maintenance of a process asset library, and reuse of process assets;

- tailor processes retrieved from the PAL and apply them to new projects (test managers).

A *tester's* role in process control and optimization includes the following:

- serve members of an SEPG/TPG (specific duties for the SEPG/TPG are described in Section 15.3);

- assist in developing policies, plans, standards, and other documents related to process control and optimization;

- participate in pilot projects for process change and technology transfer;

- enroll in training classes to learn appropriate techniques and tools for process control, optimization, and reuse;

- have an awareness of new and useful tools and technologies and identify promising candidates to the SEPG/TPG team;

- collect measurement data from projects under study by SEPG/TPG;

- help to develop control charts, identify process variations and causes, and prepare reports;

- help to identify process assets and support the process asset library;

- support integration of process changes and approved new technologies;

- serve as members of a TMM assessment team.

EXERCISES

1. Processes, like software systems, have a life cycle. Describe a set of life cycle phases that would be applicable to processes.

2. What is process control? Which groups should be involved in its implementation?

3. What are some of the reasons for process variations? How do process controllers address these variations?

4. What are some of the activities necessary for process control, and how can these be applied to control of the testing process?

5. Suppose you are a test manager. What are your specific responsibilities with respect to test process control? Use Figure 15.4 as a guide to your answer.

6. Describe some of the responsibilities that could be assigned to a Software Engineering/Test Process Group. What role can they play in test process assessment and technology transfer?

7. What are some characteristics of a reusable process?

8. What role does a process asset library (PAL) play in process reuse? What are the costs and benefits of maintaining a PAL?

9. Develop a process template using the components described in the text for a reusable unit test process whose goal is a specific degree of branch coverage.

The process will be used to unit test real-time systems. Make any necessary assumptions you need to complete the template.

10. How does achievement of the maturity goals at lower TMM levels support test process optimization at level 5?

11. Consider the situation where a new testing method and support tools are to be adopted on an organizationwide basis. Describe the technology transfer steps needed to support this goal.

12. Suppose you are a member of the training staff. What types of training modules would you prepare to support test process reuse?

13. Why is an SEPG group so necessary for support of test process optimization? Are there any other groups in an organization that might play a role in achieving this goal? If yes, then give reasons for your choices.

REFERENCES

[1] C. Hollenbach, W. Frakes, "Software process reuse in an industrial setting," *Proc. Fourth International Conf. on Software Reuse,* Orlando, FL, April 1996, pp. 22–30.

[2] M. Kellner, R. Phillip, "Practical technology for process assets," *Proc. Eighth International Software Process Workshop: State of Practice in Process Technology,* Warden, Germany, March 1993, pp. 107–112.

[3] M. Kellner, L. Briand, J. Over, "A method for designing, defining, and evolving software processes," *Proc. Fourth International Conf. on the Software Process,* Brigthon, UK, Dec. 1996, pp. 37–48.

[4] M. Paulk, C. Weber, B. Curtis, M. Chrissis, *The Capability Maturity Model,* Addison-Wesley, Reading MA., 1995.

[5] B. Affourtit, "Statistical process control applied to software," *Total Quality Management for Software,* G. Schulmeyer, J. McManus, eds., Van Nostrand Reinhold, New York, 1992.

[6] L. Zells, "Learning from Japanese TQM applications to software engineering," *Total Quality Management for Software,* G. Schulmeyer, J. McManus, eds., Van Nostrand Reinhold, New York, 1992.

[7] W. Florac, A. Carleton, J. Barnard, "Statistical process control: analyzing a space shuttle onboard software process," *IEEE Software,* Vol. 17, No. 4, 2000, pp. 97–106.

[8] E. Weller, "Practical applications of statistical process control," *IEEE Software,* Vol. 14, No. 3, 2000, pp. 48–55.

[9] D. Putman, "Using statistical process control with automated test programs," *CROSSTALK: The Journal of Defense Software Engineering,* Vol. 11, No. 8, August 1998, pp. 16–20.

[10] G. Wigle, G. Yamamura, "Practices of an SEI CMM level 5 SEPG," *CROSSTALK: The Journal of Defense Software Engineering,* Vol. 10, No. 11, Nov. 1997, pp. 19–22.

[11] G. Daich, G. Price, B. Ragland, M. Dawood, *Software Test Technologies Report,* August 1994, Software Technology Support Center (STSC) Hill Air Force Base, UT, August 1994.

[12] A. Homyen, "An assessment model to determine test process maturity," Ph.D. Thesis, Illinois Institute of Technology, Chicago, IL, 1998.

THE TESTING MATURITY
MODEL AND TEST
PROCESS ASSESSMENT

16.0 The Need for a Testing Maturity Model

The organizing framework behind this text is the Testing Maturity Model (TMM) which was developed by a research group headed by the author at the Illinois Institute of Technology [1–5]. The TMM was designed to be used by software development organizations to assess and improve their testing processes. It is also useful as a model that illustrates in stages how a testing process should grow incrementally in proficiency. This property makes it useful as an educational tool to introduce testing concepts, principles, and best practices in an evolutionary manner. Chapter 1 describes several aspects of the TMM including its basic structure and maturity levels. Chapter 14 offers more details on the maturity levels and their relationship to the tools in the Testers' Workbench.

It this chapter additional aspects of the TMM are described for those readers interested in implementing test process assessment and improvement efforts in their organizations. Among the areas discussed are the history of TMM development and the TMM assessment process. A comparison between the TMM and other existing process improvement models is made, and relationships between the models are described. Finally, some applications of the TMM in industry are given with implications for future work.

The development of the TMM was driven by the need for high-quality software and the important role that quality software systems play in our society. The central role of software-based systems has made it imperative that quality issues relating to both the software product and process be addressed. The TMM is focused on process, specifically, on the software testing process. Testing as defined in the TMM is applied in its broadest sense to encompass all software quality–related activities. Improving the testing process through application of the TMM maturity criteria has the potential to make a positive impact on software quality, software engineering productivity, and cycle time reduction efforts.

16.1 Approach to Model Development

A principle objective for developing the Testing Maturity Model was to make available a model that could be used by software development organizations to evaluate and improve their testing processes. The intended use of the TMM is to support assessment and improvement drives from within an organization. Test process assessment and improvement efforts can be carried out as an independent set of activities, or performed in conjunction with general software process improvement efforts driven by other models. In these contexts the TMM can be used by:

- an internal assessment team to identify the current testing capability state;

- upper management to initiate a testing process improvement program;

- software quality assurance engineers to develop and implement test process improvement plans;

- development/testing teams to improve testing effectiveness;

- users/clients to define their role in the testing process.

Several process evaluation and improvement models and standards have been developed over the last decade. Some examples include the Capability Maturity Model (CMM), its successor the Integrated Capability Maturity Model for Software (CMMI) [6,7], ISO 9001 [8], BOOTSTRAP [9], and SPICE [10]. Most of these models do not adequately address testing issues. For example, in the CMM:

- the concept of testing process maturity is not addressed;

- there is inadequate attention paid to the role of high-quality testing as a process/product improvement mechanism;

- testing issues are not adequately addressed in the many of the key process areas;

- quality-related issues such as testability, test adequacy criteria, test planning, and software certification are not satisfactorily addressed;

- advanced testing practices such as usage profiling, statistical testing, and quantitative control of the testing process are not described in sufficient detail.

Because of the important role of testing in software process and product quality, and the limitations of existing process assessment models, the Testing Maturity Model was developed. The following components support the objectives of TMM development:

Component 1 A set of levels that defines a testing maturity hierarchy. Each level represents a stage in the evolution of a mature testing process. The levels guide an organization to higher degrees of test proficiency and should be addressed in the order specified by the TMM. Movement to an upper level implies that lower-level practices continue to be in place.

Component 2 A set of maturity goals and subgoals for each level (except level 1). The maturity goals identify testing improvement goals that must be addressed in order to achieve maturity at that level. The subgoals define the scope, boundaries, and needed accomplishments for a particular level.

Associated with each maturity goal is also a set of Activities, Tasks, and Responsibilities (ATRs) needed to support it. The ATRs describe the practices that need to be institutionalized to achieve testing process maturity. The ATRs are assigned to the three critical groups essential to testing efforts—managers, developers/testers, and users/clients. Inclusion of the three critical groups (views) is unique to the TMM. The views specify roles for all of the stakeholders in the testing process, and promote both internal and external support for test process assessment and improvement.

Component 3 An assessment model consisting of three components: (i) a set of maturity goal-related questions designed to determine the current test process state, (ii) a set of guidelines designed to select and instruct the assessment team, and (iii) an assessment procedure with steps to guide the assessment team through test process evaluation and improvement.

The general requirements for TMM development are as follows.

1. The model must be acceptable to the software development community, and be based on agreed upon software engineering principles and practices. At the higher maturity levels it should be flexible enough to accommodate future best-test practices.
2. The model must allow for the development of testing process maturity in structured stepwise phases that follow natural process evolution.
3. There must also be a support mechanism for test process assessment and improvement.

To satisfy these requirements, four sources as shown in Figure 16.1 serve as the principal inputs to TMM development. They are the Capability Maturity Model (CMM) [6,11,12], Gelperin and Hetzel's Evolutionary Testing Model [13], Current Industrial Testing Practices [14], and, Beizer's Progressive Phases of a Testers' Mental Model [15].

Like the widely accepted CMM, the TMM is a staged model (see Section 16.2) and uses the concept of maturity levels as a script for testing process evaluation and improvement. The TMM levels have a structural framework as do the levels in the CMM. A unique component called

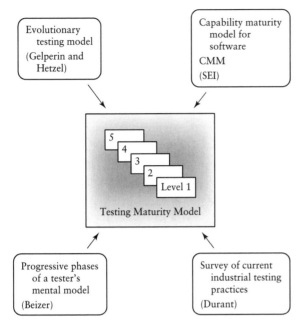

FIG. 16.1

Input sources for development of the TMM.

the "critical views" has been added to the framework in order to formally include the key groups necessary for test process evolution.

To support the self-assessment process, the TMM uses the questionnaire/interview evaluation approach of the CMM. Besides being related to the CMM through these structural similarities, the TMM can be visualized as a complement to the CMM. This view is understandable since (i) a mature testing process is dependent on general process maturity, and (ii) organizational investment in assessments can be optimized if assessments in several process areas can be carried out in parallel. TMM/CMM relationships are discussed in more detail in Section 16.8 of this chapter.

A Testing Maturity Model should reflect the evolutionary pattern of testing process maturity growth documented over the last several decades. This approach will expedite movement to higher maturity levels of the model as it will allow organizations to achieve incremental test process improvement in a way that follows natural process evolution. Designers of the CMM also considered historical evolution an important factor in process improvement model development. For example, concepts from Crosby's quality management maturity grid, which described five evolutionary stages in the adaptation of quality practices, were adjusted for the software process and used as input for development of the CMM maturity levels [6].

The historical model of testing reported in a key paper by Gelperin and Hetzel [13] provided a foundation for historical level differentiation in the TMM and served as one of the inputs to TMM development. The Gelperin/Hetzel model describes phases and test goals for the periods of the 1950s through the 1990s. The initial period in their model is described as "debugging-oriented." During that period most software development organizations did not differentiate between testing and debugging. Testing was an ad hoc activity associated with debugging to remove bugs from programs. Testing has since progressed through several additional phases according to the Gelperin/Hetzel model to culminate in a "prevention-oriented" period that encompasses best current testing practices, and reflects the optimizing level 5 of both the CMM and the TMM.

A survey of current industrial practices also provides important input to TMM level definition [14]. It illustrates the best and poorest testing environments in the software industry of 1993, and allows TMM developers to extract realistic benchmarks by which to evaluate and improve testing practices. In addition, concepts associated with Beizer's evolutionary model of the individual tester's thinking process [15] has been integrated into the TMM. Its influence on TMM development is based on the premise that a mature testing organization is built on the skills, abilities, and attitudes of individuals that work within it.

During the period in which the TMM was being developed, two other models that support testing process assessment and improvement were reported. The model proposed by Gelperin and Hayashi, called the "testability maturity model," uses a staged architecture for its framework [16,17]. Three maturity levels are described by the authors, along with six key support areas, which they reported to be analogous to key process areas in the CMM. The three levels in the model are defined loosely as weak, basic, and strong. The internal level structure is not described in detail in the report, nor is it clear where the six key support areas fit into the three-level hierarchy. A simple scorecard that covers 20 test process–related issues is provided, to be used by an organization to determine its "testability maturity model level" [17]. No formal assessment process is reported.

Koomen and Pol describe what they call a "test process improvement model (TPI)," which is based on a contiguous model architecture [18,19]. Their model contains 20 key areas each with different levels of maturity. Each level contains several checkpoints that are helpful for determining maturity. In addition, improvement suggestions to reach a target level are provided with the model. These are helpful for generating action plans.

In contrast to these two test process improvement models the TMM structure has the following advantages:

- it is more detailed and fine-grained in its level structure, key practices, and roles;

- it provides greater coverage of test-related issues;

- it is well-suited to support incremental test process maturity growth;

- it is supported by a well-defined assessment model;

- its structure is more compatible with the widely used staged version of the CMM which facilitates parallel process improvement efforts.

16.2 Process Improvement Model Representations

Process improvement models were categorized in the previous section as belonging to two major architectural groups that are called staged and continuous representations. These model groups are shown in Figure 16.2. Each type contains what are called process areas. Process areas represent aspects of a process to focus on for improvement. Each process area has a purpose or goal, and a set of practices associated with it. A staged representation for a process improvement model means that process areas are grouped into stages or maturity levels. Within a stage or level, an organization must put into place all the practices recommended

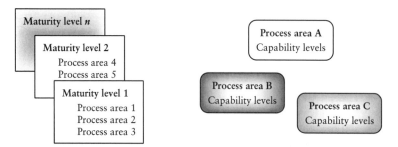

Staged process improvement models   Continuous process improvement models

FIG. 16.2

Staged and continuous process
improvement model representations.

for all the process areas contained in that level in order to successfully achieve or complete that stage or level. When an organization has achieved the goals a particular level (and all lower levels), it is said to have a process maturity at that level.

To use staged models effectively an organization should address the goals in each level in the order specified by the model. Skipping of levels is not recommended. However, an organization may begin a practice at a lower maturity level where it is not formally specified by a staged model, but when the practice is formalized at a given level the implication is that it is then documented, applied consistently, and institutionalized. For example, in the TMM it is recommended that simple measurements be collected beginning at TMM level 1; however, a formal measurement program is specified at TMM level 4. At level 4 the measurement program is supported by an institutional infrastructure that is put into place by achieving maturity goals at the lower TMM levels. It is formally documented, supported by management, practiced uniformly in all projects, and maintained by a motivated and trained staff.

The levels in staged process improvement models are usually associated with a specific numerical value, and so a process maturity level number can be assigned to an organization after its process has been evaluated with respect to achievement of the process areas in the model. The level number is a process metric that can be used as an indicator of performance for the process. Outside organizations may use that level number as a basis for selecting among competing contractors, bidders, or vendors. Processes assessed to be at the highest maturity levels are expected to perform more effectively and complete projects closer to planned schedules and budgets than those operating at the lower maturity levels. As a result of the more predictable and managed processes operating at higher maturity levels, it is more likely that product quality will be of a consistently higher level as compared to products resulting from processes assessed to be at lower maturity levels.

The CMM is a widely used example of a staged process improvement model [6,11,12]. It contains five process maturity levels each of which consists of several process areas. The process areas contain goals, common features, and practices. The TMM is also a staged model and is, as previously discussed, characterized by five testing maturity levels within a framework of goals, subgoals, activities, tasks, and responsibilities. The goals, subgoals, and activities, tasks, and responsibilities define its process areas, and describe its recommended practices [1–5].

Continuous models also contain process areas, but these are not grouped by levels. There are sets of goals and practices that are generic in nature and may apply to several process areas. Other goals and practices may be specific to individual process areas. Process areas have capability levels so that an organization when achieving all of the practices associated with an area (both generic and specific) attains a capability level for that area. The order in which an organization addresses process areas is not represented in this type of model; however, there may be recommendations for a sequence. The SPICE model (Software Process Improvement and Capability dEtermination), and the Electronics Industries Alliance Interim Standard 731 Systems Engineering Capability Model (EIA/IS-731), are examples of continuous models [10,20]. The Integrated Capability Maturity Model (CMMI) developed by the Software Engineering Institute has both a continuous and a staged version [7,21].

16.3 The TMM Structure: The Testing Maturity Levels

The TMM is defined by five maturity levels: Initial; Phase Definition; Integration; Management and Measurement; and Optimization, Defect Prevention, and Quality Control. These were shown in Figure 1.5 and are repeated in Figure 16.3 for review. Chapters 1 and 14 described the set of maturity goals associated with each maturity level.

Each maturity level has an internal structure, which was shown in Figure 1.7 and is repeated in Figure 16.4. Note that each level implies a specific testing process capability. With the exception of level 1, several maturity goals (MG) that identify key process areas are indicated at each level. The maturity goals represent testing improvement goals that must be addressed in order to achieve maturity at that level. As required by its staged model architecture, the TMM specifies that in order to be placed at a given level, an organization must satisfy the maturity goals at that level and all lower levels.

As shown in Figure 16.4 each maturity goal is supported by one or more maturity subgoals (MSG). The MSGs specify less abstract objectives and they define the scope, boundaries, and needed accomplishments for a particular level. The maturity goals and subgoals are achieved through a set of activities and tasks with responsibilities (ATRs).

The ATRs are a unique aspect of the TMM structure [1–5]. They address implementation and organizational adaptation issues at each specific level. Activities and tasks are defined in terms of actions or practices that must be performed at a given level to improve testing capability; they are linked to organizational commitments. Responsibilities are assigned for these activities and tasks to three groups that are believed to represent the key participants in the testing process—managers, developers/testers, and users/clients. In the model they are referred to as "the three critical views (CV)" [1–5].

The *manager's* view involves commitment and the ability to perform activities and tasks related to improving testing capability. Examples of managers in the context of the TMM are project managers, test group managers, test organization managers, and software quality assurance managers. Also included in this view are upper-level managers such as site or division managers.

The *developer/tester's* view encompasses the technical activities and tasks that when applied, constitute quality testing practices. Developers and testers are those staff members who are involved with specifying, designing, coding, and testing software. They may be called software engineers, test engineers, test specialists, programmers, coders, or software developers.

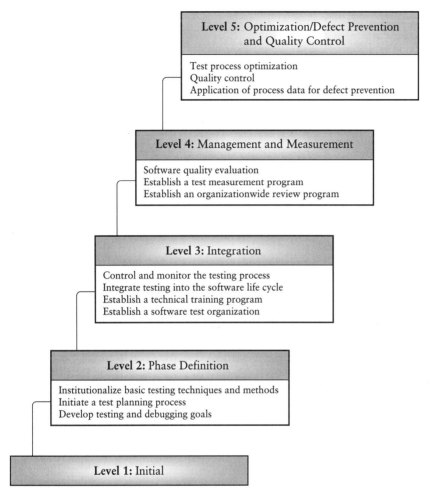

FIG. 16.3

The five-level structure of the Testing Maturity Model.

The *user's/client's* view is defined as a cooperating or supporting view. The focus is on soliciting client/user support, consensus, and participation in activities such as requirements analysis, usability testing, operational profile modeling, and acceptance test planning. The user view represents those who will be the end users of the software being developed. The client view represents those who may have initiated the project

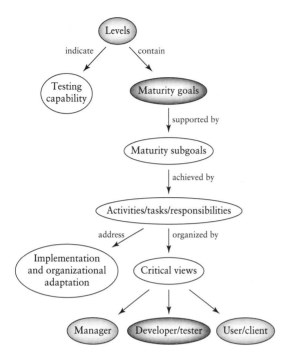

FIG. 16.4

The internal structure of TMM
maturity levels.

and/or signed the contract and/or will be providing compensation to the development organization. Clients and users may be internal or external to the organization developing the software.

A set of ATRs for the TMM is described throughout this text at the ends of relevant chapters. The complete set of ATRs appears in Appendix III.

16.4 The TMM Assessment Model (TMM-AM): Design Approach

In order for an organization to self-evaluate its testing process a formal assessment model supported by steps, activities, tasks, and forms is needed. Such a model should also provide support for process improvement actions when the evaluation is complete. The TMM Assessment

Model (TMM-AM) meets these requirements. It uses the TMM as its reference model, and measures an organization's testing process against TMM maturity goals. Unlike many other process assessment and improvement models, use of TMM-AM does not require participation of an external body to perform a certification process.

The CMM and SPICE Assessment Models were used to guide development of the TMM-AM [6,11,12,22,23]. The goal was to have the resulting TMM-AM be compliant with the Capability Maturity Model Appraisal Framework (CAF) [24] so that organizations would be able to perform parallel assessments in multiple process areas. Based on a set of 16 test process assessment principles [25], the CMM Assessment Model, SPICE, and the CAF, a set of components for the TMM-AM was developed that will be described in the subsequent sections of this text.

16.5 The TMM Assessment Model Components

The three major components of the TMM-AM are (i) team training and selection criteria, (ii) the assessment procedure, and (iii) the assessment instrument (a questionnaire). A set of inputs and outputs is also prescribed for the TMM-AM [25]. The relationship among these items is shown in Figure 16.5. A discussion of the components follows.

16.5.1 Assessment Team Selection and Training

Performing a test process assessment, gathering and interpreting data, and developing the final reports is a complex process. This process should be the responsibility of an assessment team. The team members need to be knowledgeable and motivated. A candidate for TMM assessment team membership should have TMM assessment knowledge, be well-respected in the organization, be motivated to improve the testing process, have the ability to implement change, and have several years of development/testing, and/or managerial experience (an average of 7 years is recommended) [25]. Team members may come from the projects being selected for assessment or from other projects in the organization. An assessment team should have a leader(s) who has a high level of technical and managerial expertise, experience in TMM assessments, is a problem solver, and has excellent communication skills. The team leader should

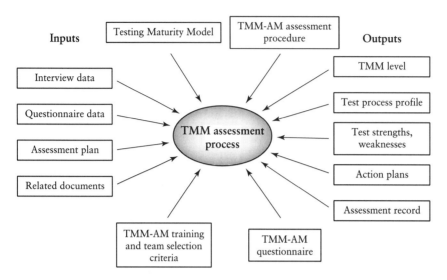

FIG. 16.5

TMM Assessment Model inputs/outputs [25].

ensure that all team members have the proper motivation and training to carry out their assessment tasks.

The size of a TMM assessment team may vary, and depends on the scope of the assessment, the experience level of the team, and the size and complexity of the organizational projects being assessed. A team size of 4–8 members is suggested.

Preparation for the assessment team should be under the direction of the assessment team leader. The training program staff in the organization should be involved in development, distribution, and discussion of the relevant materials. Training material modules should include topics such as:

- introduction to process improvement models;

- an overview of the TMM;

- interviewing techniques;

- assessment planning;

- data analysis;

- report development.

Each of these topics can be presented in a modular form perhaps as a "minicourse." Training activities also include team-building exercises, a walk through the assessment process, filling out a sample TMM questionnaire and other assessment-related forms, and learning to prepare final reports [25].

16.5.2. The Assessment Procedure

The TMM-AM assessment procedure consists of a series of steps that guide an assessment team through a testing process self-assessment. The principal goals for the TMM assessment procedure are:

1. to support the development of a test process profile and the determination of a TMM level;
2. to guide the organization in developing action plans for test process improvement;
3. to ensure the assessment is executed with efficient utilization of the organization's resources;
4. to guide the assessment team in the collection, organization, and analysis of assessment data.

The steps in the assessment procedure are shown in Figure 16.6, and a summary of each one follows [25].

Preparation

Preparing for a TMM assessment requires effort and coordination on the part of many staff members throughout the organization. There are several key activities to carry out in this step. The first task is to select the assessment team members and the team leader. The leader must ensure that the team undergoes proper training as described in the previous section. When training is completed, the assessment team develops the assessment plan. The plan should describe the scope of the assessment, as-

TMM Assessment Procedure

FIG. 16.6

Steps in the TMM assessment procedure.

sessment inputs and outputs, estimated schedules and costs, tasks and responsibilities, control mechanisms, and risk factors that could impact on the outcome of the assessment. Assessment techniques and tools should be described.

The organizational units selected for assessment are also identified in this step. These units should be prepared for participation. Preparing the units includes selecting a coordinator who will be the liaison to the assessment team, briefing the unit members on the nature of the assessment, gathering support information, developing confidentiality agreements, and selecting specific projects. Projects that are selected should:

- be representative of the software products of major concern to the organization, and have an impact on the business in terms of revenue, profit, or strategic value;

- be representative of the software and testing processes used in the organization;

- be variable in size and duration with a life cycle of at least 6 months.

The project/test managers of the selected projects should support test process assessments. It is best if selected projects are not managed by an assessment team member.

Conducting the TMM Assessment

In this step the assessment team collects and records assessment information for interviews, presentations, the TMM questionnaire, and relevant documents. A test management support system as described by Hearns and Garcia is very helpful for (i) automatically collecting and organizing test process related data, and (ii) for use in cross-checking data from multiple sources [26]. The TMM Traceability Matrix as described in Section 16.7 can also be used by the assessment team to check the accuracy, consistency, and objectivity of the data. This helps to ensure that assessment results will be reliable and reproducible.

The TMM level of the organization, which is a measure of its current testing maturity level, is determined by analysis of the collected data and use of a ranking procedure as described in Section 16.6 of this chapter.

Reporting the Assessment Outputs

The TMM-AM outputs include a test process profile, a TMM level, and an assessment record. The assessment team prepares the test process profile which gives an overall summary of the state of the organization's testing process. The profile should include the following sections as shown in Figure 16.7.

1. A table of contents.
2. An executive summary (includes maturity level rating).
3. A maturity goal and subgoal record. This is a listing of all the TMM maturity goals and subgoals and their rating.
4. A summary of test process strengths, weaknesses, and areas not rated.
5. Recommended areas for improvements, and priorities for action planning.

The TMM level is a numerical value from 1 to 5 that indicates the current testing process maturity level of the organization. Level values correspond to the testing maturity hierarchy shown in Figure 16.2.

The assessment record is also completed in this step. It is a comprehensive written account of the actual assessment that includes names of

Test Process Profile: Organization XYZ
March 2001

Table of Contents
   ...
   ...

Executive Summary
   I. Maturity Level
   II. Maturity Profile
         1. Maturity Goal Record

TMM level	Maturity goals	Satisfied	Not satisfied	Not applicable	Not rated	Notes
2						
Phase	Inititate	X				
definition	Test planning					
	Testing/debugging					
...	goals	X				
3						
...						

         2. Maturity Subgoal Record
   ...

   III. Assessment Analysis
         Areas of strengths in the testing process
               1. ...
               2. ...
         Areas of weakness in the testing process
               1. ...
               2. ...
         Areas not rated
               1. ...

         Areas selected for improvement (by priority)
               1. ...

FIG. 16.7

Sample test process profile [25].

assessment team members, assessment unit coordinators, assessment inputs and outputs, actual schedules and costs, tasks performed, task durations, persons responsible, data collected, and problems that occurred. The assessment outputs are delivered as a written report (the final assessment report), which may be accompanied by a presentation.

Analyzing the Assessment Outputs

In this step the assessment team, along with managers and software quality engineers, use the assessment outputs to identify and prioritize goals for improvement. An approach to prioritization is described by Homyen [25]. It is based on previous work in this area by Humphrey and Sweet [27]. The prioritization process begins with a selection of about five areas that are believed to be very important in improving testing process quality in the organization being assessed. Each area is assigned a value to represent its relative importance. A scale from 1 to 10 can be used. The next step is to quantify the current capability in the selected areas. A scale of 0 to 10 can be used in this step. A value of zero could indicate "we don't perform this practice at all," whereas a value of ten might indicate "we perform this practice consistently and correctly." The "degree of satisfaction" measurement for related maturity subgoals as described in Section 16.6 can provide useful information for selecting a value. A priority can be calculated by subtracting item 2 from item 1. The area with the highest positive priority value is ranked first, and so on. Action plans can be developed for the highest-ranking areas first, as described in the next step. Lower-priority areas can be addressed in future action planning sessions.

Action Planning

An action planning team develops actions plans that focus on improvements in the high-priority areas that have been identified in the previous step. This team can include assessors, software engineering process group members (SEPG), SQA staff, and/or opinion leaders chosen from the assessment participants [28]. Action planning can be implemented in workshop format. When the action plan draft is completed it should be reviewed.

The action plan describes specific activities, resources, and schedules needed to improve existing practices, and/or to add missing practices, so that the organization can move up to the next TMM level. An action plan is much like a project plan, and should be sufficiently detailed so that it can be readily executed. It should include the items shown in Figure 16.8. These include goals and improvement targets, tasks, activities, responsibilities, estimates of costs, and benefits. Risks associated with actions should be analyzed, and status tracking systems should be described. Pilot projects to which the action plan will be applied should be selected by the team. Process reuse possibilities in a the case of successful executions of the plan should also be considered by the team.

Implementing Improvement

After the action plans have been developed and approved, they are applied to the selected pilot projects. The pilot projects need to be monitored and tracked to ensure task progress, and achievement of the target goals. Favorable results with the pilot projects set the stage for organizational adaptation of the new process.

16.5.3 The TMM Assessment Questionnaire

In general, assessment instruments are used to support the collection and analysis of information from an assessment, maintain a record of results, and provide information for assessment post mortem analysis. There are several choices of assessment instruments including questionnaires, checklists and forms. The questionnaire was selected as the TMM assessment instrument for the following reasons. Use of a questionnaire supports CAF compliance [24], facilitates integration with other related process assessment instruments [23], insures assessment coverage of all activities, tasks and responsibilities identified in each maturity goal for each level of the TMM, provides a framework in which to collect and store assessment data, and provides guidelines for the assessors as to which areas should be the focus of an interview.

It should be noted that the TMM questionnaire is not the sole source of input for determination of TMM rank or for the generation of testing assessment results. The data from completed questionnaires must be augmented and confirmed using information collected from interviews and presentations, as well as by inspection of relevant documents. Section 16.7

Action Plan for Test Process Improvement

Plan Components

    I. Description of goals and improvement targets

   II. Tasks and activities

  III. Responsibilities

  IV. Resources required

   V. Estimates of costs/benefits

  VI. Schedules

 VII. Risks

VIII. Tracking and controlling systems

FIG. 16.8

Action plan components.

describes forms that support assessors in the collection and verification of data.

The TMM questionnaire consists of eight parts which are (i) instructions for use, (ii) respondent background, (iii) organizational background, (iv) maturity goal and subgoal questions, (v) testing tool use questions, (vi) testing trends questions, (vii) recommendations for questionnaire improvement, and (viii) a glossary of testing terms [25,29].

Components 2 and 3 of the questionnaire are used to gather information about the respondent (the staff member completing the questionnaire), the organization, and the units that will be involved in the TMM assessment. The maturity goal and subgoal questions in component 3 are organized by TMM version 1.1 levels, and include a developer/tester, manager, and client/user view. Questions cover issues related to all of the maturity goals and subgoals. A sample of the format of the TMM questionnaire is shown in Figure 16.9. The questions are designed to determine to what extent an organization has in place mechanisms to achieve the maturity goals, and resolve maturity issues at each TMM level. The testing tool component records the type and frequency of test tool use which can help the team make tool recommendations for the future in order to assemble a Testers' Workbench (see Chapter 14). The testing trends section was added to provide a perspective on how the testing process in the organization has been evolving over the last several years. This information is useful for preparing the assessment profile and the assessment

Question	Yes	No	Does not apply	Not known
1. Do developers follow a written organizational policy for testing? Comments				
2. Have testing policy documents been distributed to project managers and developers? Comments				
3. Is there an organizational policy for test planning? Comments				

FIG. 16.9

Format of the TMM questionnaire.

record. The recommendations component allows each respondent to give questionnaire developers feedback on the clarity, completeness, and usability of the questionnaire document. Readers can view version 1.2 of the TMM questionnaire in Appendix III of this text.

16.6 The TMM Ranking Procedure

The ranking procedure for the TMM-AM is based on a procedure described by Masters and Bothwell in their work on the Capability Maturity Model Assessment Framework [24]. In the testing domain, the TMM is the reference model for test process ranking, and the TMM questionnaire, along with other assessment information, provides the input data for the ranking. The final outputs of the ranking procedure are (i) a testing maturity level number that represents the current state of an organization's testing process, and (ii) a summary report of the areas of strength and weakness in an organization's testing process. This information becomes a part of the test process profile and assessment record.

The TMM ranking algorithm requires first a rating of the maturity subgoals, then the maturity goals, and finally the maturity level [25]. As in the ranking system of Masters and Bothwell, the TMM ranking starts with four major rating possibilities for the TMM maturity goals and subgoals.

1. *Satisfied:* A maturity goal, or subgoal is satisfied if this area has been implemented and instituted by the organization as defined by the TMM, or there is a satisfactory alternative in place.
2. *Unsatisfied:* A maturity goal, or subgoal is said to be unsatisfied if this area as defined in the TMM is weakly implemented and/or weakly instituted by the organization, and there is no satisfactory alternative in place.
3. *Not Applicable:* A maturity goal or subgoal is not applicable if it is not relevant in view of the organization's environment.
4. *Not Rated:* A maturity goal or subgoal is not rated if the associated appraisal findings do not adequately cover it, or it is beyond the scope of the current TMM appraisal.

In addition to these four major rating categories, the TMM ranking procedure offers an auxiliary level of detail which is described as "the degree of satisfaction." Using this finer rating granularity, an organization is able to rate its achievement level in terms of very high, high, medium, low, and, very, low degrees of satisfaction for the TMM maturity subgoals. The finer level of granularity provides a richer source of information on which to base final assessment results, and gives assessors additional support for the selection of weak and strong areas in the testing process. It also helps action planners prioritize test process areas that need to be addressed.

The TMM questionnaire as described in the previous section is completed by appropriate respondents for all projects/units within the scope of the assessment. The questionnaire results, confirmed by inspection of other assessment information, provide the data that allows a final assignment of the four ratings described above for each maturity goal. The following steps are applied in the TMM ranking procedure:

- rate the maturity subgoals;

- rate the maturity goals;

- determine the maturity level;

- identify strong and weak areas in the testing process.

Rating the Maturity Subgoals (MSG)

Each maturity subgoal has a set of associated questions on the TMM questionnaire [25]. The rating level is calculated as shown in Figure 16.10 using a scheme similar to Cook [30]. The "YES" answers refer to the column marked "YES" in the TMM questionnaire as shown in Figure 16.9. The number of "does not apply" and "not known" answers are also tabulated. From Figure 16.10 it can be seen that if the number of "YES" answers in a maturity subgoal (MSG) area is 50% or greater the maturity subgoal is said to be satisfied. Satisfaction can be had at three levels as shown (very high, high, and medium). If the percentage of "YES" responses is less than 50% the subgoal is said to be unsatisfied (at two possible levels). If the percent of "does not apply" responses is greater than or equal to 50, then a "not applicable value" is assigned to the maturity subgoal. If the percent of "not known" responses is greater than or equal to 50, then a rank of "not rated" is assigned.

Rating the Maturity Goals (MG)

The rating for each maturity goal is determined in manner shown in Figure 16.11. The rating for each maturity goal is dependent on consideration of the ratings of all the maturity subgoals within its scope.

Determining a Testing Maturity Level For a Project/Unit

The TMM has been described as a staged process improvement model. Therefore, the ranking procedure specifics that a testing maturity level is

Degree of satisfaction is: very high if % of "yes" answers is >90 (MSG is satisfied)
Degree of satisfaction is: high   if % of "yes" answers is 70–90 (MSG is satisfied)
Degree of satisfaction is: medium   if % of "yes" answers is 50–69 (MSG is satisfied)
Degree of satisfaction is: low   if % of "yes" answers is 30–49 (MSG is unsatisfied)
Degree of satisfaction is: very low if % of "yes" answers is <30 (MSG is unsatisfied)

FIG. 16.10

*Calculation of degree of satisfaction
for maturity subgoals.*

satisfied if *all* the testing maturity goals within the level and each lower level are satisfied. The output testing maturity level ranking is that of the highest testing maturity level satisfied [24,25].

If only one significant project (unit) is selected for assessment, then the organization can use the maturity level determined for that project as its testing maturity level. This is one example of a simple ranking case. Another simple ranking case occurs when all of the projects assessed are found to be at the same maturity level. A more complex case will occur when all assessed projects are ranked at two or more different TMM levels (a difference of more than two levels will probably be very rare). In those cases the organization will have to make decisions based on the number of assessed projects at a particular level, and the importance of the projects at each level. Conditions can also be attached to assignment of a maturity level As a simple example, if 80% of the assessed projects are at a given maturity level, then the overall organizational maturity level can be considered to be at this level. If 60–80% of the projects are at a given level, and they are highly important projects, then an organization can be considered to be at that level given the condition that it improves the deficiencies in the projects identified at a lower maturity levels [25].

Identifying Strong and Weak Areas in the Testing Process

The assessment team can use the findings from maturity subgoal/maturity goal rankings to map out the strong and weak areas in the testing process. This material should be included in the test process profile. Areas of high strength will have a "very high" degree of satisfaction that implies they

MG is satisfied if:	% of satisfied MSG is ≥ 50
MG is unsatisfied if:	% of satisfied MSG is < 50
MG is not applicable if:	% of not applicable MSG is ≥ 50
MG is not rated if:	% of not rated MSG is ≥ 50

FIG. 16.11

Calculation of maturity goal rankings.

are consistently, successfully, and completely performed by an organization as described in the TMM. Better then 90% of the required activities, tasks, and responsibilities in this area are implemented by the organization. Those areas with a "high" degree of satisfaction may also be considered areas of strength. Weakest areas will be those where the degree of satisfaction is "low" or "very low." Those are areas where the respondent answers on the TMM questionnaire indicates that they are inconsistently, incompletely, or incorrectly performed by the organization. Improvement effects should be strongly considered for these areas, that is, they should be areas of high priority for action planning.

16.7 Forms, and Tools for Assessment Support

To support an assessment team, several forms and a tool that implements a web-based version of the TMM questionnaire [25,29] have been developed. These forms and tools are important to ensure that the assessments are performed in a consistent, repeatable manner, to reduce assessor subjectivity and to ensure the validity, usability, and comparability of the assessment results. The tools and forms developed to support TMM assessments include the test process profile and test process assessment record whose roles have been described in previous sections of this chapter. Additional items are described below.

Team Training Data Recording Template

Training for a TMM assessment team is discussed in Section 16.6. The "team training and recording template" allows the assessment team leader and training program manager to record and validate team training data. Completed instances of the template can be used in future assessments to make any needed improvements to the assessment training process. An example format is shown in Figure 16.12.

Traceability Matrix

The "traceability matrix," in conjunction with the assessment team training procedure, the "team data recording template" and the traceability matrix review, were introduced to address the issue of interrater agreement and general assessment reliability [31]. The matrix, which is filled in as assessment data is collected, allows the assessors to identify sources of data, cross-check the consistency and correctness of the data from multiple sources, and resolve any data-related issues. Review of the matrix data by the assessment team supports the elimination of biases, and inaccuracies. The matrix and the matrix review process help to ensure data integrity and the reproducibility of the assessment results. A sample format is shown in Figure 16.13.

Web-Based Questionnaire

A prototype of a web-based version of the questionnaire was implemented by members of the TMM research group. It was believed that such a tool would enable assessors to easily collect assessment data from distributed sites. The data could then be organized and stored in a central data repository that could be parsed for later analysis [29]. This approach to tool design also would allow the tool implementation to run on multiple operating systems and collect data from users around the world, thus providing support for test process assessment to local and global organizations.

16.8 Relationship of the TMM to Other Process Improvement Models

The TMM is a process improvement model that specifically focuses on the testing process. The nature of the TMM allows it to be applied by an organization in many ways. Some possible applications are described below.

Training module ID	Description	Instructor	Date	Attendees	Comments

FIG. 16.12

Sample format for the team training and data recording template.

Perform parallel assessments and improvement efforts in several process areas. The TMM can be used in conjunction with staged models such as the CMM and the CMMI-SE/SW (staged version) to evaluate both the general development process and the testing process as well. Since the models are of similar structure, and the model vocabularies and goals overlap, parallel training and parallel assessments can be accomplished by an assessment team. Improvement efforts may overlap a well since there are common goals to be achieved. The TMM can also be used to address testing issues in conjunction with contiguous models such as ISO 12207. Overlapping process areas that relate to testing can be evaluated and improved using the TMM, while other process areas fall under the umbrella of the broader-scoped models.

An additional circumstance for TMM application might arise where an organization has *already* satisfied a quality standard for its overall software process but wants to focus additional efforts on testing. As a subsequent discussion of other process improvement models will show, testing issues are often underemphasized. Using the TMM as a complement to these models can result in bringing management attention to the testing process and extracting a commitment for additional testing resources to address the problem areas identified by a test assessment.

Perform assessment and improvement of the test process. The advantage of using a focused model such as the TMM is that an organization can initiate a process improvement effort in a specific process area. The narrower process scope allows for a smaller resource commitment, a faster learning curve, and a shorter time period for benefits to become apparent. Successful improvement in this one process area can provide the needed expertise and motivation to address other areas.

Activity	Result	Information Sources	Comments
Rate the MG for test planning	rating of "satisfied"	1. Questionnaire (questions #x, y, z) 2. Interviews of testers, test managers 3. Reviewed test plan template (ID #123) 4. Reviewed test policy statement (policy ID, abc-1)	Testers regularly use test plan template ID #123 for all projects

FIG. 16.13

Sample traceability matrix.

Another advantage of the TMM, especially for smaller organizations, is that a TMM assessment can be conducted by an internal assessment team; no outside certifier is required. The results are private, and the organization can use the findings as it sees fit to improve its testing process. An organization also has the option to hire an outside consulting team to perform a TMM assessment. This approach may be more feasible for a smaller company just beginning to initiate process improvement efforts. The assessment results in this case are also private and belong to the assessed organization to use as it sees fit unless otherwise specified (see the next section on industrial applications of the TMM).

Readers should note that even though it is possible to assess the testing process as an independent entity, testing and other process improvement efforts cannot be entirely decoupled. The testing process is a component, or subprocess, of the overall software development process, and certain practices in the development process are needed to support high-quality testing and successfully higher levels of test process maturity. For example, effective test planning needs support from project planning, configuration management, and requirements development/management. Test process controlling and monitoring needs support from development process controlling and monitoring.

Use as an educational and training tool. The TMM is a rich source of testing knowledge. Its maturity levels are based on the historical evolution of the testing process and current best practices. The maturity goals, subgoals, and practices described in the ATRs can be introduced incrementally as testing topics to students and practitioners in order to improve their expertise in the testing domain. This text is an example of use of the TMM in an educational context. Finally, the TMM can also be used as a guiding framework and educational tool for initiating user/client involvement in the testing process.

Applications for the TMM note its possible use in conjunction with other process improvement models. There are a growing number of process assessment and improvement models/life cycle standards that are applicable to the needs of software development organizations. Most have a broader process scope than the TMM, and apply to the software development process in its entirety. A very few focus on specific software subdomains such as documentation and design [30,32]. To apply most of these models, external auditors are required to conduct an assessment or certification procedure. Examples of broad-scoped process assessment and improvement models have already been discussed in this text. One widely used example is the Capability Maturity Model (CMM) developed at the Software Engineering Institute (SEI) [6,11]. Its successor, the Integrated Capability Maturity Model for Systems Engineering and Software Engineering (CMMI-SE/SW) [20,21,33,34], is a result of an SEI effort to ingrate its family of models into an inclusive entity that supports integrated product and process improvement efforts across an entire enterprise. The scope of what is called the CMMI project includes integration of the CMM and the Systems Engineering (SECM) and Integrated Product and Process Development (IPPD) Capability Models. The CMMI-SE/SW that resulted from this integration is broader in scope than its predecessor, and exists in both a staged and a contiguous version. It has some additional process areas and features not included in the original CMM.

Other process improvement models currently available have been developed by the joint efforts of the International Standardization Organization and International Electrotechnical Commission (ISO/IEC). Examples are SPICE [10,22], its successor ISO/IEC 15504 [35,36], and ISO/IEC 12207 [37,38]. The SPICE model, which has a contiguous architecture, was developed to satisfy several goals: (i) to help advance the state of the art for process assessment, (ii) to provide a publicly shared model for assessment based on existing models, and (iii) to integrate the efforts of model developers. It is now evolving into a standard known as the ISO/IEC 15504. ISO/IEC 12207 focuses on the entire software life cycle, from initial concept to software retirement, and includes software quality components. It is especially suited for acquisitions since it recognizes the distinct roles of acquirer and supplier.

There is also an ISO 9000 series of models [8], including ISO 9001 and ISO 9000-3 [6,39]. The ISO 9000 series focuses on management system standards and can be applied over many domains. The ISO 9001 standard was designed to be used by outside auditors as a basis for certifying that an organization can design, develop, and produce products (such as software) and services at a high quality level. ISO 9000-3 is a guide for applying ISO 9001 to the development, supply, and maintenance of software.

The models described in these series are examples of both staged and contiguous architectures, and they do cover testing issues, but in a limited manner. The approach to addressing testing issues in many of the models/standards consists of a limited number of test-related process areas distributed throughout the maturity or capability levels. These coexist with process areas that focus on many other aspects of the software process. The comprehensive presentation of testing issues and the opportunity for incremental growth of testing knowledge and expertise as promoted by the TMM is lacking. In addition, the models do not provide adequate support to an organization that wishes to add more complex and high-level testing practices in a stepwise progressive manner. Finally, the descriptions of testing goals and practices does not achieve the level of detail and attention as specified in the TMM.

As an example, software testing is addressed directly in only a small component of the "software product engineering" process area of the CMM at level 3 (see Table 16.1). Lower levels of the CMM pay little attention to testing goals and practices. Using the CMM, an organization whose goal it is to reach level 3 must implement many testing practices simultaneously at that level. In the TMM the practices are distributed over multiple levels allowing for an incremental implementation. In addition, an organization using the CMM must devote staff and resources to other process areas besides testing to satisfy the level 3 goals. An even greater number of process areas must be addressed along with testing at corresponding levels of the CMMI-SE/SW. For many organizations, especially those with limited resources, this is difficult to accomplish, and

TMM level MG	CMM level KPA	CMMI-SE/SW level KPA
2 Test planning Testing/debugging policies/goals Basic testing techinques/ methods	2 Requirements management (S) Project planning (S) Configuration management (S)	2 Requirements management (S) Project planning (S) Configuration management (S)
	3 Software product engineering (P) (particularly activities 5, 6, 7 except for independent test group, TMM level 3, statistical testing, usage profiles, TMM level 4, managing and controlling, TMM level 3)	3 Requirements development (S) Validation (P) Risk management (S)
3 Control/monitor test Integration of test Test training Test organization	2 Project tracking/ oversight (S)	2 Project monitoring and control (S) SQA (S)
	3 Organization process focus (S) (apply to test process/test group) Training (S,P) Intergroup coordation (S,P) SQA (S)	3 Organizational training Organizational process focus (S) (apply to test process/test group)

KPA, key process area; MG, maturity goal; (S), supporting role; (P), parallel role.

TABLE 16.1

Common process areas: levels 2, 3 TMM and CMM, CMMI-SE/SW.

as a consequence their testing processes may suffer from lack of adequate attention and investment. Use of software subdomain-specific models such as the TMM that focus on one vital process at a given time may be more effective for this type of organization.

Tables 16.1, 16.2, and 16.3 summarize the process areas in some of the key process improvement models that overlap with the maturity goals of the TMM. Note in the case of the CMM and the CMMI-SE/SW as shown in Tables 16.1 and 16.2, supporting areas (S) and parallel (P) areas are denoted. Supporting areas encompasses those software development goals and related practices that should be in place to support achievement of TMM maturity goals. Parallel areas (P) are those that are similar in nature in the models being compared, and that can be simultaneously pursued. Satisfying the goals and implementation of the practices in one model may lead to satisfactory implementation in the other.

16.9 Industrial Applications of the TMM

The TMM was completed in 1998, and several organizations have recently begun to apply it in an industrial setting. The organizations currently using the TMM include software test consulting firms, software training groups, large telecommunications companies, and a hardware/software enterprise. Some organizations experimenting with the TMM are domestic (U.S.); others are international. In addition, a study of TMM applications in Japan is now in progress [40]. This section will provide the reader with an overview of how the TMM has been put into practical use by a variety of organizations.

16.9.1 TMM Application I: Evaluating the Usability of the TMM Questionnaire

The initial trial usage of the TMM focused on evaluating the usability of the questionnaire, experimenting with the ranking algorithm using actual industrial data, generating sample action plans, and studying problems of testing process improvement in real-world environments [25,29,41]. The evaluation of the questionnaire and collection of the data was per-

TMM level MG	CMM level KPA	CMMI-SE/SW level KPA
4 Software quality evaluation Test measurement Review program	3 Peer reviews (S,P) 4 Software quality management (P)	3 Verification (S,P) 4 Measurement and analysis (S,P)
5 Test Process optimization Quality control Defect prevention	3 Organizational process definition (S,P) 4 Quantitative process management (S,P) 5 Defect prevention (P) Technology change management (S,P) Process change management (S,P)	3 Organizational process def (S,P) 4 Organizational proc performance (S,P) 4 Quantitative project management (S) 5 Organizational innovation & deployment (S) Casusal analysis & resolution (P)

KPA, key process area; MG, maturity goal; (S), supporting role; (P), parallel role.

TABLE 16.2

Common process areas: Levels 3, 4 TMM and CMM, CMMI-SE/SW.

formed by two software engineers who worked on different types of projects and in different companies. One engineer was employed by an organization that evaluates household hardware products (Organization I), and was manager of a team that developed internal software products to assist the hardware engineers in their testing tasks. The other engineer was employed by an organization that produced both hardware and software products for the telecommunications industry (Organization II).

The questionnaire evaluation for this study focused on (i) clarity of the questions, (ii) organization of the questions, (iii) ease of use, and (iv) coverage of TMM maturity goals and subgoals. Feedback from the evaluation enabled TMM developers to revise and reorganize the TMM ques-

TMM level	ISO-9001 areas	ISO/IEC 12207 areas
2	4.10 (test)	5.3.7 SW Test only
		5.3.8 SW Integration
		5.3.11 System qual-test
		5.3.13 SW
		Acceptance support
		6.5 Validation process
3	4.2 Quality systems	6.3 Quality assurance
	4.18 Training	7.4 Training process
4	4.10 Inspections	6.4 Verification
	4.12 Inspection, test status	6.6 Joint review process
	4.16 Quality records	6.8 Problem resolution
	4.20 Statistical techniques	
5	4.14 Defect prevention	7.1 Management process
		7.2 Infrastructure process
		7.3 Improvement process

TABLE 16.3

Common process areas: TMM/ISO-9001/ ISO/IEC 12207.

tions for better understandably and to improve question sequencing. A revised version appears in Appendix III of this text.

Both engineers involved in this study performed a limited TMM assessment on their testing groups. The assessment was limited in the sense that only the questionnaire data was used to generate a TMM rank. An interesting result of this experiment was that although the two organizations were evaluated to be at TMM level 1, the areas of testing strength and weakness of each were quite different for the projects that were evaluated. Organization I had weaknesses in two of the three maturity goals at TMM level 2, and had not addressed any testing issues at higher levels of the TMM. Organization II had a weakness in one of the TMM level 2 maturity goals, which could easily be rectified. There were indications that it could satisfy some of the maturity goals at the higher levels of the TMM. However, practices in some of these areas were informal and unstructured. Additional work would need to be done to truly achieve all of the level 3 maturity goals.

Since this application of the TMM was limited in scope, no actual improvement actions were carried out; however, sample action plans for improvement were suggested for both organizations that focused on areas of test weakness. An action plan template for use with the TMM as shown in Figure 16.14 was developed to instantiate the plans. Included items in the sample action plans were an action identifier, the planned start and end date for the action, a description of the action item, the related TMM maturity goal that the action will address, the deliverables that will result from the action, and the groups responsible for carrying out the action.

16.9.2 TMM Application II: Identifying Test Problem Areas and Risks

A preliminary application of the TMM was reported by Olsen and Stall-Vinje at a large European-based technology enterprise [42]. As described in their study, both authors were members of special-interest groups on test. Olsen was employed by the technology company under study and Stall-Vinje was president of a software test consulting firm. The TMM was applied in three different projects from different divisions of the organization to identify major problems and areas for improvement in the testing process. The projects included an integrated business system 14,000 function points in size (Project 1), a new release of a civil service system (Project 2), and a COBOL-based telecommunication billing system that was under development at three different geographical sites (Project 3). Using the TMM the authors were able to identify the strengths and weaknesses in the testing process for all three of the projects. These findings are summarized in Table 16.4.

In this study the authors found that the TMM was useful for test process evaluation especially to identify problem, or risk-prone, areas, and to predict where testing problems might occur in future projects. They also found the TMM to be a good source of knowledge and direction for test process improvements.

	Dates			Related		
Action Plan Template Summary of action plan goals						
Item ID	Start	End	Action items	TMM goal	Deliverables	Responsibilities

FIG. 16.14

Action plan template for test process improvement.

16.9.3 TMM: Application III: Software Test Consulting

The TMM has been utilized by several software test consulting firms that work with clients to evaluate and improve their testing processes. The range of clients is broad and includes those who develop software in application areas such as telecommunications and finance. Emphasis is on testing issues relating to methodologies, processes, and quality assurance. The consultants are also involved in training software quality and test professionals in areas such as test planning, test design, testing tools, defect tracking, and requirements development and tracking. One such organization located in the midwest has recently begun to offer TMM assessments to their clients [43]. For one of its clients application of the TMM Assessment Model revealed the following characteristics of their testing process:

- it was chaotic, unfocused, and undocumented;

- there was no testing group (developers performed all testing);

- test planning was very poor;

- there was an absence of testing/debugging goals.

Project ID	TMM level	Summary of weaknesses	Summary of strengths
1	2	Monitoring, measurement, vendor management*	Good test planning; a test organization
2	1	Inadequate test planning; inadequate test resources	Some testing goals, polices
3	1 (very close to level 2)	Some planning weakness; some weakness in use of basis test techniques; need for simple test measurements; need for monitoring	A test group; integration of test activities into SW life cycle; good test leadership

*Not covered by TMM maturity goals

TABLE 16.4

Summary of TMM Findings at European Technology Enterprise.

In addition, the consultants found that requirements management was very poor at this organization, and that no simple product or process measurements were being collected that could help define a test process baseline. This client group was essentially at TMM level 1.

The TMM provided support for the group to successfully implement the following test process improvement action items for this client. Similar action items were also recommended to other clients whose testing processes were subsequently evaluated with the TMM and also found to operate at low levels of test effectiveness [43]:

- design a baseline testing process (necessary for those organizations whose testing process is poor and/or ill-defined);

- improve test planning;

- improve requirements management, and traceability to test;

- recommend requirements and testing tools;

- initiate a simple defect tracking system;

- initiate a test process monitoring procedure;

- train staff in testing process issues.

There are two major risks identified by all of the consulting groups in applying the TMM. These risks (developer/tester- and manager-related) are often associated with any process improvement effort. One of the risks lies in the lack of support from developers for test process improvement. This may be true particularly for organizations at lower TMM levels (1,2) where no test organization is in place. Developers may be unfamiliar with, and lack education in, the area of testing processes. As a result, they may be uncooperative and unwilling to implement changes. It is vital in this case, as in all cases, to also have strong support from management for any test process improvement efforts. Lack of management support can also spell failure for any process assessment and improvement effort. The greatest successes in improving a development or test process usually occur when full support from management is obtained. In one instance where management support was lacking the midwest consultants report that their team was "at the mercy of the developers and project manager who resented our presence."

The midwest group continues to apply the TMM as a tool to evaluate, understand, and improve the quality of software testing processes in industry. In some cases they perform what they call "TMM mini-assessments" that are organized as follows [43]:

Preparation: The following items are prepared:

1. Executive Summary and thank you letter.
2. Hard and electronic copies of questionnaire.
3. Instruction Sheet for client participants.

Presentation to client:

4. Meet with client, make presentation, obtain approval and support.

5. Meet with participants, review instructions, identity respondents, distribute questionnaires, return these to the consultants in three days.

Analysis:

6. Analyze data.
7. Conduct interviews (scheduled by client team).

Report:

8. Develop test process assessment profile and report.
9. Deliver to client and make recommendations for improvement.

The midwest consulting group is also planning to work with the author to develop a set of automated tools and training materials to assist with TMM assessments [43].

16.9.4 TMM Application IV: The Role of Human Factors in Process Assessment

In this application the TMM was used to study the testing process at a single site of a very large international enterprise that develops both hardware and software. The engineers at this site are involved in developing software for use with hardware devices. The principal investigator participating in this TMM study is a software engineer working at the site.

The site has been certified for ISO 9000 and has won a quality award as well. These indicators of quality were very positive; however, the engineer was concerned about the possibility of complacency in the areas of product and process quality. In many cases where current quality is high, there is a tendency for an organization to rest on its laurels and to become indifferent to making further improvements. The investigating engineer wanted to identify a process evaluation/improvement system that was cost effective and efficient, and that would support the site in ongoing process evolution and improvement. The TMM was found to be an ideal model to apply for the following reasons [44].

1. There was a perception at the site that the testing process needed to be examined.

2. Management's attention needed to be focused on software test.
3. Since the TMM supports an internal testing process assessment, it could be used as a tool to continually improve testing. Improved testing would support growing businesses' needs and demands.
4. Since the TMM supports an internal assessment procedure it is more cost effective than hiring an independent assessment team.
5. The TMM is based on concepts similar to the CMM, the latter of which management was familiar with. The TMM also has overlapping areas with other process improvement models in which the organization was interested in establishing compliance.
6. Findings from a TMM assessment could be used to leverage management support for test process improvements.
7. Application of the TMM could renew efforts to focus on software product quality.

One of the useful findings that resulted from this study was the importance of considering human factors in performing a TMM assessment [44]. In order to accurately determine the state of a testing process, the participants in the assessment must provide accurate and consistent information. They must be motivated to work with the assessment team toward the goal of test process improvement. Therefore it is important for the participants to be trained and prepared, and that the assessment process be tailored so that it is a good fit with the cultural norms of the organization. In addition, it is also very important for the TMM assessment team to obtain strong management support for the assessment and the process changes that may follow. This maximizes the chances for success (see Section 16.9.3).

To address these human factor issues, the investigator in this TMM study has added phases or steps to augment the "preparation phase" of the assessment procedure as described by Homyen [25]. The new initial phase is called the "proposal phase." It is suggested by the investigator that this phase be applied to organizations new to TMM assessments, and/or those that are conservative in their approach to process changes. The proposal phase includes activities such as a study of the organizational culture, obtaining support from SEPG or other process improvement groups, enlisting volunteers to sign up for an informal assessment (filling out the TMM questionnaire), educating staff and upper management on the TMM, and having a kick-off meeting for participants. During this phase the questionnaire information is tallied and reported back to SEPG and/or upper management. The results provides a rough picture of the testing process, and can be used to motivate and initiate further actions. When this step is complete a formal proposal for a TMM assessment is developed, and potential sponsors and projects are identified. At this time, the TMM team should ensure that there is a statistically significant number of participants for the assessment. A buy-in plan for upper management is developed, and the plan and proposal are presented to this group. The TMM team uses the buy-in plan and the proposal to obtain commitment, support, and funding from upper management for the assessment. Having this commitment from management is essential for the process assessment and improvement effort to succeed.

In what is called the "human-oriented preparation phase," the TMM investigator augments the original "preparation" step of the TMM with a developer/tester buy-in plan. The buy-in plan is important to make the participants aware that process improvement is everybody's effort, that there are many benefits that result from an assessment, and that quality practices play a critical role in product quality. Note that in the midwest consulting group study, lack of developer/tester support was sited as one of the risks in applying an assessment model for process improvement. The suggested buy-in plan reduces that risk.

The investigator has suggested several tools that can be used to support the collection and processing of TMM assessment data. In this particular study commercially available tools were used to produce the questionnaire online and store the data. It was found that the participants preferred the electronic form of the questionnaire rather than a paper version. The raw data from the questionnaire was moved to a commercial program that produces spreadsheets. Fonts and colors in the spreadsheet program were used to highlight ranges of values. The spreadsheet was also used to produce the TMM rankings.

The assessment data was collected by a group of seven participants; two were SEPG leaders (SEPG1 and SEPG2) and five were test leaders (TL1–TL5). Each was responsible for a varying number of developers and testers; however, the SEPG members were responsible for larger groups than the test leaders (TL). Within these groups some of the developers had part-time testing responsibilities [44]. A summary of the TMM ranking results found in this study is shown in Table 16.5.

The rankings that resulted from this study are preliminary for this organizational site, and a more formal assessment is planned to obtain test process baseline rankings. The major lessons learned from the study are described below.

- Human factors are an important consideration in conducting an assessment, An augmented TMM "preparation phase" is useful to address human factors issues. Tools, training, and customization of work steps should be provided to support a successful assessment. As part of the training and customization process, instructors should provide a mapping of terms used by the TMM with those used by the organization. This is useful even though the TMM questionnaire has a glossary of terms. It helps to minimize the number of "don't know" and inaccurate answers.

- Performing an assessment even one that is as informal as in this study, has many benefits and is an excellent tool for gaining knowledge about the nature of a process. It is also a tool to gain management support and resources for test process improvement.

- Some the weakest test process areas found in this study were:

  —developing testing/debugging policies and goals;

  —integration of test into the software life cycle;

  —identifying test risks;

  —ensuring independence of the test group;

  —training;

  —developing an organizationwide review program;

  —developing a test measurement program.

- Satisfying TMM level 5 maturity goals may be very difficult for a particular organization or group. The investigator suggested that for this site, smaller groups of developers/testers led by test leaders who are involved in the low-level details of testing should work toward reaching TMM level 4. This may be a more practical goal for these

	TMM	
Summary of TMM Ranking Results		
Group	**Level**	**Comments on results**
TL1	1	Poor use of test plan template; poor use of requirements as input to test plan; no test risks identified for test plan; no integration of test into life cycle.
TL2	1	Absence of debugging policies/goals; lack of controlling and monitoring; no integration of test into life cycle.
TL3	1	No separation of testing and debugging; poor developer/tester ratio; poor institutionalization of basic testing techniques and methods.
TL4	2	Need tech training program; integration of test to reach level 3.
TL5	1	Many "not applicable" and "don't know" answers on questionnaire.
SEPG1	1	This group can satisfy all maturity goals at all TMM levels except for test planning and test measurement programs that have weaknesses. This group leads the test efforts at this site.
SEPG2	2	Achieves all TMM maturity goals through level 4. One weakness is in risk management for test.

TABLE 16.5

Summary of TMM ranking results for a hardware/software enterprise.

groups. Reaching TMM level 5 needs to be addressed at a more global level and involve many SEPG participants who oversee large groups of testers, and who have a more high-level view of testing. They can provide the support, expertise, and oversight needed to raise the entire group to TMM level 5.

The TMM investigator concluded that this preliminary study was very informative for the organizational site. Many testing issues were raised, and the developers, testers, and managers got a better understanding of the nature of their testing processes. For the short term the detailed results were returned to each of the participants (SEPG1, SEPG2, and TL1–5) with insights and feedback to help them improve their testing processes. In the future a formal TMM assessment is planned, with funding and support to be obtained from upper management. This preliminary study has paved the way for obtaining such support.

16.9.5 Lessons Learned from the TMM Studies

These experimental studies indicate that the TMM shows promise as a tool useful for software test process understanding, evaluation, and improvement. It is also a rich knowledge source for software engineers, test specialists, and managers who want to learn about good testing practices, and how to improve the effectiveness of their current testing process. The TMM is unique in that it provides a distinct role for all of the stakeholders in the testing process through its three critical views. Participation and communication by all interested parties is promoted. In addition, the studies show that the flexible design of the TMM allows it to be applied by different types of organizations involved in developing and testing software systems from a wide variety of problem domains.

Another useful finding that resulted from these studies is the significance of the role that human factors play in the success of an assessment and improvement effort. Human factors in these studies center around two groups—the technical staff (developers and testers) and the managerial staff (upper- and lower-level managers). The following three areas were found to be human factors focal points that should be noted by assessment teams.

1. Staff should be trained and motivated.

To support successful test process assessment and improvement efforts, an organization needs to ensure that its technical staff is properly trained, motivated, and provided with support tools to do the job. This requirement has roots in "Total Employee Involvement (TIE)" effort, which in itself was a part of the "Total Quality Management" movement in Japan [45]. Staff must be convinced that process assessment and improvement is a team project and requires participation by all. They must also be convinced that everybody benefits from the effort.

2. The assessment effort should be tailored to meet the cultural norms of the organization.

In addition to providing training and tools, the assessment leaders may also need to tailor the assessment steps, forms, and procedures so that they are a good fit for a particular organizational environment. Tailoring has been shown to promote success in process assessment and improvement efforts on the personnel level with the Personal Software Process (PSP) [46]. Assessment team members may need to perform tailoring on both a fine- and coarse-grained level. As a fine-grained example, in TMM application IV the investigator found that differences in interpretation of technical terms needed to be resolved so that the TMM questionnaire could be completed properly and accurately.

3. The assessment team should obtain commitment and support from management.

These studies illustrate the importance of management involvement and commitment for the success of any process assessment and improvement effort. Past experiences with the quality efforts such as Total Quality Management (TQM), and with process assessment/improvement efforts using the CMM, PSP, and ISO-9000, also point out the importance of this commitment. To quote from Paulk et al., "Improvement requires strong management support and a consistent long-term focus" [6]. A management buy-in plan and kick-off meeting as implemented by the TMM application IV investigator promotes this needed managerial support and commitment. The TMM assessment procedure steps can easily be augmented to include this item.

Finally, the TMM rankings placed most of the groups assessed in these initial studies at low levels of the TMM (levels 1, 2). In several cases there were weaknesses in basic areas such as testing planning and the development of testing/debugging policies. These findings parallel results obtained in initial studies using the CMM as a reference model for process assessment. Many organizations were then assessed to be at a CMM level of 1 and 2. Now that there is a broad recognition for the value of quality processes, many organizations have made significant investments in process improvements and have raised their maturity ratings. Business needs and competition promoted the proliferation of improvement efforts. When organizations become more aware of the need to focus on testing as (i) an important quality-enhancing process, and (ii) a process that adds value to their products, they will invest more resources. The best practices required of a high-quality testing process will be widely applied in industry, and as a consequence TMM levels should rise.

At this time the midwest consulting group continues to work with its industrial clients and apply the TMM to their testing processes. The investigator at the hardware/software enterprise hopes to obtain support for a planned full TMM assessment at his site. Several additional consulting, software development, and training organizations are also in the process of applying the TMM in their work The author plans to publish reports with industrial collaborators as they become available.

REFERENCES

[1] I. Burnstein, T. Suwanassart, and C. Carlson, "Developing a testing maturity model: part I," *CrossTalk: Journal of Defense Software Engineering.* Vol. 9, No. 8, 1996, pp. 21–24,

[2] I. Burnstein, T. Suwanassart, and C. Carlson, "Developing A testing maturity model: part II," *CrossTalk: Journal of Defense Software Engineering.* Vol. 9, No. 9, 1996, pp. 19–26.

[3] I. Burnstein, A. Homyen, R. Grom, C. R. Carlson, "A model for assessing testing process maturity," *CrossTalk: Journal of Department of Defense Software Engineering,* Vol. 11, No. 11, Nov. 1998, pp. 26–30.

[4] I. Burnstein, A. Homyen, T. Suwanassart, G. Saxena, R. Grom, "Using the testing maturity model to assess and improve your software testing process," *Proc. of International Quality Week Conf.* (QW'99), San Jose, CA, May 1999.

[5] I. Burnstein, A. Homyen, T, Suwanassart, G. Saxena, R. Grom, "A testing maturity model for software test process assessment and improvement," *Software Quality Professional* (American Society for Quality), Vol. 1, No. 4, Sept. 1999, pp. 8–21.

[6] M. Paulk, C. Weber, B. Curtis, and M. Chrissis, *The Capability Maturity Model,* Addison-Wesley, Reading, MA, 1995.

[7] Software Engineering Institute, www.sei.cmu.edu/cmmi/publications

[8] F. Coallier, "How ISO 9001 fits into the software world," *IEEE Software,* Vol. 11, No. 1, 1994, pp. 98–100.

[9] A. Bicego, P. Kuvaja, "BOOTSTRAP: Europe's assessment method," *IEEE Software,* Vol. 10, No. 3, 1993, pp. 93–95.

[10] M. Paulk, M. Konrad, "An overview of ISO's SPICE project," *American Programmer,* Vol. 7, No. 2, 1994, pp. 16–20.

[11] M. Paulk, B. Curtis, M. Chrissis, and C. Weber. "Capability maturity model, version 1.1," *IEEE Software,* Vol. 10, No. 4, 1993, pp. 18–27.

[12] M. Paulk, C. Weber, S. Garcia, M. Chrissis, and M. Bush, "Key practices of the capability maturity model, version 1.1," Technical Report, CMU/SEI-93-TR-25, 1993, Software Engineering Institute, Pittsburgh, PA.

[13] D. Gelperin, B. Hetzel, "The growth of software testing," *Communications of the Association of Computing Machinery,* Vol. 31, No. 6, 1988, pp. 687–695.

[14] J. Durant, "Software testing practices survey report," Technical Report, TR5-93, Software Practices Research Center, 1993.

[15] B. Beizer, *Software Testing Techniques,* second edition, Van Nostrand Reinhold, New York, 1990.

[16] D. Gelperin, A. Hayashi, "How to support better software testing," *Application Trends,* May 1996, pp. 42–48.

[17] D. Gelperin, "What's your testability maturity?" *Application Trends,* May 1996, pp. 50–53.

[18] T. Koomen, M. Pol, "Improvement of the test process using TPI," Technical Report, IQUIP Informatica B.V., Diemen, The Netherlands, 1998, http://www.iquip.nl.

[19] T. Koomen, M. Pol, *Test Process Improvement,* Addison-Wesley, Reading, MA, 1999.

[20] A. Clouse, C. Wells, "Transitioning from EIA/IS-731 to CMMI," *CrossTalk: Journal of Department of Defense Software Engineering,* Vol. 13, No. 7, July 2000, pp. 15–20.

[21] S. Shrum, "Choosing a CMMI model representation," *CrossTalk: Journal of Department of Defense Software Engineering,* Vol. 13, No. 7, July 2000, pp. 6–7.

[22] International Organization for Standardization (ISO), ISO/IEC Software Process Assessment Working Draft-Part 3: Rating processes, version 1.00; Part 5: Construction, selection and use of assessment instruments and tools, version 1.00; Part 7: Guide for use in process improvement, version 1.00, International Organization for Standardization, Geneva, 1995.

[23] D. Zubrow, W. Hayes, J. Siegel, D. Goldenson, "Maturity questionnaire," Technical Report, CMU/SEI-94-SR-7, Software Engineering Institute, Pittsburgh, PA, 1994.

[24] S. Masters, C. Bothwell, "A CMM appraisal framework, version 1.0," Technical Report, CMU/SEI-95-TR-001, Software Engineering Institute, Pittsburgh, PA, 1995.

[25] A. Homyen, "An assessment model to determine test process maturity," Ph.D. thesis, Illinois Institute of Technology, Chicago, IL, 1998.

[26] J. Hearns, S. Garcia, "Automated test team management—it works!" *Proc. of the 10th Software Eng. Process Group Conference* (SEPG'98), 6–9 March, Chicago, IL, 1998.

[27] W. Humphrey, W. Sweet, "A method for assessing the software engineering capability of contractors," Technical Report, CMU/SEI-87-TR-23, Software Engineering Institute, Pittsburgh, PA, 1987.

[28] J. Puffer, A. Litter, "Action planning," *IEEE Software Engineering Technical Council Newsletter,* Vol. 15, No. 2, 1997, pp. 7–10.

[29] R. Grom, "Report on a TMM assessment support tool," Technical Report, Illinois Institute of Technology, Chicago, IL, 1998.

[30] C. Cook, M. Visconti, "New and improved documentation model," Technical Report, Oregon State University, 1996.

[31] K. El Emam, D. Goldenson, L. Briand, P. Marshall, "Interrater agreement in SPICE-based assessments: some preliminary reports," *Proc. Fourth International Conference on the Software Process,* Brighton, UK, 1996, pp. 149–156.

[32] G. Saxena, "A framework for building and evaluating process maturity models," Ph.D. thesis, Illinois Institute of Technology, Chicago, IL, 1999.

[33] J. Weszka, P. Babel, J. Ferguson, "CMMI: evolutionary path to enterprise process improvement," *CrossTalk: Journal of Department of Defense Software Engineering,* Vol. 13, No. 7, July 2000, pp. 8–11.

[34] CMMI Product Development Team, "CMMI for systems engineering/software engineering, version 1.02 (CMMI-SE/SW, V1.02) staged representation," Technical Report, CMU/SEI-2000TR-018, ESC-TR-2000-018, Software Engineering Institute, Nov. 2000.

[35] D. Kitson, "An emerging international standard for software process assessment," *Proc. IEEE Third International Software Engineering Standards Symposium and Forum,* Walnut Creek, CA, June 1999.

[36] S. Garcia, "Evolving improvement paradigms: Capability Maturity Models and ISO/IEC 15504 (PDTR)," *Software Process Improvement and Practice,* Vol. 3, No. 1, 1998.

[37] International Organization for Standardization (ISO), "ISO/IEC 12207: Information Technology—Software Life Cycle Processes," 1995.

[38] J. Moore, "ISO 12207 and related software life cycle standards," http://www.acm.org.tsc/lifecycle.html.

[39] R. Kehoe, A. Jarvis, *ISO-9000-3*, Springer-Verlag, New York, 1995.

[40] I. Burnstein, T. Suwanassart, private correspondence, 2001.

[41] J. Hook, "Evaluation of the TMM questionnaire," Technical Report, Illinois Institute of Technology, Chicago, IL, 1997.

[42] K. Olsen, P. Stall Vinje, "Using the testing maturity model in practical test-planning and postevaluation," EuroSTAR98 Conference, Munich, Germany, 1998.

[43] I. Burnstein, L. Miller (President, Midwest Software Testing Lab, Inc.), private correspondence, 2000–2001.

[44] H. Tran, "A procedure on how to conduct a testing maturity assessment on a software development organization using the TMM assessment methodology," M.S. thesis, University of Minnesota, Rochester, MN, 2001.

[45] L. Zells, "Learning from Japanese TQM applications to software engineering," *Total Qualty Managment for Software,* G. Schulmeyer, J. McManus, eds., Van Nostrand Reinhold, New York, 1992.

[46] K. El Emam, B. Shostak, N. Madhavji, "Implementing concepts from the personal software process in an industrial setting," *Proc. Fourth International Conference on the Software Process, Improvement, and Practice,* Brighton, UK, 1996, pp. 117–130.

TEST-RELATED REFERENCES

I. Software Testing: Related Conferences

Listed below are references to test and process-related conferences of interest. This list is not meant to be exhaustive, just representative of available conferences in these areas. Some of the conference are held once per year; others are held several times per year. Locations of the conferences may vary from year to year.

Software Test Automation Conference and Expo
Software Quality Engineering
330 Corporate Way
Orange Park, FL 32073
www.sqe.com
www.stickyminds.com (*newsletter*)

Software Engineering Process Group Conference
Carnegie Mellon University
Software Engineering Institute
Pittsburgh, PA 15213-3890

International Software Test Professionals Week
Practical Software Quality Techniques, PSQT
International Institute for Software Testing
Software Dimensions
8476 Bechtel Ave
Inver Grove Heights, MN 55076
www.testinginstitute.com

Software Technology Conference
Hill Air Force Base STSC
5045 Old Main Hill
Logan, UT 84322-5045
www.stc-online.org

International Internet and Software Quality Week Conference
Software Research, Inc.
901 Minnesota Street
San Francisco, CA 94107
www.qualityweek.com

II. Web Sites for Software Process and Software Quality Information

This list contains web sites that focus on general process improvement material. Testers and test managers may find some very useful information at these sites.

1. Software Technology Support Center

    www.stsc.hill.af.mil

    This center is sponsored by the US Department of Defense. They distribute a very useful publication called *CrossTalk* which is free of charge.

2. Software Process Improvement Network (SPIN)

    www.cmu.edu/collaborating/spins/spins.html

SPIN groups offer a forum for exchanging information, experiences, and knowledge about software process improvement. In many large cities there are local SPIN groups. Associated with most local SPIN groups is a regular series of presentations by practitioners involved in process improvement efforts.

3. Software Engineering Institute

   www.sei.cmu.edu

   This is a federally funded research center that has developed the CMM family of models. Details on the CMMI project can be found at

   www.sei.cmu.edu/cmmi

4. Software Engineering Process Office (SEPO)

   http://sepo.nosc.mil

   This is the software engineering source for the Space and Naval Warfare Systems Center. It does offer consulting services for government and industry partners.

5. The Software Engineering Laboratory (SEL)

   http://sel.gsfc.nasa.gov

   The SEL has collected and analyzed software development metrics from projects within the NASA Goddard Space Flight Center.

6. Software Productivity Consortium

   www.software.org

   Partnership of industry, government, and academia. Develops process methods, tools, and support services.

7. European Software Process Improvement Foundation (ESPI)

   www.espi.co.uk

   Provides software engineering information and promotes quality software practices through process improvement.

8. EGroups

   www.egroups.com/group.spi

   Electronic forum for exchanging information relating to software process improvement.

9. Software Process Improvement and Capability dEtermination (SPICE)

   www.sqi.gu.edu.au/spice/contents.html

   Developers of SPICE process improvement model. SPICE is international initiative to develop an international standard for software process assessment.

10. American Society for Quality (ASQ)

    www.asq.org

    Publisher of *Software Quality Professional,* a journal containing high-quality papers covering aspects of software test and quality. The society is also involved in the certification of quality engineers, sponsors quality/test conferences, posts books, and has a six-sigma forum.

11. Software Engineering Body of Knowledge (SWEBOK). Developed by a joint IEEE/ACM task force.

    www.swebok.org

    SWEOK contains knowledge areas and descriptions of topics that are essential for all software engineers to know.

12. Quality Assurance Institute (QAI)

    www.qaiusa.com

    Sponsors conferences, certification, and educational activities.

III. Test-Oriented Web Sites

There are many web sites devoted to testing. Many offer testing services. The following is a list of some useful test-related web sites that contain links to papers, conferences, and services of interest to test professionals.

1. RBSCB Bibliography: Testing Object-Oriented Software

   www.rbsc.com

   Has a good listing of papers related to testing of object-oriented systems.

2. Software Quality and Testing Resource Center

www.softwareqatest.com

Has links to many testing resources and tools.

3. Society for Software Quality

www.ssq.org

This is an organization whose members work to promote quality in software development.

4. IEEE Standards Web Site

standards.ieee.org/catalog

Lists IEEE standards documents and how to order copies. The IEEE web site is:

ieee.org

5. Software Testing Institute (STI)

www.ondaweb.com

Lists publications, research documents, and services for test professionals. Also has a Software Testing Newsletter and an STI Buyer's Guide which is a directory of vendors and consultants.

6. Software Testing On-line Resources

www.mtsu.edu/~strom/

This is a good source for test-related material. It is maintained by Middle Tennessee State University. There is a list of researchers in test, reviews, monographs, and educational sources.

7. Software Testing and Quality Engineering Magazine (STQE)

www.stqemagazine.com/

This site describes a magazine that contains articles on software testing.

8. Software Research (SR Institute, Test Works)

www.soft.com

Sponsor of research conferences on testing, site has a newsletter with archives.

IV. Bibliography (Papers and Books)

This section contains a list of papers and books related to software testing that are of interest to developers, testers, and managers. The list is in alphabetical order and contains a compilation of the references mentioned in each book chapter as well as additional items that augment the material in the text.

Abramovici, M., M. Brever, A. Friedman, *Digital System Testing and Testable Design,* Computer Science Press, New York, 1990.

Abran, A., J. Moore, P. Bourque, R. Dupuis, eds., "Guide to the Software Engineering Body of Knowledge—Trial Version," IEEE Computer Society Press, Los Alamitos, CA, 2001.

Affourtit, B., "Statistical process control applied to software," *Total Quality Management for Software,* G. Schulmeyer, J. McManus, eds., Van Nostrand Reinhold, New York, 1992.

Arnold, T., W. Fuson, "Testing in a Perfect World," *Comm. of the ACM,* Vol. 37, No. 9, 1994, pp. 78–86.

Ayer, S., F. Patrinostro, *Software Configuration Management,* McGraw-Hill, New York, 1992.

Bartol, K., D. Martin, "Managing the consequences of the DP turnover: a human resources planning perspective," *Proc. 20th ACM Computer Personnel Research Conf.,* 1983, pp. 79–86.

Basili, V., D. Weiss, "A methodology for collecting valid software engineering data," *IEEE Transactions on Software Engineering,* Vol. SE-10, No. 6, 1984, pp. 728–738.

Beizer, B., *Black Box Testing,* Wiley, New York, 1995.

Beizer, B., *Software Testing Techniques,* second edition, Van Nostrand Reinhold, New York, 1990.

Beizer, B., *Software System Testing and Quality Assurance,* Van Nostrand Reinhold, New York, 1984.

Berard, E., *Essays on Object-Oriented Software Engineering, Volume 1,* Prentice Hall, Englewood Cliffs, NJ, 1993.

Bertolino, A., "Software testing," in *Guide to the Software Engineering Body of Knowledge,* version 0.7, A. Abran, J. Moore, P. Bourque, R. Dupuis, eds., April 2000.

Bicego, A., P. Kuvaja, "BOOTSTRAP: Europe's assessment method," *IEEE Software,* Vol. 10, No. 3, 1993, pp. 93–95.

Binder, R., "Design for testability in object-oriented systems," *Comm. of the ACM,* Vol. 37, No. 9, 1994, pp. 87–101.

Boehm, B., "Software risk management: principles and practices," *IEEE Software,* Jan. 1991, pp. 32–41.

Boehm, B., *Software Engineering Economics,* Prentice Hall, Englewood Cliffs, NJ, 1981.

Boehm, B., J. Brown, M. Lipow, "Quantitative evaluation of software quality," *IEEE 2nd International Conf. on Software Engineering,* San Francisco, CA, pp. 592–605, Oct. 1976.

Booth, P., *An Introduction to Human–Computer Interaction,* Lawrence Erlbaum Associates, London, 1989.

Brettschneider, R., "Is your software ready for release?" *IEEE Software,* Vol. 6, No. 4, pp. 100–108, 1989.

Burnstein, I., F. Saner, "Fuzzy reasoning to support automated program understanding," *International Journal of Software Engineering and Knowledge Engineering,* Vol. 10, No. 1, Feb. 2000, pp. 115–137.

Burnstein, I., A. Homyen, T. Suwanassart, G. Saxena, R. Grom, "A Testing Maturity Model for software test process assessment and Improvement," *Software Quality Professional* (American Society for Quality), Vol. 1, No. 4, Sept. 1999, pp. 8–21.

Burnstein, I., A. Homyen, T. Suwanassart, G. Saxena, R. Grom, "Using the Testing Maturity Model to assess and improve your software testing process," *Proc. of International Quality Week Conf.* (QW'99), San Jose, CA, May 1999.

Burnstein, I., A. Homyen, R. Grom, C. R. Carlson, "A model for assessing testing process maturity," *CrossTalk: Journal of Department of Defense Software Engineering,* Vol. 11, No. 11, Nov. 1998, pp. 26–30.

Burnstein, I., T. Suwanassart, C. R. Carlson, "Developing a Testing Maturity Model: part I," *CrossTalk: Journal of Defense Software Engineering,* Vol. 9, No. 8, August 1996, pp. 21–24.

Burnstein, I., T. Suwanassart, C. R. Carlson, "Developing a Testing Maturity Model: part II," *CrossTalk: Journal of Defense Software Engineering,* Vol. 9, No. 9, Sept. 1996, pp. 19–26.

Card, D. "Leaning from our mistakes with defect causal analysis," *IEEE Software,* Vol. 13, No. 1, 1998, pp. 56–63.

Cangussu, J., R. DeCarlo, A. Mathur, "A Formal Model of the Test Process," *IEEE Trans. Software Engineering,* Vol. 28, No. 8, August 2002, pp. 782–796.

Chen, M., M. Kao, "Investigating test effectiveness on object-oriented software: a case study," *Proc. Twelfth International Quality Week Conf.,* May 1999.

Chen, T., Y. Yu, "On the expected number of failures detected by subdomain testing and random testing," *IEEE Trans. Software Engineering,* Vol. 22, 1996, pp. 109–119.

Chernak, Y., "Validating and improving test case effectiveness," *IEEE Software,* Vol. 16, No. 1, 2001, pp. 81–86

Chilenski, J., P. Newcomb, "Formal Specification Tools for Test Coverage Analysis," Proc. IEEE Conf. on Knowledge-Based Software Engineering, Monterey, CA, 1994, pp. 59–68.

Cho, C., "Statistical methods applied to software quality control," in *Handbook of Software Quality Assurance,* second edition, G. Schulmeyer, J McManus, eds., Van Nostrand Reinhold, New York, 1992.

Clarke, L., A. Podgurski, A. Richardson, S. Zeil, "A comparison of data flow path selection criteria," *Proc. Eighth International Conf. on SW Engineering,* August 1985, pp. 244–251.

Clouse, A., C. Wells, "Transitioning from EIA/IS-731 to CMMI," *CrossTalk: Journal of Department of Defense Software Engineering,* Vol. 13, No. 7, July 2000, pp. 15–20.

CMMI Product Development Team, "CMMI for systems engineering/software engineering, version 1.02 (CMMI-SE/SW, V1.02) staged representation," Technical Report CMU/SEI-2000TR-018, ESC-TR-2000-018, Software Engineering Institute, Nov. 2000.

Coad, P., E. Yourdon, *Object-Oriented Analysis,* second edition, Yourdon Press, Englewood Cliffs, NJ, 1991.

Coallier, F., "How ISO 9001 fits into the software world," *IEEE Software,* Vol. 11, No. 1, 1994, pp. 98–100.

Cobb, R., H. Mills, "Engineering software under statistical quality control," *IEEE Software,* Vol. 7, No. 5, 1990, pp. 44–54,

Cook, C., M. Visconti, "New and improved documentation model," Technical Report, Oregon State University, 1996.

Crosby, P., *Quality Is Free: The Art of Making Quality Certain,* Mentor, New American Library, New York, 1979.

Daich, G., G. Price, B. Ragland, M. Dawood, *Software Test Technologies Report,* August 1994, Software Technology Support Center (STSC) Hill Air Force Base, UT, August 1994.

Dalal, S., C. Mallows, "Some graphical aids for deciding when to stop testing software," *IEEE Journal on Selected Areas in Communications,* Vol. 8, No. 2, 1990, pp. 169–175.

Dalal, S., C. Mallows, "When should one stop testing software?" *J. American Statistical Assoc.,* Vol. 81, No. 403, pp. 872–879, 1988.

Delamaro, M., J. Maldonado, A. Mathur, "Interface mutation: an approach for integration testing," *IEEE Transactions on Software Engineering,* Vol. 27, No. 3, March 2001, pp. 228–247.

DeMillo, R., R. Lipton, F. Sayward, "Hints on test data selection: help for the practicing programmer," *Computer,* Vol. 11, No. 4, 1978, pp. 34–41.

Deming, W., *Out of the Crisis,* MIT Center for Advanced Engineering Study, Cambridge, MA, 1986.

Dieli, M., "A problem-solving approach to usability test planning," *Proc.*

International Professional Communication Conf., Seattle, pp. 265–267, 1988.

Doong, R., P. Frankl, "The ASTOOT approach to testing object-oriented programs," ACM *Transactions of Software Engineering and Methodology,* Vol. 3, 1994, pp. 101–130.

D'Souza, R., R. LeBlanc, "Class testing by examining pointers," *J. Object Oriented Programming,* July–August 1994, pp. 33–39.

Duran, J., S. Ntafos, "An evaluation of random testing," *IEEE Trans. SW Engineering,* Vol. 10, 1984, pp. 438–444.

Durant, J., *Software Testing Practices Survey Report,* Software Practices Research Center, Technical Report, TR5-93, May 1993.

Dustin, E., J. Rashka, J. Paul, *Automated Software Testing,* Addison-Wesley, Reading, MA, 1999.

Ehrlich, W., B. Prasanna, J. Stampfel, J. Wu, "Determining the cost of a stop-test decision," *IEEE Software,* Vol. 10, No. 2, pp. 33–42, 1993.

El Emam, K., D. Goldenson, L. Briand, P. Marshall, "Interrater agreement in SPICE-based assessments: some preliminary reports," *Proc. Fourth International Conference on the Software Process,* Brighton, UK, 1996, pp. 149–156.

Endres, A., "An analysis of errors and causes in system programs," *IEEE Transactions on Software Engineering,* Vol. SE-1, No. 2, 1975.

Fagen, M., "Design and code inspections to reduce errors in program development," *IBM Systems Journal,* Vol. 15, No. 3, 1976, pp. 182–211.

Fenton, N., "Software measurement: a necessary scientific basis," *IEEE Transactions on Software Engineering,* Vol. SE-20, No. 3, pp. 199–206, 1994.

Fenton, N., *Software Metrics: A Rigorous Approach,* Chapman & Hall, London, 1991.

Fiedler, S., "Object-oriented unit testing," *Hewlett-Packard Journal,* April 1989, pp. 69–74.

Firth, R., V. Mosley, R. Pethia, L. Roberts, W. Wood, *A Guide the Classification and Assessment of Software Engineering Tools,* Technical Report, CMU/SEI-87-TR-10. ESD-TR-87-11, Software Engineering Institute, Carnegie Mellon, 1987.

Florac, W., A. Carleton, J. Barnard, "Statistical process control: analyzing a space shuttle onboard software process," *IEEE Software,* Vol. 17, No. 4, 2000, pp. 97–106.

Frankl, P., E. Weyuker, "Provable improvements on branch testing," *IEEE Trans. Software Engineering,* Vol. 19, No. 10, 1993, pp. 962–975.

Frankl, P., E. Weyuker, "A formal analysis of the fault-detecting ability of testing methods," *IEEE Trans. Software Engineering,* Vol. 19, No. 3, 1993, pp. 202–213.

Freedman, P., G. Weinberg, *Handbook of Walkthroughs, Inspections, and Technical Reviews,* Dorest House Publishing, New York, 1990.

Ganesan, K., T. Khoshgoftaar, E. Allen, "Case-based software quality prediction," *International Journal of Software Engineering and Knowledge Engineering,* Vol. 10, No. 2, 2000, pp. 139–152.

Gale, J., J. Tirso, C. Burchfiled, "Implementing the defect prevention process in the MVS interactive programming organization," *IBM Systems Journal,* Vol. 29, No. 1, 1990.

Garcia, S., "Evolving improvement paradigms: Capability Maturity Models and ISO/IEC 15504 (PDTR)," *Software Process Improvement and Practice,* Vol. 3, No. 1, 1998.

Gelperin, D., A. Hayashi, "How to support better software testing," *Application Trends,* May 1996, pp. 42–48.

Gelperin, D., "What's your testability maturity?" *Application Trends,* May 1996, pp. 50–53.

Gelperin, D., B. Hetzel, "The growth of software testing," *CACM,* Vol. 31, No. 6, 1988, pp. 687–695.

Gilb, T., *Principles of Software Engineering Management,* Addison-Wesley, Reading, MA, 1988.

Gotterbarn, D., K. Miller, S. Rogerson, "Computer society and ACM approve software engineering code of ethics," *IEEE Computer,* Vol. 32, No. 10, Oct. 1999, pp. 84–88.

Grady, R., *Practical Software Metrics for Project Management and Process Improvement,* Prentice Hall (Pearson Education), Engelwood Cliff, NJ., 1992.

Grady, R., D. Caswell, *Software Metrics: Establishing a Companywide Program,* Prentice Hall (Pearson Education), Englewood Cliff, NJ, 1987.

Graham, D., "Measuring the effectiveness and efficiency of testing," *Proc. Software Testing,* Paris, June 1996.

Gutjahr, W., "Partition testing vs. random testing: the influence of uncertainty," *IEEE Trans. Software Engineering,* Vol. 25, No. 5., Sept./Oct. 1999, pp. 661–674.

Grom, R., "Report on a TMM assessment support tool," Technical Report, Illinois Institute of Technology, Chicago, IL, 1998.

Hamlet, D., "Are we testing for true reliability?" *IEEE Software,* Vol. 9, No. 4, pp. 21–27, 1992.

Harel, D., "Statecharts: a visual formalism for complex systems," *Science of Computer Programming,* Vol. 8, 1987.

Harrold, M., G. Rothermel, "Performing data flow testing on classes," *Proc. Second ACM SIGSOFT Symposium on Foundations of Software Engineering,* Dec. 1994, pp. 154–163.

Harrold, M., J. McGregor, K. Fitzpatrick, "Incremental testing of object-oriented class structures," *Proc. 14th International Conf. on Software Engineering,* May 1992, pp. 68–80.

Hearns, J., S. Garcia, "Automated test team management: it works!!" *Proc. 10th Software Engineering Process Group Conference* (SEPG'98) Chicago, IL, March 1998.

Hetzel, B., *The Complete Guide to Software Testing,* second edition, QED Information Sciences, Inc., Wellesley, MA. 1988.

Hollenbach, C., W. Frakes, "Software process reuse in an industrial setting," *Proc. Fourth International Conf. on Software Reuse,* Orlando, FL, April 1996, pp. 22–30.

Homyen, A. "An assessment model to determine test process maturity," Ph.D. Thesis, Illinois Institute of Technology, Chicago, IL, 1998.

Hook, J., "Evaluation of the TMM questionnaire," Technical Report, Illinois Institute of Technology, Chicago, IL, 1997.

Horgan, J., S. London, M. Lyu, "Achieving software quality with testing coverage measures," *IEEE Computer,* Vol. 27, No. 9, 1994, pp. 60–68.

Horgan, J., S. London, "Data flow coverage and the C language," *Proc. ACM SIGSOFT Symposium on Testing, Analysis, and Verification,* Oct. 1991, pp. 87–97.

Howden, W., "Weak mutation testing and completeness of test sets," *IEEE Trans. Software Engineering,* Vol. 8, No. 4. 1982, pp. 371–379.

Howden, W., "A survey of dynamic analysis methods," In *Software Testing and Validation Techniques,* second edition, E. Miller, and W. Howden, eds., IEEE Computer Society Press, Los Alamitos, CA, 1981.

Humphrey, W., *A Discipline for Software Engineering,* Addison-Wesley, Reading, MA. 1995.

Humphrey, W., *Managing the Software Process,* Addison-Wesley, Reading, MA, 1990.

Humphrey, W., W. Sweet, "A method for assessing the software engineering capability of contractors," Technical Report, CMU/SEI-87-TR-23, Software Engineering Institute, Pittsburgh, PA, 1987.

Hurst, P., "Software project management: threads of control," in *Software Engineering Project Management,* second edition, R. Thayer, ed., IEEE Computer Society Press, Los Alamitos, CA, 1997, pp. 410–422.

IEEE Software, "Tools assessment," special issue, May 1992.

Institute of Electrical and Electronics Engineers, Inc., *IEEE Standards Collection for Software Engineering,* 1994 edition, New York, 1994.

Institute of Electrical and Electronics Engineers, Inc., IEEE Standard

1008-1987, *Standard for Software Unit Testing,* (Reaff 1993), 1987, all rights reserved.

Institute of Electrical and Electronics Engineers, Inc., IEEE/ANSI Standard 1016-1987, *Recommended Practices for Software Design Descriptions,* (Reaff. 1993), 1987, all rights reserved.

Institute of Electrical and Electronics Engineers, Inc., IEEE/ANSI Standard 1012-1986, (Reaff 1992), *Standard for Software Verification and Validation Plans,* 1986, all rights reserved.

Institute of Electrical and Electronics Engineers, Inc., IEEE/ANSI Standard 829-1983, (Reaff 1991), *Standard for Software Test Documentation,* 1983, all rights reserved.

International Organization for Standardization (ISO), ISO/IEC Software Process Assessment Working Draft—Part 3: Rating processes, version 1.00; Part 5: Construction, selection, and use of assessment instruments and tools, version 1.00; Part 7: Guide for use in process improvement, version 1.00, International Organization for Standardization, Geneva, 1995.

International Organization for Standardization (ISO), ISO/IEC 12207, *Information Technology: Software Life Cycle Processes,* 1995.

International Organization for Standardization (ISO), *Information Technology: Software Product Evaluation: Quality Characteristics and Guidelines for Their Use,* ISO/IEC IS 9126, Geneva, ISO, 1991.

Jacobson, I., M. Christerson, P. Jonsson, G. Overgaard, *Object-Oriented Software Engineering: A Use Case Driven Approach,* Addison-Wesley, Reading, MA, 1992.

Jorgensen, P., C. Erikson, "Object-oriented integration test," *CACM,* Vol. 37, No. 9, 1994, pp. 30–38.

Juran, J., M. Gryna, M. Frank, Jr., R. Bingham, Jr. (eds.), *Quality Control Handbook,* third edition, McGraw-Hill, New York, 1979.

Juran, J., *Managerial Breakthrough,* McGraw-Hill, New York, 1964.

Kaner, C., J. Falk, H. Nguyen, *Testing Computer Software,* second edition, Van Nostrand Reinhold, New York, 1993.

Kehoe, R., A. Jarvis, *ISO-9000-3,* Springer-Verlag, New York, 1995.

Kellner, M., L. Briand, J. Over, "A method for designing, defining, and evolving software processes," *Proc. Fourth International Conf. on the Software Process,* Brigthon, UK, Dec. 1996, pp. 37–48.

Kellner, M., R. Phillip, "Practical technology for process assets," *Proc. 8th International Software Process Workshop: State of the Practice in Process Technology,* Warden, Germany, March 1993, pp. 107–112.

Kemerer, C., "How the learning curve affects CASE tool adaptation," *IEEE Software,* pp. 23–28, May 1993.

Khoshgoftarr, T., J. Munson, "Predicting software development errors using software complexity metrics," *IEEE J. Selected Areas in Comm.,* Vol. 8, No. 2, Feb. 1990, pp. 252–261.

Kit, E., *Software Testing in the Real World,* Addison-Wesley, Reading, MA, 1995.

Kitson, D., "An emerging international standard for software process assessment," *Proc. IEEE Third International Software Engineering Standards Symposium and Forum,* Walnut Creek, CA, June 1999.

Koomen, T., M. Pol, *Test Process Improvement,* Addison-Wesley, Reading, MA, 1999.

Koomen, T., M. Pol, "Improvement of the test process using TPI," Technical Report, IQUIP Informatica B.V., Diemen, The Netherlands, 1998, http://www.iquip.nl.

Korel, B., I. Burnstein, R. Brevelle, "Postcondition–based stress testing in certification of COTS components," *Proceedings of the First International Software Assurance Certification Conference,* Washington, D.C., March 1999.

Kozaczynski, W., J. Ning, "Automated program recognition by concept recognition," *Automated Software Engineering,* Vol. 1, 1994, pp. 61–78.

Kung, D., P Hsia, J. Gao, *Testing Object-Oriented Software,* IEEE Computer Society Press, Los Alamitos, CA, 1998.

Laitenberger, O., K. El. Eman, T. Harbich, "An internally replicated quasi-experimental comparison and checklist and perspective-based reading of code documents," *IEEE Transactions on Software Engineering,* Vol. 27, No. 5, May 2001, pp. 387–421.

Laski, J., B. Korel, "A data flow oriented testing strategy," *IEEE Trans. Software Engineering,* Vol. 9, No. 3, 1983, pp. 347–354.

Lee, L., *The Day the Phones Stopped,* Primus, New York, 1992.

Legg, D., "Synopsis of COCOMO," *Software Engineering Project Management,* second edition, R. Thayer, ed., IEEE Computer Society Press, Los Alamitos, CA, 1997, pp. 230–245.

Linnenkugel, U., M. Mullerburg, "Test data selection criteria for (software) integration testing," *Proc. First International Conf. Systems Integration,* April 1990, pp. 709–717.

Lyu, M., A. Nikora, "Applying reliability models more effectively," *IEEE Software,* Vol. 9, No. 4, pp. 43–52, 1992.

Mantei, M., "The effect of programming team structures on programming tasks," *Communications of the ACM,* Vol. 24, No. 3, 1981, pp. 106–113.

Marick, B., *The Craft of Software Testing,* Prentice Hall, Englewood Cliffs, NJ, 1995.

Marks, D., *Testing Very Big Systems,* McGraw-Hill, New York, 1992.

Martin, J., W. Tsai, "N-fold inspection: a requirements analysis technique," *Comm. ACM,* Vol. 33, No. 2, 1990, pp. 225–232.

Masters, S., C. Bothwell, "A CMM appraisal framework, version 1.0," Technical Report, CMU/SEI-95-TR-001, Software Engineering Institute, Pittsburgh, PA, 1995.

Mays, R., "Defect prevention and total quality management," in *Total Quality Management For Software,* G. Schulmeyer, J. McManus, eds., Van Nostrand, Reinhold, NY, 1992.

McCabe, T., G. Schulmeyer, "The Pareto principle applied to software quality assurance," in *Handbook of Software Quality Assurance,* second edition, G. Schulmeyer, J. McManus, eds., Van Nostrand Reinhold, New York, 1992.

McCabe, T., C. Butler, "Design complexity measurement and testing," *CACM,* Vol. 32, No. 12, 1989. pp. 1415–1425.

McCabe, T., "A complexity measure," *IEEE Transactions on Software Engineering,* Vol SE-2, No. 4, 1976, pp. 308–320.

McCall, J., P. Richards, G. Walters, *Factors in Software Quality,* Technical Report 77CIS 02, General Electric, Command and Information Systems, Sunnyvale, CA, 1977.

McGregor, J., A. Kare, "Parallel architecture for component testing of object-oriented software," *Proc. Ninth International Quality Week Conf.,* May 1996.

Mills, C., "Usability testing in the real world," *SIGCHI Bulletin,* Vol. 19, No. 1, pp. 43–46, 1987.

Mills, H., M. Dyer, R. Linger, "Cleanroom software engineering," *IEEE Software,* Vol. 4, No. 5, pp. 19–24, 1987.

Mills, H., "On the statistical validation of computer programs," Technical Report, FSC-72-6015, IBM Federal Systems Division, Gaithersburg, MD, 1972.

Moore, J., "ISO 12207 and related software life cycle standards," http://www.acm.org.tsc/lifecycle.html.

Morell, L. "Theoretical insights into fault-based testing," *Proc. Second Workshop on Software Testing, Verification, and Analysis* (IEEE/ACM/SIGSOFT), Banff, Canada, 1988, pp. 45–62.

Moseley, V., "How to assess tools efficiently and quantitatively," *IEEE Software,* pp. 29–32, May 1993.

Murphy, G., P. Townsend, P. Wong, "Experiences with cluster and class testing," *CACM,* Vol. 37, No. 9, 1994, pp. 39–47.

Musa, J., "Operational profiles in software reliability engineering," *IEEE Software,* Vol. 10, No. 3, pp. 14–32, 1993.

Musa, J., A. Ackerman, "Quantifying software validation: when to stop testing," *IEEE Software,* Vol. 6, No. 3, May 1989.

Musa, J., A Iannino, K. Olomoto, *Software Reliability, Measurement, Prediction Application,* McGraw-Hill, New York, 1987.

Myers, G., "A controlled experiment in program testing and code walk-throughs/inspections," *CACM,* 1978, pp. 760–768.

Myers, G., *The Art of Software Testing,* John Wiley, New York, 1979.

Olsen, K., P. Stall Vinje, "Using the testing maturity model in practical test-planning and postevaluation," EuroSTAR98 Conference, Munich, Germany, 1998.

Osterweil, I., "Strategic directions in software quality," *ACM Computing Surveys,* Vol. 28, No. 4, 1996, pp. 738–750.

Ostrand, T., E. Weyuker, "Data flow–based test adequacy analysis for languages with pointers," *Proc. ACM SIGSOFT Symposium on Testing, Analysis, and Verification,* Oct. 1991, pp. 74–86.

Parrish, A., S. Zweben, "Analysis and refinement of software test data adequacy properties," *IEEE Trans. Software Engineering,* Vol. 17, No. 7, 1991, pp. 565–581.

Paulk, M., C. Weber, B. Curtis, M. Chrissis, *The Capability Maturity Model,* Addison-Wesley, Reading MA., 1995.

Paulk, M., M. Konrad, "An overview of ISO's SPICE project," *American Programmer,* Vol. 7, No. 2, Feb. 1994, pp. 16–20.

Paulk, M., M. Konrad, "An overview of ISO's SPICE project," *American Programmer,* Vol. 7, No. 2, 1994, pp. 16–20.

Paulk, M., B. Curtis, M. Chrissis, and C. Weber, "Capability Maturity Model, version 1.1," *IEEE Software,* Vol. 10, No. 4, 1993, pp. 18–27.

Paulk, M., C. Weber, S. Garcia, M. Chrissis, M. Bush, "Key practices of the Capability Maturity Model, version 1.1," Technical Report, CMU/SEI-93-TR-25, Software Engineering Institute, Pittsburgh, PA, 1993.

Perry. D., G. Kaiser, "Adequate testing and object-oriented programming," *J. Object Oriented Programming,* Vol. 2, No. 5, 1990, pp. 13–19.

Perry, W., *Effective Methods for Software Testing,* John Wiley, New York, 1995.

Pham, H., *Software Reliability and Testing,* IEEE Computer Society Press, Los Alamitos, CA, 1995.

Poston, R., *Automating Specification-Based Software Testing,* IEEE Computer Society Press, Los Alamitos, CA, 1996.

Poston, R., "Testing tools combine best of new and old," *IEEE Software,* Vol. 12, No. 2, 1995, pp. 122–126.

Poston, R., "Automated testing from object models," *Comm. of the ACM,* Vol. 37, No. 9, 1994, pp. 48–58.

Poston, R., M. Sexton, "Evaluating and selecting testing tools," *IEEE Software,* pp. 33–42, May 1992.

Pressman, R., *Software Engineering: A Practitioner's Approach,* fifth edition, McGraw-Hill, Boston, MA, 2001.

Prowell, S., C. Trammell, R. Linger, J. Poore, *Cleanroom Software Engineering,* Addison-Wesley, Reading, MA, 1999.

Puffer, J., A. Litter, "Action planning," *IEEE Software Engineering Technical Council Newsletter,* Vol. 15, No. 2, 1997, pp. 7–10.

Putman, D., "Using statistical process control with automated test programs," *CrossTalk: The Journal of Defense Software Engineering,* Vol. 11, No. 8, August 1998, pp. 16–20.

Quilici, A., "A memory-based approach to recognizing program plans," *CACM,* Vol. 37, No. 5, 1994, pp. 84–93.

Rakos, J., *Software Project Management for Small- to Medium-Sized Projects,* Prentice Hall, Englewood Cliffs, NJ, 1990.

Rangaraajan, K., P. Eswar, T. Ashok, "Retesting C++ classes," *Proc. Ninth International Quality Week Conf.,* May 1996.

Rapps, S., E. Weyuker, "Selecting software test data using data flow information," *IEEE Trans. Software Engineering,* Vol. 11, No. 4, 1985, pp. 367–375.

Richards, F., *Computer Software: Testing, Reliability Models and Quality Assurance,* Technical Report, NPS-55RH74071A, Naval Postgraduate School, Monterey, CA, 1974.

Roper, M., *Software Testing,* McGraw-Hill, London, 1994.

Roper, T., *Software Testing Management: Life on the Critical Path,* Prentice Hall, Englewood Cliffs, NJ, 1993.

Rubin, J., *Handbook of Usability Testing,* John Wiley, New York, 1994.

Sauer, C., D. Jeffery, L. Land, P. Yetton, "The effectiveness of software development technical reviews: a behaviorally motivated program of research," *IEEE Transactions on Software Engineering,* Vol. 26, No. 1, 2000, pp. 1–14.

Saxena, G., "A framework for building and evaluating process maturity models," Ph.D. thesis, Illinois Institute of Technology, Chicago, IL, 1999.

Schell, D., "Overview of a typical usability test," *Proc. International Professional Communications Conf.,* Winnipeg, pp. 117–125, 1987.

Schulmeyer, G., "Software quality assurance metrics," in *Handbook of Software Quality Assurance,* G. Schulmeyer and J. McManus, eds., Van Nostrand Reinhold, New York, 1992.

Schulmeyer, G., "The move to zero defect software," in *Handbook of Software Quality Assurance,* second edition, G. Schulmeyer, J. McManus, eds., Van Nostrand Reinhold, New York, 1992.

Schulmeyer, G., "Software quality lessons from the quality experts," in *Handbook of Software Quality Assurance,* second edition, G. Schulmeyer, J. McManus, eds., Van Nostrand Reinhold, New York, 1992.

Sheldon, F., K. Kavi, R. Tausworthe, J. Yu, R. Brettschneider, W. Everett, "Reliability measurement: from theory to practice," *IEEE Software,* Vol. 9, No. 4, pp. 13–20, July 1992.

Shrum, S., "Choosing a CMMI model representation," *CrossTalk: Jour-*

nal of Department of Defense Software Engineering, Vol. 13, No. 7, July 2000, pp. 6–7.

Smith, M., D. Robson, "A framework for testing object-oriented programs," *J. Object Oriented Programming,* June 1992, pp. 45–53.

Shooman, M., *Software Engineering: Design, Reliability and Management,* McGraw-Hill, New York, 1983.

Speed, J., "What do you mean I can't call myself a software engineer?" *IEEE Software,* Nov./Dec. 1999, pp. 45–50.

Spencer, B., "Software inspections at applicon," *CrossTalk: Journal of Defense Software Engineering,* Vol. 7, No. 10, Oct. 1994, pp. 11–17.

Subramaniam, B., "Effective software defect tracking: reducing project costs and enhancing quality," *CrossTalk: The Journal of Defense Software Engineering,* Vol. 12, No. 4, April, 1999, pp. 3–9.

Sullivan, P., "Beyond a narrow conception of usability testing," *IEEE Transactions on Professional Communications,* Vol. 32, No. 4, pp. 256–264, 1989.

Suwannasart, T., "Towards the development of a testing maturity model," Ph.D. thesis, Illinois Institute of Technology, Chicago, IL, 1996.

Thayer, R., ed., *Software Engineering Project Management,* second edition, IEEE Computer Society Press, Los Alamitos, CA, 1997.

Tian, J. L. Peng, "Test-execution-based reliability measurement and modeling for large commercial software," *IEEE Transactions on Software Engineering,* Vol. 21, No. 5, 1995, pp. 405–414.

Tichy, W., "Design, implementation, and evaluation of a revision control system," *Proc. Sixth International Conf. Software Engineering,* 1982, pp. 58–67.

Tsai, B., S. Stobart, N. Parrington, I. Mitchell, "A state-based testing approach providing data flow coverage in object-oriented class testing," *Proc. Twelfth International Quality Week Conf.,* May 1999.

Voas, J., "Certification: reducing the hidden costs of poor quality," *IEEE Software,* July/August 1999, pp. 22–25.

Voas, J., "Certifying off-the-shelf software components," *IEEE Computer,* June 1998, pp. 53–59.

Voas, J., "A dynamic failure model for propagation and infection analysis on computer programs," Ph.D. Thesis, College of William and Mary in Virginia, May 1990.

Wakid, S., D. Kuhn, D. Wallace, "Toward credible IT testing and certification," *IEEE Software,* July/August 1999, pp. 39–47.

Walton, G., J. Poore, C. Trammell, "Statistical testing of software based on a usage model," *Software: Practice and Experience,* Vol. 25, No. 1, 1995, pp. 97–108.

Weiser, M., "Programmers use slices when debugging," *CACM,* Vol. 25, No. 7, 1982, pp. 446–452.

Weller, E., "Using metrics to manage software projects," *IEEE Software,* Vol. 9, No. 5, 1994, pp. 27–32.

Weller, E., "Practical applications of statistical process control," *IEEE Software,* Vol. 14, No. 3, 2000, pp. 48–55.

Weszka, J., P. Babel, J. Ferguson, "CMMI: evolutionary path to enterprise process improvement," *CrossTalk: Journal of Department of Defense Software Engineering,* Vol. 13, No. 7, July 2000, pp. 8–11.

Weyuker, E., T. Ostrand, J. Brophy, R. Prasad, "Clearing a career path for software testers," *IEEE Software,* Vol. 17, No. 2, March/April 2000, pp. 76–82.

Weyuker, E., "The evaluation of program-based software test adequacy criteria," *CACM,* Vol. 31, No. 6, 1988, pp. 668–675.

Weyuker, E., "Axiomatizing software test data adequacy," *IEEE Trans. Software Engineering,* Vol. 12, No. 12, 1986, pp. 1128–1138.

Whittaker, J., "What is software testing? and why is it so hard?" *IEEE Software,* Jan./Feb. 2000, pp. 70–79.

Wilde, N., "Testing your objects," *The C Users Journal,* May 1993, pp. 25–32.

Wigle, G., G. Yamamura, "Practices of an SEI CMM level 5 SEPG," *CrossTalk: The Journal of Defense Software Engineering*, Vol. 10, No. 11, Nov. 1997, pp. 19–22.

Wilkins, B., *Principles of Testing in VSLI Circuits and Systems in Silicon*, A. Brown, ed., McGraw-Hill, New York, 1991, pp. 222–250.

Zawacki, R., "How to pick eagles," *Datamation Magazine*, Sept. 1995, pp. 115–16.

Zeitler, D., "Realistic assumptions for software reliably models," *Proc. International Symp. Software Reliability Eng.*, IEEE Press, Los Alamitos, CA, pp. 67–74, 1991.

Zells, L., "Learning from Japanese TQM applications to software engineering," *Total Quality Management for Software*, G. Schulmeyer, J. McManus, eds., Van Nostrand Reinhold, New York, 1992.

Zhu, H., "A formal analysis of the subsume relation between software test adequacy criteria," *IEEE Transactions on Software Engineering*, Vol. 22, No. 4, 1996, pp. 248–255.

Zhu, H., P. Hall, J. May, "Software unit test coverage and adequancy," *ACM Computing Surveys*, Vol. 29, No. 4, 1997, pp. 366–427.

Zubrow, D., W. Hayes, J. Siegel, D. Goldenson, "Maturity questionnaire," Technical Report, CMU/SEI-94-SR-7, Software Engineering Institute, Pittsburgh, PA, 1994.

SAMPLE TEST PLAN

This appendix contains an abbreviated version of a system test plan that was developed for instructional purposes. It will illustrate for the reader the contents of several of the major components of a typical test plan. Test plan attachments are not included in this example.

For pedagogical purposes, the software to be tested is an automated course scheduling system called the "College Course Scheduler (CCS)," which is under development for a local college. The proposed client is South Central College. The college offers bachelors and masters degree programs, and both undergraduate and graduate courses are listed in its catalog and course schedules. The dean of the college is the principle liaison to the development group called Windy City Developers Corporation. The users are departmental administrative assistants and chairpersons, and the college registrar.

Project Background

Currently the class scheduling is done manually based on college-based policies. Each instructor specifies in writing the courses he or she prefers to teach for the given semester, and his or her time-of-day preferences for lecture and laboratory sessions. The preferences as input by the instructor must be valid courses and lecture times, which are specified for each department. The written preferences are submitted to the administrative assistant in the department who does the manual scheduling. If an instructor does not submit a written list of preferences, the courses are scheduled without preferences. The final schedule lists each course offered, the instructor, the class time, and the room. Unschedulable items are listed in a separate report. Hard copies of the final schedule are sent to each instructor.

When manually scheduling, the administrative assistant must be sure that the following rules are adhered to:

1. the classroom is large enough to hold the enrolled students;
2. a slot for a room is given to only one course;
3. graduate-level courses are given preference over undergraduate courses;
4. no two graduate courses can be scheduled at the same time.

General Project Overview

Based on interviews with client groups, the automated course scheduler will operate as follows. Instructor preferences for courses, time slots, and special needs should be emailed to the administrative assistants of their respective departments in a timely manner (5 weeks into the current semester to schedule for the next semester). The administrative assistants will sort the preferences in order of the time received and store them in a formatted file. If an instructor does not respond with specific needs by the designated deadline, courses will be assigned based on past schedules, and these courses will have no time preferences.

The course scheduling system will have a database of rooms for each campus building, number of seats in each room, and special features in each room such as a pull-down screen, microphones, and TV equipment for remote broadcasting. It will also have a database of instructors (and their email addresses) and the courses they have taught over a 5-year period, the time slots (total minutes) normally allocated for each of the classes taught at the college, and estimated enrollments for the courses. When the administrative assistant (or chairperson) submits the file of preferences at the end of the fifth week of the semester (to schedule for the upcoming semester) the system produces a report listing all of the classes assigned for this semester, the instructors, the class time period, and a room number. The scheduling algorithm must adhere to the four rules described previously. Each faculty member is emailed a copy of the report and also receives a hard copy to confirm the correctness of the schedule and to address any errors. The schedules from all the departments are published in the collegewide course schedule for each semester that is distributed to all students.

Administrative assistants, department chairs, and the registrar can query the system to retrieve information on course offerings, classrooms, course time slots, and so on. Chairpersons and administrative assistants can make changes to the databases associated with their departments. Course schedules dating back through a 7-year period will also be stored in the system database, and users can query for this information as well.

The system should be user friendly; all users should be computer literate. The system should run on a work station with access to a server and print reports on all types of printers. It will have to interface with an email facility to collect preferences and to notify instructors.

System Requirements

The following is an abbreviated description of the project requirements.

CCS-REQ-1. Scheduling Reports

The CCS system should produce a schedule report for each department initiated by a request from a departmental chair or administrative assistant. The schedule should list each course, the course number, instructor, lecture times, and room number. Unscheduled courses should be listed in a separate report along with the reasons—for example, a conflict with another course, no room with proper capacity. The scheduling algorithm requires information from a database of room numbers for each department, their capacity, and special features. Databases of courses from the department catalogs, valid lecture times, and course instructors are also part of the system. The departmental schedule report should be emailed to appropriate faculty; it can be printed and is also saved in a file for use in printing the collegewide course schedule that is assembled by the college registrar.

CCS-REQ-2. Preferencing Inputs

The system should accept a file input by the departmental administrative assistant or chair, listing course numbers offered for the semester, instructors, expected enrollments, and a set of lecture time preferences.

CCS-REQ-3. Querying

Users should be able to query the system for courses, instructors, room information, and past preferences. The system should also save scheduling information over the last 7 years for inspection by users.

CCS-RE4. E-mail Notification

The system should have the ability to email a scheduling report to each faculty member in each department.

CCS-REQ-5. User Interface

The system should be menu-driven and easy to learn. A Help facility is required, and users should get feedback on system activities. The system should give helpful feedback in the case of user errors.

CCS-REQ-6. Performance

Issuing a scheduling report for 20 courses, each with up to 5 preferences, should take no longer than 1 minute. Queries should take no longer than 1 minute to retrieve system information, assuming that there are 200 courses listed in the college catalog (not all are offered each semester), 75 instructors (full and part time), 12 departments, and 200 rooms on campus. Currently there are 12 chairpersons, one registrar, and 24 administrative assistants. The maximum number of simultaneous users is estimated at 15. Only one person in each department can request a scheduling run at a given time. Updates to a departmental schedule are allowed up to the designated completion date. After that date only the registrar can make any changes.

CCS-REQ-7. Security

The system should be secure, and only authorized users be granted access. There are two levels of users: (i) the college registrar who is the system administrator, and (ii) the departmental administrative assistants and chairpersons. The registrar has all system privileges. All users may generate schedules and formulate queries. In addition, users in each department can maintain (add, delete, modify) the appropriate data in the databases associated with their respective department. Users may not alter information from outside departments. The South Central College registrar is responsible for adding, deleting, and modifying user records, and assigning user privileges.

CCS-REQ-8. Database Administration

Users should have the ability to view, modify, add, and delete information from the system databases appropriate to their departments, and access level.

CCS-REQ-9. Hardware and Software Constraints

The CCS System should run on a network of UNIX-based workstations. A central server will contain the necessary databases and querying capabilities.

COLLEGE COURSE SCHEDULER (CCS) SYSTEM TEST PLAN

for

SOUTH CENTRAL COLLEGE

PREPARED BY

Jane Smith, Test Group Manager
Windy City Development Corporation

JANUARY 15, 2001

Contents

1. Test Plan Identifier

CCS-WCD-2001-4

2. Introduction

The following sections describe the nature of the system under test, the test objectives, and the scope. A list of related documents is also provided.

2.1. Nature of the Project

The College Course Scheduler (CCS) is being developed for the client organization, South Central College. The system will automate the process of course scheduling for the college, a tedious task that previously has been performed manually by departmental administrative assistants. Course scheduling is an important task for the college that is performed every semester to place instructors and students in classrooms that meet their needs. The client expects that the CCS system will perform the task more efficiently, accurately, and securely than the current manual system. It will relieve the chairpersons and administrative assistants from a time-consuming task and allow them to devote their time to other important matters that occur before each semester begins.

Delivering a high-quality software system is important to the client, since they will be depending on the software to implement a major operation that is vital to the institution. Windy City is a relatively new software development firm (established 1990), and it is important to us to deliver a fully functional CCS system on time, within budget, and of a high quality in terms of functionally, performance, security, and robustness. A very low rate of failure is our goal.

Windy City's test process has been assessed at TMM level 3, which means that we have a dedicated and trained test group, test policies are in place, we have a test planning process, and we are familiar with basic testing techniques. We also have the staff, training, and tools in place to insure that the CCS software will be evaluated effectively with respect to the required functional and quality attributes.

2.2. System Test Objectives and Scope

This test plan describes the environment, activities, tasks, tools, costs, and schedules for system testing the College Course Scheduler (CCS) system being developed for South Central College by Windy City Development Our objective for system testing are to insure that:

- all the required functionalities, of the CCS are in place and are working correctly according to the client's requirements;

- the software meets its performance requirements;

- the software is reliable and robust; it can recover gracefully from failures;

- the software is easy to use and maintain;

- the software is secure;

- it interfaces properly with the required external software and hardware.

A full set of system tests will be performed including:

functional testing (input of preferences, scheduling with preferences, scheduling without preferences, inability to schedule, report generation, querying, database updates, communication links, system administration)

performance testing (response time for queries and reports)

stress testing (maximum number of users and maximum number of scheduling transactions)

security testing (login, and access rights).

2.3. Related Documents
The following documents are being used as sources of information for the development of this test plan.

CCS Requirements Document (CCS-REQ-1-2001)
CCS Software Quality Assurance Plan (CCS-SQA-P-1-2001)
Windy City System Test Plan Template (STP-T-5-1995)
CCS Configuration Management Plan (CCS-CMP-1-2001)
Windy City Test Policy and Procedure Document (TPP-2-1995)
CCS Project Management Plan (CCS-SPMP-2-2001)

CCS Design Specification Document (CCS-DS-3-2001)
CCS Master Test Plan (CCS-MTP-3-2001)

The following are test-related documents that will be prepared for the CCS system and can be used as information sources for the system test planners.

CCS Unit Test Plan (CCS-UTP-4-2001)
CCS Integration Test Plan (CCS-ITP-4-2001)
CCS Acceptance Test Plan (CCS-ATP-5-2001)
CCS Usability Test Plan (CCS-UTP-12-3-2001)

3. Items to Be Tested

All of items that constitute the College Course Scheduler (CCS) system will be tested during the system test to insure that they work together to implement the client's requirements. These items are listed below with their identification number, version number, and source code library. These items constitute the testable configuration for the CCS software.

NAME	IDENTIFIER	LIBRARY	VERSION NUMBER
main	CCS-1	Main_lib	2.3
get_val_input_file	CCS-2	Input_lib	1.1
validate_file	CCS-3	Input_lib	1.2
validate_rooms	CCS-4	Input_lib	1.2
validate-courses	CCS-5	Input_lib	1.3
validate_lec_times	CCS-6	Input_lib	2.1
get_course_index	CCS-7	Input_lib	2.2
get-val_preferences	CCS-8	Input_lib	2.2
form_course_record	CCS-9	Input_lib	1.3
separate-courses	CCS-10	Input_lib	1.4
schedule	CCS-11	Input_lib	1.5
get_room_index	CCS-11	Input_lib	1.5
sched_ug_prefs	CCS-12	Input_lib	2.3
sched_gr_prefs	CCS-13	Input_lib	2.4
sched_ug_no_pref	CCS-14	Input_lib	2.3
sched_gr_no_prefs	CCS-15	Input_lib	1.1
output	CCS-16	Output_lib	1.1

print_schedule	CCS-17	Output_lib	2.3
e-mail_schedule	CCS-18	Output_lib	1.5
print_no_schedule	CCS-19	Output_lib	1.5
query	CCS-20	Query_lib	2.1
form_query	CCS-21	Query_lib	2.1
database_admin	CCS-22	Database_lib	1.1
sys_admin	CCS-23	Admin_lib	1.1
login	CCS-24	Admin_lib	2.1
select_options	CCS-25	Admin_lib	2.1
help	CCS-26	Help_lib	2.2

4. Features to Be Tested

The following is a list of the features to be tested along with their design specification identifier.

FEATURE	DESIGN SPECIFICATION IDENTIFIER
Scheduling with preferences	CCS-DS-3-2001-1
Scheduling without preferences	CCS-DS-3-2001-2
Report—printing	CCS-DS-3-2001-3
Report—emailing	CCS-DS-3-2001-4
Submitting preferences	CCS-DS-3-2001-5
Preferences	CCS-DS-3-2001-6
Security	CCS-DS-3-2001-7
Querying	CCS-DS-3-2001-8
Multiple users	CCS-DS-3-2001-9
Response-time reports	CCS-DS-3-2001-10
Database administration	CCS-DS-3-2001-11
Interface	CCS-DS-3-2001-12
Help	CCS-DS-3-2001-13
System administration	CCS-DS-3-2001-14

Configuration and recovery tests will not be performed for this release due to time constraints. Future releases will undergo such tests. Usability testing is covered in the CCS-Usability Test Plan (CCS-UTP-12-3-2001).

5. Approach

Windy City Software is a TMM level 3 organization. We have a dedicated and trained testing group, and have the resources and environment necessary to test all software that we develop to insure high quality and adherence to our clients' requirements. The College Course Schedule system will be tested thoroughly on several levels (refer to related documents under Section 2.3). System-level tests will be thorough and extensive. All items will be tested to insure they work together correctly; all features and requirements will be tested to insure they meet user needs. A requirements-to-test tracer will be used to insure all requirements are covered by at least one test case. Templates for test design and test case specifications are found in the Windy City Test Policy and Procedure document TTP-2-1995. The test cases and design specifications, as well as any test scripts that are prepared, will be saved in a test repository for use in future releases.

5.1. Sources of Sample Domain Data and Test Oracles

The Dean of South Central College will assist in providing typical scheduling inputs and outputs, rooms, courses, enrollments, and other necessary college-related information for the test database. Expected usage patterns will also be described. Input data from the past six semesters will be used, and the schedules generated will be compared to the existing schedules to help in evaluating the system.

5.2. Staff

Two test engineers, Prerek Patel and Sally Jordan, will be responsible for test case design, test execution, and recording of results. They will be supervised by Jane Smith, test manager, and Jonathan Boyd, lead test engineer. All have at least 5 years experience in testing similar systems and have had in-house training in the application of test design techniques and testing tool usage.

5.3. Record Keeping

All events observed during execution will be recorded in a test log that will be associated with each test. All failures will assigned a severity level and be recorded in a test incident/problem report. A tally of the number of the latter reports will be recorded. The formats for test logs and test incident/problem reports are described in the Windy City Test Policy and Procedure document, TTP-2-1995. All defects revealed during system test will be recorded in the defect repository. The number of defects found (by type and severity level) per KLOC in each type of system test will also be recorded for quality evaluation. Tester productivity will be monitored using a measure of the number of test cases developed per week, and the number of test cases executed per week.

5.4. Test Status

System testing will be monitored through weekly test status meetings. Plots and summary reports will be prepared by Jane Smith and Jonathan Boyd. The number of requirements covered per week versus the total number of requirements will be one of the items plotted to track testing progress. Other items to be plotted include the number of defects of a specific severity level found per week. Measurements, plots and templates associated with test status reports are described in the Windy City Test Policy and Procedures standard document, TTP-2-1995. Testing costs will be monitored using earned values as described in Windy City Test Policy and Procedures document, TTP-2-1995.

5.5. Test Tools

The following tools will be used to support the system testing effort. All testing personnel involved in this project have been trained and have experience in using these tools. The role of these tools is described in the Windy City Test Policy and Procedures document, TTP-2-1995.

Support Tools for System Testing CCS

Configuration management tool
Configuration building tool
Requirements-to-test-tracer
Capture-replay tool/comparator
Defect tracker
Performance testing tool
Load generator

5.6. Stop-Test Criteria

A decision to stop system testing will be based on tracking (i) coverage of all the requirements, and (ii) the number of open incident/problem reports. We will consider system test to be completed when all the requirements have been covered by at least one test case, and no incident/problem reports with associated defect severity levels of 1–3 (catastrophic-moderate impact) are outstanding. We accept the risk that the software may still contain low severity level defects that have a minimal effect on the users.

5.7. Types of System Tests

FUNCTIONAL TESTING. All functional requirements as described in the CCS Requirements Document (CCS-REQ-1-2001) will be evaluated. The following black box test design techniques will be used:

1. equivalence class partitioning and boundary-value analysis (ECP/ BVA);
2. state transition testing.

In general, functional tests will be designed using ECP/BVA to insure that all classes of legal inputs—for example, correct courses, time preferences, and instructors—are accepted by the software and that illegal inputs are rejected. In the case of the latter, the system must remain functional. All possible classes of system outputs will be exercised and examined; for example, all types of scheduling reports of various sizes and for representative departments will be generated and printed. Test cases indicating no preferences, and those resulting in conflicts or inability to schedule, will also be designed. The ability to email schedules to faculty members from representative departments will also be tested. The help facility will be evaluated with requests for help on inputting preferences, generating queries, updating departmental databases, and generating a schedule. The system administration function will be evaluated with respect to adding, deleting and modifying user information, and proper assignment of user access rights.

All effective system states and state transitions will be exercised and examined; for example, the inputting preferences state, the report generation state, the entering a new user state. The system state transition diagram as found in CCS Requirements Document (CCS-REQ-1-2001) will be used as an information source for test design. Input data from manual scheduling operations will also serve as a source for designing test data, and schedules obtained from these manual operations will be used as oracles to evaluate the system outputs. Test design specifications and test cases are found in attachments to this test plan.

PERFORMANCE TESTING. The critical performance requirements are expressed in terms of time required for report generation and response time for queries. The system will be tested with preferences and course data from the smallest department—philosophy—and the largest department—computer science—to determine report generation time. Queries will be formulated based on typical inputs supplied by the college dean. Response times will be recorded. Average numbers of simulated scheduling transactions and queries will also be used to evaluate performance with multiple users.

SECURITY TESTING. Tests will be run using legal and illegal user names and passwords to insure that unauthorized users do not have access to the system, and that each type of user has access to the allowed system features appropriate for his/her security level. Tests representing the adding, modifying, and deleting of users will also be designed. Testers will attempt to identify any trap doors that allow unauthorized users to access the system. This will be implemented by allowing Tom White and John Li, testers not formally assigned to the test group for this project, to serve as a "tiger team." In this capacity they will attempt to "break-into" the software using any means they devise. All attempts will be documented and the results logged.

STRESS TESTING. Stress testing is important for the CCS system to uncover race conditions, deadlocks, depletion of resources in unusual or unplanned patterns, and upsets in the normal operation of the software system. System limits and threshold values will be exercised. Several departmental users may access the CCS at the same time, placing a heavy load of scheduling transactions and queries on system resources. This is most likely to occur during the fifth week of each semester, when scheduling for the next semester must be done. The average number of users is estimated to be 15. During stress testing, inputs from 25 users will be simulated and system behavior observed. Tools will monitor CPU usage, number of system calls, interrupts, and other system characteristics to determine if any abnormal events have occurred. System parameters will be tuned to maximize efficiency.

REGRESSION TESTING. This is *not* a type of system test but constitutes a retesting of code when changes are made. Regression testing for the CCS system will be conducted when changes are made due to defect repairs. The regression testing will be done by running all of the tests on the new version of the code that were run on the old version and then comparing results. A capture-replay tool will be used to run and rerun the tests where feasible, and its associated comparator will be used to compare resulting files.

6. Pass/Fail Criteria

The Windy City Test Policy and Procedure document, TTP-2-1995, describes a scale of severity levels for faults and failures. The scale ranges in values from 1 to 4 where 1 is a failure that has a catastrophic effect on the system/users to a value of 4 which indicates a minimal effect on the system/user. For the CCS software system a test will be considered as a pass if the failure observed is rated at a level of 3 or 4. That means that testing may continue; however all of the failures and associated defects must be recorded and addressed. Test incident reports and problem/defect reports are to be completed for all failures observed. All failures should be forwarded to development and prioritized for subsequent repair, followed by regression testing by the test group.

7. Suspend/Resume Criteria

Normally testing will be suspended at the end of the work day. All test-related documents must be submitted to Jane Smith. Testing is resumed the following work day morning. In addition, testing will be suspended if:

(i)   a failure of severity level 1 or 2 is observed;
(ii) the system is unable to accept a valid input file;
(iii) the system is unable to produce a schedule;
(iv) a hardware failure occurs.

When the defect causing a software failure is repaired, the new version of the software will undergo a regression test. If the new version passes the regression test, then normal testing can resume.

If during system test there is a hardware failure, the tester will notify the appropriate staff members and resume testing when the repairs are made, restarting from the beginning of the test set.

8. Test Deliverables

The following items will be generated by the system test group for this project. A detailed description of each item is contained in the Windy City Test Policy and Procedure document, TTP-2-1995.

System test plan (copy to client)
System test design specifications
System test case specifications
System test procedure specifications
System test logs
System test incident reports
System test summary report
Test scripts (from use of the capture-replay tool)
Test data

- input and output files, screens, and reports resulting from functional tests;

- input, and output data from performance and stress tests;

- security test inputs and results;

- query input screens and results.

Inputs for all tests are found in attachments to the system test plan. The test plan and test plan attachments will be placed under the control of the Windy City Configuration Management System (see CCS Configuration Management Plan, CCS-CMP-1-2001).

9. Testing Tasks

A testing task list is found in an attachment to this system test plan. It was prepared by developing a work breakdown structure for test-related tasks required by the CCS project. The attachment lists each testing task as shown below, its predecessor tasks, special skills needed to carry out the task, person responsible, effort required, and completion date.

List of Testing Tasks:

- preparing the test plan and attachments;
- preparing the test design specifications;
- preparing the test case specifications;
- interviews with the south Central College Dean to obtain examples of previous schedules, preferences, and other college-related data needed to prepare test inputs and to set up the database needed for testing;
- tracking test transmittal reports;
- preparing test scripts and setting up the tools;
- executing the functional tests and recording results;
- executing the performance and stress tests; recording results;
- executing the security and regression tests; recording results;
- regression testing; recording results;
- transmitting test-related documents to the configuration management group;
- supervising the testing staff and organizing test-related measurements;

- preparing for, and attending, test status meetings;

- preparing the test status and test summary reports.

10. The Testing Environment

HARDWARE REQUIREMENTS. Five UNIX workstations networked together; a central server with an Oracle database capability. The test database must be prepared using South Central College data relating to departments, courses offered, instructors, rooms, enrollments, and special needs.

SOFTWARE TOOL REQUIREMENTS. To test this system we will use the capture-replay tool currently in use by the testing group with a comparator capability. Software probes developed in-house will be used to monitor hardware/software system attributes during performance and stress testing. A load generator will be used to simulate interactions from multiple users.

11. Responsibilities

Since our organization is at TMM level 3 we have a dedicated testing group. The test group members responsible for system testing the College Course Scheduler system are:

- Jane Smith, test manager

- Jonathan Boyd, lead test engineer.

- Prerek Patel, test engineer

- Sally Jordan, test engineer

- Tom White and John Li are not formally associated with the testing group for this project, but will assist in security testing.

The two test engineers, Prerek Patel and Sally Jordan, will be responsible for test design specification, test case and test procedure design, test execution, and recording of results. They will be supervised by Jane Smith, test manager, and Jonathan Boyd, lead test engineer, who are also responsible for developing the test plan, supporting test case design, managing test-related documents and measurements, managing the test status meeting, and developing test status reports and the final test summary report. They will also meet with the college dean to collect the necessary course data and to identify typical usage scenarios. An attachment describes in detail the testing responsibilities for these staff members.

The CCS development group is responsible for responding to the test incident/problem reports. This group will locate, repair defects, and log defects. They will return the repaired code to the testers for regression and other required tests. The group also supports testers with the task of maintaining the defect repository,

12. Staffing and Training Needs

Staff members required for the system testing effort are listed in Section 11 of this test plan and in an attachment to this test plan. We are a TMM level 3 organization. All of our testing staff has had training in the development of test design, test case, and test procedure specifications. They have the necessary training in test tool usage, and also have had experience in test planning, so no additional training for this project is required.

13. Scheduling

Task durations and schedules are described in detail in an attachment to this test plan. The project should be ready for acceptance test by XX/YY/0Z. This will allow the system to be installed so that it is ready for scheduling for the Spring 200Z semester.

14. Risks and Contingencies

1. The college dean is required to travel extensively and may not be available to the testing group. If the college dean is not available to interface with the test team to provide data for the test database, usage information, and past schedules, then the assistant dean will be available to the group and will supply the needed information.

2. Conflict of staffing responsibilities. Jonathan Boyd, the lead test engineer, may be required to work on a more urgent project (ABC-51-17-03) currently in production. Sally Jordan has the experience and training to serve as a lead test engineer if this circumstance occurs. Sue Chan, a member of the organizational test group, will replace Sally as a test engineer.

3. Delays in the testing effort. If the testing schedule is significantly impacted by high severity level defects, an additional developer will be assigned to the project to perform fault localization. In addition, Mike Smith, an experienced tester, has a light assignment during this time period and will be available if extra tester power is needed.

15. System Test Costs

Our organization has been assessed at TMM level 3 with respect to its testing process. This implies that we have a stable and predictable testing process, a trained staff, and available testing tools. In addition, we also have an extensive database of past project test costs. The CCS project is typical of the many applications we have developed in the past, and for which we have collected relevant test-related data. We estimate that test costs impact items for the CCS project will be similar to those of past projects, and we are confident that we can use past approaches/heuristics to help estimate testing costs for the CCS system. Our confidence is based on:

- the nature of this project which is not complex (it has no mission- or safety-critical features);

- the similarity to projects we have successfully developed in the past;

- our relatively stable testing process and highly skilled testing group;

- minimal tool and training costs due to our level of testing maturity.

In the past we have had success in using the COCOMO model to estimate total costs for this type of project using a set of constants generated from internal data. We then apply the heuristic developed by our organization that system test costs for this type of project will be 34.5%

of the total cost of the project. In this case, an overall cost estimation for the entire project has been derived using the COCOMO model as well as the Delphi method. The two agree within a margin of 5.3 %. The total cost of the project is estimated to be $ABC. Therefore, the total cost for the system tests is ABC * .345 dollars.

16. Approvals

JANE SMITH

Test Manager

_____   _____
SIGNATURE   DATE

CHRIS PADILLA

Project Manager

_____   _____
SIGNATURE   DATE

TIM RUBIN

Software Quality Assurance Manager

_____   _____
SIGNATURE   DATE

APPENDIX III

TESTING MATURITY MODEL

Part 1:

THE TMM QUESTIONNAIRE

Part 2:

TMM ACTIVITIES, TASKS, AND RESPONSIBILITIES

This appendix has two parts. Part 1 contains the complete TMM Questionnaire. Part 2 contains the complete set of Activities, Tasks and Responsibilities (ATRs) recommended for each level of the TMM.

PART 1 • THE TMM QUESTIONNAIRE

This part of Appendix III contains the complete contents of the TMM Questionnaire document, version 2.0. The TMM Questionnaire has eight sections. The contents of each section are described below.

SECTION 1. Instructions for the respondent.
SECTION 2. Respondent identification and background.
SECTION 3. Organizational background.

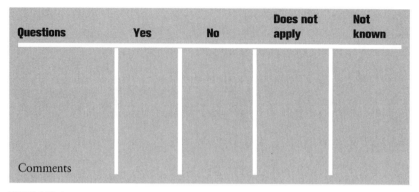

TABLE AIII.1
Questionnaire template.

SECTION 4. The TMM questions. For each TMM level there is:

    (i)   the set of maturity goals;

    (ii) the set of maturity subgoals associated with each maturity goal;

    (iii) the set of questions associated with each maturity goal.

Each question has four possible answers as shown in the questionnaire template form shown above (Table AIII.1). The respondent should answer either YES, NO, DOES NOT APPLY, OR NOT KNOWN. The respondent can also enter comments relating to each question in the space provided

SECTION 5. Testing tool questions.
SECTION 6. Testing trends questions.
SECTION 7. Comments from respondents.
SECTION 8. Glossary of terms.

Section 1. Instructions for the Respondent

Please read and answer the following questions carefully using the knowledge and experience gained from working on current projects in your organization. Many of the technical terms are defined in the glossary section of this document. If you wish to comment on any of the questions or qualify your answers, please use the comment space provided. Your answers will be held in confidence.

For the maturity goal questions found in Section 4, four possible choices are offered as follows:

1. **YES.** Check when a practice is well established and consistently performed.
2. **NO.** Check when the practice is not well established or is inconsistently performed.
3. **DOES NOT APPLY.** Check when you have the required knowledge of the project or organization, but you believe that the question does not apply to the project or organization.
4. **NOT KNOWN.** Check when you are uncertain as to how to answer this question, or you do not have the proper information or experience.

Only one of the choices for each question should be selected, and all of the questions should be considered. Please continue on to the remainder of the questionnaire, and thank you for your help.

Section 2. Respondent Identification and Background

In evaluating the TMM data it will help assessors to have information about the software engineering background, technical skills, and the current duties of each respondent.

1. Respondent Identification

    Name
    Position
    Project Name
    Telephone
    Email
    Date

2. Respondent Background
    Which best describes your current position?

    Manager
    Senior or upper management
    Project manager

Test manager
Software quality assurance group leader
Software engineering process group leader
Test-related subgroup leader (*please specify the name of the subgroup*)
Other (*please specify*)

Technical Staff
Software engineer
Test engineer
Programmer (developer)
Analyst
Software quality assurance group member
Software engineering process group member
Test-related subgroup member (*please specify*)
Other (*please specify*)

3. Current Duties and Responsibilities

Which test-related activities are you actively engaged in (you can check more than one)?

Test policy and goal development
Test planning
Test case and test procedure design
Test execution
Collection and analysis of test-related measurements
Defect data collection
Maintenance of defect database
Standards development
Reviews and audits
Status tracking
Training
Metrics definition
Hiring and recruiting
User/client communications
Process control
Defect prevention
Technology transfer
Process assessment

Process improvement
Reliability modeling and engineering
Usability testing
Tool evaluation
Process reuse

4. Have you received any TMM training?

Yes (*please describe*)
No

5. What is the extent of your experience in the software industry?

Your present organization	Number of years
Overall industry experience	Number of years
Overall testing experience	Number of years

6. Have you participated in other types of software testing appraisals?

Yes (*please describe*)
No

Section 3. Organizational Background

1. Describe as best you can the type of your organization.

Develops military software
Develops application software
Develops telecommunication software
Software quality assurance/software testing/certification
Other (*please describe*)

2. Is the majority (greater than 50%) of the software developed for internal or external use?

Internal   External   Doesn't apply

3. How many people are employed in the organization being assessed?

Total number of employees
Number engaged in software development and/or maintenance
Number engaged in software testing

4. Please describe the percent of staff engaged in testing as follows:

   Full time
   Part time
   Consultants

5. Are the people involved in process improvement in your organization well respected with regard to their technical and management skills? (Please circle one: 1 means no respect and 5 means highly respected.)

   1   2   3   4   5

6. Are the responsibilities for test process improvement clearly defined and supported? (Please circle one: 1 means not defined nor supported, and 5 means well defined and supported.)

   1   2   3   4   5

7. Does the organization under assessment have a software engineering process group or a similar unit?

   Yes   No

8. How is the testing group organized? (please select one)

   Developers do the testing
   Test group within development, report to project manager
   Separate test group, report to test manager
   Part of Software Quality Assurance group

9. How would you generally characterize the nature of your testing process?

   Ad Hoc
   Informal
   Somewhat structured
   Highly structured

10. How frequently do project managers have to meet the challenges of changing customer requirements?

    Never   Rarely   Frequently   Very frequently

Section 4. Maturity Goal Questions

Please answer each of the following questions with either a YES, NO, DOES NOT APPLY, or NOT KNOWN response. Comments may be entered after each question.

• TMM Level 2: Phase Definition

MATURITY GOAL 2.1: DEVELOP TESTING AND DEBUGGING GOALS AND POLICIES

The purpose of this goal is to differentiate clearly the processes of testing and debugging. The goals, tasks, activities, and tools for each must be identified. Responsibilities for each must be assigned. Policies must be established by management to accommodate and institutionalize both processes.

MATURITY SUBGOALS that support this goal are:

2.1.1. An organizationwide committee(s) or group on testing and debugging is formed and provided with funding and support. The committee(s) develops, documents, distributes, and supports procedures, goals, and policies for testing and debugging. The goals, policies, and procedures, once approved, are put in place and periodically reviewed.

2.1.2. Testing and debugging policies/goals are reflected in project/test plans.

2.1.3. A basic defect classification scheme is established, and a basic defect repository is put into place.

2.1.4. Simple testing and debugging measurements are identified and collected.

QUESTIONS

1. Has a committee(s) on testing and debugging been established?
2. Have policies, goals, activities, and tools for the testing process been identified, documented, and approved?
3. Have policies, goals, activities and tools for the debugging process been identified, documented, and approved?

4. Is the process of testing defined?

5. Is the process of debugging defined?

6. Have the policy documents on testing been distributed to project managers and developers (testers)?

7. Have the policy documents on debugging been distributed to project managers and developers (testers)?

8. Do the software developers (testers) follow a written organizational policy for testing when test planning?

9. Do the developers follow a written organizational policy for debugging?

10. Are basic measurements used to determine achievement of testing goals?

11. Are basic measurements used to determine achievement of debugging goals?

12. Have the testing policies and goals been developed with inputs from user/client groups with respect to their needs?

13. Have the debugging policies and goals been developed with input and feedback from user/client groups with respect to their needs?

14. Has a basic defect classification scheme been developed?

15. Has a defect repository been established?

16. Do developers/testers log defects into the repository on a consistent basis?

17. Are testing/debugging policies and goals periodically reviewed?

MATURITY GOAL 2.2: INITIATE A TEST PLANNING PROCESS

The purpose of this goal is to establish a test planning process on an organizationwide basis. Test planning involves stating test objectives, analyzing risks, outlining strategies, and developing test design specifications, and test cases. A test plan must also address the allocation of resources, the costs, and the responsibilities for testing on the unit, integration, system, and acceptance levels.

MATURITY SUBGOALS that support this goal are:

2.2.1. An organization-wide committee, or group on test planning is formed and provided with funding and support. The committee develops, documents, distributes, and supports procedures, goals, and policies for test planning. The goals, policies and procedures, once approved are put in place, and periodically reviewed.

2.2.2. Test plan templates for all levels of testing are developed, recorded and distributed to project managers and developers/testers for use in organizational projects. Other required tested-related documents are identified, and prescribed according to organizational policy.

2.2.3. Technical training is available to cover use of test plan templates and development of test plans.

2.2.4. A procedure is put in place to include user-generated requirements as inputs to the test plan.

2.2.5. Basic planning tools and test measurements are evaluated, and applied.

QUESTIONS

1. Has an organizationwide test planning committee or group been established?
2. Is there an organizational policy, and are there procedures for test planning?
3. Have the policy and procedures been distributed and approved?
4. Is there adequate support and funding for test planning for all projects?
5. Are test goals/objectives used as a basis for test planning?
6. Have test plan templates been developed and distributed to project managers?
7. Are there appropriate planning tools available for test planning?
8. Have project managers been trained in the use of templates and planning tools?
9. Have developers (testers) been trained in the use of templates and planning tools?
10. Are developers (testers) trained properly to develop test specifications, test designs, and test cases for the test plan?
11. Are test-related risks considered when developing test plans?
12. Are estimates (time, budget, tools) available from past projects for use in test planning?
13. Is test planning done at the unit level?

14. Is test planning done at the integration level?
15. Is test planning done at the system level?
16. Is test planning done at the acceptance level?
17. Is there a procedure in place for soliciting user/client input for test planning where appropriate (e.g., in acceptance test planning)?
18. Do developers (testers) have the opportunity to give inputs to the test plan at all levels?
19. Is the test planning process reviewed on a periodic and/or event-driven basis?
20. Are other test-related items such as test transmittal reports, test logs, test incident reports, and test summary reports defined in organizational documents?
21. Are other test-related items such as test transmittal reports, test logs, test incident reports, and test summary reports completed for each project?
22. Does management support interactions between project (test) managers, developers (testers), designers, and analysts to support test planning?
23. Are basic test measurements specified in the test plan at all levels?
24. Do developers (testers) collect and store basic test-related measurements?
25. Are the basic test measurements used to ensure that basic testing goals have been met?

MATURITY GOAL 2.3: INSTITUTIONALIZE BASIC TESTING TECHNIQUES AND METHODS

The purpose of this maturity goal is to improve test process capability by applying basic testing techniques and methods. How and when these techniques and methods are to be applied and any basic tool support for them should be specified clearly in testing policies and plans. Various basic techniques and methods that are often used in the testing process are black box and white box test design strategies, use of a requirements validation matrix, and the division of execution-based testing into subphases such as unit, integration, system and acceptance testing. Some testing tools that support use of these techniques and methods are static and dynamic analyzers, coverage analyzers, test data generators, and error checking tools.

MATURITY SUBGOALS that support this goal are:

2.3.1. An organizationwide committee, or group on test technology is formed and provided with funding and support. The committee studies, evaluates and recommends a set of basic testing techniques and methods, and a set of simple forms, and tools to support them. It develops relevant polices, procedures, and documents, and these are distributed. When approved, they are put in place and periodically reviewed.

2.3.2. Technical training and basic tools are available to support use of testing techniques and methods.

2.3.3. Software testing is planned and implemented at the unit, integration, system, and acceptance levels according to policy.

2.3.4. Basic testing strategies (white/black box), techniques and methods are used organizationwide to design test cases. Interaction between developers (testers) and other technical staff (e.g., designers, and requirements analysts) is promoted to identify testability issues, encourage development of software representations useful for white/black box testing methods, and to support multiple levels of testing.

QUESTIONS

1. Has a committee or group been formed to evaluate and recommend a set of basic testing techniques, methods, and tools?
2. Have the recommendations of the group been documented, distributed, and approved?
3. Have basic tools and techniques been included in test policies?
4. Have appropriate forms and templates been designed to support basic testing techniques?
5. Are adequate resources provided by upper management to support the use of basic testing techniques and methods, as well as basic testing tools?
6. Have developers (testers) been trained to apply the basic tools, forms, and methods?
7. Are basic testing techniques, and methods applied on an organizationwide basis?
8. Are basic testing tools applied on an organizationwide basis?
9. Are basic testing techniques and methods reviewed periodically?

10. Do testing policy statements include the requirement for multilevel testing?

11. Is testing planned and implemented at multiple levels (unit, integration, system, etc.)?

12. Are the basic testing techniques and tools described in policy statements applied at all levels of testing?

13. Are the testing techniques and tools to be applied described in multilevel test plans?

14. Does upper management support interaction between analysts, designers, and developers (testers) to ensure testing issues are addressed by these groups?

• TMM Level 3: Integration

MATURITY GOAL 3.1: ESTABLISH A TEST ORGANIZATION

The purpose of this maturity goal is to identify and organize a group of highly skilled people that is responsible for testing. The test group should be responsible for test planning, test execution and recording, test-related standards, test metrics, the test database, test reuse, test tracking, and evaluation. The group should also be responsible for maintaining the defect repository.

MATURITY SUBGOALS that support this goal are:

3.1.1. An organizationwide committee is formed to map out the structural framework for the test organization or group. Leadership, support and funding for the test group is provided. Roles, responsibilities, and career paths are defined for the test group.

3.1.2. An organizationwide test group is established through task force efforts and its functionality and position in the reporting hierarchy is defined. Well-trained and motivated members are assigned to the test group. Well-defined user/client, developer, and SQA communication links with the test group are established. The test group is reviewed periodically by management.

3.1.3. Training is available to ensure that the test group has the technical expertise to and apply appropriate testing tools and techniques, evaluate new tools and techniques, and plan for the testing effort.

QUESTIONS

1. Is testing recognized as a professional activity by the organization?
2. Has a committee or task force been formed to map out a framework for a test organization or test group?
3. Is there an organizationwide software test organization responsible for testing for each project?
4. Is there a career path that members of the test group can follow?
5. Are adequate resources provided for the software test organization?
6. Are members of the software test organization trained in testing methods, test planning, theory, tools and techniques?
7. Are testers adequately compensated with respect to other software engineers?
8. Are the roles and responsibilities of the group defined?
9. Are the group's activities documented and reported to upper management?
10. Does the organizational software test group coordinate with the SQA group to enhance test effectiveness and improve software quality with respect to the user's requirements?
11. Does the testing group have a communication path with developers for test planning, test design, and code repair when problems arise?
12. Are client concerns solicited as input to test organization policies?
13. Is there a formal mechanism for tester-user/client interaction?
14. Is the test group periodically reviewed by management?

MATURITY GOAL 3.2: ESTABLISH A TECHNICAL TRAINING PROGRAM

The purpose of this maturity goal from the viewpoint of the testing group is to insure that a skilled staff is available to perform testing tasks. The formal training program is based on a training policy. It calls for specifying training goals and developing specific training plans and materials. Training classes are available to all staff members. The impact of the training program on testers is to train them in state-of-the-art testing techniques, methods, and tools. It also prepares testers for test planning, for tasks involving integration of testing into the software life cycle, for the review process, and for identifying and prioritizing test-related risks. At higher TMM levels it prepares testers for test process control, a test measurement program, statistical testing, test process action planning, reliability modeling, and other higher-level testing activities.

MATURITY SUBGOALS that support this goal are:

3.2.1. An organizationwide committee or group on technical training is established with funding and resources. The technical training committee develops, gains approval for, and distributes the organizational training policy document. The training policy and program is reviewed periodically.

3.2.2. An in-house training group is established and chartered with leadership, tools, and facilities in place according to policy. The group develops a training program. Training goals and plans are developed by the group with input from project/test managers. Training materials are developed by the group and group members serve as training instructors.

QUESTIONS

1. Has a committee or group on technical training been established with funding and support?
2. Are policies and goals relating to technical training documented, distributed, and approved?
3. Does the organization follow a written organizational policy to meet its training needs?
4. Has a technical training program been established to improve skills for the technical staff?
5. Are training plans developed with input from project/test managers?
6. Are adequate resources provided to implement the technical training program?
7. Does management recommend training courses for technical staff on a regular basis?
8. Do training group members develop training materials and serve as instructors for the training courses?
9. Do participants in the test group receive the training necessary for developing the skills, and acquiring the knowledge required to perform their testing tasks?

10. Are measurements used to determine the quality and effectiveness of the training program?
11. Are training program activities reviewed on a periodic basis?

MATURITY GOAL 3.3: INTEGRATE TESTING INTO THE SOFTWARE LIFE CYCLE

The purpose of this maturity goal is to promote the performance of testing activities in parallel with other life cycle phase activities starting early in the software life cycle. A mature organization does not delay testing activities until coding is complete. Examples of good practices promoted by this goal are: master and system test planning are initiated early in the life cycle at requirements time, and integration and unit test planning are initiated at detailed design time. A variation of the V-model is used by managers, testers, and developers to guide integration activities. Resources that support the integration of the testing effort are, for example, qualified staff, supporting life cycle models, standards and policy documents, appropriate planning and scheduling.

MATURITY SUBGOALS that support this goal are:

3.3.1. An organizationwide committee, or group on the integration of testing activities is established and provided with funding and support. The committee develops, documents, distributes, and supports procedures, goals, and policies for test integration. The goals, policies and procedures, once approved, are put in place, and reviewed periodically.

3.3.2. Testing activities are integrated into the software life cycle using the adopted life cycle model following the written organizational policy. Project and test planning policies are adjusted to promote integration of testing. Standards and quality guidelines are developed for test-related work products produced at each life cycle phase.

3.3.3. Resources and training are provided to support the integration of testing activities into the software life cycle.

QUESTIONS

1. Has a group or committee been established to support integration of testing activities?

2. Has a software life cycle model that supports integration of testing activities been adopted?
3. Have testing activities and testing requirements associated with each life cycle phase been identified?
4. Has an integration policy, and a set of documented procedures based on the adopted model, been developed, approved, and distributed?
5. Is adequate training provided for the integration of testing effort?
6. Are adequate resources provided for the integration of testing effort?
7. Are the activities for integrating testing into the software life cycle reviewed on a periodic basis?
8. Have project and test planning procedures been modified to comply with, and to accommodate, integration activities?
9. Does the each project follow a written organizational policy for the integration of the testing efforts?
10. Have the test organization and SQA group developed a set of documented standards for all test work products produced in each life cycle phase?
11. Is there a policy to handle noncompliance with standards?

MATURITY GOAL 3.4: CONTROL AND MONITOR THE TESTING PROCESS

The purpose of this maturity goal is to promote development of a monitoring and controlling system for the testing process so that deviations from the test plans can be detected as soon as possible, and management is able to take effective actions to correct the deviations. Having this capability supports a testing process that is more likely to be on time and within budget. Controlling and monitoring of test also gives visibility to the testing process, supports testing as a professional activity, and can lead to higher-quality software products.

MATURITY SUBGOALS that support this goal are:

3.4.1. An organizationwide committee or group on the controlling and monitoring of testing is formed and provided with funding and support. The committee develops, documents, distributes, and supports procedures, goals, policies, and measurements for controlling and monitoring of testing. The goals, policies, procedures, and measurements, once approved, are put in place and reviewed periodically.

3.4.2. Test-related measurements for controlling and monitoring are collected for each project. Test status reporting is performed on a regular basis for each project according to policy. Contingency plans are developed, recorded, and documented along with test plans for each project for use when status tracking shows that testing deviates significantly from what was planned.

3.4.3. Training, tools and other resources are made available to support controlling and monitoring of test.

QUESTIONS

1. Has a committee or group been established to support monitoring and controlling of test?
2. Is there an organizational policy for monitoring and controlling of testing?
3. Are tools and training available to support controlling and monitoring of a test?
4. Has a set of basic measurements for tracking test progress been defined and distributed?
5. Do project managers and test managers work together on controlling and monitoring plans?
6. Does each project follow a written organizational policy for controlling and monitoring the testing process?
7. Are test-related contingency plans developed for each project to support controlling of a test?
8. Does the organization collect and store test tracking and controlling metrics for each project?
9. Is test status information based on findings from regular status meetings reported to test, project, and upper-level managers on a periodic basis?
10. Does the test organization, supported by project management, develop contingency plans for test risks?
11. Are test items under control of a configuration management system?
12. Are the activities for controlling and monitoring the testing process reviewed on a periodic basis?

• TMM Level 4: Management and Measurement

MATURITY GOAL 4.1: ESTABLISH AN ORGANIZATIONWIDE REVIEW PROGRAM

Reviews are a type of testing technique that can be used for removing defects from software artifacts. Achieving this maturity goal results in a review program that helps an organization to identity, catalog, and remove defects from software artifacts effectively, and early in the software life cycle. Reviews also support quality evaluations of software-related items. Examples of items that can be reviewed are requirements documents, design documents, test plans, and test case specifications.

MATURITY SUBGOALS that support this goal are:

4.1.1. An organizationwide committee or group focusing on developing a review program is formed and provided with funding and support. The committee develops, documents, distributes, and supports procedures, goals, policies, and measurements for reviews of software work products resulting from all software life cycle phases. The goals, policies, procedures, and measurements, once approved, are put in place, and reviewed periodically

4.1.2. Personnel are trained so that they understand, and follow, proper review policies, practices, and procedures. They are also trained in collecting, storing, and applying review measurements.

4.1.3. Software artifacts are reviewed for each project as described in the review policy and reflected in the project plan. Review measurements are collected and applied for improving product and process quality.

QUESTIONS

1. Has an organizationwide committee or group on the review process been established, with funding and resources?
2. Has an organizationwide review policy been developed, distributed, and approved?
3. Are client concerns reflected in the review policy?
4. Have review procedures, measurements, and reporting systems been defined, documented, and approved?

5. Are adequate resources (e.g., funding, review materials, tools) provided to implement the review program?
6. Are reviewers and review leaders trained?
7. Does each project follow the written organizational policy for performing reviews?
8. Do project plan schedules reflect review needs?
9. Are the reviews planned, and the results reported and documented?
10. Are the software/test work products developed at different phases of the software life cycle reviewed?
11. Are defects found during reviews stored in a defect repository?
12. Are actions related to defects identified in reviews tracked until they are resolved?
13. Are review-related measures collected and analyzed?
14. Are measurements relating to software work products collected during the reviews?
15. Is the review program evaluated on a periodic basis?

MATURITY GOAL 4.2: ESTABLISH A TEST MEASUREMENT PROGRAM

The purpose of a test measurement program is to identify, collect, analyze, and apply measurements to support an organization in determining test progress, evaluating the quality and effectiveness of its testing process, assessing the productivity of its testing staff, assessing the results of test improvement efforts, and evaluating the quality of its software products. Examples of test-related measurements are test costs, tester productivity, number of test cases executed, and number of defects detected.

MATURITY SUBGOALS that support this goals are:

4.2.1. An organizationwide committee or group focusing on developing a test measurement program is formed and provided with funding and support. The committee develops, documents, distributes, and supports procedures, goals, policies, and measurements as applied to software artifacts and the test process. The goals, policies, procedures, and measurements, once approved, are put in place and reviewed periodically.

4.2.2. A test measurement program is developed according to policy with a measurement reporting system. Measurements are collected, stored, and analyzed. They are applied organizationwide to set test/project goals and to improve product and test process quality. Test measurements are applied organizationwide to support decision making, project/test planning, and project/test tracking and monitoring and action planning.

4.2.3. Training, tools, and other resources are provided to support the test measurement program.

QUESTIONS

1. Has an organizationwide committee responsible for test measurement been established with funding and resources?
2. Has an organizationwide test measurement policy been developed, distributed, and approved?
3. Are client concerns reflected in the measurement policy/plan?
4. Have test measurement procedures and reporting systems been defined, documented, and approved?
5. Have appropriate measurements for each test life cycle phase been specified and documented?
6. Are adequate resources (e.g., funding, materials, tools) provided to implement the test measurement program?
7. Is training in measurement identification, collection, and analysis available for managers and technical staff?
8. Does each project follow the written organizational policy for performing measurements?
9. Is there a test data repository available for use by managers and technical staff?
10. Are quantitative testing goals set for each project?
11. Are measurements used to track and monitor testing?
12. Has a basic set of software quality attributes and metrics been defined?
13. Are measures of software quality attributes used to track software quality during testing?
14. Are test data items used to support action planing for test process improvement?
15. Is the measurement program evaluated on a periodic basis?

MATURITY GOAL 4.3: SOFTWARE QUALITY EVALUATION

The purpose of the software quality evaluation maturity goal is to relate software quality issues to the adequacy of the testing process, define and promote use of measurable software quality attributes, and define quality goals for evaluating software work products. Sample quality attributes are correctness, efficiency, integrity, usability, maintainability, flexibility, testability, portability, reusability, and interoperability.

MATURITY SUBGOALS that support this goal are:

4.3.1. An organizationwide committee or group focusing on software quality evaluation is formed and provided with funding and support. The committee develops, documents, distributes, and supports procedures, goals, policies, standards, and measurements for software quality evaluation. The goals, policies, procedures, standards, and measurements, once approved, are put in place, and reviewed periodically.

4.3.2. Training, tools, and other resources are provided to support software quality evaluation.

4.3.3. Quality goals are developed for each project according to policy. The testing process is structured, measured, and evaluated to ensure that quality goals are achieved. User/client input is solicited for the development of quality goals.

QUESTIONS

1. Has an organizationwide committee on software quality evaluation been established, funded, and supported?
2. Has an organizationwide policy relating to measurement-based software quality evaluation been developed and distributed by the committee and approved?
3. Are client concerns reflect in the quality policy?
4. Has a set of software quality evaluation standards and procedures been developed, documented, and approved?
5. Are adequate resources (e.g., funding, materials, tools) provided for quality programs and quality evaluations?
6. Are managers and technical staff trained so that they are able to set measurable quality goals, develop and understand quality standards,

collect quality measurements, and evaluate quality attributes for software artifacts?

7. Does each project follow the written organizational policy for evaluating software quality?

8. Are quality goals for evaluating software work products set for each project?

9. Has a set of measurable quality attributes for software products been specified, verified, distributed, and approved?

10. Are measurable quality goals set for each software product?

11. Is there a formed procedure in place for client input to the software quality evaluation process for each project?

12. Is the testing process assessed periodically to evaluate its impact on software quality?

13. Are improvements made in testing and other quality evaluation processes to increase the level of software quality?

14. Are the activities for software quality evaluation reviewed on a periodic basis?

• TMM Level 5: Optimization/Defect Prevention and Quality Control

MATURITY GOAL 5.1: DEFECT PREVENTION

The purpose of this maturity goal is encourage an organization to formally classify, log, and analyze its defects. The organization is also encouraged to use a combination of defect causal analysis and action planning to guide process change so that these defects are eliminated from its future products. Recommended defect prevention activities include defect recording and tracking, defect causal analysis, action planning, action implementation and tracking, and training in defect prevention methods.

MATURITY SUBGOALS that support this goal are:

5.1.1. An organizationwide committee or group focusing on defect prevention is formed and provided with funding and support. The committee develops, documents, distributes, and supports procedures, goals, policies, standards, and measurements for defect prevention. The goals, policies, procedures, standards, and measurements, once approved, are put in place and reviewed periodically.

5.1.2. Training, tools, and other resources are provided to support defect prevention activities.

5.1.3. Defect prevention teams are established according to policy, with management support. Responsibilities are assigned to the defect prevention teams. The teams ensure that defects injected/removed are identified and recorded for each life cycle phase, a causal analysis procedure is established to identify the root causes of defects, and that action plans are developed through the interaction of managers, developers, and testers to prevent identified defects from reoccurring. These plans are tracked, and process changes occur as a result of success in pilot projects.

QUESTIONS

1. Has an organizationwide committee or group on defect prevention been established with funding and support?
2. Have organizationwide policies, programs, and procedures to support defect prevention been developed and distributed by the committee and approved?
3. Are client concerns reflect in the defect prevention policy?
4. Are adequate resources (e.g., funding, materials, tools) provided for defect prevention activities?
5. Are managers and technical staff trained in defect prevention activities?
6. Have defect prevention teams been established (members can be part of development, testing, SQA, SEPG groups)?
7. Does each project follow the written organizational policy for defect prevention?
8. Are defect prevention activities planned?
9. For each life cycle phase, are all injected/removed defects classified and formally recorded in a defect repository?
10. Once identified, are common causes of defects analyzed and eliminated systematically?
11. Are specific action plans developed to prevent defects from recurring?
12. Are defect prevention actions measured and tracked to insure progress and to evaluate effectiveness?
13. Are effective defect prevention actions implemented across the organization in the form of documented process changes?
14. Are defect prevention activities/programs reviewed periodically?

MATURITY GOAL 5.2: QUALITY CONTROL

The purpose of this maturity goal is to develop a comprehensive set of quality control procedures and practices that support the release of high-quality software that fully meets the customer's requirements. Achievement of this goal allows an organization to incorporate advanced measurements, techniques, and tools to improve the effectiveness of its testing process, reduce software defects, improve software reliability, and increase usability. Quality control activities call for automated tools to support the running and rerunning of test cases and defect collection and analysis. Statistical techniques and usage profiles are used to support testing efforts and achievement of quality goals. Levels of confidence can be established that indicate the likelihood that the software is fault-free. The software is tested for usability. Quantitative criteria are used to determine when to stop testing. These quantitative criteria can be based on, for example, reaching a certain level of reliability or trustworthiness, or when the number of defects/unit time at a selected severity rating arrives at a certain level.

MATURITY SUBGOALS that support this goal are:

5.2.1. An organizationwide committee or group focusing on quality control is formed and provided with funding and support. The committee develops and updates documents, and distributes and supports procedures, goals, policies, standards, and measurements for quality control. The goals, policies, procedures, standards, and measurements, once approved, are put in place, and periodically reviewed

5.2.2. The software test and the SQA groups identify suitable software attributes and establish qualitative and quantitative quality goals for software products with user/client input according to policy. These goals are included in test plans. Testing tools and techniques are used to determine if quality goals have been met. Quantifiable criteria are used for making stop-test decisions.

5.2.3. The test group and related groups are trained and assigned responsibilities for use of statistical methods and other quality-related software evaluation activities such as usability testing. The test or related group interacts with users/clients to gather inputs for usage modeling and usability testing.

QUESTIONS

1. Has an organizationwide committee focused on quality control been established with funding and support?
2. Have organizationwide policies, programs, and procedures to support software quality control been developed, distributed, and approved?
3. Are client concerns reflect in the software quality control policies?
4. Are adequate resources (e.g., funding, materials, laboratories, tools) provided for quality control activities?
5. Are managers and technical staff trained in quality control activities?
6. Are statistical methods used during testing for evaluating software quality?
7. Are quantitative and qualitative quality goals for software products identified by the software test group and the SQA group with input from users/clients?
8. Are the quality goals incorporated into test plans?
9. Are quality-related attributes and measurements identified and documented?
10. Is user/client input collected for usage modeling?
11. Has responsibility for usability testing been assigned?
12. Is the software evaluated carefully for usability with respect to user needs?
13. Is there a mechanism for user participation in usability testing?
14. Is user feedback applied to make improvements in the software under development?
15. Are quantitative criteria for stop-test decisions specified in test plans?
16. Are the quality control activities reviewed periodically?

MATURITY GOAL 5.3: TEST PROCESS OPTIMIZATION

The purpose of this maturity goal is to promote continuous test process improvement and test process reuse. An organization is encouraged to identify testing practices that need to be improved, to implement the improvements, and to track improvement progress. It is also encouraged to apply process control activities to testing, to continually evaluate new test-related tools and technologies for adaptation, and to support technology transfer. Finally, an organization is encouraged to identify high-quality testing subprocesses, store them in a Process Asset Library, and tailor them for reuse in future projects.

MATURITY SUBGOALS that support this goal are:

5.3.1. An organizationwide group focused on test process improvement is chartered and provided with funding and support. It has continuing oversight responsibilities for test process issues which include test process reuse, test process control, test process assessment and improvement, and technology transfer. It provides leadership for test process improvement efforts. The group develops and updates documents, and distributes and supports procedures, goals, policies, standards, and measurements for test process improvement activities. The goals, policies, procedures, standards, and measurements once approved are put in place, and periodically reviewed.

5.3.2. Training is available for management and technical staff in the areas of action planning, test process assessment, test process control, test process reuse, and technology transfer.

5.3.3. The test process undergoes periodic evaluation according to policy, and action plans are implemented to make improvements. New tools and techniques are continuously being evaluated and integrated.

5.3.4. High-quality test process components are recognized as assets and are stored and reused organizationwide.

QUESTIONS

1. Has a group or task force focused on test process improvement been established, with funding and support?
2. Have organizationwide policies, programs, and procedures to support test process assessment, improvement, and reuse been developed, distributed, and approved?
3. Have organizationwide policies, programs, and procedures to support test process control been developed, distributed and, approved?
4. Have organizationwide policies, programs, and procedures to support technology transfer been developed, distributed, and approved?
5. Are adequate resources (e.g., funding, materials, tools) provided for technology transfer?

6. Are adequate resources (e.g., funding, materials, tools) provided for test process control?
7. Are adequate resources (e.g., funding, materials, tools) provided for test process assessment, improvement, and reuse?
8. Are managers and technical staff trained in process control?
9. Are mangers and technical staff trained in test process assessment, improvement, and reuse?
10. Are managers and technical staff trained in technology transfer?
11. Has a Process Asset Library (PAL) been established?
12. Are test processes in the PAL tailored and reused in subsequent projects?
13. Are testing tools continually being evaluated for use by the testing group?
14. Is there a procedure for adaptation/integration of new tools and technologies into the testing process (technology transfer)?
15. Is the test process assessed periodically?
16. Do results from an assessment yield improvement actions?
17. Do successful improvement actions lead to changes in the organizational test process, associated documents, and standards?
18. Are measurements defined for test process control?
19. Are test process control activities performed periodically resulting in adjustments to the testing process?
20. Is the technology transfer program reviewed periodically?
21. Is the test process assessment and improvement program reviewed periodically?
22. Is the test process control program reviewed periodically?
23. Is the test process reuse program reviewed periodically?

Section 5. Testing Tools Questions

Assessors should note that the testing tool questions have no formal impact on the ranking that results from the TMM ranking process. This section of the TMM Questionnaire is useful for assessors to gain further insight into the current state of an organization's testing process. Answers to these questions are also useful when assembling tools for the Testers'

Workbench. For each of the tool types listed below the respondent should decide whether they are applied "never," "rarely," "often," or "always."

I. TEST RESOURCE MANAGEMENT TOOLS

1. Configuration managers (monitor and control the effects of changes throughout development and maintenance and preserve the integrity of developed and released versions).
2. Project management tools (help project/managers plan, schedule, and track the development, testing, and maintenance of systems).
3. Test planners (assist developers/testers/managers in planning and defining acceptance, system, integration, and unit-level tests).

II. REQUIREMENTS AND DESIGN TEST SUPPORT TOOLS

1. Requirements and specification analyzers (evaluate specifications for consistency, completeness, and conformance to established specification standards).
2. System/prototype simulators (merge analysis and design activities with testing).
3. Requirements tracers (reduce the work effort of tracing requirements to associated design information, source code, and test cases for large projects).

III. IMPLEMENTATION AND MAINTENANCE TEST SUPPORT TOOLS

1. Compilers.
2. Source code static analyzers (examine source code without executing it).

   - Auditors (analyze code to ensure conformance to establish rules and standards).

   - Complexity measurers (compute metrics from the source code to determine various complexity attributes associated with the source code or designs written in a program design language).

   - Cross referencing tools (provide referencing between various entities).

   - Size measurers (count source lines of code, SLOC).

- Structure checkers (identify structural anomalies and develop graphical or textual representations of the code).

- Syntax and semantics analyzers (identify type conflicts in calling arguments of separately compiled subroutines).

3. Test preparation tools (support preparation of test data or test case information)

    - Data extractors (build test data from existing databases or test sets).

    - Requirements-based test case generators (help developers evaluate requirements by building test cases from requirements written following the rules of the tool's formal specification language).

    - Test data generators (support development of test inputs that are formatted or can be formatted readily in the required files).

4. Test execution tools (dynamically analyze the software being tested).

    - Assertion analyzers (instrument the code with logical expressions that specify conditions or relations among the program variables).

    - Capture replay tools (automatically record test inputs/outputs using capture scripts, replay the tests using playback scripts. Useful for retesting when changes are made.)

    - Coverage/frequency analyzers (assess the degree of coverage of test cases with respect to executed statements, branches, paths, or modules).

    - Debuggers (not strictly a testing tool; these support the location of defects revealed during testing).

    - Emulators (may be used in place of missing or unavailable system components and usually operate at the real-time speed of the components being emulated).

    - Network analyzers (analyze the traffic on the network to identify problem areas and conditions as well as allow simulation of the activities of multiple terminals).

    - Performance/timing analyzers (monitor timing characteristics of software components or entire systems).

- Run-time error checkers (monitor programs for memory referencing, memory leaking, or memory allocation errors).

- Simulators (are used in place of missing or unavailable system components).

- Status displayers/session documents (provide test status information and record selected information about a test run).

- Test execution managers (automate various functions of setting up test runs, performing a variety of tests, and cleaning up after a test to reset the system).

5. Test evaluators (perform time-consuming and error-prone functions).

- Comparators (compare entities with each other after a software test and note the differences).

- Data reducers and analyzers (convert data to a form that can be interpreted more readily and can sometimes perform various statistical analyses on the data).

- Defect/change trackers (keep track of defect information and generate defect reports).

Section 6. Testing Trends Questions

As in the case of the testing tool use questions, the testing trend questions are designed to provide a broader view of the testing process to assessors. They play no formal role in a TMM ranking. Assessors can use the responses as they see fit to assist in the assessment process.

1. From your perspective, what are the major strengths of the testing process in your organization today?
2. From your perspective, what are the major weakness of the testing process in your organization today?
3. What changes has the organization made to improve the testing process over the last 2–5 years?
4. How would you rate the overall effectiveness of the testing process today compared to 2 years ago? Please select one of the following choices: same, improved, greatly improved, little improved, worse, don't know.

5. Compare the fraction of time, and resources allocated for testing now and 2 years ago. Please select one of the following choices: same, largely increased, largely decreased, about the same, don't know.

6. Compare the current number of full-time testers in the organization to the number available 2 years ago. Please select one of the following choices: same, increased, decreased, don't know.

7. Compare the current number of part-time testers in the organization to the number available 2 years ago. Please select one of the following choices: same, increased, decreased, don't know.

8. From your perspective, over the last 2 years has communication between testers, developers, and managers: improved, stayed the same, gotten worse, don't know?

9. From your perspective has management addressed the needs of testers/developers? Yes, no, to some extent, don't know.

Section 7. Comments from Respondents

This section is reserved for a respondent to comment on the nature of the TMM Questionnaire itself. Respondents may comment on any aspect of the questionnaire, for example, on the clarity of the questions, the organization of the questions, the completeness, and usability of the document. Comments provide useful feedback for questionnaire maintainers who can then consider appropriate changes. Respondents may use the blank section provided below and/or add supplemental pages with their comments.

Section 8. Glossary of Terms

Below is a description of many of the terms used in the TMM Questionnaire to assist in understanding, and answering the TMM questions. References in the descriptions relate to the *IEEE Standard Glossary of Software Engineering Terminology*, IEEE Std. 610.12–1990.

acceptance testing. Formal testing conducted to determine whether a system satisfies specified acceptance criteria and to enable the customer to determine whether to accept the system. [IEEE-STD-610.12–1990]

activity. Any step taken or function performed, both mental and physical, toward achieving some objective. Activities include all the work that managers and technical staff do to perform project and organizational tasks.

appraisal. A generic term used in the software engineering domain to refer to either software process assessments or software capability evaluations. Any software engineering process or subprocess can undergo an appraisal or evaluation.

artifact. An object or item produced or shaped by human workmanship. As referred to in model-based process appraisals, artifacts are the products resulting from enacting a process. Some examples of software development process artifacts are software designs, code, and test cases.

assessment. *See* test process assessment.

baseline. (1) A specification or product that has been reviewed formally and agreed upon, which thereafter serves as the basis for further development and can be changed only through formal change control procedures. (2) Baselines plus approved changes from those baselines constitute the correct configuration identification for the item. [IEEE-STD-610.12–1990]

black-box testing. A basic testing strategy that considers a functional design specification to design test cases without regard to the internal program structure. This strategy supports testing the product against the end-user external specifications.

capture/replay tool. A test tool that records test inputs and outcomes (e.g., screens) and provides facilities for subsequent re-execution or replay of the test.

commitment. A pact that is freely assumed, visible, and expected to be kept by all parties.

configuration management. A process that requires technical and administrative expertise to identify and document the functional and physical characteristics of a configuration item, control changes to those characteristics, record and report change processing and implementation status, and verify compliance with specified requirements. Configuration items can be, for example, units of code, test sets, specifications, and test plans. [IEEE-STD-610.12–1990]

consensus. A method of decision making that allows team members to develop a common basis of understanding and to develop a general agreement concerning a decision.

customer (client). The individual or organization responsible for accepting the product and authorizing payment to the developing organization.

debugging. Debugging, or fault, localization, is the process of (1) locating the fault or defect, (2) repairing the code, and 3. retesting the code.

defect. A flaw in a system or system component that causes the system or component to fail to perform its required function. A defect, if encountered during execution, may cause a failure of the system.

defect prevention. The activities involved in identifying defects or potential defects and preventing them from being introduced into future products.

developer. A technically skilled software professional who is involved in the definition, design, implementation, evaluation, and maintenance of a software system.

emulator. Hardware, software, or firmware that performs the tasks of a specified hardware component.

end user. The individual or group who will use the system for its intended operational purpose when it is deployed in its environment.

event-driven review/activity. A review or activity whose implementation is based on the occurrence of an event within the project.

formal review. A formal meeting at which a product is presented to the end user, customer, or other interested parties for comment, evaluation, and approval. It can also be a meeting to present/discuss management and technical activities, or a meeting to discuss the status of a project.

goal. (1) A statement of intent, or (2) a statement of an accomplishment that an individual or an organization wants to achieve.

infrastructure. The underlying framework of an organization including organizational structures, policies, standards, training, facilities, and tools, which support its ongoing processes.

institutionalization. The building of self-sustaining infrastructure and culture that support methods, practices, and procedures that enable a mode of doing business, even after those who originally built the infrastructure are gone.

integration testing. An orderly progression of testing in which individual software elements, hardware elements, or both are combined and tested until the entire system has been integrated.

manager. A role that encompasses providing technical and administrative direction and control to individuals performing tasks or activities within the manager's area of responsibility. The traditional functions of a manager include planning, scheduling, organizing, staffing, directing, and controlling work within an area of responsibility. There may be several levels of managers in an organization depending on the type of hierarchical structure in place.

maturity level. A well-defined evolutionary plateau or stage for a process supported by a set of goals and practices which when implemented describe the state of the process.

measure. An empirical objective assignment of a number (or symbol) to an entity to characterize a particular attribute.

method. A reasonably complete set of rules and criteria that establish a precise and repeatable way of performing a task and arriving at a desired result.

organization. A unit within a company, or the entire company itself. An organization has specific responsibilities, staff, and a reporting structure. All projects within an organization usually share common top-level management and common policies.

periodic review/activity. A review or activity that occurs at specified, regular time intervals.

policy. A high-level statement of principle or course of action that is used to govern a set of activities in an organization.

procedure. A means or technique whereby the performance of a task or process is assured. The procedure may involve several organizational elements, and its documentation may include some combination of function statements, steps, and/or operating plans. The documentation defines what should be performed, how it should be performed, and who is accountable for the results.

project. An undertaking requiring concerted effort that is focused on developing and/or maintaining a specific product. The product may include hardware, software, and other components. Typically a project has its own management, funding, cost accounting, and delivery schedule.

project manager. The person with total business responsibility for a project. The individual who directs, controls, administers, plans, and regulates the development of a software system or hardware/software system. The project manager is the individual ultimately responsible to the customer.

quality. (1) The degree to which a system, component, or process meets specified requirements. (2) The degree to which a system, component, or process meets customer or user needs or expectations. [IEEE-STD-610.12–1990]

regression testing. The process of retesting software that has been modified to insure that no defects have been introduced by the modification, and that the software is still able to meet its specification.

resource. The physical, human, and economic means needed to support a process, policy, procedure, goal, or program; for example, training materials, hardware and software tools, standards documents, staff members, and travel funds.

review. A group meeting whose purpose is to evaluate a software artifact or a set of software artifacts.

risk. Possibility of suffering loss.

risk management. An approach to problem analysis that weighs risks in a situation by identifying the risks, their probabilities of occurrence, and their impact, to give a more accurate understanding of potential losses and how to avoid them. Risk management includes risk identification, analysis, prioritization, and control.

role. A unit of defined responsibilities that may be assumed by one or more individuals.

senior manager. A management role at a high level in an organization whose primary focus is the long-term vitality of the organization, rather than short-term project and contractual concerns and pressures.

simulator. A device, data processing system, or computer program that represents certain features of the behavior of a physical or abstract system.

software life cycle. The period of time that begins when a software product is conceived and ends when the software is no longer available for use. The software life cycle typically includes a concept phase, requirement phase, design phase, implementation phase, testing phase, installation and checkout phase, operation and maintenance phase, and, sometimes, a retirement phase. [IEEE-STD-610.12–1990]

software process. The set of methods, practices, standards, documents, activities, policies, and procedures that software engineers use to develop and maintain a software system, and its associated artifacts, such as project and test plans, design documents, code, and manuals.

software quality assurance. (1) A planned and systematic pattern of all actions necessary to provide adequate confidence that a software work product conforms to established technical requirements. (2) A set of activities designed to evaluate the process by which software work products are developed and/or maintained. [IEEE-STD-610.12–1990]

software tester. *See* tester.

software work product. Any artifact created as part of defining, maintaining, or using a software product. This includes design documents, test plans, user manuals, computer code, and associated documentation. Software work products may, or may not, be intended for delivery to a customer or end user.

standard. Mandatory requirements employed and enforced to prescribe a disciplined uniform approach to software development. [IEEE-STD-610.12–1990]

system testing. The process of testing an integrated hardware and software system to verify that the system meets its specified requirements.

technical requirements. Those requirements that describe what the software must do and its operational constraints. Examples of technical requirements include functional, performance, interface, and quality requirements.

test case. A test-related item that which contains the following information: (1) A set of test inputs. These are data items received from an external source by the code-under-test. The external source can be hardware, software, or human. (2) Execution conditions. These are conditions required for running the test, for example a certain state of a data base, or a configuration of a hardware device. (3) Expected outputs. These are the results to be produced by the code-under-test.

tester. A technically skilled professional who is involved in the testing and evaluation of a software system, and in the evaluation and improvement of the testing process.

testing. (1) A group of procedures carried out to evaluate some aspect of a piece of software. (2) A process used for revealing defects in software and for establishing that the software has attained a specified degree of quality with respect to selected attributes.

testing maturity questionnaire. A set of questions that supports an assessment team in determining the testing maturity level of an organization. It is concerned with the implementation of important software testing practices in a software organization.

test manager. The person with total business responsibility for testing and evaluating a software product. The individual who directs, controls, administers, plans, and regulates the evaluation of a software system or hardware/software system. The test manager works with the project manager to ensure the system is of the highest quality and meets the customers requirements.

test process assessment. An appraisal by a trained team of software/test/SQA professionals to determine the state of an organization's current testing process, to determine the high-priority testing process-related issues facing an organization, and to obtain the organizational support for test process improvement.

test tools. The software and/or hardware systems, or other instruments, that are used to measure and evaluate a software artifact.

test work product. Any artifact created as part of testing process. Examples are test plans, test cases specifications, test procedures, and test documents.

unit testing. Aggregate of technical activities involved in demonstrating that an individual software unit has been implemented correctly, that the code and the design of a unit are consistent, and that the unit design is correct.

V-model. A framework to describe the software development life cycle activities from requirement specification to maintenance. (The Modified V Model includes test development and execution activities.)

validation. The process of evaluating a software system or component during, or at the end of, the development cycle to evaluate whether it meets the customers requirements. [IEEE-STD-610.12–1990]

verification. The process of evaluating a software system or component to determine whether the products of a given development phase satisfy the conditions imposed at the start of that phase. [IEEE-STD-610.12–1990]

white-box testing. A basic testing strategy that requires knowledge of the internal structure of a program to design test cases.

PART 2 • TMM ACTIVITIES, TASKS, AND RESPONSIBILITIES (ATRs)

This part of Appendix III contains the complete set of activities, tasks, and responsibilities (ATRs) for the three critical views as described in the TMM. The section is organized by TMM level, then by the maturity goals within each level, and finally by the three critical views. For each TMM level there is:

(i)   A statement of each maturity goal;
(ii) ATRs for managers;

(iii) ATRs for developers/testers;

(iv) ATRs for users/clients.

• TMM Level 2: Phase Definition

MATURITY GOAL 2.1: DEVELOP TESTING AND DEBUGGING GOALS AND POLICIES

Recall that at TMM level 2 there is no requirement for a dedicated testing group, so ATRs are formally assigned to developers only. If an organization does have a group of test specialists, then the developer ATRs can be transferred to this group.

ATRs FOR MANAGERS (UPPER, AND PROJECT MANAGEMENT)

- Provide leadership, adequate resources, and funding to form the committee (team or task force) on testing and debugging. The committee makeup is managerial, with technical staff serving as comembers.

- Make available any pre-existing or sample testing/debugging policies and goals.

- Assume a leadership role in testing/debugging policy development.

- Support the recommendations and policies of the committee by:

    —distributing testing/debugging goal/policy documents to project managers, developers/testers, and other interested staff, and soliciting feedback from these groups;

    —appointing a permanent team to oversee compliance and policy change-making;

- Ensure necessary training, education, and tools to carry out defined testing/debugging goals and policies are made available.

- Promote the cultural changes needed to implement the testing/debugging policies.

- Assign responsibilities for testing and debugging.

- Encourage input/feedback from key users/client groups for testing/ debugging policies.

- Ensure that there is support for development of a simple defect classification scheme and a defect repository. The classification scheme and repository should be available for all project personnel to study and access.

- Ensure that developers (testers) are familiar with the defect classification scheme and record defects occurring for each project in the repository.

- Periodically review testing and debugging goals and policies.

ATRs FOR DEVELOPERS

- Work with management to develop testing and debugging policies and goals.

- Participate in the team that oversees testing/debugging policy compliance and change management.

- Become familiar with the approved set of testing/debugging goals and policies, keeping up-to-date with revisions and making suggestions for changes when appropriate.

- Set testing goals for each project at each level of test that reflect organizational testing goals and policies.

- Develop test plans that are in compliance with testing policy.

- Carry out testing activities that are in compliance with organizational policies.

- Work with project managers to develop a defect classification scheme and defect repository.

- Record defects occurring in each project in the defect repository.

- Participate in periodic reviews of testing/debugging policies and goals.

ATRs FOR USERS/CLIENTS

- Users/clients give input/feedback on testing and debugging goals and policies when solicited by management. (These groups play an indirect role in the formation of an organization's testing/debugging goals and polices since these goals and policies reflect the organization's efforts to ensure customer/client/user satisfaction. Feedback from these groups should be encouraged by management and SQA. In general, the needs of its customers and the overall marketplace will have an impact on the nature of an organization's testing/debugging goals and policies.)

MATURITY GOAL 2.2: INITIATE A TEST PLANNING PROCESS

ATRs FOR MANAGERS

- Provide leadership, funding, and resources to an organizationwide test planning committee.

- Ensure that test planning policy statements are distributed and approved.

- Promote cultural changes to support test planning.

- Ensure that the testing policy statement, quality standards, and test plan templates support test planning with commitments of resources, tools, and training.

- Ensure that the testing policy statement contains a formal mechanism for user/client input to the test planning process, especially for acceptance testing. (At higher TMM levels this will also include usability test planning.)

- Ensure that all projects are in compliance with the test planning policy.

- Ensure that test plan templates are applied uniformly for all projects.

- Ensure that all developers (testers) complete all the necessary post-test documents such as test logs and test incident reports.

- Ensure that test plans are prepared for all levels of testing: unit, integration, system, and acceptance.

- Participate in training classes for test planning, use of test plan templates, identifying/estimating test risks, planning tools (this applies to project managers and test managers when there is a test group).

- Select appropriate test planning tools.

- Prepare multilevel test plans for each project with inputs and support from developers. (This applies to project managers and test managers when there is a test group.) Project/test managers use the organizational test plan templates as a guide for preparing test plans. Test risks are identified, and simple measurements are selected and included in the test plan to ensure testing goals have been met. Defect data from past projects are used where appropriate to assist in test planning.)

- Ensure that developers (testers) prepare test plan attachments such as test cases and test procedures.

- Ensure that auxiliary test documents are prepared such as test transmittal reports and test logs.

- Review test plans with developers (testers).

- Ensure that all developers (testers) complete all the necessary post-test documents such as test logs and test incident reports.

- Prepare a test summary report (project/test managers).

- Promote interactions with developers (testers) and clients to develop acceptance test plans, and use cases and/or any other descriptions of typical user/computer interactions.

- Periodically review test planning policies with technical staff.

ATRs FOR DEVELOPERS

- Participate as members of the test planning committee.

- Attend training classes for test planning, for using planning tools and templates, and for identifying test risks.

- Assist the project (test) manager in determining test goals, test risks, and test costs for planning at all levels of testing.

- Assist the project (test) manager in selecting test methods, procedures, and tools.

- Develop test case specifications, test procedure specifications, and other test-related documents.

- Work with analysts and designers to ensure that testability issues are addressed during the requirements and design phases to support test planning and test design.

- Collect simple test-related measures to ensure testing goals have been achieved.

- Complete all the necessary pre- and post-test documents such as test transmittal reports, test incident reports, and test logs.

- Work with clients to develop use cases and/or any other descriptions of typical user/computer interaction and acceptance test plans.

- Participate in reviews of test planning policies.

ATRs FOR USERS/CLIENTS

- Articulate requirements clearly.

- Supply input and consensus to the acceptance test plan. The required functional and performance-related attributes that are expected by the client/users should be specified clearly and quantitatively if possible.

- Provide input for the development of use cases and/or any other descriptions of typical user/computer interaction.

MATURITY GOAL 2.3: INSTITUTIONALIZE BASIC TESTING TECHNIQUES AND METHODS

ATRs FOR MANAGERS

- Provide leadership, support, and funding to a committee or group responsible for identifying, evaluating, and recommending basic testing techniques, methods, and tools.

- Ensure that the group's recommendations are documented, distributed, and approved.

- Ensure that an organization's policies and standards are designed to promote the institutionalization of black/white box test design methods.

- Ensure that testing policies and standards require multilevel testing.

- Ensure developers (testers) acquire the needed education and training to understand and apply black and white box testing methods, and to develop test cases, test procedures, test logs, and test incident reports.

- Ensure that developers (testers) have the needed education and training to perform testing at multiple levels.

- Provide resources to support use of the black/white box testing methods such as tools and templates.

- Encourage cooperation among developer (testers), requirements analysts, and designers on testing issues.

- Ensure that test plans include use of black/white box test design methods.

- Ensure that multilevels of testing are covered in the test plans.

- Promote cultural changes needed to support organizationwide application of basic testing techniques and tools.

- Promote cultural changes needed to support multilevel testing.

- Allocate adequate time and resources to design and execute the black/white box tests, multilevel tests, and analyze the test results.

- Adjust project schedules so that multilevel testing can be performed adequately.

- Provide visibility for successful application of testing techniques and methods.

- Periodically review basic testing techniques and methods and tools.

ATRs FOR DEVELOPERS

- Participate as members of a committee responsible for evaluating and recommending testing techniques, method, and tools.

- Attend classes and training sessions, read materials, acquire tools, work with knowledgeable colleagues, and gain hands-on experience in the application of white box and black box test design methods.

- Attend classes and training sessions, read materials, acquire tools, work with knowledgeable colleagues, and gain hands-on experience testing at the unit, integration, system, and acceptance levels.

- Ensure that a balance of test approaches is used for test case design at all levels of testing.

- Design test cases, test specifications, and test procedures based on knowledge of testing strategies, techniques, and methods.

- Set up software/hardware environment necessary to execute tests. Shutdown facilities when tests are completed.

- Execute test cases at all levels of testing.

- Record test-related data.

- Record defect-related data.

- Interact with specifers and designers to review their representations of the software. Representations include input/output specifications, pseudo code, state diagrams, and control flow graphs which are rich sources for test case development. These representations are vital for designing white/black-based box test cases.

- Refer to defect repository to learn about past defects for similar projects to help design proper tests.

- Support (project/test) management to ensure that multilevel testing and use of black/white box testing techniques are a part of organizational policies, are incorporated into test plans, and are applied throughout the organization

- Work with project (test) managers to ensure there is time and resources to test at all levels.

- Mentor colleagues who wish to acquire the necessary background and experience to perform multilevel testing.

- Work with users/clients to develop the use cases and/or any other descriptions of typical user/computer interaction and acceptance criteria necessary for the multilevel tests.

- Work with users/clients at acceptance test time to ensure problems are resolved to their satisfaction.

- Participate in periodic reviews of basis testing techniques and methods.

ATRs FOR USERS/CLIENTS

- Provide liaison staff to interact with development (testing) staff on test-related issues.

- Work with analysts so that system requirements are complete, clear, and testable.

- Participate in acceptance and/or alpha and beta testing.

- Provide feedback and problem reports promptly so that problems can be addressed during acceptance test (and installation test).

- Participate in use case development (and usage profiles at higher levels of the TMM).

• TMM Level 3: Integration

MATURITY GOAL 3.1: ESTABLISH A TEST ORGANIZATION

ATRs FOR MANAGERS

- Provide leadership, resources and funding to a committee defining the structural framework of the test organization.

- Ensure that the role and responsibilities of the test organization are stated in the testing policy statement.

- Ensure that client concerns are reflected in the test organization policy.

- Ensure that any needed changes to support a test organization are incorporated in the organizational reporting structure.

- Establish standards, requirements, compensation levels, responsibilities, and career paths for the test professionals.

- Support necessary cultural changes needed to put into place a test organization.

- Provide resources, staff, and funding for the test organization.

- Ensure cooperation among developers, test specialists, and the SQA organization.

- Recruit and hire test specialists and test managers.

- Evaluate and supervise testing personnel.

- Periodically initiate actions to assess the maturity, effectiveness, and performance of the test organization.

- Support education and training of test group members.

- Support cultural changes needed to sustain a test organization.

- Monitor the performance of the test group.

- Support test organization growth and test process improvement efforts.

- Encourage, and provide communication pathways for tester–client interaction.

- Promote successes that result from the work of the testing organization.

ATRs FOR TESTERS

- Serve as members of the test organization committee.

- Be aware of the tasks, responsibilities, and career paths of the test specialist.

- Keep current with respect to new testing techniques, methods, and tools.

- Keep current on test planning techniques, and risk management.

- Work with analysts, designers, developers, project managers, and SQA staff to plan for testing, and to develop quality software products.

- Work with clients on issues such as acceptance test planning, use cases (or the equivalent), and usage profile (where appropriate).

- Work with project/test managers on test planning and monitoring of test efforts.

- Work with project/test managers to identify and prioritize test risks.

- Design test cases, test procedures, and execute tests.

- Prepare pre- and post-test documents.

- Collect, analyze, and apply test-related measurements.

- Contribute to test policy making.

- Maintain the test repository.

- Maintain the defect repository.

- Recruit new staff members.

- Mentor new test staff members.

- Work to establish product and process standards.

- Evaluate and apply new testing techniques and tools.

- Participate in technical reviews.

- Contribute to test process evaluation and improvement.

- Participate in periodic reviews of the test organization.

ATRs FOR USERS/CLIENTS

- Express their concerns and needs to management on testing issues and the test organization when solicited.

- Work with testers on items such as acceptance test planning, installation test planning, use cases (or the equivalent), and usage profiles (where appropriate).

MATURITY GOAL 3.2: ESTABLISH A TECHNICAL TRAINING PROGRAM

ATRs FOR MANAGERS

- Provide leadership, funding, and support to a technical training program committee.

- Develop an organizational policy for training with input from technical staff and project/test managers. Obtain approval and distribute to all relevant parties.

- Promote development of a technical training program by providing funding for the program, staff, resources, training materials, tools, and laboratories.

- Recruit and hire qualified staff for the training organization.

- Ensure that training plans are developed to support training needs and goals for all projects.

- Monitor and review the training program with technical staff to evaluate its effectiveness and to identify areas for improvement.

- Promote the cultural changes needed to support a training program.

- Provide visibility for the training program.

- Promote successes that result from the training program.

- Recommend staff members for training sessions.

ATRs FOR TESTERS

- Participate as members of the technical training program committee.

- Attend training sessions to improve their testing skills and capabilities.

- Apply newly acquired knowledge and skills to organizational projects.

- Request the development of new training sessions to acquire needed skills.

- Identify those in the testing group that could benefit from training.

- Participate in periodic reviews of the training program.

ATRs FOR USERS/CLIENTS

- If organizational policy permits, attend training sessions to promote participation in specific areas such as technical reviews, acceptance test planning, and development of use cases (or equivalent representations).

MATURITY GOAL 3.3: INTEGRATE TESTING INTO THE SOFTWARE LIFE CYCLE

ATRs FOR MANAGERS

- Provide leadership, resources, and support to a committee focused on test integration activities and models.

- Review, approve, and adopt (with input from testers and other technical staff) a test integration model (the V-model is an example of such a model).

- Ensure that integration of testing activities is a part of the testing policy and standards documents.

- Provide training to support integration activities.

- Ensure that the integration of testing activities is applied throughout the organization for all projects.

- Ensure that all testers are trained to carry out integrated testing activities.

- Promote cultural changes needed for the integration activities.

- Monitor and review the integrated testing activities and deliverables, evaluate them, and propose improvements if needed.

- Work with testers to develop standards for test work products that result from each life cycle phase.

- Ensure that work product standards are upheld.

- Promote successes of the integration efforts.

ATRs FOR TESTERS

- Serve on the committee dedicated to review, approve, and institute a test activities integration model and associated procedures.

- Attend training sessions to prepare for the integration of test activities.

- Plan the integrated test activities (test planning policies may require modification).

- Apply the documented integrated testing activities for each project.

- Perform the required test activities throughout the software life cycle as specified in the approved model, the organizational policy statement, and standards documents.

- Prepare all test deliverables that are required for each of the integrated testing activities.

- Work with management and SQA to develop standards for test deliverables and work products.

- Work with analysts, designers, developers, clients, on testing issues at designated life cycle phases.

- Ensure that each test work products/deliverable meets organizational standards.

- Participate in periodic reviews of integration activities.

ATRs FOR USERS/CLIENTS

- Provide consensus and support for integrated testing activities and early test planning. For example, provide support for acceptance test planning, use case (or equivalent representations), and usage profile development during the requirements and specifications phases.

MATURITY GOAL 3.4: CONTROL AND MONITOR THE TESTING PROCESS

ATRs FOR MANAGERS

- Provide leadership, resources, and funding to a committee or group on test process controlling and monitoring.

- Ensure that testing policy statements are modified so that mechanisms to accomplish controlling and monitoring of testing are described in detail.

- Promote cooperation between project and test managers for planning, monitoring, and controlling activities.

- Promote cultural changes needed for implementation of controlling and monitoring activities.

- Promote sharing of tools, and techniques between project and test managers for monitoring and controlling.

- Ensure that controlling and monitoring activities are part of each test plan.

- Ensure that adequate funding, training, tools, and resources are given to support controlling and monitoring activities.

- Assign responsibilities for controlling and monitoring.

- Support identification and selection of controlling/monitoring measurements.

- Participate in status and audit meetings, contribute to problem-solving sessions, and support follow-up for corrective actions.

- Periodically review the controlling and monitoring system.

- Promote successes that result from controlling and monitoring activities.

The following ATRs are assigned primarily to test managers.

- Serve on the committee to develop controlling and monitoring policies for testing.

- Develop test plans with appropriate schedules and resources set aside for controlling and monitoring.

- Cooperate with project managers to prepare contingency plans to cover risk-related areas of test.

- Select appropriate measurements to guide controlling and monitoring of tests.

- Ensure all appropriate test documents are prepared such as test logs and test incident reports.

- Collect and analyze test-related measurements, and present reports to appropriate management and staff.

- Set up periodic test status meetings, lead discussions, and present progress reports.

- Initiate and follow-up corrective actions when testing is off track.

- Assign responsibilities to testers for corrective actions that address test-related problems.

- Follow up and report on corrective actions taken.

- Support the installation of a configuration management system and play a role on the change control board.

- Prepare and present the test summary report.

- Participate in periodic reviews of the controlling and monitoring system.

ATRs FOR TESTERS

- Attend training sessions on controlling and monitoring (includes training on configuration management).

- Work with test managers to plan for controlling and monitoring of tests.

- Work with test managers to select appropriate measurements for controlling and monitoring.

- Work with project/test managers to develop contingency plans.

- Collect and analyze test measurements.

- Participate in test status meetings.

- Complete follow-up activities for corrective actions.

- Prepare test-related documents such as test logs and test incident reports.

- Contribute to a test summary report.

- Ensure that test items are under the control of a configuration management system.

- Serve as members of the change control board.

- Participate in periodic reviews of the controlling and monitoring system.

ATRs FOR USERS/CLIENTS

- Attend special test milestone meetings when appropriate. If the software is being developed for a specific client, the development organization may invite a user/client group to attend a test milestone meeting to show progress.

- Contribute necessary data for to post-test evaluations when appropriate. If an organization is measuring test-effectiveness using post-release problem reports, the users/clients will need to complete problem reports and insure they are returned to the proper personnel in the development organization.

• TMM Level 4: Management and Measurement

MATURITY GOAL 4.1: ESTABLISH AN ORGANIZATIONWIDE REVIEW PROGRAM

ATRs FOR MANAGERS

- Provide leadership, resources, and funding to a review program committee.

- Ensure that a review policy is developed, documented, approved, and available for management and technical staff.

- Provide training and resources for the review program.

- Promote cultural changes necessary to implement the review program.

- Ensure that the review requirements for the selected software items are followed.

- Upper-level managers and project/test managers work together to ensure that project/test plans provide time and resources for reviewing project deliverables.

- Ensure that review measurements are identified, collected, and applied for review process improvements.

- Ensure that defects identified during reviews are logged.

- Ensue that defects identified during reviews are processed and that corrections are carried through.

- Ensure that review data is referred to for project/test planning.

- Evaluate the review program periodically and support improvements where needed.

- Promote the successes of the review program.

ATRs FOR TESTERS

- Participate as members of the committee to develop review policies and plans.

- Attend review training sessions.

- Serve as review leaders, review instructors, and review participants as prescribed in the review policy statements.

- Ensure that review follow-up work is completed as described in the review policy and review plans.

- Work with SQA to identify classes and severity levels for review-related defects.

- Store and analyze review defect data.

- Collect review-related measurements.

- Work with SQA staff to develop checklists and other forms to support reviews.

- Refer to current and past review defect data to support test planning and test design.

- Participate in periodic evaluations of the review program.

ATRs FOR USERS/CLIENTS

- Attend review training sessions where appropriate.

- Attend review sessions as prescribed in the review policy. (For example, attendance at requirements, acceptance test plan, and user manual reviews are vital to ensure software quality and satisfaction of user needs and requirements.)

MATURITY GOAL 4.2: ESTABLISH A TEST MEASUREMENT PROGRAM

ATRs FOR MANAGERS

- Provide leadership, resources, and funding for a test measurement program committee.

- Ensure that a measurement program/policy is developed, documented, approved, and available for management and technical staff.

- Provide training and resources for the measurement program.

- Ensure that effective test process and product measurements are identified.

- Review the selected measurements periodically, and add, modify, or delete measurements when deemed appropriate.

- Assign responsibilities for defining, collecting, storing (test data repository), analyzing, and applying the measurement data. Decide when and where the data are to be applied, and by whom.

- Ensure that test plans include appropriate measurements so that the testing process can support achievement of software product quality goals.

- Work together with other managers (upper-level managers, project/test managers) to ensure that project/test plans provide time and resources for collecting product and process measurements.

- Ensure that project/process/test data is referred to for project/test planning, and to support the development of test and project goals.

- Ensure that measurement data is used to monitor, control, and improve the testing process (test managers).

- Apply the measurement data to develop appropriate action plans when measurements (and supporting assessments) indicate the testing process needs to be changed and improved (test managers).

- Work with clients to gather inputs on software quality attributes that are of importance to them.

- Apply product data collected during testing to evaluate and improve product quality.

- Review/evaluate the measurement program periodically and support improvements where needed.

- Promote successes that result from the measurement program.

- Promote the cultural changes needed for a successful measurement program.

ATRs FOR TESTERS

- Participate in the committee involved in measurement program planning and policy making.

- Assist in selecting measurement tools and methods,

- Assist in identifying product-related quality attributes and metrics.

- Assist in identifying test process-related attributes and metrics.

- Attend measurement training classes.

- Develop and maintain the test measurement database (and defect repository).

- Collect product and test process data during all levels of testing.

- Support data analysis and application of results.

- Support use of appropriate measures for test process evaluation and improvement.

- Provide input to managers and SQA staff from measurement data for each product with respect to its quality attributes.

- Support achievement of quality goals and requirements for each project.

- Participate in periodic reviews of the measurement program.

ATRs FOR USERS/CLIENTS

- Give consensus on quality attributes for products.

MATURITY GOAL 4.3: SOFTWARE QUALITY EVALUATION

ATRs FOR MANAGERS

- Provide leadership, resources, and funding to a committee on software quality evaluation.

- Ensure that software quality evaluation policies, procedures, forms, and standards are developed, distributed, and approved.

- Ensure that a full set of software quality attributes and metrics is developed, distributed, and approved.

- Promote cultural changes needed to implement software quality evaluation activities.

- Ensure that each project follows the documented software quality evaluation procedures.

- Ensure that quantitative quality goals are set for each project.

- Ensure the quality goals are met for each project.

- Provide funding, training, tools, and other resources to support software quality evaluation.

- Periodically review software quality evaluation policies, standards, metrics, and procedures with technical staff.

- Periodically review/assess the testing process to ensure that it supports evaluation of quality attributes and achievement of quality goals.

- Ensure there are mechanisms in place for client input in setting quality goals for projects.

- Ensure that client input is solicited to identify key quality attributes.

- Promote successes that result from software quality evaluation activities.

ATRs FOR TESTERS

- Attend software quality evaluation training classes.

- Participate in development of policies, procedures, forms, and standards for software quality evaluation.

- Participate in identification and application of software quality attributes and metrics.

- Work with project managers, test managers, and clients to identify quality attributes, metrics, and quality goals relevant to each project.

- Collect measurements of software quality attributes during testing and other quality evaluation procedures.

- Participate in software quality metrics validation procedures.

- Use software quality measurements and analysis techniques to evaluate the quality of the emerging software artifacts.

- Participate in testing process assessments and evaluation procedures to ensure that testing gives strong support for quality evaluation and achievement of quality goals.

- Participate in reviews of software quality evaluation standards and procedures.

- Support achievement of quality goals and requirements for each project.

ATRs FOR USERS/CLIENTS

- Give consensus on quality attributes for products.

- Provide input and approval for the quality requirements and goals that are important to them with respect to the software being developed. These appear in the requirements document.

- Provide inputs during acceptance tests to ensure that quality requirements are met.

• TMM Level 5: Optimization/Defect Prevention and Quality Control

MATURITY GOAL 5.1: DEFECT PREVENTION

ATRs FOR MANAGERS

- Provide leadership, resources, and funding to a committee focused on the development of documented defect prevention policies, procedure, and programs.

- Ensure that defect prevention documents are distributed and approved.

- Assign responsibilities for detect prevention activities.

- Ensure that training, tools and other resources are available for defect prevention activities.

- Promote the cultural changes needed for success of defect prevention activities.

- Promote visibility for successful defect prevention actions.

- Ensure that process changes that result from defect prevention activities are incorporated into documented policies and standards.

- Participate, and serve as leaders, in defect prevention activities such as action planning and monitoring. Lead project kick-off meetings.

- Select pilot projects to implement action plans for defect prevention.

- Promote discussion and distribution of lists of common defects and process change information to project team members.

- Promote the inclusion of defect prevention activities as part of the project/test plans

- Review the defect prevention program periodically.

ATRs FOR TESTERS

- Serves as members of the defect prevention policy committee.

- Attend training classes in defect prevention methods and activities.

- Collect and store update defect data from all life cycle phases.

- Serve as members of the defect causal analysis and defect prevention teams.

- Supply input for the development of defect prevention polices and procedures.

- Participate in action planning for defect prevention especially where applied to the test process.

- Serve as members of pilot project teams that implement action plans for defect prevention.

- Track and monitor changes in the test process that result from defect prevention activities.

- Ensure that test process changes that result from successful defect prevention actions are documented and followed.

- Support cultural changes necessary for defect prevention program success.

- Participate in reviews of the defect prevention program.

ATRs FOR USERS/CLIENTS

- Report defects and problems in operating software so these can be entered into the defect data base for defect tracking and causal analysis.

MATURITY GOAL 5.2: QUALITY CONTROL

ATRs FOR MANAGERS

- Provide leadership, resources, and funding for the committee focusing on development of documented quality control policies, procedure, and programs.

- Ensure that quality control-related documents are distributed and approved.

- Assign responsibilities for quality control activities.

- Ensure that training, tools, laboratories, and other resources are available for quality control activities.

- Promote the cultural changes needed for success of quality control activities.

- Promote visibility for successful quality control actions.

- Ensure that qualitative and quantitative quality goals are set for all projects, and are included in requirements documents, test plans, and project plans.

- Ensure that project and test plans allocate sufficient time and resources for software quality control activities.

- Ensure that there is a mechanism for user/client input to usage modeling.

- Plan for reliability and usability testing.

- Promote the development of usability standards.

- Assign responsibilities for statistical testing and usability testing. (The test and SQA groups may be assigned these responsibilities after the necessary training. As an alternative, management may decide to support the establishment of specialized groups in reliability and usability engineering. Hiring such a group of specialists may be called for because of the nature of software products under development, and because of the needs of the customer base.)

- Ensure that stop-test decisions are based on quantitative criteria, and include these in test plans.

- Monitor testing and other quality-related activities to ensure that software quality goals for each project are met, and that customers needs are satisfied.

- Periodically review the software quality control program.

ATRs FOR TESTERS

If an organization decides to hire reliability and usability engineering specialists then testers may have a supporting, rather then leading, role in the following ATRs.

- Participate as members of the committee on quality control.

- Attend training classes in quality control; includes training in statistical testing, development of usage profiles, and usability testing.

- Develop and maintain operational profiles with inputs and feedback from user groups.

- Develop a hierarchy of severity levels for faults and failures.

- Support planning for statistical testing.

- Perform statistical testing, and analyze results.

- Understand and apply reliability models.

- Collect and store quality-related measurements, for example, from reliability and usability tests. (These can be used to set standards for future projects.)

- Support the development of quantitative stop-test criteria and collect measurements to support their application.

- Design and execute tests to measure attributes such as correctness, portability, reliability, usability, confidence, availability, and trust-worthiness.

- Support usability test planning.

- Identity user groups for usability testing.

- Design usability tests.

- Support set up of usability testing laboratories.

- Monitor, record, analyze, and report the results of usability tests.

- Solicit user feedback from usability tests, and ensure that follow-up work is completed.

- Assist in the development usability standards for software products.

ATRs FOR USERS/CLIENTS

- Participate in development of qualitative and quantitative quality requirements for the projects they are involved in.

- Participate in development of an operational profile.

- Participate in usability testing by using the evolving software to carry out typical tasks and giving feedback to the testing team. It is important for users to state their opinions regarding the strengths and weaknesses of the developing software system.

MATURITY GOAL 5.3: TEST PROCESS OPTIMIZATION

ATRs FOR MANAGERS

- Ensure that a group or task force (SEPG/TPG) responsible for test process improvement is established, chartered, supported, funded, and trained. Take a leadership position in the group.

- Ensure that documented test process control policies, procedures, and programs are developed, distributed, and approved.

- Ensure that documented test process assessment and improvement procedures and programs are developed, distributed, and approved.

- Ensure that documented technology transfer policies, procedures, and programs are developed, distributed, and approved.

- Ensure that documented test process reuse policies, procedures, and programs are developed, distributed, and approved.

- Assign responsibilities for test process control.

- Assign responsibilities for technology transfer.

- Assign responsibilities for test process reuse.

- Assign responsibilities for test process assessment.

- Ensure that training, tools, laboratories, and other resources are available for test process control, reuse, assessment, and improvement.

- Promote the cultural changes needed for success of test process control, reuse, assessment, and improvement activities.

- Promote the cultural changes needed for success of technology transfer activities.

- Promote visibility for successful actions in test process reuse, control, and improvement.

- Select and provide support for pilot projects that are involved in process control implementation, process assessment and improvement, and trial technologies.

- Keep abreast of current tools and technologies to support test process optimization.

- Support periodic test process assessments with the TMM.

- Oversee test process improvement activities that result from TMM assessments.

- Support development and maintenance of both a Process Asset Library and reuse of process assets.

- Identify reusable processes for inclusion in the Process Asset Library.

- Tailor processes retrieved from the PAL and apply to new projects (test managers).

- Develop control charts, identify process variations and causes, and prepare reports (test managers).

- Periodically review the test process reuse, control, assessment and improvement programs.

- Periodically review the technology transfer program.

ATRs FOR TESTERS

- Serve as members of an SEPG/TPG.

- Assist in developing policies, plans, standards, and other documents related to process control, reuse, assessment and improvement, and technology transfer.

- Attend training classes in test process control, reuse, assessment, and improvement.

- Attend training classes in technology transfer.

- Keep abreast of current tools and technologies to support test process optimization and identify promising candidates to managers and the SEPG/TPG team.

- Evaluate new tools and technologies and provide feedback to management.

- Serve as members of test process assessment teams.

- Serve as members of action planning teams.

- Participate in pilot projects for process change and technology transfer.

- Collect measurement data from projects under study by SEPG/TPG.

- Assist in the development of control charts, identify process variations and causes, and prepare reports.

- Help to identify process assets, support, and maintain the Process Asset Library.

- Support integration of process changes and approved new technologies.

- Participate in reviews of the test process control, reuse, assessment, improvement and technology transfer programs.

ATRs FOR USERS/CLIENTS

Users/clients do not play any significant role in support of this maturity goal.

INDEX